COMPUTERS
IN BUSINESS
An Introduction

COMPUTERS IN BUSINESS
An Introduction

Donald H. Sanders
*Ph.D., M. J. Neeley School
of Business, Texas Christian
University*

SECOND EDITION

McGRAW-HILL BOOK COMPANY
*New York   St. Louis   San Francisco   Düsseldorf   Johannesburg
Kuala Lumpur   London   Mexico   Montreal   New Delhi   Panama
Rio de Janeiro   Singapore   Sydney   Toronto*

To my family:
Joyce, Gary, Linda, and Craig

COMPUTERS IN BUSINESS
An Introduction

Copyright © 1968, 1972 by McGraw-Hill, Inc. All rights reserved. Printed in the United States of America. No part of this publication may be reproduced, stored in a retrieval system, or transmitted, in any form or by any means, electronic, mechanical, photocopying, recording, or otherwise, without the prior written permission of the publisher.

Library of Congress Catalog Card Number 79-168463

07-054617-7

1 2 3 4 5 6 7 8 9 0   M U R M   7 9 8 7 6 5 4 3 2 1

This book was set in Optima by York Graphic Services, Inc., and printed by Murray Printing Company, and bound by Rand McNally. The designer was Howard Leiderman; the drawings were done by F. W. Taylor Company. The editors were Richard F. Dojny, Hiag Akmakjian, and Cynthia Newby. John F. Harte supervised production.

Contents

Preface

A basic objective of higher education for business is the development of potential managers and updating of the skills of practicing managers. Students pursuing collegiate programs of study designed to better prepare them for administrative positions in such functional areas of business as marketing, production, finance, accounting, and management will find their business careers (and their private lives!) greatly affected by the use of electronic computers. Therefore, present and potential managers must prepare for a successful working relationship with computerized information processing; in addition, as well-educated citizens they must acquire a knowledge of this tool and its processing capabilities so that they will be prepared to understand and cope with the expanding uses of computers in our society. The basic purpose of this book is to lay the foundation for the *continuing study* that will provide such a working relationship and understanding.

More specifically, the objectives of this text are to (1) provide a general orientation to the stored program computer—what it is, what it can and cannot do, and how it operates—and (2) provide an insight into the broad impact that computers have had, are having, and may be expected to have on managers and on the environment in which managers work.

The initial twelve chapters are devoted primarily to the first of these objectives. A brief summary of these chapters (and *an outline of some of the significant changes incorporated in this edition*) is presented below:

Chapter Subject and Revision Features

1 The subjects of *management information* and *data processing* are introduced; the need for management information, the types of information needed, the desired properties of this information, and the pressures bringing about improvements in such information are given an expanded treatment. A summary of the economic objectives and benefits of computer usage is also added.

2 The *evolution of data processing* is presented. Revision features include a discussion of the 96-column card used in IBM's System/3 computers, a revised treatment of punched card fields, an expanded section on the use of a keypunch machine, and added information on minicomputers.

3 The overview of the "information processing revolution" found in Chapter 3 of the first edition *has been expanded* to two chapters in this revision. The new Chapter 3 emphasizes the *setting for the information revolution* which is now under way. Additional emphasis is given to the rapid scientific, social, political, and economic changes that create both opportunities and problems for institutions such as business and government. Sections on hardware reliability and operating-system software have been added, and the discussion of software developments has been reorganized.

4 This chapter deals with the *developments and issues of the information revolution*. Developments in quicker-responding and broader-based management information systems that enable managers to cope with the changing environment receive closer attention. Also, such *adjustment problems* as (a) the

challenges in information systems design, (b) the issue of invasion of privacy, (c) the issues in data communication, (d) the groping for an industry pricing structure, (e) the protection of proprietary software, and (f) the shortage of computer personnel are presented and discussed. A section on the growing popularity of facilities management organizations is also inserted.

5 An *introduction to the uses and limitations of computers,* plus the functional organizations of these machines is presented here. A brief explanation of the purpose of I/O channels is added as is a treatment of the variation that may exist in the design and construction (or architecture) of the functional elements in the central processor. Multiprocessor, concurrent, and parallel designs are briefly described.

6 & 7 These chapters deal with *input/output media and devices.* A section on the nine-channel magnetic tape format is added in Chapter 6. In Chapter 7, a discussion of Computer Output to Microfilm (COM) is a new feature; the presentation of the material on online terminals is reorganized and expanded; and a section on overlapped processing and buffer storage has been completely reworked.

8 & 9 The *central processing unit* of the computer is the topic of these chapters. In Chapter 8, the material on the capacity of storage locations has been revised to give substantially increased emphasis to the byte-addressable storage organization employed by third- and fourth-generation computers. A new section on the hexadecimal numbering system has been added, and Self-check Exercises have been incorporated. In Chapter 9, the concepts of a high-speed scratch-pad memory and of a read-only control storage are introduced; the section on plated-wire storage is completely reworked; a new section on LSI circuit storage is added (using the IBM System/370, Model 145 as an example); and the discussion of the arithmetic-logic unit has been revised to give proper attention to the storage and calculation approaches employed by byte-oriented computers.

10 This chapter stresses *programming analysis* and the benefits and limitations of flowcharts and decision tables.

11 In this chapter an *orientation to program preparation* is presented. Such topics as (a) the computer instruction, (b) languages for computers, (c) program coding, (d) program debugging and

testing, (e) program documentation and maintenance, and (f) programming aids are treated. Revision features include entirely new sections on program debugging and testing and program documentation and maintenance. The "programming aids" section has been significantly expanded to incorporate those aids that make it possible to convert existing programs so that they can be used on new hardware without the necessity for reprogramming. Included are discussions on translation, emulation, and simulation techniques. In addition, a new section on firmware developments (or microprograms or stored-logic) has been added.

12 Entirely new for this edition, this chapter expands on the subject of *program coding* and which acquaints the reader with the structure and with some of the characteristics of several popular programming languages. Two simple problems were discussed and flowcharted in Chapter 10. These same problems are now coded and explained in the FORTRAN, COBOL, PL/I, BASIC, and RPG languages in this chapter.

Chapters 13 to 17 focus attention on the managerial implications of computer usage (the second of the stated objectives of this text), and Chapter 18 projects current computer-related trends into the future. A brief summary of these chapters (and *an outline of some of the significant changes incorporated in this edition*) is presented below:

Chapter Subject and Revision Features

13 This is an orientation chapter outlining some of the broad *managerial implications of computer usage*. Several topics introduced in this chapter will be expanded upon in later chapters. The chapter has been reorganized and updated, and a more thorough summary treatment of the planning and decision-making implications of computer usage has been prepared.

14 This chapter is entitled Planning for Computers and replaces Chapter 12 (The Feasibility Study) and part of Chapter 13 in the first edition. This new chapter (a) examines the essential nature of the systems study and (b) presents a general systems-study approach. A systems study may be conducted, of course,

to determine the feasibility of installing a computer; however, the systems-study approach may also be employed to revise and update existing procedures using currently available hardware, or it may be used to develop new applications for existing hardware. Thus, the systems approach outlined in this chapter is broader in applicability than the material it replaces.

15 The *organizational implications of computer usage* is the subject of this chapter. Managers should be aware of the fact that the entire organizational structure may undergo stress and alteration as a result of computer usage.

16 This chapter, entitled Staffing and the Computer, is a reorganization and reworking of personnel topics previously considered in Chapters 13 and 14 of the first edition. A new section on motivating computer personnel has been added.

17 In this chapter we are concerned with the computer's impact on *managerial and internal control.* A new section outlining the ways in which a reduction in internal control can occur in an inadequately managed computer department has been added. A new discussion of the techniques that may be employed in the "through-the-computer" auditing approach has also been included.

18 Finally, an attempt is made to project current hardware, software, and management trends a few years into the future.

The extensively revised Glossary has been excerpted from the 1970 Copyright version of the "American National Standard Vocabulary for Information Processing," X3.12-1970. This American National Standard is an updated revision of the USA Standard X3.12-1966 which was the basis for the Glossary in the first edition.

This text is designed for use in an introductory one-semester or one-quarter course in computer data processing offered at an early stage in a collegiate program. No mathematical or data processing background is required or assumed; no specific computer make or model is featured. The book may be used without access to a machine.

An issue which has yet to be resolved concerns the depth of programming instruction that a student should receive. For many introductory courses, the programming emphasis contained in this book will be quite sufficient. However, when considerable emphasis is to be placed on the writing of programs in a specific language for a specific make and model of machine, two types of instructional materials are frequently required: (1) a basic text to add breadth to the course and (2) programming manuals available from equipment manufacturers and publishers and/or notes and materials prepared by the instructor. In such situations, this book is well suited for use as the basic text.

Many individuals have contributed to and improved the quality of this publishing effort (of course, only the author is responsible for any remaining errors). A special tribute must go to those equipment manufacturers who furnished technical materials, photographs, and other visual aids. Their individual contributions are acknowledged in the body of the book. I am also indebted to the Data Processing Management Association, publisher of my book entitled "Introducing Computers to Small Business," for their contractual permission to use appropriate materials from that earlier work. Finally, the assistance of my former students Rick Teakell, David M. Jones, and Jimmy K. Fulkerson is gratefully acknowledged.

Donald H. Sanders

Introduction and Information

Computer installations are often visited by people interested in observing the machines in action. Sometimes, if the manager of the installation has been forewarned, the visitor may be treated to the sound of recognizable tunes coming from a speaker connected to the computer. Or, if it happens to be a holiday season, the visitor may observe a printing device producing appropriate pictures, e.g., Santa Claus and his sleigh. Other snappy demonstrations are also used, and the spectator is impressed as he departs.

It requires no great amount of perception, however, for our visitor to realize that such impressive machines were not installed for their entertainment features. Magazines, newspapers, and television have informed the public of dozens of examples of how computers have been used, e.g., from guiding missiles to catching income tax cheats and from writing cake-mix recipes to monitoring elections. Indeed, our visitor may have come to the conclusion that this mysterious and baffling piece of equipment can do almost anything!

It is quite possible that our visitor is a manager in a business organization. It is also possible that the visit was to his firm's new computer installation. The impact that the computer will have on his firm (and his job) in the future is cause for personal concern. He has read articles in popular business magazines with such titles as: "Is the Computer Running Wild?," "New Tool, New World," and "The Boundless Age of the Computer." But to our visitor and to many of today's managers, the Age of the Computer might more appropriately be entitled the Age of Bewilderment. The rug of familiar methods and traditional approaches to decision making has been pulled from under many managers by rapid technological change. And the computer is a prime instrument of this change. Many present managers received their formal training and initial job experience prior to the introduction of computers. Such managers must either learn to adapt their operations to this new management tool[1] or decide to spend the remainder of their careers in a race between retirement and job obsolescence.

OBJECTIVES AND ORGANIZATION

A basic objective of education for business is the development of potential managers. Students concentrating in such areas of business as marketing, finance, accounting, or management will find their future careers and their private lives greatly affected by the computer. As future managers they must prepare for a successful working relationship with computerized information processing; as well-educated citizens they must acquire an understanding of this processing so that they will be prepared to cope with the expanding uses of computers in our society. The primary purpose of this book, therefore, is to lay the foundation for the *continuing study* that will provide such a working relationship and understanding.

More specifically, the goals of this book are to

1. Provide a general orientation to the stored program computer— what it is, what it can and cannot do, and how it operates
2. Provide an insight into the broad impact that computers have had, are having, and may be expected to have on managers and on the environment in which managers work

Chapter topics in this book will reflect these goals. Chapters 2, 3, and 4 are orientation chapters dealing with the *evolution* of data processing and with the data processing *revolution* that is now under

[1]The author modestly recommends that the adaptation begin with a reading of this text.

way. A study of the computer itself—its capabilities and limitations, its component parts, and its operation—begins with Chapter 5 and continues through Chapter 12.

In Chapters 13 to 17 attention is focused on the managerial implications of computers, the economics of these machines, and the managerial problems associated with their use. The final chapter attempts to project current trends a few years into the future.

In ancient Babylon a vast public works program was started by the leaders with the objective of building a tower reaching to the heavens. Obviously, a project of such magnitude required a considerable amount of managerial skill as well as the labor of thousands of workers. The book of Genesis tells us that this ambitious project was never completed. The managers had failed to plan for an unusual development. Displeased with the haughty conduct of the people, God confused their language. Foremen could not communicate with workers; workers could not even understand each other. The project came to a standstill, and the episode has been used for centuries as an example of the consequences of a communications breakdown.

The problem of lack of communication between computer specialists and business managers is a real one today.[2] A whole new language has developed in the past decade in business data processing—a language that might be labeled "Computerese" and that must be mastered to some extent by the future manager.[3] To many of today's managers this language is a foreign one; even to computer specialists it can be confusing. Confusion results because of the lack of uniform agreement about the meaning of many of the more popular Computerese terms.

Much of the confusion, of course, comes from the rapid rate of growth of computer technology. New concepts in the design and use of computers are announced with mind-boggling frequency, and these concepts are often described with newly coined words or phrases. Thousands of new computers are now being installed each year.

TERMINOLOGY AND THE TOWER OF BABEL

[2]In a survey of 2,500 executives, a majority said that "members of data processing staffs and middle management have not been successful in bridging the communications gap in implementing new applications. Significantly, 38% state that they consider this 'one of the most important problems relating to data processing'." See John Diebold, "Bad Decisions on Computer Use," *Harvard Business Rev.*, January–February, 1969, p. 27.

[3]English words have taken on different meanings. For example, in dictionaries of a few years ago, a "computer" was a person who did computations. Now, a "computer" is a machine or group of machines.

Understanding suffers because the number of *new* terms and *acronyms* seems to be increasing at about the same rate.[4]

In the following section and throughout the book, words are defined as they are introduced. The definitions used are the ones that appear to be most generally accepted. A glossary of commonly used technical terms is included at the back of the book. The reader will find that although some Computerese terms sound quite impressive and foreboding—as is often the case with technical jargon—closer inspection will prove them to be relatively simple.

The above remarks have served to introduce you to the objectives of this book. In later chapters we will examine computer systems in some detail. At this point, however, we should place the role of computers in business in proper perspective. Computers are used in business operations *because they produce information;* were this not so, the machines would be merely expensive curiosities. Therefore, in the pages of this chapter that follow, let us examine the subject of *management information.* After first defining some terms, we will consider the *need for management information,* the *pressures bringing about management information improvement,* and the *characteristics desirable for computer processing.* Finally, the *economic objectives and benefits of computer usage* are summarized.

MANAGEMENT INFORMATION

The word *data* is the plural of *datum,* which means *fact.* Data, then, are facts, unevaluated messages, or informational raw materials, but they are not management information except in a constricted and detailed sense. Data are independent entities and are unlimited in number. Although often considered to be numerical values, data may also be defined to include nonnumerical perceptions and observations made by human beings and machines.

Management information is relevant knowledge, produced as output of data processing operations and acquired to achieve specific purposes.[5] From this definition, we see that information is the result of a transformation process. Just as raw materials are transformed into finished products by a manufacturing process (Fig. 1-1a), so, too, are

---

[4]The reader should not despair. Rather, he should fortify himself with HADACOL (the Hope that Acceptable Definitions will Appear in Computer-Oriented Language). This is an example of an *acronym*—a term formed from the first letters of related words.

[5]The above definition emphasizes management information in what might be termed the "formal" sense. Of course, managers also receive information from overheard conversations, from the actions rather than the words of others, and from other informal sources. In this informal sense, the manager processes the input data mentally and stores in his memory the information output for possible future use.

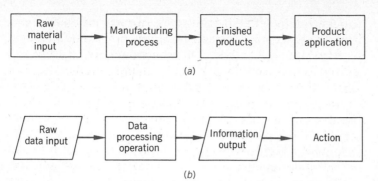

Figure 1-1 *Transformation process*

raw data transformed into information by the data processing operation (Fig. 1-1b). The products produced by the manufacturing process have little utility until they are properly applied; similarly, the information produced by data processing is of little value unless it supports meaningful decisions leading to appropriate business actions. The purpose of data processing is to evaluate and bring order to data and place them in proper perspective so that meaningful information will be produced. The primary distinction between data and information, therefore, is that while all information consists of data, not all data produce specific and meaningful information that will enable managers to plan, organize, and control their business activities.[6]

For information to be meaningful and relevant to managers, it must have such characteristics as accuracy, completeness, and timeliness; it must also provide facts that are needed and that were unknown or previously unverified. If the input data are inaccurate, incomplete, or out of date, the information that results may be of little value. For example, the *Statistical Abstract of the United States* for 1945 presents thousands of business facts. But these data are of little use to today's manager in making today's decisions.

Sources of Data

The input data used to produce information originate from internal and external sources. *Internal sources* consist of individuals and departments located within an organization. These sources may furnish facts on a regular and planned basis (i.e., on a formal basis) to support decisions if the potential user is aware that the facts are available. Internal data gathered on a formal basis typically relate to events that have already happened; they often represent feedback to

[6]It should be mentioned here, however, that what one manager might regard as irrelevant data may be interpreted by another as valuable information. The explanation of this paradox is deferred to a later section entitled What Information is Needed?

managers of the effectiveness and accuracy of earlier plans. Once the need for the data is established (and the value of supplying it is deemed to be worth the cost), a systematic data-gathering procedure is designed to produce the facts.[7]

In addition to what might be called *planned data gathering,* data may also be received from internal sources on an informal basis through casual contacts and discussions. Such facts may be quite important. For example, a sales representative for the machine-tool division of a large company may learn that one of his customers has under development an improved type of valve that may have marketing implications for the valve division of his own firm. Such information, if transmitted to the valve division, might be of great value. The *movement* of unsolicited facts to interested parties is dependent upon the possessor's willingness to transmit them and his knowledge of who the potential users are. The *value* of such data is, of course, reduced by delay in the communication channels and by distortion of the facts that may be introduced.

External, or *environmental,* sources are the generators and distributors of data located outside the organization. These sources include such categories as customers, suppliers, competitors, business publications, industry associations, and government agencies. Such sources provide the organization with environmental and/or competitive data that may give managers important clues on what is likely to happen. Government agencies, for example, furnish businesses with a wealth of environmental statistics—such as per capita income, total consumer expenditures, and population-growth estimates—which are valuable for planning purposes. Industry associations and publications furnish data on competitive performance of products and companies. Industry statistics, combined with internal data, can assist in sales planning and financial control.

Data Processing

Data processing is a relatively recent phrase, but the *activity* is as old as writing. Long before the Greek and Roman periods of history, the Babylonians had invented cuneiform writing. Cuneiform symbols were cut into damp clay, and the clay was then baked for permanence. Numerous business records on clay tablets showing such data processing outputs as sales and inventory totals have been unearthed. We no longer use clay tablets, but businesses of all sizes must still perform the data processing activity.

All data processing, whether it be done by hand or by the latest

[7]Not infrequently, a procedure for gathering and processing data continues to be followed after the need for the information no longer exists.

electronic methods, consists of one or more of the following basic steps:

1. *Originating—recording.* Data must be captured or originated in some form for processing. The first step in the data processing operation is often to include handwritten or typed forms such as sales tickets, checks, deposit slips, and customer invoices. Data originally recorded in one form may later be converted into machine-usable form for further processing. Some recording operations produce a machine-usable output directly or as a by-product.

2. *Classifying.* Identifying and arranging items with like characteristics into groups or classes is called *classifying*. Sales data taken from a sales ticket may be classified by product sold, location of sales point, customer, sales clerk, or any other classification that the processing cycle may require.

    Classifying is usually done by a shortened, predetermined method of abbreviation known as *coding*. The three types of codes used are numeric, alphabetic, and alphanumeric. Code *numbers* are used to designate persons (Social Security number, payroll number, timecard number), places (Zip code, sales district number), and things (part numbers). *Alphabetic* codes are used to classify such diverse things as vitamins (A, B, and C), financial condition (AAA, BB, and C), and astronaut status (A-OK). Combinations of letters and numbers give such *alphanumeric* codes as military service numbers (AF17341256), further classification of vitamins (B_1 and B_2), automobile license plates (AB-1234), and mail-order catalog items (XMB2973).

3. *Sorting.* After the data are classified, it is then usually necessary to arrange or rearrange them in a predetermined sequence to facilitate processing. This arranging procedure is called *sorting*. For example, insurance agents are classified in the yellow pages of the telephone directory by type of insurance sold (auto, fire and casualty, life, etc.); within each insurance category the agents are then sorted into an alphabetic sequence. Sorting is done by number as well as by letter. Sales invoices may be sorted by invoice number or by customer name. Numeric sorting usually requires less time than alphabetic sorting in machine-based processing systems and is therefore generally used.

4. *Calculating.* Arithmetic manipulation of the data is known as *calculating*. In the calculation of an employee's pay, for example, the total of hours worked multiplied by the hourly wage rate would give the taxable gross earnings. Payroll deductions such

as taxes and insurance are then computed and subtracted from gross earnings to leave net or take-home earnings. The calculating step is an important one involving a great deal of effort if done manually.

5. *Summarizing.* To be of value, data must often be condensed or sifted so that the resulting reports will be concise and effective. Reducing masses of data to a more usable form is called *summarizing.* A sales manager may be interested only in the total sales of a particular store. Thus, it would be wasteful in time and resources if he were given a report that broke sales down by department, product, and sales clerk.

6. *Storing.* Placing similar data into files for future reference is *storing.* In the payroll example cited above, the data on hours worked early in the pay period had to be stored until the payroll was prepared. Such a storage period, of course, is quite short. Other data may be stored for years. Obviously, facts should be stored only if the value of having them in the future exceeds the storage cost. Storage may take a variety of forms. Storage *media* that are frequently used include paper documents, microfilm, magnetizable media and devices, and punched paper media.

7. *Retrieving.* Recovering stored data and/or information when needed is the *retrieving* step. Retrieval methods range from searches made by file clerks to the use of quick-responding inquiry terminals that are connected directly (i.e., they are *online*) to a computer. The computer, in turn, is connected directly to a mass-storage device that contains the information. The computer is programmed to retrieve the information and relay it to the inquiry station at electronic speeds. The station may be in the room next to the computer, or it may be thousands of miles away. The subject of quick-response information systems will be covered in Chapter 4.

8. *Reproducing.* It is sometimes necessary or desirable to copy or duplicate data. This operation is known as data *reproduction* and may be done by hand or by machine. Some machines (e.g., Xerox equipment) produce a humanly readable or *hard copy document;* others reproduce the data in machine-readable form on such media as punched cards, punched paper tape, and magnetic tape, so that it is difficult or impossible for man to read it directly.

9. *Communicating.* As we have seen, data may go through many steps after they have been originated. The transfer of data from one operation to another for use or for further processing is known as data *communication.* The communication process continues until the information, in a usable form, reaches the final user's location. (Communication of a different nature, of course, will

PROCESSING METHODS	STEPS IN THE DATA PROCESSING OPERATION								
	Originating-Recording	Classifying	Sorting	Calculating	Summarization	Storing	Retrieving	Reproducing	Communicating
Manual methods	Human observation; handwritten records; pegboards	Hand posting; pegboards	Hand posting; pegboards; edge-notched cards	Human brain	Pegboards; hand calculations	Paper in files, journals, ledgers, etc.	File clerk; bookkeeper	Clerical; carbon paper	Written reports; hand-carried messages; telephone
Manual with machine assistance	Typewriter; cash register; manual	Cash register; bookkeeping machine	Mechanical collators	Adding machines; calculators; cash registers	Accounting machines; adding machines; cash registers	Motorized rotary files; microfilm		Xerox machines; duplicators; addressing machines	Documents prepared by machines; message conveyors
Electro-mechanical punched card methods	Prepunched cards; keypunched cards; mark-sensed cards; manual	Determined by card field design; sorter; collator	Card sorter	Accounting machines (tabulators) calculating punch		Trays of cards	Manual tray movement	Reproducing punch	Printed documents; interpreter
Electronic methods	Magnetic tape encoder; magnetic and optical character readers; card and tape punches; on-line terminals; manual	Determined by systems design; computer	Offline card sorter; computer sorting	Computer		Magnetizable media and devices; punched media; computer	Online inquiry with direct access devices; manual movement of storage media to computer	Multiple copies from printers	Online data transmission; printed output; visual display; voice output

Figure 1-2   Tools and techniques for data processing

often result at this point.) Output information may be in the form of a vital printed managerial report; but output can also be in the form of an electric bill on a punched card, an updated deck of payroll record cards, or an updated reel of magnetic tape. When the electric bill is paid by the customer, the card is returned and becomes the input for another processing cycle—the updating of accounts-receivable records.

These, then, are the basic steps in data processing. Figure 1-2 presents these steps and indicates some of the ways in which they are accomplished. The means of performing the steps vary according to whether *manual, electromechanical,* or *electronic* processing methods are used. Many businesses find that the best solution to their processing requirements is to use a combination of methods; e.g., manual methods may be used for small-volume jobs while computers may be used for large-volume tasks. Of course, every processing step may not be required for every piece of useful information produced.

The above brief remarks on the sources of data and the nature of data processing now make it possible to expand Fig. 1-1b. In Fig. 1-3 we see that data input is divided into sources and that data processing is broken down into operational steps. The solid lines represent the possible communication of data and information in a single processing cycle; the dashed lines represent the feedback communication required to obtain additional data and recycle the data base for future processing.

NEED FOR MANAGEMENT INFORMATION

All managers must perform certain basic management tasks or functions in order to achieve company goals. The objectives pursued differ, of course, but the basic tasks are common to all. In other words, the

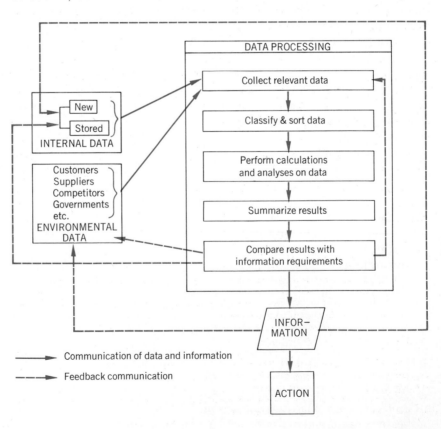

Figure 1-3

functions of *planning, organizing, staffing,* and *controlling* are performed by all managers.[8] The success of any business is determined by how well its executives perform these activities. And how well these functions are carried out is dependent, in part, upon how well the information needs of managers are being met.[9] Why is this? It is because each function involves decision making, and decision making must be supported by information that is accurate, timely, complete, concise, and relevant. If a manager's information does not possess these characteristics, the quality of the decisions that he makes will probably suffer and the business (at best) will not achieve the success it might otherwise have had. When viewed in this light, it is evident that information is a competitive tool.

In summary, as shown in Fig. 1-4, quality information in the hands of those who can effectively use it will support good decisions; good decisions will lead to effective performance of managerial activities; and effective managerial performance will lead to successful attainment of organizational goals. Thus, as Sisson and Canning have observed, ". . .information is the cement that holds together any organization."[10] Fig. 1-5 graphically demonstrates the "cementing" role of, and the need for, information in a business organization.

The *demand for information,* like the sources of supply of data input, originates from both internal and external locations. As we have just seen, managers within the organization need information for the performance of managerial functions. Information is also required, however, to meet demands originating from the environment in which the business operates. Reports of various kinds are required by government bodies;[11] dues reports are prepared for labor unions; annual and interim reports giving financial information are expected by creditors, stockholders, and lending institutions; and market and product information may be desired by customers and suppliers of raw materials.

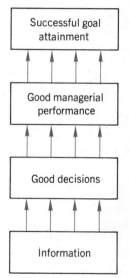

Figure 1-4

[8]We shall examine these functions in Chapter 13.

[9]It is necessary to add that the manager must have the ability to effectively use the information that he receives. If he can't use it, either the information in its present form is wrong for the manager or the manager will have to be trained to use it properly. Merely providing a manager with *needed* information is no guarantee that it will be (or can be) effectively used.

[10]Roger L. Sisson and Richard G. Canning, *A Manager's Guide to Computer Processing,* John Wiley & Sons, Inc., New York, 1967, p. 1.

[11]A *Time* magazine article in 1964 announced that the U.S. government required that the business community file 5,455 different reports during the year. In one extreme example, a farm-products firm handled 173 different federal forms in a single year. Various reports were sent in at different intervals ranging from daily to annually. A final total of 37,683 reports, involving 48,285 man-hours of work, was submitted! In addition, businesses must also satisfy state- and local-government requirements.

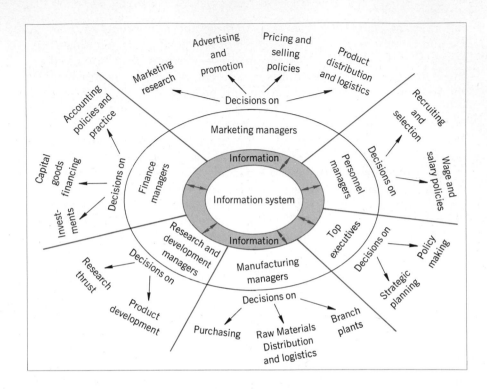

Figure 1-5

**What Information
Is Needed?**

What information does the manager need to manage effectively? A common need basic to all managers is an understanding of the purpose of the organization, i.e., its policies, its programs, its plans, and its goals. But beyond these basic informational requirements, the question of what information is needed can only be answered in broad general terms because individual managers differ in the ways in which they view information, in their analytical approaches in using it, and in their conceptual organization of relevant facts. An additional factor that complicates the subject of the information needed by managers is the organizational level of the managerial job. Managers at the lower operating levels need information to help them make the day-to-day operating decisions. At the top levels, however, information is needed to support long-range planning and policy decisions. Thus, because of the types of decisions they must make, managers at the top and lower levels generally *utilize time* differently, tend to need different degrees of *information summarization,* and are inclined to use information obtained from *different sources.*

In Fig. 1-6*a* we see that at the lower managerial levels more time is generally spent in performing control activities (e.g., checking to make sure that production schedules are being met) while at the upper levels more time is spent on planning (e.g., determining the location and specifications of a new production plant). Fig. 1-6*b* shows that although lower-level managers need detailed information relating to daily operations of specific departments, top executives are best served with information that summarizes trends and indicates exceptions to what was expected. A final generalization is that the higher one is in the management hierarchy, the more he needs and is likely to use information obtained from external sources (see Fig. 1-6*c*). A foreman uses internally generated feedback information to control production processes, but a president studying the feasibility of a new plant needs information about customer product acceptance, locality tax structures, competitive reactions, availability of labor and suppliers, etc., and this information is environmental in nature.

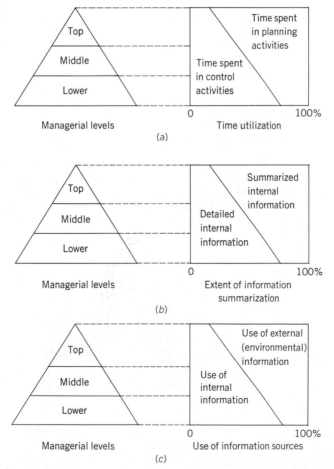

Figure 1-6

In summary, the types of decisions vary, and the information needs also vary. Thus, as Dr. Eugene Kozik, a General Electric planner, writes:

> *We do not believe it is possible to design an information system on the basis of even the most exhaustive task analysis of the managerial jobs involved with any reasonable expectation that the system design will be uniformly suitable or desirable for all managers associated with the complex.*[12]

The specific information needed by a particular manager includes everything that manager must have to (1) establish, evaluate, and adjust goals, (2) develop plans and standards and initiate action, (3) measure actual performance and take appropriate action when performance varies from the standard, and (4) assess achievements.

To carry the generalization of the preceding paragraph a step further, a manager should perform the following analysis to acquire the information he needs:

1. He should identify those factors that are critical to the success of his contribution to the organization's goals.
2. He should determine how these critical factors can be measured.
3. He should determine, for each critical factor, what quantifiable measurement constitutes success.
4. He should take steps to acquire information that will be needed to ensure achievement of "success measurements."

By following this general procedure, the manager will have the quality information which *he* needs to manage effectively.

Desired Properties of Management Information

As noted earlier, output reports, taken by themselves, generally have little or no value to an organization unless they can be *used* to make decisions that lead to profitable business actions.[13] As a general rule, the more information serves to reduce the element of uncertainty in decision making, the greater is its value. But information is a business resource, and like any other business resource it is not free. It is therefore necessary that the cost of acquiring the resource be compared with the value to be obtained from its availability. Just as it would be economically foolish for an organization to spend $100 to

---

[12]Eugene Kozik, "Computer Augmentation of Managerial Reasoning," *Management Accounting,* vol. 48, p. 40, December, 1966.

[13]Reports required by government agencies are often costly to prepare and *may not* result in decisions that lead to profitable business actions. In such situations, however, the stalwart civil servant may be counted on to specify a penalty for not producing the information that will exceed the cost of report preparation.

mine $75 worth of coal, so, too, would it be unsound to produce information costing $100 if this information did not lead to actions that yielded a net return. In other words, information should be prepared if its cost is less than the additional revenues produced or if it serves to reduce other expenses by a more than proportionate amount. In some cases the actual costs of preparing information can be compared with the *tangible* economic benefits obtained from its use. Frequently, however, the cost of producing information with characteristics generally considered to be desirable must be compared with benefits of an *intangible* nature. For example, whether or not revenue will be raised enough to justify additional costs that are frequently incurred to give managers more accurate, more timely, and more complete information with which to make operating and control decisions is something that must be considered by information-system designers.

The overview of information economics just presented should be kept in mind as we look at the desirability of information that possesses the characteristics of *accuracy, timeliness, completeness, conciseness,* and *relevancy.* Up to a certain point, information that possesses these properties may be expected to be more valuable than information lacking one or more of these characteristics.

Accuracy   Accuracy may be defined as the ratio of correct information to the total amount of information produced over a period of time. If, for example, 1,000 items of information are produced and 950 of these items give a correct report of the actual situation, then the level of accuracy is 0.95. Whether or not this level is high enough depends upon the information being produced. Fifty incorrect bank balances in a mailing of 1,000 bank statements would hardly be acceptable to depositors or to the bank. On the other hand, if physical inventory records kept on large quantities of inexpensive parts achieve an accuracy level of 0.95, this might be acceptable. In the case of bank statements, greater accuracy *must* be obtained; in the case of the parts inventory, greater accuracy *could* be obtained, but the additional value to managers of having more accurate inventory information might be less than the additional costs required.

Inaccuracies are the result of *human errors* and/or *machine malfunctions.* Human error (in system design, machine operation, the preparation of input data, and in other ways) is the primary cause of inaccuracy. Computer equipment malfunctions occur only infrequently, and the machine failures that do appear are usually traceable to input/output devices. However, programmed error checks and built-in error-detecting features can often discover input/output malfunctions. An important benefit of well-designed computer information systems is their ability to provide much greater accuracy than the manual or electromechanical systems that they replace.

Timeliness   Timeliness is another important information characteristic. It is of little consolation to a manager to know that information that arrived too late to be of use was accurate. Accuracy alone is not enough. An interesting fact is that in the past a tradeoff between timeliness and accuracy was often required; i.e., greater accuracy might require more input data control points, which could slow down the processing speed and therefore reduce the timeliness of the output information. Computer usage, however, reduces the significance of this conflict between accuracy and processing speed.

How fast must be the *response time* of the information system? Unfortunately, it is once again impossible to give an answer which will satisfy all situations. In the case of *regular reports,* an immediate response time following each relevant business transaction would involve a steady outpouring of documents, each of which would cover a very brief time interval. The result might well be a costly avalanche of paper. Report contents could not possibly be assimilated by the manager; and even if they could be, the time period involved would be too short to reveal meaningful trends, although superficial events could be blown up out of proportion to their importance.

Thus, in the case of periodic reports, a compromise is often required. The response interval should be short enough so that the information does not lose its freshness and value and so that fewer expensive data-storage devices will be needed. On the other hand, the response interval should be long enough to reduce report volume (and associated costs) and reveal important trends that signal the need for action. Figure 1-7 summarizes the general relationship of information cost and value over time. The most appropriate information interval is therefore a matter which must be determined by each organization. It should also be noted that once the cutoff date for

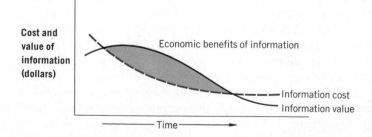

Figure 1-7   Relationship of information cost and value over time

the report period has arrived, further compromise is usually required. Generally speaking, the shorter the delay in getting the information into the hands of the manager, the higher will be the costs involved.

In Chapter 4 we shall look at new computer-based information systems that provide quick-response times to managers. Systems have been developed that give access to records within a fraction of a second after an inquiry has been made. How current this information is depends upon the degree of quickness in updating the records. In some quick-response installations, the information may be updated periodically—e.g., daily or weekly—while in others it may be updated immediately after the completion of a transaction.

Completeness Most managers faced with a decision to make have been frustrated at some time by having supporting information that is accurate, timely—and *incomplete*. A report is complete if it gives the manager all the information he needs to make the decision. Admittedly, this is a rare document. But more complete information can often be provided through the design of systems that do a better job of integrating and consolidating available facts. A dramatic historical example of the consequences of failure to consolidate related pieces of information occurred at Pearl Harbor in 1941. Historians tell us that data available, in bits and pieces and at scattered points, if integrated, would have signaled the danger of a Japanese attack. Better integration of the facts available at scattered points in a business for the purpose of furnishing managers with more complete information is a goal of information systems designers. We shall look at the emphasis now being placed on these *broader systems* in Chapter 4.

Conciseness As we have just seen, information completeness is a desirable characteristic. Many systems have been designed on the assumption that lack of completeness is the most critical deficiency of managerial information. Too often in the past, though, the solution has been to employ an ineffective shotgun approach, peppering the manager with more information than can possibly be used. Important information, along with relatively useless data, is buried in stacks of detailed and unrefined reports. The manager (if he uses the reports at all) is then faced with the problem of extracting those items of information that he needs. Concise information that summarizes (perhaps through the use of tables and charts) the relevant data and that points out areas of exception to normal or planned activities is what is often needed by—but less often supplied to—today's managers.

Relevancy   Relevant information is "need-to-know" information that leads to action. "Nice-to-know" information placed in the hands of a manager who is not in a position to influence the events reported is not relevant information to that particular manager and thus it generally has no dollar value. Likewise, reports that were once valuable but that no longer lead to action are not relevant and should be discontinued. In other words, information is relevant and is worth producing only if it will *"identify and support necessary action by responsible individuals within the organization."*[14]

PRESSURES FOR MANAGEMENT INFORMATION IMPROVEMENT

As a competitive weapon, management information improvement has not normally received primary emphasis in the past. Product and/or service changes and improvements, marketing efforts such as advertising and sales promotion, production economies—all of these areas have usually been given attention before managerial consideration was given to information preparation. However, in recent years managerial awareness has been drawn to the need for information improvement by the following factors:

1. *Increased paperwork volume.* Data processing capability in many firms has been strained by (1) the growth in size and complexity of the firm, (2) the increased requirements for data from external sources such as local, state and federal governmental agencies, and (3) the demand of managers for more information. More than a million new pages of data are generated each minute of the day in our offices—an increase of 300 percent in the last three decades.
2. *Demand for timeliness.* As we have seen, meaningful information is timely information. But with an increase in volume, there is often a reduction in the speed of processing. Managers demand timely information. Unfortunately, although they may receive information about areas of virtual certainty in short order, information that reduces the element of uncertainty is often delayed until such time as it is merely collaborative.
3. *Demand for quality.* Many marketing managers are responsible for supervising the sales activities of a large number of branches scattered throughout the nation. They must have accurate information if they are to control such an effort properly. But if a data processing operation is strained to and beyond the capacity for which it was originally planned (if there was an original plan),

[14]Richard Werling, "Action-Oriented Information Systems," *Datamation,* June, 1967, p. 59.

inaccuracies will begin to appear. Inadequate control will permit inadequate performance. Thus, the marketing manager will logically demand better quality in the information he receives.

4. *Pressure from outside changes.* Rapid changes are taking place in the world socially, economically, and technically. These outside changes will be discussed in some detail in Chapter 3. Such changes, however, have a significant impact on the environment in which businesses must operate, on the planning that managers must do, and on the information that they must have.

5. *Costs.* The increasing costs of clerical labor, materials, and other expenses associated with the data processing operation require eventual managerial attention. Often, when a top executive realizes the magnitude of the office expense, pressure will be exerted to get "more processing for a buck."

Management information can be improved in a variety of ways. Better information may be obtained by using improved manual methods, noncomputer machine methods, computerized techniques, or some combination of any or all of these. This book, however, is primarily concerned with the computer. What type of operations are best suited for computer processing? The following section deals with this question.

CHARACTERISTICS DESIRABLE FOR COMPUTER PROCESSING

A computer is used most efficiently in processing operations that have one or more of the following characteristics:

1. *Large volume of input.* The greater the volume of data that must be processed to produce *needed* information, the more economical computer processing becomes relative to other possible methods.

2. *Repetition of projects.* Because of the expense involved in preparing a task for computer processing, it is frequently most economical to use the computer for repetitive projects.

3. *Desired and necessary greater speed in processing.* The greater the *need* for timely information, the greater will be the value of a computer relative to alternative (and slower) methods.

4. *Desired and necessary greater accuracy.* Computer processing will be quite accurate if the task to be performed has been properly prepared.

5. *Processing complexities that require electronic help.* In some situations when large numbers of interacting variables are present, there is *no* alternative to the computer. For example, decision

making with complex managerial tools[15] such as linear programming and business simulation generally requires the use of a computer. And certainly it is hard to conceive of anything but a computer being used to process mission control information for a spacecraft while it is in flight. Possibly by now the reader has compared the characteristics outlined in this section with the factors (described in the previous section) that have caused managers to seek improved management information. Business paperwork volume is increasing, and the computer thrives on volume; speed in processing is needed, and the computer is fast. There is little wonder, then, that computers have been chosen for use by many businesses. The objectives sought by businesses can often be achieved with a computer.

ECONOMIC OBJECTIVES AND BENEFITS

In our economy, a primary objective of business is to earn a sufficient profit in the long run. Profit may be defined as the difference between revenue and expenses (profit = revenue − expenses). A convenient way of considering the economic objectives and benefits of computers is to examine the effects of computer utilization on profit.

Computer usage may enhance the profit picture of the firm by *cost displacement, operational improvement,* or *revenue improvement.* The objectives of most firms in using computers can be attributed to one or more of these three approaches.

Cost Displacement

Compared to other processing methods, the use of computers may make it possible for certain administrative costs to be reduced while the level of business activity remains stable. Of course, when computers are substituted for other methods mainly to reduce expenses, it is expected that the costs of computer hardware, software, and personnel will be less than the costs of precomputer labor and equipment.

Figure 1-8 gives a general idea of the cost relationships existing between computer processing methods and alternative methods.[16] Fixed costs associated with a computer installation are relatively high; therefore, when small-volume applications are all that must be processed, the total cost for computer processing may exceed other methods. Point A shows the breakeven total cost position between

[15]These tools will be discussed in Chapter 13.
[16]Figures 1-8 and 1-9 are adapted from Donald H. Sanders, *Introducing Computers to Small Business,* Data Processing Management Association, Park Ridge, Ill., 1966, pp. 60–61.

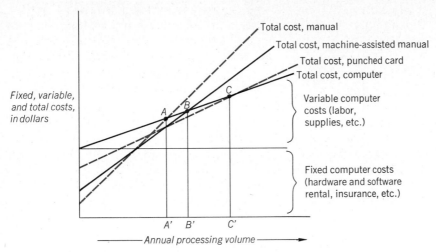

Fixed, variable, and total costs, in dollars

Total cost, manual
Total cost, machine-assisted manual
Total cost, punched card
Total cost, computer

Variable computer costs (labor, supplies, etc.)

Fixed computer costs (hardware and software rental, insurance, etc.)

A' B'   C'

—— Annual processing volume ——→

Figure 1-8   Total cost relationships

manual and computer processing at a volume of A'. When volume is less than A', it would be more economical to use manual methods than a computer. Points B and C show other breakeven positions. Can you explain the significance of volumes B' and C'?

A comparison of cost relationships between alternative processing methods can also be made on the basis of the average cost required to process a typical document or record. Figure 1-9 shows average cost curves for different processing techniques. Points, A, B, and C are the breakeven points referred to in Fig. 1-8. Unfortunately for information systems planners, the cost curves in Fig. 1-8 and 1-9 do not remain constant. Each increase in clerical labor rates and the cost of clerical office supplies, for example, shifts the manual method

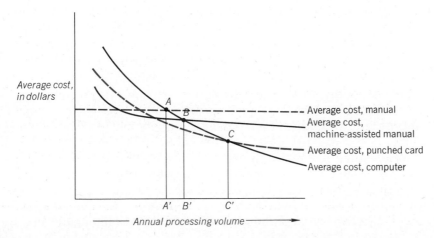

Average cost, in dollars

Average cost, manual
Average cost, machine-assisted manual
Average cost, punched card
Average cost, computer

A' B'   C'

—— Annual processing volume ——→

Figure 1-9   Average cost relationships

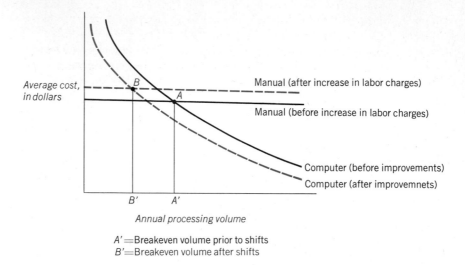

Average cost, in dollars

Manual (after increase in labor charges)

Manual (before increase in labor charges)

Computer (before improvements)

Computer (after improvemnets)

Annual processing volume

A'=Breakeven volume prior to shifts
B'=Breakeven volume after shifts

Figure 1-10

curves, while each new hardware innovation may serve to reduce computer costs and thus shift the computer curve. Figure 1-10 illustrates the effects these shifts can have on volume breakeven points.

Operational Improvements

The computer may provide information that will lead to some improvements in reaction time and operating efficiency. The cost of goods sold may be reduced, and inventory carrying charges may be cut without in any way affecting the quality of products or services offered to customers.

Revenue Improvement

Another way the profit outlook may be improved is to apply the computer in such a way that revenue increases at a faster rate than expenses. This general objective may be achieved by (1) having faster, more complete, and more accurate dealings with present customers, (2) making it possible (with increased processing capacity) to expand marketing efforts to include new customers, and (3) providing managers with more timely, more comprehensive, and more accurate information with which to improve their operating and control decisions.

Computer benefits are sometimes classified as *tangible* (a dollar-and-cents value can be assigned) or *intangible* (not subject to precise quantitative measurement). Cost displacement and operational improvement goals should lead to tangible benefits. Revenue improvement objectives often produce benefits of a real but intangible nature.

It is quite possible, of course, for a firm to seek and receive both tangible and intangible benefits from its computer.

The objectives originally sought by managers when a computer is ordered and the benefits that are ultimately received may not be the same. Some goals may not be achieved, while some unexpected benefits may appear.

Future managers must prepare for a successful working relationship with computerized information processing. The objective of this text is to provide an orientation to computers and their impact on the business community.

SUMMARY

Management information is relevant knowledge produced as output of data processing operations. Although data are not, strictly speaking, information, they are the input from which information is produced. Data are received from internal and external sources and are needed in the operation of businesses of all sizes, from the corner grocery to the giant corporation. The data processing operation, in its entirety, requires nine steps; however, some steps may be omitted in specific situations. Manual methods, manual with machine assistance, electromechanical punched card methods, and computer methods may be used to perform the steps in the data processing operation.

Information is needed by managers to plan, organize, staff, and control business activities. But it is impossible to state specifically what information a manager will need because managers differ in the ways they view information and in their analytical approaches in using it. Furthermore, because of the types of decisions they must make, managers at the top and lower managerial levels generally utilize time differently, tend to need different degrees of information summarization, and are inclined to use information obtained from different sources.

Regardless of the nature of the information needed, that information should possess the characteristics of accuracy, timeliness, completeness, conciseness, and relevancy. In recent years, managerial awareness has been drawn to the need for information improvement by reports lacking one or more of these characteristics and by increased paperwork volume, rising costs, and pressures from outside changes. Fortunately, computers thrive on repetitive large-volume processing tasks, are fast and accurate, and can do jobs that could not otherwise be attempted.

Business computer goals generally center around the means for profit improvement. Computer usage may provide economic benefits of a tangible and intangible nature by making possible cost displacement, operational improvement, and revenue improvement. Of course, such benefits can brighten the profit picture. Economic gains, however, are not received automatically when the computer is installed, as we shall see in later chapters.

DISCUSSION QUESTIONS

1. Why may there be lack of communication between computer specialists and business managers?
2. (a) What is management information?
   (b) What is the difference between data and information?
   (c) Compare the manufacturing process with the information-producing process.
3. Identify and explain the sources of business data.
4. (a) How does data processing affect the operations of a business?
   (b) Identify and explain the basic data processing steps.
   (c) What processing methods may be used to perform these steps?
5. "Information is the cement that holds together any organization." Explain this sentence.
6. "Beyond certain basic informational requirements, the question of what information is needed by managers can only be answered in broad general terms." Discuss this statement.
7. (a) Why does the organizational level of the managerial job affect the information needed?
   (b) How do informational needs differ?
8. Identify and discuss the desired properties of management information.
9. What factors have focused attention on the need for management information improvement in recent years?
10. Identify and explain the characteristics desirable for computer processing.
11. "The total cost for computer processing may exceed other methods when the processing volume is small." Discuss this statement.
12. Explain how computer acquisition may improve a firm's profit picture.
13. "Revenue improvement goals often produce benefits of an intangible nature." Explain this sentence.

Ackoff, Russell L.: "Management Misinformation Systems," *Management Science* (Application Ser.), December, 1967, pp. B147–B156.

Nichols, Gerald E.: "On the Nature of Management Information," *Management Accounting,* April, 1969, pp. 9–13ff.

Norton, John H.: "Information Systems: Some Basic Considerations," *Management Review,* September, 1969, pp. 2–8.

The Data
Processing
Evolution

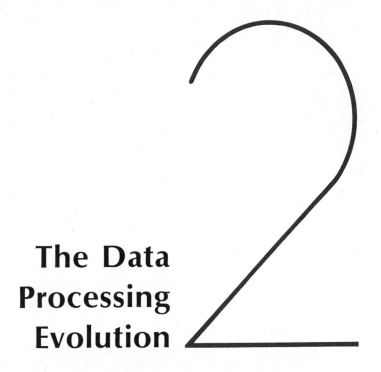

In this chapter we shall discuss the data processing *evolution,* while in Chapters 3 and 4 we shall be concerned with a survey of the information processing *revolution.* It is, of course, not change or the absence of change that distinguishes evolution from revolution, for we are interested in the process of change in all of these chapters. Rather, the distinction we are making is in the rapidity with which change occurs. In biology, *evolution* implies gradual change over long periods of time, and it is in this gradual change context that we are using the term. *Revolution,* on the other hand, implies significant change of a much swifter nature. Thus, this chapter deals with a brief survey of data processing techniques and equipment from earliest times to about 1964. Chapters 3 and 4 present an overview of some of the more significant developments occurring since 1964.

The following discussion of the evolution of data processing is organized around the processing methods identified in the last chapter;[1] i.e., we shall consider developments in (1) *manual,* (2) *machine-assisted manual,* (3) *electromechanical punched card,* and (4) *computer* methods of data processing.

THE MANUAL STAGE

For centuries, man lived on earth without keeping records. But as social organizations such as tribes began to form, it became necessary for man to adjust. The complexities of tribal life required man to remember more details. Methods of counting, based on the biological fact that man has fingers, were thus developed. However, the limited number of digits combined with the need to remember more facts posed problems. For example, if a shepherd were tending a large tribal flock and if he had a short memory, how was he to keep control of his inventory? Problems bring solutions, and the shepherd's solution might have been to let a stone, a stick, a scratch on a rock, or a knot in a string represent each sheep in the flock.

As tribes grew into nations, trade and commerce developed. Stones and sticks, however, were not satisfactory for early traders. In 3500 B.C., the ancient Babylonian merchants were keeping records on clay tablets. At about the same time (give or take a few centuries) the ancient Egyptians made a great improvement in record keeping possible when they developed *papyrus* (the forerunner of paper) and a sharp-pointed pen called a *calmus.*

An early manual calculating device was the *abacus,* which, although over 2,000 years old, may still be the most widely used calculator in the world. Its origin is unknown; indeed, it may have originated in several places, for it has appeared with different names throughout many parts of the world. Figure 2-1 represents an abacus of the type used in the Orient since the thirteenth century. Skilled abacus operators have won speed races in competition with clerks using desk calculators.

Manual record-keeping techniques continued to develop through the centuries, with such innovations as record audits (the Greeks), banking systems and budgets (the Romans), and double-entry bookkeeping (the Italians in Florence, Genoa, and Venice). In the United States, in the twenty years following the Civil War, the main tools of data processing were pencils, pens, rulers, work sheets (for classifying, calculating, and summarizing), journals (for storing), and ledgers (for storing and communicating). The data processor was (or so the cartoons and literature of the time would have us believe) a clerk of

---

[1]See Fig. 1-2, page 9.

*Figure 2-1   An abacus
(courtesy IBM Corporation
Antique Calculator
Collection)*

unenviable status, toiling through the day in a dim corner, wearing an eyeshade, and sitting on a tall stool. Less than 1 percent of the processing work was machine aided.

The volume of business and government processing during this period was expanding rapidly, and, as might be expected, such complete reliance upon manual methods resulted in information that was relatively inaccurate and often late. To the consternation of the Census Bureau, for example, the 1880 census was not finished until it was almost time to begin the 1890 count! In spite of accuracy and timeliness limitations, however, manual processing methods have the following *advantages:* (1) information is in a humanly readable form; (2) changes and corrections are easily accomplished; (3) no minimum economic processing volume is generally required; and (4) manual methods are easily adapted to changing conditions.

The evolution of machine-assisted manual processing methods has gone through several stages. The first stage was the improvement in performance of a *single* processing step through the use of mechanical devices. The second, and more advanced, stage was the development of machines that could *combine* certain steps in a single operation. A third stage is emerging from these mechanical developments, which combines computer or electronic features with earlier mechanical developments. This third stage tends to defy classification—the machines are not strictly mechanical nor are they strictly computers.

**MACHINE-ASSISTED
MANUAL DEVELOPMENT**

The First Stage

The typewriter is a *recording* aid that was first introduced around the turn of the last century and that quickly proved to be an important office asset. Writing speeds were doubled, and legibility was improved.

Mechanical *calculating* aids have a long history. In 1642, in Paris, a brilliant young (eighteen year old) Frenchman named Blaise Pascal decided to help ease the computation load of his father, who was Superintendent of Taxes. Pascal's effort resulted in the world's first mechanical adding machine (Fig. 2-2). Gears with one tooth for each digit from 0 to 9 were connected in a series. When one gear was rotated past the tooth representing the 9 digit, the next gear to the left would be advanced by one tooth or digit. The result was a machine that was capable of *carrying*. Although this principle is used today in many mechanical office machines, it was not until well into the 1800s that the "grandfather" of present-day desk calculators was developed.

In the late 1800s and early 1900s, many machines to aid in the calculating step were developed and introduced to businesses. These strictly mechanical machines were later replaced by motor-driven calculators. Recently, however, developments in computer technology have made it possible to produce totally electronic desk calculators (see Fig. 2-3) that weigh only a few pounds. Although no programming is required, these new calculators have, in common with computers, integrated circuits and built-in storage elements that can be used to accumulate totals or store constants or intermediate results for later recall.

The Second Stage

Machines that calculate and print the results were first produced around 1890. They combine calculating and recording steps and produce a printed tape record suitable for storing data.

After World War I, specialized accounting machines first appeared.

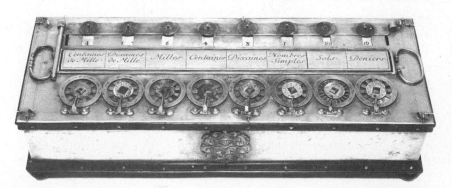

Figure 2-2 Pascal's adding machine (courtesy IBM Corporation)

Figure 2-3   Electronic calculator (courtesy NCR)

These machines are designed for special purposes, e.g., billing, retail sales, payroll, and they also enable an operator to combine steps. They often contain several adding *registers* or *counters* to permit the accumulation of totals for different classifications. For example, a typical supermarket accounting machine is the cash register, which will have separate registers to sort and total (summarize) the day's sales of meats, produce, and groceries. Figure 2-4 shows two of the types of modern accounting machines available.

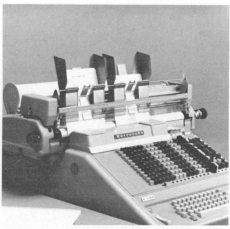

Figure 2-4(a)   Cash register (courtesy NCR), (b) electronic accounting machine (courtesy Burroughs Corporation)

(a)   (b)

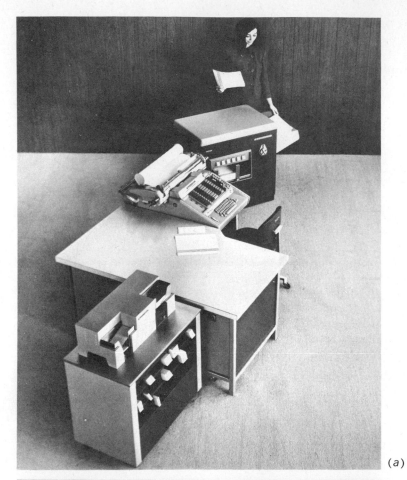

(a)

(b)

Figure 2-5(a)   Burroughs E4000 electronic accounting machine (courtesy Burroughs Corporation), (b) NCR 400 electronic accounting machine (courtesy NCR)

Many of the business machines that started as pieces of mechanical equipment are now powered by electric motors and thus might be classed as electromechanical devices. Yet most of them merely use electricity to turn gears and other mechanical parts, and all of them require manual keyboards to enter the data for processing.

Office equipment manufacturers, however, have begun to take steps to ensure that accounting machines are not made obsolete by the computer. Features of accounting machines are being combined with features taken from punch card equipment and from computers to create an entirely new class of desk-size hardware—not quite as sophisticated, perhaps, as computers, but not traditional accounting or punch card machines either. These new devices (see Fig. 2-5) are making it difficult to distinguish between computer and noncomputer systems.

When compared with the manual processing of the late 1800s, machine-assisted manual methods have the advantages of greater speed and accuracy. However, a higher processing volume is generally required to justify equipment costs, there is some reduction in the flexibility of the processing techniques, and it is relatively more difficult to (1) correct or change data once it has entered the processing system and (2) implement changes in machine-assisted procedures.

Tradeoffs between accuracy and timeliness, on the one hand, and procedural flexibility, on the other, are not uncommon. Figure 2-6 summarizes the place in the processing spectrum of the equipment just surveyed. As processing volume advances up the scale from low to high levels, the level of equipment sophistication increases,[2] greater accuracy and faster processing speeds may be expected, but the more rigorously defined and standardized the procedures are likely to become.

Punched card methods have been in *widespread* business use only since the 1930s, but the history of the punched card dates back to about the end of the American Revolution when a French weaver named Jacquard used them to control his looms.

Although punched cards continued to be used in process control,

ELECTROMECHANICAL PUNCHED CARD DEVELOPMENT

History

[2]Figure 2-6 deals in generalizations. Possibly an electronics engineer would consider a recently developed electronic accounting machine technically more "sophisticated" than punched card equipment; perhaps one firm will do a larger volume of processing with electronic accounting machines than will others with punched card equipment or a minicomputer. Alas, the safe generalizations of yesterday become the *faux pas* of tomorrow because of the ingenious application of computer hardware elements to "lesser" office machines.

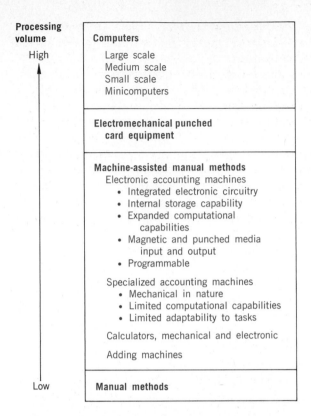

Processing volume

High

Computers

  Large scale
  Medium scale
  Small scale
  Minicomputers

**Electromechanical punched
card equipment**

Machine-assisted manual methods
Electronic accounting machines
- Integrated electronic circuitry
- Internal storage capability
- Expanded computational
  capabilities
- Magnetic and punched media
  input and output
- Programmable

Specialized accounting machines
- Mechanical in nature
- Limited computational capabilities
- Limited adaptability to tasks

Calculators, mechanical and electronic

Adding machines

Low

Manual methods

Figure 2-6

it was not until the use of manual methods resulted in the problem of completing the 1880 census count that they began to be considered as a medium for data processing. The inventor of modern punched card techniques was Dr. Herman Hollerith, a statistician. He was hired by the Census Bureau as a special agent to help find a solution to the census problem. In 1887, Hollerith developed his machine-readable card concept and designed a device known as the *"census machine,"* which could handle 50 to 80 cards per minute. Tabulating time with Hollerith's methods was only one-eighth of that previously required, and so his techniques were adopted for use in the 1890 count. Although population had increased from 50 to 63 million people in the decade after 1880, the 1890 count was completed in less than three years. (Of course, this would be considered intolerably slow by today's standards,[3] but the alternative in 1890 would have been to continue the count beyond 1900 and violate the Consti-

[3]The 1950 census, using punched card equipment, took about two years to produce; the 1970 census yielded figures in a few months.

tutional provision that congressional seats be reapportioned every ten years on the basis of census data.) Figure 2-7 shows an early card sorter developed by Dr. Hollerith.

Following the 1890 census, Hollerith converted his equipment to business use and set up freight statistics systems for two railroads. In 1896, he founded the Tabulating Machine Company to make and sell his invention. Later, this firm merged with others to form what is now known as International Business Machines Corporation (IBM).

By the time it became necessary to begin planning for the 1910 census, it also became obvious to officials that additional equipment would be required. James Powers was hired by the Census Bureau. He designed some new punched card machines with desirable characteristics, and they were used in the 1910 count. The next year Powers

Figure 2-7 The vertical sorter developed by Dr. Herman Hollerith (courtesy IBM Corporation)

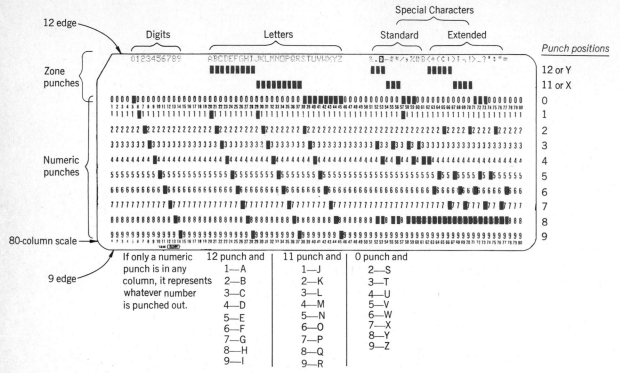

Figure 2-8 The punched card and the Hollerith code

If only a numeric punch is in any column, it represents whatever number is punched out.	12 punch and	11 punch and	0 punch and
	1—A	1—J	2—S
	2—B	2—K	3—T
	3—C	3—L	4—U
	4—D	4—M	5—V
	5—E	5—N	6—W
	6—F	6—O	7—X
	7—G	7—P	8—Y
	8—H	8—Q	9—Z
	9—I	9—R	

formed the Powers Accounting Machine Company, which was later merged into the Remington Rand Corporation.[4]

Punched Cards and Codes

The 80-column card Early Hollerith cards measured 3 by 5 inches; the typical 80-column punched card used in business today measures $7\frac{3}{8}$ inches long by $3\frac{1}{4}$ inches wide. Special card paper stock is used. One corner is usually trimmed to help maintain proper positioning during processing (see Fig. 2-8).

The card is divided, from left to right, into 80 consecutively numbered vertical *columns*. These columns, in turn, have 12 horizontal positions, or *rows*. By appropriate coding, each column can record one character of information, i.e., a numerical digit, a letter, or a special character. Columns 5 to 14 in Fig. 2-8 illustrate the digit punches. Notice that only a *single* hole is punched in each column to record the desired *numeral*.

[4]Still later, Remington Rand and The Sperry Corporation merged to form Sperry Rand.

When *letters* of the alphabet are recorded, *two* holes must be punched. Along the top of the card are three *zone* punching positions—the 0 row and the blank area at the top of the card, which is designated as punching positions 11 and 12 (or as areas X and Y). A logical combination of zone and digit punches is required for letters in the Hollerith code. For example, letters A to I are coded by using a 12-zone punch and digit punches 1 to 9. Special characters are coded by using one, two, or three holes. Figure 2-8 shows special characters classified into *standard* and *extended* categories. The coding of the characters in the extended category were added by IBM for use with their System/360 family of computers.

IBM's 96-column card　In July, 1969, IBM announced the System/3 (see Fig. 2-9), a small business computer that features a new punched card. The new 96-column card shown in Fig. 2-10 is only one-third the size of the traditional 80-column card just described. The 96 columns are separated into three sections (columns 1 to 32 are in the upper section, columns 33 to 64 are in the middle, and columns 65 to 96 are in the lower section). The upper third of the card contains 128 positions for the printing of characters.

Differences other than mere size and the number and arrangement of columns exist between 80- and 96-column cards. One obvious difference is that the holes are round rather than rectangular; another

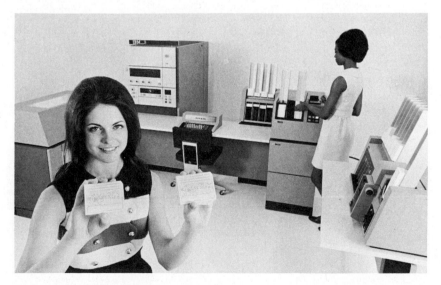

*Figure 2-9　IBM System/3
(courtesy IBM Corporation)*

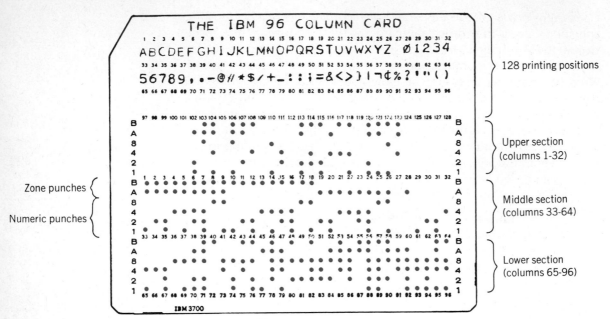

Figure 2-10　IBM 96-column card (courtesy IBM Corporation)

is that 96 columns will hold 20 percent more data than 80 columns. A more significant difference is in the coding methods employed. The rows of the small card are divided into A and B zone positions and 1, 2, 4, and 8 numeric positions.[5] Columns 60 to 69 in Fig. 2-10 illustrate the coding of digits. The numeral 1 is represented by a single hole punched in the 1 row of column 61. Column 62 codes the numeral 2. But in columns 63, 65, 66, 67, and 69, the numerals are represented by the *sum* of the rows punched; e.g., in column 67 the digit 7 is represented by holes punched in the 4, 2, and 1 rows.

Alphabetic characters are represented by combinations of holes punched in the zone and numeric rows. The nine letters A to I, for example, are coded by holes punched in the A and B rows plus the combination of holes used to represent the numerals 1 to 9. To illustrate, the seventh letter G is coded by holes in the A and B zone positions plus the combination of holes in rows 1, 2, and 4, which add to seven (see column 39 in Fig. 2-10). The special characters represented in columns 70 to 96 are coded by various combinations of holes punched in the six rows.

[5]We shall have more to say in Chapter 8 about this *binary coded decimal* (BCD) method of data representation.

Card columns are laid out in consecutive groups called *fields* for specific business purposes. Fields are carefully planned by the application designer and may be of any width from 1 column to 80.

Fields

Figure 2-11 shows a customer invoice—a detailed description of what has been shipped—which serves as the source document for the sales accounting card. The card is divided into 11 fields, which contain *reference* data (customer name and number, and invoice date and number), *classification* data (location of sale, trade classification, sales branch, and salesman number), and *quantitative* data used in calculations (quantity sold of a particular item and the item amount).

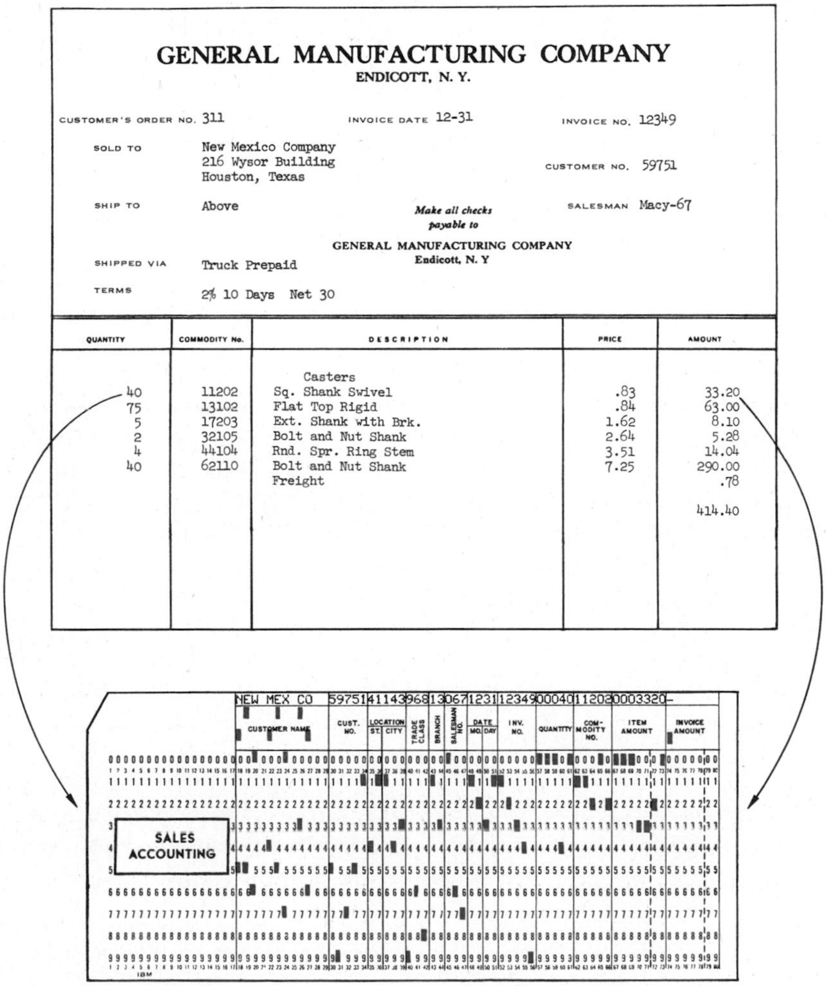

Figure 2-11 Data fields
(courtesy IBM Corporation)

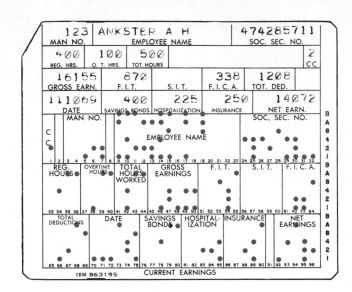

Figure 2-12   Data fields
(courtesy IBM Corporation)

The card contains (1) the descriptive data at the top of the invoice and (2) the data on the first line of the body of the invoice. The *item amount* field is seven columns wide, which means that the maximum amount that can be recorded is $99,999.99 (columns are not used to punch the dollar sign, comma, and decimal point). The card in Fig. 2-11 is often classified as a *detail* card. In preparing the five *additional* detail cards that would be required to capture the invoice data, columns 18 to 56 would be automatically duplicated and columns 74 to 80 would perhaps be punched in the last card. In subsequent processing of the detail cards, *summary* cards may be automatically produced, which will contain such information as total sales made to the particular customer and total sales credited to the salesman and sales branch during a specified time period.

Figure 2-12 shows a 96-column payroll record card with several fields. Employee Ankster has a gross pay of $161.55 for working 50.0 hours. After tax deductions and other assessments, his net pay is $140.72 for the period.[6]

The Equipment

A punched card is often referred to as a *unit of record* because data recorded in most cards deal with only one business transaction. Once the data are punched, the card may be combined with many other

---

[6]Before leaving this subject, it should be noted that judgment and compromises are required in determining field width. The 15-column employee-name field in Fig. 2-12 will be satisfactory in most cases—until the personnel department hires Agamemnon Southwesterfield.

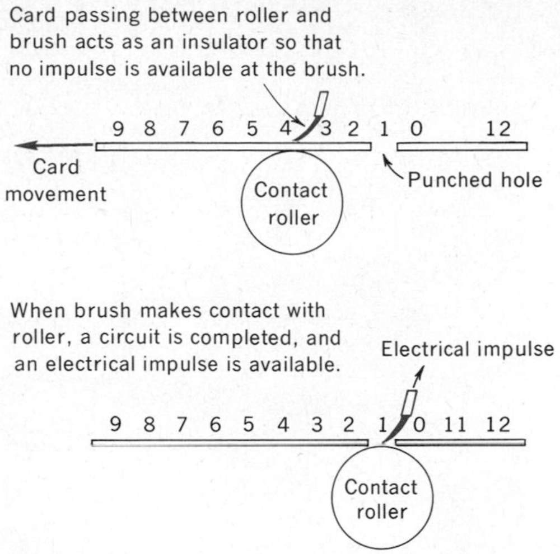

Card passing between roller and
brush acts as an insulator so that
no impulse is available at the brush.

9 8 7 6 5 4 3 2 1 0   12

Card
movement

Contact
roller

Punched hole

When brush makes contact with
roller, a circuit is completed, and
an electrical impulse is available.

Electrical impulse

9 8 7 6 5 4 3 2 1 0 11 12

Contact
roller

Figure 2-13 (Courtesy IBM Corporation)

different cards containing related data to produce a wide variety of reports. The card in Fig. 2-11, for example, deals only with the first invoice transaction, but this card may be used in (1) sales analyses to determine profitability of territories, accounts, and products, (2) calculations of bonuses and commissions for salesmen, and (3) billing and accounts-receivable operations.

The remainder of this section will be devoted to a brief survey of punched card (or *unit record*) machines which perform the steps in the data processing operation. In these devices, the card passes through a *reading* station. This station is equipped with special brushes and a contact roller to convert the holes in a card into electric impulses (see Fig. 2-13). The electric pulses are then processed by the particular machine to obtain the desired output.

Recording devices The most common way of recording data in punched card form is through the use of a keypunch or card punch machine (see Fig. 2-14). When a key is depressed, the correct combination of holes is produced in the card. Keypunching is similar, in many ways, to typing with an electric typewriter. The path followed by cards through the keypunch may be summarized as follows.[7]

1. Blank cards are loaded into the *card hopper* at the upper right of the machine.

[7]Since students may be expected to do some punching of *computer* program and/or data cards, familiarity with keypunch operation is needed.

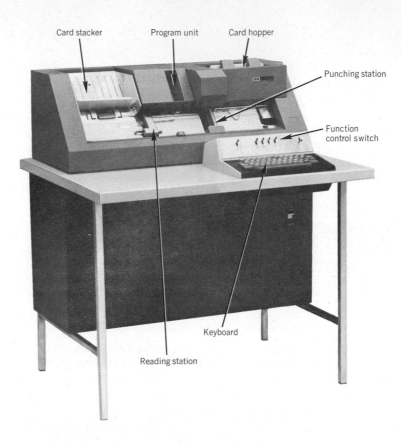

Card stacker   Program unit   Card hopper

Punching station

Function
control switch

Keyboard

Reading station

*Figure 2-14   Model 29
keypunch* (*courtesy IBM
Corporation*)

2. By depressing the FEED key, the operator moves a card from the hopper to the entrance to the *punching station*. Keying the FEED button a second time will drop a second card and properly align the first card at the punching station. (If only a single card is to be punched, depressing the REGister key will align the card under the punches.)

3. The punching station, as might be expected, has 12 blades (one for each card row), which are positioned over a card column. As a key is depressed during punching, one or a combination of blades punches the Hollerith code in the column aligned under the punching station.

4. After the punching has been completed and after column 80 has passed the punching station, the first card is released to the *reading station,* the second card is positioned at the punching station, and an AUTO FEED provision may be used to automatically drop a third from the card hopper.

5. The first and second cards move together through the reading and

punching stations; i.e., as columns 1, 2, 3, etc., of the first card pass under the reading station, the *same columns* of the second card are being positioned under the punching station. This synchronization feature permits duplication of data in common fields into the second card. For example, if the first card punched was the card in Fig. 2-11, the data in columns 18 to 56 would also be needed in the second card. By depressing a DUPlicate key, the data sensed in columns 18 to 56 at the reading station would be automatically reproduced in the same columns of the second card.[8] The operator would then key in the different invoice data in the second card.

6. When the first card is released from the reading station, it moves to the *card stacker* at the upper left of the machine, the second card moves to the reading station, etc.

To check keypunching accuracy, *verifiers* are used. The verifier is similar to the keypunch (see Fig. 2-15); but instead of punching holes, it merely senses whether or not the holes in the card being tested correspond with the key being depressed.

[8]When a considerable amount of repetition is called for, the keypunch has a program control device, which utilizes a program card and a control drum to automatically perform the repetitive operations.

Figure 2-15   Model 59 verifier (courtesy IBM Corporation)

In addition to mechanical keypunching, data may be recorded on cards through the use of portable manual punches. Data may also be recorded on cards *automatically*. For example, a master card may be reproduced any desired number of times (*gangpunching*); a group of *different* cards may be automatically duplicated (*reproducing*); cards marked with a special graphite pencil in designated places can be punched automatically (*mark sensing*); and cards may be produced automatically as by-products of other machine operations and as outputs of other activities.

Sorting and classifying devices   Arranging the cards according to some desired order or sequence is the function of the *sorter* (Fig. 2-16). The 13 pockets in the sorter correspond to the 12 rows in the card (0 to 9, 11, and 12) and a thirteenth or *reject* pocket for cards that do not belong in any other pocket (e.g., because there is no hole in the column). Sorting (which generally moves from the right column to the left column of the data field) is done *one* column at a time in each sorting *pass*. Thus, the sorting procedure in a data field of five digits would take five passes before the cards would be in the proper numerical *sequence*.

In addition to numerical and alphabetical sequencing, the sorter is used to *group* like fields together. Sales to customers in a particular geographic region, for example, might be grouped for marketing analyses. Or, a sorter can be used to *select* from a card file the card records of sales made to a particular customer. Various sorters can

*Figure 2-16   The sorter
(courtesy IBM Corporation)*

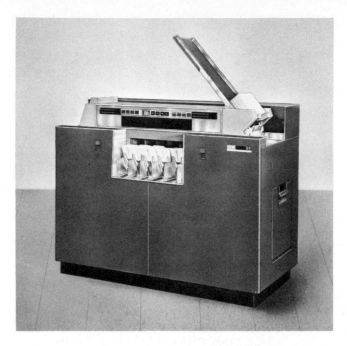

Figure 2-17   Model 88 collator (courtesy IBM Corporation)

operate during a pass at speeds ranging from 450 to 2,000 cards per minute.

The *collator* (Fig. 2-17) is a machine that can combine two decks of sequenced cards into a single sequenced deck (*merging*). It can also compare agreement between two sets of cards without combining them (*matching*). Other manipulations are possible with two decks of sequenced cards. The collator can check a tray of cards to determine correct ascending or descending order. After the arrangement of the cards in the proper order, they are usually then taken to a machine that can perform calculations on the data.

Calculating and summarizing devices   As is the case with many punched card machines, the *calculator* or *calculating punch* (Fig. 2-18) is directed in its operation by an externally wired control panel (Fig. 2-19). It reads data from input cards, performs (according to the wiring arrangements in the control panel) the arithmetic operations of addition, subtraction, multiplication, and division, and punches the results into (1) the input card that supplied the data or (2) a following card.

The *accounting machine* or *tabulator* (Fig. 2-20) is used to summarize data from input cards and print the desired reports. It can add and subtract during summarization and has several registers or counters for this purpose.

*Figure 2-18   Model 609
calculator (courtesy IBM
Corporation)*

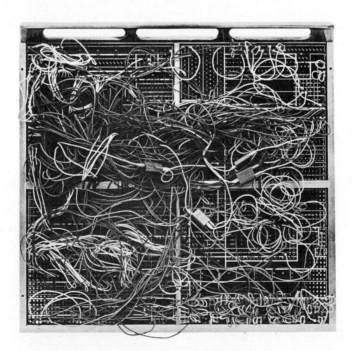

*Figure 2-19   Externally
wired control panel
(courtesy IBM Corporation)*

Figure 2-20   Model 407 accounting machine (courtesy IBM Corporation)

Reproducing and communicating devices   The *reproducer* (Fig. 2-21) is used to *duplicate* or reproduce the data found in a large number of cards. The cards to be duplicated are placed in a reading unit hopper; blank cards are placed in the input hopper of the punching unit. At speeds up to 100 cards per minute, the reproducer carries

Figure 2-21   Model 519 reproducer (courtesy IBM Corporation)

out the process of duplicating in the blank cards the required data sensed by the reading unit. The reproducer is also used for gang-punching, i.e., copying data from a master card into any desired number of detail cards, and for punching the holes in mark-sensed cards. Finally, the reproducer may be connected to the accounting machine to punch accumulated *summary* information into cards. For example, the customer number, invoice number, and invoice total might be punched into a summary card as the accounting machine prepared the invoice.

If it is necessary to use the card for visual reference, the *interpreter* is needed to translate the machine code into humanly readable form. The machine interprets the data represented by the holes in a card and then prints the data directly on the card. The printing order need not follow the order in which the holes appear in the card—any desired printing sequence may be used. Generally, the data are printed at the top of the card.

From this very brief survey of punched card data processing, it is obvious that significant improvement was possible over manual methods previously used. Gains in speed and accuracy were made. Punch card equipment proved effective in performing many of the individual steps necessary, e.g., sorting, calculating, and summarizing. But it is still necessary to have people handle trays of cards between each step. Separate machines must be fed, started, and stopped. This *limited intercommunication* between processing stages requiring manual intervention is a major disadvantage. With the computer this disadvantage is eliminated; no manual interference between data input and information output is required. What sets the computer apart from any other type of data processing machine is the concept of storing, within the machine itself, alterable instructions that will direct the machine to perform automatically the necessary processing steps. Let us now, in the remainder of this chapter, look at the history and development of the computer.

COMPUTER DEVELOPMENT

History

The history of computer development, like any history, may be divided into arbitrary time periods. For our purposes we shall use four periods; (1) Ancient History (1833–1937); (2) the Middle Ages (1937–1954); (3) the Victorian Period (1954–1964); and (4) the Recent Period (1964–present). The Recent Period will be discussed in Chapters 3 and 4.

Ancient History (1833–1937)   In 1833, Charles Babbage, Lucasian Professor of Mathematics at Cambridge University in England, proposed a machine, which he named the *analytical engine*. Babbage's dream—to many of his contemporaries it was "Babbage's folly"—would have incorporated a punched card input, a memory unit, or *store,* an arithmetic unit, or *mill,* automatic printout, sequential program control, and 20-place accuracy. In short, Babbage had designed a machine that was a prototype computer and that was a hundred years ahead of its time. Although his ideas were beyond the technical capabilities (and the human imagination) of the day, he continued to spend much of his time (and £17,000 of Her Majesty's funds) working on the analytical engine until his death in 1871. Little additional progress was made until 1937.

Babbage was a very colorful and eccentric individual who sought to analyze and then alleviate the "stupidities" of his day. His work was interrupted by feuds with organ grinders, who disturbed his privacy, and by disputes with neighborhood children, who undoubtedly enjoyed annoying him. His life makes for very interesting reading.[9]

The Middle Ages (1937–1954) The twenty years between 1937 and 1957 produced the following important events:

1. The first large-scale *electromechanical* computer was built (1944).
2. The first *electronic* computer was completed (1946).
3. A basic philosophy of computer design was formulated (1946).
4. The first *stored program electronic* computer was finished (1949).
5. The first computer acquired for business data processing was installed (1954).
6. The competitive structure of an industry was established (1950–1957).

Beginning in 1937, Harvard professor Howard Aiken set out to build an automatic calculating machine that would combine established technology with the punched cards of Hollerith and Powers. With the help of graduate students and IBM engineers, the project was completed in 1944. The completed device was known as the Mark I digital computer. (A *digital* computer is one that essentially does counting operations.) Internal operations were controlled automatically with electromagnetic relays; arithmetic counters were mechanical. The Mark I was thus not an *electronic* computer but was rather an *electromechanical* one. In many respects the Mark I was the

---

[9]He was also something of a literary critic. In "The Vision of Sin," Tennyson wrote: "Every moment dies a man/Every moment one is born." Babbage wrote Tennyson and pointed out to the poet that since the population of the world was increasing, it would be more accurate to have the verse read: "Every moment dies a man, Every moment one and one-sixteenth is born." What he lacked in aesthetic taste he compensated for with mathematical precision!

realization of Babbage's dream. However, the Mark I was nearly completed before Aiken became aware of Babbage's work—an example of a breakdown in information retrieval. Appropriately, this "medieval" machine is now on display at Harvard University.

The first *electronic* digital computer was created as a secret wartime project between 1939 and 1946 at the University of Pennsylvania's Moore School of Electrical Engineering. The team of John W. Mauchly and J. Presper Eckert, Jr., was responsible for its construction. Vacuum tubes (19,000 of them!) were used in place of relays. The ENIAC (Electronic Numerical Integrator And Calculator), as it was called, weighed about 30 tons, took up about 1,500 square feet of floor space, and was built for the U.S. Army for the purpose of calculating artillery trajectory tables. ENIAC could do in one day what a manual operation would require 300 days to perform; it could do 300 multiplications in one second while the fastest electromechanical devices of the day could perform only one multiplication per second.[10] Instructions to ENIAC were fed through externally located plugboards and switches. In 1956, ENIAC was placed in the Smithsonian Institution.

In 1946, in collaboration with H. H. Goldstine and A. W. Burks, John von Neumann, a mathematical genius and member of the Institute for Advanced Study in Princeton, New Jersey, suggested in a paper that (1) *binary* numbering systems be used in building computers and (2) computer *instructions* as well as the *data* being manipulated could be stored internally in the machine. These suggestions became a basic part of the philosophy of computer design. The binary numbering system is represented by only two digits (0 and 1) rather than the 10 digits (0 to 9) of the familiar decimal system. Since electronic components are typically in one of two conditions (on or off, conducting or not conducting, magnetized or not magnetized), the binary concept facilitated equipment design. A more thorough discussion of the binary concept will be left to a later chapter. In the mid-1940s, von Neumann demonstrated how computer instructions could be coded as numbers and thus stored internally in the machine along with the data.

These design considerations came too late to be incorporated in ENIAC, but with the aid of these new concepts, Mauchly, Eckert, and others at the University of Pennsylvania set out to construct a machine with a *stored program,* i.e., with the instructions for operation stored

[10]William Shanks, an Englishman, spent twenty years of his life computing π to 707 decimal places. In 1949, ENIAC computed π to 2,000 places in just over seventy hours and showed that Shanks had made an error in the 528th decimal place. Fortunately, Shanks was spared the knowledge that he had been both slow and inaccurate, for he preceded ENIAC by 100 years.

internally. Their next effort was EDVAC (Electronic Discrete Variable Automatic Computer). Design of the EDVAC had actually begun prior to the completion of ENIAC, but EDVAC was not completed until 1952. EDVAC was then the prototype stored program computer in the United States. It is still being used by the Army at the Aberdeen (Maryland) Proving Ground. To the EDSAC, finished in 1949 at Cambridge University, must go the distinction of being the first stored program electronic computer.

One reason for the delay in EDVAC was that Eckert and Mauchly founded their own company in 1946. From this firm came the first commercially available computer—the UNIVAC-I (UNIVersal Automatic Computer). In 1949 Remington Rand acquired the Eckert-Mauchly Computer Corporation, and in early 1951 the first UNIVAC became operational at the Bureau of the Census. This "medieval" relic was used until 1963 when it, too, went to the Smithsonian Institution. The first computer acquired for *business data processing* was another UNIVAC-I, which was installed in 1954 at General Electric's Appliance Park in Louisville, Kentucky.

The Victorian Period (1954–1964) The Victorian Period begins with this first business installation. There was initial reluctance on the part of IBM to enter the computer market, but the loss of Census Bureau business changed this attitude. IBM reacted to produce new commercial machines.[11] Other computer manufacturers were not idle.

In the period from 1954 to 1959, many businesses acquired computers for data processing purposes even though these *first-generation* machines had been designed for scientific uses.[12] In the design of early equipment, emphasis was placed on computational capability with little attention being given to the input/output capacity of the machines. But since business data processing generally involves large volumes of record input and output with relatively little computation per record, the equipment available for data processing left something to be desired. Nevertheless, the early uses of computers left even more to be desired. Managers generally considered the computer to be an accounting tool, and the first applications were designed to process routine tasks such as payrolls and customer billing. Unfortunately, in most cases little or no attempt was made to modify and redesign existing accounting procedures in order to produce more effective managerial information. The potential of the computer was consist-

[11]The IBM 650 first saw service in Boston in December, 1954. It was an all-purpose machine, comparatively inexpensive, and was widely accepted. It gave IBM the leadership in computer production in 1955, and this leadership has never been challenged.
[12]By 1960 there were about thirty-five hundred computers in the United States.

ently underestimated; more than a few were acquired for no other reason than prestige.

But we should not judge the early users of electronic data processing too harshly. They were pioneering in the use of a new tool not designed specifically for their needs; they had to staff their computer installations with a new breed of workers; and they initially had to cope with the necessity of preparing programs in a tedious machine language until improvements in programming methods could be developed to speed up the coding process. In spite of these obstacles, the computer was found to be a fast, accurate, and untiring processor of mountains of paper.

The computers of the *second generation* were introduced around 1959–1960 and were made smaller, faster, and with greater computing capacity through such improvements as the use of small, magnetizable rings or cores for internal storage of data and instructions. The vacuum tube, with its heat, bulk, and relatively short life, gave way to compact *solid state* components such as diodes and transistors. Unlike earlier computers. some second-generation machines were designed from the beginning with business processing requirements in mind. The IBM 1400 series were the most popular second-generation machines—nearly 15,000 of them were produced.

In 1964, IBM ushered in the *third generation* of computing hardware when it announced its System/360 family of computers. This announcement marks the beginning of the Recent Period. The third generation continued the trend toward miniaturization of circuit components; further improvements in speed, cost, and storage capacity were realized. In the next chapter we shall look in more detail at some of the developments in computer technology that have occurred since 1964.

Size and Scope of Computer Industry

Over a hundred different computer models have been designed and built since 1954; thousands of machines have been installed. Yet in 1950 it was generally agreed by most businessmen (including the top executives of firms producing data processing equipment) that eight or ten of the big "electronic brains" would satisfy the entire demand for such devices! This monumental blunder in prognostication today boggles the mind; it must go down in history as one of the worst market forecasts of all time.

Number of computers Although IBM initially expected to sell 50 of their 650 computers, about 2,000 were produced in the 1950s. In 1956, however, there were only about 600 computers installed in the United

States; a decade later there were over 30,000 in operation; in 1970 the number had risen to 90,000; and by 1975 the number is expected to be approaching 200,000. In 1970, it was estimated that 18,500 new computers were shipped to users; by 1975 the number of annual shipments is expected to grow to 46,000—a 650 percent increase in just ten years.[13]

Value of computer systems The nearly 600 computers installed in 1956 had a total value of about $350 million. By the end of 1968 the total investment in installed computer systems had exceeded this earlier figure by over $17 *billion*. In 1970, the cumulative value of computer systems had risen to over $26 billion, and this figure is likely to double by 1975. Also, in 1970 the *annual* industry sales of computers, peripheral equipment, programs, and services had grown to over $12 billion—a figure that represented over 10 percent of the nation's investment in new plant and equipment. (By 1975 the $12 billion annual sales figure will likely have grown to over $27 billion.) An additional $15 billion (give or take a few hundred million) was spent in 1970 for internal programming, personnel, and operating costs. Let us summarize all of these mind-crunching statistics with this final observation: Since the computing industry is currently growing at about a 20 percent annual rate and since there are no immediate signs of market saturation, it may not be too many years until this industry represents one-fifth of the nation's gross national product. Thus, the computing industry would then have the same economic impact as the auto industry has today.

Computer manufacturers There are several dozen computer manufacturers, many of whom specialize in scientific, process control, and very small general purpose machines. Of the larger firms, most were initially business-machine manufacturers (e.g., IBM, UNIVAC Division of Sperry Rand, NCR and Burroughs Corporation), or they manufactured electronic equipment (e.g., Honeywell and RCA).[14] Exceptions are such firms as Control Data Corporation (CDC) and Xerox Data Systems (formerly Scientific Data Systems), which were founded to produce computers. The industry leader is IBM, with about 65 percent of the market; Honeywell ranks second, with about 10 percent

---

[13]Statistics are taken from a report issued by The Diebold Group, Inc. Another source has predicted 350,000 computers in use in the United States by 1980. Past and present figures are estimates because most manufacturers do not officially release installation data.

[14]On May 20, 1970, Honeywell and General Electric announced an agreement in principle to form a new computer company. The merger was finalized a few months later, and the new firm is called Honeywell Information Systems, Inc.

of the sales. American manufacturers and their foreign subsidiaries produce 95 percent of the Western world's computers.

Computer size categories   Computers, of course, come in various sizes, from the very large to the cash-register-size models that can

Figure 2-22(a)   Atron 501 minicomputer (courtesy Atron Corporation), (b) PDP—8/E minicomputer (courtesy Digital Equipment Corporation)

(a)

(*b*)

sit on a desk. Systems may be arbitrarily classified in terms of relative computing power and cost as *minisized, small, medium,* or *large.* Although we will not go into any discussion of equipment at this time, perhaps it is appropriate here to present an overview of typical computer installations.

Minicomputers (see Fig. 2-22) are, naturally, very small machines that perform the same arithmetic and logic functions, use several of the same programming languages, and have many of the same circuitry features of larger computers. Although they are general purpose devices, some are used for special or dedicated purposes such as controlling a machine tool or a process (see Fig. 2-23). Others are (1) used for business data processing purposes, (2) connected to larger computers and act as input/output and message-switching terminals, (3) used in school systems for educational purposes, and (4) used in laboratories for scientific computation purposes. In short, minicomputers may be economically used for processing tasks that do not require considerable access to large masses of stored data. The versatility of minicomputers, combined with their low cost (they range in price from about $5,000 to $50,000 and rent for $300 to $1,200 per month), account for their rapid acceptance. Growth in the number of mini-computer installations between 1971 and 1975 will be dramatic.

Small business computers may be the *punched-card-oriented* successors to unit record machines described in earlier pages (see Figs. 2-9 and 2-24). These computers accept data stored in cards, manipulate and update these facts, and produce information in the form of new punched cards and printed documents. Rental charges for such machines vary from about $1,200 to $4,000 per month; selling prices

Figure 2-23 Minicomputer used in process control (courtesy Digital Equipment Corporation)

vary in a range from about $50,000 to $150,000. In addition to small card-oriented computers, other small systems exist that substitute magnetic tapes (resembling large sound-recorder tapes) and magnetic disks (resembling large phonograph records) for cards as data storage

Figure 2-24 Small card-oriented computer— UNIVAC 9200 (courtesy UNIVAC Division, Sperry Rand Corporation)

(a)

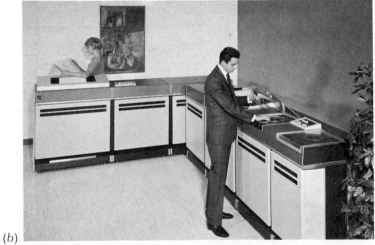

(b)

Figure 2-25(a) *Small tape-oriented computer (courtesy UNIVAC Division, Sperry Rand Corporation),* (b) *Small disk-oriented computer—NCR Century 100 (courtesy NCR)*

media (see Fig. 2-25).[15] These *tape-* and *disk-oriented* systems are faster, generally have a greater internal capacity to store data, and are more expensive—they rent for $2,500 to $5,000 per month and generally sell in the $125,000 to $250,000 range.

Medium-sized computers rent for $5,000 to $20,000 per month and sell for $250,000 to $1 million (see Fig. 2-26). *Larger systems* (Fig. 2-27)

[15]Punched cards may continue to be used in these systems for data input and output purposes. We shall have much more to say about magnetizable media in later chapters.

Figure 2-26 RCA medium-scale computer (courtesy RCA)

exceed these price ranges. In return for these higher prices, users receive faster processing speeds, greater data storage capacity, wider selection of optional equipment from which to choose, and a lower cost-per-calculation figure.[16] Figure 2-28 shows the large-scale UNI-

[16]This assumes that the volume of work is sufficient to keep a large machine occupied. If a man can compute the answer to a multiplication problem in one minute, and there are 125 million such problems to be solved, the total cost to do the calculations manually would exceed $10 million. The UNIVAC I (which in terms of computing power is a very small machine by today's standards) could have done the job for $4,300. However, the CDC 6600, which rents for well over $100,000 per month, could do the job for $4.

Figure 2-27 Large-scale computer—IBM System/370, model 165 (courtesy IBM Corporation)

*Figure 2-28   UNIVAC 1108
computers at NASA
(courtesy UNIVAC Division,
Sperry Rand Corporation)*

VAC 1108 computers installed at NASA's Manned Spacecraft Center in Houston. These machines played a vital role in returning the stricken Apollo 13 spacecraft safely to Earth.

In terms of *number* of installations (not value), large-scale systems represent about 3 percent of the total, medium-scale systems account for 14 percent, and small and minicomputers make up the remainder. Computers are rented in about three-fourths of all business installations.

For several years, computers were available only to the larger businesses for economic reasons. But developments in the last decade have brought computer capability to an ever-expanding circle of smaller organizations. One such development, of course, has been the creation of efficient and low-cost minicomputers and small business computers. Other developments include: (1) the establishment by small concerns of member-owned cooperative computer centers; (2) the willingness (even eagerness) of larger firms to sell unused time on their machines; (3) the availability of timesharing services for small subscribers (to be discussed in Chapter 4); and (4) the rapid increase in the number of commercial *computer centers* (or *service bureaus,* as they are sometimes called).[17]

Computer center organizations may be subsidiaries of computer

**Computer
Service Centers**

---

[17] Commercial banks process such customer jobs as payrolls, accounts-receivable accounting, sales and expense analyses, etc. Their fees for these services exceed $100 million annually.

manufacturers (most of the larger ones have such affiliates), independent (i.e., not affiliated with a manufacturer) national service chains, or independent local firms. Some specialize in a particular industry's processing problems, while others offer a general service. They all perform a data processing service to outside clients for a fee. Thus, they differ from organizations that only sell excess computer time on a do-it-yourself basis. The computer center will, for example, assume the responsibility for performing a specific task by a certain time for a specified fee. This service may involve any or all of the following: (1) analyzing the client's information needs, (2) preparing computer programs to perform the needed processing, (3) converting the client's input data into machine-acceptable form, and (4) producing the output information from the input data.

Although computer centers serve many small clients, their service is not limited to small organizations. Many firms with their own computing equipment use centers during peak or overload work periods and at other times when special equipment and assistance may be needed. Also, companies planning to acquire their own equipment or convert to newer equipment have used center facilities on an interim basis to gain experience.

SUMMARY

Data processing techniques have been undergoing evolutionary change since the beginning of mankind. This evolution has advanced through four stages, from manual methods to the development of the computer. However, none of these stages should be considered obsolete, for each has its place.

Manual methods can be traced from ancient civilizations. These methods were later supplemented by machines that extended man's capabilities in performing specific data processing steps. Further advances in office equipment made it possible to combine steps in a single operation. Earlier mechanical concepts are today being combined with electronic features, which give accounting machines many of the characteristics of computers. Manual methods are well suited to low-volume processing tasks. As volume increases, however, the equipment needed to economically perform the tasks increases in sophistication, greater accuracy and faster processing speeds may be expected, but procedures are likely to become the more rigorously defined and standardized.

Development of punched card methods and equipment may be traced from the nineteenth century. Two types of cards, the 80- and 96-column cards are in widespread use today. The more popular

80-column card uses the Hollerith code to represent digits, letters, and special characters; the smaller System/3 card uses combinations of holes punched in six rows to represent data. Regardless of the coding method employed, card columns are laid out in consecutive groups called *fields* for specific business purposes. A number of punched card machines have been developed. These separate machines must be fed, started, and stopped by human operators, who must also carry trays of cards between machines. This limited intercommunication between processing steps is a limitation that is overcome by computer methods.

The computer, with its ability to store and act upon its own instructions, makes possible automatic communication between processing steps. Although Charles Babbage dreamed of building a computer in the 1800s, the first electronic machine was not completed until 1946. Ten years later it was placed in the Smithsonian Institution, an indication of the rapid progress made in computer development. By 1970, four generations of computing hardware had been designed, the number of systems in operation had risen to 90,000, and the value of these systems exceeded $26 billion. Future developments in the computer industry will continue to be dramatic.

There can be little doubt that the computer is responsible, in large measure, for the significant and sweeping change that is now taking place in the field of information processing. The next chapter examines some of the causes and effects of this revolution.

DISCUSSION QUESTIONS

1. Trace the evolution of manual methods of data processing.
2. What are the advantages and limitations of manual data processing methods?
3. (a) Who invented the first mechanical adding machine?
   (b) How did it operate?
4. "Trade-offs between accuracy and timeliness, on the one hand, and procedural flexibility, on the other, are not uncommon." Discuss this statement.
5. (a) Why was Dr. Herman Hollerith hired by the U.S. Census Bureau?
   (b) What were the results of his work?
6. Describe the 80-column punched card and the Hollerith code.
7. Describe the 96-column punched card and the coding employed.
8. What is a field?
9. (a) How many business transactions are recorded in a typical detail card?

(b) What is the difference between detail cards and summary cards?

10. Explain the path followed by cards through the keypunch.

11. Explain the function of the following unit record machines:
    (a) Verifier
    (b) Sorter
    (c) Collator
    (d) Calculator
    (e) Tabulator
    (f) Reproducer

12. "Limited intercommunication is a disadvantage of unit record processing systems." Explain this sentence.

13. (a) What was the analytical engine?
    (b) What features would it have had in common with modern computers?
    (c) Why wasn't it built?

14. (a) What was the Mark I?
    (b) Was it an electronic computer?

15. (a) What was the ENIAC?
    (b) Why was it built?
    (c) How did it differ from the Mark I?

16. What important contributions to computer design were proposed by John von Neumann?

17. Distinguish between first- and second-generation computing hardware.

18. Discuss the size and scope of the computer industry.

19. (a) What is a computer service center?
    (b) What services might a center perform for a client?

SELECTED REFERENCES

Jequier, Nicolas: "Computer Industry Gaps," *Science & Technology,* September, 1969, pp. 30–39.

Kluchman, Allen Z.: "Minicomputers on the Move," *Computers and Automation,* December, 1969, pp. 24–26.

Roy, John L.: "The Changing Role of the Service Bureau," *Datamation,* March, 1970, pp. 52–53ff.

Schussel, George: "IBM vs REMRAND," *Datamation,* May, 1965, pp. 54–57.

Thomas, Donald R.: "Data Processing Service Bureaus," *Management Accounting,* March, 1970, pp. 25–27ff.

The Information Revolution: Its Setting

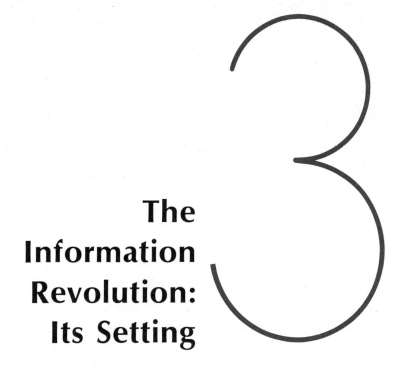

History records, in a relatively unfavorable light, periods in which the tempo of change has diminished. For example, we are told that, during the centuries known as the Dark Ages following the fall of the Roman Empire, an attempt to preserve the status quo against change was made by European political and religious leaders. But there were also periods of dynamic change as well as men and nations who were able to meet the resulting challenges. The Dark Ages eventually gave way to that period of reawakening and accomplishment known as the Renaissance and the Age of Exploration. The pages of history are filled with accounts of men of courage and foresight who, during the dynamic periods, emerged to create change or to meet the challenges brought by changing conditions.

Unfortunately, the footnotes of these pages often contain accounts of men who failed to respond to the changes taking place around them. At the turn of the nineteenth century, some members of the British Parliament argued that since the important inventions had all been made, there was no further need to keep the Royal Patent Office open. Since, of the top 25 United States businesses at the time of this British debate, only two are still ranked that high, it is apparent that the business managers of that time, on the whole, possessed no greater foresight than did the politicians. To illustrate, Vincent Learson notes that in the early 1900s the keynote speaker at the annual meeting of the National Association of Carriage Builders delivered the following encouraging message to the assembled buggy manufacturers:

> Eighty-five percent of the horse-drawn vehicle industry of the country is untouched by the automobile. In proof of the foregoing permit me to say that in 1906-7, and coincident with an enormous demand for automobiles, the demand for buggies reached the highest tide of its history. The man who predicts the downfall of the automobile is a fool; the man who denies its great necessity and general adoption for many uses is a bigger fool; and the man who predicts the general annihilation of the horse and his vehicle is the greatest fool of all.[1]

Nor were the buggy builders the only ones in the transportation industry to be surprised. A top executive for the leading steam-locomotive manufacturer was quite certain thirty years ago that the diesel locomotive had only limited application. In his words, "the field of probably profitable application of the diesel locomotive is pretty generally indicated at work speeds not exceeding 10 miles an hour."

These examples point out to business managers the importance of being prepared to cope with environmental changes. Yet the *scope* and *pace* of the environmental changes occurring today are *unprecedented* in history. Revolutionary technological, social, and economic forces are at work; managerial techniques that were adequate in the past may not continue to be effective; the risks of failure and the rewards of success are probably higher than they have ever been. The basic challenge to the managers of today is to foresee and manage (and not be swept along by) the flood of changes facing their organizations, within a democratic framework, for the benefit of society as well as for the benefit of customers, employees, and owners. The names of managers failing to meet this challenge may someday be placed in the footnotes of business history books in company with the spokesmen for the buggy and steam-locomotive builders.

In this chapter dealing with the factors contributing to the information revolution that is now under way, we will first examine the *revolutionary environmental changes* facing business in scientific,

---

[1] Quoted in T. Vincent Learson, "The Management of Change," *Columbia J. World Business,* vol. 3, p. 59, January-February, 1968.

social, and economic areas. Obviously, coping with accelerating change requires higher-quality managerial information. We will then look at the *revolution in computer technology,* which is constantly improving the information processing capability of this management tool. Next, we will consider some of the concepts that have been developed to help the computer-user *make the transition* to these more powerful computing systems. Finally, we will (1) define what is meant by *management information systems* and (2) point out how *traditional information systems have failed* to adequately respond to the rapidly changing needs of managers.

To briefly summarize the theme of the following pages, rapid environmental changes create a need for better information; revolutionary changes in computer technology make better information possible; and since traditional methods are often inadequate, revolutionary new systems are thus being developed to employ the tool to satisfy the need. The nature of these new management information systems is the subject of the next chapter.

REVOLUTIONARY ENVIRONMENTAL CHANGES

We are witnessing today rapid scientific and technological changes taking place over a broad front. These scientific changes and developments may sweep aside current practices, open new opportunities, and create new problems for institutions such as business and government. Such results are possible because scientific changes are accompanied by pervasive social and economic changes—and problems. Often, of course, changing social and political values determine the direction, significance, and timing of technological changes. The growing awareness of the importance of ecological conditions, for example, blocks the construction of nuclear power plants and places greater importance on antipollution research. Let us now look more closely at some of the revolutionary changes that are occurring in the environment in which businesses must function.

Scientific Changes

World War II and the cold (and hot) war years that have followed have provided much impetus for scientific discovery and technological change. During World War II, for example, the multibillion-dollar Manhattan Project led to the atomic bomb, ballistic missiles were produced, research in the realm of electronics led to radar and improved communications and weapons systems, and ENIAC was built for the U.S. Army by Mauchly and Eckert to compute artillery trajectory tables. Since World War II, these breakthroughs, in turn, have led to computer-based early warning command and control systems, the development of new electronic circuitry, and the beginning steps in the conquest and exploration of space. The Russian Sputnik satellite success brought about a public demand in this country for faster progress in missile and space technology and related areas. Computer technology has benefited from, and has contributed to, this expanded space effort. And peaceful applications of defense-inspired discoveries have resulted in new commercial materials and products.

In short, during an extremely short span of time in the history of man, the *broadening scope* of scientific inquiry has resulted in movement along such paths as space exploration, increasing use of nuclear power, laser experimentation, and molecular biological research probing toward the secrets of life itself. As a result of an expanding scope of scientific inquiry, there has been an explosion in the amount of available scientific knowledge. (After all, 90 percent of all the scientists and engineers ever formally trained are alive today!) The output of scientific information is doubling every eight and one-half years; the average volume of such information reached 120 million pages by 1970, and the new information available every twenty-four hours would pack seven sets of a 24-volume encyclopedia.[2]

Information retrieval has therefore become a major problem in many scientific and business areas. Researchers may spend considerable time and money on problems that, unknown to them, have been solved and published elsewhere. No one knows how much is spent each year in such duplication (what researcher wants to admit that his pet—and expensive—project was published in an obscure journal last year?), but the figure runs into the hundreds of millions of dollars.[3] Much work is currently being done in the field of computer-assisted information retrieval systems. In the U.S. Patent Office, for example, retrieval systems are being studied to aid examiners in their file search of previously patented ideas. Since there are 3.5 million United States patents and 5 million foreign patents on file, this is a formidable retrieval problem. Automated information retrieval systems are also being developed in the fields of law enforcement

[2]See George Schussel, "Advent of Information and Inquiry Services," *J. Data Manage.*, September, 1969, p. 24.

[3]In the September 1960 issue of *Fortune*, Francis Bello wrote that a major electronics firm had paid $8 million for two patented inventions only to discover that they had no value. Buried in the Patent Office files were documents which proved that both ideas had been anticipated earlier. One study of aeronautical and electronic societies in southern California revealed that between 30 and 85 percent of scientific man-hours were wasted because existing information was not available to the right person when it was needed. See Schussel, *op. cit.*, p. 24.

Figure 3-1   Information retrieval system for law enforcement (courtesy Ampex Corporation)

and health. For example, a new system, which combines television and computer technologies to automatically retrieve law enforcement records, was installed in Los Angeles County in 1970 (see Fig. 3-1). Another system, which combines microfilm and television devices and which may be linked to a computer, enables a physician to review patient-history information within seconds (Fig. 3-2).

In addition to an expansion in the scope of scientific inquiry, there has also been a great acceleration in the *speed or rate* with which new knowledge is put to use. The Department of Commerce estimates that prior to World War I there was an average wait of thirty-three years between an invention and its application; by World War II, the lag time had dropped to ten years; and now the delay has been further reduced. For example, the laser was invented in 1958 and was being applied seven years later for manufacturing and surgical purposes. And four computer generations have been introduced since 1950. The

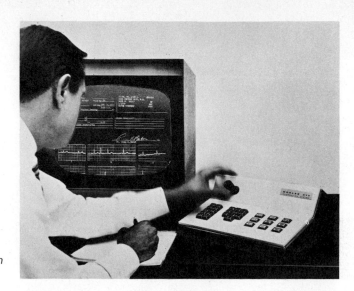

Figure 3-2 Information retrieval of medical records (courtesy Mosler Information Services Division)

implications of an accelerating rate of change are obvious to managers: A major change, which might have required five years to implement a decade ago, must now be completed in a shorter period if the firm is to remain competitive. On the one hand, management reaction time is constantly shrinking, while, on the other hand, each decision made involves more risk and is valid for a shorter time span. Furthermore, as reaction time diminishes, opportunities for profitable action are lost because preoccupied managers fail to reach out and grasp them (see Fig. 3-3).

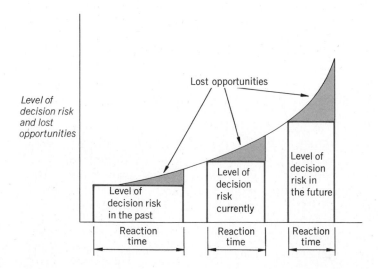

Figure 3-3

Recent scientific change affects the way people live, think, and asso-ciate with each other; it also has profound economic implications. In the wake of technological change has come a wave of *social* and *political problems*. Creeping urban decay exists in many cities in the midst of wealth; the air and water become more polluted; irritating noise levels move ever higher; traffic congestion becomes more in-tense. Increasingly effective communications media tell of the rapid advances being made in space exploration and in other scientific areas. The story of improving living standards is also presented in direct and subtle ways to citizens who have not shared adequately in past progress. The rising expectations that these progress reports engender then come into conflict with the harsh reality of poverty, inadequate housing, lack of opportunity, lack of preparation, and chronic un-employment. The resulting despair often leads to violence and rioting.

A continuing mass migration of unskilled and uneducated farm workers to the cities compounds the urban difficulties and increases the already overcrowded situation. In the relatively brief twelve-year period between 1955 and 1967, agricultural employment dropped 40 percent (from 6.7 million to 4.0 million)! A large proportion of these displaced workers sought jobs in urban areas. As a result of this farm-to-city migration, 70 percent of the population now lives in metropolitan areas on 1 percent of the nation's land area. This popu-lation percentage in urban areas is increasing.

These and other social problems call for concerted government action. They will also require that business executives take a more active future role in helping to provide solutions to these social difficulties. The business community can, for example, make a positive contribution by training unskilled workers and giving them job op-portunities and by making sure that its firms are not contributing to environmental pollution. Regardless of the actions taken, it will be necessary to plan carefully to achieve clear objectives. (The last cities left completely to God's will were Sodom and Gomorrah.) New information will be needed by managers to cope with these unsolved ailments.

In addition to contributing to the solution of social problems, managers will also have to carefully assess the effects of changes in the *size and composition of the population*. If the number of people in the world continues to grow at the present rate, population will double between 1970 and 2000. Late in 1967, the United States popu-lation passed the 200-million mark; in 1910 we numbered only 90 million. By 1980, it is expected that our population will be in the region of 231 million. These additional millions must be fed, housed, clothed, educated, transported, and eventually employed. Business activity

**Social and
Economic Changes**

obviously must expand to meet (1) the demands of additional population at home, (2) the demands from abroad for American goods and services, and (3) the demands brought about by an improvement in the overall standard of living (which is brought about, in part, by the increased productivity resulting from technological innovations).

The fastest-growing segment of the population in the 1970s will be the 20 to 35 age category. In the early 1970s, the median age will be 26; i.e., half the population will be under 26. Not too long ago the median age was 29. The age category that typically supplies a large percentage of business executives—the 35 to 55 group—will change very little, and there will even be a decline in the number at the higher ages. Peter Drucker colorfully explains the implication of this fact to top executives in these words: "The age structure of our population is such that in the next 20 years, like it or not, we are going to have to promote people we wouldn't have thought old enough, a few years ago, to find their way to the water cooler."[4] Other implications are that products will be developed or redesigned for (and advertising will be aimed at) the large young market. And the creation of an additional 15 to 20 million new families during the 1970s will bring a significant increase in the demand for housing.

Mass *education* is part of our social picture and is a leading contributor to spiralling change. Why is this? It is because education leads to knowledge; knowledge creates the tools which lead to higher productivity and rising standards of living; and higher standards of living enable man to devote more time to education. Thus the cycle begins anew but at a progressively higher plane (see Fig. 3-4).

Educational attainment, as measured by years of formal schooling, will continue to rise. In 1952, one out of twelve in the labor force had attended college for at least four years; in 1975, the comparable figure will be about one out of six (one out of four will have had some higher education). The knowledge explosion in many fields makes continuing education beyond graduation a necessity. One-third of all university students in the world are Americans.

A better-educated population is potentially more productive and more mobile and will have more leisure time and more money to spend in the future. There is also a tendency for well-educated workers to place professional standards above loyalty to, and the values of, the organizations that employ them. Top executives will have to adjust to accommodate and motivate a more independent type of subordinate in the future. What are some of the other business implications

---

[4] Peter F. Drucker, "The Manager and the Moron," condensed from *The McKinsey Quarterly*, Spring, 1967, and appearing in *Management Rev.*, vol. 56, p. 22, July, 1967.

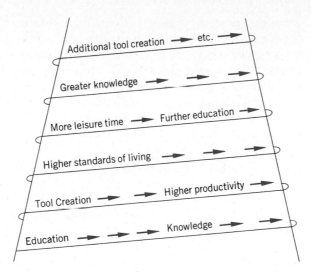

Figure 3-4

of these changes? In the past, increased mobility has brought changes in product-distribution methods. Suburbs have grown and new shopping centers have sprung up. Changes of this type will continue as the labor force reacts to changing geographical demands for labor services. Population mobility is a matter that must be considered by marketing managers. Also, increasing leisure time improves the markets for boats, camping equipment, and travel-oriented businesses.

We noted that future consumers would have more money to spend. This will be true because the value of the tools of production that lead to higher productivity will expand from a 1965 level of $700 billion to a 1975 level of about $1,200 billion. In addition to an absolute growth in productive facilities, existing facilities will be upgraded with newer and more productive capital equipment. The result will be that in the decade from 1970 to 1980, the GNP (gross national product measured in constant dollars) will expand by about 50 percent. The fact that consumers will earn significantly more in the future has obvious implications for business.

The implications of rapid scientific, social, political, and economic changes are clear—the business manager must be prepared to make continuous readjustments in his plans. He must make more and better decisions about new products and existing products because of their shorter profitable lifespan; he must make decisions about product prices, new markets, and channels of distribution to use; he must be prepared to face increasingly aggressive foreign and domestic competition; and he must decide on matters of finance. Furthermore, he must make these decisions within a time span that is constantly shrinking; he must attempt to anticipate and plan for environmental changes; and he must take a more active role in seeking solutions to the social ills which exist in the environment in which he lives and works. To compete profitably in the future will require information of the highest possible quality. The computer, which is undergoing rapid technological improvement, is a tool that can provide the needed information to managers who must operate in a dynamic environment.

REVOLUTION IN COMPUTER TECHNOLOGY

The computer is a tool that is *contributing* to advances in virtually all fields. Computer-hardware technology is also benefiting from new discoveries in the fields of electronics and physics. Computer *hardware* consists of all the machines that make up a functioning computer system. Basically, these machines accept data input, store data, perform calculations and other processing steps, and prepare information output.

Hardware alone, however, is merely a box of electronic parts that represents a business expense; an equally important (perhaps more important) consideration in the effective business use of computers is the *software*. Software is the name given to the multitude of instructions, i.e., the name given to *programs* and *routines,* that have been written to cause the hardware to function in a desired way. Let us now briefly look at the technological advances that have occurred in computer hardware and software.

Hardware Developments

Hardware technological development has been incredibly rapid, as may be seen by an examination of the factors of (1) *size,* (2) *speed,* (3) *cost,* (4) *information storage capacity,* and (5) *reliability.*

Size The earliest computers were large enough to store grain in (ENIAC, you will recall, weighed about 30 tons). The tubes used in this equipment produced considerable heat, which made it necessary to air-condition the room where the machine was located. Using transistors instead of tubes, the second-generation computers were greatly reduced in size. For example, compact tube equipment contained an average of 5,000 *components* per cubic foot. Second-generation machines, however, could pack an average of 100,000 *circuits* into a similar space—and each circuit would contain a number of separate components. Also, transistors were more reliable than tubes and generated little heat.

The *third-generation* computers, introduced in 1964, make use of microelectronic, or *integrated, circuits* on a large scale. Such circuits may be almost microscopic, but they contain the equivalent of many transistors. (Instead of 100,000 circuits per cubic foot, third-generation technology allowed packing 10 million circuits in the same space.)

During the summer and fall of 1970, IBM, RCA, NCR, Burroughs, and others introduced new hardware lines. For example, IBM announced the first models (the 145, 155, and 165) of its new System/370 line of computers. Touted by IBM officials as the computing "landmark for the 1970s," these *fourth-generation*[5] models make use of extended microelectronic concepts to achieve further circuit packing densities (see Fig. 3-5). The greatly magnified chip of silicon on the nib of the pen in Fig. 3-5 contains 64 complete memory circuits. Furthermore, a chip is now in production for the University of Illinois' advanced ILLIAC IV supercomputer that employs large-scale integration (LSI) to squeeze about 1,200 transistors, 1,200 resistors, and 71

[5] Hardware generation designations are applied to computers in a rather arbitrary manner by the computer industry. Although IBM does not claim that the System/370 is the fourth generation, many in the industry have considered it in that light. See *Business Week,* July 4, 1970, p. 21. Certainly from a marketing point of view, if not entirely from a technical point of view, the new lines probably do represent a new generation.

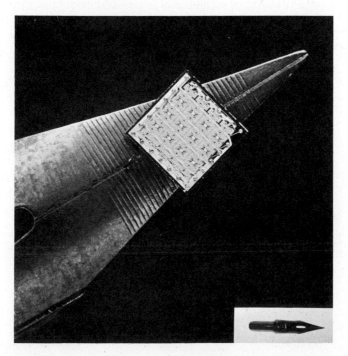

Figure 3-5 (Courtesy IBM Corporation)

diodes on a surface $\frac{1}{10}$ inch square.[6] The packing density of this chip is 160,000 components per square inch.

Has the end been reached in the feasible size reduction of computer circuitry? Hardly. As just noted, it is now possible to pack over 100,000 components on a thin *square* inch wafer. One scientist recently speculated that in a decade or so it may be possible to achieve such packing density *throughout* a *cubic* inch of material. The density of electronic components would then be "about a fourth the density of nerve cells in the human brain."[7]

These size reductions make it possible to produce, in an extremely small package, a device with the computing power of the earlier monsters. That many currently produced computers are also rather large merely gives an indication of the growth in computing capability.

Speed　Circuit miniaturization has brought increased speed of operation to the latest computers. Why is this? It is because size reduction means shorter distances for electric pulses to travel, and thus processor speed has increased. Third-generation machines were 900 times faster than 1950 models. A job taking one hour to finish in 1950 could be completed in three or four seconds in the mid-1960s. Fourth-generation hardware, of course, further reduces the time required.[8]

Early computer speed was expressed in *milliseconds* (thousandths of a second); second-generation speed was measured in *microseconds* (millionths of a second); third- and fourth-generation hardware has internal operating speeds measured in *nanoseconds* (billionths of a second). Since circuit speeds are likely to increase by five times between 1970 and 1975, future machines may have speeds measured in *picoseconds* (trillionths of a second).[9]

Cost　We have seen the rapid growth in the number of computer installations. Linked with this rapid expansion—in fact, a significant

---

[6]LSI refers to circuits which pack from 50,000 to 100,000 components in a square inch space.

[7]F. G. Heath, "Large-Scale Integration in Electronics," *Sci. Amer.*, February, 1970, p. 22. An article in the June 22, 1970, issue of the *Wall Street Journal* reported that in the not-too-distant future it may be possible to fit 12 *billion* circuits into a small 3-pound package—a packaging feat "that would approximate the density and complexity of the circuits in the human brain."

[8]The IBM System/370, model 165, is up to five times faster than the large-scale 360/65. The 165's basic machine cycle time, i.e., the time it takes to execute an instruction, is 80 billionths of a second. Electricity traveling at 186,000 miles per second can move only about 80 feet in that time.

[9]Such speeds are difficult to comprehend. A space ship traveling toward the moon at 100,000 miles per hour would move less than 2 *inches* in 1 microsecond; it would move only the length of 10 fat germs in a nanosecond. More antiseptically speaking, there are as many nanoseconds in one second as there are seconds in thirty years, or as many nanoseconds in a minute as there are minutes in 1100 *centuries*. Electricity travels about 1 foot per nanosecond, and this fact imposes an ultimate limit to internal computer speed.

cause of it—is the dramatic reduction in the cost of performing a specific number of operations. In 1950, for example, 35 *thousand* basic computer instructions could be processed for $1; in the mid-1960s, using third-generation hardware, $1 would process 35 *million* instructions. Thus, the cost of raw computing power was reduced to one-thousandth of its previous level in less than two decades. Furthermore, fourth-generation technology has carried this cost-reduction trend forward. If automobile costs were reduced to the same degree that computation costs have been, you would now be able to buy for less than $5 a luxury car costing $5,000 in 1950,[10] and a home purchased for $20,000 in 1950 would now represent an investment of about $15.

Nor does it appear that the end is in sight in computational cost reduction. The cost of certain basic components will continue to decline while their speed and performance increases. Fabricating 100,000 transistors on a wafer the size of a postage stamp is expected to be no more expensive than fabricating 100 or 1,000 transistors on the same chip.[11] In 1965 the average cost to provide internal storage capacity for one binary number was about 20 cents (down from 85 cents in 1960 and $2.61 in 1950). The comparable cost in 1970 was about 5 cents, while the 1975 figure is expected to be $\frac{1}{2}$ cent.

Information storage capacity   Information may be stored for use by a computer in a number of ways. The central processing unit (CPU) of the computer holds data and the instructions needed to manipulate the data internally in its *primary storage,* or *main memory,* section. In early computers this primary storage capacity was quite small (2,000 to 4,000 "words"). With second-generation hardware, internal storage that exceeded 30,000 words was available; third-generation computers can store hundreds of thousands of words in primary storage; and fourth-generation technology permits a million or more words to be so retained.

Perhaps even more impressive than the increase in central processor primary storage capacity has been the improvement in mass *external online* (or *secondary*) storage devices. These devices are connected directly to, i.e., they are online to, the CPU. Utilizing magnetizable disks, drums, cards, and strips, these storage devices serve as *reference libraries* by accepting data directly from and returning data directly to the CPU without human intervention. We have seen, of course, that data which the computer may use are also stored

---

[10]Carrying this fantasy a step further, you might not wash a dirty car—you would merely throw it away and buy another. It has been predicted that future portable radios made on a single inexpensive silicon chip will be discarded when the original power supply is exhausted.
[11]See Heath, *op. cit.,* p. 22.

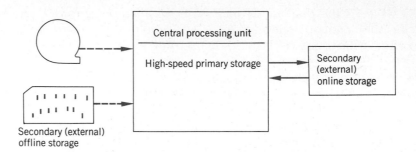

Figure 3-6   Computer information storage

outside the CPU in the form of punched cards and magnetic tape. These facts, however, are *offline* since the CPU does not have direct access to them (see Fig. 3-6).

Wide variation exists (1) in the time required for the storage and retrieval of data from online storage devices and (2) in the storage capacity of such devices. Speed is generally sacrificed (but the cost per character stored is frequently reduced) as online storage capacity is increased.[12] However, the time required for data to go from the slowest online storage device to the CPU, although much slower than the nanosecond access time of primary storage, is still measured in milliseconds.

In 1956 maximum online storage capacity was about 10 million alphanumeric characters. By 1961, this capacity had doubled, and the next year saw capacity increase to 100 million characters. But with the arrival of third-generation hardware also came the ability to store online over 100 billion characters—a growth factor of 10,000 in a decade![13] Current research holds forth the promise that by 1975 between five and ten times as many characters can be packed on magnetizable surfaces of the size being used today.

Reliability   The reliability of hardware has improved substantially with the substitution of long-life solid state components for the early vacuum tubes. Much of the research effort directed toward achieving greater reliability has been sponsored by the U.S. government for space and missile programs. That the trend toward greater hardware reliability is continuing is shown by the fact that while in 1962 the "average" *aerospace* computing system had an airborne mean time between failure (MTBF) of 330 hours, by 1970 the MTBF had risen to thousands of hours.[14]

In 1967, IBM scientists prepared a plan for a *self-repairing* com-

[12]Characteristics of various storage devices will be covered in Chapter 9.
[13]See Richard G. Canning, *EDP Analyzer*, November, 1966, p. 2.
[14]J. S. Butz, Jr., "As Computers Shrink, Their Uses Grow," *Air Force Space Digest*, January, 1970, p. 30.

puter that (997 times out of 1,000 attempts) could be expected to operate correctly on a ten-thousand-hour space mission. The self-repairing concept essentially involves partitioning the computer into functional blocks and building identical components into each block. Some of the parts are used for processing immediately; others serve as standby spares. A failure occurring in one component or subsystem would be detected by a status-sensing device, and the faulty part would be electronically and automatically replaced with a spare. Assuming that those sections with a reduced number of standby spares were replaced during periodic preventive maintenance, the MTBF would likely be measured in years rather than in weeks or a few months as is often the case today. The self-repairing *commercial* computer is still on the drawing boards because of the additional cost of redundant parts.[15] However, as LSI circuit technology produces lower costs, this obstacle may be overcome in the not-too-distant future.

Software Developments

Software is the general name given to all the programs and routines associated with the use of computer hardware. Unfortunately, when compared with the tremendous hardware advances, the developments in the software area seem less impressive. Furthermore, as anticipated hardware improvements are realized, an overwhelming proportion of the problems experienced in utilizing the computer to produce managerial information will be traceable to software difficulties. Today, in fact, it is quite likely that good supporting software takes longer to produce than the hardware; also, the pace of software production generally determines the speed with which computer-based projects are completed. As a result, it is a generally accepted fact that the investment in programming and systems personnel and in the software they create now far exceeds the investment in hardware in most installations.[16] The trend will undoubtedly continue in this direction because hardware production is automated while increasingly complex software must still be written on an artisan basis.[17]

[15] In space missions and in other areas where reliability is of paramount importance, the higher cost is, of course, more acceptable. A self-repairing computer (like "HAL" in the film *2001: A Space Odyssey*) is currently being designed for an eleven-year journey to the outermost fringes of our solar system.

[16] Earl Joseph, a UNIVAC Division scientist, estimates that although in 1950 only 5 percent of total computer-system cost was for software, the figure had risen to 50 percent by 1965 and was about 80 percent in 1970. See E. Joseph, "Trends Toward Tomorrow's Computers," *Automation,* June, 1969, p. 70.

[17] Thus, with hardware computation costs declining and with software development costs becoming proportionately larger, programming techniques that are less efficient in terms of machine time have been (and will continue to be) implemented if they help to reduce program preparation time.

Yet there have been significant gains in the development of software. The three basic software categories are (1) *translation programs,* (2) *applications programs,* and (3) *operating-system programs.* Let us look at the developments in each of these categories.

Translation programs   In the early 1950s, users had to translate problem-solving instructions into special machine codes for each computer. Such instructions typically consisted of strings of numbers (sometimes in a binary form), which were quite tedious to prepare. In addition to remembering dozens of operation code numbers (21 might mean add), the employee performing the task of instructing the computer (a *programmer*) was also required to keep track of the locations in the central processor where the instructions and data items were stored. Initial program coding often took many months; checking instructions to locate errors was about as difficult as writing the instructions in the first place; and modifying programs was often a nightmare. In short, machine language coding was fine for the machine, but man found it awkward to use.

To ease the programmer's burden, a compromise approach between man and machine was developed, which resulted in the introduction of special coding *languages* that save time and are more convenient to use. In using these languages, the programmer writes his instructions in a form that he finds easier to understand—e.g., he may print the word ADD or use the plus symbol rather than use the number 21. Unfortunately, this code is not in the machine's language, and so it does not directly understand the orders. How, then, can the machine execute instructions it cannot understand? It merely takes over the translation task from the programmer and converts his instructions into machine-usable form by means of separate translation software.

The *translating program* is stored on cards or on a magnetizable medium and is read into the computer where it has control over the translation procedure (see Fig. 3-7). The *source program* written by the programmer is converted to a machine-readable form (e.g., punched cards) and is then read into the computer a card at a time under the control of the translating program. The output of this operation is a machine language, or *object program,* which can then be read into the computer to control the processing of problem data. A majority of the programs written today are prepared in higher-level translatable languages.[18]

Continuing efforts are being made to produce software that will

---

[18] Several of these languages are presented in Chapter 12.

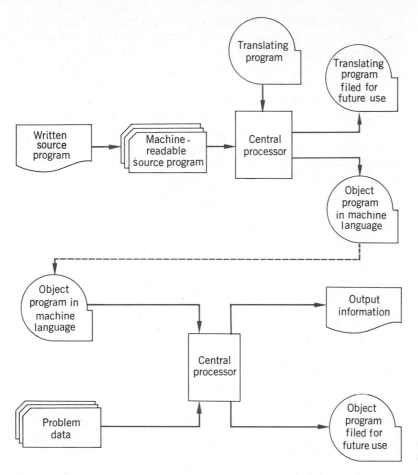

Figure 3-7 Program translation process

permit easier man-machine communication. For example, efforts are being made to develop software that will give the ultimate users of the processed information the ability to prepare programs in languages that are more familiar to them.

Application programs The programs written in translatable or machine languages for the purpose of solving particular processing jobs also come under the heading of software. These programs are commonly prepared by each using organization to process such applications as payroll, billing and accounts receivable, inventory control, project scheduling, and other tasks. Many applications programs must, of course, be prepared by users to process tasks that are unique to their particular needs. In the past, however, much programmer time (a scarce and expensive resource) has been spent in duplicating programs prepared in other companies. Recognizing the wastefulness of such duplication, equipment manufacturers and independent software companies have prepared generalized *applications packages* (or *packaged programs*) for widely used applications. Retail stores, for example, sell on credit and thus maintain credit records and perform billing operations. Since many retail firms employ essentially the same accounting procedures in such cases, a billing and accounts-receivable application package may be used with a minimum of modification. Packages are equally feasible in other industries such as manufacturing, insurance, and transportation.

The *use of application packages is increasing for a number of reasons,* including the following:

1. Several of the higher-level translatable languages, e.g., FORTRAN and COBOL, have been adapted for use with a large number of computers. Thus, programs prepared in these languages are essentially machine independent and can be used with many different hardware makes and models with little or no modification. This software *compatibility* has furnished added incentive for the development of better packaged programs since these programs can now be usefully employed by a much larger number of installations.
2. Commercial computer centers have been active in promoting the use of these packages by smaller firms. A small retailer, for example, can send specially printed cash-register tapes to a commercial computer center for processing (see Fig. 3-8). The tape data may provide the input for sales reports and analyses. The computer center could use the same application package to provide similar information to other retailing clients.
3. The packaged program, prepared by excellent programmer specialists, may be more efficient than a run-of-the-mill program prepared by the user; furthermore, it may be less expensive to buy than to make the program package.
4. The speed with which applications can be converted to the computer may be substantially reduced. It may, in fact, be cheaper and faster to use certain packaged programs than to reprogram existing applications for a conversion to new hardware.
5. Because of the current shortage of programmers, the using firm may not have the programming personnel available to write the needed package.

Among the possible *limitations of applications packages are* the following:

Figure 3-8 Cash register tape input for computer (courtesy NCR)

1. Available packages will not fit the needs of the potential user without extensive initial modification.
2. User programmers may have difficulty making needed changes to a relatively unfamiliar package.
3. In attempting to create a package with universal applicability, the designer may have sacrificed operating efficiency in areas important to the potential user.

Operating-system programs Computer-users today are not merely buying hardware when they install a computer. Rather, they are acquiring an *interface;* i.e., they are purchasing rules, regulations, controls, and equipment that will permit them to accomplish, through applications programs, the desired information output. The interface package includes, of course, the necessary hardware, but to effectively use the hardware it also includes translating programs and the operating-system software.

As the name implies, the *operating system* (OS) was initially a set of programs, or routines, prepared by equipment manufacturers and users to assist the computer operator. It is the function of the operator to load data input devices with cards and tapes, to set switches on the computer console, to start the processing run, and to prepare and unload output devices. It should not be his job, however, to waste his (and the machine's) time doing things that the computer could do more quickly and reliably. Housekeeping duties such as loading and unloading input and output equipment, clearing central processor storage locations between jobs, and loading into storage the next job program and data from the jobs stacked up in a waiting queue are now controlled by the software. Shifting control to specially prepared operating programs thus reduced the operator's work, cut down on the programmer's drudgery (by eliminating the need to rewrite certain input and output instructions for each program), provided relatively nonstop operation, and therefore speeded up the amount of processing that could be accomplished. The name given to the software that aids in performing the housekeeping duties just described is the input/output control system (IOCS)—an important segment of a modern operating system.

The objective of current operating systems is still to operate the computer with a minimum of idle time and in the most efficient and economical way during the execution of application and translation programs. But the operating software is now vastly more complex. More sophisticated software has been required to keep faster and more powerful hardware occupied. An example is the development of *multiprogramming,* the name given to the *interleaved* execution of two or more different and independent programs by the same computer.[19]

Multiprogramming *is not* generally defined to mean that the computer is executing instructions from several programs at the same instant in time;[20] instead, it *does mean* that there are a number of

---

[19] The mechanically inclined readers know that the automobile distributor head rotates, makes electrical contact with, and zaps a pulse of electricity to each spark plug in one revolution. Similarly, the computer may allocate a small amount, or *slice,* of time—say, 150 milliseconds per second—to each program being executed. Fifteen-hundredths of a second may not seem like much time to you, but as Harris Hyman noted in the February, 1967, issue of *Datamation* (p. 53): "That is enough to solve 20 simultaneous equations, sort 200 numbers into order, calculate the prices of 300 municipal bonds, perform 500 Runge-Kutta integrations, calculate 850 payrolls—all kinds of useful things." The result of such speed is that each user has the illusion that he has the undivided attention of the computer.

[20] The term *multiprocessing* is used to describe interconnected computer configurations or computers with multiple arithmetic-logic units that have the ability to *simultaneously* execute several programs.

programs stored in primary and/or online storage and a portion of one is executed, then a segment of another, etc. The processor switches from one program to another almost instantaneously. Since internal operating speeds of CPU's are much faster than are the means of getting data into and out of the processor, the CPU can allocate time to several programs instead of remaining idle when one is bringing in data or printing out information. With multiprogramming, it is thus possible for several user stations to share the time of the CPU. This *timesharing* feature may permit more efficient use of the capacity of the processor.

The incorporation of multiprogramming into the OS has, of course, complicated matters. For example, software must keep track of the locations in storage of each of the several programs, must remember at what point it should return to in an interrupted program, and must, perhaps, assign job priorities to the several tasks waiting to be completed. Operating systems of multiprogrammed computers are integrated collections of processing programs and a master control program that are expected to perform the *scheduling, control, loading,* and *program call-up* functions described below:

1. The *scheduling* function involves the selection of jobs to be run on a priority basis from a table or list of jobs to be processed. Available storage space and the most suitable peripheral hardware to use is allocated to the job or jobs being processed. Whenever possible, jobs are selected to balance input/output and processing requirements. They are added to and deleted from the job table as required.
2. The *control* function consists of a number of activities including (a) the control of input and output housekeeping operations, (b) the proper handling, shifting, and protection of data, instructions, and intermediate processing results when a high-priority program interrupts the processing of a lower-priority program, (c) the timing of each job processed and the allocation of processor time to user stations, and (d) the communication of error and control messages to human operators.
3. The *loading* function includes reading in and assigning storage locations to object programs and data. Checks are also made to prevent the loading and processing of incorrect files.
4. The *program call-up* function emphasizes the overall control of the OS master program (referred to by such names as *monitor, executive routine,* and *supervisor*) over other software elements including *translating programs, service programs,* or *utility routines* (for loading programs, clearing storage, sorting and merging data, diagnostic testing of new programs, etc.), and the installation's

stored file of *applications programs*. The monitor integrates this assorted software into a single consistent system. The system monitor generally remains in primary storage where it may occupy 25 to 60 percent of the available space; in installations with online storage capability, many of the other programs and routines are kept online and are called up and temporarily stored in the CPU as needed.

Figure 3-9 summarizes the relationship existing between the hardware and software categories discussed in the above pages. In view of the advances described in these pages, it is not surprising that many firms have exchanged earlier computing systems for newer versions one or more times. Let us now consider, in the following section, developments that may smooth the transition to more powerful systems.

SMOOTHING SYSTEMS TRANSITION

Bridging the "generation gap" can be traumatic for parents, their progeny—and computer-users. (In the case of computer-users, moving about within a hardware generation in the past was not without hazards.) Too often, the change to a new system made it necessary to completely rewrite proved and satisfactory applications programs for use with the new equipment. The development of *compatibility* and *modularity* concepts has served to ease systems-transition problems.[21]

Compatibility Developments

As noted earlier, *compatibility* is a term that may be associated with the software of a computer. If the programming aids, data, and instructions prepared for one machine can be used by another without conversion or program modification, the machines are said to be *compatible*. Many manufacturers of third- and fourth-generation computers have designed "families" of machines to provide compatibility for the user. The IBM System/360 family of machines, for example, consists of several models differing in size and power. Yet some of these models are both hardware compatible, i.e., the basic machine language instructions of one model will run on others, and software compatible, i.e., the higher-level language programs are interchangeable with little or no modification needed. Furthermore, Sys-

---

[21]Systems transition is also eased significantly by the use of such program conversion techniques as *translation, simulation,* and *emulation* (using *microprogramming* or *firmware* concepts). These topics are discussed in Chapter 11.

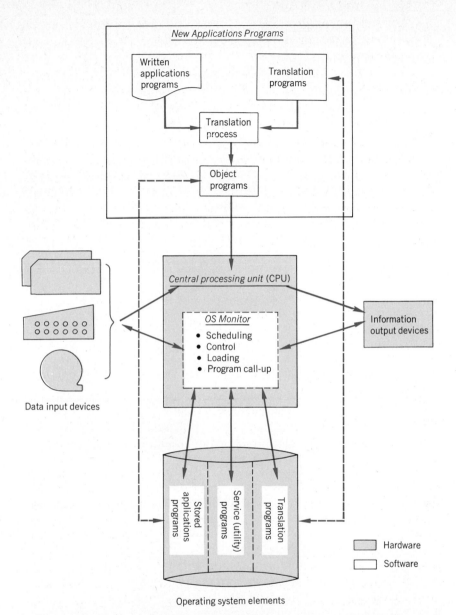

New Applications Programs

Written applications programs

Translation programs

Translation process

Object programs

Central processing unit (CPU)

OS Monitor
- Scheduling
- Control
- Loading
- Program call-up

Information output devices

Data input devices

Stored applications programs

Service (utility) programs

Translation programs

Hardware

Software

Operating system elements

Figure 3-9

tem/370 models are compatible with each other and will run many existing 360 programs without change.

In addition to making machines that are compatible with their other products, some manufacturers are also making their machines compatible with the equipment produced by others. (Compatibility exists, to a large extent, between certain models of the IBM System/360, the RCA Spectra/70, and the UNIVAC 9000 series of computers.) Thus, compatibility may exist both *within* a product line and *among* product lines.

The need for compatibility has been apparent for several years. Consider, for example, the plight of the expanding firm with an older machine that must process (as its longest program) a payroll requiring 7,000 characters in internal storage. The machine has an 8,000-character storage capacity, and so all is well. But as the firm grows, new employees are added, and new pay scales are created. The payroll program eventually requires storage capacity of 9,000 characters. Several alternatives are open to the company's managers, but let us first assume that they elect to acquire a new and larger machine.

All too often in the past, such a decision has required a costly rewriting of the programs developed for the old machine because of the lack of compatibility between it and its replacement. With upward compatible machines, however, a user may start with a small model geared to his requirements and convert to more powerful models as his workload expands.[22] The need to convert programs is substantially reduced. Also, greater exchange of programs, information, and data between users is possible.

The federal government, as the largest single user of computers (10 percent of the market), has suffered because of past lack of compatibility. Various economic indicators, for example, are gathered by different agencies. Rapid consolidation of such data is desirable in economic planning. But data and program incompatibility have hindered the effort in the past. Thus, the federal government has actively pushed the development of the compatibility concept.

Modularity Developments

If, in the above example of the payroll program grown too large, the firm could have expanded the storage capacity of its machine to, say, 16,000 characters, this might have been a more attractive alternative than acquiring a new system. Although not available with early hardware generations, the concept of *modularity* (also called *open-ended design* and *upgrading*) allows a computer installation to change and grow. To the original CPU can be attached additional units as the need arises, just as additional freight cars can be hooked onto a freight train. Users can begin with small systems and build up the installation gradually; it is not necessary that final capacity be provided at the

---

[22] Programs written for large machines may not run on smaller models without modification. But since computer systems have a tendency to expand, *upward* compatibility is generally a more important consideration than *downward* compatibility.

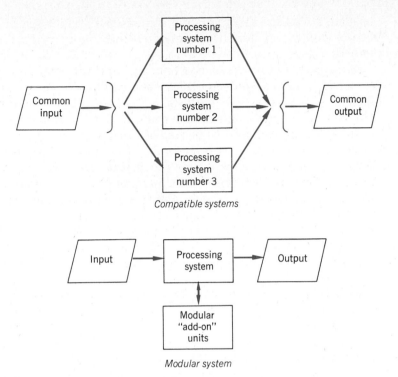

Compatible systems

Modular system

Figure 3-10

outset. In addition to *adding on,* true modularity also makes it possible to replace smaller components with larger versions while other hardware remains unchanged.

How does the modularity concept differ, then, from compatibility? *Two or more different* machine systems are compatible if they can accept the same input data and programs and produce the same output. A *single* system has modular capability if it can grow (see Fig. 3-10). Thus, a given installation may be both modular and compatible, may possess only one feature, or may have neither.

The technological advances in computer hardware and software discussed in the above pages have both contributed to and been stimulated by the rapid environmental changes mentioned earlier. Because of these rapidly changing conditions, managers have sought to implement computer-oriented management information systems that will enable them to cope with their changing environment. In the remainder of this chapter, let us (1) define what is meant by *management information systems* and (2) point out the factors that have made it difficult for traditional systems to continue to satisfy management needs.

**MANAGEMENT
INFORMATION SYSTEMS**

What are management information systems (MIS)? Strangely enough, it is not easy to pin down these innocent-looking words for they are defined in dozens of different ways and the definitions vary in scope and breadth.[23] For our purposes, *management information systems* are networks of data processing procedures developed in the organization *and integrated as necessary* for the purpose of providing managers with timely and effective information. A *procedure* is a related group of data processing steps, or *methods* (usually involving a number of people in one or more departments), which have been established to perform a recurring processing operation. Figure 3-11 illustrates these definitions in the narrow context of information needed by personnel managers. Each line represents a procedure (consisting of a series of steps, or methods, indicated by the squares) that is directed toward achieving the objective of more effective personnel management. Each procedure produces needed information, and several procedures cut across departmental lines. The *evalu-*

[23]Systems specialists even have difficulty agreeing on the definition of the word *systems*. At one meeting of these specialists, definitions offered "ranged from 'helping administrators ease decision-making when faced with multidirectional functional alternatives' to 'presenting a synthesis of a very diverse network of homogeneous complexities.' As *The New York Times* dryly reported: 'Jargon came into its own that day'." See George Berkwitt, "Systems: Too Much too Soon?" *Dun's Rev.*, June, 1968, p. 42.

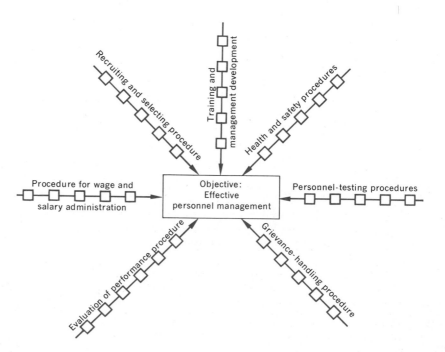

Figure 3-11   Personnel information system

ation of performance procedure, for example, may require the co-operation of supervisors throughout the firm.

Our personnel information system is, of course, only one of several information producing activities in a business.[24] Other activities typically included are those in the areas of accounting and finance, production, and marketing. Thus, information is produced in a number of systems, and the past success of these systems in consolidating this information within an appropriate time frame may or may not have satisfied the total needs of the business. In too many companies in the past, the information needs have not been met.

Traditional business information systems have often been found wanting because they do not provide information with the desired properties mentioned in Chapter 1. More specifically, traditional systems often fail in the following respects:

Difficulties with Traditional Systems

1. *Information is not timely.* Information arrives too late to be of value in planning and making decisions. Therefore the ability to take corrective action to prevent out-of-control situations is hampered. Part of the problem is due to the inability of older systems to cope with increased paperwork loads.
2. *Information is not properly integrated.* Potential users may be unaware of the availability of valuable information produced by internal departments and external sources. The information presented to managers is thus *not as complete as it could be.* As a result, significant past internal relationships are not analyzed; external social, economic, political, and technological factors that influence competitive actions and the business climate are inadequately considered.
3. *Information lacks conciseness.* Too much detail obscures clarity and prevents managers from focusing attention on those areas of significance that deviate from planned performance.
4. *Information is not available in the proper format.* Sales reports may be presented in terms of company departments and divisions when a more valuable classification might be to present the information in terms of products and customers. Report formats

[24]Some writers treat the entire business as a single *system* and the component parts of the business as *subsystems*. In this case our personnel system would be labeled a subsystem within the overall business system. We have no quarrel with this treatment since the difference is primarily one of semantics. Some also treat the entire business as a single information system. When total integration is required, a single system would result from our definition. It should be pointed out, however, that the degree to which information systems (or subsystems) can and should be integrated is rather controversial at this time.

often lack *consistency*. Analyses are frequently presented in monetary terms when another unit of measure might be more appropriate.

5. *Information costs too much to produce*. This is especially true when the information is wanted infrequently and at different times. Optimum use has often not been made of personnel and available data processing equipment. The financial returns obtained from the information produced frequently does not measure up to returns expected from investment in other areas of the organization.

6. *Information produced is not relevant*. Managers receive information they do not need because they are not in a position to take action that will influence the events reported. And, as noted above, relevant information that would assist the manager in recognizing significant external factors and events is generally not available.

To reduce the difficulties experienced with traditional approaches, new computer-oriented systems concepts have been developed (and are now emerging). These new concepts are the subject of the next exciting chapter—don't miss it!

SUMMARY

An information revolution is quietly taking place. Rapid developments in scientific, social, and economic areas have stimulated and contributed to significant changes in computer hardware and software (and vice versa) in the decade of the 1960s. Hardware advances include (1) substantial reduction in the size, weight, and cost of equipment compared with the same features of earlier machines and (2) significant increases in speed, storage capacity, and reliability. Advances in software include (1) more efficient and effective translating programs, which reduce tedious coding, (2) the development of better applications packages, and (3) the creation of sophisticated multiprogramming concepts and complex operating systems.

In the past, the decision to move from an old computing system to a larger and more efficient one often led to traumatic reprogramming experiences. Such a transition may still be fraught with peril, but hardware and software compatibility between computer families has benefited users by permitting them to exchange programs and update equipment without having to completely rewrite existing programs. The use of modular equipment may reduce the need to replace old equipment since it is then possible to extend the capabilities of existing systems.

Because of the unprecedented scope and pace of environmental changes, business managers have been forced to plan better and make swifter readjustments in their plans. As a result of difficulties experienced with traditional systems, they have been forced to support the development of computer-oriented management information systems. These new developments are the subject of the next chapter.

DISCUSSION QUESTIONS

1. Discuss this statement: "The basic challenge to the managers of today is to foresee and manage (and not be swept along by) the flood of changes facing their organizations, within a democratic framework, for the benefit of society as well as for the benefit of customers, employees, and owners."

2. (a) Describe several of the scientific discoveries that have been made since the beginning of World War II.
   (b) Comment on the broadening scope of scientific inquiry and on the rate with which new knowledge is put to use.
   (c) What effects do scientific changes have on business management?

3. (a) Identify and discuss the social and economic changes that are taking place today.
   (b) What effects will these changes have on business management?

4. Discuss this statement: "To compete profitably in the future, a manager must have information of the highest quality."

5. (a) What changes have taken place in computer hardware?
   (b) In computer software?

6. (a) What are the three basic software categories?
   (b) Discuss the developments in each of these categories.

7. What functions are performed by operating systems?

8. Define the following terms:
   (a) Millisecond
   (b) Microsecond
   (c) Nanosecond
   (d) Primary storage
   (e) Secondary online storage
   (f) Self-repairing computer
   (g) LSI
   (h) Source program
   (i) Object program
   (j) Compatibility
   (k) IOCS

      (l) Multiprogramming
      (m) Multiprocessing
      (n) Monitor

9. Differentiate between compatibility and modularity.
10. (a) What are management information systems?
     (b) What is a procedure?
     (c) What is a method?
11. What difficulties have managers experienced with traditional management information systems?

SELECTED REFERENCES

Bright, James R.: "Evaluating Signals of Technological Change," *Harvard Business Review,* January-February, 1970, pp. 62–70.

Heath, F. G.: "Large-Scale Integration in Electronics," *Scientific American,* February, 1970, pp. 22–31.

Joseph, Earl C.: "The Coming Age of Management Information Systems," *Financial Executive,* August, 1969, pp. 45–46ff.

Lenihan, John F.: "Applied Programming Packages are Growing in Importance," *Management Accounting,* January, 1970, pp. 12–14.

Rathe, Alex W.: "Projection 1976: New Demands on Management," *Michigan Business Review,* May, 1968, pp. 20–24.

"The Seventies: Super but Seething," *Business Week,* December, 6, 1969, pp. 77ff.

"Where the Action Is in Electronics," *Business Week,* October 4, 1969, pp. 86–91ff.

Withington, Frederic G.: "Trends in MIS Technology," *Datamation,* February, 1970, pp. 108–110ff.

The Information Revolution: Developments and Issues

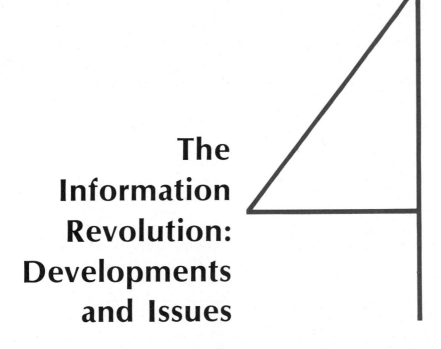

To reduce difficulties experienced with traditional approaches, new *computer-based* management-information-systems concepts have been (and are being) developed. These new concepts may be characterized as being (1) *quicker responding* and (2) *broader in scope* than traditional systems. New systems possessing these characteristics are discussed below and are manifestations of rapidly developing computer technology combined with the desire of managers to use this technology to meet increasingly demanding information requirements. It is possible, of course, for a specific business to make use of management information systems utilizing several of the concepts that will be presented at the beginning of this chapter.

In addition to new approaches, however, have come new issues and problems which must be considered. In the latter pages of the chapter we shall consider some of the *problems of adjustment* which are accompanying the information revolution.

QUICK-RESPONSE SYSTEMS

Information is time dependent; it must be collected, manipulated, communicated, stored, retrieved, and presented in a time frame that is appropriate to the problem being considered. *Quick-response systems,* as the name implies, have been developed to increase the timeliness, effectiveness, and availability of business information. *Quick-response systems have the following advantages:*

1. *They allow managers to react more rapidly.* Information from field representatives, customers, suppliers, creditors, and competitors can be more speedily assimilated. Managers may make direct inquiry and promptly receive infrequently needed internal information. And they may "converse" with the system in searching for answers to poorly structured questions.
2. *They reduce waste in the use of business resources.* Waiting time of customers, creditors, suppliers, managers, and employees can be trimmed; more efficient control of valuable and perishable inventories, such as seats on an airplane, can be obtained.
3. *They permit quick follow-up on creative ideas.* For example, by having direct access to a central processor, product research scientists may follow up on ideas that they might otherwise neglect if they had to wait for a long time to use the equipment. Furthermore, it would be possible for them to make quick experiments with different approaches for implementing the idea. Also, programmers may quickly check to see if there are "bugs" in programs or program segments which they are preparing.

Quick-response systems may be described by a bewildering variety of Computerese terms. A glance through a few current management and data processing periodicals shows the subject to be a veritable semantic jungle with many "experts" swinging from different definition vines. We shall attempt to cut through the foliage by examining the concepts of (1) *online processing,* (2) *real time processing,* and (3) *timesharing.*

Online Processing

The term *online* is used in several different ways. We have seen that a peripheral machine connected directly to and capable of unassisted communication with the central processor is said to be an online device. Online also describes the status of a person who is communicating directly with (i.e., he has *direct access* to) the central processor without the use of media such as punched cards or magnetic tape. Finally, online refers to a *method of processing data.* However, before looking at the concept of *online processing,* we should pause to describe the characteristics of the *batch processing* approach.

Batch processing (it is also called *serial, sequential,* or *offline* processing) is the evolutionary predecessor of online methods and accounts for the bulk of the work performed in current installations. Perhaps an illustration will best explain batch methods. Let us trace the activities that follow Zelda Zilch's credit purchase of a zither in a department store. The sales slip for this *transaction* is routed to the accounting office where it and others are collected for several days until a large batch accumulates. The data on the slips may be recorded on a machine input medium such as punched cards. The cards are then sorted by customer name or charge-account number into the proper sequence for processing. Processing consists of adding the item description and price of all the recent transactions to the customer's other purchases for the month. Thus, a customer accounts-receivable master file, perhaps in the form of magnetic tape, must be updated to reflect the additional charges. The sequence in which the new transactions are sorted is an ordered one and corresponds to the sequence on the master file. Figure 4-1 illustrates this batch processing procedure. At the end of the accounting period, the master file is used to prepare the customer statements.

Other files are periodically updated in similar fashion. A *file,* then, is a collection of related records and items treated as a unit. In our example, the zither purchase was one *item* on Zelda's bill; Zelda's bill would represent one charge-account *record;* and the purchase records of all credit customers would comprise the accounts-receivable *file.*

Batches may be collected at a central computer site or at other locations. One *other* location might be a small business that is a client of a computer service center; another might be a branch office of a large firm. In either case, batches may be collected and converted into the appropriate input medium. These ordered transactions may then be sent to the computer center through the mail, by messenger, or by the use of *remote batch processing stations* (see Fig. 4-2), which

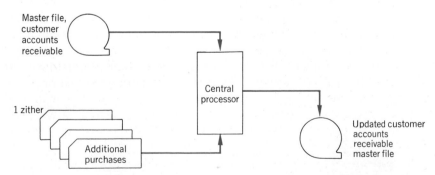

Figure 4-1   Batch processing

Figure 4-2 Remote batch processing station (courtesy Honeywell Information Systems)

often employ telephone circuits to transmit data directly into the central computer system. Depending on the type of user and the nature of the input data, the central computer may (1) update online files, (2) process the data and transmit the output information back by mail or messenger, or (3) process the data and transmit the output information back to a printer at the remote station.[1]

Batch processing has certain advantages:

1. *It is economical.* In general, a large throughput volume results in a low processing cost per record and makes efficient use of computing equipment. Accumulating transactions for large-volume processing permits economies of scale resulting from labor specialization and concentration of effort. The input/output devices used in batch processing generally operate at faster speeds than do the keyboard terminals used with other processing methods.

2. *It is the most appropriate method for many types of applications.* In batch processing, transactions are submitted in a group and several results are obtained from processing. This is quite appropriate for important applications such as payroll and the preparation of customer statements. It is not necessary to update employee pay records or to send statements to customers every day. In these examples, the delay brought about by accumulating data into batches does not reduce the value of the information.

[1] The time lapse here is typically greater than is the case with the methods of online processing we will consider. It may be minutes, hours, or days before the output information is received back at the station. Although priorities may be established, the remote batch job is stored in a queue of jobs waiting to be processed, and when its turn comes, it is executed consecutively to completion. It should be noted, however, that some commercial computer centers (e.g., Control Data Corporation's network) provide fast remote batch processing service to clients.

On the other hand, *batch processing has certain inherent disad-vantages:*

1. *It requires sorting.* Input data and master files must be arranged in some ordered sequence prior to processing. This sorting may be rather expensive in terms of time and money. In addition to sorting, it is also necessary to take time to set up the equipment for each batch job to be processed.
2. *It reduces timeliness in some cases.* The time required to accumulate data into batches, in some instances, destroys much of the value of the data. The information that results from eventual processing is no longer timely.
3. *It requires sequential file organization, and this can be a handicap.* To answer inquiries about the current status of the account of Zelda Zilch *between* processing periods is most difficult. If we assume that a magnetic tape master file and an alphabetic sequence are used, Zelda's record will obviously be near the end of the file and the entire file would have to be searched. Considering the trouble involved and the number of batch jobs waiting to be run, the inquiry might go unanswered until the next processing cycle—and by then, of course, some unwise credit authorizations might have been made.

Online processing has been developed for certain uses as an answer to the batch processing deficiencies noted above. In contrast to batching, online (or *direct access* or *random access*) processing permits transaction data to be fed under CPU control directly into secondary online storage devices from the point of origin without first being sorted. These data may be keyed in by the use of a typewriter-like terminal (see Fig. 4-3), or they may be produced by a variety of other data collection and transaction recording devices. The CPU can make programmed input control checks during this process. Appropriate records (which may be *organized* in the secondary storage unit in either a sequential or random fashion) may therefore be quickly updated. Information contained in any record is accessible to managers without the necessity of a sequential search of the file and within a fraction of a second after the inquiry message has been transmitted. Thus, online processing systems may feature *random* and rapid input of transactions and immediate and *direct access* to record contents as needed (see Fig. 4-4).

Direct access to records may permit executives to probe and query the file contents of advanced systems in order to ultimately obtain answers to questions that initially were vague and/or poorly defined. The success of such systems will depend upon (1) the availability of

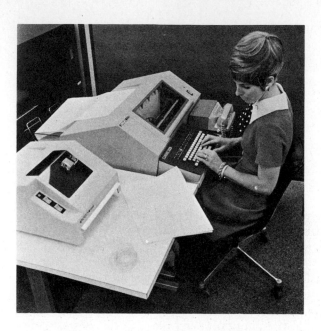

Figure 4-3   UNIVAC DCT 1000 data terminal (courtesy UNIVAC Division, Sperry Rand Corporation)

a common *data base* (or *data bank*), which will be developed as basic company data are commonly defined and consistently organized throughout the organization, and (2) the successful implementation of file processing software[2] that will "manage" the stored data items and assemble those items needed from the common base in response to the query or instruction of a manager who is not a programming specialist. Direct access to the central processor from an online station may also encourage managers to make more use of the decision-making techniques that will be discussed in Chapter 13.

Online processing and direct access to records *requires unique hardware and software.* For example, the capacity of the primary storage unit of the CPU must be adequate to (1) handle the complex online operating-system executive or master-control program and (2) serve a variety of other storage uses. Also, since many online users

[2]Among the names given by the developers of this type of software are Data Management System (Systems Development Corporation), Data Manager-1 (Auerbach Corporation), Integrated Data Store (General Electric Company), MARK IV File Management System (Informatics, Inc.), and Generalized Information Systems (IBM).

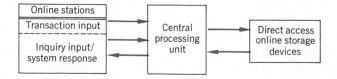

Figure 4-4   Online processing

may have access to stored records, software security provisions are necessary to (1) prevent confidential information from falling into unauthorized hands and (2) prevent deliberate or accidental tampering with data and program files. Furthermore, in many cases, processors must be fast enough to respond to multiple online stations operating simultaneously in a multiprogramming mode; and large-capacity peripheral online storage units are required to store additional operating-system elements, user data, and programs. Finally, data transmission facilities must be provided to communicate with online terminals located in the next room, on the next block, or thousands of miles away. Data transmission techniques make use of leased or public telegraph, telephone, and microwave radio facilities. The transmission of data over these facilities is increasing so fast that it is estimated that by 1975 ". . . the traffic between computers will be occupying as much communication capacity as all the traffic between people."[3]

It should be noted here, however, that online processing systems may differ considerably in level of complexity. Some systems may have only a few terminals, and the volume of transactions to be processed may thus be low; these transactions may be processed on a first-come, first-served basis with no attempt being made to use multiprogramming, and the system may employ relatively simple data communication facilities. At the other extreme are online systems that have hundreds of remote stations and communication lines; their operating systems may require hundreds of thousands of program instructions, and multiprogramming will be used to interleave the processing of transactions arriving simultaneously from a number of stations.

The speed of processing needed by a business varies with the particular application. As we have seen, batch processing is appropriate for many jobs. Online processing, although quicker responding than traditional methods, may involve different degrees of quickness in the needed response. For example, a system may combine immediate access to records for inquiry purposes with *periodic* (perhaps daily) transaction input and updating of records from a central collecting source. Such a system would meet many needs and would be simpler and less expensive than an online real time system.

Real Time Processing

The words *real time* represent a semantic bucket of worms—you can choose from over 30 definitions that have appeared in the literature. (This has led a few authorities to recommend that the words be

[3] Ervin K. Dorff, "Computers and Communications: Complementing Technologies," *Computers and Automation*, May, 1969, p. 22.

dropped altogether.) Some writers maintain that a system is responding in real time if it furnishes information to a manager in time for him to take effective action. Using this definition, a manual processing system might be operating in real time for some applications. The consensus of opinion is, however, that a *real time processing* operation is (1) in a parallel time relationship with an ongoing activity and (2) producing information quickly enough to be useful in controlling this current live and dynamic activity. Thus, we shall use the words *real time* to describe an online processing system with severe time limitations. A real time system is generally considered to be online; an online processing system, however, *need not* be operating in real time.

Real time processing requires *immediate* (not periodic) transaction input from all input-originating terminals. Many remote stations may be tied directly by high-speed communications equipment into the central processor; several stations may be operating simultaneously. Files may be updated each minute, and inquiries may be answered by split-second access to up-to-the-minute records. Some examples of business real time processing are the systems designed to keep track of the availability of motel and hotel rooms (e.g., the system of the Holiday Inn chain), the systems that provide for immediate updating of customer records in savings banks, and the systems that provide up-to-the-minute information on stock prices.

Another excellent example of a business real time processing installation is the SABRE system of American Airlines, which controls the inventory of airline seats available. A central computing center 30 miles north of New York City acts as a warehouse by receiving transaction data and inquiries directly (by over 31,000 miles of communications lines) from remote stations at over 1,000 reservation and ticket sales desks across the nation. In seconds, a customer may request and receive information about flights and available seats. If a reservation is made, the transaction is fed into the computer immediately and the inventory of available seats is reduced. The reverse, of course, occurs in the event of a cancellation. What if a flight is fully booked? If the customer desires to be placed on a waiting list, data such as customer name and telephone number are maintained by the computer. If cancellations occur, waiting-list customers are notified by agents.

But there is yet another facet to the SABRE system. It is tied in with similar systems of many other airlines to provide an exchange of information on seat availability. Thus, an agent for any of the participating companies may sell space on *any* of the airlines if the system shows it is available.

Real time processing is required and cooperation is necessary among airlines because of the perishability of the service sold—when an airplane takes off, vacant seats have no value until the next landing. It would be a mistake, however, to assume that real time processing should be universally applied to all data processing applications. A quick-response system can be designed to fit the needs of the business. Some applications can be processed on a lower-priority, or "background," basis using batch methods (e.g., payroll); some can be online with periodic (not immediate) updating of records; and some can utilize real time methods. Figure 4-5 illustrates some of the systems possibilities. In Fig. 4-5a transactions are collected and processed periodically using batch techniques while inquiry stations are used to obtain stored information. Figure 4-5b shows a real time system with immediate terminal input of selected types of transactions combined with background batch processing capability. Such a computer configuration might be programmed to follow the priority logic depicted in Fig. 4-6.

Timesharing

Managers cannot bear to see an idle computer—it is too expensive. For this reason, timesharing has always existed in computer installations in the sense that different departments in a company shared the total time of the hardware by requesting and receiving processed information. Generally, the jobs to be run for these departments receive a priority rating, and a job queue develops. Low-priority jobs may not be completed for days. In the quick-response context, however, there is a *much shorter* time scale involved, although the time restrictions may be less severe than those of the real time systems described above.

Timesharing is a term used to describe a processing system with a number of independent, relatively low-speed, online, *simultaneously usable* stations (see Fig. 4-7). Each station provides direct access to the central processor. As noted in the previous chapter, the speed of the system and the use of multiprogramming allows the central processor to switch from one using station to another and to do a part of each job in the allocated "time slice" until the work is completed. The speed is frequently such that the user has the illusion that he alone is using the computer. Timesharing systems vary from those that are designed for special purposes by a *single* organization (e.g., an airline reservation system) to those that are intended to provide services to a *multitude* of different organizations seeking to process a broad range of business and scientific jobs. Much of the contemporary literature dealing with timesharing emphasizes the latter type of system.

The number of special purpose timesharing systems is growing.

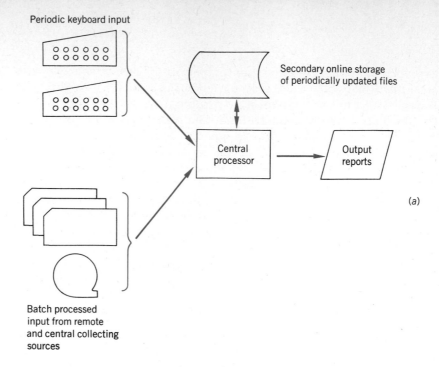

Periodic keyboard input

Secondary online storage
of periodically updated files

Central
processor

Output
reports

(a)

Batch processed
input from remote
and central collecting
sources

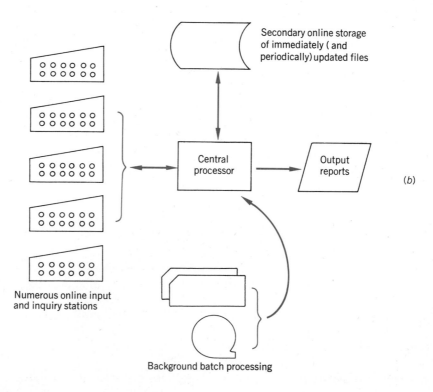

Secondary online storage
of immediately (and
periodically) updated files

Central
processor

Output
reports

(b)

Numerous online input
and inquiry stations

Background batch processing

Figure 4-5

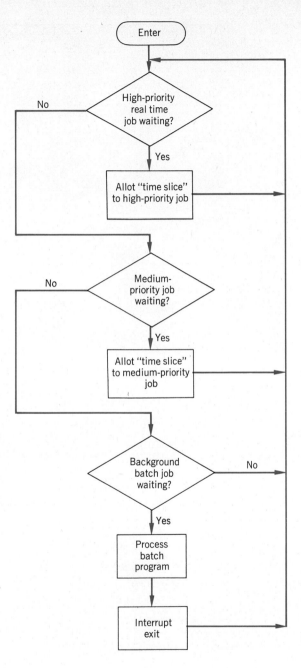

Figure 4-6

Figure 4-7 Timesharing terminal (courtesy General Electric)

More dramatic, however, is the growth of general purpose, multisubscriber installations, which have been established to service the needs of different organizations. In contrast to the typical arrangements made with a commercial computer center (which usually assumes the responsibility for performing a task), the control of processing in a timesharing operation generally remains with the using business. Transactions are initiated from, and output is delivered to, the premises of the using firm at electronic speeds. The subscriber pays for the processing service in much the same way he pays for his telephone service: There is an initial installation charge; there are certain basic monthly charges; and, perhaps largest of all, there are transaction charges (like long-distance calls), which vary according to usage. These variable charges are generally based on the time the terminal is connected to the central processing system and/or on the seconds of CPU time used.

 Because of similarities with public utilities (such as telephone companies), such timesharing[4] services have been called *information*

---

[4] *Resource sharing* might be a more appropriate term because commercial services permit users to share not only the time of the central processor but applications programs, storage space, and other facilities as well.

utilities and *computing utilities,* to the chagrin of industry spokesmen who feel the term *utility* suggests monopoly power and invites unwanted governmental regulation. The first completely commercial information utility was dedicated in November, 1965, in Cambridge, Massachusetts. Founded by Charles W. Adams, a former M.I.T. professor, Keydata Corporation was providing quick-response online service to 30 subscribers and 60 stations within a year. At least one subscriber replaced its own computer with the service. At the beginning of 1968, there were less than 50 general purpose timesharing installations in the United States. By 1970, however, General Electric alone had over 75 systems in operation, serving an estimated 100,000 individual users in over 20 countries. And it is expected that by 1974 there will be more than 1,200,000 terminals linked by data transmission facilities to computers.

The following *advantages of timesharing* help explain its expected rapid growth:

1. *Timesharing can reduce central processor idle time.* It is wasteful (and expensive) for the CPU to be effectively utilized less than 30 percent of the time. Yet this is what happens in a conventional batch processing installation as the CPU waits during setup times and during input/output operations. Timesharing can significantly increase CPU utilization.
2. *Timesharing offers computing capability to small users.* Small businesses can gain direct access to much more sophisticated hardware and software than they could otherwise justify or afford. They merely pay a fee for resources used and are relieved of the hardware, software, and personnel problems associated with acquiring and maintaining their own installations.
3. *Timesharing can provide the quick-response advantages noted earlier.* It allows managers to react more rapidly; furthermore, it permits them to *interact* or *converse* with the system in seeking solutions to unusual problems and answers to poorly defined questions. Timesharing may also reduce waste in the use of business resources, and it can permit quick follow-up on creative ideas. Answers to "what if?" questions may be quickly received. In short, user efficiency is often improved.
4. *Timesharing can improve input accuracy.* Inserting data into a file as they are originated eliminates errors that might occur during keypunching, sorting, etc. Also, programmed checks can verify the reasonableness of input data before they are accepted.
5. *Timesharing can reduce the output of paper.* If a manager can retrieve at any time the specific information he needs from an

online file, he does not need a bulky report that contains much of the file information.

6. *Timesharing is relatively easy to acquire and use.* A terminal may be quickly installed wherever there is a telephone line and a source of electric power. Special programming languages may be learned in a relatively short time. One such language—BASIC—is presented in Chapter 12.

7. *Timesharing permits use of applications programs.* A user need not write his own program instructions when performing many processing tasks. He need only call up the needed program stored online at the computer site and supply the data.

But the following *timesharing problems remain to be considered:*

1. *The question of economics.* From a strict cost standpoint, a small firm with enough batch processing volume to use about two days a week of computer time would likely find it less expensive at this time to acquire its own small in-house installation.[5] Input/output terminals are generally slow and inefficient when compared with the equipment used in batch processing. Thus, jobs with relatively large input and output requirements tend to be processed using on-site or remote batch techniques.

2. *The problems of data communications.* The *cost* of data communication has been declining but not nearly so rapidly as the cost of processing data. Thus, data transmission charges make up an increasing portion of the total timesharing cost package. In addition, telephone lines were designed for voice communication rather than data communication, with the result that current transmission equipment is not considered adequate by many timesharing spokesmen. We shall consider this data communications problem again later in the chapter.

3. *The question of security.* Provision must be made to protect the security and integrity of user data and programs maintained in online storage. This is currently being accomplished by such methods as (a) assigning certain areas of storage to only one user and to only his terminals and (b) requiring hierarchies of passwords or lockwords from users prior to file access. In spite of such precautions, however, skilled penetrators can bypass the programmed controls of current timesharing systems with distressing frequency. For example, Professor E. L. Glaser of Case Western Reserve University is a security expert and penetrator who is hired by timesharing developers to try to circumvent their security

[5]See David H. Li, *Accounting/Computers/Management Information Systems,* McGraw-Hill Book Company, New York, 1968, p. 281.

precautions. "After learning the standard operating procedures for the system, and thinking about the matter for a time, it is not unusual for him to be able to break through the security measures within five minutes time at a terminal."[6] The purpose of such a breakthrough might be to discover the names of passwords and their owners or to bring the entire system to an abrupt and disorganized halt—Professor Glaser has succeeded in doing both to systems he has tested.[7] The problem of securing user programs and data will receive greater attention in the future; at the present time there is an element of risk associated with storing valuable and/or highly confidential data at timesharing facilities.

4. *The problem of reliability.* There will be less margin for equipment downtime as more users come to rely on timeshared services. Provisions will have to be made to provide dependable and continuous service. The mean time between failure of complex timesharing systems is currently measured in days or—at most— weeks. The self-repairing computer mentioned earlier may ultimately help overcome the reliability problem, but troubles that occur now are not so much with the CPU as they are with online devices and software.

5. *The lack of certified applications programs.* There have been cases where timesharing library programs that purport to perform the same task have yielded *different results* when supplied with the same input data. Obviously, such inconsistency could result in users making unfortunate decisions.

The quick-response-system concepts that we have now considered are improving the timeliness, effectiveness, and availability of information. In addition, many of these emerging quick-response systems are taking a broader approach to the needs of the firm by attempting to provide better integration of information-producing activities. In the following section we shall briefly examine this trend.

Better integration of information-producing activities can lead to information that is more complete and relevant. Traditionally, business data processing has been organized by departments and by applications. Many computers were originally installed to process a large-volume job such as payroll or customer billing. Other applications, treated independently, followed, but it soon became clear that this

BROADER SYSTEMS

---

[6] Richard G. Canning, *EDP Analyzer*, May, 1970, p. 2.
[7] *Ibid.*

approach was unsatisfactory. In some cases, basic company data were defined and organized differently for each application; thus, the data were often expensively duplicated (with an increase in the possibility of error) because it was impossible to integrate these facts in meaningful ways. For example, information from the payroll file and the personnel file could not be combined because of different methods of classifying employees.

Dissatisfied with such conditions, some businesses began looking for ways to consolidate activities. Various names are given to these efforts. Among the terms used are (1) *integrated systems,* (2) *data-base systems,* and (3) *total systems.*

Integrated Systems

Integrated systems have as their objective the single recording of basic data into a common classifying code for the purpose of making maximum use of the data with a minimum number of human operations. A common example of this approach is found in the handling of sales orders. An order is received and confirmed on a special typewriter, which produces a punched paper tape as a by-product. The sales data (customer name, address, items ordered, etc.) are punched on this tape, which may then be used as a computer input to prepare shipping orders and the customer invoice. The same data are also used to update inventory, product sales, and accounts-receivable files. Obviously, the same common classifying code must be used to represent the data in the several files.

Data-base Systems

Data-base, or single-flow, systems are designed around a *single* integrated information file or *data bank*. This file is located in directly accessible online storage. Transactions are introduced into the system only once; all data-bank records that these transactions affect are updated at the time of input. The total file is not subdivided into applications. The single-flow concept requires that input data be commonly defined and consistently organized and presented throughout the business. And this requirement, in turn, calls for rigid input discipline; it also means that someone in the organization must be given the overall authority to standardize (and approve any necessary changes to) data with companywide usefulness, such as part numbers and customer and employee identification codes, in order to ensure that inconsistencies in data definitions are not introduced into the system.[8]

[8]Several authorities believe that although a closely integrated system might not now be planned, it is important for firms to begin now to achieve this standardization so that at a later time they will have the *option* of introducing broader systems.

As noted earlier, such a data base, combined with the successful implementation of data management software that will organize, process, and present the necessary data elements, will enable managers to probe and query file contents in order to extract the needed information. In the past, if a manager wished to have a special report prepared using information stored in the data base, he would probably communicate his needs to a programmer, who, when he had time, would write one or more programs to prepare the report. The availability of data management software, however, offers the user a much faster alternative communications path (see Fig. 4-8).

In addition to having direct access to data generated within the organization, a manager may also have externally produced information at his fingertips. It is anticipated that the sale of raw data will grow rapidly in the future. Such data will be produced by the data supplier's computer in a form to be used as input by the customer's system. Of course, this will necessitate an agreement on data format if effective use of purchased data is to be obtained. Industry data standards will develop because of this fact. In the future, firms may have to decide whether to "make" their own data or "buy" them from external data banks, just as they have often had to make similar decisions about physical products.[9] Presented below are a few examples of (1) data currently being sold in machine-sensible form, and (2) data-base services that are available.

1. *Marketing data*. Data about products sold in its stores are available from the Kroger Company. *Sales Management* magazine provides

[9] This statement applies now to software.

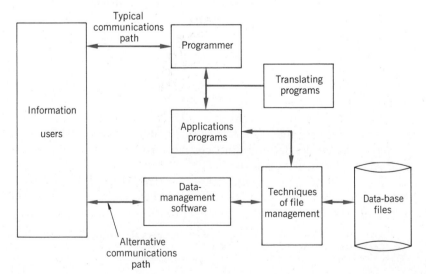

Figure 4-8

information on income and consumption patterns by geographic area. The F. W. Dodge Company, a McGraw-Hill subsidiary, sells data about the construction market. And there is a data bank for real estate agents, which contains listings on available property across the nation.

2. *Financial data.* Dun and Bradstreet provides a financial file on nearly 400,000 firms. Another McGraw-Hill subsidiary, Standard & Poor, offers a COMPUSTAT file, which contains sales and earnings figures on about 2,500 companies. White Weld and Company, New York investment bankers, offers a timesharing service to banks, pension funds, insurance companies, and other financial institutions. A twenty-year record of financial information—income statements and balance sheets—on over a thousand United States corporations is stored in online computer files. By the use of terminals and a specially developed inquiry language, White Weld's customers can have immediate access to this information.

3. *Economic data.* Economic statistics are available from a number of government agencies including the Bureau of the Census and the Department of Commerce.

4. *Personnel data.* Several employment agencies are tied into data banks, which match the characteristics of job applicants with the needs of employers.

Total Systems

Although the term *total systems* has been used in so many ways that it is now too ambiguous to be of much value, it has been described as the ultimate result of the consolidation of integrated subsystems. Thus, the words have been used to describe a single information system—a *total* system—which makes use of quick-response tools and techniques such as online mass storage, immediate updating of records from remote stations, and online inquiry.

A total system is an ideal that has been sought; unfortunately, it has seldom (if ever) been achieved. The management consulting firm of McKinsey & Company concluded after a careful study that "in terms of economic payoff and operational feasibility [total systems] are as yet ill-defined, and certainly they are a long way from practical utilization in business."[10]

It is not at all clear to what extent systems should be broadened. As a *philosophy*, however, the total systems concept has made a contribution. Computers *do* make certain consolidations possible;

[10] McKinsey & Company, Inc., "Unlocking the Computer's Profit Potential," *Computers and Automation*, April, 1969, p. 32.

most of the older systems *were* too narrow. Many businesses are now working toward gradual integration of information-producing systems and the creation of data banks. The approach is generally somewhat conservative because: (1) broad studies take a long time, are quite complex, require the efforts of highly paid employees who are in short supply, and often do not show any prospect of immediate tangible benefits; (2) substantial gains are still possible by placing new applications on the computer; (3) resistance is often encountered from managers who do not want to experiment with the familiar system; and (4) the planning and coordination of such a study is complicated since in many cases no single individual can really understand the total system.

The previous chapter and the above pages have shown some of the revolutionary changes taking place in technology and in the uses of this technology for information processing purposes. As might be expected, however, rapid change is often accompanied by problems of adjustment.

The growth in the development and use of computers in the 1960s made it possible for computer-users to obtain more timely and more complete information. But this uncontrolled growth brought adjustment problems, which affect individuals, computer-users, and the computer industry. These issues must be dealt with in the 1970s. In the following pages let us briefly describe the nature of such adjustment problems as: (1) the *challenges in information systems design;* (2) the *issue of invasion of privacy;* (3) the *issues in data communication;* (4) the *groping for an industry pricing structure;* (5) the adequate *protection of proprietary software;* and (6) the *shortage of computer personnel.*

PROBLEMS OF ADJUSTMENT

Challenges in Information Systems Design[11]

Many individuals are at work today on the design and development of a computer-based MIS that will be quick responding and comprehensive. The progress that pioneering designers have made in achieving these ends in the last decade has been most impressive. But progress has not yet measured up to the predictions made several years ago by a few zealots who envisioned a totally integrated, all-

[11] The purpose of this section is merely to present an overview of some of the problem areas currently being studied by systems designers. Although it is beyond the scope of this book to attempt an in-depth treatment of most of these design controversies, a few of the topics introduced here will be considered again in later chapters.

pervasive single information system that would employ a gigantic online data base and that would instantly give managers all the information they needed to make their decisions. What problems have prevented systems designers from achieving such "far-out" predictions? Let us first develop a few background ideas before we attempt to answer this question.

The management of medium-sized and larger organizations is a complicated process, which takes place on at least three managerial levels. Top executives perform the vital *strategic* planning and decision-making activities of the firm. They are charged with weighing the risks and making the major policy decisions on such matters as new product development, new plant authorizations and locations, corporate mergers and acquisitions, etc. They must also consider future technological developments in planning the firm's long-range strategy. Thus, as we saw in Chapter 1, the key factors that must be considered by top executives as they study a problem often are of an external nature—e.g., consumer preferences, labor union constraints, reactions of competitors to new products, and the reaction of a community to a new plant.

The *tactical* management decisions made by middle managers deal with the implementation of strategic decisions. Resources are allocated, authority is delegated, and control is maintained so that the strategic plans will be carried out. Lower-level *operating* managers make the day-to-day scheduling and control decisions that are needed if specific tasks are to be accomplished. Actual results of an operation are carefully checked against planned expectations, and corrective actions are taken as needed. Certain types of internal information resulting from operating decisions are summarized and fed back to upper managerial levels by existing information systems. The information flow to support decision making may be generalized as shown in Fig. 4-9.

Figure 4-10*a* depicts the three management levels, each with its own information needs. In addition to what might be termed the *horizontal* structure shown in Fig. 4-10*a*, an organization is also divided *vertically* into different business specialities or functions, which generate separate information flows (see Fig. 4-10*b*). Combining the horizontal managerial levels with the vertical business specialities produces the complex organizational structure shown in Fig. 4-10*c*. Underlying this structure in Fig. 4-10*c* we have a data base consisting, ideally, of internally and externally produced data relating to past, present, and predicted future events.

With the above concepts in mind, we are now in a position to better appreciate the problems and challenges that MIS designers face.

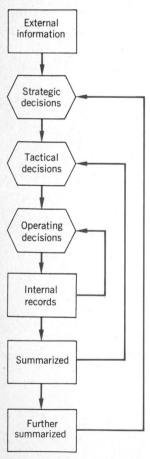

Figure 4-9

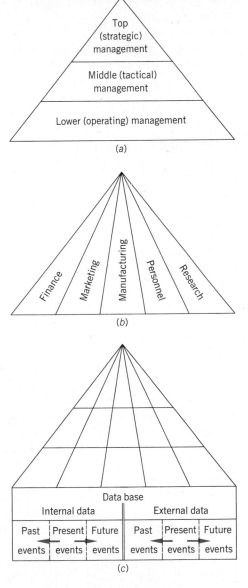

Figure 4-10

More specifically, systems designers are currently grappling with the following questions:

1. *Can a single data base be created to satisfy the differing information needs of the three managerial levels?* Most information systems today serve the needs of operating managers and, to a

lesser extent, middle managers. They provide internally produced data dealing with past and current activities. Although some firms are using internal data and carefully developed planning models incorporating assumptions about external conditions to *simulate* responses to the "what if?" questions of top executives,[12] the fact remains that most current systems focus on internal and historic events and produce output of only limited use in strategic planning. Whether to attempt to organize and structure a *single* data base to meet varying needs or to create *different* bases for different horizontal levels is a problem facing designers. Figure 4-11 depicts the alternatives.

2. *Can different business specialities share the same data base?* Can the system supply from a single data base the information needed by marketing, production, finance, and personnel managers at different levels, or must separate vertically oriented data bases be designed for each speciality? Different business functions have generally had their own information systems. Attempting to integrate these separate systems into one or more corporate data bases that will serve the broader needs of many managers is a formidable challenge, but the effort is being made.

3. *Can externally produced data be incorporated into the data base?* To be of value to managers at the higher echelons, an MIS must supply information about the external world, and this information must be complete, timely, and accurate. But the quality of externally produced data is more difficult to control than internal data quality, and external data has been expensive to obtain. The growing availability of external data in machine-sensible form and/or the use of external data banks will make more data avail-

---

[12]We shall look at simulation in more detail in Chapter 13.

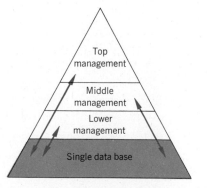

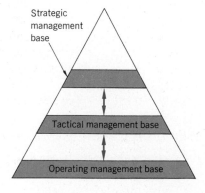

Figure 4-11

able to the firm's data bank. It is the designer's problem to see that these new facts are incorporated into the MIS in meaningful ways.

4. *Can suitable flexibility be built into the system?* Different managers occupying the same position over a period of time will have different information needs, and the system should not have to be redesigned to meet these changing needs. Executive A may want highly condensed reports with little detail; executive B, on the other hand, may wish to delve into a detailed data base and seek many facts before making a decision. Robert Head notes that President Eisenhower was the type of executive who wanted fewer details while former Secretary of Defense Robert McNamara was the executive B type who sought numerous facts.[13] The problem of the systems designer is to make it possible for executive B to succeed executive A without requiring that the system be restructured. The use of the data-management software described earlier may make it possible to supply executive B with greater detail.

5. *Should we attempt to "solve the triangle"?* That is, should the designers attempt to create an overall system that would simultaneously satisfy the information needs of all the segments shown in Fig. 4-10c, or should they select a subset and concentrate on it? Although the tendency of some organizations may be to attempt the triangle solution, "unless the organization is very small, it will take many, many years to 'solve the triangle,' and by the time the solution is operational, the solution will also be obsolete."[14] The complexity of the problems involved in developing an integrated MIS are such that even IBM, with its resources, is taking a gradual and controllable approach in designing its own MIS.

We may summarize the discussion in this section with the observation that although significant progress has been made in designing computer-based systems that, when compared with traditional methods, are quicker responding and better integrated, much unfinished business and many unanswered questions remain. The full potential of the computer has yet to be realized by businesses, but several are now in the process of moving out of a period of learning (though learning, of course, continues) into a period of innovation.

---

[13] See Robert V. Head, "Structuring the Data Base for Management Information Systems," *J. Syst. Manage.*, January, 1969, p. 11.
[14] James M. McKeever, "Building a Computer-Based MIS," *J. Syst. Manage.*, September, 1969, p. 13.

The Invasion of Privacy Issue

For years private and governmental agencies have been building separate files containing information about those with whom they come in contact. For example, credit bureaus, banks, and other financial institutions have files showing the credit and financial status of millions of people. Files on individuals are also maintained by schools (academic records), physicians (health records), courts (legal and criminal records), companies (customer and employee records), the FBI and the CIA (fingerprint records, security records, and ??), the Internal Revenue Service (tax records), state motor vehicle bureaus (driving records), the Veterans Administration (service records)—the list seems to be endless!

The keeping of these separate files has led to many abuses of an individual's legitimate right to privacy, i.e., his right to keep to himself (or to have kept on a confidential basis) those facts, beliefs, thoughts, and feelings that he does not wish to publically divulge. But many of these files are incomplete and are poorly maintained. Thus, the value of their contents may give unauthorized persons little incentive to snoop. The development of computer data banks, however, has changed the situation. Files maintained in these large integrated banks may be more complete, less subject to deterioration, and therefore more worthy targets for unscrupulous persons bent on ferreting out information of a private and confidential nature. Proposals for the creation of data banks that would be national in scope have touched off a significant—and as yet unresolved—controversy. Although privately sponsored national banks may be created which would raise serious privacy questions, e.g., a system to tie the records of all credit bureaus into a central bank, most of the controversy has focused on a federal government proposal.

Late in 1966, after eleven months of study, a special government Task Force on the Storage of and Access to Government Statistics recommended to the Bureau of the Budget that a National Data Center be established. This center would consolidate all data compiled by about twenty federal agencies.[15] Budget Bureau officials maintain that such a center would lead to *more efficient and effective economic and social analyses* by (1) improving the comparability of interrelated statistical data and (2) making these data more readily available. By building on the Budget Bureau proposal and by incorporating other available local and state government files, other proponents of a broad national data bank see the following *additional* advantages: (1) *law enforcement benefits*—the problems brought about by mobile crimi-

---

[15] As you may know, many agencies have the power to force individuals to supply information. For example, the penalty for failing to answer the 1970 Census question on the number of flush toilets owned was the same as that for indecent exposure.

nals and lack of communication between fixed law enforcement jurisdictions could be reduced; (2) *convenience to the individual*—a national data bank would eliminate the need to fill out so many information forms; (3) *greater privacy through better control*—a legally recognized national center, policed and controlled under legal safeguards, is preferable to the many semisecret and often misleading files in existence today.

In spite of the merits that such a data bank might have, a number of opponents are concerned about the threat that it might eventually present to an individual. Their concern was perhaps best summarized in a *Saturday Review* cartoon, which showed a distressed executive listening to a telephone message. The message was: "This is the Computer Data Bank. Leave $100,000.00 in small bills in locker 287 at the Port Authority Bus Terminal or I'll print out your complete dossier and send it to your wife." Among the more specific objections which have been voiced are:[16] (1) *information may be obtained* from confidential sources for the national bank *without the knowledge or consent* of the individual; (2) there may be *no means of verifying the accuracy, completeness, or subjective quality of the dossier*—factual errors or misleading information may seriously damage an individual's reputation; (3) there is *lack of security*—sensitive and confidential personal information will likely be obtained and used by unauthorized and unscrupulous personnel who will find ways to penetrate the safeguards of an online system;[17] and (4) there may be *eventual loss of personal freedom*—the creation of a federal government superbank with a complete computer-based dossier on every individual would give considerable power to those in charge of the bank, and this development might be the beginning of a drift toward the "big brother" state created by George Orwell in his book *1984*.

At this writing the National Data Center has not been implemented. But the importance of the invasion of privacy issue justifies the serious consideration that it is currently receiving.

The Data Communications Problem

The importance of data communications in timeshared information systems was noted earlier. Telephone lines are used extensively to connect remote terminals to central computers. In fact, it has been estimated that in the middle or late 1970s well over 50 percent of the revenue of the American Telephone and Telegraph Company (AT&T)

[16] Many of these same objections have been directed toward existing information files.
[17] Fred Gruenberger has described how it is that a programmer may not be sure of the consequences of what he has programmed. He also notes that it is impossible to assume that any network is secure, particularly if it utilizes telephone lines. See "The Unpredictable Computer," *Datamation*, March, 1967, pp. 59ff.

will be generated by data transmission rather than by voice transmission. Yet there have been questions raised by computer-industry spokesmen and computer-users about the ability of the telephone network to adequately handle this jump in demand caused by the rapid spread of remote computing.

Why the concern? It is because, as telephone critics point out, the telephone system was designed for voice transmission rather than for the transmission of data. A certain amount of line noise, fading, *crosstalk,* and other inconveniences can be tolerated in voice communication, but this is not true when data are being transmitted. There are four main types of message switching circuits used today in the telephone system,[18] and the two older switching mechanisms have often proved to be too "noisy" to handle data communication. (The line noise may change the meaning of a character being transmitted to the computer, or it may be interpreted as a character when none was intended—an unsettling thought!) Since the telephone-user generally has no control over the line circuits that handle his data communications, he may receive satisfactory circuits during one hookup and noisy and undesirable circuits during the next. Also, a severe mismatch often exists between computer speed and the slower capabilities of the locally available transmission equipment.

In attempting to come to grips with the anticipated interrelated problems of the computing and communications industries, the Federal Communications Commission (FCC) began a series of hearings in the mid-1960s. Among the results of these hearings (which at this writing are still being conducted) are the following:

1. *An easing of the "foreign attachments" rule.* The position of the telephone companies for years had been that in order to protect their network and maintain the quality and reliability of their service, they had to produce and/or have control over any attachments, e.g., switchboards, to that network. Subscribers were thus required to rent such equipment from the phone company. In June, 1968, in the *Carterfone* case, the FCC ruled that subscribers could connect their mobile radio systems to the phone network through the use of "foreign" converters produced by Carter Electronics Corp. This ruling thus opened the door for the use of peripheral data processing equipment, which many computer users felt would be more satisfactory and/or less expensive than telephone company equipment.

---

[18] The telephone companies are currently replacing the older crossbar, panel, and rotary switching equipment with an electronic switching system, but the conversion may not be completed until the year 2000. The computing community, of course, is not pleased with this prospect.

2. *Approval of new interstate data communications service.* In August, 1969, Microwave Communications, Inc., received FCC approval to operate a data communications service between Chicago, Ill., and St. Louis, Mo. This new service will charge rates significantly below those previously quoted by AT&T, and it opens the door to the possible establishment of an additional national communications network, which would compete with existing facilities.

At this writing there are numerous skirmishes taking place in the battle between the regulated telephone and telegraph carriers and the data processing community for the upper hand in future developments in data communication. Among the sticky public-policy questions that must be considered in the 1970s are the following: (1) Should the regulated carriers be allowed to offer computing services in a package along with their transmission services? And if this is permitted, might not this give the carriers an unfair competitive edge over computing-oriented firms? (2) Should nonregulated data processing organizations be allowed to offer communications services in densely populated low-cost areas, which would "skim the cream" of revenue from the carriers' markets and leave them to provide high-cost service to sparsely settled regions?

Computer Industry Pricing Changes

During the 1960s, computer manufacturers had specific sales and rental prices for their hardware, but no *explicit* charges were generally made for the software and technical assistance that they provided to their customers. The high cost incurred by the manufacturer in providing software and supporting services was, of course, passed along to the customer as part of the hardware charges, but to computer-users this was a hidden cost. There was, in other words, a *bundle* of goods and services provided in return for a charge placed only on hardware. Because of this pricing policy, many users became accustomed to considering the software and services of their supplier as being "free." Thus, they tended to limit their choice of software and services to what was provided in the manufacturers' bundle. (After all, they generally still paid the same price even if they did not avail themselves of all the available "free" features provided, and if they decided to obtain computing software and services from independent sources, there would be additional expenses incurred.)

Because IBM is the dominant firm in the computing industry, with control of about two-thirds of the market, and because (its competitors claimed) its bundled price policies tended to keep customers from searching for alternative sources of supply, several lawsuits[19] charging unfair competitive practices and attacking IBM's policy of furnishing software and systems engineering services without charge were filed against the company in late 1968 and 1969.

Partially in reaction to the antitrust suits, IBM announced on June 23, 1969, that effective January 1, 1970, it would begin to place separate charges on: (1) a broad range of *program products;* (2) *systems engineering services,* i.e., the services of systems specialists who are available to help the user in the installation and application of his information system; (3) *custom contract services,* i.e., contracts where IBM will assume responsibility for the performance of specified tasks in the areas of systems design and analysis, application and program development, and systems installation and evaluation; and (4) *customer education,* i.e., formal courses offered by IBM education centers to train user employees and others who meet course prerequisites. A 3 percent reduction in hardware prices was also announced.

The industry reaction to this *unbundling* was "varied, optimistic, diverse, pessimistic, dissimilar, and cautious."[20] During late 1969 and 1970, other manufacturers groped for a pricing policy. Some remained bundled (UNIVAC, Honeywell, and NCR); some followed the unbundling route (Control Data and Burroughs); and one firm (RCA) gave customers a bundled or unbundled option. Although at this writing the effects of these changes in the computer industry marketplace are confused and uncertain, it is likely that they will be felt for years to come. Most authorities believe that unbundling (1) has raised the total data processing bill of the typical user (estimates range from 5 to over 25 percent) and (2) has opened up the market for independent software, service, and educational organizations.

The Problem of Software Protection

When a central processor is rented to a customer, the title remains with the manufacturer and the user seldom has the economic incentive or the capability to secretly build and use a copy. Patent laws safeguard the manufacturer against those few who might be tempted. When software is rented, however, it may be easily copied. A program in punched card or magnetic tape form can be quickly and inexpensively duplicated; documents may be reproduced without difficulty. A program taking man-years to prepare at a cost of $500,000 might be rented on a one-time basis by an unethical customer, copied for $50, and secretly used thereafter. Thus, software developers need legal

---

[19] Included are suits by Control Data Corporation and the U.S. Department of Justice.
[20] Aubrey Dahl, "1969: An Overview of the News," *Datamation,* January, 1970, p. 91.

safeguards to protect against the unauthorized use of their proprietary programs.

The software industry has thus far failed to agree on the most appropriate means of program protection, but this protection problem is one that must be resolved in the future. Among the legal protective measures advocated are: (1) patent protection;[21] (2) copyright protection; (3) trade-secret protection, i.e., treating the program and supporting documents as a trade secret; and (4) contractual protection, i.e., using written agreements between developer and user.

The rapid expansion in the number of computer-oriented information systems during the 1960s has produced a serious shortage of qualified computer personnel. The current demand for skilled people greatly exceeds the available supply. Thus, salary levels are in five figures and have been rapidly increasing. Employment opportunities in the computer field are excellent. Furthermore, the number of people needed in the areas of *information systems management, information systems analysis and design,* and *program preparation* will expand significantly in the next few years for the following reasons.

The Shortage of (and Employment Opportunities for) Computer Personnel

1. As we have seen, the number of computers will increase substantially in the span of a very few years. These computers must be staffed.
2. The workload in existing installations will be increased as additional applications in all business areas are converted to the computer.
3. Many existing applications programs will be redesigned and reprogrammed to some extent during conversion to new equipment in order to make more efficient use of technological advances in hardware and software.
4. New and quicker-responding information systems will be designed to integrate existing and proposed applications in order to provide higher-quality information.

Information systems management   The information systems manager performs the administrative duties of all managers. That is, he *plans* the activities of his department so that it will provide a quality product, a timely product, and an economical product; he *organizes* the human and physical resources of his department to achieve a smooth

[21] Prior to August, 1969, the federal government's general position was that programs were not patentable. At that time, however, the U.S. Court of Customs and Patent Appeals ruled that programs meeting certain conditions could be patented.

and efficient operation; and he *controls* these very expensive resources to achieve his planned objectives. Increasingly, people planning to seek a career in business computer management must first acquire a college education. Courses in business administration, economics, data processing, mathematics, and statistics are desirable. Also, the importance of being able to work with people cannot be overemphasized.

According to estimates, there were 30,000 qualified managers and supervisors in data processing installations in 1966. This figure fell about 10,000 *short* of the need at that time. In 1970, about 85,000 managers were needed—an increase of 55,000 in a four-year time span! The shortage of qualified managers is growing more acute every year. (One source has placed the *shortage* figure at over 50,000 in 1971.) Keeping pace with demand, salaries have increased rapidly for good managers during the last few years. This trend will obviously continue. Managers can now expect to earn, on the average, between $15,000 and $30,000 annually.

Systems analysis and design   Although there are often several grades of *systems analyst* (senior, junior, etc.), the job basically consists of (1) examining the basic methods and procedures of current information systems and (2) modifying, redesigning, and integrating these existing procedures into new systems specifications as required to provide the needed information. Typically, the analyst must know a great deal about the particular firm and the industry as well as about the uses and limitations of computers. Educational backgrounds vary, but many analysts have a college background in business administration, economics, or the liberal arts. The analyst is often a prime candidate for promotion to more responsible management positions both in and out of data processing because of his broad knowledge of the business.

There were approximately 60,000 qualified analysts available in 1966—a figure that fell 35,000 short of the need. By 1970 the number available had risen to about 85,000 but—alas—about 185,000 were then needed. By 1973 it is estimated that there will be 200,000 analysts available with an unfilled demand for an additional 300,000! Thus, the employment opportunities in this area are apparent. The good analyst can expect to earn an average of between $13,000 and $25,000 per year.[22]

[22] In at least one instance, a textile manufacturer was forced to abandon plans for a sophisticated MIS because the salaries required to obtain the needed senior analysts would have exceeded the incomes of vice presidents.

Program preparation   The job of the applications programmer[23] is to take the systems designs of the analyst and transform these specifications into machine instructions or programs. In most cases the programmer will work very closely with the analyst during the systems-design phase. In smaller organizations the systems analysis and program preparation functions are often combined. As with analysts there are different job grades of applications programmers. In scientific programming a strong mathematics background is required; in business programming the educational requirements depend on such factors as system complexity, the industry, and standards of the employer. Logical reasoning ability and attention to detail are required. A college degree, however, is not necessarily a condition for employment, although many businesses use a degree as a means of screening applicants. According to estimates made by Control Data Institute, approximately 20 percent of all computer programmers today are women.

In 1950 there were only a few hundred programmers, while in 1966 the number had grown to 120,000 (about 50,000 short of the need). In 1970 the programming ranks had grown to 145,000 and the need had grown to 235,000. By 1973, over 500,000 will be needed but only 260,000 will be available.[24] A skilled applications programmer can expect to earn on the average between $12,000 and $20,000 per year. Junior programmers with college degrees earned *starting* salaries from $10,000 to over $13,000 in 1970, according to a survey compiled by the Robert Half Personnel Agencies, Inc.

Facilities Management Organizations

The problem areas discussed in the preceeding pages are, of course, directly affecting computer-using organizations. For example, new systems concepts must be designed and implemented, but qualified personnel are in very short supply and are expensive. Also, the structure and pricing policies of the computer industry are in a state of flux at the same time that the economic justification of new systems through the use of tangible cost-displacement techniques is often becoming more difficult to establish. Rather than deal with one or more of these problem areas, several computer users have contracted to turn over the management and operation of their computer installations to *facilities management* organizations.

---

[23] *Systems programmers* are those who write the complex operating system software and translating programs referred to in Chapter 3. As might be expected, there has never been enough of these highly skilled specialists to fill the need.

[24] These and earlier figures are based on those released by John M. Scandalios. See "Facilities Management," *IEEE Computer Group News*, March–April, 1970, p. 14.

These organizations are specialists in data processing and have been able to attract and retain highly qualified people by offering excellent salaries and a variety of challenging client job assignments. From the client's point of view, the arrangement has appeal because (1) he contracts to receive, at a fixed price for a relatively long period, a service beset with spiraling costs and (2) he receives, during a time of severe shortage, the talents of skilled people to achieve his information and processing needs.[25] When the facilities management firm consolidates the processing jobs of several clients at a single large installation in order to achieve economies of scale, the distinction between the services offered by the facilities management company and the commercial computer-center company tends to become blurred.

SUMMARY

As a result of difficulties experienced with traditional information processing techniques, businesses have developed (and are currently working on) quicker-responding and more integrated systems to meet the informational needs of managers.

Quick-response systems enable managers to react more rapidly, reduce waste in the use of business resources, and permit quick follow-up on creative ideas. The speed of processing needed by a business, however, varies with the particular application. Batch processing is appropriate for many jobs. Where quicker response is needed, a system might combine immediate access to online records for inquiry purposes with periodic (but not immediate) updating of records. When immediate updating of records from all transaction-originating terminals is required, a real time system must be installed. *Timesharing* is a term that describes a quick-response system with a number of online, simultaneously usable terminals that are connected to the central processor. Although growth in the number of general purpose timesharing installations is expected to be rapid in the 1970s, this growth will be hindered to some extent by data communications problems.

Many quick-response systems are taking a broader approach to the needs of businesses by attempting to provide better integration of information-producing activities. Difficult problems and challenges

[25]For more information on the facilities-management concept, see Scandalios, *op. cit.*, pp. 12–17; Douglass M. Parnell, Jr., "EDP Facilities Management: Abdication or Salvation," *Computers and Automation*, October, 1970, pp. 23–27; and "When EDP Goes Back to the Experts," *Business Week*, October 18, 1969, pp. 114–116.

face designers, but many are working hard to create online data-base systems that will cut across traditional departmental lines. However, the potential creation of national data banks containing dossiers about citizens raises serious questions about whether or not the individual's right to privacy will be safeguarded.

A critical shortage of qualified managers, systems analysts, and programmers exists now and will become more severe in the next few years. For persons trained in these areas, employment opportunities appear to be unlimited.

DISCUSSION QUESTIONS

1. (a) Why have quick-response systems been developed?
   (b) What are the advantages of such systems?
   (c) What is the distinction between online processing and real time processing?
2. (a) What is batch processing?
   (b) How does it differ from online processing?
   (c) What are the advantages and disadvantages of batch processing?
3. "Online processing and direct access to records requires unique hardware and software." Discuss this statement.
4. (a) What is meant by *timesharing?*
   (b) What is an *information utility?*
   (c) What are some of the advantages and current limitations of timesharing?
5. Identify and discuss the broader systems approaches that have been used to consolidate information processing activities.
6. "A total system is an ideal that has been sought; unfortunately, it has seldom (if ever) been achieved." Discuss this statement.
7. "Growth in the development and use of computers in the 1960s brought adjustment problems that affect individuals, computer users, and the computer industry." What problems may be identified?
8. Identify and discuss four challenges currently facing MIS designers.
9. (a) What advantages might be obtained through the creation of a National Data Center?
   (b) What objections have been voiced to such a center?
   (c) Would you be in favor of such a center?
10. Identify and discuss the *data communications problem.*
11. What is meant by *unbundling?*

12. What is a facilities management organization?
13. Has the computer-personnel shortage been a factor in the creation of facilities management firms? Why?
14. What are the job functions of (a) the information systems manager, (b) the systems analyst, (c) the applications programmer?

SELECTED REFERENCES

Allen, Brandt: "Time Sharing Takes Off" *Harvard Business Review,* March–April, 1969, pp. 128–136.

Berkeley, Edmund C.: "The Invasion of Privacy," *Computers and Automation,* April, 1970, pp. 6ff.

Brunow, Gordon P.: "Computers: More Problems?" *S.A.M. Advanced Management Journal,* April, 1970, pp. 35–40.

Canning, Richard G.: "Technical Support for an MIS," *EDP Analyzer,* November, 1969, pp. 1–12.

Head, Robert V.: "Protecting Packaged Programs," *Journal of Systems Management,* October, 1969, pp. 40–41.

Rhind, C. Ridley: "The Computer and Functions of Management," *Datamation,* June, 1969, pp. 43–46.

Sprague, Richard E.: "The Invasion of Privacy and a National Information Utility for Individuals," *Computers and Automation,* January, 1970, pp. 48–49.

"The Wide-Open Market that IBM Unbundled," *Business Week,* May 2, 1970, pp. 84ff.

Wilson, John L.: "Separate Pricing for Computer Support Services," *Business Horizons,* June, 1970, pp. 79–85.

Introduction to Computers

In earlier pages we have dealt with computers in general terms. In this chapter, however, we begin the closer examination of this exciting business tool. More specifically, in the next few pages we shall consider: (1) the *classes* of computers, (2) their *capabilities,* (3) their *limitations,* (4) their *learning* ability, and (5) their *functional organization*.

COMPUTER CLASSIFICATIONS

As you know, many firms offer tours of their facilities to interested parties. Let us assume that you are in a group visiting an insurance company. In the course of your visit, the tour guide asks you to identify the equipment located in a large room. Because you are an intelligent person, you respond that this is the firm's computer. The guide replies, "Yes, this is our medium-sized, fourth-generation, electronic, stored program, digital (a gasp for breath), general purpose computer used for business purposes."

You recognize what he meant by the terms *medium-sized, fourth-generation, electronic,* and *stored program.* Computers are sometimes classified by size into large, medium, small, and mini categories on the basis of computing power and cost. A medium-sized system might cost from $250,000 to $1 million. The fourth-generation age classification is arbitrary and may refer to equipment produced in the first half of the 1970s, while the term electronic distinguishes the equipment from mechanical and electromechanical processing machines that are much slower in their operation. The stored program concept is vital to the modern computer and refers to the ability of the machine to store internally a list of sequenced instructions that will guide it automatically through a series of operations leading to a completion of the task. We will come back to this concept in later chapters.

But what about the other classifying terms used by the guide—what exactly did he mean by *digital, general purpose,* and *business purposes?* Let us look at each of these items.

Analog and Digital Computers

There are two broad classes of computing devices—the analog and the digital. The *analog* machine does not compute directly with numbers; rather, it measures continuous physical magnitudes (e.g., pressure, temperature, voltage, current, shaft rotations, length), which represent, or are *analogous* to, the numbers under consideration. The service station gasoline pump, for example, contains an analog computer that converts the flow of pumped fuel into two measurements—the price of the delivered gasoline to the nearest penny and the quantity of pumped fuel to the nearest tenth of a gallon. Other examples of analog computers are (1) the widely used slide rule, which permits computations by the movement of one length along another; and (2) the automobile speedometer, which converts drive-shaft rotational motion into a numerical indication by the speedometer pointer.

Analog computers are used for scientific, engineering, and process control purposes. Because they deal with quantities that are continuously variable, they give only approximate results. The speedometer pointer, for example, might give a reading of 45 miles per hour. But if the pointer were lengthened and sharpened, if the speedometer were calibrated more precisely, and if the cable were given closer attention, the reading might then be 44 miles per hour. Further refinements might give a reading of 44.5 miles per hour. A well-known soap product has claimed for years to be "99 and 44/100 percent pure." Under the best circumstances, an analog computer can achieve a somewhat higher degree of precision than this figure. But in a problem involving $1 million, an analog device might give answers only to the nearest hundred or thousand dollars.

The *digital* computer operates by *counting* numbers. It operates directly on numbers expressed as digits in the familiar decimal system or some other numbering system. The ancient shepherd, it will be recalled, used stones to represent sheep, and these were counted one by one to determine the total number of sheep in the flock. Nothing was measured as an analogous representation of the number of sheep; they were counted directly, and their total was exact. Stones have been replaced by adding machines, desk calculators, and digital computers, but all employ the same counting rules we learned in grade school.

Digital computation results in greater accuracy. While analog computers may, under ideal conditions, be accurate to within 0.1 percent of the correct value, digital computers can obtain whatever degree of accuracy is required simply by adding *places* to the right of the reference or decimal point. Every youngster who has worked arithmetic problems dealing with circles knows that pi (π) has a value of 3.1416. Actually, however, the value is 3.14159. . . . In 1959, a digital computer worked the value of π out to 10,000 decimal places in a short period of time![1]

Digital computers, unlike analog machines, are used for both business data processing and scientific purposes. In special situations (e.g., to simulate a guided missile system or a new aircraft design), desirable features of analog and digital machines have been combined to create a *hybrid* computer.

Digital computers may be produced for either special or general uses. A *special purpose* computer, as the name implies, is designed to perform one specific task. The program of instructions is built into the machine. Specialization results in the given task being performed economically, quickly, and efficiently. A disadvantage, however, is that the machine lacks versatility; it is inflexible and cannot be used to perform other operations. Special purpose computers designed for the sole purpose of solving complex navigational problems are installed aboard our atomic submarines, but they could not be used for other purposes unless their circuits were redesigned.

Special Purpose and General Purpose Computers

---

[1]Alas, later more accurate work showed that this computer had made an error in the 7,480th decimal place.

A *general purpose* computer is one that has the ability to store *different* programs of instructions and thus to perform a variety of operations. In short, the stored program concept makes the machine a general purpose device—one that has the versatility to make possible the processing of a payroll one minute and an inventory control application the next. New programs can be prepared, and old programs can be changed or dropped. Because it is designed to do a wide variety of jobs rather than perform a specific activity, the general purpose machine typically compromises certain aspects of speed and efficiency—a small enough price to pay in most cases for the advantage of flexibility.

Scientific and Business Applications

A single general purpose central processor is now frequently used for both scientific and business applications. There is nothing new about this arrangement. The IBM 650 model, introduced late in 1954, was also widely used for scientific and business jobs. But the earliest equipment was designed primarily to meet the needs of the scientific community, and it soon became apparent that the processing needs differed between scientific and business jobs. Let us pause briefly here to examine the processing characteristics of scientific and business applications.

Scientific processing applications   A research laboratory may wish to analyze and evaluate a product formula involving 3 variables and 15 terms (which results in 45 different values for each variable). The computer *input* would be the 15-term formula, the 135 values for the 3 variables, and the set of instructions to be followed in processing. The input is thus quite small. The *processing* involved, however, may well consist of hundreds of thousands of different computations—computations that may represent many months of labor if performed by other methods. The *output* necessary for a problem of this type may consist of a few typed lines giving a single evaluation or a few alternatives.

In short, the volume of input/output in scientific data processing is relatively small, and the speed with which these operations are performed is usually not too important. Computational speed, on the other hand, is a critical consideration since the bulk of the total processing job involves complex calculation. Storage capacity need only be sufficient to hold instructions, input data, and intermediate and final computational results.

Business processing applications   In contrast to scientifically oriented applications, business tasks generally require faster input and output of data and larger storage capacity. An examination of a typical business application will usually show that the volume of data input and information output is quite large. For example, the billing operation associated with the credit card purchases of an oil company's products involves thousands of customers and hundreds of thousands of sales transactions each month. Each transaction represents input data, while each customer represents an output statement. The running time required by the computer to complete such a business application is usually determined by the input/output speeds obtainable.

Computational speed is less critical in business applications because (1) arithmetic operations performed on each input record represent a relatively small proportion of the total job and (2) the internal arithmetic speed of the slowest computer is frequently much greater than the speed of input/output devices.

Greater storage capacity is required for business applications. Internal storage must be available for instruction programs, which are often quite lengthy, as well as for the manipulation and maintenance of large masses of data. The relatively high cost of internal storage combined with increased business demand for economical storage capacity has resulted in the development of the online mass storage devices mentioned earlier.

To summarize (see Fig. 5-1), scientific and business applications typically differ with respect to (1) input/output volume, (2) input/output speed needed, (3) amount of computation, (4) importance of computational speed, and (5) storage requirements. As a result of these differences, second-generation computers were frequently oriented toward either scientific or business use. Of course, many companies used business-oriented computers for scientific applications and vice versa. But computer running time (an obvious expense) is de-

Processing characteristics	Scientific applications	Business applications
Input/output volume	Low	Very high
Input/output speed	Relatively unimportant	Very important
Ratio of computations to input	Very high	Low
Computation speed	Very important	Relatively unimportant
Storage requirements	Modest	High

Figure 5-1

termined by the *total* time required for input, processing, and output operations, and so this dual use led to inefficiency. In short, the *throughput,* i.e., the total amount of useful work performed by a computer system in a given period of time, suffered when computers oriented toward one type of application were used to process another type of application.

The distinction between business- and scientific-oriented computers became blurred in the last half of the 1960s with the introduction of third-generation families of computers. Although some models in a line still tend to be used primarily for one type of application or the other, certain software and hardware control features together with a wide range of peripheral equipment (such as input/output devices) and modular *add-on* units (to provide, for example, greater storage capacity) permit many central processors to flexibly and efficiently serve both types of applications. Furthermore, a fast central processor that might remain idle much of the time during the completion of a business application can, through the use of multiprogramming and timesharing concepts, allocate resources to other business and scientific tasks.

The stored program, digital, general purpose computer used for business purposes (henceforth called *computer* for apparent reasons) possesses certain capabilities, which are summarized in the next section.

COMPUTER CAPABILITIES

The popular press has tended, in past years, to view the computer in several roles. In one article a computer system will be viewed as having *human* characteristics, e.g., as a device which can play checkers and verbally answer inquiries. In another article (or in a movie), the computer is placed in a *superhuman* role (remember the spaceship computer "HAL" in the movie *2001: A Space Odyssey?*). And in a third article, the impression may be conveyed that the computer is *extra-human;* e.g., it is the tireless teaching machine of infinite patience.

Such characterizations may tend to stimulate a variety of emotions (excitement, uneasiness, even fear?). Although articles may not contain specific inaccuracies, many tend to exaggerate certain computer capabilities. Yet it is clear that the computer *is* a powerful *tool* for extending man's brainpower. Peter Drucker has pointed out that man has developed two types of tools: (1) those that add to his capabilities and enable him to do something that he otherwise could *not* do (e.g., the airplane) and (2) those that multiply his capacity to do that which he is *already capable* of doing (e.g., the hammer).[2]

The computer falls into the latter category. It is an intelligence amplifier. It can enlarge brainpower because of the properties presented below. These properties have led to the human, superhuman, and extrahuman images.[3]

1. *The ability to provide new time dimensions.* The machine works one step at a time; it adds and subtracts numbers; it multiplies and divides numbers (in most cases merely by a repetitive process of addition and subtraction); and it can be designed or programmed to perform other mathematical operations such as finding a square root. There is nothing profound in these operations—even the author can perform them! What is significant, as we know, is the speed with which the machine functions. Thus, man is freed from calculations to use his time more creatively. His time dimension has been broadened; he can obtain now information that could not have been produced at all a few years ago or that could not have been produced in time to be of any value. Karl Gauss, a German mathematician, at a young age had ideas that might have reshaped the study of mathematics in his time. Twenty years of his life were spent, however, in calculating the orbits of various heavenly objects. Were Gauss alive today, he could duplicate his calculations on a computer in a few hours and then be free to follow more creative pursuits. A more recent illustration will serve to conclude this discussion of computer speed. John Kemeny of Dartmouth College has estimated that the calculations it took a year to complete working around the clock at the atomic laboratories at Los Alamos in 1945 could be duplicated in one afternoon by an undergraduate student while sharing the computer's time with 30 others.

2. *The ability to perform certain logic operations.* When two values, A and B, are *compared,* there are only three possible outcomes: (1) A is *equal* to B ($A = B$); (2) A is *greater than* B ($A > B$); or (3) A is *less than* B ($A < B$).[4] The computer is able to perform a simple comparison and then, depending on the result, follow

---

[2] See Peter F. Drucker, "What the Computers Will Be Telling You," *Nation's Business,* August, 1966, pp. 84–90.

[3] Of course, the computer has also been characterized as being *inhuman,* e.g., the source of heartless decisions made without regard for human feelings, and *subhuman,* e.g., the moron responsible for stupid and infuriating errors in billing. In the next section we shall look at the computer limitations responsible for these illusions.

[4] The possible outcomes form what logicians forebodingly call the *law of trichotomy.* Computers also compare numbers to see whether they are positive, negative, or equal to zero.

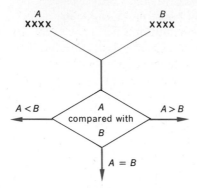

Figure 5-2

one of three *predetermined branches,* or courses of action, in the completion of that portion of its work. (See Fig. 5-2.) Thus, the computer has made a "decision" by choosing between alternate possible courses of action. Actually, however, it might be more appropriate to say that the computer has *followed* decisions made earlier by the programmer. But this simple ability to compare is an important computer property because more sophisticated questions can be answered by using combinations of comparison decisions.

3. *The ability to store and retrieve information.* We know that the computer places in internal storage both facts and instructions. The ease with which instruction programs can be changed gives the computer great flexibility. The *access time* required for information to be recalled from internal storage and be available for use is measured in microseconds or more precise units. Few machines used by man have this stored program ability—the instructions generally reside in man's mind and thus are outside the machine. Instructions and data are in a coded form that the machine has been designed to accept. The machine is also designed to perform automatically and in sequence certain operations on the data (add, write, move, store, halt) called for by the instructions. The number of operations that can be performed varies among computer models. The stored program may, as we have just seen, allow the computer to select a branch of instructions to follow from several alternate sequences. The program may also allow the computer to *repeat* or *modify* instructions as required. Computers communicate with human operators by using input and output devices, and they communicate with other machines.

4. *The ability to control error.* It is estimated that you or I would make one error in every 500 to 1,000 operations with a desk

calculator. A computer, on the other hand, can perform hundreds of thousands of arithmetic operations every second and can run errorless for hours and days at a time. Computers also have the ability to check their own work. By a method known as *parity checking,* computers check on data when they enter storage, when they are moved internally, and when they leave in the form of output. Each character (e.g., number or letter) fed into the computer is represented in a coded form by several binary digits (0s and 1s) called *bits,* just as each number or letter in a punched card is usually represented by the Hollerith code. The parity check performed by the computer involves the examination of each character's code to determine whether bits have been added or lost by mistake. More will be said about parity checking in a later chapter.

It should not be assumed, however, that computers have unlimited capabilities or that they are free of error. They do have their limitations, and they have been involved in some classic mistakes.

Jack and Jill
Went up the hill
With great anticipating
Jack came down
And with a frown
Gave up computer dating[5]

**COMPUTER
LIMITATIONS**

A publishing company customer received a computer-produced invoice requesting that he pay his bill in the amount of "W-2.C." The customer promptly forwarded his check for W-2.C as directed with a note saying, "Out here in the sticks, we dig this crazy new currency you folks have invented."[6] Billing operations have produced other computer goofs. For example, an insurance company kept sending a policy holder a bill for $0.00 and demanding payment, and in Fort Worth, Texas, a man was surprised a few months ago to receive a brief, rather cool, letter from an oil company telling him that his account was past due by $34.32. The man can be excused his surprise because he had never received a credit card from any oil company. Six weeks passed before the error was discovered, during which time the man kept protesting and the form letters (getting less and less cordial) kept coming in.

[5] Edmund Conti, *Datamation,* April, 1970, p. 89.
[6] Reported in *The Long Island Commercial Review,* May, 1966.

Or consider the case of the Michigan GI who, as a result of computer record processing, was mistakenly shipped back to Vietnam for a second tour of duty and somehow wound up in Thailand. By the time the error was discovered and the Army began to look for him in Thailand, he had been transferred back home. These victims, along with the Phoenix man who was treated for pneumonia and charged for the use of the nursery and the delivery room, perhaps felt as did another victim who said: "The computer is a complete revolution in the ways of doing business, . . . and as in any revolution some innocent people always get slaughtered."[7]

That such stories are carried in newspapers is indication enough that they occur only infrequently. Perhaps in most cases the errors may be traced to humans who failed to give proper attention to the following limitations:

1. *Application programs must always be prepared.* The machine does what it is programmed to do and *nothing else.* It can only operate on data; i.e., it can accept data, process it, and communicate results, but it cannot directly perform physical activities such as bending metal. (The processed information may be used, however, to control metal-bending machines.) Furthermore, a program may *seem* to be flawless and operate satisfactorily for some months and then produce nonsense (a bill for $0.00 for instance) because some rare combination of events has presented the computer with a situation (1) for which there may be no programmed course of action or (2) where the course of action provided by the programmer contains an error that is just being discovered. Of course, a truly flawless program, supplied with incorrect data, may also produce nonsense. And once incorrect facts are entered into a computer system they are usually not as easy to purge as is the case when manual methods are used.

2. *Applications must be able to be quantified and dealt with logically.* The computer will not help the manager in areas where *qualitative* considerations are important. It will not, for example, signal a change in a trend until after the fact. It will not tell the manager whether or not a new product will be successful if marketed. The ultimate decision is of a qualitative nature because it is involved with future social, political, technological, and economic events; and sales volume levels are thus impossible to predict with certainty. The computer will *by simulation* let a manager know how a new product will fare under *assumed* price,

[7] Lee Berton, "Zip, Buzz, Whir, Clonk: Computers Botch Some of Their Jobs," *The Wall Street Journal,* July 6, 1966.

cost, and sales volume conditions. The computer, in short, is limited to those applications that have precisely defined goals; furthermore, it must be possible to reach these goals by a logical series of instructions, which consist of a specific number of steps. If the steps in the solution of the problem cannot be precisely written down, the application cannot be performed on today's commercial computers. And, as you know, each time the computer must make a choice the appropriate alternate steps must have been foreseen and provided for by the programmer.

3. *Applications must weigh resources.* Merely because a computer *can* be programmed to do a job does not always mean that it *should.* Writing programs, although less tedious than in the past because of developments in software, is still a time-consuming and expensive human operation. Thus, nonrecurring tasks or jobs that are seldom processed are often not efficient areas for computer application at the present time. In business data processing, it is usually most economical to have programmers (a scarce resource) prepare programs for large-volume, repetitive operations that will be used many times and that promise fast returns on the time invested in program preparations.[8]

Much has been written in the past few years pro and con about the question of whether computers can be programmed to "think" and "learn." Most of the controversy probably stems from (1) a lack of understanding about the processes involved in human thinking and learning and (2) the absence of acceptable definitions of such words as *think* and *learn*.

EXPERIMENTS IN LEARNING

Although the computer can only do what it is instructed to do, research and experiments are being conducted in the use of computers to solve relatively ill-structured problems. For example, a machine has been programmed to play checkers and to modify its program on the basis of success and failure with moves used in the past against human opponents. The computer has continually improved its game to the point where it regularly defeats the author of the program. Thus, the machine has "learned" what not to do through trial and error.

Computers have also been programmed to play chess, prove mathematical theorems, and compose music, but thus far such re-

[8] In engineering and scientific computing, the importance of a nonrecurring task often warrants the necessary investment in programming time. An example might be the engineering planning and construction scheduling, by computer, of a single multimillion-dollar office building.

search activities are limited and involve "thinking" on the part of the machine in a most limited sense.

Heuristic[9] is a word that means *serving to discover.* It is used to describe the judgmental, or *common sense,* part of problem solving. That is, it describes that part of problem solving which deals with the definition of the problem, the selection of reasonable strategies to be followed, which may or may not lead to optimum solutions, and the formulation of hypotheses and hunches. Man is *far superior* to the computer in the heuristic area of intellectual work. As man's thinking and learning processes become better understood, however, it may be possible to develop new programs and machines with improved heuristic abilities. Certainly, some very able researchers are working toward this end. However, the role of the computer will continue to be that of an intelligence amplifier.

COMPUTER ORGANIZATION

The computer solves problems and produces information in much the same way that you do. Let us illustrate this fact by first making a most disagreeable assumption: that in the near future you will have to take a written examination on the material covered in the first few chapters of an accounting book. For the past few days you have been reading the text, trying to catch up on your homework problems, and listening to your professor's lectures. You have written several pages of notes and have memorized various facts, concepts, and procedures. Finally, the examination period arrives, and you begin to work the test problems. Transactions are noted, and proper (?) accounts receive debits and credits. Procedures are followed, you hope, in the correct order. As time runs out, you turn your paper in to the professor and leave, resolving to pay somewhat closer attention to what he has to say in the future.

Five functions were performed in the above illustration (see Fig. 5-3). These functions are:

1. *Input.* The input function involves the receipt of facts that can be used. You received data from your accounting textbook and from your professor.
2. *Storage.* Facts received must be stored until they are needed. Your notebook (offline storage) and your brain (online storage) were used to store accounting information and the procedures to use for solving problems.

[9] Pronounced *hew-ris' tik.*

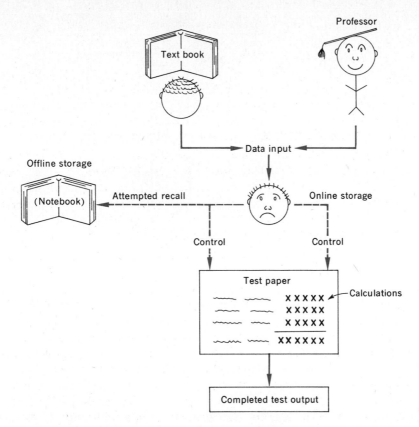

Figure 5-3

3. *Calculation.* On your test you performed the arithmetic operations of addition, subtraction, multiplication, and division, either manually or with the help of a desk calculator.

4. *Control.* On the exam it was necessary to follow certain procedures in the proper order, or sequence; i.e., you could not total an account until all transactions had been recorded, and you did not record the last transaction of the month first because it might have been based on transactions occurring earlier in the month. Control, then, simply means doing things in the correct sequence.

5. *Output.* Your finished test was the output—the result of your data processing operations. It will provide your professor with part of the information needed to arrive at a decision about your final grade.

All computer installations perform these five functions. Figure 5-4 illustrates the *functional* organization of a computer. Let us briefly examine each part of this diagram.

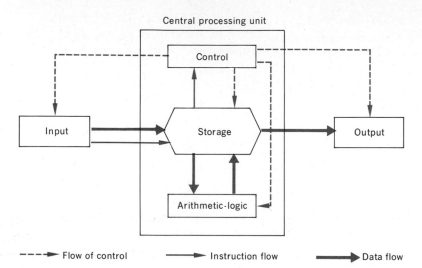

Figure 5-4   Computer functional organization

Input

Computers, obviously, must also receive facts to solve problems. Data and instructions must be put into the computer system in a form that it can use. There are a number of devices that will perform this input function, as we shall see in the following chapter. They may allow direct man-machine communication without the necessity of an input medium (e.g., the keyboard of a timesharing remote station), or they may present information that typically has been produced offline in batches on an input medium (e.g., punched cards). Regardless of the type of device used, they are all instruments of interpretation and communication between man and the machine.

Storage

The heart of any computer installation is the *central processing unit* (CPU), which we have referred to in earlier chapters. Within this unit are generally located the storage, control, and arithmetic-logic units. It is this central processor (see Fig. 5-5) that makes comparisons, performs calculations, and selects, interprets, and controls the execution of instructions.

The storage section of the central processor is used for *four purposes,* three of which relate to the data being processed. First, data are fed into the storage area where they are held until ready to be processed. Second, additional storage space is used to hold data being processed and the intermediate results of such processing. Third, the storage unit holds the finished product of the processing operations until it can be released in the form of output information. Fourth, in addition to these data-related purposes, the storage unit also holds the program instructions until they are needed.

Arithmetic-logic

All calculations are performed and all comparisons (decisions) are made in the arithmetic-logic section of the central processor. Data flow between this section and the storage unit during processing operations; i.e., data are received from storage, manipulated, and returned to storage. No processing is performed in the storage section. The number of arithmetic and logic operations that can be performed is determined by the engineering design of the machine.

To briefly summarize, data are fed into the storage unit from the input devices. Once in storage, they are held and transferred as needed to the arithmetic-logic unit where processing takes place. Data may move from storage to the arithmetic-logic unit and back again to storage many times before the processing is finished. Once completed, the information is released from the central processor to the output device.

Control

How does the input unit know when to feed data into storage? How does the arithmetic-logic unit obtain the needed data from storage, and how does it know what should be done with them once they are received? And how is the output unit able to obtain finished information instead of raw data from storage? It is by selecting, interpreting, and executing the program instructions that the control unit of the central processor is able to maintain order and direct the operation of the entire installation. It thus acts as a central nervous

Figure 5-5   RCA 3 processor (courtesy RCA)

system for the component parts of the computer. Instructions are *selected* and fed in sequence into the control unit from storage; there they are *interpreted;* and from there signals are sent to *other* machine units to *execute* program steps. The control unit itself does not perform actual processing operations on the data.

Output

Output devices, like input units, are instruments of interpretation and communication between man and machine. They take information in machine-coded form and convert it typically into a form that can be used (1) by humans (e.g., a printed report) or (2) as machine input in another processing operation (e.g., magnetic tape). In the following chapter we shall take a closer look at several output devices.

Extensive Variations Possible

All computer systems are similar in that they perform the basic functions just described. However, computers vary widely in their external configurations. Some computers are housed in three boxes, as implied in Fig. 5-4; some are in a single cabinet; some have multiple units for the input and output functions; some distribute parts of the storage and control functions to equipment peripheral to the CPU; and some use a single cabinet to house both input and output functions. Figure 5-6 illustrates some of the possible machine combinations. (The input/output hardware and media shown will be surveyed in the next two chapters; a closer look at the CPU will be the subject of Chapters 8 and 9.) The boxes labeled "channels" in Fig. 5-6 require a brief explanation here.

A *channel* consists of hardware that, along with other associated monitoring and connecting elements, controls and provides the path for the movement of data between relatively slow input/output (I/O) devices, on the one hand, and high-speed central processor primary storage, on the other. Because of the differences in operating speeds, the CPU would be idle much of the time if it had to hold up processing during the periods that input was being received and output was being produced. Fortunately, most computers built since the mid-1960s have features that make it possible to *overlap* input, processing, and output operations in order to make more efficient use of computing resources. Once the channel has received appropriate instruction signals from the central processor, it can operate independently and without supervision while the CPU is engaged in performing computations. For example, at the same time that the CPU is processing one group of records, one channel can be receiving another group for subsequent processing while a second channel can be

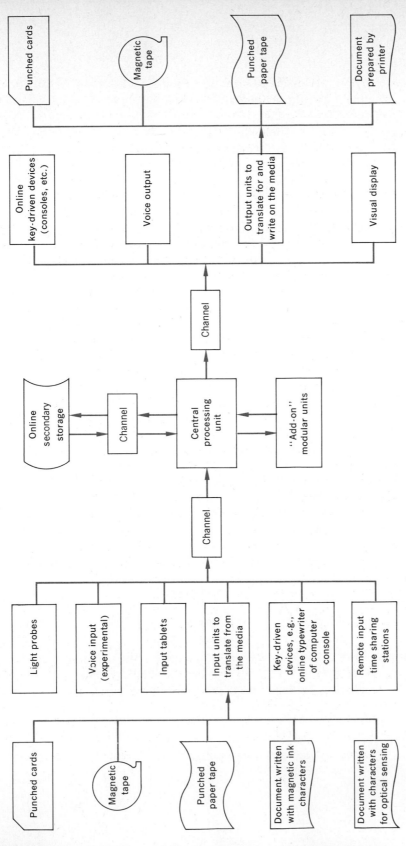

Figure 5-6 Input/output hardware and media

supplying processed information to the appropriate output device. We shall have more to say about overlap operations in Chapter 7.

The channel may be a separate small special purpose control computer located near the CPU, or it may be a physical part of the CPU which is accessible to both I/O devices and other elements of the CPU. Multiple channels may be used to serve a large number of peripheral I/O devices, e.g., a large number of terminals used in a timesharing system.

Before concluding this section, it might be appropriate here to mention another type of variation that can exist in computer systems— the variation in the design and construction (or architecture) of the functional elements in the CPU. Figure 5-4 shows the *traditional* and currently most popular design. This design features *single* control, storage, and arithmetic-logic units in the CPU. But there are several ways this traditional design can be modified in order to achieve even greater computing speeds. Among the possible alternative designs used by the *largest* computer systems are the following: [10]

1. *The multiprocessor design.* By adding additional control and arithmetic-logic units (see Fig. 5-7a), several instructions can be processed at the same instant in time. "What is the difference between multiprogramming and multiprocessing?" you might ask. A cavalier response could be to refer you back to Chapter 3, but at the risk of redundancy we may point out here that multi-programming involves executing a portion of one program, then a segment of another, etc., in brief *consecutive* time periods. Multiprocessor design, however, makes it possible for the system to *simultaneously* work on several program segments. Thus, this design represents, in effect, a system with two or more central processors.

2. *The concurrent design.* Computing speed can also be increased by separating the arithmetic-logic unit into functional subunits, each of which can operate independently under the direction of the control unit (see Fig. 5-7b). When, for example, consecutive and independent program instructions call for the use of separate subunits (e.g., addition, multiplication, and division), the control unit will signal the proper elements to proceed *concurrently* to process all of these instructions. Lacking functionally independent subunits, a traditionally designed arithmetic-logic unit will take the first instruction in the sequence and execute it before moving to the next instruction.

3. *The parallel design.* The ILLIAC IV, a "supercomputer" developed

---

[10] For further details on these design variations, see the April, 1970, issue of *Datamation*.

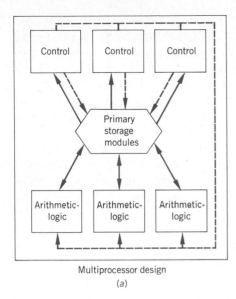

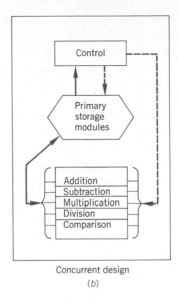

Multiprocessor design
(a)

Concurrent design
(b)

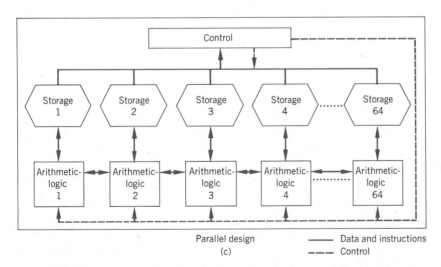

Parallel design
(c)

———— Data and instructions
- - - - Control

Figure 5-7

in the late 1960s and early 1970s at the University of Illinois with funds provided by the U.S. Department of Defense, is a massive number-cruncher consisting of four control units, *each* of which directs the operations of 64 arithmetic-logic units. Each arithmetic-logic unit has its own storage unit. Thus, there are a total of 256 arithmetic-logic and storage units in four controlled quadrants. One such quadrant is shown in Fig. 5-7c.

These variations from traditional design result in faster computation speed, which is important in processing scientific applications, but the more complicated circuitry required in these faster designs is obviously more expensive.

SUMMARY

Electronic computers may be classified in a number of ways. In this book we are interested in digital machines that count sequentially and very accurately; we are interested in general purpose equipment that can do a variety of jobs; and we are interested primarily in hardware that is used to process business-oriented tasks.

Computers extend man's brainpower; they are intelligence amplifiers that provide new dimensions in the time available for creative work. They are able to perform certain logic operations. Sophisticated questions can be answered by the combination of many simple machine "decisions." Computers can store and retrieve information rapidly and accurately.

But machines, like humans (especially like humans) are not infallible. They make errors, and they must be told exactly and precisely what to do. Although experiments are being conducted by extremely able researchers in the attempt to improve the machine's heuristic capabilities, they are restricted in practical use to applications that can be quantified and structured into a finite number of steps to achieve a specific goal. The writing of machine instructions is still an expensive and time-consuming operation, and it is for this reason that it is usually not feasible to process many nonrecurring business jobs with a computer.

Computers are organized to perform the functional activities of input, storage, arithmetic-logic, control, and output. A multitude of machine configurations and media are used in the performance of these functions. The composition of the CPU is subject to design variation; the most powerful computers generally depart in some way from the traditional design, which features single control, storage, and arithmetic-logic units in the CPU.

DISCUSSION QUESTIONS

1. Discuss the various ways in which computers may be classified.
2. (a) What is an analog computer? (b) How does it differ from a digital computer?
3. How does a special purpose computer differ from a general purpose machine?

4. Compare and contrast the processing characteristics typically found in business and scientific applications.
5. Why is it possible to say that the computer is an intelligence amplifier?
6. Identify and discuss the limitations of computer usage.
7. Why does controversy surround the question of whether or not computers can be programmed to "think"?
8. Identify and discuss the five functions which are performed by computers.
9. "The storage section of the central processor is used for four purposes." What are these four purposes?
10. (a) What functions are performed in the arithmetic-logic section of the central processor? (b) In the control section?
11. What is the role of a data channel?
12. Differentiate between traditional CPU design and (a) multiprocessor design, (b) concurrent design, and (c) parallel design.

SELECTED REFERENCES

Bartee, Thomas C.: *Digital Computer Fundamentals,* 2d ed., chap. 1, McGraw-Hill Book Company, New York, 1966.

Graham, William R.: "The Parallel and the Pipeline Computers," *Datamation,* April, 1970, pp. 68–71.

Licklider, J. C. R.: "Computers: Thinking Machines or Thinking Aids?," *Management Review,* July, 1965, pp. 40–43.

McIntyre, David E.: "An Introduction to the ILLIAC IV Computer," *Datamation,* April, 1970, pp. 60–67.

Surface, Bill: "What Computers Cannot Do," *Saturday Review,* July 13, 1968, pp. 57–58ff.

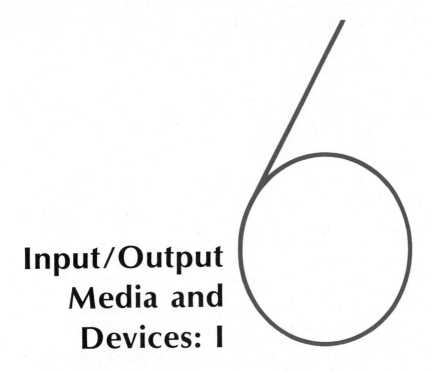

Input/Output Media and Devices: I

Why have input/output (I/O) media and devices? The answer to this question, of course, is that they make it possible for data processing to occur; i.e., they make it possible for man to place data into and receive information out of the central processor. To illustrate, the general sequence of input activities followed in a typical business computer system is:

1. The control unit in the CPU receives instructions to read data from a specific input device.
2. The message is relayed to activate the device.
3. The device converts the input data into electric pulses, and, after appropriate checks are made, the data are transferred to primary storage locations in the CPU. A channel usually provides the path for data movement.
4. A signal to the central processor indicates that the input operation is completed.

The output activities followed are similar but reversed; i.e., output is available in primary storage and must be transferred, in the form of electric signals, to an output device for translation into more usable form.

The computer installation thus performs the necessary processing steps and communicates with man only through the I/O equipment. In this chapter we will study some of the ways in which communication is accomplished. But before moving on to specific media and machines, let us look briefly at (1) *data organization concepts* and (2) *selection considerations*, which have an important bearing on I/O activities.

DATA ORGANIZATION CONCEPTS

It is important to understand that to perform efficiently and economically the data processing steps (classifying, sorting, calculating, etc.) mentioned in Chapter 1, data must first be grouped or organized in some logical arrangement. In business information systems, data are generally organized into *files;* files consist of a number of related *records;* records are made up of groups of data items arranged into *fields* (or words); and, as we saw in Chapter 2, fields consist of one or more consecutive data *characters*. We thus have in business information systems the data hierarchy shown in Fig. 6-1. Obviously, then, business data processing involves operations on records and files. Since our I/O activities will be concerned primarily with the maintenance of records and files, let us make sure we have a clear understanding of these data organization concepts.

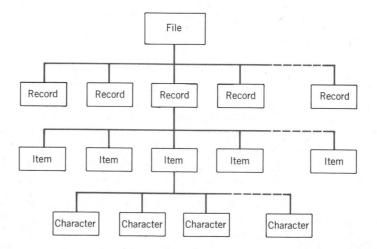

Figure 6-1   Data hierarchy

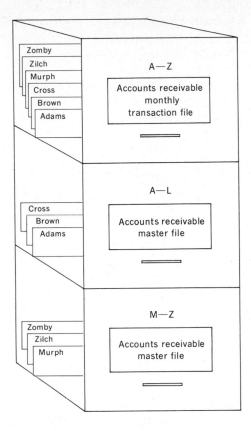

Figure 6-2

A hypothetical accounts-receivable application in a manual accounting system will be used to illustrate data organization. The accounts-receivable file contains records for each customer showing such information as customer name, account number, address, amount owed, and credit limit. Each record is filed alphabetically, by customer name, in the *transaction file* drawer, as shown in Fig. 6-2. Each record folder contains credit sales transaction tickets (items), which have been (1) *recorded* and *classified* by customer name, (2) *sorted* alphabetically, and (3) *stored* in the file drawer until the end of the month.

At the end of the month, the record folders are removed from the transaction file drawer, and the following processing steps are performed:

1. *Calculations* are made to determine the total amount purchased by each customer during the month.
2. The monthly transactions are used to revise and update the infor-

mation contained in the *master file* in the bottom two drawers of the file cabinet.

3. The total amount owed is *communicated* to the customer in the form of a bill.

4. A report is prepared that *summarizes* for managers the pertinent information contained in the files, e.g., the total credit sales for the month, records that show slow payment, etc.

Processing is done sequentially (in alphabetical order) beginning with Adams and ending with Zomby. Thus, the data processing functions and the I/O activities take place within the organizational framework of the accounts-receivable files. The master file has a degree of permanency, while transaction file data are emptied each month.

Computers replace manual methods, but files still must be maintained that continually receive and transmit information. Figure 6-3 charts the general flow of activities involved in file processing. Files may be sequentially organized and stored offline on such media as punched cards, punched paper tape, or magnetic tape. Or they may be randomly organized in online, mass storage units.

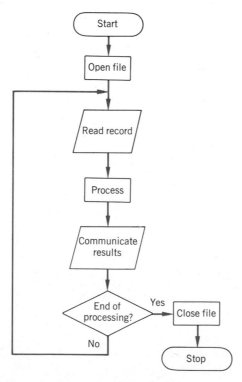

Figure 6-3

Records may be sequentially *processed* (batch processing), or they may be immediately accessed and updated by random access *processing*. Since it is quite easy to become confused about the meaning of the terms *sequential* and *random* when they are used with the words *processing* and *organization,* let us pause to clarify this semantic entanglement.

When master files are stored offline, they are almost always sequentially *organized*. And when such files are updated, sequential *processing,* by means of appropriate I/O devices, is used. But when files are located in online storage, they may be organized sequentially *or* randomly. Thus, as Fig. 6-4 shows, random access *processing* is possible with files organized *both* sequentially and/or randomly.

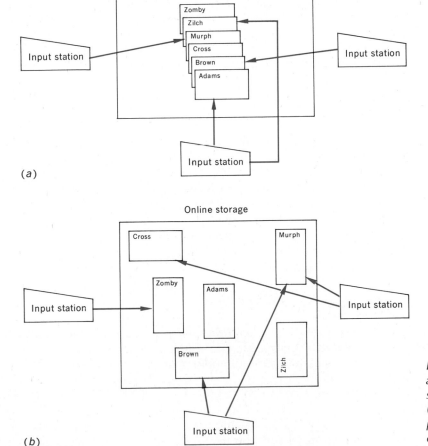

Figure 6-4(a) *Random access processing with sequential file organization,* (b) *Random access processing with random file organization*

Figure 6-4a shows conceptually the random selection and processing of records from a sequentially organized master file, while Fig. 6-4b shows random file organization *and* random processing.

SELECTION OF MEDIA AND DEVICES

Because files vary in character, size, and location (online or offline), a wide variety of I/O media and devices has been developed. Managers thus must choose from a number of alternatives. A compromise is often necessary: Certain advantages are obtained only by the acceptance of certain drawbacks. There are a number of factors to consider in making the selection including:

1. *The volume of data to be processed.* In addition to considerations of equipment speed and capacity, the manager may also have to make provisions for processing peak volumes during certain periods of the year.
2. *The frequency of processing needed.* The total volume of data processing is, of course, affected by the frequency with which records must be updated. If records must be updated as transactions occur, then batch processing techniques must obviously give way to random processing techniques.
3. *The quality requirements.* To what extent can errors be tolerated in the information output? The higher the accuracy requirements, the greater the need may be to replace humans with machines that can "read" the source documents.
4. *The type and quality of output required.* Will the output be used by man, or will it be reused by the computer at a later time? How many reports will be needed? How frequently are they required? How many copies are needed? Answers to such questions have a direct bearing on the I/O selections.
5. *The nature of the source documents.* The methods for originating data, the types of source documents used, the message length, and the data form (alphabetic, numeric, or alphanumeric) must be considered.
6. *The economic considerations.* Greater accuracy and faster response are usually desirable, but are these benefits worth the higher costs for I/O equipment that may be incurred?

The time required to complete a processing job is determined by the speed of input, processing, and output operations. The input and output of data have for several years been a bottleneck in a computerized system. In addition to slowing down the processing operation, input methods have often been costly and subject to errors. Duplication of effort has often been required to transfer data from source documents to a machine-acceptable form.

In the following pages of this chapter we shall examine media and related devices possessing most of the following characteristics:

1. Processing is accomplished with media that tangibly record data by the use of (a) holes in paper or (b) magnetized spots or patterns.
2. Batch processing methods are generally employed.
3. Input data preparation is offline relative to the central processor.
4. Data are frequently recorded in some humanly usable form before or at the same time the input media is prepared.
5. The media store the files (with proper care) for an indefinite period of time. The file storage is offline.
6. The volume of processing is often quite high.

PUNCHED CARDS

The punched card is the most familiar I/O medium. It performs a *dual purpose:* it is used to enter data into and receive information out of the central processor. You will recall that in Chapter 2 we considered the 80-column Hollerith-coded card and IBM's System/3 96-column card. Illustrations of small, card-oriented computer systems were also presented there. Unless otherwise indicated, the discussion in this section refers to the more widely used 80-column card.

The typical card is 0.007 inch thick. This thickness is a compromise between processing speed (thicker cards can generally be processed faster) and storage space (but they take up more room). A small triangular piece is removed from a corner of each card. This corner cut is usually not made for any machine purpose. Rather, it merely helps the operator arrange the cards for processing. Cards from different file decks may also be colored or striped in some way for human identification. Also, the operator may make notes on the cards (e.g., "first card in file," "last card," "accounts-receivable master file") since the machines will ignore the writing.

Although it is called a *unit record,* the card does not necessarily contain all the data of a particular file record. It may merely contain data about one record item, and the complete record may thus consist of several cards. Files are organized sequentially in card trays. Batch processing methods are employed.

The cards must be properly stored when not in use. The humidity maintained in the storage room is important since cards lose moisture, shrink, and become brittle and buckled if the air is too dry. When the relative humidity is high, the cards gain moisture, swell, and warp. In either case, difficulties are likely to be encountered when the cards are processed. Cards are best stored standing on edge and under some pressure in compact trays designed for that purpose.

Punched Card Equipment

Manually operated keypunch machines, as we saw in Chapter 2, are the primary means of preparing punched cards. Although this is a tedious and expensive operation, the use of keypunch equipment has through the years remained the most popular data input method. Various approaches have been developed in an attempt to reduce the limitations of card preparation: (1) mark sensing can be used in some applications to eliminate manual keying; (2) prepunching into cards data used repeatedly (such as a customer's name and address) reduces keypunching, improves accuracy, and speeds preparation time; (3) typing operations can be designed that will produce punched cards as a by-product, thus combining processing steps; and (4) data recording can be done directly on cards at the source (Fig. 6-5).

Once the data are punched into the cards, they are fed into the central processor by means of a *card reader* (Fig. 6-6). Cards are placed into a read hopper from where, on command from the program in the central processor, they are moved through the card feed unit past either brush-type or photoelectric-cell reading stations. Figure 6-7 shows the two reading stations used in the brush-type reader. These stations sense the presence or absence of holes in each card column

Figure 6-5　Source record punch (courtesy Standard Register Company)

*Figure 6-6   Card reader
(courtesy RCA)*

and convert this information into electric pulses that the computer can accept. The reading brush rides on top of each card and makes contact with a roller beneath the card when a hole appears. This contact completes an electric circuit.

The reading stations may use photoelectric-cell readers in place

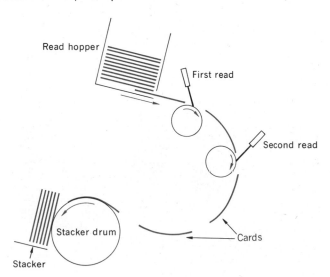

Figure 6-7

of the brush-type devices. Photoelectric cells give off electric energy when activated by light. Light shines on the card (and through the holes) as it passes the station. Photoelectric cells behind the cards are then activated by the bursts of passing light.

The card reader may compare the pulses received from each reading station as a check on the accuracy of the operation, or the pulses may be transmitted directly to the central processor where the check can be made. After the cards have been read, they are fed into the stacker hopper. The maximum reading speed varies from 100 to 2,000 cards per minute depending on the machine used. (The reading speed with System/3 cards varies from 250 to 500 cards per minute.) When all 80 columns of the card are punched, a machine reading 2,000 cards per minute has a CPU input of 2,667 characters per second, a figure that is relatively slow for machine input although quite favorable when compared with a good typist's production of about five characters per second. In addition to reading-speed variations, card readers also come in several sizes, from the large, on-site readers such as the one shown in Fig. 6-6 to small desk-sized readers (Fig. 6-8) that are suitable for remote batch processing operations.

Cards may also serve as an output medium through the use of a *card punch* machine (Fig. 6-9). Blank cards are placed in a punch hopper (Fig. 6-10). Upon command from the program, they are moved, one at a time, to a punch station where processed information is received. After being punched, the holes in the card are compared at a second station with the punching instructions. If no error is detected, the card is then moved to a stacker. When errors are sensed in either reading or punching operations, the device will stop until the error is corrected.

Figure 6-8 Card reader (courtesy Data Products Corporation)

Figure 6-9   Card punch (courtesy RCA)

The card punching function is frequently housed with the card reading activity in a machine called a *read punch* (Fig. 6-11). In small card-oriented computer systems, a single *multifunction card machine* (Fig. 6-12, right foreground) is used to perform most of the functions of the unit record devices described in Chapter 2. Cards placed in either of the two input hoppers can be read or punched and stacked in any of the five output hoppers. This device can be used to merge,

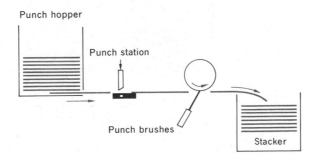

Figure 6-10

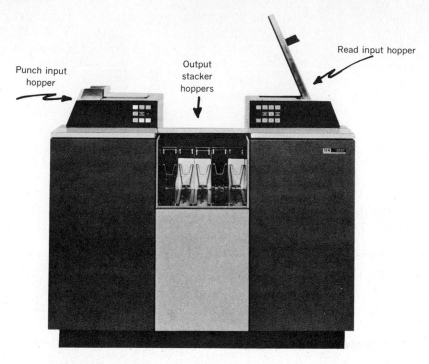

Punch input hopper

Output stacker hoppers

Read input hopper

Figure 6-11 IBM 2540 read punch (courtesy IBM Corporation)

match, reproduce, interpret, sort, summary-punch, and gangpunch cards under program control. In short, many of the functions of the five unit record machines in the background of Fig. 6-12 are performed by a single multifunction card device.

Output speeds are much slower than reading speeds owing to the slow electromechanical movement of the die punches. Cards are punched at the rate of 60 to 500 per minute. Because of this bottleneck in the processing operation, system analysts often try to keep the volume of punched card output to a minimum. Card punches have proven to be very useful, however, in producing documents that are later reentered into processing operations. An example of such a *turnaround* application is the billing approach used by many public utilities. Bills sent to customers are in the form of cards prepared as computer output. Appropriate data are punched into this card. When a part or all of the card is returned by the customer with his payment, it may then be used as an input that requires no keypunching.

Advantages and Limitations of Punched Cards

Many businesses use punched cards as an I/O medium because they were used with the firm's unit record equipment prior to the intro- duction of the computer. But cards possess advantages other than merely being an old, reliable, and available medium. For one thing, they are complete records of transactions and are thus easily understood. Particular records can be sorted, deleted, and replaced without disturbing other cards. It may be possible to add more data to the cards if necessary. Magnetic and paper tapes lack these advantages. Also, as we have just seen, a card can be used as a humanly readable turnaround document as well as a processing medium. Tape media also lack this feature. Finally, cards are useful as an external storage medium for permanent records.

But cards have certain inherent disadvantages that may limit their use in or exclude them from use in a particular application. For example, the number of data characters (80) that can be punched per card is quite low—much less than the number of characters (2,000) that can be typed on the card with a typewriter. *Data density* is low

Figure 6-12 (courtesy IBM Corporation)

because of the code used and the hole size required even when all 80 columns are punched. But in most business applications all the columns will *not* be punched, and data density is thus further reduced. For example, if the dollar amount of credit sales transactions in an exclusive retail store may reach or exceed $10,000.00, then the purchase amount field on each card must provide seven columns of space even though most purchases will be for much less (e.g., three columns would be unused if a purchase were made for $75.00).

Cards are fixed in length. If 85 characters are required, an additional card must be used. The size of the card deck is increased as is the time required to process it. Because tapes are continuous in length, they do not have this drawback.

The above paragraphs have implied that cards are bulky and slow to process—and they are. One-hundred cards, laid end to end, would extend more than 60 feet. But they could not store the data contained in less than a foot of magnetic tape. And while the *fastest* card reader can achieve a maximum input of 2,667 characters per second, an average input speed with magnetic tape might easily be 100,000 characters per second.

Cards may sometimes be misplaced or separated from their proper file deck. Also, as everyone knows, they cannot be folded, stapled, or mutilated. A bent corner or a warped card can jam equipment and further slow the processing. And obviously, the data in a card cannot be erased so that the card may be used again.

PUNCHED PAPER TAPE

Punched paper tape, like cards, is a dual-purpose medium that is suitable for computer input and output operations. It has long been used in wire communication systems where messages are punched on the tape offline at the sending station. The tape is then edited and corrected, and the data are sent to the receiving station at maximum transmitting speed.

Paper tape is often used with small scientific computers where the I/O volume is modest. It is used in business applications to record, reproduce, and communicate information. Perhaps its most popular business use is to capture data as by-products of some other processing activity. Time and labor are thus saved. In Chapter 4 we saw punched tape used in this way in an integrated sales-order application. Also, paper tape attachments on many timesharing terminals permanently capture input data and output information on tape (Fig. 6-13). Small businesses frequently send tapes produced by special adding machines, accounting machines, and cash registers (Fig. 6-14) to

Figure 6-13   Paper tape attachment on timesharing terminal (courtesy General Electric)

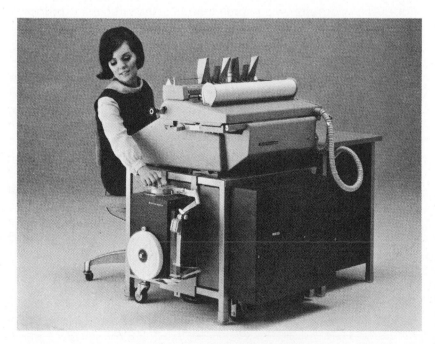

Figure 6-14   Paper tape by-product of electronic accounting machine operations (courtesy Burroughs Corporation)

computer centers where they are used as inputs for computer-prepared reports and analyses. Similarly, many firms have regional offices that must supply data to the central headquarters computer. The expense of online remote stations is often not justified, and quite frequently paper tape is used for communication purposes. It may be sent through the mail since it is light, or wire communication facilities may be used. In the latter case, a machine at the receiving headquarters produces a duplicate of the tape being read at the sending station.

Data are recorded on the tape by punching round holes into it. The tape varies from about 0.75 to 1 inch wide and is generally from 300 to 1,000 feet in length. It is usually stored on reels, although unreeled strips may also be used. Tape, like the punched card, is laid out in rows and columns. The width of the tape depends on the number of parallel *channels* (or rows) along the length of the tape into which data can be punched. As is true with punched cards, a character of information is represented by a punch or combination of punches in a vertical column or *frame* across the width of the tape. Since there are 10 frames in each inch of tape, it is possible to record 10 characters in that space.

The most commonly used sizes are five-channel tape used in teletype communications systems and eight-channel tape used by more recently developed equipment for business processing purposes. We shall consider only the eight-channel tape and its code.

Tape Coding

Figure 6-15 illustrates the coding system employed with eight-channel tape. The bottom four channels are labeled to the left of the tape with the numerical values 1, 2, 4, and 8. (The series of holes between channels 4 and 8 are sprocket holes used to feed the tape through the machines and are not considered in the code.) Decimal digits 1 to 9 can be represented by a hole or a combination of holes in these bottom channels. For example, a single hole punched in channel 2 has a decimal value of 2, while holes punched in channels 4, 2, and 1 denote a decimal 7. The X and 0 channels serve the same purpose as zone punches in cards; i.e., they are used in combination with numerical punches to form alphabetic and special characters. Channel

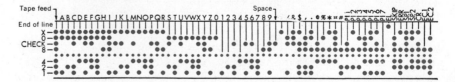

Figure 6-15 Eight-channel paper tape code

0 used alone, of course, is the code for zero. The letter A is represented by zone punches in X and 0 plus numerical 1 hole. The letter B has the same zone punches plus numerical 2, etc. The reader can examine the remainder of the letters to see the code pattern.

Thus far, the coding approaches of cards and tape have been similar. The check and end-of-the-line (EL) channels, however, perform special functions. You will notice that there is an odd number of holes punched in each frame. When the basic code requires an even number of holes, there will be an additional hole punched in the check channel. For example, the number 3 consists of punches in channels 1 and 2, thus giving an even number of holes. In this case there is also a punch in the check channel to raise the total to an odd number of holes. The reader can identify similar situations. Thus, all valid characters are formed with an odd number of holes, and this becomes the basis for checking the accuracy of the tape. This concept is known as *parity checking*. In this situation an *odd-parity* code is used, but even-parity checking is used in other data processing systems.

A punch in the EL channel occurs to signal the machine of a record on the tape—not required with the unit record punched card, but a necessity with continuous length I/O media. Blank character positions (tape feed) are indicated by holes punched in all but the EL channel.

Input/Output Equipment

The data coded on punched tape are fed into the central processor by means of a *paper tape reader* (Fig. 6-16). Tape readers, like card readers, sense the presence or absence of holes and deliver this information to the CPU. Sensing is accomplished at reading stations by the use of (1) electromechanical brushes or sensing pins or (2) photoelectric cells. The reading operation is similar to that of punched cards, and so we need not dwell on it here. Electromechanical reading speed is quite slow—from less than fifty to only a few hundred characters per second. Photoelectric reading is faster, with speeds ranging from several hundred to almost two-thousand frames per second. About one-thousand characters per second are the rule, however, because of the mechanical problems associated with the movement of tape at speeds exceeding 100 inches per second (10 characters per inch $\times$ 100 inches = reading of 1,000 characters per second).

Paper tape punches record information received from the CPU in the form of holes punched in blank tape (Fig. 6-17). Punching is a mechanical operation and is thus quite slow. The speed of this

Figure 6-16 Paper tape reader (courtesy NCR)

operation ranges from about ten to three-hundred characters per second. Tape readers and punches are sometimes combined.

Advantages and Limitations of Punched Tape

Punched paper tape provides certain advantages over punched cards. First, because it is a continuous-length medium, there is no upper-limit restriction on the length of records and no wasted space when records are short. Tape thus provides greater data density, which makes for easier handling and storage. Also, it is more economical than cards. The tape required to store 120,000 characters would cost only about one-third of the card figure if *all* columns were punched in the cards—an unlikely assumption in most cases. The equipment required for paper tape punching and reading is small, light, relatively simple in design (thus reducing maintenance costs), and less expensive than comparable card machines. As a result, tape machines can be combined with a variety of other business machines to produce by-product output. Because of this fact, tape has sometimes been referred to as the *common language* medium.

But punched tapes have their faults. It is more difficult to verify the accuracy of tape output than is the case with cards. Errors that are discovered cannot be corrected as easily as in the case of cards. An error in a card record requires repunching only one or a few cards, while an error in a tape means that the tape must be spliced or entirely repunched. Similarly, changes such as the addition to or deletion of records are more difficult with tape than with cards. These problems, of course, result from the continuous length of tape—a feature that may be an asset for some applications and a liability for others. Some firms use tape-to-card *converters* when necessary (Fig. 6-18). Like cards, tape is easily torn and mutilated.

Figure 6-17 Paper tape punch (courtesy NCR)

Figure 6-18   Tape to card punch (courtesy IBM Corporation)

MAGNETIC TAPE

Because of its relatively fast *transfer rate* (the speed at which data can be transferred from the input medium to CPU storage), magnetic tape is the most popular I/O medium being used today for high-speed, large-volume applications. In addition to providing rapid input and output, it is the most widely used offline computer storage medium. The tape contained in a typical reel would be $\frac{1}{2}$ inch in width and 2,400 feet in length. Other sizes are available. One standard $10\frac{1}{2}$-inch reel (costing about $25 and weighing about 4 pounds) is capable of storing over 20 million characters—the equivalent of more than 250,000 fully punched cards! And while the *maximum* card-input transfer rate is 2,667 characters per second, magnetic tape can achieve transfer at the rate of over 350,000 characters in the same amount of time. The transfer rate for magnetic tape depends on such factors as (1) the data density of the magnetized marks (which varies) and (2) the speed with which the tape moves (usually about 100 inches per second).

The tape itself is quite similar to the kind used in a sound tape recorder. It is a plastic ribbon coated on one side with an iron-oxide material that can be magnetized. By electromagnetic pulses, business data are recorded in the form of tiny invisible spots on the iron-oxide side of the tape, just as sound waves form magnetic patterns on the tape of a sound recorder. Both the data and the sound can be played back as many times as desired. And like the tape used on a recorder, computer tape can be erased and reused indefinitely (tape manufacturers claim that 20,000 to 50,000 passes are possible). Data contained in a tape are automatically erased as new data are being recorded. Thus, careful control and identification procedures are required to prevent important file tapes from being mistakenly used to accept computer output. Since people are unable to read information stored in the tape, it is difficult for a machine operator to distinguish between reels. *Tape librarians* are employed in large installations to maintain tape controls. When not in use, the tape reels are stored in protective, dust-resistant plastic cases.

Although it is possible to directly encode magnetic tape from source data manually (Fig. 6-19), it may not always be practical. How, then, are new transactions placed on the tape? Frequently, new input data are captured in punched card or punched tape form and are then transcribed on magnetic tape by a special offline *data converter*. In very large installations, input and output data transcription may be performed by a smaller, general purpose computer system.[1]

[1] In 1969 and 1970, several small firms were developing keyboard-to-magnetic tape data input systems utilizing multiple keyboards tied through a minicomputer to one or more magnetic tape devices. One new firm, in an attempt to establish a name for itself and for its product, sent homing pigeons to computer managers with an interest card attached. After filling out the card, the manager was to return it by the pigeon to the enterprising firm's office. Unfortunately, there was one little oversight: the pigeons had not been trained to home anywhere. At last report, many had established homesteads atop the managers' office buildings and were dropping ill will upon the potential customers below.

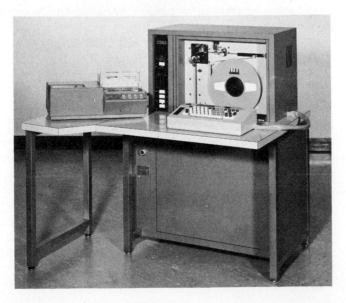

Figure 6-19 Magnetic tape encoder (courtesy NCR)

Magnetic Tape Coding

The coding philosophy of magnetic tape is similar to that of punched paper tape. Magnetic tape is divided horizontally into rows (called *channels,* or *tracks*) and vertically into columns or frames. The most commonly used tape codes employ seven and nine channels. Figure 6-20 illustrates the seven-channel-tape format. You will note that channel designations are quite similar to those used in eight-channel punched tape. Data are represented in a coded form.[2] The presence of a mark in Fig. 6-20 indicates that the channel value is "on" while the absence of a magnetized spot signifies an "off" condition. Each vertical frame represents one data character. (Unlike punched cards and tape, the number of characters per inch *can vary* with magnetic tape. Tape density ranges from 200 to 1,600 frames per inch.)

The code is easily deciphered by one who understands the paper tape system. Let us ignore for a moment the parity check channel. The numerical values are determined by one or a combination of the bottom four channels, while the A and B zone tracks are used in conjunction with the numeric channels to represent letters and special characters. For example, the decimal 7 is represented by an on condition in channels 4, 2, and 1. You can test your understanding by observing the coding pattern used for the other alphanumeric characters. By now you may also have noticed the difference between this parity checking method and the one illustrated in the punched tape example. Here we have an *even-parity* check; i.e., all valid characters must have an even number of similarly magnetized spots. The parity check channel has a mark when necessary to achieve this condition.

There is one other difference between this seven-channel code and the eight-channel code of punched tape. One of our channels is obviously missing! Magnetic tape, like paper tape, is a continuous-length, sequential file medium. How then can the computer distinguish between different records on the tape? Paper tape had an end-of-the-line channel for this purpose, but that track is missing here.

Figure 6-21 shows an accounts receivable file organized on mag-

---

[2]The code used here is called *binary coded decimal* (BCD). In Chapter 8 we will become better acquainted with BCD. We will also examine an extended version of BCD at that time.

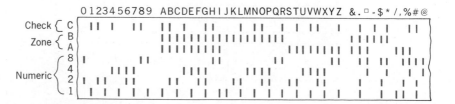

Figure 6-20 Seven-channel magnetic tape code

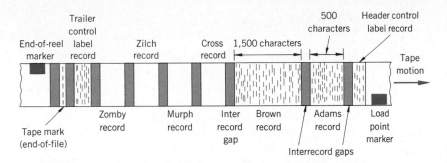

Figure 6-21

netic tape. Customer records may be of varying length. They may also be combined into tape *blocks* of several records (Fig. 6-22). For our purposes, however, it is convenient to think in terms of single-record blocks. The records are separated by blank spaces in the tape called *interrecord gaps,* which perform the end-of-line function. Interrecord gaps are automatically created by the computer system after the last character in a record (or block of records) has been recorded. These blank sections vary in width from about $\frac{1}{4}$ to 1 inch, with 0.6- and 0.75-inch gaps being most common.

The first several feet of tape are unrecorded to allow for threading on the equipment. A reflective marker known as the *load point* indicates to the equipment the beginning of usable tape, while a similar *end-of-reel* marker signals the end of usable tape. The markers are placed on opposite edges of the tape for machine identification purposes. Between the load-point marker and the first data record is a *header control label,* which identifies the tape contents, gives the number of the program to be used when the tape is processed, and supplies other control information that helps to prevent an important

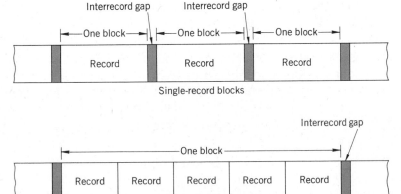

Figure 6-22 Fewer interrecord gaps save tape and speed data input. This is important when record lengths are short. The program of instructions separates the records within a block for processing.

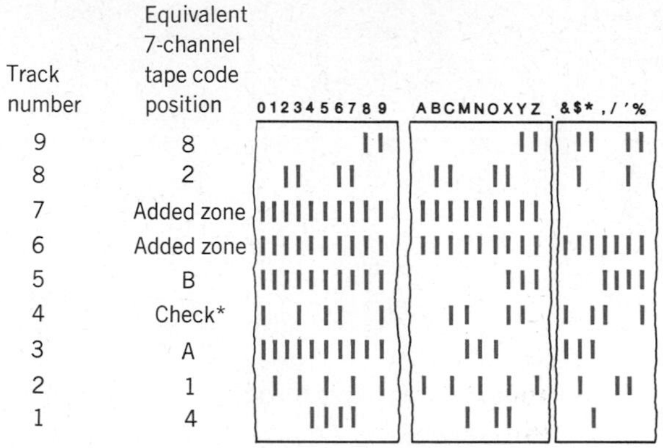

Track number	Equivalent 7-channel tape code position	0 1 2 3 4 5 6 7 8 9	A B C M N O X Y Z	& $ * , / ' %
9	8				
8	2				
7	Added zone				
6	Added zone				
5	B				
4	Check*				
3	A				
2	1				
1	4				

Figure 6-23 Nine-channel extended magnetic tape code

*The check position here produces odd parity.

tape from accidently being erased. Following the last data record in a file is a *trailer control label,* which contains a count of the number of blocks in a file. A comparison between the number of blocks processed and the number in the file may be made to determine that all have been accounted for. The end of a file may be signaled by a special one-character record. This special character is called a *tape mark.* Some systems use other control means such a $3\frac{3}{4}$-inch end-of-file gap to serve the same purpose.

Most third-generation computers use an extended version of the seven-channel tape code described above. As with seven-track tape, this nine-channel format employs four numeric tracks and a parity check channel. However, *four* (rather than two) zone positions are available. The additional zone tracks make it possible to extend the code to include lowercase alphabetical and other special characters. Figure 6-23 shows a few characters coded in the nine-channel format. The most frequently used tracks are grouped near the center of the tape so as to reduce the chances of losing data owing to the physical deterioration of the outer edges of the tape. This arrangement gives the code format a peculiar appearance. The equivalent seven-channel tape code positions are shown in Fig. 6-23 to aid in interpretation. For example, the numeral 7 is represented here by an "on" condition in the four zone positions and in the channels equivalent to 4, 2, and 1. Note that odd parity checking is employed.

Magnetic Tape Equipment   The magnetic tape units shown in Fig. 6-24 are used for both data input (*reading*) and output (recording or *writing*). Called by such names as *tape drives* and *tape transports,* these machines read and write data on the tape by the use of *read-write heads* (Fig. 6-25). There

Figure 6-24 Magnetic tape units (courtesy NCR)

is one read-write head for each tape channel. Each head is a small electromagnet with minute gaps between the poles. In the writing operation, the tape moves over the gaps while electric pulses from the CPU flow through the write coils of the appropriate heads causing the iron-oxide coating of the tape to be magnetized in the proper pattern. When the tape is being read, the magnetized patterns induce pulses of current in the read coils that feed the data into the CPU.

The tape is loaded onto the tape drive in much the same way that a movie projector is threaded (Fig. 6-26). The tape movement during processing is from the supply reel past the read-write heads to the take-up reel. Tapes may move at speeds up to 200 inches per second, and they achieve this rate in a few milliseconds. Several

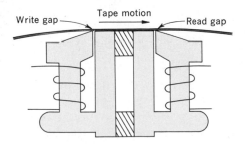

Figure 6-25 Two-gap read-write head

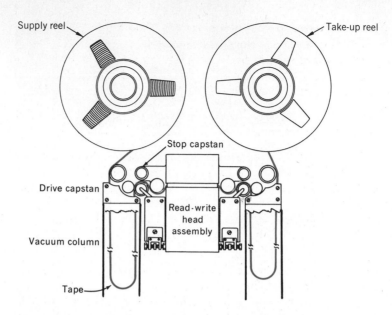

Supply reel · Take-up reel

Stop capstan

Drive capstan

Read-write
head
assembly

Vacuum column

Tape

Figure 6-26

methods are used to prevent tape damage from sudden bursts of speed. One such method is to use vacuum columns to hold slack tape, thus damping the inertial effect of the tape reels.

There are usually several tape drives used in an installation. In most applications, a tape is either read or written in a single pass. Therefore, if we wish to update our master accounts-receivable file, we may have one unit reading in the old master file, another feeding in recent transactions, a third introducing the processing instructions, and a fourth writing the updated master file. Small installations may have up to about six transports, while very large processors can handle over two hundred.

Advantages and Limitations of Magnetic Tape

The *advantages* of magnetic tape can be summarized as follows.

1. *Unlimited length of records.* Unlike cards, any number of characters can be placed in a record. Files can be as long as necessary.
2. *Compact storage.* The data density, as we have seen, is far greater than that of cards and paper tape. Data handling is facilitated. Many firms keep their tapes in special air-conditioned vaults and thus provide safer storage for their records than is practicable with paper media and documents.
3. *Reduced cost.* A tape costs less than the hundreds of thousands of cards that it can replace. Storage space is reduced, and the tape can be reused many times.

4. *Rapid transfer rate*. Neither cards nor punched tape can compare with magnetic tape in input/output speed.

5. *Protection against record loss*. In card systems, there is always the danger of losing or misplacing one or more cards from a file. The use of magnetic tape is a protection against this danger.

Magnetic tape, however, has several *disadvantages*. Included among these are:

1. *Need for machine interpretation*. Since the magnetized spots are invisible, they cannot, of course, be read by humans. A printing operation must be performed if it is necessary to check or verify tape data.

2. *Lack of random accessibility*. Because of the sequential nature of tape file processing, it is not generally suitable for jobs that require rapid and random access to particular records. Tape file processing is also not efficient when the job being processed calls for the use of only a small proportion of the total tape records. In either situation, too much time is wasted in reading records that will not be used.

3. *Environmental problems*. Specks of dust on a tape can be read as data characters or can cause an improper reading. Special dust-resistant cases must be used to store the tapes. The humidity of the storage area must be controlled. Care must be taken to keep the tape transports and the computer room as free of dust as possible. Careful control procedures must be followed to prevent an important file from being erased by mistake. (Instead of losing a card or two, the entire file might be lost—a revolting development!) External descriptive reel labels and internal header control labels help to prevent such a disaster. Stray magnetic fields caused by sparking electric motors in close proximity to stored tapes can alter the tape contents. A diligent janitor (with a faulty electric vacuum cleaner) intent on cleaning the tape storage area of potentially harmful dust particles could do more harm than good.

SUMMARY

Data are organized into files of related records and fed into computers for processing. The information needed by managers is the output obtained by processing files. These files may be organized in two ways—either sequentially or randomly. Batch processing is possible with files organized in either way. A wide variety of I/O media and devices is available. The business manager must consider many factors in choosing the best approach for his firm.

Punched cards are the most familiar medium. They are easily understood, and they possess advantages because of their fixed length and unit record nature; e.g., some cards can be deleted, added to, sorted, etc., without disturbing the others. However, their data density is low, they are bulky, and they represent a slow means of input and output.

Punched paper tape is a popular means of capturing data as a by-product of another processing activity. Round holes are punched to represent data. Several coding systems are employed. Certain advantages accrue to paper tape because of its continuous length. There is no upper-limit restriction on the length of records and no wasted space when records are short. Paper tape is also more economical than cards. But error correction, additions, and deletions are more difficult than is the case with cards. And like cards, paper tape is a relatively slow I/O medium.

Magnetic tape is much faster. Its transfer rate is significantly improved by its high data density. It can be erased and reused many times and is thus very economical. Data are usually represented by either a seven- or nine-channel code, and parity checking is used to reduce the chance of error. However, the coded magnetized spots are invisible, and thus a printing operation is required to check or verify tape data. Tape records lack random accessibility. The following table summarizes the I/O speeds obtained by the media presented in this chapter.

Medium	Input Device Used	Output Device Used	I/O Speed Range, Characters/Second	
			Input	Output
Punched card	Card reader	Card punch	150–2,667	80–650
Paper tape	Tape reader	Tape punch	50–1,800	10–300
Magnetic tape	Tape drive	Tape drive	15,000–350,000	15,000–350,000

DISCUSSION QUESTIONS

1. How are data organized in business information systems; i.e., what organizational hierarchy is employed?
2. Discuss the factors to be considered in selecting the alternate I/O media and devices.

3. A punched card is a dual-purpose medium. (a) What is the meaning of dual purpose? (b) What other media are dual purpose in nature?
4. Define the following terms:
   (a) Turnaround document
   (b) read punch
   (c) data density
   (d) channels
   (e) frame
   (f) parity checking
   (g) transfer rate
   (h) tape-recording density
   (i) interrecord gaps
   (j) load-point marker
   (k) header label
   (l) trailer label
   (m) record
   (n) item
   (o) multifunction card machine
5. Discuss the advantages and limitations of punched cards.
6. Discuss the advantages and limitations of punched paper tape.
7. Explain how data are read from and written on magnetic tape.
8. Discuss the advantages and limitations of magnetic tape.

SELECTED REFERENCES

Feidelman, Lawrence: "A Primer on Source Data Automation," *Data Processing Magazine,* September, 1969, pp. 26–29ff.

Schwab, Bernhard, and Robert Sitter: "Economic Aspects of Computer Input/Output Equipment," *Financial Executive,* September, 1969, pp. 75–76ff.

Stender, Robert C.: "The Future Role of Keyboards in Data Entry," *Datamation,* June, 1970, pp. 60–72.

Input/Output Media and Devices: II

In spite of advances made in many areas of processing technology, input preparation in a majority of installations has not changed significantly in the past decade. Data are still taken from printed documents and recorded in machine-acceptable form by a manual keying operation. In many cases a further manual verification step is required to check the accuracy of the initial keying. Several devices, however, have been designed to eliminate manual keying by reading the characters printed on the source documents and converting the data *directly* into computer-usable input. In the first pages of this chapter we shall look at these *character readers,* which are generally used in high-volume, batch processing applications. *High-speed printers* are also considered.

The latter part of the chapter is devoted to (1) some I/O devices that are frequently found in online, random access processing situations and (2) complementary tools and concepts that facilitate I/O operations.

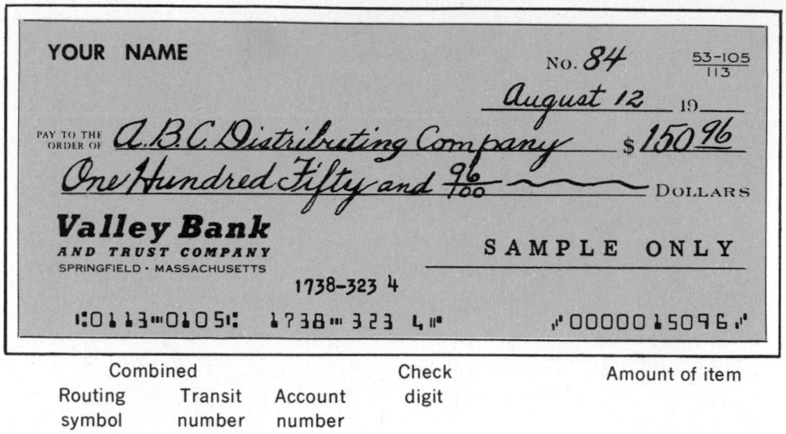

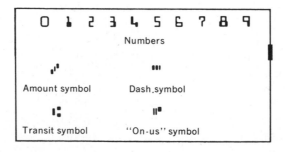

	Combined		Check	
Routing	Transit	Account	digit	Amount of item
symbol	number	number		

Figure 7-1 (Courtesy NCR)   Numbers at bottom of check are printed in approved E-13-B character shape

MAGNETIC INK CHARACTER RECOGNITION

Use and Development

The magnetic ink character recognition (MICR) concept is widely used by banking and financial institutions as a means of processing the tremendous volume of checks being written.[1] Figure 7-1 shows a sample check coded with a special ink, which contains tiny iron-oxide magnetizable particles. The code number of the bank to which the check will be written and the depositor's account number are pre-coded on the checks. The first bank to receive the check after it has been written encodes the amount in the lower right corner. The check at this point is a unit record and, like punched cards, may then be handled automatically through regular bank collection channels—e.g., from (1) the initial bank receiving the check to, perhaps, (2) the Federal Reserve bank to (3) the depositor's bank to (4) the depositor's account. The type font used (Fig. 7-2) permits the reading equipment to distinguish between symbols.

[1] It is estimated that 20 *billion* checks were written in 1970. And the typical check may pass through two to four banks and be handled and read up to seven times before it is finally cleared.

Figure 7-2   E-13B type font approved by the American Bankers Association

Because of the nature of bank collection channels, any approach to automatic check processing must receive the support of the entire banking industry. In 1955, the American Bankers Association began to study the problem of how to improve check processing. The result of this study was the recommendation that magnetic ink characters become the common language for checks. The development of MICR (although not painless) was possible only through the coordinated efforts of the American Bankers Association, check printers, equipment manufacturers, the Federal Reserve System, and the individual banks and their customers. The success of the MICR approach was illustrated when on September 1, 1967, Federal Reserve banks stopped handling, through the regular clearing channels, checks not encoded with magnetic ink (see Fig. 7-3 for an announcement made earlier in 1967). The magnetic ink characters have also been accepted as a standard by the British Bank Association. Thus, the concept has now become international in scope.

Equipment

Magnetic ink character *reader-sorter* units (Fig. 7-4) interpret the encoded data on checks (which vary in length, width, and thickness) and transfer this information to the CPU. They also sort the checks by account number, bank number, etc., into pockets. Input speed ranges from about 180 to nearly 2,000 paper documents each minute; a maximum of from 700 to 3,200 characters may be read each second.

As checks enter the reading unit and immediately prior to the reading operation, they pass through a strong magnetic field, which causes the iron-oxide particles to become magnetized. The read heads are then able to produce electric signals as the magnetized characters pass beneath them. Each character pattern is divided into many segments and analyzed by built-in recognition circuits to determine

---

FEDERAL RESERVE BANKS WILL NOT HANDLE CHECKS
RECEIVED WITHOUT MAGNETIC INK NUMBERS
EFFECTIVE SEPTEMBER 1, 1967

Effective September 1, 1967, checks and drafts deposited with Federal Reserve banks will not be handled through regular bank collection channels if received without the magnetic ink (MICR) transit number. The new electronic processing demands such magnetic ink encoding.

To avoid the delays of special handling of your checks, please use only the printed checks which your bank furnishes. (If not convenient to carry your checkbook, keep a few blank checks with you.) **Do not use customer's draft forms or "changed" checks.**

You may be required to pay a service charge for collecting a check which cannot be processed electronically by the Federal Reserve banks.

TR-402 1-67

Figure 7-3

Figure 7-4 MICR reader-sorter (courtesy Honeywell Information Systems)

which of the 14 characters has been sensed. Valid characters may then be fed directly into a general purpose computer, or they may be transferred to magnetic tape for later processing. The number of sorting pockets varies from 2 to 32.

Advantages and Limitations of MICR

There are several *advantages* associated with the use of MICR:

1. *High reading accuracy.* Checks may be roughly handled, folded, smeared, stamped, endorsed, and covered with extraneous markings. Yet, this does not prevent recognition with a high degree of accuracy. Portions of characters can be missing, and the characters may still be readable.
2. *Direct input with source document.* Processing is speeded because checks can be fed directly into the input device. In addition, the checks can vary in size and still be acceptable as input.
3. *Humanly readable data.* The type font used is easily recognized and read, if necessary, by clerical personnel.
4. *Reduction in bad check losses.* In the past merchants kept blank customer draft or courtesy check forms available for customers to fill in with the name of their bank, its location, etc., in addition to the amount of the check. Occasionally, honest people would make errors in filling in the information, their accounts could not

be located, and the merchant might not have enough information to trace the customer. When people are required to use their own checks properly encoded, there is much less chance of this type of error. It is, of course, still possible for fraudulent checks to be written, but there is less likelihood that a merchant will find himself in the embarrassing position of having cashed a check drawn on an imaginary institution such as The East Bank of the Trinity River.

The primary *limitation* of MICR is that only a *small number of characters* are used. Since it was designed by and for the banking industry, MICR uses only the characters needed for bank processing. No alphabetic characters are available. Thus MICR has not been found suitable for general business applications. Also, clerical processing is still required to handle (1) damaged documents, (2) checks not encoded with the proper amount of ink, and (3) checks not encoded in the proper position. In spite of Federal Reserve policies, checks are written on uncoded forms and on forms where the writer has substituted the name of one bank for another—still a nuisance to the banking community.

OPTICAL CHARACTER RECOGNITION

Optical character recognition (OCR) may well become to businesses in general what MICR is to the banking community. The basic differences between MICR and OCR are: (1) the MICR process requires encoding with special ink while OCR techniques make possible the reading of any printed character; and (2) the magnetic ink reader is limited to 14 characters while an optical reader may include alphabetic as well as numeric characters. Thus, the flexibility of OCR may make it possible for many businesses to eliminate or reduce the input keying bottleneck.

Uses of OCR

Although machines are available that will read handwritten numbers (Fig. 7-5), the automatic reading of handwritten script is still some years in the future. (While your penmanship is undoubtedly beautiful, the author's presents a formidable challenge to the equipment designers.) Most OCR devices being used in business are designed to read *machine-printed* characters and simple handmade marks. A standard type font (OCR-A) recognized by the American National Standards Institute is used in the United States (Fig. 7-6).

One popular use of OCR is in credit card billing. Many credit card systems use embossed plastic plates bearing the holder's account

Figure 7-5 IBM 1287 optical reader (courtesy IBM Corporation)

Alphabet (upper case)

ABCDEFGHIJKLMNOPQRSTUVWXYZ

Alphabet (lower case)

abcdefghijklmnopqrstuvwxyz

Numerics

0123456789

Symbols

■ Period	━ Minus or hyphen	⊓ Quotation mark
⌐ Comma	⋮ Colon	✳ Asterisk
? Question mark	✚ Plus sign	═ Equals sign
/ Slant or slash	⁒ Percent sign	⌐ Semi colon
⌐ Left parenthesis	⅊ Dollar sign	▼ Apostrophe
⌐ Right parenthesis	& Ampersand	

Abstract symbols

| ⌐ Hook |
| ⌐ Chair |
| ⌐ Fork |
| ⌐ Field separator |

Figure 7-6 American National Standards Institute OCR type font

Figure 7-7 Addressograph 1455 data recorder (courtesy Addressograph Multigraph Corporation)

number in specially designed characters. When a credit sale is made at a gasoline station, for example, the attendant uses an inexpensive imprinter (Fig. 7-7) to record the data from the customer's card and the amount of the transaction onto a form that is then forwarded to a central processing point. There the document is read automatically by an optical instrument. The data may then be entered directly into the CPU, or they may be transferred to punched cards, punched tape, or magnetic tape for later processing. The 14 largest United States oil companies now use OCR in their monthly credit billing operations.

Public utilities also use OCR in their billing activities. A water department, for example, may print the customer's name and account number on the meter-reading forms with characters that can be optically interpreted. The meter reader than makes pencil marks in appropriate columns on the forms to designate the quantities used (an optical version, without special pencils, of the mark-sensing process used with punched cards). The completed forms are then optically processed, and the monthly bill is prepared by a high-speed printer connected to the CPU. The customer returns the bill with the payment; a clerk checks the amount of payment against the billed amount and notes partial payments by making the appropriate marks on the left side of the form; and the bill then becomes the machine input to update the customer's account record. Thus, the desirable turnaround character of utility billing is still maintained with OCR processing.

Other OCR uses include (1) the reading of school documents such as registration forms, attendance rosters, and grade reports to maintain student records in large metropolitan school systems and (2) the reading of adding machine and cash register tapes for accounting and

Figure 7-8   (Courtesy NCR)   (a)   (b)

inventory control purposes. For example, the specially printed tape produced by the adding machine in Fig. 7-8*a* may be read directly into the computer system by the *optical reader* shown in Fig. 7-8*b*. Also, the post offices in large cities use optical recognition equipment to read typed addresses and sort mail geographically. The use of Zip codes improves this sorting procedure.

Equipment

The ideal optical reader would be one that could read any character written in any form. It could accept documents of all sizes, and it would not be confused by smudges and other defects. Alas, the ideal machine is not yet available.

However, several types of optical readers are available. Some are limited to mark reading; some are designed for reading turnaround documents and have alphanumeric capability, although the character locations, number of lines to be read, type font used, etc., permit only limited flexibility; and some are capable of reading entire pages of printed matter (upper- and lowercase letters, numbers, and punctuation marks). In all readers the printed marks and/or characters must be scanned by some type of photoelectric device, which recognizes characters by the absorption or reflectance of light on the document (characters to be read are nonreflective).[2] Reflected light patterns are converted into electric impulses, which are transmitted to recognition logic circuits. There they are compared with the characters that the machine has been programmed to recognize and, if valid, are then recorded for input into the CPU. If no suitable comparison is possible, the document may be rejected. Reading speed generally varies from about 100 to 2,400 characters per second.[3]

[2]Some machines break the scanned character down into distinguishable segments, or spots, for recognition purposes while others scan the entire character without segmentation.
[3]An exception is the Bank of America machine developed by Control Data Corporation, which reads 14,000 characters per second.

The primary *advantage* of OCR is that it eliminates some of the duplication of human effort required to get data into the computer. This reduction in human effort (1) can *improve the quality* (*accuracy*) of input data and (2) can *improve the timeliness of information processed*. Also, OCR helps businesses cope with the paperwork explosion. If volume of processing is sufficiently high, OCR will result in cost savings. Typed input documents are easily read by humans, and typists are easier to locate and hire than keypunch operators. Input preparation at remote stations requires only the use of an imprinter, a typewriter, an adding machine, etc.—devices that are less expensive than other input preparation machines.

Advantages and Limitations of OCR

Among the *limitations* of OCR are the following:

1. There are usually specific (and rather inflexible) requirements for type font and size of characters to be used.
2. The difficulty of controlling print quality causes reading problems in some applications; e.g., in typing there is the problem of uneven spacing, strikeovers, smudges, and erasures.
3. Forms design, ink specifications, paper quality, etc., become more critical and must be more standardized than is the case when keypunch source documents are prepared.
4. Most optical readers are not economically feasible unless the daily volume of transactions is relatively high (some multifont page readers are as expensive as medium-sized computers). But smaller readers with lower price tags have recently been introduced. And furture development work on optical readers is expected to improve their technical capabilities and reduce their cost.

HIGH-SPEED PRINTERS

High-speed printers (Fig. 7-9) provide information *output* from the CPU in the form of permanently printed characters which have meaning to humans. They are the primary output device when the information is to be used by man rather than by machine.

Printer Progress (and a Problem)

Significant improvements have been made in printers in the past few years. Because the earlier computers were scientifically oriented, the printed output was expected to be small. Therefore, many earlier printers were merely souped-up, one-character-at-a-time versions of electric typewriters. Such printed output facilities proved to be completely inadequate for business purposes. In fact, printing was a major bottleneck of the early business processing systems.

Figure 7-9 High-speed
printer (courtesy NCR)

But with the introduction of second-generation equipment designed specifically for business use came greatly improved printing capability. Character-at-a-time printing gave way to *line-at-a-time* printing. Speed increased from about five 120-character lines per minute for typewriters to over 1,200 similar lines per minute for high-speed impact printers.[4] Progress in printer development has continued so that printers are now available which will print two-thousand 132-character lines per minute. In other words, printing speed has gone from 600 to over 260,000 characters per minute.

However, as you will recall, some magnetic tape drives can write characters at a rate of over 300,000 per *second*. Thus, there is still a substantial mismatch between output by printing and output by magnetic tape. Several approaches have been used to reduce the problem of CPU idleness during printing. Some large computer systems, for example, write the CPU output on tapes, and the printing operation is then controlled offline from the large system by smaller computers. Other large multiprogrammed systems have multiple printers (Fig. 7-10), and only a small portion of the time of the CPU need be allocated to driving these devices. A third approach is to reduce the role of the printer by replacing paper output documents

---

[4]The two basic types of high-speed printers are *impact* and *nonimpact* devices. Impact printing is performed by the familiar method of pressing a typeface against paper and inked ribbon. Nonimpact (or electrostatic) printers generally form images by means of electrical and chemical processes. Nonimpact printing, while capable of producing over 5,000 lines per minute, produces only one copy, and the quality of that copy is not too good. Since the vast majority of printers used today are of the impact type, we shall limit our study to these machines. Future advances are expected in nonimpact methods.

Figure 7-10   IBM System/370, Model 165, with three high-speed printers. The IBM 3211 Printer in the left foreground operates at 2,000 lines per minute. (courtesy IBM Corporation)

with *microfilm*. The Computer-Output-to-Microfilm (COM) approach is shown in Fig. 7-11. Output information may be read onto magnetic tape and then, in an offline operation, recorded on microfilm. Or, the *microfilm recorder* (Fig. 7-12) may receive the information directly from the CPU. Most microfilm recorders project the characters of output information onto the screen of a *cathode ray tube*, which is similar to a television picture tube. A high-speed microfilm camera then films the displayed information. Up to 100,000 characters per second may be placed on film in this way—a rate of speed about twenty times faster than the fastest impact printer. After being developed, the film can be viewed directly through special readers (Fig. 7-13) by the users of the information; when necessary, paper documents can be produced from the film by a special printer.[5]

[5]For more information on COM, see the June, 1970, issue of *EDP Analyzer,* and the December, 1969, issue of *Datamation.*

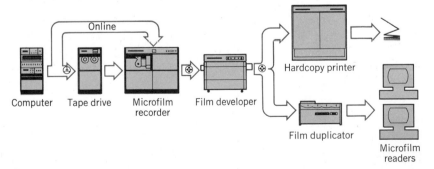

Figure 7-11   Computer output to microfilm (courtesy Stromberg DatagraphiX, Inc.)

Figure 7-12 DatagraphiX microfilm recorder (courtesy Stromberg DatagraphiX, Inc.)

Overcoming the CPU-printer mismatch by means of multiple processor, multiple printer, or COM approaches is, of course, not economically feasible in smaller computer installations where printed output is accomplished by a single online device.

Equipment

High-speed line printers vary in size from the large ones shown in Figs. 7-9 and 7-10 to the small table-top units used for remote online printing (Fig. 7-14). Line printers do not have movable carriages. Rather, they use rapidly moving chains (or trains) of printing slugs or some form of a print *cylinder* to print lines of information on paper moving past the printing station. Figure 7-15 illustrates the *print chain* concept. The links in the chain are engraved character-printing slugs. The chain is capable of producing 48 different characters, and there are five sections of 48 characters each in the length of the chain. The chain moves at a constant and rapid speed past the printing positions. Magnetically controlled hammers behind the paper are timed to force the paper against the proper print slugs. The ribbon between the paper and the character leaves an imprint on the paper as a result of the impact. Obviously, careful timing is required to actuate the hammers in each printing position at the precise moment the desired character is passing. Printing speeds of 2,000 lines per minute are possible with chain devices.

The *drum printer* uses a solid cylinder. Raised characters extend the length of the drum (Fig. 7-16). There are as many circular *bands* of type as there are printing positions. Each band contains all the possible characters. The drum turns at a constant speed, with one revolution being required to print each line. A fast-acting hammer opposite each band picks out the proper character and strikes the paper against that character. Thus, in one rotation, hammers of *several* printing positions may "fire" when the A row appears; several others may strike to imprint D's, etc. At the end of the rotation, all necessary positions on the paper are printed. The paper then moves to the next

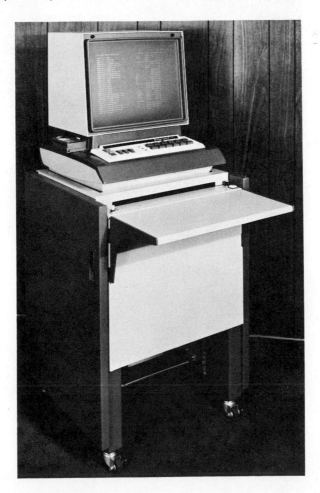

Figure 7-13   Microfilm reader (courtesy Stromberg DatagraphiX, Inc.)

Figure 7-14 (Courtesy Data Products Corporation)

line. This procedure may be repeated from 350 to over 1,500 times in a single minute. Figure 7-17 shows an exposed print drum.

Most of the tremendous volume of data and information that enters and leaves business computers each year is processed by the I/O media and machines that have now been introduced. However,

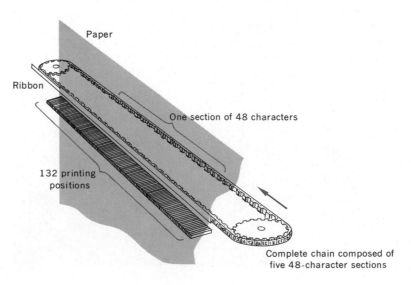

Figure 7-15

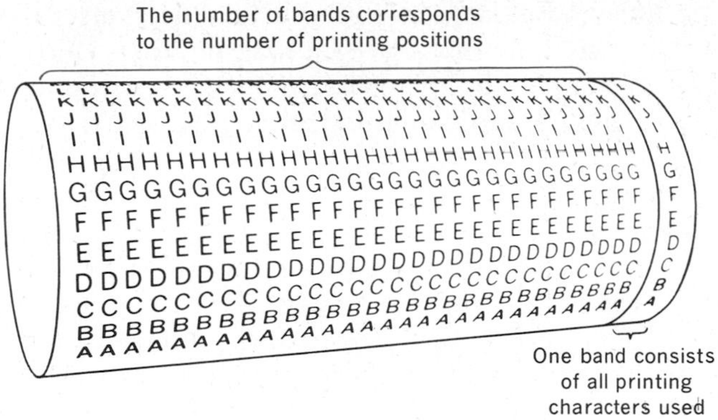

The number of bands corresponds
to the number of printing positions

One band consists
of all printing
characters used

Figure 7-16   A print drum

other means of communication between man and machine are possible. In the following pages we shall examine some I/O devices
possessing one or more of the following characteristics:

1. Direct manual input/output of information may be possible
    without data-recording media being *required;* i.e., a direct man-
    machine *interface* is possible.
2. The relationship between user and machine is thus of an online
    nature.

*Figure 7-17   An exposed
print drum (courtesy Data
Products Corporation)*

3. Random access processing is common; file storage is online.
4. The volume of input data may be lower and/or more irregular than is the case with data processed by the means described in Chapter 6 and earlier in this chapter.

ONLINE TERMINALS

The *console control panel* of a computer (Fig. 7-18) appears to most observers as a confusing array of lights, switches, and buttons; it is used to load programs, display the contents of a number of special CPU storage locations during program execution, determine the causes of certain equipment malfunctions, and reset the computer after malfunctions have been corrected. Often associated with the control panel is the *console typewriter* (Fig. 7-19), a commonly encountered online terminal that enables the computer operator to enter data directly into and receive information directly from the storage

Figure 7-18 IBM System/370, Model 155 control panel (courtesy IBM Corporation)

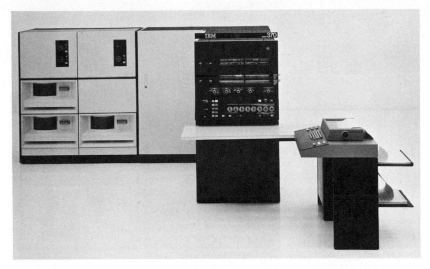

Figure 7-19 Console typewriter for IBM System/370, Model 145 computer (courtesy IBM Corporation)

unit of the central processor. When the keys of the typewriter are depressed, the code designation of the keyed characters is entered into storage. A visual record is also typed. in addition, the console typewriter may be used to (1) modify a portion of the program instructions, (2) test the program of instructions, (3) inquire about the contents of certain storage areas, (4) alter the data content of specific storage locations, (5) determine intermediate computing results, and (6) receive and type output information. Console typewriters, because of the slowness of their I/O operations, are seldom used if volume is significant.

The online terminals used in timesharing are usually (1) *typewriter-like devices,* (2) *multiunit data stations,* or (3) *visual display units.*

Typewriter Terminals

The typewriter terminals (Fig. 7-20) may be quite similar to console typewriters, but they are located away from the computer room. They may be in the next office, in a nearby building, or in the next state. And they may be connected to the CPU by a short cable or by a complex data communications system. Since we have illustrated the use of such stations by airlines and others in Chapter 4 in the discussion of timesharing and real time processing, we need not dwell further here on the subject. Of course, remote stations, like main console typewriters, produce input data and receive output information very slowly. But with many such timesharing stations online (and perhaps with batch processing jobs to perform) the CPU can be kept busy.

Figure 7-20   IBM 2740
communications terminal
(courtesy IBM Corporation)

Multiunit Data Stations

The term *multiunit data station* may refer to a remote installation consisting of a wide variety of I/O devices. Data in the form of punched cards, punched paper tape, magnetic tape, and magnetic characters may be read into a distant CPU by appropriate station units; manual keyboard input may be used; and visually displayed and printed output information may be received at the data station. The system shown in Fig. 7-21 can accomodate all of these options; however, only four are shown—a card reader (upper right), a visual display unit and keyboard (center), and a printer (foreground).

Another type of multiunit data station system makes use of a number of scattered online terminals to perform such limited functions as *data collecting* or *transaction recording*. These systems have been developed in an effort to bypass the preparation of punched cards, paper tapes, or magnetic tapes. Although data collection systems vary according to the application, they are all designed to perform a similar function—to get data from remote points into the computer as quickly as possible.

Transaction recorders are often found in factories (Fig. 7-22) to keep control of the inventory of parts and materials used in production. Let us assume, for example, that an employee needs a dozen hinges to complete a job. He gets the hinges and an identification card from a supply station. The card identifies the hinges by part number and contains any other *fixed* information (such as unit price) that is necessary. The worker inserts the card into a transaction recorder and then keys or moves levers to indicate the *variable* part of the transaction—the number of hinges taken, the job number, etc. He then pushes a transmit button to send the data to the computer where they are checked for accuracy and then accepted to update the proper record in the inventory file. If an error is detected, a signal is relayed back to the recording station. It is obvious, of course, that such a system requires random access processing.

Many savings institutions are also making use of online transaction-recording devices. Let us assume that a deposit is to be made by a customer. The customer presents his bankbook and the amount of his deposit to the teller, who inserts the book into a recorder and keys in the transaction data. The data are then sent to the computer,

Figure 7-21   IBM 2770 data communication system (courtesy IBM Corporation)

Figure 7-22   Area station, IBM 2790 data communication system (courtesy IBM Corporation)

which adjusts the customer's savings balance. The updated information is relayed back to the remote station where it is entered in the customer's bankbook. The entire transaction is accounted for in a matter of seconds.

Visual Display Terminals

Terminals using a typewriter or keyboard approach are relatively inexpensive and familiar to users. In addition, they provide a *hard copy* paper printout, which can be referred to as needed. Many will also produce a punched-paper-tape copy of data transmitted and information received. But such terminals are often very slow character-at-a-time output devices; moreover, they may be very noisy, and since they have many mechanical moving parts, they are subject to wear and relatively frequent breakdowns.

As a result of these disadvantages, considerable emphasis is now being placed on visual display terminals, which look like small television sets equipped with a manual keyboard. Although input by means of the keyboard may be no faster than with typing, output is silent and very fast—the screen of the terminal's cathode ray tube (CRT) can be instantly covered with hundreds of characters of displayed information. Also, since a display terminal is essentially an electronic device, many of the maintenance problems associated with mechanical instruments can be eliminated or reduced. The absence of a paper document output may be a disadvantage of CRT devices in some applications, but photographic equipment and optional printer attachments are sometimes used to make a permanent record of a display. The Diebold Group, Inc., a respected professional organization in the computer industry, has predicted that over 700,000 visual display units will be in use by 1975 (up from less than 4,000 in 1965 and about 75,000 in 1970!). Many modern computer systems are now employing operator consoles with visual displays (Fig. 7-23).

There are two basic classes of CRT display terminals. In the *first* category are lower-cost units, which display *only alphanumeric* information (Fig. 7-24). In the *second* class are expensive units, which are capable of projecting graphs, charts, and designs as well as alphanumeric characters (Fig. 7-25). The first category might be considered a clever, "paperless electronic typewriter"; the second class of display units possesses graphic art capabilities not available with typewriter devices. Let us briefly look at some of the ways in which these display units are currently being used.

Figure 7-23 Operator console with visual displays (courtesy Burroughs Corporation)

Figure 7-24   (Courtesy NCR)

Alphanumeric display applications   Terminals that display only alphanumeric information are well suited for the following purposes:

1. *Obtaining quick response to inquiries.* The visual display unit
    provides a window into the computer's data base. Status of a
    customer's credit, prices quoted on stock exchanges, current
    inventory levels, availability of airline seats, locations of truck
    shipments and railroad freight cars, locations of unsold seats in
    a theater or stadium, location and telephone number of students
    and employees of a university—information such as this is being
    kept current by various organizations in online files so that it is
    instantly available for display upon inquiry. The keyboard can be
    used to update files in order to reflect any transaction that may
    be made at a display station, e.g., when airplane and theater tickets
    are sold, when credit purchases are authorized, when an order
    for additional inventory is placed, etc.
2. *Providing convenient man-machine interaction.* We saw in Chap-
    ter 4 that data management software would enable a manager to

probe and query files in order to obtain information relevant to some unique problem. The combination of an easy-to-use inquiry language and a visual display unit facilitates this process. The manager, in effect, carries on a "conversation" with the computer system by supplying data and key phrases, while the system responds with displayed end results, intermediate results, or questions. The questions may be in a multiple-choice format so that the manager need only key in the number indicating his response. Because of the output speed of the display unit, the interaction between man and machine is faster than would be the case with a typewriter terminal.

Graphical display applications   Preliminary sketches, design drawings, and engineering drawings are generally required in the design and development of new products and projects. When the designer first gets a new-product thought, he makes some preliminary sketches to get his idea down on paper so that it may be more thoroughly analyzed. As the design is modified, additional drawings may be required;

Figure 7-25   IBM 2250 display unit (courtesy IBM Corporation)

when the idea is approved, further detailed production drawings are prepared. Thus, the preparation of drawings may occupy a substantial portion of the designer's time. Although it is possible to convert graphical material into numerical coordinates for purposes of computer analysis, this is a very time-consuming process if done manually.

In recent years, visual *input* instruments have been developed which make it possible for the computer to receive human sketching directly.[6] One such instrument is an *input tablet,* which may be made of glass or plastic and is about the size of a sheet of paper. The tablet contains hundreds of copper lines, which form a fine grid that is connected with the computer. Each copper line receives electric impulses. A special pen or stylus attached to the tablet is sensitive to these impulses and is used to form the sketches. However, the pen does not mark directly on the tablet. To communicate with the machine, the designer merely draws on a piece of paper placed on the glass or plastic. The tablet grid then senses the exact position of the stylus as it is moved and transmits this information to the computer.

As the designer draws, the computer may display the developing sketch on the CRT. However, there is a difference between the drawing and the display. Poorly sketched lines are displayed as straight; poor lettering is replaced by neat printing; and poorly formed corners become mathematically precise. Changes and modifications in the drawing can be quickly made; e.g., a line can be "erased" from (or shifted on) the display unit with a movement of the stylus. Once the initial sketching is finished and displayed on the CRT to the satisfaction of the designer, he may then instruct the computer to analyze the design and report on certain characteristics. For example, the computer might be asked to work out the acoustical characteristics of a theater that the designer has sketched. The sketch may then be modified by the designer on the basis of the computer analysis, or the machine may be instructed to display a theater with more desirable acoustics. Such direct man-machine graphical communication enables the designer to (1) learn what effect certain changes have on the project and (2) save valuable time for more creative work.

Another graphical input instrument is the electronic *light pen*. This pen is a photocell placed in a small, easily handled tube (Fig. 7-26). It may be used to "write" on the surface of the CRT. When the pen is moved by the user over the screen, it is able to detect the light coming from a limited field of view. The light from the CRT causes the photocell to respond when the pen is pointed directly at a lighted

[6]For an excellent discussion of graphical devices, see Ivan E. Sutherland, "Computer Inputs and Outputs," *Sci. Amer.,* vol. 215, pp. 86–96, September, 1966, Also, see Sutherland, "Computer Displays," *Sci. Amer.,* vol. 222, pp. 56–60ff., June, 1970.

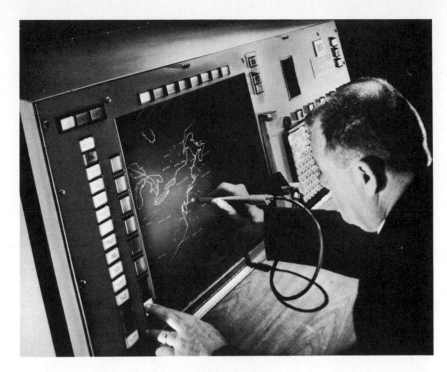

Figure 7-26   Light-pen input (courtesy Burroughs Corporation)

area. These electric responses are transmitted to the computer, which is able to determine that part of the displayed drawing that is triggering the photocell response. Under program control, the pen can be used to modify a displayed image or add or delete lines. By using a light pen, an executive could experiment with displayed operating charts (e.g., charts portraying revenue and cost curves) to determine the effects of changes in such variables as prices and quantities produced.[7]

Input units, basically, do nothing more than convert human language into machine language. Why, then, doesn't someone invent a machine that will enable a person to talk to the computer in English? As a matter of fact, a few manufacturers have done just that on an experimental basis. Although the vocabulary is quite small, sound waves have been converted into machine language. Speech recognition, however, will not become an economical input technique for some time.

VOICE COMMUNICATION

[7]For further details on this interesting use of light pens, see Irvin M. Miller, "Computer Graphics for Decision Making," *Harvard Business Rev.*, November–December, 1969, pp. 121–132.

Figure 7-27   RCA Spectra
70/510 voice response unit
(courtesy RCA)

When we look at the *output* side of verbal communication,
however, we find that computers are now being used to give English
responses in reply to human inquiries transmitted to a central computer over regular telephone lines. All the spoken words needed to
process the possible inquiries are generally prerecorded on a magnetic

or photographic film drum. Each word is given a code. When inquiries are received, the processor composes a reply message in a coded form. This coded message is then transmitted to an *audio-response* device (Fig. 7-27), which assembles the words in the proper sequence and transmits the audio message back to the station requesting the information.

Audio-response units are now being used by many organizations, including Southwestern Bell Telephone Company and the New York Stock Exchange. The telephone company uses audio response in the processing of intercepted calls, i.e., calls that are automatically given special handling because they are made to numbers which have been changed. The operator who receives the intercepted call asks for the number being dialed. She keys this number into the computer system, presses a start button, and is then free to handle the next intercepted call. The new number is automatically transmitted to the customer by the audio-response unit. The reply is so fast that the system is instructed to remain silent for an initial short period of time!

The New York Stock Exchange uses verbal output to direct inquiries from subscribers to the Exchange's quotation service. To receive up-to-the-minute information about a stock, the broker dials the code number of the stock over a private station phone. The dialed inquiry goes to the Exchange's computer, where it is processed. The broker immediately receives the latest information on stock prices and the volume of trading. About 400,000 inquiries a day can be handled by this system.

We may conclude this section with the observation that audio-response techniques, combined with briefcase-sized keyboard devices, turn every standard telephone into a potential computer terminal. An equipment salesman, for example, can use any available phone (Fig. 7-28) to check on product availability prior to contacting an important customer. He can type his inquiry directly into the home-office computer system and receive a computer-compiled audio response. If his sales efforts lead to success, he can later use the same phone booth to enter an order directly into the information system.

DATA COMMUNICATIONS

Numerous references have been made in the above paragraphs and in earlier pages to I/O stations that are connected to a central processor located at some distant point. In this section let us take a closer look at the data communications techniques that facilitate remote I/O operations and that are available to businesses. *Data communication,* of course, simply refers to the means and methods whereby data are transferred between processing locations.

Figure 7-28   IBM 2721 portable audio terminal (courtesy IBM Corporation)

There is, certainly, nothing new about data communications. Human runners and messengers have been used since the beginning of recorded history. The Greek runner carrying the message of victory on the plains of Marathon has inspired a present-day athletic event. The Pony Express won the admiration of a nation in the brief period of time before it was replaced by telegraph service. Railroads were using telegraph equipment for business data communications in the early 1900s. And the U.S. Post Office transmits an enormous quantity of business data each week.

We have seen that there is a wide variety of I/O equipment from which the business manager can choose. Not surprisingly, there is also a wide range of data transmission services available from firms such as Western Union and American Telephone and Telegraph (the Bell Telephone System parent). Figure 7-29 shows some of the media and devices that can be used to achieve communication between remote and central points. The remote stations may be online or offline. Figure 7-29 also shows the most commonly used transmission *channels,* or

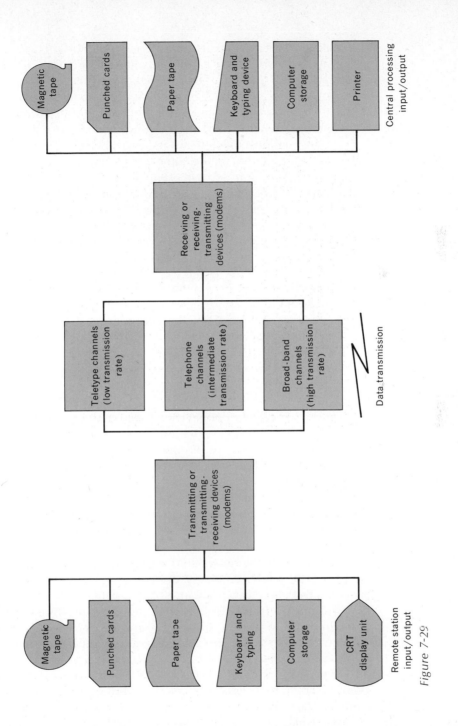

Magnetic tape

Punched cards

Paper tape

Keyboard and typing device

Computer storage

Printer

Central processing input/output

Receiving or receiving-transmitting devices (modems)

Teletype channels (low transmission rate)

Telephone channels (intermediate transmission rate)

Broad-band channels (high transmission rate)

Data transmission

Transmitting or transmitting-receiving devices (modems)

Magnetic tape

Punched cards

Paper tape

Keyboard and typing

Computer storage

CRT display unit

Remote station input/output

Figure 7-29

207

highways, for carrying data from one location to another. These channels are wire lines, cables, or microwave radio circuits, which, like I/O techniques, vary in data handling speed.

You will recall from Chapter 4 that the data transmission channels now in use were designed primarily for voice communications. Therefore, between the computing equipment in Fig. 7-29 and the data transmission channels are located devices called *modems*[8] (or *data sets*), which convert the computing equipment digital signals into signals that can be used by the voice-oriented transmission systems.

The *teletype* channels transmit data at speeds of about five to twenty characters per second—speeds that may be quite adequate for input by means of manual keying or punched paper tape. If a business has a moderate data volume, it may prove economical to lease an exclusive teletype circuit. Such a circuit may be leased for night use only, for the entire day, etc.

Standard voice-grade *telephone* channels permit more rapid transmission. Data may be sent at speeds of over three-hundred characters per second. The actual maximum rate depends on the type of telephone service used; e.g., private (leased) lines may be somewhat faster than public lines. Telephone circuits are used to communicate large amounts of data originating in the form of punched cards, punched tape, and magnetic tape. A popular means of transmission is through the use of the Bell Telephone System's *Data-Phone* modem (Fig. 7-30). The Data-Phone is connected to I/O equipment at the sending and receiving points and may be used for both voice and data transmission. Let us assume, for example, that a branch sales office is ready to transmit sales orders to the main plant. A clerk at the branch office dials the proper number at the main plant to notify it of a transmission. When the employee at the receiving station is ready to accept the message, both parties push a data button, at which point the voice communication cuts off and the data transmission begins.

If the data volume is sufficient between locations, it may be economical for the company to acquire leased lines, which can be used for both voice and data purposes. If data volume will not support a private line, however, then the regular long-distance telephone network should be used. The Data-Phones are leased full time, but the cost of data messages, like long-distance calls, is determined by time use.

Broadband channels use very high-frequency electric signals to carry the data message at maximum speeds of around 100,000 charac-

---

[8]MODEM stands for MOdulator-DEModulator. As a result of the easing of the foreign attachment rule discussed in Chapter 4, several manufacturers are now producing modems.

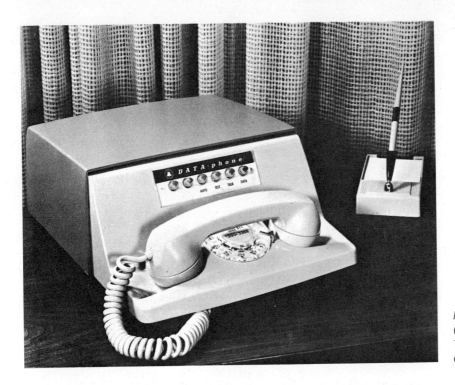

Figure 7-30 Data-Phone (courtesy American Telephone and Telegraph Company)

ters per second. These broadband circuits may be groups of voice-grade wire channels, or they may be microwave radio circuits.

Such transmission facilities are expensive and are now required by only the largest companies. Broadband facilities are used for transmitting data between magnetic tape units or from one computer storage unit to another. North American Aviation, Inc., for example, balances workloads among the computers in several divisions by transferring data from overloaded to "available-time" installations at the rate of 62,500 characters per second. And General Electric has broadband circuits installed to connect computer centers at Schenectady and Syracuse, New York, and Valley Forge, Pennsylvania.[9]

With increased emphasis being placed on broader and faster-responding business information systems, the trend is definitely toward greater use of data transmission facilities. An estimate quoted in Chapter 4 was that the traffic between machines would be occupying as much communications capacity by 1975 as all the traffic between people. And Western Union has predicted that 60 percent of the computers sold by 1975 will be linked in some way to a data communications network. A considerable amount of research is being

[9] General Electric is using a Telpak service provided by the Bell Telephone System.

directed toward the improvement of data communications; e.g., satellites, sometimes with laser beams, are being used to transmit data halfway round the world.

The wide range of data transmission services and the wide variety of I/O techniques present the business manager with an almost limitless number of alternatives. If he assumes that it is needed, what type of data communication would be best for his company? It is possible only to deal in generalities here, but the manager should consider the following factors in arriving at his decision:

1. *The number and location of I/O stations.* Is it necessary only to provide communication between two points, or is the scope of the data transmission operation broader? Do all stations transmit *and* receive data, or do some perform only one function?
2. *The accuracy requirements.* How accurate must the transmission be? Errors can occur. But various technical alternatives exist to achieve required degrees of reliability. A compromise between cost and accuracy is involved in the manager's decision.
3. *The volume of data to be communicated.* It is necessary to consider both the number of messages and the length of each message to arrive at the number of characters to be transmitted.
4. *The timing of messages.* Are messages transmitted at predictable intervals, or do they occur in a random manner? Are there peak load periods? If so, when? Are delays permissible; i.e., can the data load be scheduled to maintain a steady message flow and thus avoid peaks and valleys?
5. *The speed requirements.* Speed requirements are closely related to the above factors of volume and timing. Generally speaking, the greater the volume, the faster the data communication facility must be, and the greater the cost. Of course, a faster transmission line can do more work, and thus the cost per character transmitted may well be reduced. It is obviously inefficient, however, to contract for fast facilities when the data volume and the needs of the firm could be satisfied at a slower (and less expensive) level.

OVERLAPPED PROCESSING AND BUFFER STORAGE

Earlier computers employed *serial processing* methods to complete a task. In other words, during a processing cycle a record would be read into the CPU from an input device, processing would take place, and the information would then be supplied to an output device. The control unit of the central processor selects and interprets program input, processing, and output instructions. But since it operated on one instruction at a time (or serially), there was substantial idle time

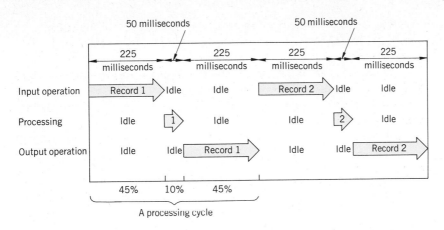

Figure 7-31 Serial (non-overlapped) processing

among earlier computer system components. In the hypothetical example shown in Fig. 7-31, the processing unit is busy only 10 percent of the time while each of the I/O devices are idle 55 percent of the time.

Obviously, performing the input-process-output cycle in a serial fashion wastes time. But why can't operations be continued while computations are being made, i.e., why can't activities be overlapped and performed simultaneously? The answer, as we know, is that activities *can* be performed concurrently on today's computers. Earlier discussions have pointed out, for example, that multiprogrammed computers could be processing the data of one program while other programs were reading in data or printing out information.

As we noted in Chapter 5, computers capable of performing *overlapped processing* have devices called *channels,* which (1) receive appropriate instruction signals from the central processor and then (2) proceed to operate independently and without supervision to bring in data and/or to write out information while the CPU is engaged in performing computations. In short, at the same time the CPU is processing, one channel can be controlling an input operation while another channel can be controlling output activities.

Buffers are high-speed storage elements, which play an important role in overlapped processing. Buffers may be found in some I/O devices; they may be in separate intermediate storage units; or they may consist of a section of the CPU main storage, which has been reserved for buffering purposes. To summarize the difference between serial and overlapped processing and to explain the use of buffer storage, let us refer to Fig. 7-32.

Data from input equipment are fed under channel control into input buffer storage, as shown in Fig. 7-32a. This input buffer has an

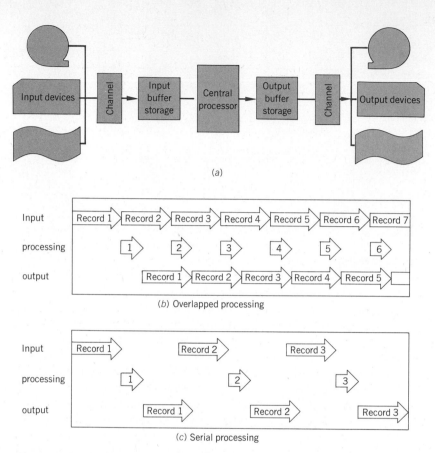

Figure 7-32

(a)

(b) Overlapped processing

(c) Serial processing

important characteristic: it can accept data at slow input speeds and release them at electronic speeds. (The reverse is true of the output buffer.) The first input record is entered into the buffer and then, under program control, to the main storage unit where processing begins immediately. While the first record is being processed, the input unit is automatically reading a second record into buffer storage (Fig. 7-32b). The processed information for the first record is transferred under program control to the output buffer and then under channel control to an output device where the writing operation begins. As soon as the first record is released, the program instructs the buffer to transmit the second record for processing. Thus, at this point in time in a synchronized system,[10] record 3 is being fed into the input buffer, record 2 is being processed, and record 1 is being written by an output device. The procedure continues until the task is finished.

[10] Although a *perfectly* synchronized system is rare, the use of buffering permits a much closer balance.

When compared with serial processing (Fig. 7-32c), overlapped processing is much more efficient.

Data may be fed simultaneously into buffers from a number of stations. Timesharing, of course, requires sophisticated buffering techniques. In addition to performing speed-changing and timesharing functions, buffers also help in translating the various human and machine codes into usable forms, i.e., one machine code into another, human language into machine code, or machine code into human language.

SUMMARY

Character readers offer businesses a way of reducing the manual effort involved in data input operations. Financial institutions have supported the development of MICR as a means of handling billions of transactions each year. The magnetic ink characters can be read even when they are smeared, stamped, or otherwise abused. The characters are humanly readable. Unfortunately for many firms outside the banking community, there are no alphabetic characters available in MICR. Optical character readers, however, have alphabetic as well as numeric capability and perform efficiently in a growing number of applications.

A high-speed printer is the primary output device when the information is to be used by man rather than by machine. Such printers have been improved significantly in the last decade. Character-at-a-time printers have been replaced by machines that print hundreds of lines each minute. When compared to magnetic tape output, however, printers are still very slow. In some cases printed output has been replaced with microfilm output.

Console typewriters, remote multiunit data stations, transaction recorders, input tablets and light pens, CRT-equipped display stations—all these online instruments—may enable man to communicate directly and randomly with any record stored in the computer. Console typewriters are used to modify and test programs and to enter and receive short messages. Inquiry and data stations may consist only of units similar to console typewriters, or they may have several types of I/O equipment; they are remotely located and are commonly used in timesharing. Transaction recorders are designed to enter data directly from the point of origin, thus bypassing the need for media preparation. Visual communication devices may only possess alphanumeric capabilities, or they may be able to display graphical information in addition to letters and numerals. They have been used quite successfully for business, scientific, and engineering purposes. Audio communication from computer to man has proven practical. The following table summarizes the range of I/O speeds permitted with some of the equipment presented in this chapter.

Medium	Input Device Used	Output Device Used	I/O Speed Range, Characters/Second	
			Input	Output
Magnetic ink	MICR reader		700–3,200	
Paper documents	OCR reader		100–2,400	
	keyboard	Character printer	2–20	2–20
		Line printer		440–4,400
Microfilm		Recorder		25,000–100,000
None		CRT visual display		250–10,000

Data communications facilities relay information between remote points. A wide range of data transmission services is available. These services vary in data-handling speed and cost. The manager must plan carefully in choosing among the alternatives. The use of overlapped processing (made possible by channels and buffer storage) permits the processing system to work at greater efficiency. Channels and buffers synchronize the I/O equipment with the CPU and permit simultaneous and overlapping processing cycles.

DISCUSSION QUESTIONS

1. Obtain a cancelled check and explain the magnetic ink coding along the bottom of the check.
2. How do MICR reader-sorter units interpret the encoded data on checks?
3. Discuss the advantages and limitations of MICR.
4. Compare and contrast MICR and OCR.
5. Give some examples of how OCR might be used.
6. Discuss the advantages and limitations of OCR.
7. Define the following terms:
   (a) Character-at-a-time printing
   (b) line-at-a-time printing
   (c) print chain
   (d) impact printer
   (e) nonimpact printer
   (f) drum printer

(g) man-machine interface

(h) cathode ray tube

(i) light pen

(j) data communication

(k) microfilm recorder

(l) console control panel

(m) multiunit data station

(n) modem

(o) buffer storage

8. How may the console typewriter be used?

9. (a) What is the purpose of a multiunit data station?

   (b) Of data collection stations?

   (c) Of display stations?

10. (a) What two basic classes of CRT display terminals are available?

    (b) How may each category be used?

11. How may audio-response units be used? Give examples.

12. Identify and discuss the most commonly used transmission channels for carrying data from one location to another.

13. What factors should be considered by managers in determining the best means of data communication?

14. (a) What is serial processing?

    (b) What is overlapped processing?

15. "The use of overlapped processing (made possible by I/O channels and buffer storage) permits the processing system to work at greater efficiency." Explain this statement.

SELECTED REFERENCES

Andersson, P. L.: "Optical Character Recognition—A Survey," *Datamation*, July, 1969, pp. 43–48.

Canning, Richard G.: "Computer Output to Microfilm," *EDP Analyzer*, June, 1970, pp. 1–14.

————: "Optical Scanning: It's on the Move," *EDP Analyzer*, June, 1969, pp. 1–13.

————: "Future Trends in Data Communications," *EDP Analyzer*, April, 1969, pp. 1–13.

Feidelman, Lawrence: "A Primer on Source Data Automation," *Data Processing Magazine*, September, 1969, pp. 26–29ff.

Kamman, Alan B.: "The Uses of Display Terminals for Business Applications," *Computers and Automation*, April, 1970, pp. 15–17.

Miller, Irvin M.: "Computer Graphics for Decision Making," *Harvard Business Review*, November–December, 1969, pp. 121–132.

Schwab, Bernhard, and Robert Sitter: "Economic Aspects of Computer Input-Output Equipment," *Financial Executive,* September, 1969, pp. 75–76ff.

Stender, Robert C.: "The Future Role of Keyboards in Data Entry," *Datamation,* June, 1970, pp. 60–72.

Yerkes, Charles P.: "Microfilm—A New Dimension for Computers," *Datamation,* December, 1969, pp. 94–97.

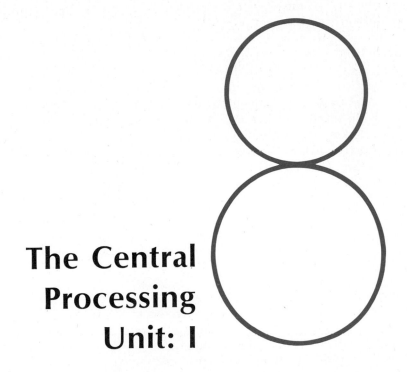

The Central Processing Unit: I

It is now time to take a closer look at the central processor. As you will remember, the typical CPU contains the storage unit, the arithmetic-logic unit, and the control unit. In this chapter we shall be concerned primarily with the *storage unit and related topics*. More specifically, we shall examine (1) the *conceptual areas* of the storage unit, (2) the *locations* in the storage unit, (3) the *capacity* of storage locations, (4) the *numbering systems* associated with computers, and (5) the methods of *data representation* used. In the first part of the next chapter, we shall continue the examination of the storage unit; in the latter part we shall turn our attention to the arithmetic-logic and control units.

We know that the storage unit contains the data to be processed and the program of instructions. As a general rule, any storage location

CONCEPTUAL STORAGE AREAS

217

in the central processor has the ability to store *either* data or instructions; i.e., a specific physical space may be used to store data for one operation and instructions for another. The programmer (or the software prepared by the programmer) determines how the location will be used for each program (Fig. 8-1).[1]

For each program, there will be, typically, four areas assigned to group related types of information. These conceptual areas are shown in Fig. 8-2. They are referred to as *conceptual areas* because it is important to remember that they are *not fixed* by built-in physical boundaries in storage. Rather, they vary (thus the broken lines in Fig. 8-2) at the discretion of the programmer. Three of the four areas (input, working, and output) are used for *data* storage purposes. The *input storage* area, as the name indicates, receives the data coming from the input media and devices. The *working storage* space corresponds to a blackboard or a sheet of scratch paper; it is space used by the program to hold data being processed as well as the intermediate results of such processing. The *output storage* section contains processed information that is awaiting a writing (or *read-out*) operation. The *program storage* area, of course, contains the processing instructions.

A typical *data-flow* pattern is indicated in Fig. 8-2. Data remain in the input area until needed. Since the actual processing occurs in the arithmetic-logic unit, data are delivered to this unit from input storage and processed and the final results move through the output storage area to the user. Intermediate figures, generated in the arithmetic-logic unit, are temporarily placed in a designated working storage area until needed at a later time. Data may move back and

[1]There are exceptions to this statement. Some "read-only" storage elements, for example, have predetermined functions and are not available to the programmer.

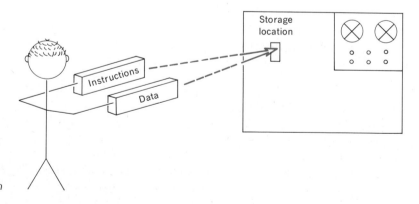

Figure 8-1   Either data or instructions may be placed in a specific storage location

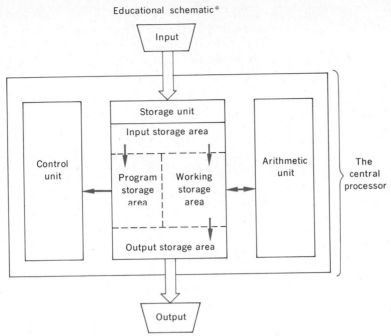

Educational schematic*

Figure 8-2   Conceptual areas
[*Source:* Orientation to
Electronic Data Processing
(*Sperry Rand Corporation,
UNIVAC Division, 1966*),
*p. 64. Copyright material
used through the courtesy of
Sperry Rand Corporation,
UNIVAC Division.*]

*The specific areas of storage used for a particular purpose (input storage, program storage, etc.) are not *fixed* but rather *vary* from program to program. The programmer defines the limits of these reserved areas for each of his programs. Therefore, broken lines (rather than solid ones) are used in the diagram to indicate this flexibility of area boundaries.

forth between working storage and the arithmetic-logic unit a number of times before the processing is completed.

Instructions move from the program storage area to the control unit. The first program instruction is sent to the control unit to begin the step-by-step processing procedure. Other instructions move into the control unit at the proper time until the job is completed. Of course, the number of instructions and therefore the size of the program storage area depend on the length and complexity of the processing problem.

The locations in the computer storage unit have been compared to such familiar things as post office boxes, hotel rooms, message boxes at hotel front desks, bins in a stock room, package deposit boxes in transportation stations, and the storage facilities of hat-check services. Figure 8-3 illustrates what each of the above things has in common—

STORAGE LOCATIONS

00	01	02	03	04	05
06	07	08	09	10	11
12	13	14	15	16	17
18	19	20	21	22	23

Figure 8-3

storage locations identified by a specific number and capable of holding many different items. The numbers may be post office box numbers, hotel room numbers, or part bin numbers. For example, a letter placed in a post office box yesterday may contain instructions on how to build a birdhouse; the card placed in the same box today may be an electric bill for $22.12. Instructions are stored one day and numerical quantities the next; contents change, but the box and the box number remain the same. The boxes differ only in their identification numbers.

In the computer there are also numbered storage locations for holding both data and instructions. These "boxes," or "cells," are referred to as *addresses*. Like a post office box number, the address number remains the same and is independent of the contents. But unlike a post office box, which can hold several different messages at the same time, an address stores only one unit of data at a time. The addresses in a storage unit containing 4,096 locations would be numbered from 0000 to 4095. Thus, one unique address will be designated 1776. It is necessary to emphasize that *there is an important distinction between the address number and the contents of the address*. Why is this distinction important? It is important because one of the basic principles of programming is that machine language instructions deal directly with address numbers rather than with the contents of the address. For example, suppose that $155 is stored in address 1776. If the programmer wants that amount printed, he will not instruct the computer to print $155. Rather, he will order the machine to print 1776, and the computer will interpret this instruction to mean that it should *print the contents of address 1776*. Just as you can locate a friend in a strange city if you know that his home address is 4009 Sarita Drive, so, too, can the computer locate the desired information if it knows the location number. But it is the programmer's responsibility (or the function of software prepared by programmers) to keep track of the contents of each address.

Perhaps an example illustrating some of the concepts that have been introduced would be appropriate at this time. In our example let us consider "a atlas aardvark." What is "a atlas aardvark"? Well, A. Atlas Aardvark is not a "what," he is a "who"—he is the Zoology Editor for Imprint Publishing Company. He is also the first person paid each week (Atlas has gone through life being first in line). Let's look at how his paycheck might be processed by Imprint's PAC (Peculiar Automatic Computer).

The payroll *data* are prepared on punched cards each week for each employee. Last week the following data were punched into Atlas's card: (1) he worked forty hours; (2) he receives $5 an hour; (3) he has 20 percent of his total income taken out for taxes; and (4) he has hospitalization insurance, which costs him $5 each week.

Instructions have been prepared by Imprint's programmer to direct the computer in the payroll operation. The following steps must be performed:

1. The machine must be started.
2. An employee's payroll data must be read into storage for processing.
3. Hours worked must be multiplied by the hourly rate to find the *total earnings*.
4. Total earnings must be multiplied by the withholding percentage figure to find the amount of tax deduction.
5. To the tax withheld must be added the hospitalization insurance deduction to arrive at the *total deduction* figure.
6. The total deduction must be subtracted from the total earnings to find the take-home earnings.
7. A check must be printed for the amount of the take-home earnings, and it must be payable to the correct employee.
8. The machine must be stopped at the end of the processing operation.

Program instructions are also presented to the PAC in the form of punched cards.

Figure 8-4 shows the PAC storage locations. Although the programmer may assign the instructions to any *section* of the storage unit, he has chosen to read them into addresses 06 to 18. These locations thus become the *program storage* area. His first instruction (in address 06) identifies the locations for the payroll data (00, 01, 02, 03, and

Figure 8-4 PAC storage

00	01	02	03	04	05
06 Read payroll data card into addresses 00, 01, 02, 03, and 04.	07 Write contents of address 01 into arithmetic unit.	08 Multiply contents of arithmetic unit by contents of address 02.	09 Duplicate preceding answer in address 05.	10 Multiply contents of address 03 by preceding answer in arithmetic unit.	11 Add contents of address 04 to preceding answer in arithmetic unit.
12 Subtract preceding answer in arithmetic unit from contents of address 05.	13 Move preceding answer to address 23.	14 Write check for amount in address 23.	15 Make check payable to contents of address 00.	16 If last card, then go to address 18.	17 Go to address 06.
18 Stop processing.	19	20	21	22	23

04). The data could just as well have been placed in addresses 19 to 23, and so this is also an arbitrary decision.[2]

Let us use Fig. 8-5 to follow through the process that is required to prepare Atlas's paycheck. (The circled address numbers represent each step in the process.) After the computer operator has loaded the instructions into storage, he places the payroll data cards into the card reader and sets the PAC controls to begin the processing at address 06, and the processing begins. This initial control setting feeds the first instruction into the control unit where it is interpreted. Signals are sent to the card reader, which carries out the command. Atlas's card is read, and the data are transferred to *input storage*. The control unit will execute the instructions automatically *in sequence* after the initial control setting until it is directed by a specific instruction to do otherwise. Therefore, as soon as the instruction in address 06 has been complied with, the control unit automatically begins interpreting the contents of address 07.

The next command instructs the control unit to copy the contents of address 01 into the arithmetic-logic unit. The control unit is not interested that the contents of 01 are 40 hours (the next employee's time may differ). It is merely concerned with carrying out orders, and so 40 hours is placed in the arithmetic unit. And, in sequence, the processing continues: The 40-hour figure is multiplied by $5 per hour to find total earnings (instruction in address 08); this total earnings figure is duplicated (instruction, 09) in address 05, which is the *working storage* area; the tax deduction is found to be $40 (instruction, 10); the total deduction figure is $45 (instruction, 11); and Atlas's take-home pay is $155 (instruction, 12). The $155 is transferred to address 23 by the next order in the sequence. (It could just as easily have been placed in any of the unused locations.) From this *output storage* area, the information is sent to the printer, which, under program control, prints the paycheck. If Atlas's card had been the last one in the deck, the instructions in addresses 16 and 18 would have halted the process. Since other cards follow, however, the control unit receives the next order in the sequence. This instruction tells the control unit to reset itself to address 06. And so the process automatically begins again.

To summarize, several important concepts have been demonstrated in this example:

---

[2]Obviously, the data could not go into addresses 06 to 18 since these locations are now occupied by instructions. If a payroll item were mistakenly entered into a program section location, it would "erase" the instruction properly located in the address. At some later time the item would enter the control unit where it would be interpreted as an instruction. If such an error should occur, the result would be quite unpredictable but invariably disastrous.

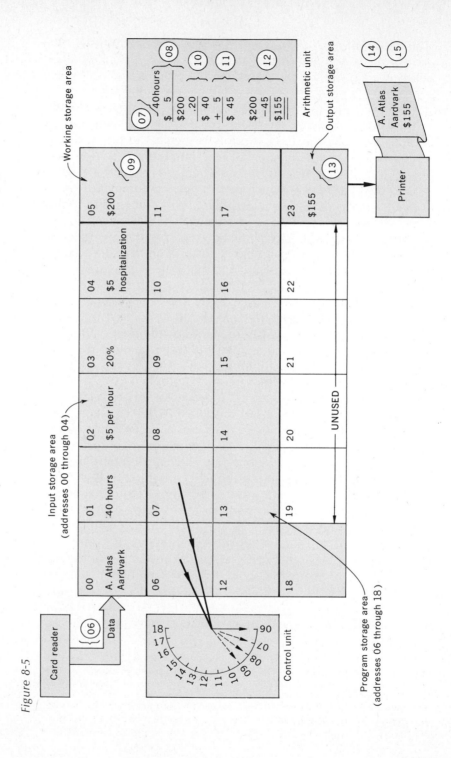

Figure 8-5

224

1. Input, working, output, and program storage areas are required, but they are not fixed in the PAC. Rather, they are determined by Imprint's programmer, and he had considerable freedom in the way in which he positioned the data and instructions.

2. The PAC is able to obey several *commands,* e.g., READ, WRITE, ADD, SUBTRACT, MULTIPLY, MOVE, GO TO. This ability to execute specific orders is *designed and built into* the machine. Every computer has a particular set, or *repertoire,* of commands, that it is able to obey. Small computers may have only a few basic commands in their repertoires, while large machines have 100 or more.

3. The output information desired by managers is produced by manipulating the facts and figures held in the storage locations. But the *instructions* that produce this output deal directly with the address numbers in the processing rather than with the contents of the addresses.

4. Computers execute one instruction at a time. They follow sequentially the series of directions until explicitly told to do otherwise. Figure 8-6 is a diagram, or *flowchart,* of the payroll procedure. The computer moves through the instructions in sequence until it comes to a *branchpoint* and is required to answer a question: Have data from the last card been fed into storage? The answer to the question determines which path or branch the computer will follow. If the answer is no, then the procedure is automatically repeated by the use of the technique known as *looping;* if the answer is yes the processing stops. Instructions that result in the transfer of program control to an instruction stored at some arbitrary location rather than to the next location in storage may be *conditional* or *unconditional* transfer commands. If the change in sequence is based on the outcome of some test (e.g., has the last card been processed?), then it is a conditional transfer; if not, it is an unconditional branch. Can you identify the conditional and unconditional transfer instructions in Fig. 8-6?

Up to this point we have not bothered to define the storage capacity of *each address.* All we have said is that an address holds a specific unit of data. Actually, the storage capacity of an address is *built into* the machine. In some machines each address may contain only a *single character* (9, A, $, *). These systems are said to be *character addressable.* Other machines are designed to store a *fixed number of characters* in each address (JONES, XY1234, GO TO 06). These

CAPACITY OF STORAGE LOCATIONS

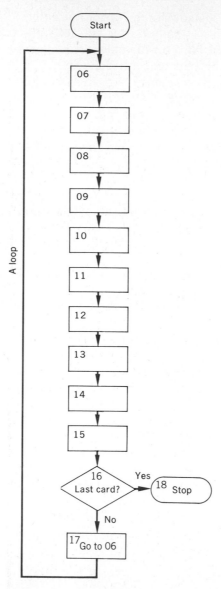

Figure 8-6

characters are treated as a single entity or unit; i.e., the computer treats them as a single data *word* or instruction *word*. Thus, machines designed to store a specified number of characters in an address are said to be *word addressable*. Figure 8-7 shows character-addressable and word-addressable storage. Character-addressable machines, on the one hand, are said to have *variable word-length storage*. Word-addressable machines, on the other hand, are said to have *fixed word-length storage*.

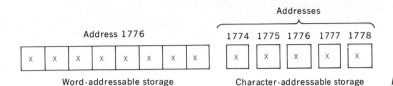

Figure 8-7

Perhaps an example will help clarify the differences between fixed and variable word-length storage. Let us assume that we are again going to place payroll data into PAC storage. The following data concern Mr. Cy ("Crab") Grass, the Botany Editor at Imprint Publishing Company:

Employee Hours worked Hourly rate Tax deduction Hospitalization
Cy Grass   40 $4   15% $5

Is PAC a fixed or a variable word-length machine? For illustration purposes and for reasons to be explained shortly, we will consider it to be both (after all, it is a Peculiar Company product).

Fixed Word-length Storage

We'll assume that each PAC address will store eight characters.[3] Figure 8-8a shows how the payroll data might be organized into 40 byte-sized cells in storage.[4] Addresses 00 to 04 are used. Figure 8-8a also shows a disadvantage of fixed word-length storage. Each word must be eight characters long, and these eight characters must be moved and operated on as a unit. If, as in address 01, only two characters are needed, the other six spaces in the word will be filled with zeroes or will be blank.[5]

Variable Word-length Storage

To realize more efficient use of storage space, variable word-length machines were developed for business purposes. Figure 8-8b shows how the payroll data might be stored if PAC were a variable word-length computer. Space to store 22 additional characters is now available. Each space has an address. The intersections of the numbers at the top and in the column to the left designate the address numbers. The name "Cy," for example, is stored in addresses 00 and 01. The

[3] The number of characters that various machines can store depends on the machine design. Eight characters has been arbitrarily selected, although eight is a common word (or double word) length.
[4] No, *byte* is not, in this case, an example of the author's spelling prowess. A byte is a character or unit of information consisting of eight binary digits. We will discuss this matter further later in the chapter.
[5] It is possible for a programmer to *pack* several data items into a single fixed-length word by using proper instructions. Of course, extra steps are required in the processing.

Address 00	C	Y		G	R	A	S	S
Address 01							4	0
Address 02						4	0	0
Address 03							1	5
Address 04						5	0	0

(a) Fixed word-length storage

	0	1	2	3	4	5	6	7	8	9
0	C	Y		G	R	A	S	S	4	0
1	4	0	0	1	5	5	0	0		
2										
3					X		Y			

Figure 8-8

(b) Variable word-length storage

letters X and Y have been placed in addresses 34 and 36, respectively, to show the addressing approach.

A fixed word-length computer identifies the stored word it is looking for by simply referring to an address number. But how can a variable word-length machine identify the particular word it is seeking when an eight-character word such as "Cy Grass" has eight addresses? There are two common approaches used to resolve this dilemma:

1. *The wordmark approach.* The underlining marks in addresses 00, 08, 10, 13, and 15 in Fig. 8-8b represent *wordmarks,* which have been set there by the programmer. Although the marks may be viewed by us as the leftmost position or the beginning of each word since we customarily read from left to right, to some popular business computers (e.g., the Honeywell 200 and the IBM 1401) the marks represent the end or *termination* of a word. Just as you move from right to left in adding columns of figures, so, too, do many computers move from right to left when processing a word. If the computer *stops* processing a word when the presence of a wordmark is sensed and if the mark identifies the leftmost position of the word, what address number must be used to identify the beginning of that word? The answer obviously is the rightmost address in the word or field.[6] Figure 8-9 shows how a

[6]You will recall from Chapter 2 that punched cards are laid out in fields for business applications. These fields are established by the application designer and may vary in width from 1 column to 80. A variable word-length computer might just as easily have been termed a *variable field-length machine;* there is little or no distinction between the terms in this situation.

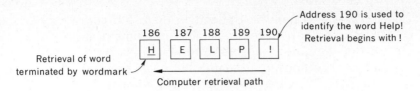

Figure 8-9   Wordmark retrieval

data word is retrieved from storage for printing purposes. The command is the *instruction word* "PRINT 190." The machine automatically moves from address 190 serially to the left until a wordmark is encountered. The same command—PRINT 190—in a word-addressable machine would yield the same results (assuming that HELP! was located in that address) except that the machine would retrieve all the characters as a single unit.

2. *The length-specification approach.* Some machines (e.g., the models in the IBM System/360 and System/370 families and the models in the RCA Spectra 70 family of computers) specify a variable-length word with an *instruction,* which (1) identifies the *leftmost* address in the word and (2) indicates the number of address locations to be included in the word. A wordmark is thus not needed. Figure 8-10 illustrates this approach. Retrieval begins with address 186 and continues for the specified number of locations.

A Comparison

To review our understanding of the above paragraphs, let us compare fixed and variable word-length storage systems:

1. *Storage efficiency.* Generally speaking, variable word-length equipment makes the most efficient use of available space for business purposes.

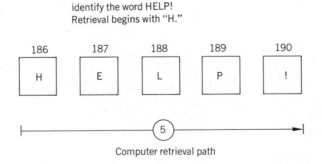

Figure 8-10   Length specification retrieval

2. *Internal data transfer*. Depending upon the computer, data are transferred or retrieved a character at a time or a word at a time.

3. *Arithmetic speed*. Variable word-length machines perform arithmetic operations in a *serial* fashion, i.e., one position at a time. For example, when two eight-digit numbers are added, eight processing cycles are required. Fixed word-length computers, however, are classified as *parallel* calculators; i.e., they can add any two data words in a *single* step without regard to the number of digits in the words (Fig. 8-11). Obviously, then, machines operating with fixed word lengths have faster calculating capability. But this faster speed must be paid for since the necessary circuitry is more complex and thus more expensive.

4. *Size and usage*. Many popular small- and middle-sized second-generation business computers are variable word-length machines. This is not surprising if you remember that business applications place greater emphasis on I/O speed and storage capacity than on speed of computation. Variable word-length machines gave managers what they wanted at the least possible cost. Large-scale second-generation computers used fixed word-length storage. These machines were typically used at least part time and often exclusively for scientific purposes, and such applications required the faster calculating and data transfer speeds provided.

A Flexible Combination

It is apparent that each method of organizing the storage unit has advantages and drawbacks. Recognizing this fact, the ingenious Peculiar Company designers of the PAC (and, incidentally, the designers of (1) the IBM Systems/360 and /370 families, (2) the RCA Spectra 70 family, (3) the UNIVAC 9000 series, (4) the XDS Sigma series, etc.) developed a third-generation machine that could be operated as *either* a variable or a fixed word-length computer. Program control, in effect, organizes the computer for either business (using variable-length

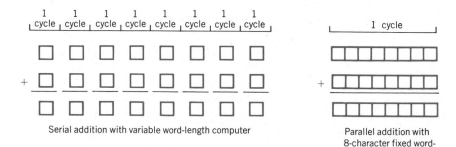

Serial addition with variable word-length computer

Parallel addition with 8-character fixed word-length computer

Figure 8-11   Arithmetic speed

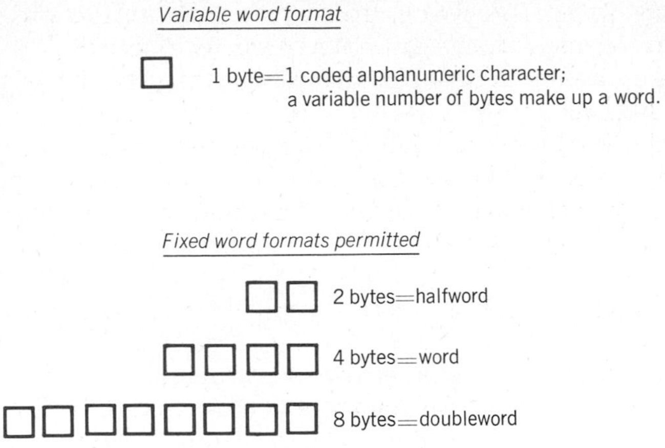

Variable word format

☐ 1 byte═1 coded alphanumeric character;
a variable number of bytes make up a word.

Fixed word formats permitted

☐☐ 2 bytes═halfword

☐☐☐ 4 bytes═word

☐☐☐☐☐☐☐ 8 bytes═doubleword

Figure 8-12 Address formats

words) or scientific (using fixed-length words) applications. How is this possible? Let us look at the storage organizational structure for the answer to this question.

Each alphanumeric character placed in storage is represented by a code consisting of 8 <u>binary digits</u> (bits);[7] and *each* of these coded characters, or *bytes,* is identified in storage by a *specific address number.* Thus, by using an appropriate set of instructions, the programmer can manipulate these characters into words of varying lengths as needed. The *length-specification approach* described above and in Fig. 8-10 is used to identify the variable-length words retained in storage. With each byte or character having an address, it is easy to see how variable-length words can be created.

But bytes can also be *grouped together and operated on as a unit.* The programmer can elect to use, for example, other available instructions that will cause the computer to automatically retrieve, manipulate, and store as a single unit a fixed word of *four* bytes. Or, he may choose to group 8 bytes into a *double word* and have the machine function in this fixed-word format. Figure 8-12 illustrates the word formats possible with most currently used computers.

Without getting bogged down here in the details of computer design, we may summarize the above comments by repeating that third- and fourth-generation machines use (1) a built-in instruction set to operate on variable-length words, with the instruction itself specifying the number of characters in the word, and (2) additional instruction sets that operate automatically on fixed amounts of data—either halfwords (2 bytes), full words (4 bytes), or doublewords

[7]We will discuss bits at some length in the next section.

(8 bytes). This ability, through program instructions, to manipulate different groupings gives PAC users with both business and scientific applications a great deal of flexibility. Maybe the PAC isn't so peculiar after all!

Regardless of whether each address contains a single data character or a data or instruction word consisting of numbers, letters, special characters, or some combination, these facts must be in the coded form that the computer can use.

COMPUTER NUMBERING SYSTEMS

The business computer represents data in a code that is related to a *binary numbering system*. It is thus necessary to understand numbering systems. In the first part of this section we shall review the familiar decimal system in order to present certain basic concepts. We shall follow this presentation with a discussion of (1) binary numbers, (2) binary arithmetic, (3) octal numbers, (4) hexadecimal numbers, and (5) a binary coded decimal system.

Decimal Numbers

We tend to take the decimal numbering system for granted because of the years of close association with it. Yet man existed on earth for centuries without it. The first systems were of an *additive* nature. That is, they consisted of symbols such as | for one, ‖ for two, ‖| for three, etc. Each symbol represented the *same value* regardless of the position it occupied in the number. Early Hebrew, Greek, and Egyptian numbers were additive. Roman numerals are also essentially additive. As you know, the symbol V represents the decimal 5 and does not change in value (even though its position changes) in the following numbers: V, VI, VII, and VIII (VI = V + I; VII = V + I + I; etc.). As Thomas Bartee writes:

> The only importance of position in Roman numerals lies in whether a symbol precedes or follows another symbol (IV = 4, while VI = 6). The clumsiness of this system can easily be seen if we try to multiply XII by XIV. Calculating with Roman numerals was so difficult that early mathematicians were forced to perform arithmetic operations almost entirely on abaci or counting boards, translating their results back into Roman-number form. Pencil and paper computations are unbelievably intricate and difficult in such systems. In fact, the ability to perform such operations as addition and multiplication was considered a great accomplishment in earlier civilizations.[8]

[8] Thomas C. Bartee, *Digital Computer Fundamentals*, 2d ed., McGraw-Hill Book Company, New York, 1966, p. 40.

Youngsters today can calculate answers to problems that would have baffled wise men of earlier centuries. A big factor in this advancement has been the development of *positional* numbering systems. In such systems there are only a limited number of symbols, and the symbols represent different values according to the position they occupy in the number (5 = V, but 51 does not equal VI because the meaning of 5 has changed with the change in its position). The number of symbols used depends on the *base* or *radix* of the particular system. The decimal system, of course, has a base of 10 and has 10 symbols (0 to 9). The *highest* numerical symbol will always have a value of one *less* than the base.

There is nothing particularly sacred about a base of 10. Probably the only reason it was originally developed and is now in widespread use is that man happens to have 10 fingers. Other systems have been created.[9] For example, the Babylonians had a base of 60 (of course, they also did their writing on mud pies); the Mayas of Yucatán used a base of 20 (a warm climate and a group of barefooted mathematicians?); and a base of five is still used by natives in New Hebrides (one hand is wrapped around a spear and is thus not available for counting?). The Duodecimal Society of America advocates a change from base 10 to a radix of 12. It is pointed out in support of their position that not only would computations be easier since 12 is divisible by 2, 3, 4, and 6, but also such a base is compatible with inches in a foot, numbers in a dozen, etc.

By the arrangement of the numerical symbols[10] in various positions, any number may be represented. We know that in the decimal system each successive position to the left of the decimal point represents units, tens, hundreds, thousands, ten thousands, etc. We sometimes fail to remember, however, that what this means is that each position represents a particular *power* of the base. Figure 8-13a points out this characteristic. The digits of any number that might be placed in the blank spaces would be multiplied by an appropriate power of 10 to arrive at the total value. For example, the number 15,236 is shown in Fig. 8-13b to represent the sum of[11]

$$(1 \times 10^4) + (\underline{5} \times 10^3) + (\underline{2} \times 10^2) + (\underline{3} \times 10^1) + (\underline{6} \times 10^0)$$

[9] For an interesting account of the history of numbering systems, see Donald E. Knuth, "The Evolution of Number Systems," *Datamation,* February, 1969, pp. 93–97.

[10] There is also nothing sacred about the shape of the symbols we use to represent quantities. We know that the symbol 2 has a certain meaning, but any number of other marks could be defined to serve the same purpose. A version of the Arabic numerals we use is thought to have originated in India around 200 B.C.

[11] Students occasionally forget their algebra and have to be reminded that n^0 is, by definition, 1; i.e., any number raised to the zero power equals 1.

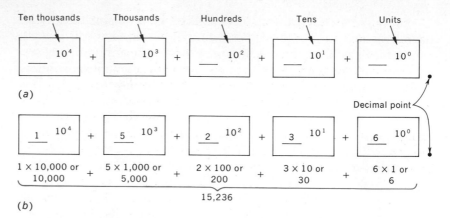

Figure 8-13

(b)

In *any* positional numbering system, *the value of each position represents a specific power of the base.* To test your understanding of the concepts that have now been introduced, let us look at the following problems:

1. What is the decimal equivalent of 463_8? (The subscript 8 following the number 463 indicates that this is an *octal* base number.) Since the *base* is *now eight* rather than 10, the possible symbols are 0 to 7 (the symbols 8 and 9 do not exist in this case). Each position in the number 463_8 represents a power of its base. Therefore,

    $(\underline{4} \times 8^2) + (\underline{6} \times 8^1) + (\underline{3} \times 8^0)$. ← Octal point

    or $(4 \times 64) + (6 \times 8) + (3 \times 1)$.

    or $(256) + (48) + (3). = 307_{10}$ The decimal equivalent

2. What is the decimal equivalent of 4221_5? (We have now shifted to a base-five numbering system.) The possible symbols in base five are 0 to 4. Each position in the number 4221_5 represents a power of its base. Therefore,

    $(\underline{4} \times 5^3) + (\underline{2} \times 5^2) + (\underline{2} \times 5^1) + (\underline{1} \times 5^0)$. ←Quinary point

    or $(4 \times 125) + (2 \times 25) + (2 \times 5) + (1 \times 1)$.

    or $(500) + (50) + (10) + (1). = 561_{10}$ The decimal equivalent

3. What is the decimal equivalent of 1001_2? (We are now using a base of two.) With a base of two, the only possible symbols are 0 and 1. Again, each position in the number 1001_2 represents a power of its base. Therefore,

    $(\underline{1} \times 2^3) + (\underline{0} \times 2^2) + (\underline{0} \times 2^1) + (\underline{1} \times 2^0)$. ← Binary point

    or $(1 \times 8) + (0 \times 4) + (0 \times 2) + (1 \times 1)$.

    or $(8) + (0) + (0) + (1). = 9_{10}$ The decimal equivalent

We now have progressed downward in this section from a numbering system using a base of 10 to one using a base of 2. We might just as easily have moved in the other direction. (In fact, we will later in the chapter.) What have these problems demonstrated? For one thing, we have seen that the lower the numbering base, the fewer the possible symbols that must be remembered. And with fewer symbols, there are smaller multiplication tables and fewer addition facts to memorize. But, as we have also seen, the smaller the base, the more positions there must be to represent a given quantity. Four digits (1001) are required in base two to equal a single decimal digit (9). You may also have observed that the decimal point becomes the *octal point* in a base-eight system, the *quinary point* in base five, and the *binary point* in base two.[12] It would thus appear that we have sneaked up on the *binary* or *base-two* numbering system used by digital computers.

Self-check Exercise 8-1

In order to test your understanding of the concepts presented above, pause for a few minutes to work the following exercise. (You will find the answers at the end of the chapter.)

Convert the numbers below to their decimal equivalents.

1. $234_8 = $ ——————$_{10}$
2. $234_5 = $ ——————$_{10}$
3. $345_5 = $ ——————$_{10}$
4. $1011_2 = $ ——————$_{10}$

Binary Numbers

It was pointed out in Chapter 2 that John von Neumann suggested in a paper written in 1946 that binary numbering systems be incorporated in computers. Although the paper came too late to prevent the very first machines from using the decimal system, von Neumann's suggestions were quickly adopted in subsequent designs.[13]

Why the rush to binary? There are several very good reasons:

1. It is necessary that circuitry be designed only to handle 2 binary digits (bits) rather than 10. Design is simplified,[14] cost is reduced, and performance is improved.

[12]The point, of course, merely serves to separate the whole from the fractional part of a number. It may be called the *radix point*, or *real point*, regardless of the numbering system being used.

[13]The pioneering work in binary numbers was done by the German mathematician Gottfried Leibniz (1646–1716). Leibniz, in addition to being an inventor of the calculus, was also known to have suggested that binary rather than decimal arithmetic be taught in the schools. He would have approved of "new math" which does introduce public school children to binary numbers.

[14]The binary system is quite adaptable to the Boolean algebra concepts used in computer design.

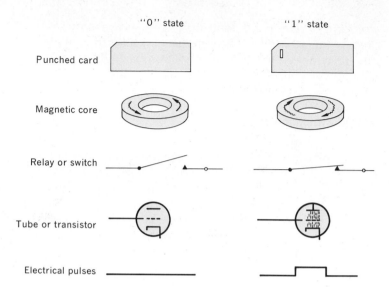

Figure 8-14

2. Electronic components, by their very nature, operate in a binary mode. As Fig. 8-14 demonstrates, a switch is either open (0 state) or closed (1 state); a tube or transistor either is not conducting (0) or is (1); electric pulses are either absent (0) or present (1); and small magnetizable rings are magnetized to represent either 0 or 1.

3. Everything that can be done with a base of 10 can be done with the binary system.

Binary counting begins, just as with any number base, with 0 followed by 1. But now we have run out of symbols. How do we represent 2 when there is no such symbol? Just as we represent the next highest value in any base when we have used our highest number in the first position to the left of the real point, we use a zero place marker in the first position and put the next lowest symbol in the next position to the left. Thus, 2 in decimal is the same as 10 in binary. Or,

$(\underline{1} \times 2^1) + (\underline{0} \times 2^0).$

$(2) + (0) = 2_{10}$

Of course, 10_2 *is not pronounced "ten,"* for it is certainly not what we have been taught to associate with the word *ten*. Names such as *toon* and *twin* have been given to 10_2, but they have not caught on. Perhaps *one zero* is as good a name as any.

Binary-to-decimal conversion The important thing to remember in counting in the binary system is that the place positions, instead of representing units, tens, hundreds, thousands, etc., now represent unit, 2, 4, 8, 16, 32, etc. Thus, the decimal value of 110011_2 is:

Power of base	2^7	2^6	2^5	2^4	2^3	2^2	2^1	2^0
Decimal equivalent	128	64	32	16	8	4	2	1
Binary number			1	1	0	0	1	1

Or $32 + 16 + 2 + 1 = 51_{10}$

To test your understanding of counting in various bases, see if you can fill in the blanks in Fig. 8-15.

Decimal-to-binary conversion We have been converting binary numbers to their decimal equivalents. Let us now, by means of a *remainder method,* perform the reverse operation; i.e., let us convert a decimal number into binary form. For illustration purposes, the

Base 2	Base 5	Base 8	Base 10
0	0	0	0
1	1	1	1
10	2	2	2
11	3	3	3
100	4	4	4
101	10	5	5
110	11	6	6
111	12	7	7
1000	13	10	8
1001	14	11	9
1010	20	12	10
1011	21	13	11
1100	22	14	12
1101	23	15	13
——	——	——	14
——	——	——	15
——	——	——	16

Figure 8-15 Equivalent numbers

number 250_{10} is chosen. The conversion procedure simply consists of dividing the original decimal number by 2 and all successive answers by 2 until the process can continue no further. The binary value is read from the successive remainder values. For example,

Remainder

$$
\begin{array}{r}
125 \\
2\overline{)250}
\end{array} \qquad 0
$$

$$
\begin{array}{r}
62 \\
2\overline{)125}
\end{array} \qquad 1
$$

$$
\begin{array}{r}
31 \\
2\overline{)62}
\end{array} \qquad 0
$$

$$
\begin{array}{r}
15 \\
2\overline{)31}
\end{array} \qquad 1
$$

$$
\begin{array}{r}
7 \\
2\overline{)15}
\end{array} \qquad 1
$$

$$
\begin{array}{r}
3 \\
2\overline{)7}
\end{array} \qquad 1
$$

$$
\begin{array}{r}
1 \\
2\overline{)3}
\end{array} \qquad 1
$$

$$
\begin{array}{r}
0 \\
2\overline{)1}
\end{array} \qquad ①
$$

— Read upward —

Binary number, with final remainder being the *most significant digit,* is equal to:

① 1111010

Thus, $250_{10} = 11111010_2$

We may test the accuracy of this method by converting the binary number back to decimal form.

Power of the base	2^7	2^6	2^5	2^4	2^3	2^2	2^1	2^0
Decimal equivalent	128	64	32	16	8	4	2	1
Binary number	1	1	1	1	1	0	1	0

Or $128 + 64 + 32 + 16 + 8 + 2 = 250_{10}$

Self-check Exercise 8-2

1. Convert the following binary numbers to their decimal equivalent values:
    (a) $111011_2 = $ _____ $_{10}$
    (b) $100000000_2 = $ _____ $_{10}$
2. What is the binary number of each of the following decimal values?

(a) $257_{10} =$ —————— $_2$
(b) $64_{10} =$ —————— $_2$
(c) $15_{10} =$ —————— $_2$

Binary Arithmetic*

Addition Binary arithmetic is simplicity itself. There are only four addition rules to remember:

$$0 + 0 = 0$$
$$1 + 0 = 1$$
$$0 + 1 = 1$$
$$1 + 1 = 0 \quad \text{and "carry" a 1}$$

We may demonstrate these rules by adding the binary equivalents of 15 and 10:

$$\text{"carries"} \longrightarrow 111$$
$$1111 = (15_{10})$$
$$\underline{1010 = (10_{10})}$$
$$11001 = (25_{10}?)$$

In the first column, $1 + 0$ is 1, and so we bring down that value and move to column 2. There $1 + 1$ is 10, and so we put down the 0 in the answer and carry the 1 to column 3. In column 3, the 1 carried plus the 1 in the column is again 10, and so we repeat the previous step. In column 4, the 1 carried plus the 1 in the top number is 10, necessitating a carry. The 1 in the bottom number plus the 0 is 1, which is put in the answer. A fifth column has the carried 1, and so it is brought down to the answer. A check may be made by converting the binary value of the answer into decimal form. Does it equal 25?

Multiplication Multiplication tables in base two are the answer to a third-grader's prayers:

$$0 \times 0 = 0$$
$$0 \times 1 = 0$$
$$1 \times 0 = 0$$
$$1 \times 1 = 1$$

Let's multiply the following binary values:

$$1101 = (13_{10})$$
$$\underline{\times 101 = (\ 5_{10})}$$
$$1101$$
$$1101$$
$$\text{"carries"} \longrightarrow \underline{1111}$$
$$1000001 = (65_{10}?)$$

*This discussion of binary arithmetic and the treatment of octal and hexadecimal numbers that follows may be omitted without loss of continuity.

As you can see, multiplication quickly becomes a problem in addition after you observe the customary procedure for arranging partial products. Does the answer equal 65_{10}?

Subtraction   Subtraction is done by a method known as *complementation*. This approach may be used with *any* positional numbering system. To explain complementation, we shall follow a three-step procedure.

The *first step* in the procedure is to complement the subtrahend (the number being subtracted). This sounds grim, but it is really quite simple. The complement of a particular digit is found by subtracting that digit from another value which is *one less than the base*.[15] For example, the complement of the decimal 6 is 3 (6 is subtracted from 9 which is one less than the base of 10). The complement of the decimal number 3,540 is

$$
\begin{array}{r}
9999 \\
-3540 \\
\hline
6459
\end{array}
$$

Once the subtrahend is complemented, the *second step* is to *add* the complemented number to the minuend. As a decimal example, let us subtract 3,540 (subtrahend) from 8,261 (minuend). As we have just seen, the complement of 3,540 is 6,459. Thus, we *add* this value to the minuend as follows:

$$
\begin{array}{r}
8,261 \\
+6,459 \\
\hline
14,720
\end{array}
$$

The *third step* is to perform the *end-around carry*. Although this sounds like a football play, it merely means that the digit in the most significant position is moved and added to the value of the least significant digit. For example,

$$
\begin{array}{r}
8,2\,6\,1 \\
+\ 6,4\,5\,9 \\
\hline
\end{array}
$$

Most significant digit $\longrightarrow$ ①4,7 2⓪ $\longleftarrow$ Least significant digit

$$
\begin{array}{r}
\longrightarrow ① \\
\hline
4,7\,2\,1
\end{array}
$$

[15] A radix complement rather than the radix-minus-one complement may be used for subtraction purposes. The radix-minus-one approach is more common.

Thus, the answer to our problem (8,261 less 3,540) is 4,721 by the complementation method. (Does this check with traditional methods of subtraction?)

Now let us follow the same three steps to solve a binary problem. We shall subtract from 110101 (53_{10}) the value 101011 (43_{10}) as follows:

1. The first step is to complement the subtrahend. Since the base is now two, we shall subtract each value in the subtrahend from 1. That is,

    ```
      111111
    −101011
    ───────
      010100
    ```

   Notice, however, that all we have done is change the 1s in the subtrahend to 0s and the 0s to 1s. Thus, all the computer needs to do to the subtrahend is replace 1s with 0s and vice versa and then add. (If by now you have come to the conclusion that about all a computer basically does is add, you are correct.)

2. The second step is to add the complemented subtrahend to the minuend:

    ```
      110101
    +010100
    ───────
     1001001
    ```

3. The third step is to perform the end-around carry operation:

    ```
      1 1 0 1 0 1
    + 0 1 0 1 0 0
    ─────────────
    ①0 0 1 0 0 1       Is the problem answer of 1010 correct? Con-
         ──────→ ①     vert the answer to a decimal figure to see.
    ─────────────
      1 0 1 0
    ```

   It is as simple as that. Division basically involves repeated shifting and subtraction, and we need not be concerned with it here.

Perform the following binary arithmetic operations:

1.
```
  1110
+ 111
─────
```

2.
```
111001
  1001
+ 111
──────
```

3.
```
  1101
−1010
─────
```

4.
```
1000
−101
────
```

5.
```
10001
× 110
─────
```

6.
```
111001
×  111
──────
```

Octal Numbers

Humans use decimal numbers, but data are represented in computer storage by coded or uncoded strings of binary digits. We mentioned briefly in an earlier section that characters in most third-generation models are represented by 8-bit units of information called *bytes*. We also saw that 4 bytes can be grouped and treated as a fixed-length word by the programmer. Such a 4-byte word, of course, would be represented in storage by a set of 32 bits. Now it is often necessary for the programmer or computer operator to determine the contents of particular storage locations. If they had to deal exclusively with 32-bit strings such as this one—11101110100111001000010100010101— the chances of interpretation errors would understandably be large. Fortunately, the *octal* (base-8) and *hexadecimal* (base-16) numbering systems provide the programmer and operator with a convenient method of expressing the same data in a more accurate and efficient manner. We shall consider the hexadecimal system in the next section.

The octal numbering system possesses properties that make it a valuable shorthand or intermediate system. Programmers (and especially those programming on scientific machines) use it to help bridge the gap between decimal and binary. In fact, there are desk calculators for programmers that operate in the octal mode. The helpful properties of the octal system are:

1. Octal numbers (0 to 7) resemble decimal numbers more closely than do binary representations.
2. It is often quicker to convert a number from a decimal base to an octal base and then to binary (and vice versa) than it is to shift directly from decimal to binary.
3. It is much easier to convert numbers between binary and octal than it is to shift between binary and decimal.

We have seen earlier that to move from *octal to decimal* one need only convert the octal number into units, 8s, 64s, etc. The number 661_8 corresponds to 433_{10} ($\underline{6} \times 8^2 + \underline{6} \times 8^1 + \underline{1} \times 8^0$). But how do we move from *decimal to the octal* equivalent? We simply use the remainder method in the same way we did to convert decimal to binary, except that now we divide successively by 8 rather than by 2. To demonstrate, let's convert 433_{10} back to octal:

Remainder

$$\begin{array}{r} 54 \\ \hline 8\overline{)433} \end{array} \qquad 1$$

$$\begin{array}{r} 6 \\ \hline 8\overline{)54} \end{array} \qquad 6$$

Again, the final remainder is the most significant digit.

$$661_8 = 433_{10}$$

$$\begin{array}{r} 0 \\ \hline 8\overline{)6} \end{array} \qquad 6$$

Obviously, there are fewer division steps required in moving from decimal to octal than there would be in converting directly to binary. But octal is also convenient because of its simple relationship to binary. (The base eight is a power of the base two—$8 = 2^3$—and one octal digit is always equal to three binary bits.) To convert from octal to binary (or vice versa), one need only determine the 3-bit binary representation for each octal digit. These 3-bit binary values are as shown at the right.

Binary		Octal
000	=	0
001	=	1
010	=	2
011	=	3
100	=	4
101	=	5
110	=	6
111	=	7

Therefore, to convert from *octal to binary* is as simple as this:[16]

$$\underset{111}{7} \quad \underset{010}{2} \quad \underset{101}{5} \quad \text{or} \quad 725_8 = 111010101_2$$

And converting from *binary to octal* is equally simple. We merely divide the bits into groups of three, beginning at the binary point. For example, 1001100101, when properly divided, becomes 1/001/100/101, and this is quickly found to be 1145_8. In both cases the decimal equivalent is 613.

Convert these octal numbers to the equivalent binary values:

1. $234_8 =$ _____ $_2$
2. $1675_8 =$ _____ $_2$

Convert these binary numbers into octal:

3. $111001110101_2 =$ _____ $_8$
4. $11101110100011001000010100010101_2$ (the 32-bit string printed in the first paragraph of this section) $=$ _____ $_8$

The hexadecimal numbering system has a base of 16. The first 10 hexadecimal symbols (0 to 9) are the familiar ones of the decimal system. But what about the remaining six? What symbols, in other words, will we use to represent the equivalent values of the decimal numbers 10, 11, 12, 13, 14, and 15? We must have a *single* hexadecimal character to represent these decimal quantities. The hexadecimal characters used by computers to represent the decimal values 10 to 15 are A to F. Thus, the 16 hexadecimal characters and their equivalent decimal values are as shown to the right.

Hexadecimal Numbers

Hexadecimal Symbol	Decimal Value
0	0
↓	↓
9	9
A	10
B	11
C	12
D	13
E	14
F	15

The decimal equivalent of $12F1_{16}$ may be found in the usual way by (1) multiplying each symbol by the appropriate power of the base

[16] You can verify the figures by converting both bases to decimal. The common decimal value is 469.

16 and (2) adding these products to get the decimal equivalent. Thus, 12F1 represents:

$$(\underline{1} \times 16^3) + (\underline{2} \times 16^2) + (\underline{F}\ or\ "15" \times 16^1) + (\underline{1} \times 16^0)$$
Or, $4096 + 512 + 240 + 1 = 4849_{10}$

To convert from *decimal to hexadecimal* is not difficult either—we again simply follow a *remainder method* procedure. Converting the decimal value 4849 back into hexadecimal would yield the following result:

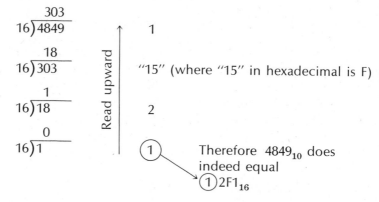

Binary	Hexadecimal
0000	0
0001	1
0010	2
0011	3
0100	4
0101	5
0110	6
0111	7
1000	8
1001	9
1010	A
1011	B
1100	C
1101	D
1110	E
1111	F

When you worked the last problem in Self-check Exercise 8-4, you found that a 32-bit number could be represented with 11 octal digits. With the hexadecimal numbering system, however, the same 32-bit value can be coded with only 8 characters. The hexadecimal base of 16 (like the octal base of 8) is a power of the binary base, that is, $16 = 2^4$, and one hexadecimal numeral is always equal to 4 bits. To convert from *hexadecimal to binary* (or vice versa), one need only determine the 4-bit binary representation for each hexadecimal numeral. These 4-bit binary values are as shown to the left.

Therefore, to convert from hexadecimal to binary is as simple as this:

$$\underset{1000}{8}\quad\underset{1010}{A}\quad\underset{0111}{7}\quad\underset{1001}{9}\qquad or\qquad 8A79_{16} = 1000101001111001_2$$

Furthermore, converting from *binary to hexadecimal* is equally simple. We merely divide the bits into groups of four, beginning at the binary point. For example, 10011010010, when properly divided, becomes 100/1101/0010, and this is quickly found to be $4D2_{16}$. In both cases, the decimal equivalent is 1,234.

1. What is the decimal equivalent of $7A2_{16}$?
2. What is the hexadecimal value of 1000_{10}?
3. Convert $7A2_{16}$ to binary.
4. What is the hexadecimal value of $11101110100111001000010\text{-}100010101_2$? (This is the same 32-bit value found in Self-check Exercise 8-4.)

Up to this point we have been discussing "pure" binary numbers. Although computers designed strictly for scientific purposes may use pure binary in their operations, business-oriented machines (or computers which are designed to process both business and scientific applications) use some *coded,* or *modified,* version of pure binary to represent decimal numbers internally. Numerous data representation formats have been developed. The most popular for business purposes, however, are the *binary coded decimal* (BCD) codes.[17]

With BCD it is possible to convert *each* decimal digit into its binary equivalent rather than convert the entire decimal number into a pure binary form. The BCD equivalent of each possible decimal digit is shown in Fig. 8-16. Because the digits 8 and 9 require 4 bits, *all*

COMPUTER DATA REPRESENTATION

Binary Coded Decimal System

---

[17]Many modern computers use both BCD and pure binary forms of data representation. For example, input data are received and stored in the CPU in a BCD format. Prior to computations, those numbers that are to be used in arithmetic operations *may* be converted to a pure binary form by the computer. Following binary arithmetic operations, the results are converted back to a BCD format before being written out.

Decimal digit	Place value			
	8	4	2	1
0	0	0	0	0
1	0	0	0	1
2	0	0	1	0
3	0	0	1	1
4	0	1	0	0
5	0	1	0	1
6	0	1	1	0
7	0	1	1	1
8	1	0	0	0
9	1	0	0	1

Figure 8-16   Binary coded decimal numeric bit configurations

decimal digits are represented by 4 bits. Let us now see how much easier it is to work with BCD by converting 405_{10} into *both* BCD and straight binary:

405_{10} in BCD = $\underbrace{0100}_{4}/\underbrace{0000}_{0}/\underbrace{0101}_{5}$ or 010000000101

405_{10} in pure binary:

$$\underline{Remainder}$$

$$\begin{array}{c} \dfrac{202}{2)\overline{405}} \quad 1 \\[2ex] \dfrac{101}{2)\overline{202}} \quad 0 \\[2ex] \dfrac{50}{2)\overline{101}} \quad 1 \\[2ex] \dfrac{25}{2)\overline{50}} \quad 0 \\[2ex] \dfrac{12}{2)\overline{25}} \quad 1 \\[2ex] \dfrac{6}{2)\overline{12}} \quad 0 \\[2ex] \dfrac{3}{2)\overline{6}} \quad 0 \\[2ex] \dfrac{1}{2)\overline{3}} \quad 1 \\[2ex] \dfrac{0}{2)\overline{1}} \quad 1 \end{array} \Bigg\} = 110010101$$

With 4 bits there are 16 different possible configurations (2^4). The first 10 of these configurations are, of course, used to represent decimal digits. The other six arrangements (1010, 1011, 1100, 1101, 1110, and 1111) have decimal values from 10 to 15. These six arrangements are *not used* in BCD coding; i.e., 1111 *does not* represent 15_{10} in BCD. Rather, the proper BCD code for 15_{10} is 0001/0101. The "extra" six configurations are used by programmers for other purposes, which we need not dwell on here.

We have seen that BCD is a convenient and fast way to convert numbers from decimal to binary. But it is hardly sufficient for business purposes to have only 16 characters available. The following section

Check bit	Zone bits		Numeric bits			
C	B	A	8	4	2	1

Figure 8-17

explains how additional characters are represented in the central processor.

Instead of using 4 bits with only 16 possible characters, equipment designers commonly use 6 or 8 bits to represent characters in *alphanumeric versions* of BCD. Since the four BCD *numeric* place positions ('1, 2, 4, and 8) are retained, these alphanumeric versions are also frequently referred to as BCD. Two *zone* positions are added to the four BCD positions in the 6-bit code. With 6 bits it is thus possible to represent 64 different characters (2^6). A seventh parity checking position is commonly added (Fig. 8-17). We have already seen examples of 6-bit alphanumeric BCD code being used to represent data in paper tape and seven-channel magnetic tape. Now that the binary numbering system has been introduced, it becomes clearer why the bottom rows of tape are labeled 8, 4, 2, and 1. These values merely represent positions to the left of the binary point. It was pointed out in the discussion of magnetic tape coding that the decimal 7 is represented by an on condition in the numeric channels marked 4, 2, and 1. It is now apparent that being "on" means that a 1 bit is represented in these positions, i.e., that 7 = 0111 in BCD.

Data are generally stored internally by the use of tiny doughnut-shaped "cores," which may be magnetized in either of two directions.[18] These cores are thus capable of representing a 1 or a 0. Seven cores, stacked in a vertical column are used in second-generation computers to represent a number, letter, or special character. Figure 8-18 shows how the decimal 7 is represented. An imaginary line passes through the cores. The shaded cores are magnetized in a direction that corresponds to a 1 bit. Like a switch, they may be considered in an on state. The unshaded cores are in an off state and represent a 0 bit. The A and B cores are the zone cores. A combination of zone (A and B) and numeric (8, 4, 2, and 1) cores may be used to represent alphabetic and special characters just as they do in tape coding. The parity check core is also shown in the off state, indicating that odd parity is used in this particular code.[19]

Six-bit Alphanumeric Code

[18] We shall have more to say about core storage in the next chapter.
[19] The code represented here is called the Standard BCD Interchange code and is used to represent data internally in many second generation computers. Seven-channel tape code differs slightly in that even parity may be used.

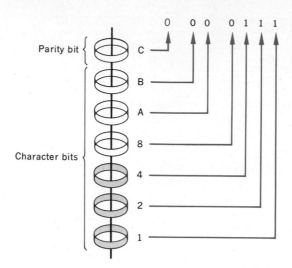

Figure 8-18 Alphanumeric BCD character location

The 6 bits permit 64 different coding arrangements. This number is sufficient to code the decimal digits (10), capital letters (26), and a number of punctuation marks and machine control characters. Six bits are *not sufficient,* however, to provide lowercase letters, capital letters, and a greatly expanded number of special and control characters.

Eight-bit Alphanumeric Codes

To permit greater flexibility in data representation, equipment designers have *extended* the 6-bit alphanumeric BCD code to 8 bits. With 8-bit coding, it is possible to provide 256 different arrangements (2^8). Each 8-bit unit of information, you will remember, is called a *byte.* Bytes may be used to represent a single character, or the programmer may use the eight cores to "pack" two decimal digits into one byte.

The nine-channel magnetic tape format discussed in Chapter 6 utilizes an 8-bit extended version of BCD. There are four (rather than two) zone bit positions available in an 8-bit code (Fig. 8-19). Eight data cores plus a check bit core are again stacked in a column and used internally in many CPUs to represent a coded character.

Selected characters are presented in Fig. 8-20 in the four most commonly encountered codes found in data processing. (Parity check bits are excluded.) These codes include the Hollerith punched card code, explained in Chapter 2, and the 6-bit Standard BCD Interchange code, mentioned above. In addition, there are *two* 8-bit codes currently being used in third- and fourth-generation computers. One, the

Check bit	Zone bits				Numeric bits			
C	Z̄	Z̄	Z̄	Z̄	8	4	2	1

Figure 8-19

Extended Binary Coded Decimal Interchange Code (EBCDIC) developed by IBM, is used in that firm's System/360 and /370 computer models and in other machines including the RCA Spectra 70 series. Another code, the American Standard Code for Information Interchange (ASCII), is popular in data communications and is used to

Character	Hollerith card code	Standard BCD interchange code	Extended BCD interchange code (EBCDIC)	ASCII-8
0	0	00 1010	1111 0000	0101 0000
1	1	00 0001	1111 0001	0101 0001
2	2	00 0010	1111 0010	0101 0010
3	3	00 0011	1111 0011	0101 0011
4	4	00 0100	1111 0100	0101 0100
5	5	00 0101	1111 0101	0101 0101
6	6	00 0110	1111 0110	0101 0110
7	7	00 0111	1111 0111	0101 0111
8	8	00 1000	1111 1000	0101 1000
9	9	00 1001	1111 1001	0101 1001
A	12-1	11 0001	1100 0001	1010 0001
B	12-2	11 0010	1100 0010	1010 0010
C	12-3	11 0011	1100 0011	1010 0011
D	12-4	11 0100	1100 0100	1010 0100
E	12-5	11 0101	1100 0101	1010 0101
F	12-6	11 0110	1100 0110	1010 0110
G	12-7	11 0111	1100 0111	1010 0111
H	12-8	11 1000	1100 1000	1010 1000
I	12-9	11 1001	1100 1001	1010 1001
J	11-1	10 0001	1101 0001	1010 1010
K	11-2	10 0010	1101 0010	1010 1011
L	11-3	10 0011	1101 0011	1010 1100
M	11-4	10 0100	1101 0100	1010 1101
N	11-5	10 0101	1101 0101	1010 1110
O	11-6	10 0110	1101 0110	1010 1111
P	11-7	10 0111	1101 0111	1011 0000
Q	11-8	10 1000	1101 1000	1011 0001
R	11-9	10 1001	1101 1001	1011 0010
S	0-2	01 0010	1110 0010	1011 0011
T	0-3	01 0011	1110 0011	1011 0100
U	0-4	01 0100	1110 0100	1011 0101
V	0-5	01 0101	1110 0101	1011 0110
W	0-6	01 0110	1110 0110	1011 0111
X	0-7	01 0111	1110 0111	1011 1000
Y	0-8	01 1000	1110 1000	1011 1001
Z	0-9	01 1001	1110 1001	1011 1010

Figure 8-20 Common methods of representing data

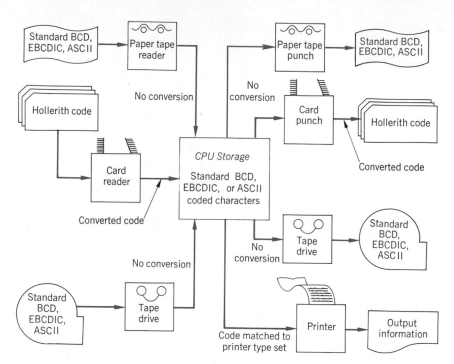

Figure 8-21   Multiple code usage

represent data internally in the NCR Century line of computers.[20] You will note that the Standard BCD code and EBCDIC differ primarily in the zone bit coding.

From the preceding paragraphs, it is now obvious that several data representation methods may be substituted for pure binary in business computer systems. Fortunately, a single computer system can make use of multiple codes. As we see in Fig. 8-21, for example, a card reader may be accepting Hollerith coded cards, but the code on these cards can be converted into Standard BCD, EBCDIC, or ASCII codes prior to being stored in the CPU. Data recorded on paper and magnetic tape may be in the code format used by the CPU, and thus no conversion may be required during input or output. Output to a card punch is generally converted from the CPU format to the Hollerith code prior to punching. Also, the internal CPU code is matched to the printer character set prior to printing.

---

[20] ASCII is also referred to as USASCII and ANSCII. The confusion is caused by changes in the name of the organization that developed the code. The code was developed by the American Standards Association (which later became the United States of America Standards Institute, and is now known as the American National Standards Institute, Inc.) in cooperation with users of communications and data processing equipment. The purpose of the developers of ASCII was to establish a standard interchange code that could be used to provide machine-to-machine and/or system-to-system communication both directly and through the data transmission network. There are both 7- and 8-bit versions of ASCII.

Storage locations may contain either data or instructions. For each **SUMMARY** program, data are typically stored in three conceptual areas—the input storage area, the working storage area, and the output storage area. Instructions are held in a program storage area. These areas are assigned by the programmer and vary in size and location depending upon the particular job being processed.

Locations in storage are identified by address numbers. The programmer (or software prepared by programmers) keeps track of address contents because when instructions are written to manipulate these contents, they must indicate in some way the address locations. The programmer has a fixed number of instruction commands at his disposal. These commands are built into the particular machine being used. When running a program, the machine is set at the first instruction and it then follows sequentially the series of directions until told to do otherwise.

Each address may contain either a single character or a word consisting of a fixed number of characters. Character-addressable machines also store words (fields), but instead of being fixed in length, these words are of variable length. Fixed word-length computers perform computations faster than variable word-length equipment and are therefore preferred in scientific installations. Most large-scale computers are organized with fixed word-length capability. Since calculations represent a lesser part of the business processing job, many small- and medium-sized business computers have been built with variable word-length design for more efficient storage utilization. Most third- and fourth-generation models may be operated as either variable or fixed word-length machines.

Binary numbers are used to simplify computer design and take advantage of the two states that electronic components may be in. Scientific computers may use a straight binary means of representing data. Computers designed to process business applications, on the other hand, use a binary-related code to designate numbers, letters, and special characters. Six- and eight-bit character codes are a popular means of representing alphanumeric data. Such codes are often alphanumeric versions of the 4-bit binary coded decimal system. The data bits plus a parity check bit may be represented internally in the CPU by tiny magnetic cores stacked in a vertical column. The cores are magnetized in one of two possible ways and thus are capable of storing an electrical representation of 0 or 1.

Although 64 characters are represented with 6 bits, it may be desirable to have a larger number of bit configurations. Most third- and fourth-generation computers use 8 bits (bytes) to code up to 256 different bit combinations.

1. (a) Identify and discuss the four conceptual storage areas. (b) What is the typical data-flow pattern in the storage unit?
2. Define the following terms:
   (a) Address
   (b) Command repertoire
   (c) Branchpoint
   (d) Looping
   (e) Wordmark
   (f) Data word
   (g) Instruction word
   (h) Conditional transfer
   (i) Unconditional transfer
   (j) Byte
3. Explain the distinction between the address number and the contents of the address.
4. (a) Distinguish between word-addressable and character-addressable computers. (b) Compare fixed and variable word-length storage systems.
5. (a) What is the difference between an additive and a positional numbering system? (b) Give examples of both types of numbering system.
6. "Many third-generation computers can be operated as either a variable word-length or as a fixed word-length machine." Discuss this comment.
7. "The highest numerical symbol will always have a value of one less than the base." Explain and give examples.
8. "In any positional numbering system, the value of each position represents a specific power of the base." Explain and give examples.
9. Why have computers been designed to use the binary numbering system?
10. (a) What is the binary equivalent of 85_{10}? (b) What is the decimal equivalent of 1110011_2?
11. (a) What is the octal equivalent of 1101011010100010_2?
    (b) The hexadecimal equivalent?
    (c) Why have octal and hexadecimal numbering systems been found useful?
12. (a) What is 150_{10} in BCD?
    (b) What is the straight binary equivalent of 150_{10}?
    (c) Compare BCD and straight binary coding.
13. Why has the 6-bit Standard BCD code been extended to 8 bits?
14. (a) What are the two popular 8-bit codes?
    (b) Who developed these codes?

1. $(2 \times 8^2) + (3 \times 8^1) + (4 \times 8^0) = 156_{10}$
2. $(2 \times 5^2) + (3 \times 5^1) + (4 \times 5^0) = 69_{10}$
3. No, the answer is not 100_{10}. Since the highest numerical symbol will always have a value of 1 less than the base, the symbol 5 is undefined and does not exist in the base-five system. Although this example may not do much to test understanding of conversion procedures, the author occasionally uses it to maintain his reputation as a "chicken professor."
4. $(1 \times 2^3) + (0 \times 2^2) + (1 \times 2^1) + (1 \times 2^0) = 11_{10}$

8-1

1. (a) $(1 \times 2^5) + (1 \times 2^4) + (1 \times 2^3) + (0 \times 2^2) + (1 \times 2^1) +$
   $(1 \times 2^0) = 59_{10}$
   (b) $(1 \times 2^8) = 256_{10}$
2. (a) $257_{10} = 100000001_2$
   (b) $64_{10} = 1000000_2$
   (c) $15_{10} = 1111_2$

8-2

```
     111  ←—— (carries)
1.  1110        (14)
   +111          (7)
   ─────        ────
   10101        (21)

   1111111  ←—— (carries)
2.  111001       (57)
     1001         (9)
    +111          (7)
   ───────      ────
   1001001       (73)

3.  1101
   +0101    (Complemented subtrahend)
   ──────
   ①0010
      ↘→1
   ─────
     11

4.  1000
   +010     (Complemented subtrahend)
   ──────
   ①010
      ↘→1
   ─────
     11
```

8-3

5.
$$\begin{array}{r} 10001 \\ \times 110 \\ \hline 100010 \\ 10001 \\ \hline 1100110 \end{array}$$
(17)
(6)

1100110   (102)

6.
$$\begin{array}{r} 111001 \\ \times 111 \\ \hline 111001 \\ 111001 \\ 111001 \end{array}$$
(57)
(7)

carries $\longrightarrow \left\{ \begin{array}{l} 111 \\ 111 \end{array} \right.$

$$\begin{array}{r} \hline 110001111 \end{array}$$ (399)

8-4

1. $234_8 = 10/011/100_2$
2. $1675_8 = 1/110/111/101_2$
3. $111/001/110/101_2 = 7165_8$
4. $11/101/110/100/111/001/000/010/100/010/101 = 35647102425_8$

8-5

1. $(7 \times 16^2) + (A \text{ or } ``10" \times 16^1) + (2 \times 16^0) = 1954_{10}$

                 <u>Remainder</u>

2.
$$\begin{array}{r} 62 \\ 16\overline{)1000} \end{array}$$ 8

$$\begin{array}{r} 3 \\ 16\overline{)62} \end{array}$$ 14 (Read E)

$$\begin{array}{r} 0 \\ 16\overline{)3} \end{array}$$ 3

     Therefore, $1000_{10} = 3E8_{16}$

3. $7A2_{16} = 111/1010/0010_2$
4. $1110/1110/1001/1100/1000/0101/0001/0101_2 = EE9C8515_{16}$

SELECTED REFERENCES

Knuth, Donald E.: "The Evolution of Number Systems," *Datamation,* February, 1969, pp. 93–97.

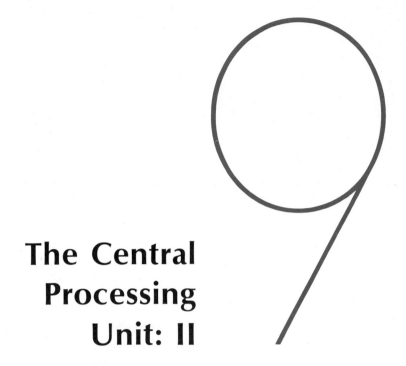

The Central
Processing
Unit: II

We continue our survey of the CPU in this chapter with an examination of storage devices in terms of the *properties* that they possess. We shall then be in a position to study the *types of storage devices* that are available. In the final pages of the chapter we shall turn our attention to the CPU's *arithmetic-logic and control units*.

PROPERTIES OF STORAGE DEVICES

A storage device, of course, is any instrument that can accept entering data, hold them as long as necessary, and produce them when necessary. Storage capability may be *classified* as either primary (internal) or secondary (external), as shown in Fig. 9-1. *Primary storage* is nothing more than the built-in storage section of the CPU. It is referred to by a number of other terms, including *internal storage, high-speed storage,* and *main memory*. A primary, or internal, storage section is

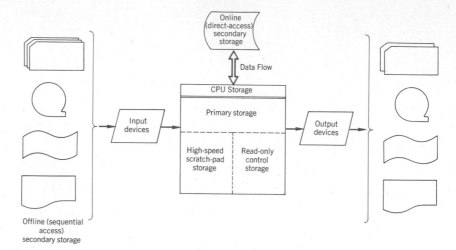

Figure 9-1 Primary and secondary storage classifications

basic to all computers and is used to hold data and program instructions.

Although our attention in this chapter will be focused on the primary storage section of the CPU and on online storage concepts, it should be noted here that many CPU's also contain other small storage elements, which perform special operating functions. One such storage element shown in Fig. 9-1 is a small high-speed *scratch-pad memory,* which is used to temporarily store data and instructions during *processing* operations. Another special *read-only storage* section found in some processors contains *control* routines, or *microprograms,* which interpret program instructions and decode them into elementary machine steps.[1] The Model 145 computer (Fig. 9-2) in the IBM System/370 line, for example, has a 32,000-byte control storage section. Microprograms prepared by IBM may be loaded into this control storage section to perform specific tasks, e.g., to enable the 145 to run programs prepared for IBM 1400 series computers. Although the contents of this control storage section may be altered, it is used as a read-only unit during data processing and will not accept input data and instructions from applications programmers.

Secondary storage is a catch-all classification. If data are not stored internally in the CPU, then they must be contained in some secondary external form. Secondary storage may be by means of *online* devices, or it may be *offline* in the form of cards, paper tape, paper documents, or magnetic tape. It is often called *external storage, high-capacity* (or *mass) storage,* and *auxiliary* memory. Online equipment provides

---

[1]We will discuss some of the uses of read-only storage and microprograms in Chapter 11.

direct access to records; records in offline storage are usually sequentially organized.

Business data processing managers are generally faced (sooner or later) with difficult decisions in determining the primary and secondary storage requirements of their companies. In making their decisions, managers should consider data storage facilities in terms of *their measurable properties of speed, capacity, safety,* and *record accessibility.* Another consideration should be that of making an *economical* choice. In short, the following questions should be considered:

1. *What processing speeds are required?* Processing speed is affected by many factors, including *access time.* Access time is defined as (1) the time interval between the instant when data are called for from a storage device and the instant the data are available for processing (i.e., the read time) and (2) the time interval between the instant when data are ready to be stored and the instant when storage is effectively completed (i.e., the write time). The *fastest* access time is available from internal (high-speed) storage. Speeds vary, of course, but some processors may retrieve or store a character in less than a microsecond. Secondary direct-access storage units are slower, with access speeds measured in milliseconds. The unattainable ideal would be an access time of zero. To the human mind, however, the nanosecond speed of some internal storage units is virtually zero. If processing speed is the

Figure 9-2   IBM System/370, Model 145 (courtesy IBM Corporation)

paramount consideration and cost is secondary, then the manager may choose a CPU with sufficient internal storage to hold all the necessary data. The amount of "necessary data" brings us to the subject of storage capacity.

2. *What storage capacity is needed?* The amount of data to be stored now and in the future must be considered by the data processing manager. He also must determine the storage capacity properties of various pieces of hardware, and this is not always as easy as it sounds. For example, a manufacturer's literature may advertise a machine with 16,000 addressable storage locations. [This figure is usually abbreviated 16K where K (or kilo) represents thousands.] But is the machine word, character, or byte addressable? If it is word addressable, how many characters are there in the fixed word? And if it is character addressable, what is the number of bits in the character? (An 8-bit byte provides greater storage than a 6-bit character because two decimal digits may be packed in a byte.) A fixed word-length storage of 16K may be considerably larger than a variable word-length storage of 24K. And, converting storage capacity of word- and character-addressable machines to the number of characters that each may hold is not altogether reliable because fixed word-length storage may result in some unused capacity. Some fourth-generation computers can store over three-million bytes of data internally. Online secondary devices have much greater storage capability and may store hundreds of millions of characters. Also, the amount of data that can be stored on magnetic tape is limited only by the space available to store the tape reels.

3. *How safe are the data?* Most businesses consider it highly desirable not to lose data stored internally or in direct-access devices in the event of a power failure in the equipment room. Commercial storage equipment is able to hold data permanently in the absence of power and is therefore said to be *nonvolatile*. However, some CPUs used for military purposes have been designed with volatile storage for reasons of security. Data recorded in punched cards are as permanent as the cards themselves. But it usually is more economical if storage space can be *erased* and reused when the need for the original data no longer exists. We have already seen how old data are erased on magnetic tape when new data are being written. Similarly, old data held in internal and online external storage are erased as new data are read into the location. This is sometimes referred to as *destructive read-in*. But it is generally best for stored data *not* to be erased from their original address when they are being recorded in another storage

location. Such *destructive read-out* would occur in magnetic core storage were it not for built-in circuitry that automatically restores the data in the original location. The data processing manager should be interested in storage facilities that are not only safe but as durable and as compact as possible.

4. *What type of record accessibility is required?* If all the needs of the business can be satisfied by batch processing methods performed on sequentially organized files, then the data processing manager should not be interested in online storage devices. On the other hand, should direct-access capability be indicated, then the data processing manager must determine which of the several alternatives best meets his needs.

5. *What is the most economical choice?* The business manager is frequently faced with the need to accept reduced performance in one area to reduce cost. Compromises between the storage properties of speed, capacity, and record accessibility are required in the interest of economy. For example, internal storage provides the fastest access time and random access capability, but the cost is highest per character stored; the use of magnetic tape provides the least expensive means of storage, but because of serial record accessibility the time required to process a particular record may be measured in minutes.

When direct-access is needed, the manager must ask himself the question, "Can I substitute in place of high-speed storage slower but less-expensive online equipment which will meet my needs?" For business purposes the answer to this question is usually yes. Direct-access units store data on magnetic drums, magnetic disks, or magnetic cards or strips. Although these units will be studied later in the chapter, it should be mentioned here that selection among these auxiliary storage units also involves compromise. Magnetic drums have fast access times, but they generally do not have the storage capacity of disks and cards or strips. In fact, with auxiliary units there is frequently an inverse relationship between speed and cost per character stored, on the one hand, and storage capacity, on the other. That is, as storage capacity increases, the access time becomes slower but the cost per character stored is reduced.

We have seen that primary and secondary storage units vary with respect to such properties as speed, capacity, permanence, record accessibility, and cost. Managers often find that it is desirable to *combine* different means of storage to get the best package. In the following sections we shall examine more closely the types of primary and secondary storage devices.

Types of storage	Uses of storage devices		
	Primary	Online secondary	Offline secondary
Magnetic drum	x	x	
Magnetic cores	x	x	
Thin films	x		
Plated wire	x		
LSI circuits	x		
Magnetic tape			x
Punched cards			x
Punched paper tape			x
Paper documents			x
Magnetic disks		x	x
Magnetic cards/strips		x	x

Figure 9-3   Uses of storage devices

TYPES OF PRIMARY STORAGE DEVICES

Figure 9-3 shows the more common means of computer storage and the way or ways in which these storage facilities have been and are being used. In the following pages we will consider each of these approaches.

Early Primary Storage

The ENIAC used vacuum tube storage. Each tube was able to hold a single bit. Storage capacity was tiny by present standards, and ENIAC was huge and therefore quite slow in operation. The most popular computer in the mid-1950s (the IBM 650) used a magnetic drum as the internal storage instrument. The drum is a metal cylinder that is coated with a magnetizable material such as iron oxide or a nickel-cobalt alloy. Although drums may still be used for primary storage in small processors, their relatively slow access times (when compared with magnetic cores and thin films) prevent them from being used in this manner in most cases. But when compared with other auxiliary storage units, they are quite fast. They are thus used extensively when fast auxiliary storage of modest capacity is needed. We shall postpone further discussion of drums to the section on secondary storage units.

During the mid-1950s magnetic core storage appeared in large-scale vacuum tube computers such as the IBM 704. Since that time internal core storage has been improved and production techniques have been refined to the point where magnetic cores are used in most current commercial computers.

In the last chapter we saw that magnetic cores are tiny doughnut-shaped rings, which can be magnetized in either of two directions. These rings are pressed from a ferromagnetic and ceramic mixture and are then baked in an oven. Early cores had an outside diameter of about $\frac{1}{12}$ inch. Access time was in the 10- to 20-microsecond range. But pressure to improve the properties of speed, capacity, and cost resulted in the development of highly automatic production tech-

Magnetic Core Storage

Figure 9-4   Miniworld of magnetic cores (courtesy Ampex Corporation)

Current is applied   Current is removed;
core remains magnetized

Figure 9-5 Magnetizing a core

niques for pressing, baking, testing, and assembling the cores. The core size has been reduced, access time has been improved, storage capacity has increased to over a million bytes (with each byte represented by eight data cores and a parity check core), and the cost per bit of storage has been reduced. Figure 9-4 compares cores of different age with the tip of a ball-point pen. The largest rings are older cores, measuring about $\frac{1}{8}$ inch in outside diameter; the smallest (and newest) cores measure $\frac{18}{1,000}$ inch. Access speeds now range from less than 300 nanoseconds to 2 microseconds.

In 1820, Hans Christian Oersted, a Danish scientist, noticed that when a small compass was placed near a current-carrying wire, there was a deflection of the compass needle. Furthermore, Oersted found that the needle was responding to a magnetic field that was produced by the current flow, and when the direction of current flow changed, so did the direction of the magnetic field. It was later discovered that a changing (expanding or collapsing) magnetic field would induce a current flow in a wire. These principles, discovered years ago, are employed in the internal core storage of computers.

Figure 9-5 shows that if a wire carrying a sufficiently strong electric current passes through a core, the core will be magnetized by the magnetic field created around the wire. Perhaps you have wrapped a wire around a nail and connected the ends of the wire to a battery to make an electromagnet. You might have been surprised when you disconnected the battery to find that the nail still had the ability to act as a magnet. As Fig. 9-5 shows, the core, like the nail, remains magnetized after the current stops.

In Fig. 9-6, the current flow from left to right has magnetized the core in a counterclockwise (0-bit) direction. But when the current flows in the opposite direction, the core becomes magnetized in a clockwise (1-bit) fashion. A core can be quickly changed from an off or 0-bit condition to an on or 1-bit state simply by reversing the current flow passing through the core (Fig. 9-7).

Figure 9-6 Two-state data representation

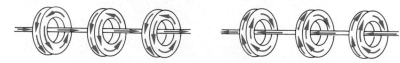

Current is applied   Core is magnetized   Current is reversed;
                                          the core reverses
                                          its magnetic state   *Figure 9-7   Flipping a core*

A large number of cores is strung on a screen of wires to form a core *plane*. Figure 9-8 shows a manufacturing operation on one such plane. These planes, resembling square tennis rackets, are then arranged vertically to represent data. The final testing of multiple stacks that contain a total of five million cores is shown in Fig. 9-9. These stacks will be combined with others to form a large core storage unit. As we saw in the last chapter, seven cores are needed to code 6-bit

Figure 9-8   Core plane assembly (courtesy Ampex Corporation)

Figure 9-9 Check-out of core storage stacks (courtesy Ampex Corporation)

characters in internal storage and provide for a parity check. Some storage planes are 128 cores wide and 128 cores long, thus giving a total of 16,384 cores per plane. A stack of seven (6-bit code) or nine (8-bit code) planes is needed to store 16,384 alphabetic characters. The imaginary line drawn through the cores in the nine planes in Fig. 9-10 shows the physical location of a letter as it might be temporarily stored.

A question frequently asked by students is how, among the hundreds of thousands of cores, is it possible to select and properly magnetize just seven or nine in such a way that the desired character is *read into* storage? Let us use an imaginary plane with only 81 cores to see how 1 bit in a character is selected (Fig. 9-11). The other bits making up the character are similarly chosen in the other planes. To make selection possible, two wires must pass through each core at right angles. If the total current needed to magnetize a core were sent along a single wire, every core through which the wire passed in getting to and from the selected core would also be magnetized—a most undesirable situation. But by sending only *half* the necessary current through each of two wires, only the core at the intersection of the wires is affected. All other cores in the plane either receive

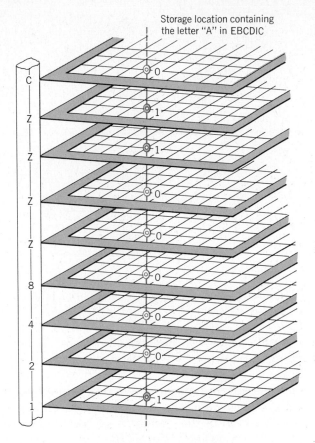

Storage location containing
the letter "A" in EBCDIC

Figure 9-10

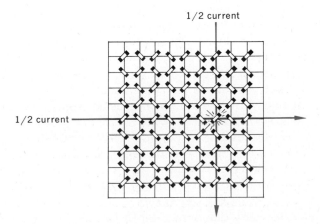

1/2 current

1/2 current

Figure 9-11 Core selection

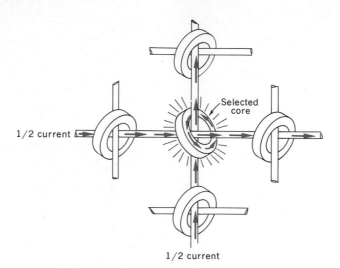

1/2 current

Selected core

1/2 current

Figure 9-12 Closeup of selected core

no current effects at all or receive only half the amount needed to magnetize. Figure 9-12 shows a closeup of a selected core magnetized to represent a 0 bit.

With a character now read into core storage, how does the computer *retrieve* it? For retrieval a third *sense* wire must be threaded diagonally through each core in a plane (Fig. 9-13). The computer tests, or reads-out, the magnetic state of a core by again sending electric current pulses through the two wires used in the read-in operation. The direction of this current is such that it causes a 0 to be written at that core position. If the core is magnetized in an on or 1 state, the writing of a 0 will abruptly *flip* the magnetic condition of the core and the changing magnetic field will induce a current into the sense wire. The reaction picked up by the sense wire tells the computer that the core contained a 1 bit. If *no reaction* is sensed, the computer will know that the core is already magnetized in the 0 state. Since only one core is being read at any given instant in a plane, only a *single* sense wire need be threaded through all the cores.

But wait a minute! If all cores storing a character have been changed from a 1 to a 0 state as a result of the reading, haven't we destroyed the character in its original location? The answer to this is usually yes, but only momentarily. Fortunately, by means of a fourth *inhibit* wire[2] the cores containing 1 bits are restored to their original state following destructive read-out. Simply stated, the processor now tries to write back 1 s in every core read an instant earlier. If the core

[2]This wire, like the sense wire, runs through every core in a plane because only one core at a time in a plane is being restored.

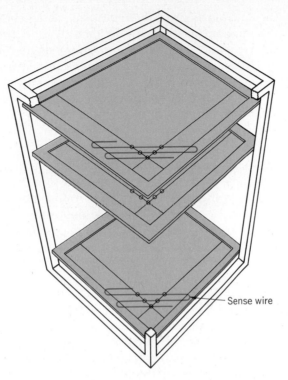

Figure 9-13 Sense wire in core plane

in the plane was originally a 1, it will be restored; if it was originally a 0, it will remain that way, and a pulse of current will be sent through the inhibit wire in the plane to cancel out the attempt to write a 1 (Fig. 9-14).

Today magnetic cores dominate the internal storage picture for several reasons: (1) they are durable; (2) they provide safe, nonvolatile storage; (3) they provide access time measured in nanoseconds; (4)

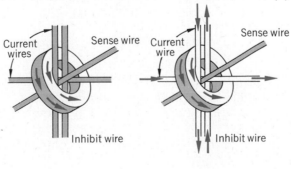

Figure 9-14 Core inhibit wire

they are inexpensive in their operation and erasable; (5) they provide fast random accessibility to records; and (6) they are compact in size—millions can be packed into a single cabinet.

Magnetic core *secondary online storage* is available but expensive when compared with other slower, online alternatives. In the future, however, the cost of core plane fabrication and the circuitry necessarily associated with magnetic cores may make them less desirable.

Planar Thin Film Storage

Primary storage units made from thin films arranged in flat planes (thus the name *planar*) may be expected to increase in popularity in the future. In the early 1950s, it was found that a tiny rectangle or circle of magnetic material could be deposited on an insulating glass or plastic base so that it could be magnetized in either of two stable preferred directions. Such film spots possess *potential*[3] cost advantages over cores. They are made directly from bulk materials rather than from individual components, which must be stamped, baked, hand threaded, and tested.

The film itself is only a few millionths of an inch thick and may be made of alloys containing nickel and iron. The circuitry required for moving data to and from storage spots usually consists of strips of conductive material etched on a nonconductor. The thin film storage plane may then be sandwiched between circuit-carrying overlays—an operation requiring careful attention. Nondestructive read-out is possible when thin film storage is used; access time is often improved when compared with core storage; and resistance to temperature change and shock is excellent. These last properties are of interest to designers of military computers.

Figure 9-15 shows a planar thin film storage frame now being used in the Burroughs B6500 computer. Tiny rectangular storage locations are used, and access time is about 300 nanoseconds. The frame shown provides the computer with 245,000 bits of storage.

Plated-wire Storage

Thin film storage cells do not have to be in the form of flat spots or rectangles. Instead, they may be in a plated-wire form. Plated-wire storage has nondestructive read-out and fast access time. Manufacturing cost per bit of storage capacity is low because of the automatic production techniques employed. Plated-wire primary storage is currently used in UNIVAC 9000 series computers and in NCR Century models.

---

[3] At this time, cores still are generally less expensive per bit of storage provided.

Figure 9-15 *Thin-film storage frame (courtesy Burroughs Corporation)*

In the NCR approach, a thin metallic film is deposited on 5-mil copper wire, which is then cut into 0.110-inch lengths. Each tiny length (or rod) is capable of storing 1 bit. A storage plane is formed by inserting the bit rods into coiled wires, which act as activating and sensing elements (Fig. 9-16). After the fabrication process is completed, the entire plane is sealed in plastic. Plating the wire, winding the coils (Fig. 9-17), cutting and inserting the rods in the coils, and sealing the planes are all automatic manufacturing operations. As with

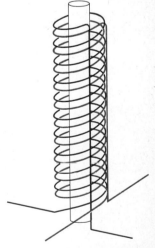

Figure 9-16 *(Courtesy NCR)*

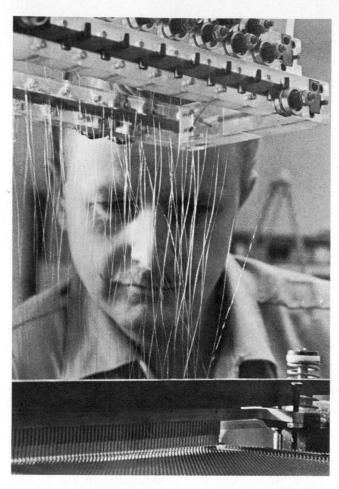

Figure 9-17   (Courtesy NCR)

core planes, the plated-wire planes are assembled into stacks. A number of these stacks are then used in systems such as the one shown in Fig. 9-18 to provide primary storage for from 32,000 to over half a million characters.

LSI Circuit Storage

With access times below 50 nanoseconds and with the potential to generally *outperform* other primary storage approaches, large-scale integrated (LSI) circuit storage elements will become increasingly popular in the future. Each LSI circuit storage chip contains many fast microscopic switches, which, for our purposes, can be considered the electronic equivalents of mechanical toggle switches. Like a toggle switch, each electronic switch can be in an "on" or "off" condition and can thus be used to represent a binary 1 or 0.

Until the fall of 1970, LSI circuit storage was not generally used as primary storage; rather, it was used mainly to replace thin films and cores in small special storage elements used in processing and control operations. In September, 1970, however, IBM officials announced that their Model 145 computer would use a primary storage unit made entirely of integrated circuits. Silicon chips, with more than 1,400 circuit elements on each $\frac{1}{8}$-inch chip, are used. The space required is only one-half that needed for conventional magnetic core storage (the CPU shown in Fig. 9-19 has a storage capacity of over a half-million characters). The Model 145 was the first commercial machine with this type of primary storage to be announced by a major manufacturer. (The University of Illinois' ILLIAC IV computer, discussed in Chapter 5, uses LSI circuits $\frac{1}{10}$ inch square in its multiple primary storage units, but this is a special $24 million project.)

The principal reason for the still-modest use of integrated circuits for primary storage purposes is their cost. It has been estimated that the cost per bit of storage capacity using LSI circuits will be around 10 cents in 1972 (down from 50 cents in 1967).[4] But this cost figure is still several times larger than the cost per bit of storage using slower magnetic recording approaches. Nevertheless, as we saw in Chapter 3, costs associated with the manufacture of LSI circuits are expected to be substantially reduced in the 1970s. More machines will use LSI primary storage as a result, and in the meantime solid state circuits will continue to be used in the special high-speed operating sections, e.g., in the scratch-pad and read-only memory sections mentioned earlier.

[4]See David W. Brown and James L. Burkhardt, "The Computer Memory Market," *Computers and Automation*, January, 1969, p. 24.

Figure 9-18 NCR Century 200 computer system (courtesy NCR)

Figure 9-19   IBM System/370, Model 145 (courtesy IBM Corporation)

TYPES OF SECONDARY STORAGE DEVICES

Offline Secondary Storage[5]

We have already dealt elsewhere with the means of providing offline secondary storage through the use of punched cards, punched paper tape, paper documents, and magnetic tape, and so we need not dwell long on these media here. It should be remembered, however, that many firms find that their *total* data processing needs are being met quite satisfactorily through the use of offline storage media. In spite of the pronouncements to the contrary by a few of the more enthusiastic boosters of broader and faster-responding business systems, sequentially organized files will be stored on tapes and cards in the foreseeable future. This is true because:

[5] Offline secondary storage may be referred to as *nonaddressable bulk storage*. The term *nonaddressable* refers to the fact that records are not directly addressable. In other words, direct-access processing is not economically feasible with these media. As might be expected, online secondary storage is sometimes called *addressable bulk storage*.

1. An unlimited amount of data may be safely retained in this way.
2. Batch processing is acceptable—perhaps even preferable—for some jobs.
3. Offline media often provide the least expensive means of data storage.
4. Magnetic tape processing, in situations where sequentially organized files are feasible, is frequently less expensive than direct-access processing.

In the remainder of this section we shall look at different types of popular direct-access storage units. It is interesting to note that some of these devices are *flexible* in the sense that the storage instruments associated with their use may be either online or offline. Magnetic disks, for example, resemble large phonograph records, have mass storage capability, and can be used indefinitely for online purposes. But the disks (and the data contained) can be removed and stored offline just like tapes and cards.

Magnetic Drums

Magnetic drums were an early means of primary storage. Now, however, they are generally used as auxiliary storage when fast response is of greater importance than large capacity. For example, they may be used to store mathematical tables, data, or program modifications that are frequently referred to during processing operations.

A magnetic drum is a cylinder that has an outer surface plated with a metallic magnetizable film. (Figure 9-20 shows three large UNIVAC Fastrand drums being tested prior to final assembly.) A motor rotates the drum on its axis at a constant and rapid rate. Data are *recorded on* the rotating drum and *read from* the drum by *read-write heads,* which are positioned a fraction of an inch from the drum surface (Fig. 9-21). As is the case with magnetic tape, data are recorded on the drum surface when pulses of current flow through the tiny wires of the write coils and set up magnetic fields. Current flow in one write coil produces a 1 bit; current in the other produces a 0-bit magnetic field. The writing of new data on the drum erases data previously stored at the location. The magnetic spots written on the drum surface remain indefinitely until they, too, are erased at a future time. Reading of data recorded on the drum is accomplished as the magnetized spots pass under the read heads and induce electric pulses in the read coils. Because millisecond time is desired in the reading and writing operations, the drum rotates several thousand times each minute.

Figure 9-20 UNIVAC Fastrand Drums (courtesy UNIVAC Division, Sperry Rand Corporation)

The binary coded data spots are arranged in *bands* or *tracks* around the circumference of the drum. A *fixed* read-write head is often employed for *each* band. Bands vary in width depending upon whether a character or fixed-length word is being stored. Some drums (e.g., the Fastrand drum shown in Fig. 9-20) may have thousands of bands. To reduce the circuitry costs associated with a large number of read-write heads, some drum units have a *single* horizontally movable head to serve *all* bands (Fig. 9-22a), while other drum devices

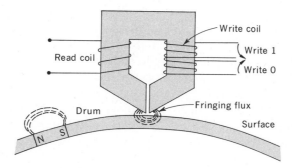

Figure 9-21   Read-write head

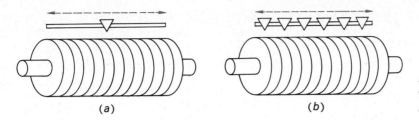

Figure 9-22(a) *Single read-write head, (b) multiple read-write heads*

(including Fastrand) have multiple heads, each of which serves a number of adjacent bands (Fig. 9-22b).[6]

The computer is able to access stored records directly because each drum has a specific number of addressable locations. A band may be divided into sections, and each section may be given an identifying number, as shown in Fig. 9-23. The width and number of

[6]The Fastrand drum, for example, uses 32 read-write heads; each head serves 96 adjacent bands, and all heads move horizontally together.

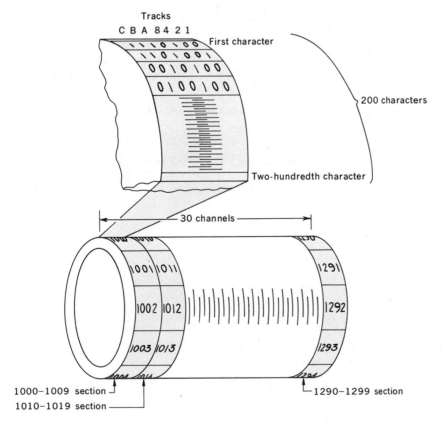

Figure 9-23

bands, the number of characters that may be stored in a section, and the number of addressable sections varies among hardware lines.

Direct-access time is basically determined by the delay time required for an addressed location to be positioned under a read-write head.[7] Although several factors are involved, let us consider only two:

1. *Number of read-write heads.* The most rapid access is achieved when there is a head for *each* band on the drum. The *rotational delay* of the drum then determines the access time. If the address containing the data to be read has just passed the head when the CPU sends a reading signal, there will be a delay while the drum makes a complete revolution. The measured time in this case is the *maximum* access time. If the address to be read were just passing under the head when the signal arrived, the *minimum* access time would be achieved. The *average* access speed is equal to about half the time required for the drum to make a revolution. If a single head is used to serve *all* bands, costs will be reduced but access time will be slower. Not only will rotational delay continue, but a new factor—*positional delay*—will be introduced. Time will now be required to locate and position the head over the proper band. Multiple head units that allocate one head to serve several adjacent bands are a compromise between speed and cost. Although they are not as fast as units with heads for each band, they are less expensive. Yet they have less positional delay than single head units.

2. *Speed of drum rotation.* A drum moving at 2,000 revolutions per minute takes 30 milliseconds to complete a single revolution. Any increase in rotational speed serves to decrease the rotational delay.

   Average drum access times range from 10 milliseconds for highspeed, limited-capacity units to about 100 milliseconds for the larger-capacity hardware. The faster drums are small in circumference (and therefore have limited space for storage), have high rotational speeds, and are the most expensive per volume of storage. The larger drums have more surface area for storage but slower access time. Drum units typically store 130,000 to 20 million characters, although the UNIVAC Fastrand II equipment has a capacity in excess of 100 million characters in a single cabinet.

[7] Technically speaking, magnetic cores and thin films have *random* access storage capability, while most online external devices including drums have *direct* but not *random* access to records. *Random access* refers to a storage device in which the access time is independent of the physical location of the data. Since the drum access time varies with the physical location of stored data, it is more technically correct to say that drums provide direct access. The distinction is often not observed, however, and the online units presented here are often described as being random access equipment.

Figure 9-24   NCR magnetic disk assembly (courtesy NCR)

Magnetic Disks

Magnetic disks resemble oversized phonograph records and are the most popular online storage medium. Unlike plastic phonograph records, however, disks are made of thin metal plates that will not warp and that are coated on both sides with a magnetizable recording material. Several disks (the number varies) are permanently mounted on a vertical shaft (Fig. 9-24), which rotates at a high, constant speed (usually over 1,000 revolutions per minute). A space is left between the spinning disks to allow small read-write heads to move to any storage location. Data are organized into a number of concentric circles or *tracks,* each of which has a designated location number.

Reading and writing operations are similar to those of drums. Data are recorded in specific locations as magnetized spots. Read-in is destructive; read-out is nondestructive. Figure 9-25 shows one type of read-write head arrangement. Arms, resembling teeth in a comb, move horizontally among the individual disks. The two heads mounted on each arm service two disk surfaces. On command from the CPU, the proper head moves to the specified track and the desired data are read as soon as they spin under the head.

Other reading-writing arrangements are possible. Figure 9-26, for example, shows disk storage devices with *multiple* read-write heads on each arm. The arm servicing the top disk surface in Fig. 9-26a contains 12 heads. Some of the older units contain stacks of 25 or 50 disks mounted on a single shaft and served by a *single access arm.*

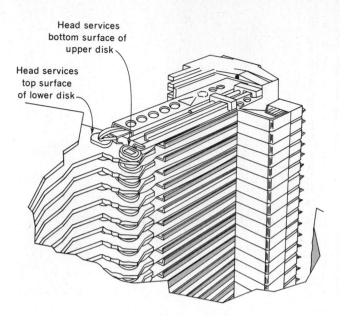

Head services
bottom surface of
upper disk

Head services
top surface
of lower disk

*Figure 9-25   Read-write
heads*

To locate data, the arm must move vertically to the proper disk and then horizontally to the proper track. Access times are, of course, quite slow. Multiple arms eliminate the vertical movement. The disks in the first units were supposed to remain permanently in their cabinets. Since that time, however, smaller disks have been developed, which can be removed and stored much like magnetic tape. (They are, however, much more expensive than a reel of tape.)

Interchangeable *disk packs* come in various sizes and storage capacities. The pack held by the operator in Fig. 9-27, for example, contains 12 disks and 20 recording surfaces (the top and bottom disks of the pack are used to protect the data surfaces). Storage capacity of the pack is 100 million bytes. It may be housed in the unit shown in Fig. 9-27 with seven others to provide a total of 800 million bytes of storage. It takes only a minute to replace a pack and thus replace 100 million characters. Smaller packs of six disks (with ten recording and two protective surfaces) are used by the disk drive in Fig. 9-28 to store over 7 million bytes of data.

The access time required for data to be transferred from a disk to primary storage (and vice versa) is determined by such factors as: (1) the number of access arms (if only a single arm is used, there is a *vertical* positional delay); (2) the amount of *horizontal* movement required for the arm to position a head over the proper track (multiple heads on each arm reduce the average length of movement and thus increase the access time, but they are more expensive); and (3) the

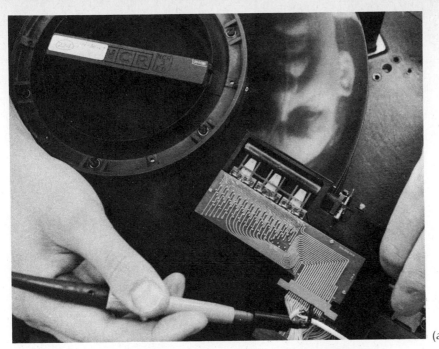

(a)

(b)

Figure 9-26(a) NCR
Century computer disk
(courtesy NCR), (b) Large
disk storage (courtesy Data
Products Corporation)

279

Figure 9-27 IBM 3330 disk storage facility (courtesy IBM Corporation)

rotational delay encountered, i.e., the time required to move the needed data under the read-write head.

In summary, the average access time of representative disk hardware ranges from 20 to 600 milliseconds; storage capacity varies from 500,000 to 800 million characters online (there is no limit to the number of disk packs that can be stored offline). Generally speaking, disk units have greater storage capability than drums but are not as fast. One can, of course, find exceptions to this generalization.

Magnetic Cards and Strips

Wouldn't it be nice to combine the magnetic tape advantages of low-cost, high-storage capacity with the advantages of rapid and direct record accessibility? This is essentially the objective of magnetic cards and strips. A magnetic card or strip may be considered to be a length of flexible plastic material upon which short pieces of magnetic tape have been mounted in a side-by-side arrangement. A number of cards are placed in a cartridge. Like disk packs, these cartridges are removable in a minute or less. Card and strip equipment generally has high-storage capability, and the cost per character stored is low. Data are erasable, but access speed is relatively slow when compared with drums and disks. This type of storage approach is used with such equipment as the National Cash Register CRAM (Card Random Access Memory), the IBM Data Cell, and the RCA Mass Storage Unit.

The CRAM unit (Fig. 9-29) contains a cartridge that holds 384 cards. Each card is 14 inches long but is much wider than a strip of magnetic tape. The cards in a cartridge and a number of tracks on each card are addressable by the CRAM unit. The cards are suspended from rods in the cartridge (Fig. 9-30). When data are to be written on or read from a particular card, the CPU sends a signal to drop the proper card into a vacuum handling device. It then is wrapped around a rapidly rotating drum, which moves it past read-write heads. After the read-write operation, the card is returned to the cartridge and the other 383 cards. The average access time is 235 milliseconds; storage capacity of a *single* cartridge is 145 million alphanumeric characters.

Figure 9-28   RCA 70/564 disk storage unit (courtesy RCA)

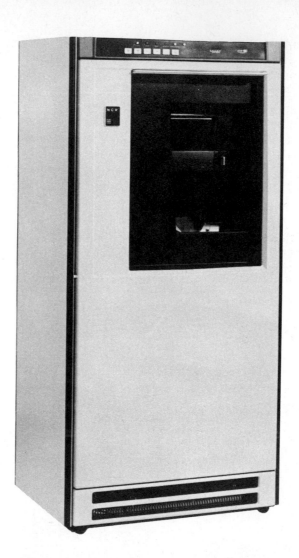

Figure 9-29   NCR CRAM unit (courtesy NCR)

A number of CRAM units may be connected to a single CPU to provide online storage for additional millions of characters.

The IBM Data Cell Drive (Fig. 9-31) provides virtually unlimited large-bulk storage and direct access to records. *Each* Data Cell unit has a storage capacity of 400 million bytes; *eight* such Data Cell units may be attached to a single control unit to provide 3.2 *billion* bytes of storage; and up to 48 control units may be attached to a large System/360 computer. You will notice in Fig. 9-32 that the Data Cell cartridge is a cylinder that resembles a snare drum. There are 10 replaceable *cells* in this cylinder. Each of the 10 cells contains 20 subcells and 200 magnetizable strips; each strip is 13 inches long and $2\frac{1}{4}$ inches wide. On one side of the strip is an iron-oxide magnetizable coating, while on the other side there is an antistatic carbon coating. The strip is divided into 100 data tracks and has an identifying coding tab.

Let us assume that the CPU is instructed to retrieve data from a specific strip. A signal is sent to the Data Cell Drive, which rotates the storage cartridge until the proper cell is positioned beneath the drive's access station. At the station the particular strip is located, withdrawn, pulled upward by a revolving drum past the read-write heads, and then returned to its original position. The strip pickup process is illustrated in Fig. 9-33. The time for this procedure averages about 450 milliseconds. A writing operation is similarly performed.

The RCA Mass Storage Unit (Fig. 9-34) is similar in concept to the above equipment; it uses eight magazines, each of which contains 256 magnetic cards. Storage capacity exceeds half a billion bytes, and cost per bit stored is very low.

All the bulk storage units introduced in this chapter have been magnetic devices. New high-resolution *photographic* media, however, are being developed to store trillions of bits of data. Data density is

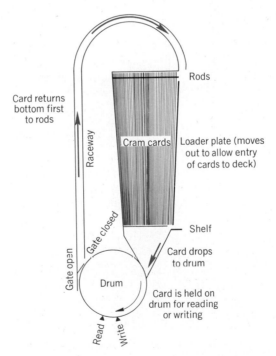

Figure 9-30 Path of a CRAM card (courtesy NCR)

Figure 9-31 IBM 2321 data cell drive (courtesy IBM Corporation)

many times greater with photographic material,[8] and although film is generally not erasable, it may play a more important role in future storage techniques. In addition to the storage function, every CPU must have components to perform the arithmetic-logic and control functions. In the remainder of the chapter we shall study these units.

THE ARITHMETIC-LOGIC UNIT

In preceding pages we noted that the arithmetic-logic unit is where the actual data processing occurs. All calculations are performed and all logical comparisons are made in this unit. In Chapter 8 we traced through a simplified program to process Editor Aardvark's weekly

[8] A piece of film $1\frac{3}{8}$ by $2\frac{3}{4}$ inches has been developed which can store several million bits.

paycheck. Some of the program instructions used then are reproduced in Fig. 9-35.

The instruction in address 07 calls for the computer to write the contents of address 01 into the arithmetic unit. Implicit in this instruction is the requirement that the arithmetic-logic unit have storage capability. It must be able to store temporarily the data contained in address 01. Such a special purpose storage location is called a *register*. Several registers will be discussed in the following paragraphs because they are basic to the functioning of the arithmetic-logic and control units.[9] The number of registers varies among computers as does the data-flow pattern. Before briefly examining some variations, let us trace the instructions in Fig. 9-35 through the PAC computer.

Up to this point we have written the instructions in addresses 07 to 11 so that we would understand them. Figure 9-36 shows how these

[9]The computer operator is able to determine the contents of the several registers in the CPU by observing small console display lights designed for the purpose.

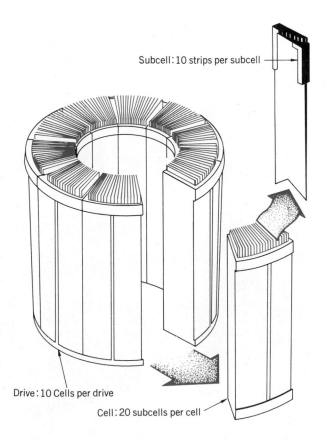

Subcell: 10 strips per subcell

Drive: 10 Cells per drive

Cell: 20 subcells per cell

Figure 9-32   (Courtesy IBM Corporation)

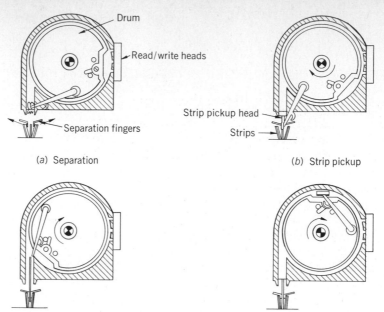

(a) Separation

(b) Strip pickup

(c) Strip withdrawal

(d) Pickup head latched to drum

Figure 9-33 Strip pickup cycle (courtesy IBM Corporation)

Figure 9-34 RCA mass storage unit (courtesy RCA)

07	08	09	10	11
Write contents of address 01 into arithmetic unit	Multiply contents of arithmetic unit by contents of address 02	Duplicate preceding answer in address 05	Multiply contents of address 03 by preceding answer in arithmetic unit	Add contents of address 04 to preceding answer in arithmetic unit

Figure 9-35 (*Source: Figure 8-4*)

same instructions may be coded and stored for PAC's convenience. The first processing instruction, CLA 01, tells PAC to <u>CL</u>ear the contents of the arithmetic-logic unit of all data and to <u>A</u>dd (store) the contents of address 01 to a register known as the *accumulator*. Thus, 40 hours—the contents of address 01—are now held in both address 01 and the accumulator (Fig. 9-37a).

The second instruction in address 08 is MUL 02. The computer interprets this instruction to mean that the contents of address 02 ($5) are to be <u>MUL</u>tiplied by the contents in the accumulator (40 hours) to get Aardvark's gross pay. Execution of this instruction may take the following form (Fig. 9-37b):

1. The contents of address 02 are read into a storage register[10] in the arithmetic-logic unit.
2. The contents of the accumulator and the contents of the storage register are given to the *adder*. The *adder* (and its associated circuits) is the primary arithmetic element because it also performs subtraction, multiplication, and division on binary digits.
3. The product of the multiplication *is stored in the accumulator.* The 40 hours previously there has been erased by the arithmetic operation.

The third instruction in the processing sequence is STO 05. The contents in the accumulator are <u>STO</u>red in address 05. The read-in to address 05 is destructive to any information that might be there. The read-out from the accumulator is nondestructive (Fig. 9-37c). The fourth instruction, MUL 03, is handled exactly like the second instruction, so we need not repeat the execution.

The fifth instruction in the sequence, ADD 04, simply tells the computer to ADD the contents of address 04 to the contents of the

---

[10]This register is sometimes called a *distributor*. Some machines move data directly from storage to the adder. We will say more about this in a few paragraphs.

07	08	09	10	11
CLA 01	MUL 02	STO 05	MUL 03	ADD 04

Figure 9-36

Figure 9-37

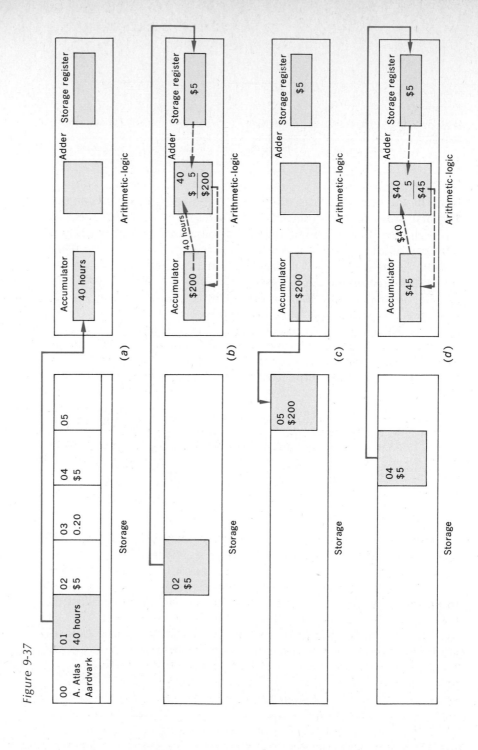

accumulator. The hospitalization insurance deduction of $5 is the contents of 04; the tax deduction of $40 is now the contents of the accumulator. Why? Because when the fourth instruction is carried out, the $200 in the accumulator is multiplied by 20 percent (the contents of 03) to get a product, which is then stored in the accumulator. As Fig. 9-37*d* shows, the contents of 04 are read into the storage register (thus erasing the previous contents); the adder totals the contents of the accumulator and the storage register; and the sum is stored in the accumulator.

It is apparent that every arithmetic operation requires two numbers and some result. Subtraction, for example, requires a minuend and a subtrahend to find a difference; multiplication uses a multiplicand and a multiplier to find a product. Although obviously two numbers and a result are handled by every computer arithmetic-logic unit, different processing and storage approaches have been developed to manage the two data words and the result.

You may recall from Chapter 8 that computations in variable word-length machines are on two digits at a time (in a serial fashion) while fixed word-length processors operate on two *groups* of digits at a time (in a parallel mode). A variable word-length business computer may perform calculations through a *storage-to-storage* approach; i.e., a digit or byte from each of two variable-length data words A and B may be moved from *primary storage* to the arithmetic-logic unit, operated on, and the result may be *returned* to the primary storage location originally occupied by data word A (Fig. 9-38). This approach, as we have seen in Chapter 8, is slower, but less expensive circuitry may be used and more flexible use of storage may be possible.

Fixed word-length computers may transfer data words from primary storage to a varying number of registers. Data from two such registers, e.g., the storage register and accumulator, may be operated on in parallel. The result may be stored in a register or moved back to a primary storage location, as shown in Fig. 9-37. Current processors that use both variable-length words for business applications and fixed-length words for scientific applications must have, of course, arithmetic-logic circuitry and registers that permit the handling of either type of application. The IBM System/360 series, for example, permits the use of the storage-to-storage approach for business processing but also makes 16 general purpose registers available for fixed word-length applications.

Logic operations usually consist of comparisons. The arithmetic-logic unit may compare two numbers by subtracting one from the other. The sign (negative or positive) and the value of the difference

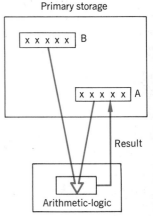

Figure 9-38 Storage-to-storage approach

tell the processor that the first number is equal to, less than, or greater than the second number. Three branches may be provided in the program for the computer to follow, depending on the result of such a comparison. Many processors are designed with a *comparer* in the arithmetic-logic unit. Data from an accumulator and a storage register may be examined by the comparer to yield the logic decision. Alphabetic data may also be compared according to an order sequence.

THE CONTROL UNIT

The control unit of the processor *selects, interprets,* and *executes* the program instructions. The arithmetic-logic unit responds to commands coming from the control unit. There are at least two parts to any instruction: the *operation,* or *command,* that is to be followed (for example, ADD, SUB, MUL, and GO TO) and the *address,* which locates the data or instructions to be manipulated. The basic components contained in the PAC control unit are the *instruction register, sequence register,*[11] *address register,* and *decoder.*

Let us trace an instruction through the PAC control unit to see how it is handled. We shall again use Aardvark's pay data along with the payroll program shown in Fig. 9-36. Let us assume that the instruction in address 07 has just been executed and that forty hours is the contents of the accumulator. The following steps are performed in the next *operating cycle* (the circled numbers in Fig. 9-39 correspond to these steps):

1. The instruction in address 08 (MUL 02) is *selected* by the *sequence register* and read into the *instruction register* in the control unit. (The sequence register does not store the instruction. We shall have more to say about the sequence register in step 5 below.)
2. The operation part of the instruction (MUL) and the address part (02) are *separated.* The operation is sent to the decoder where it is *interpreted.* The computer is built to respond to a limited number of commands, and it now knows that it is to multiply.
3. The address part of the instruction is sent to the *address register.*
4. The signal to move the contents of address 02 into the arithmetic-logic unit is sent; the command to multiply goes to the arithmetic-logic unit where the instruction is *executed.*
5. As the multiplication is being executed, the sequence register in the control unit is increased by one to indicate the location of the next instruction address. When the program was started, the

---

[11] The instruction register is also called the *operation register* and the *control register,* while the sequence register is sometimes referred to as the *control counter* or *instruction counter.*

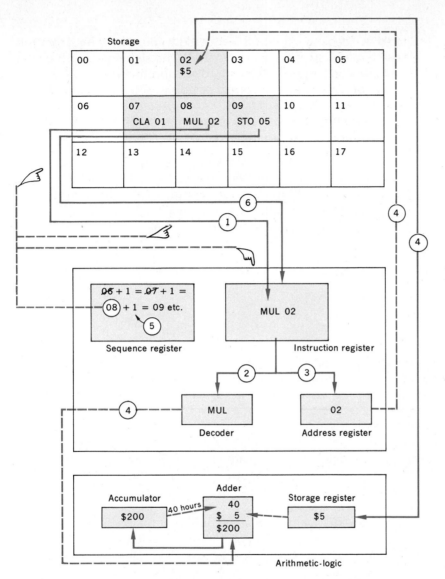

Figure 9-39

sequence register was set to the address of the first instruction by the programmer. By the time the first program instruction was finished, the contents of the sequence register had automatically been advanced to the next instruction address number. In other words, the first address in the payroll program was 06 (read data in), and the sequence register was set to 06. As that instruction was being executed, the sequence register automatically moved to 07 and then to 08, and now it is again automatically moved to 09. It keeps this up until instructed to do otherwise. From the last chapter you will recall that when the sequence register gets to address 17, it encounters an instruction that reads GO TO 06. This command alters the normal stepping of the sequence register and resets it at address 06.

6.   The instruction at address 09 moves into the instruction register, and the above steps are repeated.

We may identify separate processor phases, or cycles, in the above procedure. Step 4 is the *execution cycle*. The other steps comprise the *instruction cycle*. Thus, there are two phases in the performance of each instruction. Computers are generally *synchronous;* i.e., the various operations are synchronized by an electronic clock, which emits millions of regularly spaced electronic pulses each second. Commands are interpreted and executed at proper intervals, and the intervals are timed by a specified number of these pulses.

SUMMARY

Primary and secondary storage devices may be measured and evaluated in terms of their speed, storage capacity, safety, record accessibility, and cost. Business managers often find it desirable to combine several approaches to get a package that suits the needs of their company.

The fastest storage units are typically found internally in the CPU. Primary storage is often provided by planes of magnetic cores; however, planar thin films and plated-wire units are also available in high-speed computers. In the future, thin films and LSI circuit storage are likely to replace cores in popularity. Primary storage is the most expensive per character stored.

Secondary storage units may be online or offline. Speed is generally sacrificed and cost per character stored is frequently reduced as mass storage capacity is increased. Offline secondary storage is usually preferred by business managers when serial or batch processing methods are suitable. When direct, rapid accessibility to any file record is most desirable, online secondary storage is chosen. A manager may choose among the magnetic drums, disks, and cards or strips equipment that offers the best characteristics of speed, capacity, and cost for his particular needs.

The arithmetic-logic unit does the actual processing under program control. During the execution cycle, data stored in primary storage or in registers are moved to the arithmetic-logic unit. There they are manipulated by adder circuits to yield a result that may be stored in a register (e.g., the accumulator) or transferred to some other storage location. The control unit selects, interprets, and sees to the execution of instructions in their proper sequence. Several basic registers are required to perform the control function.

1. Distinguish between online and offline external storage.
2. Define the following terms:
    (a) Access time
    (b) Nonvolatile storage
    (c) Destructive read-in
    (d) Sense wire
    (e) Inhibit wire
    (f) Addressable bulk storage
    (g) Random access time
    (h) Disk pack
    (i) Register
    (j) Synchronous computer
    (k) Read-only storage
    (l) 16K storage capacity
    (m) Execution cycle
3. What factors should be considered in determining the data storage facilities that are needed?
4. "With auxiliary storage units there is frequently an inverse relationship between speed and cost per character stored, on the one hand, and storage capacity, on the other." Explain and give examples.
5. (a) How is information stored in ferromagnetic cores? (b) Once stored, how is it retrieved?
6. Why may core storage become less popular in the future?
7. (a) What factors determine direct-access time of magnetic drums?
    (b) What factors determine direct-access time of magnetic disks?
8. Compare magnetic cards or strips with magnetic tape.
9. (a) What is the accumulator?
    (b) What is the adder?
10. "Current processors permit the use of the *storage-to-storage approach* for business processing." Explain this sentence.
11. Define and explain the function of (a) the instruction register, (b) the sequence register, (c) the address register, and (d) the decoder.

DISCUSSION QUESTIONS

SELECTED REFERENCES   Brown, David W., and James L. Burkhardt: "The Computer Memory Market," *Computers and Automation,* January, 1969, pp. 24ff.

Evans, David C.: "Computer Logic and Memory," *Scientific American,* September, 1966, pp. 75–85.

Withington, Frederic G.: "Trends in MIS Technology," *Datamation,* February, 1970, pp. 108–110ff.

Programming
Analysis

In the past four chapters, attention has been focused primarily on computer hardware. But hardware alone does not solve a single business problem. As Fig. 10-1 indicates, there are usually many activities that lie between the realization of a need for information and the use of computer hardware to satisfy the need on a regular basis. Until the processor is given a detailed set of problem-solving instructions, it is merely an expensive and space-consuming curiosity.

The procedure to be followed in using computers to process business problems involves a number of steps:

1. *Definition of the problem and the objectives.* The particular problem to be solved, or the tasks to be accomplished, must be clearly identified; the objectives of managers in having the tasks performed must be known. Identifying the problem and the objectives seems to be an obvious step, but it is sometimes overlooked with unfortunate results.

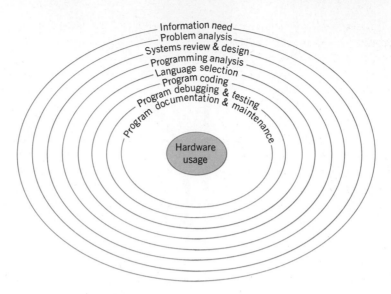

Figure 10-1

2. *Problem analysis*. Data pertaining to the problem must be gathered, organized, and interpreted. Tasks currently being performed by noncomputer methods should be examined. From this analysis may come a recognition of computer potential, i.e., a recognition that the problem could justifiably be processed with a computer.

3. *System review and design*. The present procedures should be reviewed to determine what improvements are possible. These procedures should be redesigned to meet the current needs of the business. Broad system specifications should outline the scope of the problem, the form and type of input data to be used, and the form and type of output required.

4. *Programming analysis*. The broadly defined system specifications must be broken down into the specific arithmetic and logic operations required to solve the problem.

5. *Program preparation*. The specific steps must next be translated or coded into a language and form acceptable to the processor.

6. *Program debugging and testing*. The coded program must be checked for errors and tested prior to being used on a routine basis to ensure that the correct problem is being solved and that correct results are being produced.

7. *Program documentation and maintenance*. Conversion to the new approach must be made; the program must be properly stored when not in use; it must be described in writing (and supporting written documents must also be developed and kept on file); and it must be revised and maintained as company needs change.

The purpose of this chapter and the two that follow is to survey the process of programming briefly. As used in this text, *programming* is defined as the *process* of converting broad system specifications into usable machine programs of instruction. In short, programming consists of the final four steps in the above procedure.[1] In this chapter we will look at *programming analysis;* in Chapters 11 and 12 *program preparation, debugging and testing,* and *documentation and maintenance* will be examined. It is assumed that the first three steps of the above procedure—the *systems analysis* phase—have been completed. We shall look more closely at these three very important steps in Chapter 14. Figure 10-2 summarizes (1) the steps involved in using computers to process business problems and (2) the organizational outline of the text in discussing these steps.

Two common tools used for analysis purposes are the *flowchart* and the *decision table.*

INTRODUCTION TO COMMON TOOLS OF ANALYSIS

Flowcharts

Flowcharts have existed for a number of years and have been used for a variety of purposes. For example, Figure 10-3 shows in graphical form the logic that might be involved in getting a haircut. As used in business data processing, however, a flowchart is a graphic tool

[1] Sometimes the term *programming* is used to refer only to program preparation, or *coding* (step 5 above). But programming here is considered as a problem-solving series of steps. It is a time-consuming and error-prone process that does not begin and end with the writing of lines of code on a sheet of paper. In larger organizations the systems specifications are prepared by systems analysts and the later steps are generally handled by programmers and computer operators. Close cooperation is, of course, required.

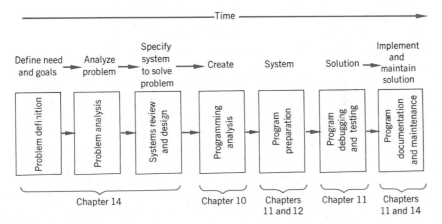

Figure 10-2   Procedure for solving problems with computers

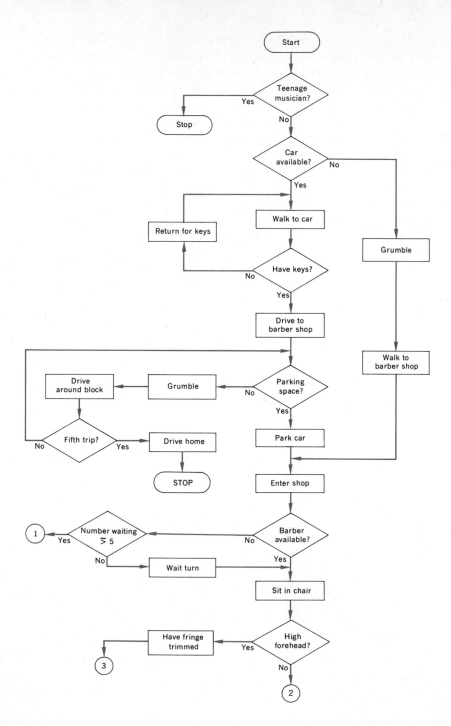

Figure 10-3   How to get a haircut

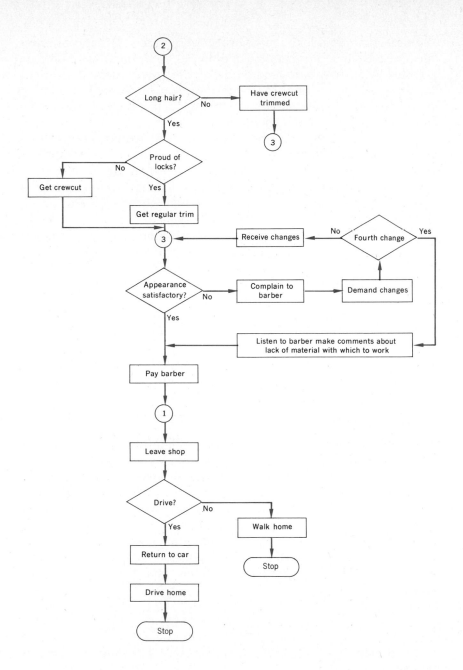

or model that provides a means of recording, analyzing, and communicating problem information. For example, appropriate symbols may be used by an analyst to *record* quickly the flow of data in a current business procedure from the originating source, through a number of processing operations and machines, to the output report. The flowchart *picture,* or schematic, may assist the analyst in acquiring a better understanding of the procedure than would otherwise be possible. It may also aid in procedure *analysis* and then in improvement, e.g., it may point out bottlenecks that may be eliminated in the flow of data. Flowcharts are frequently used to *communicate* the essential facts of a business problem to others whose skills are needed in the solution.

Here we shall be interested in two basic kinds of flowcharts. The *system flowchart* provides a broad overview of the processing operations that are to be accomplished. Primary emphasis is placed on data flow among machines, i.e., on input documents and output reports. The amount of detail furnished about *how* a machine is to convert the data on input documents into the desired output is limited. A *program flowchart,* on the other hand, does present a detailed graphical representation of how steps are to be performed *within* the machine to produce the needed output. Thus, the program flowchart evolves from the system chart. In a following section we shall take a closer look at these two types of charts.

Decision Tables

A table that presents all the conditions or contingencies that are to be considered in the solution of a problem together with all the actions or decisions that may be taken is known as a *decision table.* Simply stated, a decision table is used to present the logic of a program. And because it does present program logic, it may be used as a substitute for or supplement to a *program* flowchart. Decision tables are especially useful when the program logic is such that a number of alternate paths, or branches, must be considered before the ultimate action can be taken. We shall return to the subject of decision tables later in the chapter.

FLOWCHARTING

System Flowcharts

In the design of all flowcharts it is necessary that standard *symbols* be used to record and communicate problem information clearly. In the past (and even today) a variety of shapes were used to represent the same concept, while users sometimes attached different meanings to the same symbol. In June, 1966, the American National Standards

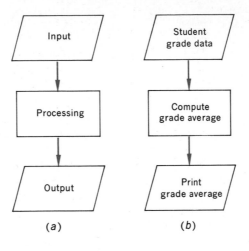

Figure 10-4 Basic system charting symbols

Institute,[2] as a means of reducing confusion, approved a set of symbols that could be used for systems and program flowcharts. These are the symbols that will be used in the remainder of the text.

Since system flowcharts emphasize inputs and outputs and are primarily designed to show the flow of data through the entire data processing system, symbols representing input, output, and general processing (Fig. 10-4a) are frequently used in them. The same basic I/O symbol may be used to show *any* type of media or data. The arrows connecting the shapes indicate the direction of data flow. The main flow is generally charted from top to bottom and from left to right. The *shape* of the symbol and *not its size* identifies the meaning. For example, the rectangular processing box may vary in size, but the shape still designates that processing is being performed. Notation within the charting symbol further explains what is being done (Fig. 10-4b).

Frequently, the basic I/O symbol is *replaced* in system flowcharts by other I/O symbols whose shape suggests the type of media or device being employed (Fig. 10-5). These symbols are familiar to us since they have been used in earlier chapters. Additional commonly used system flowchart symbols are shown and described in Fig. 10-6. With these additional shapes, we may define in greater detail the chart shown in Fig. 10-4b. The problem involved is a simple one:[3] Professor Balford Sheet, an accounting professor, wishes to compute an average

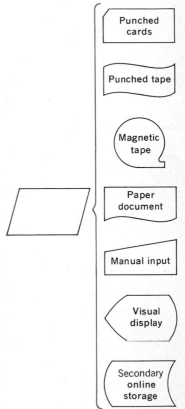

Figure 10-5 I/O substitution symbols

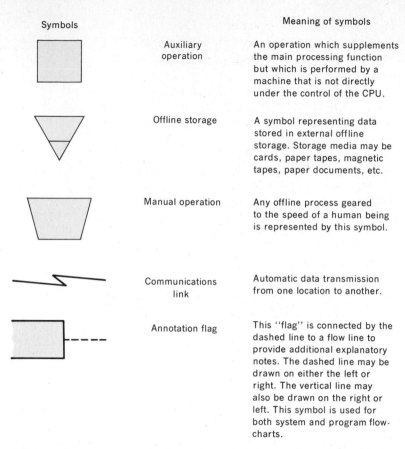

Symbols		Meaning of symbols
	Auxiliary operation	An operation which supplements the main processing function but which is performed by a machine that is not directly under the control of the CPU.
	Offline storage	A symbol representing data stored in external offline storage. Storage media may be cards, paper tapes, magnetic tapes, paper documents, etc.
	Manual operation	Any offline process geared to the speed of a human being is represented by this symbol.
	Communications link	Automatic data transmission from one location to another.
	Annotation flag	This "flag" is connected by the dashed line to a flow line to provide additional explanatory notes. The dashed line may be drawn on either the left or right. The vertical line may also be drawn on the right or left. This symbol is used for both system and program flowcharts.

Figure 10-6 Additional system flowchart symbols

(arithmetic mean) grade for a beginning accounting student based on the 35 tests he has given during the semester. (Professor Sheet teaches a rigorous course!) In Fig. 10-7 we see that the system followed by Bal Sheet is one in which the grade data for the student are punched into cards that are then fed into a computer for processing. The computed average is printed, and Professor Sheet manually updates his grade book and then prepares his final grade report on the student. We shall be concerned with only one student, but, of course, any number of student grade averages could easily be automatically processed by the computer.

Program Flowcharting

As we noted earlier, program flowcharts evolve from system flowcharts. In Bal Sheet's grade preparation diagram, a single processing box is labeled "compute grade average." Unfortunately, such an instruction is not sufficient for the computer. Thus, as a part of the programming process the programmer must specify each step needed to compute the average grade. In short, the *single* processing box labeled "compute grade average" becomes the basis for a detailed *program* flowchart.

Only a few symbols, when properly arranged, are needed in program charting to define the necessary steps. These symbols are illustrated in Fig. 10-8 and are described below.

Input/Output   The basic I/O symbol is also used in program flowcharting to represent any I/O function. The specific symbols designating cards, tapes, etc., are generally not used with program diagrams. Figure 10-9 presents a portion of a program chart (the total chart shows the steps required to compute the average grade by Professor Sheet). The I/O symbol designates that a punched card containing a student grade is to be read into the computer. The same symbol, of course, could be used to represent any output form.

Processing   Again, the rectangle represents processing operations. But now the processing described is a *small segment* of the major processing step called for in the system chart. Arithmetic and data movement instructions are generally placed in these boxes. Two processing symbols are shown in Fig. 10-9. The upper box provides for the accumulation of the total number of points in the CPU arithmetic-logic unit. Thus, when the last grade card has been read, the total of all the test scores will be stored in the accumulator. To get an average grade, as everyone knows, the total number of points must be divided by the number of tests taken. The lower processing box in Fig. 10-9 gives the denominator; the upper box, the numerator.

Termination   The terminal symbol, as the name suggests, represents the beginning and the end of a program. It may also be used to signal a program interruption point when information may enter or leave. For example, to detect certain errors in input data the programmer may provide a special program branch ending in a terminal symbol labeled "HALT."

Decision   The I/O and processing symbols, typically, have two flow lines (one entry and one exit), while the terminal has a single entrance or exit line. The diamond-shaped decision symbol, on the other hand, has one entrance line and *at least* two exit paths or branches. As Fig. 10-9 shows, exit paths may be determined by a yes or no answer to some stated condition—in this case, the condition to be determined is whether or not the last grade card has been processed. If the answer

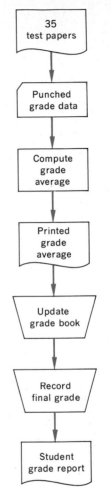

Figure 10-7 Grade preparation system

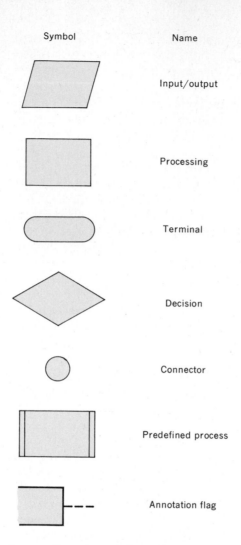

Symbol   Name

Input/output

Processing

Terminal

Decision

Connector

Predefined process

Annotation flag

Figure 10-8 Program flowchart symbols

is yes, then the total of all test scores is contained in the accumulator and the program can branch away from the *loop* that it has been following by reading cards and totaling scores successively. If the answer is no, the program continues to process the grade cards until they are all accounted for. Decision boxes are also used to show the result of a *test* or a *comparison* (Fig. 10-10).

Connector The *circular connector* symbol is used when additional flow lines might cause confusion and reduce understanding. Two connectors with identical labels serve the same function as a long flow line; i.e., they show an entry from another part of the chart, or

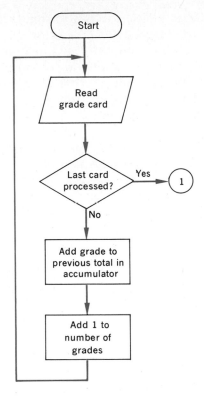

Figure 10-9

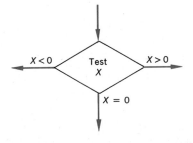

The number X is shown being tested to determine whether it is equal to zero, greater than ($>$) zero, or less than ($<$) zero, i.e., a negative value.

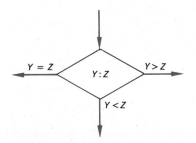

In this case, the two variables Y and Z are compared ("$Y:Z$" means to "compare Y to Z").

Figure 10-10   Decision symbol examples

they indicate an exit to some other chart section. How is it possible to determine if a connector is used as an entry point or an exit point? It is very simple: If an arrow *enters but does not leave a connector,* it is an exit point and program flow is transferred to that identically labeled connector that *does* have an outlet. Two connector symbols labeled "3" were used in the haircut example chart earlier in the chapter to represent a junction point and eliminate confusing lengthy flow lines.

Figure 10-11 completes the chart begun in Fig. 10-9 and shows the program steps that must be performed by Professor Bal Sheet to compute the average grade. This chart also illustrates the use of connector symbols. As we have seen, when the last card is processed, the computer is ready to figure the average grade. This step is per-

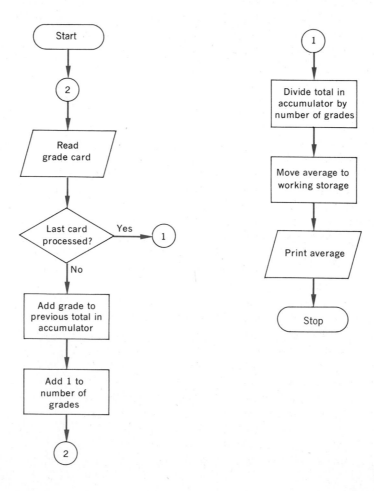

Figure 10-11   Program flowchart to average grades

formed by the first processing instruction below the upper connector labeled "1." The remaining steps in the chart are self-explanatory.

Predefined process   Programmers frequently find that certain kinds of processing operations are repeated in one or more of the programs used by their company. For example, a department store programmer may find that the steps needed to compute cash discounts are being repeated several times in some programs and used in a number of different programs. Instead of rewriting this small subordinate routine each time it is needed, the programmer can prepare it once and then integrate it into the program or programs as required. *Libraries* of these predefined processes, or *subroutines,* are often maintained to reduce the cost and time of programming. Thus, a single predefined process symbol replaces a number of operations that are not detailed at that particular point in the chart. In short, the subroutine receives input from the primary program, performs its limited task, and then returns the output to the primary program.

Annotation flag   The comments made in Fig. 10-6 also apply to program flowcharts.

The following *benefits* may be obtained through the use of flowcharts:

Benefits and Limitations of Flowcharts

1. *Quicker grasp of relationships*. Before any problem can be solved, it must be understood. The relationships that exist among problem elements must be identified. Current and proposed procedures may be understood more rapidly through the use of charts. It is usually quicker and easier for an analyst or programmer to chart a lengthy procedure than it is for him to describe it by means of pages of written notes. Thus, more time may be devoted to acquiring understanding.
2. *Effective analysis*. The flowchart becomes a model of a program or system that can be broken down into detailed parts for study. Problems may be identified; new approaches may be suggested.
3. *Effective synthesis*. Synthesis is the opposite of analysis; it is the combination of the various parts into a whole entity. Flowcharts may be used as working models in the design of new programs and systems. Elements of old approaches may be combined with new design ideas to give an effective processing plan.
4. *Communication*. Flowcharts aid in communicating the facts of a business problem to those whose skills are needed in the solution. The old adage that "a picture is worth a thousand words"

contains an element of truth when the pictures happen to be flowchart symbols.

5. *Proper program documentation.* Program *documentation* involves collecting, organizing, storing, and otherwise maintaining a complete historical record of programs and the other business documents associated with the firm's data processing systems. Proper program documentation is needed for the following reasons:

(a) Documented knowledge belongs to an organization and does not disappear with the departure of a programmer.

(b) If projects are postponed, proper documentation, which indicates the problem definition, task objective, extent of prior work, etc., will not have to be duplicated.

(c) If programs are modified in the future (and modification occurs in many cases), proper documentation will brief the programmer on what was originally done and will thus help him to understand the problem better.

(d) When staff changes occur, proper documentation serves a training function by helping new employees understand existing programs.

(e) Proper documentation will aid greatly in future program conversion when new hardware/software packages are acquired.

(f) Poor documentation represents a fundamental weakness in internal control and is an indication of poor management.

From what we have seen of the nature of flowcharts, it is obvious that they provide valuable documentation support for all but the simplest of programs.

6. *Efficient coding.* The program flowchart acts as a guide or blueprint during the program preparation phase. Instructions coded in a programming language may be checked against the flowchart to make sure that no steps are omitted.

7. *Orderly debugging and testing of programs.* If the program fails to run to completion when submitted to the computer for execution, the flowchart may help in the *debugging* process; i.e., it may help in detecting, locating, and removing mistakes. The programmer can refer to the chart as he rechecks the coding steps and logic of the written instructions. If, during a test utilizing data that produce known answers, the program runs but delivers incorrect results, the flowchart may again help to detect errors and oversights.

8. *Efficient program maintenance.* The maintenance (through necessary modification) of operating programs is facilitated by flowcharts. The chart helps the programmer concentrate his attention on that part of the information flow which is to be modified.

In spite of their many obvious advantages, flowcharts have a few *limitations*. The first is that complex and detailed charts are sometimes laborious to plan and draw, especially when a large number of decision paths are involved.[4] A second limitation in such a situation is that although branches from a *single* decision symbol are easy to follow, the actions to be taken given certain specified conditions would be difficult to follow if there were *several* paths.

The flowchart in Fig. 10-12 shows how a department store handles the billing of *overdue* accounts. A late payment penalty is charged to accounts thirty or more days overdue.[5] The amount of the penalty is based on the unpaid balance in the account: If the balance is *over* $200, i.e., if the balance is *not* equal to or less than ($\leq$) $200, the penalty is 3 percent; otherwise a 2 percent charge is levied. The amount of the penalty must be added to the next bill sent to the customer. If the account is sixty days or more overdue ($\geq$60), a warning message is printed on the bill. Accounts which are *less than* thirty days overdue ($<$30) are not included in this procedure. But in the event that such an account is entered by mistake, provision is made to prevent it from being processed. The store's credit manager handles, on an individual basis, those accounts that remain unpaid after a certain time.[6]

Although the procedure in Fig. 10-12 is relatively simple, it is not immediately obvious, for example, what actions would be taken if a particular account with a balance of $300 were sixty days or more overdue. (What actions *would* be taken?) Of course, with more complex problems the appropriate actions become much more obscure when flowcharts are used. Under such circumstances, flowcharts may be replaced or supplemented by decision tables.

DECISION TABLES

A *decision table* can be a powerful tool for defining complex program logic. Figure 10-13 shows the basic table format. The table is divided by the bottom horizontal heavy line into two main parts: the upper part, which contains the *conditions and questions* that are to be considered in reaching a decision; and the lower part, which contains

[4]During the program preparation stage, sections of original charts may be added to, deleted, patched, and otherwise marked up to the point where they become nearly illegible. Since considerable time and effort could be required to manually redraw complex charts, special automatic flowcharting programs have been developed, which use a high-speed printer to produce the charts in good form.

[5]In Fig. 10-12, the symbol $\geq$ means *equal to or greater than*. Therefore $\geq$ 30 refers to accounts equal to or greater than thirty days overdue. Similarly, $\leq$ means *equal to or less than*.

[6]This accounts-receivable penalty procedure will also be traced through further steps in the programming process.

the prescribed *action* to be taken when a given set of conditions is present.

The conditions and questions are written in the *condition stub* to the left of the vertical heavy line. The contents of the condition stub correspond to the statements and questions contained in the

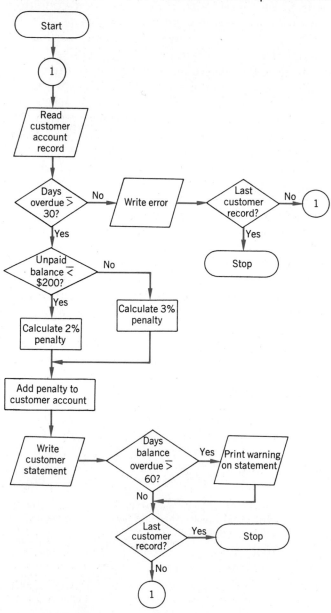

Figure 10-12   Accounts receivable penalty procedure

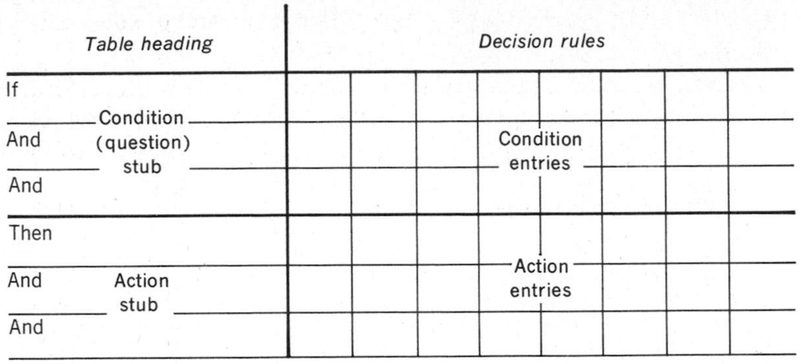

Figure 10-13   Decision table format

decision *symbols* of the flowchart; the *condition entries* to the right of the heavy vertical line in the figure correspond to the branches or *paths* going out from decision symbols in a flowchart. Thus a condition entry may be a simple yes (Y) or no (N); it may be a symbol which shows relationship between variables ($>$, $<$, $=$, $\geq$, etc.); or it may be the outcome of certain tests (code 1, code 2, etc.). The *action statements,* which correspond to the action statements located in nondecision symbols of a flowchart, are written in the *action stub.* The conditions may be listed in any convenient order; the actions are listed in the order in which they are normally executed. To briefly summarize, the upper (condition) parts of a decision table are generally concerned with "IF" statements (which are made or implied) and with the responses to those IF statements, while the lower (action) quadrants deal with "THEN" statements and responses to the specified conditions. In short, IF certain conditions exist, THEN specified actions should be taken.

A maze of possible flow paths may exist between START and STOP in a program. *Each* of the columns in the table *body* is the equivalent of *one* path through the flowchart and is called a *rule.* When a table is completed, each rule column which is used contains one or more condition entries. An example should help clarify matters.

Figure 10-14 shows the decision table for the accounts-receivable penalty procedure charted in Fig. 10-12. You will notice that the statements in the condition stub correspond to the questions being asked in the flowchart decision symbols. You will also note that the action statements correspond to the directions given or implied by the other flowchart symbols. A few paragraphs earlier this question was asked: What actions would be taken if an account with a balance of $300 were sixty days or more overdue? Let us now look at column 6 (which follows that particular path through the flowchart) to check the answer. The first entry in the column shows that the account is

		Decision *Rule number*						
Accounts receivable penalty procedure		1	2	3	4	5	6	7
Condition	Number days balance overdue	< 30	< 30	⩾ 30	⩾ 30	⩾ 60	⩾ 60	
	Number days balance overdue			< 60	< 60			
	Unpaid balance ⩽ $200?			Y	N	Y	N	
	Last customer account record?	N	Y	N	N	N	N	Y
Action	Calculate 2% penalty			x		x		
	Calculate 3% penalty				x		x	
	Add penalty to customer account			x	x	x	x	
	Write customer statement			x	x	x	x	
	Print warning on statement					x	x	
	Write error	x	x					
	Go to next account record	x		x	x	x	x	
	Stop		x					x

Figure 10-14   Decision table for accounts receivable penalty procedure (Source: Figure 10-12)

sixty days or more overdue. The second condition is irrelevant in this case, and so the space in rule 6 is left blank. The second entry tells us that the unpaid balance is not equal to or less than $200, and so therefore it must be greater than that figure. The third entry merely shows that the last record has not yet been processed. Thus, the set of conditions in rule 6 has defined our problem! (The other condition sets have defined all the other feasible paths or situations.)

Now what about the *answer* to the problem? An x has been placed in column 6 opposite each appropriate action that helps satisfy the given set of conditions. You can compare your answer with the one indicated in Fig. 10-14. You may also want to trace through the table and the flowchart to see what actions are taken when other possible conditions occur.

In our simple example we have compared a decision table with the flowchart of the problem. But in actual practice, tables are not necessarily compared with charts. Why? Simply because there may be no flowchart. As noted earlier, tables may be used as chart substitutes. A number of small interconnected tables may be quickly constructed to express the logic required to solve complex problems.

The following benefits may be obtained through the use of decision tables:

1. *Less danger of omitting a logical possibility.* Tables force the analyst to think the problem through. For example, if there are three conditions to be considered, each of which can be answered yes or no, then there are 2^3 or 8 possible paths or rules.[7] Some of these conceivable paths may not, of course, be pertinent to the problem. But by knowing the total number of paths, the analyst lessens the danger of forgetting one.

2. *Better communication between interested parties.* Tables can perform a valuable communication function. An analyst may design a new system and present it in the form of a table or tables to other analysts, programmers, and managers and executives. The table format is easily followed by others. Flowchart symbols, on the other hand, are not always standardized, and this factor may hinder their communication value. Tables appear to be easier for many managers to follow than flowcharts. An operating manager can quickly trace and verify those paths in the procedure that are of greatest interest to him.

3. *Easier construction and adaptability.* Tables are easier to draw up than comparable flowcharts. They are also easier to change since it is a relatively simple matter to add conditions, rules, and actions to a table.

4. *More compact program documentation.* Several pages of flow charting may be condensed into one small table. And, of course, it is easier to follow a particular flow path down one column than it is to follow the same path through several flowchart pages.

5. *Direct conversion into computer programs.* It is possible for the contents of a decision table to be coded directly into a language that the computer understands. For example, DETAB/65 (DETAB stands for DEcision TABle, while 65 refers to 1965) is a software aid that converts table contents directly into programs written in the COBOL language.[8]

Decision tables appear to have an edge over flowcharts in expressing complex decision logic. However, they are not as widely used as flowcharts because (1) many problems are simple, have few branches, and lend themselves to charting; (2) charts are able to

---

[7]These rules contain the following entries:

(1)	(2)	(3)	(4)	(5)	(6)	(7)	(8)
Y	Y	Y	N	Y	N	N	N
Y	Y	N	Y	N	Y	N	N
Y	N	Y	Y	N	N	Y	N

[8]COBOL stands for COmmon Business Oriented Language and will be discussed in the next two chapters.

express the *total sequence* of events better; and (3) charts are familiar to, and preferred by, many programmers who resist changing to the use of tables.[9]

SUMMARY

Before a computer can be used to solve a business problem, the problem itself must be defined. Problem data must be gathered, organized, and analyzed. From problem analysis may come ideas for improvement of old methods. New approaches to problem solving may be designed. Once broad system specifications have been determined, the programming process may begin. The first step in programming is to break the broad specifications down into specific arithmetic and logic operations. The remaining steps are to (1) prepare programs in a form that the processor can accept, (2) test the new programs, and (3) implement and maintain them as needed. These remaining steps will be considered in the next two chapters.

The basic tools of programming analysis are flowcharts and decision tables. System flowcharts provide the broad overview required for programming analysis to begin. Program flowcharts evolve from the system charts. A set of standardized charting symbols is presented in Figs. 10-4 to 10-6. When compared with pages of written notes, flowcharts help the programmer obtain a quicker grasp of relationships. Charts also aid in communication, provide valuable documentation support, and contribute to more efficient coding and program maintenance.

A decision table is an excellent means of defining complex program logic. In this respect it has an edge over flowcharts. A table is easy to construct and change. It is more compact, provides excellent program documentation, and is an aid in communication.

DISCUSSION
QUESTIONS

1. Identify and discuss the steps that must be followed to use computers to process business data.
2. (a) What is a system flowchart? (b) How is it used?
3. (a) What symbols are used in system flowcharts to represent input and output? (b) To represent a manual operation?
4. (a) What is the purpose of a program flowchart? (b) How does it differ from a systems flowchart?

[9]There are a number of reasons for such resistance. One is that if tables were used, new techniques and habits would have to be acquired and programmers, like the rest of us, prefer to stay with familiar methods. Also, it is easy to see that some programmers, familiar with such software aids as DETAB/65, might feel that tables were a threat to their position.

5. (a) What symbols are used in a program flowchart to represent input and output, processing, decision, terminal, and connector? (b) Construct a flowchart on a problem of your choice using these symbols.
6. What is a subroutine?
7. Discuss the benefits and limitations of flowcharts.
8. Why is proper documentation required?
9. (a) What is a decision table? (b) Explain the basic parts of the decision table. (c) What is a rule?
10. What benefits may be obtained from the use of decision tables?

SELECTED REFERENCES

Chesebrough, Wilfred C.: "Decision Tables as a Systems Technique," *Computers and Automation,* April, 1970, pp. 30–33.

Honeywell Information Systems, Inc.: *An Introduction to Decision Tables,* Wellesley Hills, Mass., 1969.

Rudolph, Harley H., Jr.: "Flow Charting: A Systems and Control Technique," *Management Services,* September-October, 1966, pp. 24–30.

Program
Preparation

As we saw in the last chapter, the programming process begins with the broad systems specifications. The programmer analyzes these specifications in terms of (1) the *output solution* needed, (2) the *operations and procedures* required to achieve the necessary output, and (3) the *input data* that are necessary to produce the output. In connection with this analysis, the programmer develops a programming plan and prepares program flowcharts and/or decision tables which detail the procedures for converting input data into output information. Once the analysis phase is completed, the next step is to prepare the written instructions that will control the computer during the processing. These instructions must be coded in a language that the computer can accept and according to a specific set of rules. Once the instructions have been prepared, they must be tested prior to use on a routine basis. All supporting documents pertaining to the problem and the program solution must be assembled and put in good

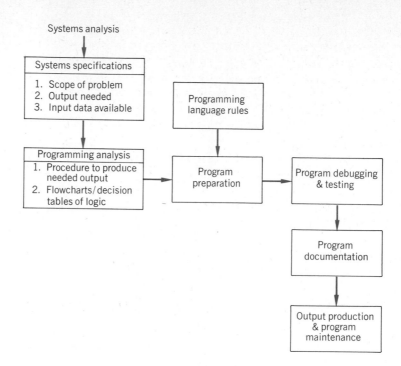

Figure 11-1   Programming process

order. Figure 11-1 summarizes this brief review of the programming process.

The purpose of this chapter and the one that follows is not, of course, to make a programmer of the reader; entire books have been written that have this as their objective. Rather, the purpose here is to give the reader an idea of what a programming language is and what is involved in expressing problems in a language that is acceptable to a computer. Therefore, in the following pages we shall look at (1) the *computer instruction,* (2) *languages for computers,* (3) *program coding,* (4) *program debugging and testing,* (5) *program documentation and maintenance,* and (6) *programming aids.* In the next chapter we shall expand on the program coding topic by showing how simple problems (which are now familiar to us) might be prepared for computer processing using several of the most popular programming languages.

THE COMPUTER INSTRUCTION

A program, we know, is a complete set of written instructions that enables the computer to process a particular application. Thus, the instruction is the fundamental component in program preparation.

Like a sentence, an instruction prepared in a basic form consists of a subject and a predicate. The subject, however, is usually *not* specifically mentioned; it is, instead, some *implied* part of the computer system that is directed to execute the command that is given. For example, if a teacher tells a student to "read the book," the student will interpret this instruction correctly even though the subject "you" is omitted. Similarly, if the machine is told to "ADD 0184," the control unit may interpret this to mean that the arithmetic-logic unit is to add the contents of address 0184 to the contents of the accumulator.

In addition to an implied subject, every basic computer instruction has an explicit predicate consisting of at least two parts. The *first* part is referred to as the *command,* or *operation;* it answers the question "what?"; i.e., it tells the computer what operation it is to perform. Each machine has a limited number of built-in operations that it is capable of executing. An *operation code* is used to communicate the programmer's intent to the machine. Operation codes vary from one machine line to another. In the IBM System/360 line, for example, the machine "op codes" for ADD, LOAD, and STORE are 5A, 58, and 50.

The *second* explicit part of the instruction, known as the *operand,* names the object of the operation. In general terms, the operand answers the question "where?"; i.e., it tells the computer where to find or store the data or other instructions that are to be manipulated. Thus, an operand may indicate:

1. The location where data to be processed are to be found.
2. The location where the result of processing is to be stored.
3. The location where the next instruction to be executed is to be found. (When this type of operand is not specified, the instructions are taken in sequence.)

The *number* of operands and therefore the structure or format of the instruction *vary* from one computer to another. Up to this point we have dealt only with instructions having a *single* operand. But in addition to the *single-address* format there are also *two-* and *three-address* command structures.

In earlier chapters we have seen that several instructions may be required to complete an arithmetic operation when a single-address format is used. For example, Fig. 11-2a shows the procedure that may be required to add two numbers and store the result. Figure 11-2b shows how an addition may be handled in a two-address machine, while Fig. 11-2c demonstrates a three-address instruction format. The three-address design is well suited to arithmetic operations, which, by their nature, normally require two values to yield a third. Yet for

Command Code	Meaning	Operand	Explanation
(1) XX	(CLA)	0184	Three steps are used to perform an addition
(2) XX	(ADD)	8672	and a storage operation. The accumulator is
(3) XX	(STO)	1273	cleared of previous data, and the number in

Three steps are used to perform an addition and a storage operation. The accumulator is cleared of previous data, and the number in address 0184 is then put in that register (1). The number in address 8672 is added to the first number. The result is now in the accumulator (2). The result in the accumulator is stored in address 1273 (3).

(a)

Command Code	Meaning	First operand	Second operand
(1) XX	(ADD)	0184	8672
(2) XX	(MOVE)	0184	0185
(3) XX	(ADD)	0184	8672

Explanation

The number in address 8672 is added to the number in location 0184. The result may automatically be stored in address 0184 by the computer circuitry. Of course, this erases the original number contained in 0184, so if that number is to be saved, it must be duplicated elsewhere *prior* to the add instruction. Instructions (2) and (3) show how this could be done. Instruction (2) duplicates the contents of 0184 in 0185 prior to the addition order (3).

(b)

Command Code	Meaning	First operand	Second operand	Third operand
(1) XX	(ADD)	0184	8672	1273

Explanation

The number in address 8672 is added to the number in 0184, and the result is stored in address 1273.

Figure 11-2 Command structures: (a) *single-address,* (b) *two-address,* (c) *three-address*

(c)

nonarithmetic operations, three operands may not be needed, and thus the design may waste storage space. Newer computers frequently have the ability to vary the length of the instruction word just as they have the ability to deal effectively with both fixed- and variable-length data words. However, the command always comes first in the instruction and is followed by the operand(s). Of course, the programmer must prepare his instructions according to the format required by the machine with which he is working.

The *execution* of program instructions was traced through the arithmetic-logic and control units in Chapter 9, and so we need not repeat that topic here. It is worth noting, however, that the number of registers in the arithmetic-logic and control units varies with the design of the instruction format.

The number of commands in a machine's repertoire may range from less than 30 to more than 100. These commands may be classified into input/output, data movement and manipulation, arithmetic, logic, and transfer of control categories. *Input/output* instructions are required to permit communication between I/O devices and the central processor. A number of *data movement and manipulation* commands are typically designed into the computer. These instructions involve the copying of data from one storage location to another and the rearranging and changing of data elements in some prescribed manner. An example of a data movement command is shown in Fig. 11-2*b*. If the programmer of the two-address processor wishes to preserve the number in address 0184 for future use, he must copy the number in another location prior to the add instruction. Data manipulation commands may also be provided that will combine several processing operations in a single instruction for the convenience of the programmer; e.g., a LOAD AND TEST command may combine data movement and logical operations.

The *arithmetic* commands to permit addition, subtraction, multiplication, and division are, of course, common in all digital computers. *Logic* instructions are available to permit comparison between variables. *Transfer of control* instructions may then be used to branch or change the sequence of program control, depending on the outcome of the comparison. Of course, some transfer instructions are not based on the outcome of comparisons. As we saw in Chapter 8, transfer commands may be *conditional* or *unconditional*. If the change in sequence is based on the outcome of a test or comparison, then it is a conditional transfer; if not, it is an unconditional branch.

Figure 11-3 presents a standard command repertoire for the IBM System/360 computer series. Instruction sets for several other lines have similarities. The operation codes are shown for each instruction. A symbolic code used by programmers to represent each instruction is also presented in Fig. 11-3.

Command Repertoire

In writing his program instructions, the programmer must use a language that can be understood by the computer. There are several approaches that can achieve man-machine communication. To illustrate these approaches, let us assume that the computer only understands Russian while the programmer's language is English. How can communication occur? One approach is for the programmer to code laboriously, with the help of a translating dictionary, each of his

LANGUAGES FOR COMPUTERS

Command name	OP code	Symbolic code	Type* of Command
Input/output commands			
Start I/O	9C	SIO	SI
Test I/O	9D	TIO	SI
Halt I/O	9E	HIO	SI
Test Channel	9F	TCH	SI
Data movement/manipulation commands			
Insert Character	43	IC	RX
Load Register	18	LR	RR
Load	58	L	RX
Load Address	41	LA	RX
Load and Test	12	LTR	RR
Load Complement	13	LCR	RR
Load Halfword	48	LH	RX
Load Multiple	98	LM	RS
Load Negative	11	LNR	RR
Load Positive	10	LPR	RR
Load PSW	82	LPSW	SI
Move Immediate	92	MVI	SI
Move Characters	D2	MVC	SS
Move Numerics	D1	MVN	SS
Move with Offset	F1	MVO	SS
Move Zones	D3	MVZ	SS
Pack	F2	PACK	SS
Unpack	F3	UNPK	SS
Shift Left Double	8F	SLDA	RS
Shift Left Single	8B	SLA	RS
Shift Left Double Logical	8D	SLDL	RS
Shift Left Single Logical	89	SLL	RS
Shift Right Double	8E	SRDA	RS
Shift Right Single	8A	SRA	RS
Shift Right Double Logical	8C	SRDL	RS
Shift Right Single Logical	88	SRL	RS
Store	50	ST	RX
Store Character	42	STC	RX
Store Halfword	40	STH	RX
Store Multiple	90	STM	RS
Test and Set	93	TS	SI
Test Under Mask	91	TM	SI
Translate	DC	TR	SS
Translate and Test	DD	TRT	SS
Edit	DE	ED	SS
Edit and Mark	DF	EDMK	SS
AND	54	N	RX
AND	14	NR	RR
AND	94	NI	SI
AND	D4	NC	SS

Figure 11-3   Command repertoire, IBM System/360 computers

instructions into Russian prior to giving them to the processor. This approach is fine from the machine's standpoint, but the programmer finds it awkward.

Another approach is a compromise between man and machine. The programmer first writes his instructions in a code that is easier

Command name	OP code	Symbolic code	Type* of Command
Data movement/manipulation commands			
(continued)			
Convert to Binary	4F	CVB	RX
Convert to Decimal	4E	CVD	RX
OR	16	OR	RR
OR	56	O	RX
OR	96	OI	SI
OR	D6	OC	SS
Exclusive OR	17	XR	RR
Exclusive OR	57	X	RX
Exclusive OR	97	XI	SI
Exclusive OR	D7	XC	SS
Execute	44	EX	RX
Arithmetic commands			
Add Register	1A	AR	RR
Add	5A	A	RX
Add Halfword	4A	AH	RX
Add Logical Register	1E	ALR	RR
Add Logical	5E	AL	RX
Subtract Register	1B	SR	RR
Subtract	5B	S	RX
Subtract Halfword	4B	SH	RX
Subtract Logical Register	1F	SLR	RR
Subtract Logical	5F	SL	RX
Multiply Register	1C	MR	RR
Multiply	5C	M	RX
Multiply Halfword	4C	MH	RX
Divide Register	1D	DR	RR
Divide	5D	D	RX
Add Decimal	FA	AP	SS
Subtract Decimal	FB	SP	SS
Multiply Decimal	FC	MP	SS
Divide Decimal	FD	DP	SS
Zero and Add	F8	ZAP	SS
Logic commands			
Compare Register	19	CR	RR
Compare	59	C	RX
Compare Halfword	49	CH	RX
Compare Logical Register	15	CLR	RR
Compare Logical	55	CL	RX
Compare Logical Character	D5	CLC	SS
Compare Logical Immediate	95	CLI	SI
Compare Decimal	F9	CP	SS

Figure 11-3 (Continued)

for him to relate to English. Unfortunately, this code is not the machine's language (Russian), and so it does not understand the orders. However, the programmer has an answer to the dilemma. When he gives the computer the coded instructions, he also gives it another program—one that enables it to translate the instruction code into its own language. In other words, the translating program corresponds

Command name	OP code	Symbolic code	Type* of Command
Transfer of control commands			
Branch and Link Register	05	BALR	RR
Branch and Link	45	BAL	RX
Branch on Condition	07	BCR	RR
Branch on Condition	47	BC	RX
Branch on Count	06	BCTR	RR
Branch on Count	46	BCT	RX
Branch on Index High	86	BXH	RS
Branch on Index Low or Equal	87	BXLE	RS
Supervisor Call	OA	SVC	RR

*You will recall that computers such as the System/360 models may be used for both business and scientific applications. As we saw in chapter 9, scientific applications using fixed-length data words make use of registers; business applications using variable-length words use a storage-to-storage approach during processing. Instructions are classified in this table into types on the basis of register and storage usage: some are normally used in one type of application but not in the other. Thus, RR indicates an instruction which is used in a register-to-register operation; RS and RX instructions deal with situations where one operand is in a register and another is in primary storage; SS commands involve storage-to-storage operations; and SI commands deal with instruction-to-storage situations. For further details, see Ned Chapin, **360 Programming in Assembly Language.** (New York: McGraw-Hill Book Company, 1968).

Figure 11-3   (*Continued*)

in our example to an English-to-Russian dictionary, and the translating job is turned over to the machine. The programmer finds this approach much more to his liking; the machine—being a machine—has no objection. The compromise approach between man and machine is the one that is followed in business programming.

A third approach, and a most desirable one from man's point of view, is for the machine to accept and interpret instructions written (without constraints) in everyday English terms.[1] The semantic problems involved in this approach, however, are formidable. John Pfeiffer points out that while the sentence "Time flies like an arrow" may seem clear to man, it is subject to several machine interpretations. One incorrect translation, for example, might be: "Time the speed of flies as quickly as you can." ("Time" is considered a verb.) Another false interpretation might be that "certain flies enjoy an arrow." ("Time" is now considered an adjective, while "like" is interpreted as a verb.)[2]

In this section we shall consider the following three language categories: *machine language, symbolic language,* and *procedure-oriented language.* We shall deal primarily with categories here rather

[1] As we shall soon see, the COBOL language uses English words, but there are a number of constraints imposed on the way these words are employed.
[2] See John Pfeiffer, "Machines That Men Can Talk With," *Fortune,* vol. 69, pp. 153–156ff. May, 1964.

than with specific languages used with specific machines for very simple reasons: There are probably more than 1,000 programming languages, and some of these languages have dozens of dialects![3] Some languages can be used only with a single machine; some can be used with several models of the same manufacturer but cannot be used with other makes; and some can be used with more than one make and model.

Machine Language

Early computers were quite intolerant—the programmer had to translate his instructions into the machine language form that the computers understood. Of course, this language was not Russian. Rather, it was a string of numbers that represented the command code and operand address. To compound the difficulty for the programmer, the string of numbers was often not even in decimal form. For example, the instruction to ADD 0184 looks like this in the IBM 7040 machine language:[4]

$$000100000000000000000000000010111000$$

In addition to remembering the dozens of code numbers for the commands in the machine's repertoire, the programmer was also forced to keep track of the storage locations of data and instructions. The initial coding often took months, was therefore quite expensive, and often resulted in error. Checking instructions to locate errors was about as tedious as writing them initially because their code numbers became as meaningless to the programmer within minutes after he had prepared them as they appear to us. And if a written program had to be modified at a later date, the work involved could take weeks to finish.

Symbolic Language

To ease the programmer's burden, *mnemonic* command codes and *symbolic* addresses were developed in the early 1950s. The word *mnemonic* (pronounced *ne-mon-ik*) refers to a memory aid. One of the first steps to improve the program preparation process was to substitute letter symbols for basic machine language command codes. Figure 11-3 shows both the mnemonic (symbolic) and machine operation codes used in IBM System/360 computers. Each business computer now has a mnemonic code, although, of course, the actual

---

[3] COBOL is a business-oriented language that is somewhat standardized. Yet there can be a number of different COBOL dialects, depending on the make and model of the processor being used.

[4] In this case, the last 8 bits represent 0184.

symbols vary among makes and models.[5] For example, erasing old data in the accumulator and then adding the contents of an address to it is a common command. The mnemonic code used in the Honeywell 200 is ZA (Zero and Add). In other machines the symbol for the same operation may be CLA (CLear accumulator and Add) or RAD (Reset accumulator and ADd). Machine language is *still used* by the computer in the actual processing of the data, but it first translates the specified command code symbol into its machine language equivalent.

The improvement in the writing of command codes set the stage for further advances. It was reasoned that if the computer could be used to translate convenient symbols into basic commands, why couldn't it also be used to perform other clerical coding functions such as assigning storage addresses to data? This question led to *symbolic addressing;* i.e., it led to the practice of expressing an address, not in terms of its absolute numerical location, but rather in terms of symbols convenient to the programmer.

In the early stages of symbolic addressing, the programmer initially assigned a symbolic name and an actual address to a data item. For example, the total value of merchandise purchased during a month by a department store customer might be assigned to address 0063 by the programmer and given the symbolic name of TOTAL. Also, the value of merchandise returned unused during the month might be assigned to address 2047 and given the symbolic name of CREDIT. Then, for the remainder of the program, the programmer would refer to the *symbolic names rather than to the addresses* when such items were to be processed. Thus, an instruction might be written "S CREDIT, TOTAL" to subtract the value of returned goods from the total amount purchased to find the amount of the customer's monthly bill. The computer might then translate this symbolic instruction into the following machine language string of bits:[6]

<u>011111</u>	<u>011111111111</u>	<u>000000111111</u>
Operation or command code	2047	0063
(S)	(CREDIT)	(TOTAL)

Another improvement was that the programmer turned the task of assigning and keeping track of instruction addresses over to the computer. The programmer merely told the machine the storage

[5]Some examples of symbolic programming languages are IBM's Basic Assembly Language, Honeywell's Easycoder, and UNIVAC's Sleuth.
[6]This example uses a format and machine language of the Honeywell 200.

address number of the *first* program instruction, and then all others were automatically stored in sequence from that point by the processor. If another instruction were to be added later to the program, it was not then necessary to modify the addresses of all instructions that followed the point of insertion (as would have to be done in the case of programs written in machine language). In such a case, the processor automatically adjusted storage locations the next time the program was used.

The programmer no longer assigns actual address numbers to symbolic data items as he did initially. "In fact, all the coder has to do is specify where he wants the first location in his program. The assembly program will take it from there, allocating a location for each instruction and each word of data."[7]

The *assembly program* is the software aid that translates the symbolic-language *source program* into a machine language *object program*. Figure 11-4 may help to clear up any confusion about the three different programs. The following steps (numbered in Fig. 11-4) take place during the *assembly* and *production* runs:[8]

1. The *assembly program* is read into the computer, where it has complete control over the translating procedure. This program is generally supplied by the manufacturer of the machine as part of the total hardware-software package.
2. The *source program* written by the programmer in the symbolic language of the machine is recorded on an input medium such as punched cards.
3. During the assembly the source program is treated as data and is read into the CPU an instruction at a time under the control of the assembly program.
4. The assembly program translates the source program into a machine language *object program,* which is recorded on tapes or cards as the output of the assembly run. It is important to remember that during the *assembly run* no problem data are processed. That is, the source program is *not being executed;* it is merely being converted into a form so that it *can* be executed. After the assembly run, the assembly program is filed for future use.
5. The object program is read into the CPU as the first step in the *production run.*
6. Problem data, recorded on a suitable input medium, are read into the CPU under object program control.

[7] Herbert D. Leeds and Gerald M. Weinberg, *Computer Programming Fundamentals,* 2d ed., McGraw-Hill Book Company, New York, 1966, p. 64.
[8] This general procedure was briefly mentioned in Chapter 3.

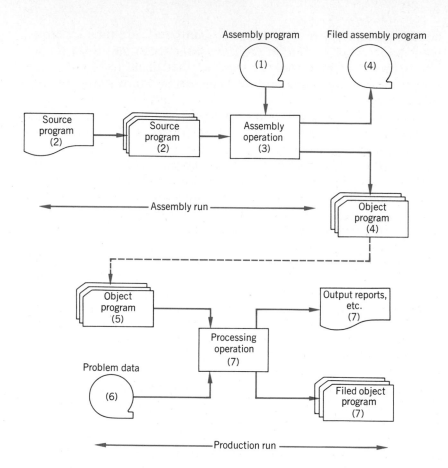

Figure 11-4 Converting
symbolic language to
machine language

7. The application is processed, the information output is properly
    received, and the object program is filed for future repetitive use.

To summarize, symbolic languages possess many advantages over
machine language coding. Much time is saved (in some cases coding
time has been reduced by 60 percent); detail is reduced; fewer errors
are made (and those which are made are easier to find); and programs
are much easier to modify.

**Procedure-oriented
Languages**

Up to this point we have generally been using symbolic language
concepts for illustration purposes. But coding in symbolic language
is still time-consuming. Also, symbolic languages are *machine
oriented;* i.e., they are designed for the specific make and model of
processor being used. Programs would have to be recoded if the

company acquired a different machine. Furthermore, the programmer writing instructions in a machine's symbolic language must have an intimate knowledge of the workings of that processor. Finally, the earlier assembly programs produced *one* machine instruction for each source program instruction.

To speed up coding, later assembly programs were developed that could produce a *variable* amount of machine language code for *each* source program instruction. In other words, a single *macro instruction* might produce *several* lines of machine language code. For example, the programmer might write "READ FILE," and the translating software might then automatically provide the detailed series of previously prepared machine language instructions, which would copy a record into primary storage from the file of data being read by the input device. Thus, the programmer was relieved of the task of writing an instruction for every machine operation performed. Input/output control systems (IOCS) employing macro instruction routines were developed to (1) handle the complex programming problems associated with overlap operations, (2) schedule operations, (3) identify errors, and (4) provide greater efficiency in reading and writing records. In spite of significant advances, however, assembly programs were still machine oriented; they were still written to meet the requirements of a specific equipment line.

The development of mnemonic techniques and macro instructions led, in turn, to the development of *procedure-oriented languages*.[9] As the name implies, languages have been created that are oriented toward a specific class of processing problems. In other words, a class of similar problems is isolated, and a language is developed to process these types of applications. A number of languages have been designed to process problems of a scientific-mathematic nature. Other languages have appeared that emphasize the processing of business applications. It is estimated that by 1974 programs written in procedure-oriented languages will be used to process 90 percent of the existing computer workload.[10]

Unlike symbolic programs, procedure-oriented programs may be used with a number of different hardware makes and models with little or no modification. Thus, reprogramming expense is greatly reduced when new equipment is acquired. Other advantages of procedure-oriented languages are: (1) they are easier to learn than symbolic languages; (2) they require less time to write; (3) they provide

[9] These are also called *high-level languages* and *problem-oriented languages*.
[10] See Jerome Kanter, *Management Guide to Computer System Selection and Use*, Prentice-Hall, Inc., Englewood Cliffs, N.J., 1970, p. 111.

better documentation; and (4) they are easier to maintain. Also, a programmer skilled in writing programs in such a language is not restricted to using a single machine.[11]

Naturally, a source program written in a procedural language must also be translated into a machine-usable code. The translating program that performs this operation is called a *compiler*. Compilers, like advanced assembly programs, may generate many lines of machine code for each source program statement.[12] A *compiling run* is required before problem data can be processed. With the exception that a compiler program is substituted for an assembly program, the procedures are the same as those shown in Fig. 11-4. The production run follows the compiling run.

Common Procedural Languages

The first compiler had the name A-2 and was developed in 1952 by UNIVAC's Dr. Grace M. Hopper. Since that time, many procedural languages have been produced—generally by equipment manufacturers and/or by committees of interested parties. In 1956, UNIVAC also produced a language to solve mathematical problems (MATH-MATIC) and one to process commercial problems (FLOW-MATIC). Most procedural languages have emphasized one of these two paths. Slightly later, the IT (Internal Translator) was developed, which could be used by both the IBM 650 and the Burroughs 205 Datatron. This marked the first time that a compiler was used with equipment produced by different manufacturers.

FORTRAN   In 1954, an IBM-sponsored committee headed by John Backus began work on a scientific-mathematic language. The result of this effort was FORTRAN (FORmula TRANslator), which was introduced in 1957 for the IBM 704 computer. It has been estimated that the cost to produce the 25,000 lines of detailed machine instructions that went into the first FORTRAN compiler was $2.5 million. Since its introduction, FORTRAN has been widely accepted and has been revised a number of times. Most IBM computers designed since 1957 have had a FORTRAN compiler. In fact, the overwhelming majority of *all* makes and models now in use have FORTRAN capability.

[11]Sometimes these advantages must be traded off against some loss of efficiency in the compiler object program. Certainly, a programmer *skilled* in the machine oriented language of a particular processor should be able to produce a more efficient object program, i.e., one that takes less storage space, runs faster, etc., than the average programmer working with a procedural language. Whether it would be economical for him to do so, however, is another matter.

[12]Some use the word *statement* to refer to a line of code in a high-level language and the word *instruction* to refer to a line of machine or symbolic language code that will produce a single machine operation.

Because of this widespread acceptance, the forerunner of the American National Standards Institute began work in 1962 on FORTRAN standard languages. These standards were approved in 1966.[13]

Like other higher-level languages, a single FORTRAN statement may be translated into multiple lines of machine language instructions. In statistical sampling procedures, for example, a commonly used measure is the standard deviation, which has the following formula:

$$\sqrt{\frac{\Sigma X^2 - (\Sigma X)^2/N}{N - 1}}$$

where Σ represents the *sum of* a value, X represents the variable being sampled, and N represents the size of the sample. A single FORTRAN statement to instruct the processor to compute a standard deviation might then look like this:

STDEV = SQRT [(SUMSQ — SUM**2/SIZE)/(SIZE — 1.0)]

We shall consider FORTRAN again in the next chapter.

ALGOL   In 1957, a group of international mathematicians met to begin the design of a language suited to their needs. ALGOL (ALGOrithmic Language) was the eventual result of this effort. Like FORTRAN, ALGOL has been revised several times in the past few years. While it is used extensively in Europe, its "competitor," FORTRAN, is the dominant scientific language in the United States.

COBOL   The COBOL (COmmon Business Oriented Language) language, written by a committee, was designed to serve two purposes. The first was that COBOL was specifically to be a tool of the business data processing community. The second purpose was that COBOL was to help users achieve program compatibility. The design group gathered at the Pentagon in Washington, D.C., in May, 1959, with the official sanction of the U.S. Department of Defense—the world's largest single user of computers. Members of the COnference of DAta SYstems Languages (CODASYL) represented computer manufacturers, government agencies, user organizations, and universities. The CODASYL Short Range Committee, which prepared the COBOL framework, consisted of representatives from federal government agencies (the Air Material Command, the Bureau of Ships, and the Bureau of

---

[13]There are two published standards. The ANSI Basic FORTRAN version is a subset of the "full" FORTRAN standard and does not have some of the additional features of the more extensive version. They do not differ, however, in their structure. The ANSI Basic FORTRAN standard is similar to FORTRAN II; ANSI FORTRAN corresponds to FORTRAN IV.

Standards) and from computer manufacturers (IBM, Honeywell, Burroughs, RCA, UNIVAC Division of Sperry Rand, and Sylvania). From June to December, 1959, this committee worked on the language specifications. Their final report was approved in January, 1960, and the language specifications were published a few months later by the Government Printing Office.

Also in 1960, the Department of Defense announced that it would not purchase or lease any computer that did not have an available COBOL compiler unless the manufacturer could prove that such software would not enhance machine performance. Early in 1961, Westinghouse Electric Corporation followed this lead by stating that all new equipment that they installed would have to have COBOL capability. Other large corporations followed with similar policies. With such backing, it is not surprising that since 1961 COBOL compilers have been prepared for all but the smallest commercial processors. Other CODASYL committees have continued to maintain, revise, and extend the initial specifications. COBOL has been used extensively for the past few years. There is also a published ANSI COBOL standard, which was approved in 1968. We shall look at simple COBOL examples in the next chapter.

PL/I Developed in the mid-1960s by IBM and a committee of users for the IBM System/360 family of computers, PL/I (Programming Language I, where I stands for *one*) is being promoted as a universal language; i.e., it is reputed to be a single high-level language that can be used to solve all types of business and scientific problems efficiently. As a scientific language, PL/I appears to be an extension of FORTRAN; however, COBOL-type data description is also used. Because there is the possibility that PL/I could replace both FORTRAN and COBOL, it has caused a great deal of controversy. Computer users are naturally anxious to protect the gigantic investment they have in FORTRAN and COBOL programs, and some fear the PL/I development will come at the expense of continued improvement in both of these languages. The measure of success of a language, of course, is determined by its use. Although the ultimate success of PL/I remains to be determined, it is expected that its usage will increase in the future. We shall look at this major language again in the next chapter.

BASIC Not to be confused with the Basic FORTRAN language standard referred to earlier, BASIC (Beginner's All-purpose Symbolic Instruction Code) is a popular *timesharing* language that has wide appeal because of its simplicity and ease of usage.[14] A problem solver with little or no knowledge of computers or programming can learn to write BASIC programs at a remote terminal in a short period of time.

BASIC was developed in 1963–1964 at Dartmouth College under the direction of Professors John Kemeny and Thomas Kurtz. The purpose of this effort was to produce a language that undergraduate students in all fields of study (1) would find easy to learn and (2) would thus be encouraged to use on a regular basis. BASIC was a success at Dartmouth on both counts. The Dartmouth timesharing system was implemented on General Electric equipment with the assistance of G.E. engineers. Recognizing the advantages of BASIC, G.E. quickly made the language (along with FORTRAN and ALGOL) available for the use of commercial timesharing customers. "BASIC is now offered, in one way or another, by *every* major computer manufacturer and almost every independent supplier of time-sharing."[15] Users of BASIC range from public school students to aerospace engineers. Figure 11-5 shows an IBM System/360 user interacting with a program written in BASIC. The user's instructions to the prepared BASIC program are underlined; the computer's responses are printed in capital letters. We will look at BASIC coding in the next chapter.

REPORT PROGRAM GENERATOR (RPG) An RPG language is generally available for small computers, which are used primarily for business processing applications. There is, however, no RPG published standard, and so the several versions differ in some respects. Four coding sheets, or forms, are typically used by programmers to prepare the problem for processing. The programmer writes the file description, input, calculation, and output format specifications on the coding forms; the RPG compiler then uses these specifications to prepare a detailed report-writing object program.

The primary programming language for IBM's small System/3 business processor is RPG II, a language based on the System/360 RPG, which is widely used in model 20 installations to produce customized

[14]FORTRAN and BASIC are the two most popular timesharing languages, probably accounting for about 70 percent of the timesharing programs written. See Bohdan Szuprowicz, "The Time-Sharing Users: Who Are They?" *Datamation*, August, 1969, pp. 55–59. Many other user languages are, of course, available, including PL/I, APL, and JOSS. Among the more interesting names are DDT, LAFFF, SYNFUL, FRED, and PENELOPE. One can't help but speculate about whether synful FRED and PENELOPE would be allowed alone in core together.

[15]Michael F. Lipp, "The Language BASIC and its Role in Time Sharing," *Computers and Automation*, October, 1969, p. 42.

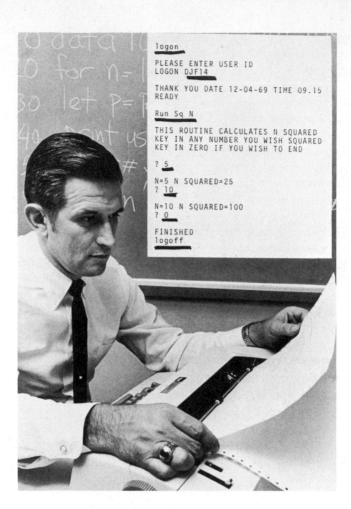

```
logon

PLEASE ENTER USER ID
LOGON DJF14

THANK YOU DATE 12-04-69 TIME 09.15
READY

Run Sq N

THIS ROUTINE CALCULATES N SQUARED
KEY IN ANY NUMBER YOU WISH SQUARED
KEY IN ZERO IF YOU WISH TO END

? 5

N=5 N SQUARED=25
? 10

N=10 N SQUARED=100
? 0

FINISHED
logoff
```

Figure 11-5 Interacting with a BASIC program (courtesy IBM Corporation)

and easy-to-read business reports. An RPG example will be coded in the next chapter.

Language Selection

The large number of programming languages, the differences in compiler performance, the vast range of types of computing problems, the needs and hardware of the particular user, and the abilities of different programmers—all these factors combine to make language selection unbelievably complex. Yet the data processing manager must often evaluate and choose among the language alternatives available. Obtaining answers to the following questions may help in this evaluation.

1. *Are company programmers familiar with the language?* In many cases, the language used is simply the one that is best known to the programmers. If a language is not familiar, can it be learned quickly? Is it easy to use?

2. *What is the nature of the application?* Does the language perform well in applications of this type? Was it designed for such applications?

3. *Is a satisfactory compiler available?* There is an important distinction between a language and a compiler. A procedural language is a humanly convenient set of rules, conventions, and representations used to convey information from man to machine, while a compiler is a translator written by one or more programmers. It is entirely possible that a good language, when used with an inefficient compiler, will yield unsatisfactory results.

4. *What is the cost of the compiler?* Unbundled manufacturers may now charge a monthly fee at each user installation for the use of new or enhanced compilers that were formerly supplied without charge. For example, an improved PL/I compiler designed for the IBM System/370 (and made available in the fall of 1971) carries a monthly license fee of $250. Compiler acquisition cost is a factor that must now be considered in language selection.

5. *How frequently will the application be processed?* If an application is processed repeatedly, attention must be given to operating speed, i.e., the time required to complete a production run. A symbolic language program usually has a shorter operating time than does a program of the same application written in a higher-level language. If the job is run frequently enough, the value of the operating time saved may be more than enough to offset the cost of additional time spent in program preparation. For limited-life jobs, however, the faster the possible programming time is (with procedural languages), the more economical the approach.

6. *Will the program be changed frequently?* The ease of program modification varies with different languages. A higher-level language is typically easier to modify than a symbolic language.

7. *Is a hardware change anticipated during the life of the application?* Conversion of procedure-oriented programs is easier and faster; machine-oriented programs may have to be completely rewritten.

8. *Is the language being periodically improved and updated?* Will new machines continue to accept the language source programs? Who is sponsoring the language and what is their commitment to it?

PROGRAM CODING

Coding is the actual writing of the computer program of instructions. It follows the systems design and programming analysis stages in the programming process. Although instructions could be written in the machine language of the available computer, this is seldom (if ever) the language used by the applications programmer. The symbolic assembly language is often used by systems programmers; however, the tendency is for applications programs to be written in higher-level procedural languages such as those identified above. Regardless of the language used, the programmer must follow strict rules with respect to punctuation and statement structure. (It has been reported that a missing comma in a guidance program caused a space probe to veer so badly off course that it had to be destroyed by a signal from the ground control station.)

Special coding forms, organized to help the programmer comply with the language rules, are used with many languages. Examples of these coding forms are presented in the next chapter. Simple programs coded in five popular languages (FORTRAN, COBOL, PL/I, BASIC, and RPG) are presented. A brief overview is given to acquaint you with (1) the general structure of each language and (2) some of the characteristics of each language. Since the entire next chapter is, in fact, devoted to program coding, we will postpone further discussion of this topic to those pages.

PROGRAM DEBUGGING AND TESTING

Debugging

Clerical mistakes and errors caused by faulty logic are inelegantly referred to as *bugs*. Eliminating these mistakes and errors that prevent the program from running and producing correct results is appropriately called *debugging*. It is unusual for complex programs to run to completion in the first attempt. In fact, time spent in debugging and testing often equals or exceeds the time spent in program coding. Failure to provide for a possible program path, or branch, keypunching errors, mistakes in coding punctuation, incorrect operation codes, transposed characters—these are but a few of the bugs that can thwart the programmer.

To reduce the number of clerical and logical errors, the programmer should carefully check his coding sheets before they are turned over to the keypunch operator. This *desk-checking* process should include an examination for program completeness; furthermore, typical input data should be manually traced through the program processing paths to identify possible errors. In short, the programmer attempts to play the role of the computer.

After program cards are punched and desk checked for accuracy, an attempt is made to assemble or compile the source program into object program form. Assembly and compiler programs contain error diagnostic features, which detect (and print messages about) certain types of mistakes in the source program, e.g., undefined symbols and incorrect operation codes. Detected mistakes, of course, must be remedied by the programmer. An error-free pass of the program through the assembly or compiler run *does not* mean that the program is perfected or that all bugs have been eliminated. It usually does mean, however, that the program is ready for testing.

A program to be tested has generally demonstrated that it will run and produce results. The purpose of *testing* is to determine if the results are correct. The testing procedure involves using the program to process input test data that will produce known results. The test deck should contain (1) typical data, which will test the generally used program paths, (2) unusual but valid data, which will test the program paths used to handle exceptions; and (3) incorrect, incomplete, or inappropriate data, which will test the program error-handling capabilities. If the program passes the test, the programmer may release it for implementation;[16] it it does not, he may do the following: **Testing**

1. Trace through the program, a step at a time, at the computer console. Errors may be discovered by noting register contents after each program operation. Such an approach may be permissible with a few minicomputer and small computer systems, but it is hardly appropriate to tie up an expensive large computer for such purposes.
2. Call for a *trace program* run. The trace program prints out the status of registers after each operation and thus is comparable to console checking. However, less machine time is required.
3. Call for a *storage dump* when the program "hangs up" during a test run, i.e., obtain a printout of the contents of primary storage and registers at the time of the hangup. The programmer can then study this listing for possible clues to the cause of the programming error(s).

[16]It should be noted here, however, that bugs may still remain undetected. In complex programs there may be tens of thousands of different possible paths through the program. It simply is not practical (and maybe not even possible) to trace through all the different paths during testing. This explains why nonsense may suddenly be produced by programs months after they have been released for production use. Some unique and unanticipated series of events has produced input or circumstances that turn up a bug for the first time. The error was always there; it simply remained undetected. Very complex systems are considered to be *undebuggable* by professional programmers.

After the program appears to be running properly and producing correct results, there is frequently a transitionary cutover period during which the job application is processed both by the old method and by the new program. The purpose of this period, of course, is to verify processing accuracy and completeness.

PROGRAM DOCUMENTATION AND MAINTENANCE

Documentation, as stated in Chapter 10, involves collecting, organizing, storing, and otherwise maintaining a complete record of the programs and other documents associated with the firm's data processing systems. The need for documentation was explained in Chapter 10.

The documentation package for a particular program should include:

1. *A definition of the problem.* Why was the program prepared? What were the objectives? Who requested the program and who approved it? Questions such as these should be answered.
2. *A description of the system.* The system or subsystem environment in which the program functions should be described; systems flowcharts should be included. Broad systems specifications outlining the scope of the problem, the form and type of input data to be used, and the form and type of output required should be clearly stated.
3. *A description of the program.* Program flowcharts, decision tables, program listings, test decks and test results, storage dumps, trace program printouts—these and other documents that describe the program and give an historical record of difficulties and/or changes should be available.
4. *A recitation of operator instructions.* Among the items covered should be computer switch settings, loading and unloading procedures, and starting, running, and terminating procedures.
5. *A description of program controls.* Controls may be incorporated in a program in a number of ways. For example, programmed controls may be used to check on the reasonableness and propriety of input data. A description of such controls should be a part of the documentation. We shall consider this matter of control again in Chapter 18.

Production-run programs are continuously being modified and improved. Sometimes the object program can be patched to include small modifications so that a compiling run is not necessary. (A danger of this approach, however, is that the small changes may not be incorporated in the supporting documents.) Program *maintenance* is an important duty of the programmer and may involve all steps from problem definition through analysis, design, and program preparation. It is not unusual to find a programmer spending 25 percent of his time on this activity. In some installations there are programmers who do nothing but maintain production programs.

Although it is still a time-consuming and expensive process, considerable improvement has been made in programming since the early days of computers. Programming aids are available to assist the programmer in the *initial preparation* of applications programs. There have also been developments that make it possible to *convert existing programs* so that they can be used on new hardware without the necessity for reprogramming. Let us briefly look at each of these topics.

PROGRAMMING AIDS

A listing of factors that have improved programming performance in the initial preparation of applications programs includes the following aids:

Initial Preparation Aids

1. *Translating and operating system programs.* We have already seen how these aids improve program-preparation time while reducing error.
2. *Subroutine libraries.* A subroutine, you will remember, is a well-defined set of instructions that performs a specific arithmetic or logic operation. Subroutines are classified as open or closed (Fig. 11-6). An *open subroutine* is inserted or spliced directly into the main program at any point where it may be needed. The *closed subroutine,* on the other hand, remains a separate program that is typically used several times during the processing. An instruction in the main program branches program control to the subroutine location. When the subroutine operation is completed, another branch instruction transfers control back to the main program. It is obvious that a good library of tested subroutines (which are prepared by equipment manufacturers and furnished to their customers) can often speed the writing of new programs.
3. *Application programs.* Application or packaged programs were introduced in Chapter 3. In addition to subroutines, manufacturers have prepared entire programs for applications that are of a general nature and that are common to the needs of many firms in an industry. For example, IBM and Honeywell have prepared

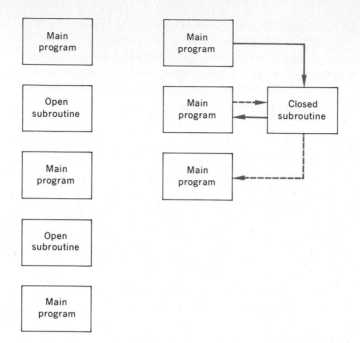

Figure 11-6 Open and closed subroutines

programs to suit the needs of a number of businesses in the areas of banking, insurance, distribution, and manufacturing. Other manufacturers have similar packages available. These "canned" programs can reduce programming time and expense since they are readily available and have been debugged. Of necessity however, they must be broad enough to cover a number of contingencies. Thus, they may not be as efficient as a specially prepared program in terms of storage space used and running time required.

4. *User groups.* Users of similar machines have formed associations to share experiences and to exchange information and programs. In 1955, for example, a number of organizations using large-scale IBM machines met to form a user group known as SHARE, an acronym said to mean the Society to Help Alleviate Redundant Effort.[17] Meetings are held biannually, with IBM paying part of the expenses. Members of the group have access to a library of contributed programs. Other manufacturers help sponsor groups that use their equipment; e.g., USE is a UNIVAC organization, and SWAP is a Control Data Corporation group.

5. *Software consultants.* A number of independent software consulting companies have been formed to help businesses with their programming problems. The better of these consulting firms can

[17]Other groups known as GUIDE and COMMON, are also partially sponsored by IBM.

often provide specialized software to their clients that is not available from the manufacturer or that is more efficient than the software provided by the manufacturer. Consultants, for a fee, can supplement a firm's own programming staff during overload periods created by conversion to a new machine or by preparation of complex new system programs.

We saw in Chapter 3 that the development of compatibility and modularity concepts has served to ease systems transition problems. But is there any alternative to completely rewriting proved and satisfactory programs before a new computer can be utilized if the existing computer system (1) is no longer adequate, (2) is not compatible with other models, and (3) does not have modular units to extend its capabilities? Considering the tremendous investment in such programs, the answer, fortunately, is yes. The transition from an old system (computer O) to a new one (computer N) can be made less painful by the use of the following techniques, which permit existing programs to run on computer N without the necessity for initial reprogramming.[18]

Program Conversion Developments

1. *Writing programs in a machine-independent language.* As discussed earlier, if computer O programs have been prepared in a higher-level standardized language that is essentially machine independent, computer N will have translating software available to accept existing programs directly with a minimum of reprogramming needed.
2. *Using translation techniques.* The machine-level language of a particular computer is a collection of all the acceptable instructions it can understand and execute. The machine-level languages of different-generation computers vary because of design and technology changes. Several special programs called *translators* have been developed to translate the "foreign" machine language of machine O into the machine language of computer N. The new machine language program produced can be used thereafter without reference to the original program.[19]
3. *Using emulation techniques.* Emulation involves software features and the use of a special purpose read only storage device. The

[18] On frequently used programs some subsequent reprogramming will likely be necessary to realize the full potential of computer N, but the conversion pace need not be so frantic.
[19] An example of a translator is EXODUS II, developed by Boise Cascade programmers to convert IBM 1401 autocoder and SPS programs into System/360 Basic Assembly Language. The reader is cautioned not to confuse the admittedly confusing terms *translator* and *translating programs*. The latter term is associated with language translation for a single machine and was discussed earlier.

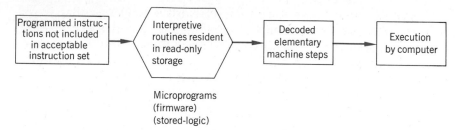

Figure 11-7

contents of this special hardware unit may be altered, for example, by mechanical or other means, but unlike other storage devices it will not accept input data and instructions from applications programmers. Computer O program instructions are channeled through this *emulator,* which interprets them, converts them into computer N equivalent instructions, and thus permits their execution by computer N. This process (see Fig. 11-7) is repeated each time the program is run. Computer N is thus made to act like computer O—a role that fails to utilize its full potential. System/370 machines will emulate second-generation IBM models such as those in the 1400 and 7000 series.

4. *Using simulation techniques.* A *simulator* is software that performs the same functions as an emulator. Under the direction of the simulator, instructions from the old program are fed into computer N where they are interpreted, converted into computer N equivalent instructions, and executed. Simulation is generally slower than emulation.

Firmware Developments

It might be appropriate here to further discuss a concept used in program conversion. The special purpose read-only storage unit used in emulation has interpretative routines, or *microprograms,* which are wired into or plugged into the unit. As shown in Fig. 11-7, these routines accept foreign instructions, analyze them, and decode them into the elementary operations that the CPU is designed to execute. In short, such microprograms (which are also referred to as *firmware,* or *stored-logic*) are the control elements that direct the computer to carry out a series of decoded elementary machine operations in order to execute each foreign instruction.

The usefulness of the firmware concept extends beyond emulation. In third-generation hardware, in fact, microprograms are used to make the small models in a family of machines hardware compatible with the larger models. In the System/360, for example, larger models have a more extensive built-in set of instructions that they can execute than do the smaller models. But by using microprograms the smaller models are able to execute instructions even though the instructions are basically foreign to the circuitry of the smaller models.

Computer technology in the 1970s will likely make much greater use of firmware. By converting functions currently being performed with software into circuit elements[20] (which are becoming less expensive), the need for some of the detailed (and very expensive) programming currently being done may be reduced. For example, in performing its functions of scheduling, control, etc., the operating system (OS) software discussed in Chapter 3 uses storage space in and the time of the CPU—space and time resources that might otherwise have been used for mathematical or data processing tasks. To reduce this OS overhead, resident microprograms operating at hardware speeds may be substituted for some of the tasks currently being accomplished at relatively slow speeds with a series of OS program instructions. It may also be feasible to use various combinations of plug-in microprogrammed elements with generalized central processors to create "custom-built" systems for specific users.

SUMMARY

Although computers vary with respect to the number of commands that they can execute, they are all similar in that they must ultimately receive their instructions in a machine-language form. Early programmers had to code instructions laboriously into this machine language.

To ease the programmer's burden, mnemonic operation codes and symbolic addresses were developed in the early 1950s. The development of machine-oriented symbolic languages led to further programming improvement first in the form of macro instructions and then in the form of procedure-oriented languages. Many procedural languages are directed toward either scientific or commercial problems. Some languages, e.g., PL/I, are used with both types of applications. The selection of a language, like the selection of hardware, is a complex task. Among the most popular high-level languages are FORTRAN, COBOL, PL/I, BASIC, and RPG.

A program must be debugged as much as possible and tested before it can be used. These activities often take as much time as is required to perform the initial coding; sometimes they can take much longer. A program cannot be considered completed until the documentation package is put in good order. Maintenance of production run programs is an important part of the programming job.

[20] The term *firmware,* coined by Ascher Opler, refers to this intermediate position between the traditional roles of hardware and software. See "Fourth-Generation Software," *Datamation,* January, 1967, pp. 22–24.

In preparing initial programs, programmers are aided by translating software, subroutine libraries, and packaged programs. User groups and consultants are the source of valuable information and assistance. Program conversion aids such as translators, simulators, and emulators (using firmware concepts) have reduced the necessity for rewriting satisfactory programs when new equipment is obtained.

DISCUSSION QUESTIONS

1. Identify the steps in the programming process.
2. "Every computer instruction has an explicit predicate consisting of at least two parts." Identify and explain these two parts.
3. Compare the command structures of single-, two-, and three-address machines.
4. What types of commands are found in a computer's repertoire?
5. What are the differences among machine, symbolic, and procedure-oriented languages?
6. (a) What is an assembly program? (b) What is a source program? (c) What is an object program? (d) Explain the relationship among these three programs.
7. (a) What is FORTRAN? (b) For what type of problems was FORTRAN designed?
8. (a) What is COBOL? (b) How did it originate? (c) For what purposes was COBOL designed?
9. (a) What is PL/I? (b) How did it originate? (c) How may PL/I represent a threat to FORTRAN and COBOL?
10. (a) What is BASIC? (b) Where did it originate? (c) For what purpose was BASIC designed?
11. (a) What is RPG? (b) For what is it used?
12. Discuss the factors to consider in language selection.
13. Define the following terms.
    (a) Macro instruction
    (b) Machine-oriented language
    (c) Compiler
    (d) Debugging
    (e) Open subroutine
    (f) Closed subroutine
    (g) IOCS
    (h) Translator
    (i) Emulation
    (j) Microprogram
    (k) Firmware
    (l) Read-only storage

(m) Desk checking

(n) Simulator

14. What steps can be taken during debugging and testing to locate and remove program errors?

15. What information should be included in a program documentation package?

16. Discuss the factors that have improved programming performance in the initial preparation of applications programs.

17. Differentiate between emulation and simulation.

18. What function is performed by firmware (microprograms)?

SELECTED REFERENCES

Flores, Ivan: "Computer Software," *Science & Technology,* May, 1969, pp. 16–25.

Harrison, William L.: "Program Testing," *Journal of Data Management,* December, 1969, pp. 30–33.

Judd, D. R.: "Program Testing and Validation," *Computer Bulletin,* March, 1967, pp. 28–32.

Naftaly, Stanley M.: "How to Pick a Programming Language," *Data Processing Digest,* November, 1966, pp. 1–14.

Opler, Ascher: "Fourth-Generation Software," *Datamation,* January, 1967, pp. 22–24.

Riggs, Robert: "Computer Systems Maintenance," *Datamation,* November, 1969, pp. 227ff.

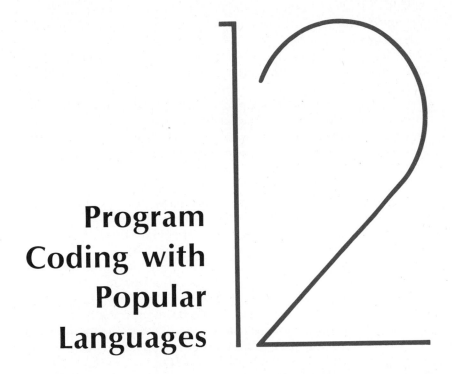

Program Coding with Popular Languages

The purpose of this chapter is to present a brief overview of five popular programming languages (FORTRAN, COBOL, PL/I, BASIC, and RPG), which are used here to code two simple programs. Since entire volumes are available on each of these languages, little more than a brief outline of each is possible in a single chapter.[1] Nevertheless, the material presented here will acquaint you with (1) the general structure and (2) some of the characteristics of each language. Before beginning the language discussions, however, it might be appropriate to pause here long enough to describe the problems that are coded.

THE PROBLEMS

The same two simple problems are coded in the five languages.[2] Simple problems have been selected so that problem details will not

NAME   A.V. STUDENT

TEST RESULTS
75
50
55
0
100
100
75
100
100
50
0
75
100
67
63
97
63
93
57
67
83
0
100
100
72
75
63
87
93
75
100
100
100
100
90
2,625

AVERAGE   75

Figure 12-1

confuse the issue while introductory language and coding concepts are presented. The two problems were introduced earlier.

Because of his propensity to test and his willingness to incur low ratings in student opinion polls, Professor Balford Sheet of Chapter 10 fame has presented us with the *first problem*. This problem (which was shown in flowchart form in Fig. 10-11, page 306) is to determine the average (arithmetic mean) grade of Mr. A. Valiant Student—the sole survivor in Professor Sheet's accounting course. Each of the 35 grades recorded for Mr. Student represents a single record. Each grade score (or record) is punched into a card and read into a computer for processing. The processing operation involves adding together the individual grade scores. After each grade record is processed, it is then written on an output report by a high-speed printer.[3] This written report is the output file on Val Student. When all records are processed, the machine then computes and prints a summary measure— the average score—which becomes the basis for Val's course grade. The output report (regardless of the programming language employed) will have the appearance of Fig. 12-1. The 35 input grade scores, of course, are also indicated in Fig. 12-1.

The *second problem* to be coded deals with the accounts-receivable penalty procedure, which was also introduced in Chapter 10. Figures 10-12 (flowchart) and 10-14 (decision table) describe the program logic. To briefly review, a late-payment penalty is charged to credit customers whose accounts are 30 days or more *overdue*. The amount of the penalty is based on the unpaid account balance: if the balance is over $200, i.e., if the balance is *not* equal to or less than ($\leq$) $200, the penalty is 3 percent; otherwise, a 2 percent charge is levied. The amount of the penalty is added to the next statement sent to the customer. If the account is sixty days or more overdue ($\geq$60), a warning message is printed. Accounts that are *less than* ($<$) 30 days overdue are not to be included in this penalty procedure process. But in the event that such an account is entered by mistake, provision is made to prevent it from being processed.

For illustration purposes, we will use the following input data:

Days Overdue	Unpaid Balance	Customer Name
25	$150.00	John Smith
45	200.00	A. V. Student
65	250.00	Randy Johnson
30	300.00	Beverly Bivens
60	350.00	Alexandre Dumas

[3]In the case of the BASIC language examples, a character-at-a-time online terminal typewriter produced the outputs and data entry was by paper tape and/or keyboard rather than by punched cards.

```
CUSTOMER STATEMENT FOR JOHN SMITH
ACCOUNT NOT INCLUDED


CUSTOMER STATEMENT FOR A.V. STUDENT
BALANCE DUE      $ 204.00


CUSTOMER STATEMENT FOR RANDY JOHNSON
BALANCE DUE      $ 257.50
ACCOUNT IS 65 DAYS OVERDUE


CUSTOMER STATEMENT FOR BEVERLY BIVENS
BALANCE DUE      $ 309.00


CUSTOMER STATEMENT FOR ALEXANDRE DUMAS
BALANCE DUE      $ 360.50
ACCOUNT IS 60 DAYS OVERDUE
```

Figure 12-2

Can you figure out the appropriate response that should be made in each of these situations? You may check your answers (and your understanding of the problem) by referring to Fig. 12-2.[4] The output of the penalty-procedure programs (again regardless of the language used) will have the appearance of Fig. 12-2.

In the remaining pages of this chapter we shall look at the way programs written in the FORTRAN, COBOL, PL/I, BASIC, and RPG languages use the same input data to produce the same output information.

FORTRAN[5]

FORTRAN was developed primarily for scientific and engineering purposes, but it is also used in some business applications where extensive files are not being manipulated. Figure 12-3 shows the coding for Bal Sheet's average grade problem.

Program Statements

The FORTRAN source program shown in Fig. 12-3 is composed of several types of *statements,* which may be classified into the following

[4] In the interests of simplicity, a single document rather than separate customer statement forms are used in this problem solution.
[5] The FORTRAN IV version is used in the examples shown in this section.

IBM FORTRAN Coding Form

X28-7327-6 U/M050
Printed in U. S. A.

PROGRAM	AVERAGE OF TEST SCORES		PUNCHING INSTRUCTIONS	GRAPHIC	PAGE 1 OF 1
PROGRAMMER	JOHN Q. PROGRAMMER	DATE 1/26/70		PUNCH	CARD ELECTRO NUMBER*

COMM. | STATEMENT NUMBER | CONT. | FORTRAN STATEMENT | IDENTIFICATION SEQUENCE

```
      READ (1,10)N,ANAME1,ANAME2
   10 FORMAT(I2,2X,2A10)
      IF(N)100,100,20
   20 ITOTAL=0
      WRITE (3,30) ANAME1,ANAME2
   30 FORMAT(10X,4HNAME,2X,2A10/)
      WRITE (3,40)
   40 FORMAT(21X,12HTEST RESULTS)
      DO 70 I=1,N,1
      READ (1,50)ISCORE
   50 FORMAT(I3)
      WRITE (3,60)ISCORE
   60 FORMAT(23X,I4)
      ITOTAL=ITOTAL+ISCORE
   70 CONTINUE
      IAVE=(ITOTAL+(N+1)/2)/N
      WRITE (3,80)ITOTAL
   80 FORMAT(122X,I5/)
      WRITE (3,90)IAVE
   90 FORMAT(5X,7HAVERAGE,11X,I4)
  100 STOP
      END
```

*A standard card form, IBM electro 888157, is available for punching statements from this form

Figure 12-3

categories: (1) *input/output,* (2) *arithmetic assignment and compu-tation,* and (3) *program control.* Those statements that are referred to in other parts of the program are assigned arbitrary numbers on the left side of the coding sheet by the programmer. Each statement is punched on one or more cards. The numbers below the "FOR-TRAN STATEMENT" heading on the coding sheet refer to columns of a punched card. Thus, the first statement in Fig. 12-3 would be punched in columns 7 to 32 of the first card in the source program deck. A *comment* card may be included in a program to provide an explanatory note by punching a C in column 1 and then by punching the message in the remaining columns. Such a card would not be processed during compilation. When a statement will not fit on a single card (or line), it may be continued on a following card through the use of a character, e.g., 1 to 9, in column 6 of the continuation card.

Input data may, of course, be in alphabetical or numerical form. In FORTRAN, numerical data are commonly classified into *integer* and *real* numbers. An integer number is a decimal value *without a deci-mal point;* for example, 35,262 and 75 are integer numbers. A real number is simply a decimal value that *does have a decimal point;* for example, 6.25, 0.325, and −0.987 are real numbers. A real number may also be presented in an exponential, *scientific notation,* or *float-ing-point notation* form. How? I'm glad you asked. It may be done by simply expressing the number as a value between 1 and 10 multi-plied by an exponent (E) or power of 10. For example, the floating decimal expression 3.68E+02 means 3.68×10^2, which is 368 in fixed decimal notation.[6] And 1.26E − 02 means $1.26 \times 1/10^2$ or .0126 in customary form. Also, the decimal values 123000 and −.0000123 may become 1.23E+05 and −1.23E−05 in floating-point notation. Float-ing-point notation is conveniently used to express very large or very small quantities.

The first line of code in Fig. 12-3 is a READ statement, which is used to read input data from an input device (generally a card reader) into primary storage. The fifth line of code is a WRITE statement, which is used to write output information from primary storage to an output device (generally a printer). The form of READ and WRITE statements is

Input/Output Statements

| READ (i,n) list | WRITE (i,n) list |

[6]Alternatively, the value could be expressed as a decimal fraction between 0.1 and 1.0 multiplied by a power of 10. Thus, the *normal form* floating-point numeral .368E+03 means 0.368×10^3, which is also 368 in fixed decimal notation.

where i refers to the input or output device that will be used in the operation; n indicates the statement number of an appropriate FORMAT[7] statement; and "list" refers to the variable names that are to be read or written. Thus, in the first statement of Fig. 12-3, the programmer is indicating that a card reader (1) is to be used to input the *variable names* N, ANAME1, and ANAME2 according to the format specified in statement number 10. And in the WRITE statement in the fifth line of Fig. 12-3, the programmer is specifying that a printer (3) is to be used to print ANAME1 and ANAME2 in accordance with FORMAT statement number 30.

The variable names are symbols invented by the programmer to represent quantities that may have different values. Certain rules must be followed in assigning variable names. The variable name N, for example, is an integer quantity that represents the number of test grades being averaged. The letter G, however, could not have been used for this purpose because variable names that represent integer values must begin with the letters I, J, K, L, M, and N. Names beginning with other letters represent real numbers. When the first READ statement is executed, specific values from the data card will be assigned to the three variable names listed; i.e., N will be assigned a two-digit integer number while ANAME1 and ANAME2 (the variable tags used to identify the name of the student in storage) may each accommodate 10 alphanumeric characters. How does the computer know this? Because this information is contained in FORMAT statement number 10. The I2 in this statement refers to a two-digit integer value (for the storage location to be labeled N); the 2X specifies 2 blank spaces; and the 2A10 specification means that the two storage locations labeled ANAME1 and ANAME2 may each accomodate 10 alphanumeric characters.

The general form of the FORMAT statement is

$$n \text{ FORMAT } (s_1, s_2, \ldots, s_m)$$

where n is a statement number and s represents a specification that describes the type and arrangement of an item in the order in which it appears on the input or output record. Some commonly encountered data specifications are presented in Fig. 12-4.

Arithmetic Assignment and Computation Statements

The form of the *arithmetic assignment* statement resembles a mathematical formula. The statement ITOTAL = 0 means that zero is assigned to the variable name ITOTAL (which must represent an

---

[7]Because the letters O, I, and Z resemble the digits 0, 1, and 2, they are often written O, I, and Z on coding sheets to reduce keypunching errors.

Specification	Description	Examples
Iw	An interger value which is w characters in width	I4 might refer to 2625 I2 might refer to 35
Fw.d	A real number having w characters, with d digits to the right of the decimal point	F8.2 might refer to 12345.25 (where the decimal point is counted as a character)
Ew.d	A real number written in floating point notation having w characters, with d digits to the right of the decimal point	E8.2 might refer to a value of 1.67E+06 (counting the decimal point as a character) which is 1.67×10^6 or 1670000. in customary notation.
wX	Skip over w characters	10X means to skip 10 characters.
nAw	Alphanumeric data having w characters may be read or written into each of n fields.	2A10 means two fields may each accommodate up to 10 alphanumeric characters.
wH	Print exactly as written the next w characters in the FORMAT statement.	12HTEST RESULTS means to print TEST RESULTS on the output document.

Figure 12-4 FORMAT statement specifications

integer quantity because the first letter is I). IN FORTRAN the "equals" sign *does not* necessarily mean equality; rather, it means that the value of the expression to the right of the sign is assigned to the storage location having the name of the variable to the left of the sign. Thus, as we see in Fig. 12-3 in the line below statement number 60, ITOTAL = ITOTAL + ISCORE obviously is not a mathematical equation. What this line does mean is that the values stored in ITOTAL and ISCORE will be added and the result will be assigned to the ITOTAL location (thus erasing the previous ITOTAL contents).

The five basic arithmetic operations performed in FORTRAN are:

Operation	FORTRAN Symbol
Addition	+
Subtraction	−
Multiplication	*
Division	/
Exponentiation	**

The *order* of computations performed in an arithmetic operation follows specific rules. Parentheses are often used to designate the order of operations. Moving from left to right in an arithmetic expression without parentheses,

1. All exponentiation (raising to a power) is performed first.
2. All multiplication and division operations are then completed.
3. Finally, all addition and subtraction takes place.

If parentheses are used, the computations within the parentheses are handled first using the above order rules. If several sets of parentheses are nested within one another, the operations in the innermost group are performed first. To illustrate, let us consider the following statement found in Fig. 12-3, which computes Val Student's average grade for the 35 test scores:

$$IAVE = (ITOTAL + (N + 1)/2)/N$$

The first part of the expression evaluated would be $(N + 1)$ in the innermost set of parentheses. The result in our problem would be

$$IAVE = (ITOTAL + 36/2)/N .$$

Within the remaining set of parentheses, the division operation would be performed first and the resulting value of 18 would be added to the contents of the storage location labeled ITOTAL.[8] This total would then be divided by the number of test scores (35).

Program Control Statements

FORTRAN statements are executed sequentially until the sequence is altered by an unconditional or conditional branch instruction. An example of an acceptable FORTRAN *unconditional* branching statement is GO TO 100, where 100 refers to a statement number. An example of a *conditional* branch statement is IF (N) 100,100,20, which is on the third line of Fig. 12-3. The general form of the IF statement is

$$IF (a)n_1, n_2, n_3$$

where a refers to an arithmetic computation to be performed or a variable name. *If* the value of a turns out to be *negative*, program control will be transferred to statement number n_1; *if* a is *zero*, control

---

[8]Since integer values are used in this averaging program, the purpose of $(N + 1)/2$ is to round off computations of the average grade to the nearest integer value.

moves to statement number n_2; and *if* a is a *positive* value, control transfers to n_3. In our example in Fig. 12-3, control will branch to statement number 100 (STOP) in the event that N is mistakenly entered as a negative value or as zero. Normally, of course, statement number 20 will be executed in sequence.

An additional program control statement is illustrated in Fig. 12-3. The line that reads

$$DO\ 70\ I = 1,N,1$$

controls a program *loop*. The general form of such a DO statement is

$$DO\ n\ i = m_1,\ m_2,\ m_3$$

where the DO n portion of the statement indicates the instructions included in the DO loop; i.e., all statements down to and including the last one numbered n constitute the DO loop. Thus, in our program example the *range* of the loop goes from the DO statement down to and including statement number 70 (CONTINUE). In this loop the program will:

1. Read a test score data card from the card reader and store the value in a storage location named ISCORE, which can accept a three-digit integer number. Or

$$READ\ (1,\ 50)\ ISCORE$$
$$50\quad FORMAT\ (I3)$$

2. Print the score value in a column that is 23 spaces to the right of the left margin of the output document (see Fig. 12-1). Or

$$WRITE\ (3,60)\ ISCORE$$
$$60\quad FORMAT\ (23X,I4)$$

3. Add the test score (ISCORE) to the value stored in ITOTAL and return the accumulated total to ITOTAL. Or

$$ITOTAL = ITOTAL + ISCORE$$

4. Return to the beginning of the loop or branch away, depending on the number of iterations that have been made.

How does the computer know when to stop the loop? This is determined by the remainder of the DO statement. The i portion sets up an integer variable name, which acts as an *index*. The value of m_1 is the *initial value* given to the index; the value of m_2 is the value of the index when the looping should be *completed;* and the value of m_3 is the amount by which the index should be increased after each iteration through the loop (if this value is 1 it may be omitted). In our example, the index (I) is initially set at 1 (m_1). After each pass through the loop, the index is tested to see if m_2 (in this case 35) has been reached. If it has not been reached, the index is increased by 1 (m_3) and another iteration occurs; if it has, program control moves to the statement *following* the one specified in the DO instruction. In our example, the average grade would be computed following the termination of the DO loop.

As a result of our studying FORTRAN language characteristics, we have just about completed the description of the grade averaging program. Let us summarize this program by referring to Fig. 12-5, a flowchart that graphically presents the program logic using the terminology of the statements coded in Fig. 12-3. The numbers in parentheses in Fig. 12-5 refer to the lines of code in Fig. 12-3.

The first two lines of code—a READ statement and an associated FORMAT statement—provide the processor with data about the number of grades and name of the student. Following a test for reasonableness of input data (line 3), a variable name (ITOTAL) is identified and given a temporary integer value of zero (line 4). The first two printed lines on the output report (see Fig. 12-1, page 348) are prepared using the WRITE and FORMAT statements coded in lines 5 to 8 of Fig. 12-3 (the slash character at the end of FORMAT statement number 30 caused the printer to space between the first and second print lines). The DO loop just discussed is found in lines 9 to 15 of the coding sheet. At the termination of the looping, ITOTAL contains the accumulated test score points. The average grade is computed to the nearest integer value in line 16. This grade is 75. The last two printed lines on the output report are prepared using the program statements on lines 17 to 20. STOP and END statements are used to conclude FORTRAN programs.

Accounts-receivable Penalty Procedure Coding

Figure 12-6 shows a computer listing of the 28 lines of FORTRAN code used to prepare the output shown in Fig. 12-2 on page 349. The line numbers are indicated in the left column of Fig. 12-6, but they are not written on the coding sheets. A flowchart indicating the program logic is presented in Fig. 12-7. Again, the numbers in parentheses refer to lines of code. Let us briefly trace through the program using Figs. 12-6 and 12-7.

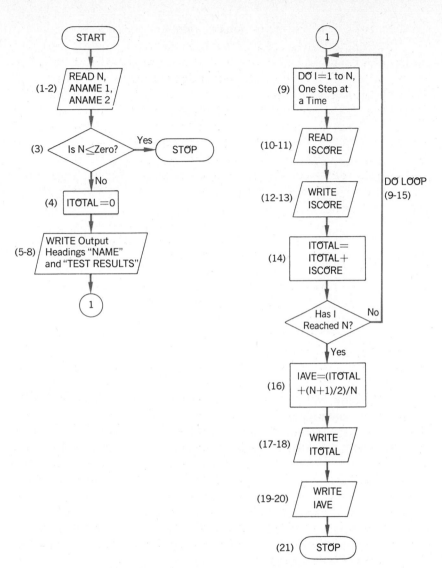

Figure 12-5 Grade averaging (FORTRAN) flowchart (numbers in parentheses refer to the lines of code in Figure 12-3)

A record counter (M) is assigned a value of zero in line 001, and the number of records to be processed (N) is read into the computer (lines 002 and 003). As you can see in line 003, N may be a five-digit integer number. Coding line 004 advances the record counter by one (M=M+1), so that when the first record has been processed, the counter will have a value of 1. Each time program control branches back to read another record, the counter is advanced by one. When all records have been processed, the values of M and N will be equal

```
                              FORTRAN    RUN
FORTRAN COMPILATION   VER 2 MOD 2
$OBJECT MACHINE SIZE = 15999
001          M=0
002          READ(1,10)N
C03      10 FORMAT(I5)
004      20 M=M+1
005          READ(1,30)NDAYS,UNBAL,ANAME1,ANAME2
006      30 FORMAT(I3,2X,F10.2,5X,2A10)
C07          WRITE(3,40)ANAME1,ANAME2
008      40 FORMAT(1X,22HCUSTOMER STATEMENT FOR,1X,2A10/)
009          IF(NDAYS-30)50,70,70
010      50 WRITE(3,60)
011      60 FORMAT(1X,20HACCOUNT NOT INCLUDED///)
012          IF(M-N)20,170,170
013      70 IF(UNBAL-200.)90,90,80
014      80 PENLTY=.03*UNBAL
015          GO TO 100
016      90 PENLTY=.02*UNBAL
017     1CO CACCNT=UNBAL+PENLTY
018          WRITE(3,110)CACCNT
019     110 FORMAT(1X,11HBALANCE DUE,5X,1H$,F7.2/)
020          IF(NDAYS-60)140,120,120
021     120 WRITE(3,130)NDAYS
022     130 FORMAT(1X,10HACCOUNT IS,I3,1X,12HDAYS OVERDUE///)
023          GO TO 160
024     140 WRITE(3,150)
025     150 FORMAT(1H0)
026     160 IF(M-N)20,170,170
027     170 STOP
028          END
```

Figure 12-6

and processing will be terminated. As long as M remains less than N, however, processing will continue.

A customer account record containing the number of days overdue (NDAYS), the unpaid balance (UNBAL), and the customer's name (ANAME1 and ANAME2) is read into storage by lines 005-006. You should now be able to read the FORMAT statement in line 006 with understanding: it specifies that NDAYS may be a three-digit integer number, that UNBAL is a real number having 10 characters with 2 digits to the right of the decimal point, and that a total of 20 alphanumeric characters may be stored to identify a customer. Lines 007 and 008 write the heading "CUSTOMER STATEMENT FOR . . . ." on the output document (Fig. 12-2).

Line 009 tests to determine if NDAYS is <30. This normally *should not* be the case, but if it is (1) an error message is written (lines 010 and 011), (2) a check is made to see if the last customer record has been processed (line 012), and (3) control branches to STOP or back to read another record, depending on the outcome of the check. If NDAYS ≥ 30, a test is made to determine if UNBAL is ≤ $200 (line 013). If UNBAL is > $200, that is, is not ≤ $200, a PENLTY is computed by multiplying UNBAL by .03 (line 014); if UNBAL is $200 or less, the PENLTY = .02 * UNBAL (line 016). The customer's current account (CACCNT) value is then computed by adding UNBAL and PENLTY (line 017).

The heading on the output report "BALANCE DUE . . . ." is prepared by lines 018 and 019. If NDAYS $\geq$ 60 (line 020), another heading ("ACCOUNT IS . . . . DAYS OVERDUE") is printed on the report (lines 021 and 022); if NDAYS < 60, the output document is advanced in the printer but no printing occurs (lines 024 and 025). Finally, another check is made to determine if the last customer record has been processed (line 026). If the answer is yes, i.e., if M — N does not yield a negative value, the processing stops (line 027); otherwise, program control branches back to advance the record counter and read the next customer record.

This completes our brief introduction of FORTRAN, a language that is relatively easy to learn and widely accepted. Although not well suited for processing large business files, it is often used for business statistical analysis purposes.

COBOL

Let us now examine the grade averaging program prepared by Professor Bal Sheet in the COBOL language. Figure 12-8 is the written source program prepared on special COBOL coding sheets. The heading information is self-explanatory. Each page has 24 lines and is designed to facilitate keypunching (the numbers at the top of the sheet correspond to columns in an 80-column card). Each line is numbered by the programmer to indicate proper card sequences after the punching is completed. The first three spaces in a line indicate the *page number* (001, 002, etc.), while the next three spaces give the *line number* (010, 020, 030, etc.). Lines may be numbered by increments of 10 so that insertions may be made later in the program if needed, e.g., so that a line labeled 160 may be followed later by 161, 162, 163, etc. A dash (-) is written in column 7 if a *word* is continued from the previous line. The letters A and B directly over columns 8 and 12 indicate *margins* are that used in COBOL "punctuation."

There are two types of COBOL words—*reserved words* and *supplied words* (or *names*). Reserved words such as SELECT, ASSIGN, READ, USAGE, COMPUTATIONAL, and PICTURE have special meaning to the compiler and *must* be used according to COBOL language rules. Supplied words or names such as GRADE-CARDS, GRADE-RECORD, NO-GRADES, REPORT, and HEADING-ROUTINE, are as-

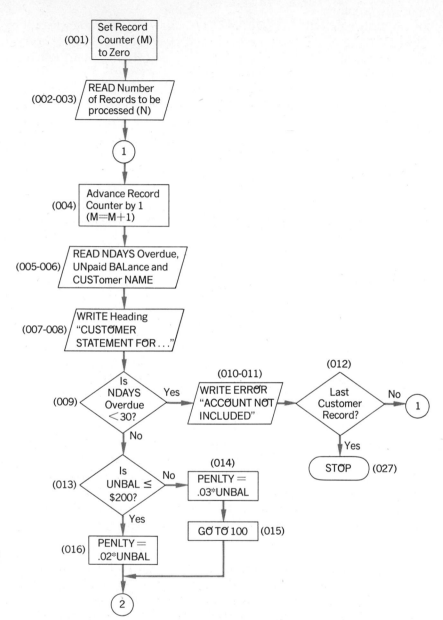

Figure 12-7 Accounts receivable penalty procedure FORTRAN program flowchart (numbers in parentheses refer to the lines of code in Figure 12-6)

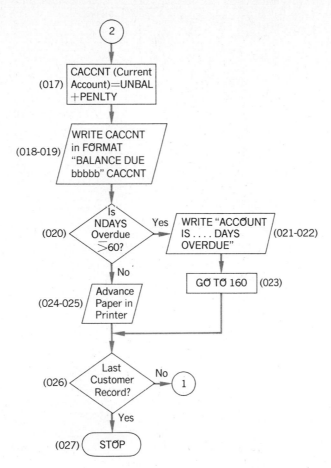

Figure 12-7   (Continued)

signed by the programmer. In other words, a supplied word may be anything that has meaning to the programmer and that does not violate any of the language rules.[9]

Identification Division

In Fig. 12-8, the first entry (page 001, line 010) is IDENTIFICATION DIVISION. This is the *first* of *four* basic *divisions* in a COBOL source program. This division consists of one required *paragraph*, which identifies the program (line 020). Additional optional paragraphs (with reserved names) may be included to identify the program author (line

---

[9]Supplied words may be made up of combinations of characters taken from the 26 letters of the alphabet, the numerals 0 to 9, and the dash or hyphen (-). No blank spaces are permissible within a word. INVENTORY-ON-HAND is a valid supplied word because the dashes replace blank spaces. No more than 30 characters may be used in a word, nor may a word *begin* or *end* with a dash.

COBOL Coding Form

SYSTEM		
PROGRAM	AVERAGE GRADE	
PROGRAMMER	BAL SHEET	DATE 10/13/1999

PUNCHING INSTRUCTIONS — GRAPHIC / PUNCH — CARD FORM #

SEQUENCE (PAGE) / (SERIAL)	CONT	A B	COBOL STATEMENT	IDENTIFICATION
001 010			IDENTIFICATION DIVISION.	AVERAGES
020			PROGRAM-ID. 'AVERAGES'.	
030			AUTHOR. BAL SHEET.	
040			DATE-WRITTEN. OCTOBER 13, 1999.	
050			DATE-COMPILED. OCTOBER 13, 1999.	
060			ENVIRONMENT DIVISION.	
070			CONFIGURATION SECTION.	
080			SOURCE-COMPUTER. IBM-360 F30.	
090			OBJECT-COMPUTER. IBM-360 F30.	
100			INPUT-OUTPUT SECTION.	
110			FILE-CONTROL.	
120			SELECT GRADE-CARDS ASSIGN TO UNIT-RECORD 2540R.	
130			SELECT REPORT ASSIGN TO UNIT-RECORD 1403.	
140			DATA DIVISION.	
150			FILE SECTION.	
160		FD	GRADE-CARDS, DATA RECORD IS GRADE-RECORD	
170			LABEL RECORDS ARE OMITTED.	
180		01	GRADE-RECORD.	
190		02	INITIALS-1 PICTURE IS A.	
200		02	INITIALS-2 PICTURE IS A.	
210		02	LAST-NAME PICTURE IS A(12).	
220		02	SCORE PICTURE IS 999.	
230		02	FILLER PICTURE IS X(63).	

Figure 12-8

IBM

COBOL Coding Form

SYSTEM			PUNCHING INSTRUCTIONS		
PROGRAM			GRAPHIC		CARD FORM #
PROGRAMMER	DATE		PUNCH		

IDENTIFICATION: `AVERAGES` (cols 73–80)

```
SEQUENCE
(PAGE)(SERIAL) CONT A  B
002 010        FD REPORT, DATA RECORD IS PRINT-LINE
    020              LABEL RECORDS ARE OMITTED.
    030           01 PRINT-LINE    PICTURE IS X(132).
    040           WORKING-STORAGE SECTION.
    050           77 ONE           PICTURE IS 9    USAGE IS COMPUTATIONAL-3   VALUE IS 1.
    060           77 ACCUMULATOR   PICTURE IS S9999  USAGE IS COMPUTATIONAL-3
    061              VALUE IS ZERO.
    070           77 NO-GRADES     PICTURE IS 99   USAGE IS COMPUTATIONAL-3
    071              VALUE IS ZERO.
    080           77 AVERAGE       PICTURE IS 999  USAGE IS COMPUTATIONAL-3
    081              VALUE IS ZERO.
    090           01 HEADING-LINE.
    100           02 FILLER        PICTURE IS X(10)  VALUE IS SPACES.
    110           02 FILLER        PICTURE IS X(6)   VALUE IS 'NAME'.
    120           02 INITIAL-P1    PICTURE IS A.
    130           02 FILLER        PICTURE IS X      VALUE IS '.'.
    140           02 INITIAL-P2    PICTURE IS A.
    150           02 FILLER        PICTURE IS XX     VALUE IS '.'.
    160           02 LAST-NAME-P   PICTURE IS A(12).
    170           02 FILLER        PICTURE IS X(99)  VALUE IS SPACES.
    180           01 HEAD-LINE-2.
    190           02 FILLER        PICTURE IS X(21)  VALUE IS SPACES.
    200           02 FILLER        PICTURE IS X(12)  VALUE IS 'TEST RESULTS'.
    210           02 FILLER        PICTURE IS X(99)  VALUE IS SPACES.
```

*A standard card form, IBM Electro C61897, is available for punching source statements from this form.
Instructions for using this form are given in any IBM COBOL reference manual.
Address comments concerning this form to IBM Corporation, Programming Publications, 1271 Avenue of the Americas, New York, New York 10020.

GX28-1464-5 U/M 050
Printed in U.S.A.

Figure 12-8 (Continued)

IBM

SYSTEM		
PROGRAM		
PROGRAMMER	DATE	

PUNCHING INSTRUCTIONS — GRAPHIC / PUNCH — CARD FORM # — *

IDENTIFICATION: A V E R A G E S

```
SEQUENCE  CONT  A  B   COBOL STATEMENT
003 010         01  DATA-LINE.
    020         02  FILLER    PICTURE IS X(5)   VALUE IS SPACES.
    030         02  LABEL     PICTURE IS X(7)   VALUE IS SPACES.
    040         02  FILLER    PICTURE IS X(9)   VALUE IS SPACES.
    050         02  SCORE     PICTURE IS ZZ,ZZ9.
    060         02  FILLER    PICTURE IS X(105) VALUE IS SPACES.
    070     PROCEDURE DIVISION.
    080     OPEN-PARA.
    090         OPEN INPUT GRADE-CARDS OUTPUT REPORT.
    091         READ GRADE-CARDS AT END GO TO TOTAL-PARA.
    100     INITILIZ-PARA.
    110         PERFORM HEADING-ROUTINE.
    111         GO TO A1.
    120     PROCESS-PARA.
    130         READ GRADE-CARDS AT END GO TO TOTAL-PARA.
    150     A1. ADD SCORE OF GRADE-RECORD TO ACCUMULATOR.
    140         ADD ONE TO NO-GRADES.
    160         MOVE SCORE OF GRADE-RECORD TO SCORE OF DATA-LINE.
    170         WRITE REPORT FROM DATA-LINE AFTER ADVANCING 1 LINES.
    180         GO TO PROCESS-PARA.
    190     TOTAL-PARA.
    200         MOVE ACCUMULATOR TO SCORE OF DATA-LINE.
    210         WRITE REPORT FROM DATA-LINE AFTER ADVANCING 2 LINES.
    220         DIVIDE NO-GRADES INTO ACCUMULATOR GIVING AVERAGE ROUNDED.
```

*A standard card form, IBM Electro C61897, is available for punching source statements from this form.
Instructions for using this form are given in any IBM COBOL reference manual.
Address comments concerning this form to IBM Corporation, Programming Publications, 1271 Avenue of the Americas, New York, New York 10020.

GX28-1464-5 U/M 050
Printed in U.S.A.

Figure 12-8 (Continued)

COBOL Coding Form

IBM

SYSTEM

PROGRAM

PROGRAMMER

DATE

PUNCHING INSTRUCTIONS — GRAPHIC / PUNCH

CARD FORM #

IDENTIFICATION: AVERAGES

SEQUENCE	COBOL STATEMENT
004010	MOVE AVERAGE TO SCORE OF DATA-LINE.
020	MOVE 'AVERAGE' TO LABEL.
030	WRITE REPORT FROM DATA-LINE AFTER ADVANCING 2 LINES.
040	CLOSE GRADE-CARDS REPORT. STOP RUN.
050	HEADING-ROUTINE.
060	MOVE INITIALS-1 TO INITIAL-P1.
070	MOVE INITIALS-2 TO INITIAL-P2.
080	MOVE LAST-NAME TO LAST-NAME-D.
090	WRITE REPORT FROM HEADING-LINE AFTER ADVANCING 0 LINES.
100	WRITE REPORT FROM HEAD-LINE-2 AFTER ADVANCING 2 LINES.

* A standard card form, IBM Electro C61897, is available for punching source statements from this form.
Instructions for using this form are given in any IBM COBOL reference manual.
Address comments concerning this form to IBM Corporation, Programming Publications, 1271 Avenue of the Americas, New York, New York 10020.

GX28-1464-5 U/M 050
Printed in U.S.A.

Figure 12-8 (Continued)

030), show the dates when the program is written and compiled (lines 040 and 050), and furnish other desirable information. Like this sentence, division and paragraph headings must end with a period.

Environment Division

The second COBOL division is the *environment division* (line 001060). This division describes the specific hardware being used and is therefore machine oriented. Since Professor Sheet has access to an IBM System/360 model 30 computer, the required *configuration section* of the environment division must reflect this fact. Lines 080 and 090 tell us that the program is compiled and run on this particular machine. The "F30" refers to the internal storage capacity (F) and the model number (30). The required *input/output section* describes the online I/O devices that are used in the processing. Lines 120 and 130 tell us that the input data cards (containing Val Student's individual test grades) are read by an IBM model 2540 card read-punch. The output report is printed by an IBM model 1403 printer. The environment division of a COBOL program must be rewritten any time the program is to be processed on different equipment. This rewriting, however, usually presents no problem.

Data Division

The *data division* (line 001140) is the third of the four COBOL divisions. In our example, there are two sections—the *file section* and the *working storage section*. The function of the file section (line 150) is to describe all data that enter or leave the CPU storage unit. Since business data are organized into files of records that consist of items, the file section entries are also grouped into these organizational levels, as shown in Fig. 12-9. Every file to be processed is identified by a file description (and the letters FD) on the COBOL coding sheet.

In our example we have only two simple files—an input GRADE-CARD file and an output REPORT file. The description of the GRADE-CARD file begins on line 001160 of Fig. 12-8. There is only a single

```
DATA DIVISION
  File section
    FD  File name.......................................
        01  Record name................................
            02  Description of record item.................
            02  Description of record item.................
            02  Description of record item.................
        01  Record name................................
    FD  File name.......................................
        01  Record name................................
            02  Description of record item.................
            02  Etc.........................................
```

Figure 12-9 File section organization

EXAMPLE	MEANING
PICTURE IS 999999.	The data item may consist of six unsigned numeric characters.
PICTURE IS 9(6).	Another way of expressing the preceding example.
PICTURE IS ZZ999.	The data item may consist of five unsigned numeric characters, and zeroes will be suppressed—i.e., replaced by blank spaces—if they appear in the two leftmost positions.
PICTURE IS 99V99.	The data item may have four unsigned numeric characters with a decimal point between the second and third characters.
PICTURE IS S99V99.	Same as the preceding example except that an operational sign (+ or —) will be present.
PICTURE IS AAAAA.	There may be five alphabetic characters in the data item.
PICTURE IS XXXX.	Four alphanumeric characters are reserved for this data item.

Figure 12-10

type of record in the input file, and this type of record is given the name of GRADE-RECORD in line 160. The description of the items included in this type of record (an 80-column card) begins on line 190. In lines 190 to 220 we see that provision is made on the input cards for two initials, a last name, and a grade score. The COBOL words "INITIALS-1," "INITIALS-2," "LAST-NAME," and "SCORE" are names that have been coined by Programmer Bal Sheet; they will be referred to again in the last division of the program.[10]

The word "PICTURE," used in lines 190 to 230, is a reserved word that describes the data items. (Fig. 12-10 shows the form and meaning of representative PICTURE clauses.) For example, the PICTURE IS A description tells the CPU the *size and class* of the words "INITIALS-1" and "INITIALS-2"; i.e., a *single* character tells the CPU that the size is one, and the character A also tells it that the class is *alphabetic*. The contents of the word "LAST-NAME" occupy 12 alphabetic character spaces. On line 220, the PICTURE IS 999 description indicates to the CPU that SCORE occupies three spaces and that the data class is *numeric*. Line 230 is used to absorb unused space in the input records. The symbol X, when used in a PICTURE clause, specifies to the CPU that the character may be anything available in the machine's

[10] *Every supplied name mentioned in the procedure division must be described in the data division.*

character set. On line 230, X(63) refers to 63 blank spaces. You will note that a total of 80 character spaces have been accounted for in lines 190 to 230. These 80 characters, of course, correspond to the 80 columns in the input record cards.

The output REPORT file is described in Fig. 12-8 (page 363) by lines 002010 to 002030. The output record is named "PRINT-LINE," and a printer with 132 characters per line is being used. The detailed description of the printed output format is left to the working storage section.

The second major component of the data division is the working storage section. In Chapter 8 we saw that the working storage area of the CPU is a portion of internal storage set aside temporarily to hold data being processed and also to hold intermediate results of that processing. As might be expected, entries in the working storage section of the data division specify the memory locations that are needed during processing to hold (1) intermediate results, (2) exact record descriptions, and (3) other frequently used independent items.

The intermediate results and other items that are independent of any record are assigned a special level number (77) and must appear first in the working storage section. Following these entries come record descriptions (with a level code of 01). In our example, there are four independent items that are assigned specific working storage locations by the compiler program. The names and descriptions of these items are as follows:

1. ONE (line 002050). The word "ONE" is used in the final COBOL division and is therefore defined and assigned to working storage. The number 1 occupies the *location named* "ONE." This word is used for computational purposes.
2. ACCUMULATOR (lines 060 and 061). The word "ACCUMU-LATOR" identifies the location that stores Val Student's total test points during the processing; i.e., as the score on each test is read into the computer, it is added to the previous points and the total is kept in ACCUMULATOR storage. The initial value of ACCU-MULATOR is 0. Provision is made to store five numeric characters.
3. NO-GRADES (lines 070 and 071). The word "NO-GRADES" has been created by Programmer Sheet to represent the number of test grades processed. The initial value of this word is set at 0, but when the processing is completed, the number 35 is stored in the NO-GRADES location. When Val's average grade is computed, the amount stored in ACCUMULATOR is divided by the number stored in NO-GRADES.
4. AVERAGE (lines 080 and 081). The *result* of dividing NO-GRADES

into ACCUMULATOR is stored in the working storage location named "AVERAGE." Space is provided for three numeric characters. (Unfortunately, no student has ever come close to an average grade of 100 in Professor Sheet's course, but it *is* possible.)

The remainder of the working storage section describes the format of the printed output report shown in Fig. 12-1, page 348. Program lines 100 to 170 describe the top line of print in Fig. 12-1, while program lines 190 to 210 define the contents and location of the second printed line. In this second printed line (HEAD-LINE-2), for example, the first 21 spaces are blank. Then, beginning with space number 22, the 12 fixed characters (TEST RESULTS) between the quotation marks[11] in program line 200 are printed. The remaining 99 spaces across the output report page are blank. The first six lines of the COBOL program sheet (Fig. 12-8, page 364) describe the format of the last two printed lines on the output report.

Procedure Division

The remaining lines of the COBOL example (Fig. 12-8, pages 364 and 365) specify the steps that the computer follows in processing the application. The steps in this final *procedure division* make use of the names of records and independent items, which are so precisely defined in the data division. The flowchart in Fig. 12-11 may help us trace through the necessary steps. The numbers beside each flowchart symbol correspond to the line numbers of the COBOL example (Fig. 12-8, pages 364 and 365).

The first paragraph in the procedure division (OPEN-PARA) is used to open the input and output files. The second paragraph (INITILIZ-PARA) instructs the printer to PERFORM the HEADING-ROUTINE, which results in the first two lines being printed on the output report. Instructions in the HEADING-ROUTINE paragraph tell the computer to move two initials and a last name from the CPU input storage area to specifically named locations (INITIAL-P1, INITIAL-P2, and LAST-NAME-P) in the working storage area. The printer then follows the format prescribed in line 002090 to 002210 of the program to print the two heading lines on the output report.

Processing steps are given in the third and fourth paragraphs (PROCESS-PARA and A1).

1. The *first* grade (a 75) is added to the contents of ACCU-MULATOR, and the total value (initially 75) is stored in ACCU-MULATOR.

---

[11] A COBOL word bounded by quotation marks is known as a *literal constant*.

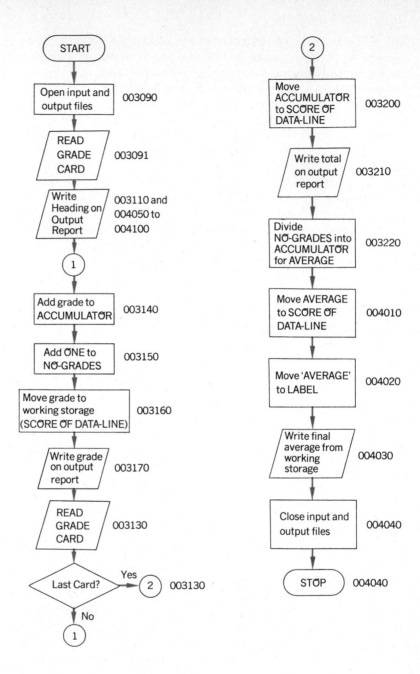

Figure 12-11   Procedure division flowchart

2. The contents of working storage location ONE are added to the contents of working storage location NO-GRADES; that is, 1 is initially added to 0.

3. The grade of 75 is moved to working storage location SCORE in the DATA-LINE record (see line 003050).

4. The contents of the DATA-LINE record, containing at this time only the grade of 75, are printed on the output report. The program then loops back, another card is read, and the procedure is repeated.

When the last grade record is processed, the program branches from PROCESS-PARA to TOTAL-PARA to compute the summary grade average. In 35 tests, Val Student scored 2,625 points.[12] When the last card is processed, this total is stored in the ACCUMULATOR location. To write this figure on the output report, the figure is first read into the SCORE location in the DATA-LINE record and from there it is moved to the printer. The total still remains in ACCUMULATOR, however, because read-out is nondestructive. To compute the average grade, the contents of NO-GRADES (35) are divided into the ACCUMULATOR contents (2,625). The resulting average of 75 is stored in location AVERAGE. From there it also is moved to the SCORE location in the working storage area. The instruction on line 004020 replaces the seven blank spaces in location LABEL in the DATA-LINE record with the seven characters between the quotation marks, i.e., with 'AVERAGE.'[13] The contents of the DATA-LINE record are then printed as the last line of the output report by the instruction on line 004030. The job is now completed, and so the files are closed and the run is stopped.

A computer listing of the penalty procedure program is shown in Fig. 12-12. Entries in the first two divisions require little explanation. Some remarks have been added in the identification division for explanation purposes.

Accounts-receivable Penalty Procedure Coding

The file section of the data division describes the AR-CARDS file and the output REPORT file. The AR-CARDS file has only a single type of record (AR-RECORD), which is described in lines 25 to 29. Thus, the input format for the number of days overdue, the amount of the unpaid balance, and the customer's name are described in these lines. The REPORT file description is similar to the one found in the grade averaging program.

[12] The breakdown of the test scores, of course, is shown in Fig. 12-1. Val finished strong.
[13] Data location AVERAGE should not be confused with the literal constant 'AVERAGE.'

```
LINE NO. SEQ. NO.        SOURCE STATEMENT                    CRD CL3-5 06/29/70          PAGE   1
      1    00101  IDENTIFICATION DIVISION.                                            ARPENALT
      2    00102  PROGRAM-ID. 'ARPENALT'.                                             ARPENALT
      3    00103  AUTHOR. HAL COMPUT.                                                 ARPENALT
  S   4    00100  REMARKS.  COMPUTE BILLING OF ACCOUNTS RECEIVABLES WITH PENALTY.     ARPENALT
      5    00105        OVER DUE BY 30 DAYS OR MORE -                                 ARPENALT
      6    00106           UNPAID BALANCE - $200 OR LESS    PENALTY OF 2%             ARPENALT
      7    00107                          MORE THAN $200 PENALTY OF 3%.               ARPENALT
      8    00108        OVER DUE BY 60 DAYS OR MORE - PRINT WARNING STATEMENT.        ARPENALT
      9    00109  DATE-WRITTEN. OCTOBER 13, 1999.                                     ARPENALT
     10    00110  DATE-COMPILED. OCTOBER 13, 1999.                                    ARPENALT
     11    00111                                                                      ARPENALT
     12    00112  ENVIRONMENT DIVISION.                                               ARPENALT
     13    00113  CONFIGURATION SECTION.                                              ARPENALT
     14    00114  SOURCE-COMPUTER. IBM-360 F30.                                       ARPENALT
     15    00115  OBJECT-COMPUTER. IBM-360 F30.                                       ARPENALT
     16    00116  INPUT-OUTPUT SECTION.                                               ARPENALT
     17    00117  FILE-CONTROL.                                                       ARPENALT
     18    00118        SELECT AR-CARDS ASSIGN TO 'SYS001' UNIT-RECORD 2540R.         ARPENALT
     19    00119        SELECT REPORT ASSIGN TO 'SYS002' UNIT-RECORD 1403.            ARPENALT
     20    00120                                                                      ARPENALT
     21    00201  DATA DIVISION.                                                      ARPENALT
     22    00202  FILE SECTION.                                                       ARPENALT
     23    00203  FD  AR-CARDS, DATA RECORD IS AR-RECORD, LABEL RECORDS ARE           ARPENALT
     24    00204        OMITTED, RECORDING MODE IS F.                                 ARPENALT
     25    00205  01  AR-RECORD.                                                      ARPENALT
     26    00206      02  AR-OVER-DUE-DAYS     PICTURE IS 99.                         ARPENALT
     27    00207      02  AR-AMOUNT            PICTURE IS 9(6)V99.                     ARPENALT
     28    00208      02  AR-NAME              PICTURE IS X(40).                       ARPENALT
     29    00209      02  FILLER               PICTURE IS X(30).                       ARPENALT
     30    00210  FD  REPORT, DATA RECORD IS PRINT-LINE, LABEL RECORDS ARE            ARPENALT
     31    00211  .     OMITTED, RECORDING MODE IS F.                                 ARPENALT
     32    00212  01  PRINT-LINE  PICTURE X(132).                                     ARPENALT
     33    00213                                                                      ARPENALT
     34    00214  WORKING-STORAGE SECTION.                                            ARPENALT
     35    00215  77  PENALTY  PICTURE IS S9(6)V99  USAGE IS COMPUTATIONAL-3.         ARPENALT
     36    00216  01  HEADING-LINE.                                                   ARPENALT
     37    00217      02  FILLER          PICTURE IS X(10)  VALUE IS SPACES.          ARPENALT
     38    00218      02  FILLER          PICTURE IS X(23)                            ARPENALT
     39    00219          VALUE IS 'CUSTOMER STATEMENT FOR '.                         ARPENALT
     40    00220      02  PL-NAME          PICTURE IS X(40)                           ARPENALT
     41    00301      02  FILLER          PICTURE IS X(59)   VALUE IS SPACES.         ARPENALT
     42    00302  01  AMOUNT-LINE.                                                    ARPENALT
     43    00303      02  FILLER          PICTURE IS X(10)  VALUE IS SPACES.          ARPENALT
     44    00304      02  FILLER          PICTURE IS X(14)                            ARPENALT
     45    00305          VALUE IS 'BALANCE DUE  '.                                   ARPENALT
     46    00306      02  PL-AMOUNT        PICTURE IS $Z(5)9.99.                       ARPENALT
     47    00307      02  FILLER          PICTURE IS X(98)   VALUE IS SPACES.         ARPENALT
     48    00308  01  WARNING-LINE.                                                   ARPENALT
     49    00309      02  FILLER          PICTURE IS X(10)  VALUE IS SPACES.          ARPENALT
     50    00310      02  FILLER          PICTURE IS X(11)                            ARPENALT
     51    00311          VALUE IS 'ACCOUNT IS '.                                     ARPENALT
     52    00312      02  PL-OVER-DUE-DAYS PICTURE IS 99.                             ARPENALT
     53    00313      02  FILLER          PICTURE IS X(13)                            ARPENALT
     54    00314          VALUE IS ' DAYS OVERDUE'.                                   ARPENALT
     55    00315      02  FILLER          PICTURE IS X(96)   VALUE IS SPACES.         ARPENALT
     56    00316  01  NOTOVER-LINE.                                                   ARPENALT
     57    00317      02  FILLER          PICTURE IS X(10)  VALUE IS SPACES.          ARPENALT
     58    00318      02  FILLER          PICTURE IS X(20)                            ARPENALT
     59    00319          VALUE IS 'ACCOUNT NOT INCLUDED'.                            ARPENALT
     60    00320      02  FILLER          PICTURE IS X(102)  VALUE IS SPACES.         ARPENALT
     61    00401                                                                      ARPENALT
     62    00402  PROCEDURE DIVISION.                                                 ARPENALT
     63    00403  OPEN-HOUSEKEEPING.                                                  ARPENALT
     64    00404      OPEN INPUT AR-CARDS   OUTPUT REPORT.                            ARPENALT
     65    00405      MOVE SPACES TO PRINT-LINE.                                      ARPENALT
     66    00406      WRITE PRINT-LINE AFTER ADVANCING 0 LINES.                       ARPENALT
     67    00407  READ-CUSTOMER-RECORD.                                               ARPENALT
     68    00408      READ AR-CARDS   AT END GO TO END-OF-JOB.                        ARPENALT
     69    00409      MOVE AR-NAME TO PL-NAME.                                        ARPENALT
     70    00410      WRITE PRINT-LINE FROM HEADING-LINE AFTER ADVANCING 3 LINES.     ARPENALT
     71    00411      IF AR-OVER-DUE-DAYS LESS THAN 30                                ARPENALT
     72    00412          WRITE PRINT-LINE FROM NOTOVER-LINE AFTER ADVANCING          ARPENALT
     73    00413            2 LINES                                                   ARPENALT
     74    00414          GO TO READ-CUSTOMER-RECORD.                                 ARPENALT
     75    00415      IF AR-AMOUNT GREATER THAN 200.00                               ARPENALT
     76    00416          COMPUTE PENALTY ROUNDED = AR-AMOUNT + AR-AMOUNT * .03       ARPENALT
     77    00417      ELSE COMPUTE PENALTY ROUNDED = AR-AMOUNT + AR-AMOUNT * .02.     ARPENALT
     78    00418      MOVE PENALTY TO PL-AMOUNT.                                       ARPENALT
     79    00419      WRITE PRINT-LINE FROM AMOUNT-LINE AFTER ADVANCING 2 LINES.      ARPENALT
     80    00420      IF AR-OVER-DUE-DAYS LESS THAN 60 GO TO READ-CUSTOMER-RECORD.    ARPENALT
     81    00501      MOVE AR-OVER-DUE-DAYS TO PL-OVER-DUE-DAYS.                      ARPENALT
     82    00502      WRITE PRINT-LINE FROM WARNING-LINE AFTER ADVANCING 2 LINES.     ARPENALT
     83    00503      GO TO READ-CUSTOMER-RECORD.                                     ARPENALT
     84    00504  END-OF-JOB.                                                         ARPENALT
     85    00505      CLOSE AR-CARDS  REPORT.                                         ARPENALT
     86    00506      STOP RUN.                                                       ARPENALT
```

Figure 12-12

In the processing of the program, intermediate results will be given the name PENALTY; therefore, PENALTY is defined in the first line of the working storage section of the data division (line 35). The remaining lines of the working storage section (lines 36 to 60) define the format of the printed output report shown in Fig. 12-2 (page 349). You should now be able to understand each of these entries. For example, the name HEADING-LINE refers to the first line to be printed for each customer account. This printed line has 10 blank spaces followed by CUSTOMER STATEMENT FOR . . . . , and then the customer's name (PL-NAME) is inserted. Forty characters may be used in the customer's name. The remaining 59 spaces in the 132-character print line are left blank.

A flowchart of the procedure division is presented in Fig. 12-13. The numbers in parentheses refer to the lines of code in Fig. 12-12. A study of Figs. 12-12 and 12-13 should enable you to trace through the remainder of the program. Since the flowchart is quite comparable to Fig. 10-12, we need not devote further attention to it here.

Although COBOL may be more difficult to learn than FORTRAN, it is currently the most popular language for business data processing applications where large files must be updated on a regular basis. The documentation provided in COBOL source programs is generally better than that provided by other languages.

PL/I

As noted earlier, PL/I is a language that combines features of both FORTRAN and COBOL. In addition, it has features not to be found in either of those languages. Because of its numerous features and facilities, PL/I is organized into "building blocks," or modules, which meet the needs found in particular application areas.

Some PL/I Statement Concepts

The coding for the grade averaging problem is shown in Fig. 12-14. A general purpose form is used because PL/I requires no special coding sheets; the programmer has considerable latitude in the way he writes his instructions. For example, it is possible to have more than one statement on a line, and it is also possible to use *multiple* variable names in a single arithmetic assignment statement. That is, in the PL/I statement

$$\text{EGAD, ZOUNDS, UGH} = X/Y + Z;$$

where X is 6, Y is 3, and Z is 8, the result of this statement would be to assign the value 10 to each of the three variable names to the

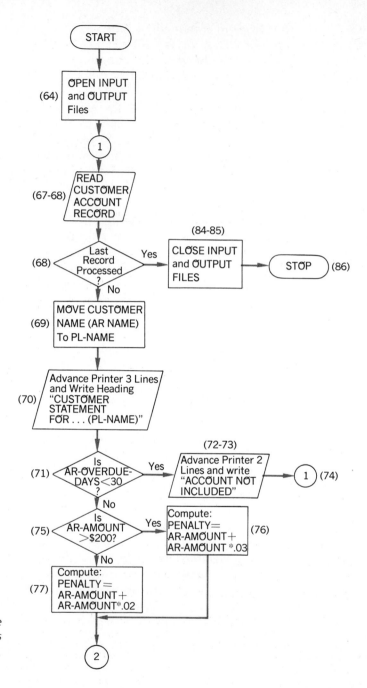

Figure 12-13 Accounts receivable penalty procedure COBOL flowchart (numbers in parentheses refer to line numbers in Figure 12-12)

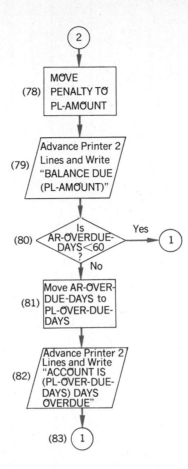

Figure 12-13   (*Continued*)

left of the assignment (=) sign. Such a statement would not be possible in FORTRAN. Program statements in PL/I use FORTRAN symbols for arithmetic operations,[14] programmer-defined *identifiers* (similar to COBOL supplied words), and PL/I defined *keywords*.[15]

Each PL/I statement is concluded with a semicolon, and statements are combined into *groups* and *blocks* to form the program. A group is similar to a COBOL paragraph; a block may represent an entire small program or a subroutine of a more complex program.

---

[14] See the FORTRAN symbols on page 353. Additional operation symbols used in PL/I include $>$, $<$, L (not equal to), $>=$ (greater than or equal to), $<=$ (less than or equal to), etc.
[15] An identifier may have up to 31 alphanumeric characters, must begin with a letter, and must have no blank spaces (an underscore or break character is used to fill blank spaces rather than the hyphen used in COBOL). Keywords have specific meanings to the compiler when used in the proper context, but they are not "reserved" like the reserved words in COBOL. A programmer may use a keyword as an identifier, and the compiler will detect the difference by the *position* or context of the characters in the statement.

GENERAL PURPOSE CARD PUNCHING FORM

PUNCHING INSTRUCTIONS

JOB	AVERAGE OF TEST SCORES	WRITTEN AS:
BY	JOHN Q PROGRAMMER	DATE 1/26/70	PUNCH AS:

NOTES: PL/I

FIELD IDENTIFICATION

	1-10	11-20	21-30	31-40	41-50	51-60	61-70	71-80

```
1   AVERAGE: PROCEDURE OPTIONS (MAIN);
2   DECLARE
3     N FIXED (2),
4     NAME CHARACTER (15),
5     SCORE FIXED (3),
6     TOTAL FIXED (4),
7     AVE FIXED (3),
8     SWT FIXED (1),
9     WORK FILE,
10    NWORK FILE PRINT;
11    TOTAL = 0;
12    N = 0;
13    SWT = 0;
14    OPEN FILE (WORK) INPUT, FILE (NWORK) OUTPUT;
15    READ: GET FILE (WORK) EDIT (NAME, SCORE) (X(60),A(15),X(2),F(3));
16    ON ENDFILE (WORK) GO TO OUTPUT;
17    IF SWT = 1 THEN GO TO CONTINUE;
18    SWT = 1;
19    PUT FILE (NWORK) EDIT ('NAME    ',NAME) (PAGE,X(10),A(6),A(15));
20    PUT FILE (NWORK) EDIT ('TEST RESULTS') (SKIP(2),X(21),A(12));
```

Figure 12-14

376

GENERAL PURPOSE CARD PUNCHING FORM

PUNCHING INSTRUCTIONS

WRITTEN AS:		
PUNCH AS:		

JOB AVERAGE OF TEST SCORES

BY JOHN Q. PROGRAMMER   DATE 1/26/70

NOTES: PL/1

```
     FIELD IDENTIFICATION
     1-10        11-20        21-30        31-40        41-50        51-60        61-70        71-80
1    CONTINUE: PUT FILE (NWORK) EDIT (SCORE) (SKIP(1),X(24),P'ZZ9',);
2    N = N + 1;
3    TOTAL = TOTAL + SCORE;
4    GO TO READ;
5    OUTPUT: PUT FILE (NWORK) EDIT (TOTAL) (SKIP(2),X(22),P'9,999',);
6    AVE = TOTAL / N;
7    PUT FILE (NWORK) EDIT ('AVERAGE',AVE) (SKIP(2),X(5),A(7),X(12),P'Z99',);
8    CLOSE FILE (WORK), FILE (NWORK);
9    END AVERAGE;
10
11
12
13
14
15
16
17
18
19
20
```

PAGE 2 OF 2

Figure 12-14 (Continued)

377

The Procedure Block

Every PL/I program must have at least one *external procedure block*. On the first line of Fig. 12-14 is AVERAGE: PROCEDURE OPTIONS (MAIN);—a line that heads the required block and that identifies our program by a label (AVERAGE).[16] The block (and in our case the program) is terminated by the word END followed by the block label or identifier, i.e., END AVERAGE;.

The DECLARE statement (page 1, lines 2 to 10 of Fig. 12-14) specifies the attributes of the identifiers that will be used in the program. We see, for example, that N will be an integer (FIXED) number from 0 to 99. Other identifiers (SCORE, TOTAL, AVE, and SWT) are also fixed-point numbers. The identifier NAME may represent a string of 15 characters (line 4, Fig. 12-14). The last two lines of the DECLARE statement identify WORK and NWORK as files, with NWORK being an output PRINT file.

Figure 12-15 is the PL/I grade averaging flowchart. The numbers in parentheses refer to (page)-(line) numbers in Fig. 12-14. Following the assignment statements on lines 1-11 to 1-13, the program calls for the OPEN statement to be executed. WORK is specified as an INPUT file, and NWORK is an OUTPUT file. A PL/I "GET EDIT" statement used for input purposes is illustrated on line 1-15. (The statement itself is identified by the label READ, which is supplied by the programmer for program control purposes.) The general form of the GET EDIT statement is

GET . . . EDIT (data-list) (format-list);

where the *input* data items to be read into primary storage are listed and the format for each data item is specified. On line 1-15, NAME may be a 15-character string of alphabetic data, and SCORE may be a three-digit integer value. The X(60) and X(2) indicates blank spaces.

When all data have been processed, the program will branch to the statement labeled OUTPUT (on line 2-5) to compute the average grade. When the first test score is being processed, however, the program continues in sequence to the conditional branch "IF" statement found on line 1-17. Initially, a value of zero was assigned to SWT. Therefore, when the first card is processed SWT will *not* = 1. This condition will result in program control moving to the instruction on line 1-18. After SWT has been assigned a value of 1 (line 1-18), the first two printed lines on Fig. 12-1, page 348, will be prepared by the "PUT EDIT" statements on lines 1-19 and 1-20.

---

[16] If the procedure block represented a subroutine, the first word or label would be used as a reference for the main entry point to the procedure.

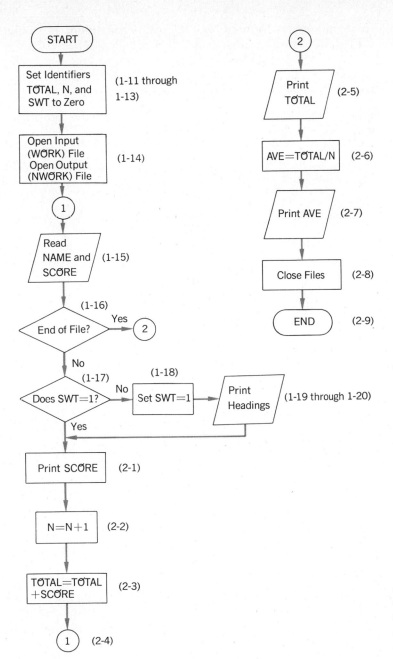

Figure 12-15 Grade
averaging (PL/I) flowchart
(numbers in parentheses
refer to page and line
numbers in Figure 12-14)

The general form of the PUT EDIT statement is similar to the GET EDIT statement; i.e., it is

PUT . . . EDIT (data-list) (format-list);

where the *output* data items are listed and the output format is specified. On line 1-19, the word bounded by quotation marks will be reproduced exactly and will be followed by the contents of the storage location identified as NAME. The specification PAGE in the format-list section tells the printer to begin on the top line of a new page; X(10) skips 10 spaces on the line; and the printing then begins. The code on line 1-20 writes the heading TEST RESULTS on the output document after skipping two lines. The statement identified by the label CONTINUE (on line 2-1) then prints the test score after advancing the printer one line;[17] the value of N is stepped up by one (line 2-2); the value of SCORE is added to TOTAL (line 2-3); and the program unconditionally branches back to the statement labeled READ to obtain the next test score. When the last score has been processed, TOTAL will be printed (line 2-5), AVE will be computed (line 2-6) and printed (line 2-7), and the files will be closed (line 2-8).

Accounts-receivable Penalty Procedure Coding

The PL/I statements used to code the accounts-receivable penalty procedure problem are listed in Fig. 12-16. The program flowchart is shown in Fig. 12-17, with the numbers in parentheses corresponding to the statement numbers printed in Fig. 12-16.[18] In the DECLARE statement, UNBAL FIXED (6,2) means (1) that up to six digits may be stored and (2) that two of the digits are to be treated as fractional; i.e., they will be placed to the right of the decimal point. Since there are no significant additional features of PL/I presented in this program, no further comments need be made here. After studying Figs. 12-16 and 12-17, you should be able to describe the essential characteristics of the program. Remember that the PUT EDIT statements refer to output operations performed on Fig. 12-2.

PL/I is a flexible and sophisticated language with features found in both FORTRAN and COBOL. It is more difficult to learn in its entirety than either of those languages. But because of its building block or modular structure, one need not learn the entire language in order to prepare applications programs of a particular type. Also,

[17] The P'ZZ9' on line 2-1 is a PL/I adaptation of the COBOL PICTURE clause. In this case, of course, the value of SCORE may be three digits, and the first two digits will have unnecessary zeros suppressed.

[18] Several statement *numbers* (but not statements) have been omitted by the compiler.

```
        PENLTY: PROCEDURE OPTIONS (MAIN);

STMT LEVEL NEST
  1                   PENLTY: PROCEDURE OPTIONS (MAIN);
  2      1            DECLARE
                         ANAME CHARACTER (15),
                         NDAYS FIXED (3),
                         UNBAL FIXED (6,2),
                         PENLTY FIXED (6,2),
                         CACCNT FIXED (6,2),
                         WORK FILE,
                         NWORK FILE PRINT;
  3      1            OPEN FILE (WORK) INPUT, FILE (NWORK) OUTPUT;
  4      1            READ: GET FILE (WORK) EDIT (NDAYS,UNBAL,ANAME) (X(49),F(3),X(2),F(6,2),
                      X(5),A(15));
  5      1            ON ENDFILE (WORK) GO TO FINISH;
  7      1            PUT FILE (NWORK) EDIT (' CUSTOMER STATEMENT FOR ',ANAME) (A(24),A(15));
  8      1            IF NDAYS >= 30 THEN GO TO TEST;
 10      1            PUT FILE (NWORK) EDIT (' ACCOUNT NOT INCLUDED') (SKIP(2),A(21));
 11      1            PUT FILE (NWORK) SKIP(4);
 12      1            GO TO READ;
 13      1            TEST: IF UNBAL <= 200 THEN GO TO MULT;
 15      1            PENLTY = .03 * UNBAL;
 16      1            GO TO ADD;
 17      1            MULT: PENLTY = .02 * UNBAL;
 18      1            ADD: CACCNT = UNBAL + PENLTY;
 19      1            PUT FILE (NWORK) EDIT (' BALANCE DUE      ',CACCNT) (SKIP(2),A(17),
                      P'$ZZZZV.99');
 20      1            IF NDAYS >= 60 THEN GO TO DAYS;
 22      1            PUT FILE (NWORK) SKIP(4);
 23      1            GO TO READ;
 24      1            DAYS: PUT FILE (NWORK) EDIT (' ACCOUNT IS',NDAYS,' DAYS OVERDUE')
                      (SKIP(2),A(11),P'Z99',A(13));
 25      1            PUT FILE (NWORK) SKIP(4);
 26      1            GO TO READ;
 27      1            FINISH: CLOSE FILE (WORK), FILE (NWORK);
 28      1            END PENLTY;
```

Figure 12-16

modular procedure blocks identified by program control labels are efficiently handled by the operating system in a multiprogramming environment.

BASIC

BASIC is an easy-to-learn language that is widely used by problem-solvers working at remote timesharing terminals. Engineers, managers, secretaries, teachers, students—these and many others have been introduced to programs and computers through the use of BASIC.

Basic Program Statements

We can consider some of the more commonly used BASIC statements by referring to Fig. 12-18, the program for the grade averaging problem, and Fig. 12-19, the output resulting from this program. The program was typed on (and the output was produced by) a terminal similar to the one shown in Fig. 4-7 (page 104).

Although all BASIC program statements must have *line numbers* assigned by the programmer, *system commands* do not require them. System commands enable the user to communicate with the operating system of the computer. Thus, the command RUN at the bottom of Fig. 12-18 is a system command that instructs the computer to process the program. Figure 12-19 is the computer's response to RUN.

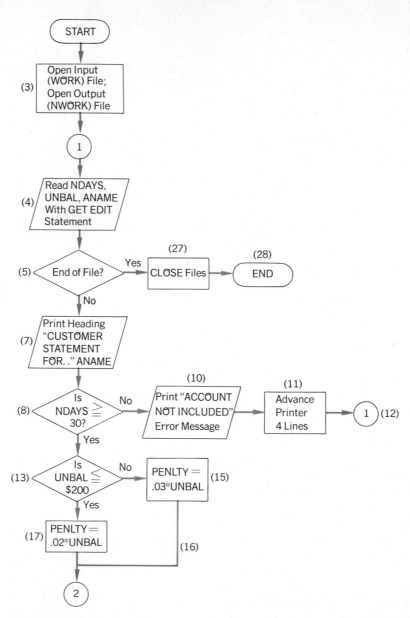

Figure 12-17 Accounts receivable penalty procedure (PL/I) flowchart (numbers in parentheses refer to statement numbers in Figure 12-16)

The first statement in the program is an input READ statement, which must be combined with a DATA statement. The general form of these statements is

| In READ list of variable names | In DATA list of data values |

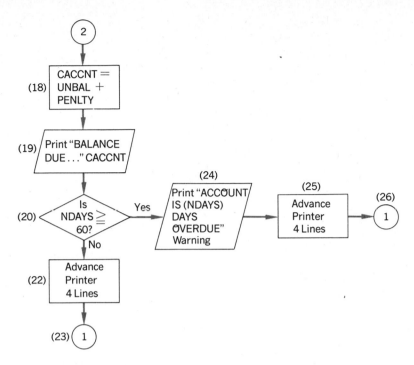

Figure 12-17   (Continued)

where ln is the line number and the values to be assigned to the variable names identified in a READ statement are found in a DATA statement. Thus,

```
010 READ A, N$
```

means that the computer will locate the *first* DATA statement and assign to the variable name A the first value encountered. In this case, A will be assigned the value of 35, which is the first item found on line number 170. In BASIC, a variable name is *limited* to a single letter or a letter followed by a digit or special character. If the second character is a dollar sign—as in N$ in our first READ statement—the variable name will be assigned a string of alphanumeric characters from the DATA statement. Therefore, "A. V. STUDENT" (line 170) is assigned to N$. Although DATA statements may be typed anywhere in the program except after the END statement, it is standard practice to locate them near the end of the program as shown in Fig. 12-18. Before executing the program, the processor will arrange *in order,* in a single long list, *all* of the data values contained in the DATA statements. A *pointer* is set internally in the system at the *first* value in the list, and the first variable name encountered in a READ statement

```
010 READ A,N$
020 IF A<=0 THEN 250
030 LET T=0
040 PRINT TAB(11);"NAME";TAB(17);N$
050 PRINT
060 PRINT TAB(22);"TEST RESULTS"
070 FOR I=1 TO A
080 READ S1
090 PRINT USING 95,S1
095:                              ####
100 LET T=T+S1
110 NEXT I
120 LET M1=T/A
130 PRINT
140 PRINT TAB(23);T
150 PRINT
160 PRINT TAB(6);"AVERAGE";TAB(25);M1
170 DATA 35,A.V. STUDENT
180 DATA 075,050,055,000,100,
190 DATA 100,075,100,100,050,
200 DATA 000,075,100,067,063,
210 DATA 097,063,093,057,067,
220 DATA 083,000,100,100,072,
230 DATA 075,063,087,093,075,
240 DATA 100,100,100,100,090
250 END
```

Figure 12-18   RUN

during program execution is assigned the value indicated by the pointer. The pointer then shifts to the next value, which will be supplied to the next variable name encountered in a READ statement, etc.

On line number 020 we find a conditional IF . . . THEN *branching* statement, which tells the computer that IF A is less than or equal to zero ($<=0$) THEN branch to line 250 (END); otherwise, continue to line 030.[19] On lines 030, 100, and 120, we find BASIC *arithmetic assignment* statements. The word LET is used to introduce this type of statement. On line 030, the variable T (for TOTAL) is assigned a value of zero; on line 100, the quantity identified by the name S1 is added to T and the result is assigned to T; and on line 120 the result of dividing A into T is assigned to M1. The BASIC symbols used in arithmetic operations are similar to those used in the other languages we have examined; i.e., $+$, $-$, $*$, and $/$ refer to addition, subtraction,

---

[19] This statement is included for input error control purposes. In short, the IF part of a statement describes a condition, and the THEN part branches program control to another line number if the condition is true.

multiplication, and division—except that exponentiation may be indicated by the symbol ↑.

The word PRINT is used in output operations to display program results. A statement that reads

> 015 PRINT A,B,C,D,E

would cause the values of the five variable names to be printed across the page, with A beginning at the *left margin,* B beginning 15 spaces to the right, C beginning 30 spaces to the right, etc. The width of many terminal printers is 75 characters, and the use of commas in the PRINT statement *automatically* establishes a format of 5 columns of 15 characters each. This implicit format specification feature of BASIC is especially appreciated by problem-solvers who are not professional programmers. But specifying output format is also possible in BASIC. On lines 040, 060, 090 to 095, 140, and 160 of Fig. 12-18 we have examples of PRINT statements that indicate the desired format. Line 040 prints the top heading line of Fig. 12-19. The TAB(11) portion of the statement directs the printer to move 11 spaces *from the left margin;* the word in the quotation marks is then printed exactly as it appears on the statement line; TAB(17) directs the printer to 17 spaces *from the left margin* (not from NAME); and N$ (A. V. STUDENT) is then printed. The statement

> 050 PRINT

is used to advance the print page one line.[20] Line 060 then prints the second line of Fig. 12-19 beginning 23 spaces from the left margin. On line 090, the program instructs the printer to use the format specified on line 095 to print the value of S1. Lines 140 and 160 require no further explanation.

Lines 070 to 110 put the program into a looping or iterative process. The BASIC FOR/NEXT statements are always used together and are similar to the DO statement discussed in the FORTRAN section. The general form of these statements is

> ln FOR v = n_1 TO n_2 STEP n_3
> ln   .
> ln   .
> ln   .
> ln NEXT v

```
NAME   A.V. STUDENT

               TEST RESULTS
                   75
                   50
                   55
                    0
                  100
                  100
                   75
                  100
                  100
                   50
                    0
                   75
                  100
                   67
                   63
                   97
                   63
                   93
                   57
                   67
                   83
                    0
                  100
                  100
                   72
                   75
                   63
                   87
                   93
                   75
                  100
                  100
                  100
                  100
                   90

                 2625

AVERAGE           75
```
Figure 12-19

---

[20]The printer does what it is told to do; it fills the line with blank spaces.

where ln is the line number, v is a variable name acting as an index, n_1 is the initial value given to the index, n_2 is the value of the index when the looping is completed, and n_3 is the amount by which the index should be *stepped up,* or increased, after each iteration through the loop (if the step is 1, this portion of the statement may be omitted as it is on line 070). In our example, the index (I) is initially set at 1 (n_1) and the program steps called for in lines 080 to 110 are executed. The statement on line 080 reads the first test score (075) from DATA line 180;[21] this score is printed according to the format specified on lines 090 and 095; the value of the score is added to the value stored in T and the result is stored in T (line 100); and the end of the loop is reached (line 110). If a test shows that A (in this case 35) has not been reached, the index is increased by 1 and the *next* pass through the loop occurs. When the looping has been completed and all 35 test scores have been read, printed on Fig. 12-19, and totaled, program control moves to line 120. The average grade (M1) is computed (line 120), a line is skipped on the output document (line 130), the total of the test score points is printed (line 140), another line is skipped (line 150), and the final line on Fig. 12-19 is produced (line 160). Figure 12-20 is the flowchart for this BASIC program.

Accounts-receivable Penalty Procedure Coding

The BASIC statements used to code the accounts-receivable penalty procedure problem are listed in Fig. 12-21, the output of this program is shown in Fig. 12-22, and the program flowchart is presented in Fig. 12-23. With the help of these illustrations you should now be able to trace through this program.

BASIC is the easiest to learn of the languages discussed in this chapter. The problem solver need not be confused about output formats because the PRINT statement may automatically provide a usable format. As we have seen, however, format specification is possible. No distinction need be made between integer and real numbers. But, on the other hand, there is as yet no standard version of BASIC, its file handling capabilities are limited, and it lacks some of the advanced features that professional programmers might want to use.

REPORT PROGRAM GENERATOR (RPG)

Because RPG is a limited purpose language that is used for certain types of business data processing applications, we shall restrict our

[21]The score of 075 is the third value in the total list of data values stored in the computer. Since the first two values were read when the READ statement on line 010 was encountered, the pointer was at 075 when the next READ command was received. After assigning 075 to S1, the pointer moved to 050, the next data item.

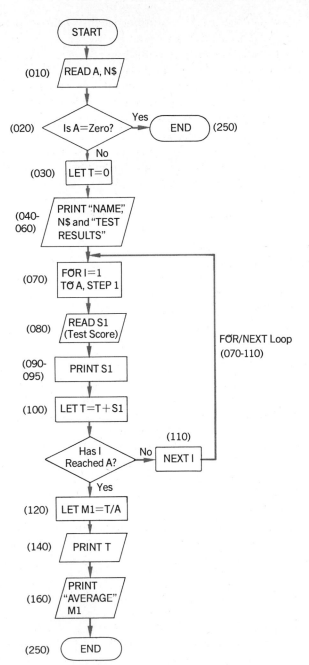

Figure 12-20 Grade averaging (BASIC) flowchart (numbers in parentheses refer to line numbers in Figure 12-18)

```
010 LET M=0
020 READ N
030 LET M=M+1
040 READ N1,N2,N$
050 PRINT TAB(2);"CUSTOMER STATEMENT FOR ";TAB(25);N$
060 PRINT
070 IF N1>=30 THEN 140
080 PRINT TAB(2);"ACCOUNT NOT INCLUDED"
090 PRINT
100 PRINT
110 PRINT
120 IF M>=N THEN 370
130 IF M<N THEN 30
140 IF N2<=200.00 THEN 170
150 LET P=.03*N2
160 GO TO 180
170 LET P=.02*N2
180 LET C=N2+P
190 PRINT USING 195," BALANCE DUE","$",C
195: "           "     '####.##
200 IF N1<60 THEN 270
210 PRINT
220 PRINT TAB(2);"ACCOUNT IS";TAB(12);N1;TAB(15);" DAYS OVERDUE"
230 PRINT
240 PRINT
250 PRINT
260 GO TO 300
270 PRINT
280 PRINT
290 PRINT
300 IF M<N THEN 30
310 DATA 5
320 DATA 25,150.00,JOHN SMITH
330 DATA 45,200.00,A.V. STUDENT
340 DATA 65,250.00,RANDY JOHNSON
350 DATA 30,300.00,BEVERLY BIVENS
360 DATA 60,350.00,ALEXANDRE DUMAS
370 END

RUN
```

Figure 12-21

discussion here to a brief consideration of only the accounts-receivable penalty procedure problem. There is no standardized version of RPG, but the version presented here is a popular one used with the IBM System/360, model 20, computer. Why is RPG a limited purpose language? It is because *every* object program generated from source programs by the RPG compiler follows a basic processing cycle from which it *never* deviates. The general form of this cycle is illustrated in Fig. 12-24.

Since the general processing logic never varies, the RPG programmer concerns himself with *file description* and with specifications about *input, calculations,* and *output format.* Figure 12-25 shows the coding sheets used in our example problem; it also illustrates the extent to which RPG relies on rigorously described specification sheets. Let us examine each of these sheets.

The name used by the programmer to define the input (I) file is CARD;[22] the name given to the output (O) file is OUTPUT. An IBM 2560 multifunction card machine found in model 20 installations is used to read the input file, and the model 20 printer is the device used for output operations.

File-description Specifications

The input data fields are defined on this sheet on lines 020 to 040. Card columns 1 and 2 are for the number of days the account is overdue (NDAYS), with no decimal positions; columns 3 to 10 are for the unpaid balance (UNBAL), which will have two digits to the right of the decimal position; and columns 11 to 25 are specified for a 15-character customer NAME.

Input Specifications

On the first two lines of the *calculation sheet* (lines 010 and 020), *resulting indicators* 02, 03, 04, and 05 are set in an "off" position (SETOF). These indicators are programmed switches that, when "on,"

Calculation and Output-format Specifications

[22] The P in column 16 indicates that CARD is a primary file.

```
CUSTOMER STATEMENT FOR JOHN SMITH

ACCOUNT NOT INCLUDED


CUSTOMER STATEMENT FOR A.V. STUDENT

BALANCE DUE       $ 204.00


CUSTOMER STATEMENT FOR RANDY JOHNSON

BALANCE DUE       $ 257.50

ACCOUNT IS 65 DAYS OVERDUE


CUSTOMER STATEMENT FOR BEVERLY BIVENS

BALANCE DUE       $ 309.00


CUSTOMER STATEMENT FOR ALEXANDRE DUMAS

BALANCE DUE       $ 360.50

ACCOUNT IS 60 DAYS OVERDUE
```

Figure 12-22

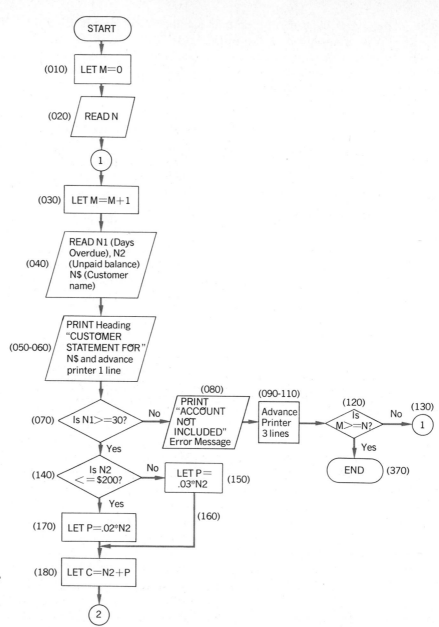

Figure 12-23 Accounts receivable penalty procedure (BASIC) flowchart (numbers in parentheses refer to line numbers in Figure 12-21)

Figure 12-23   (Continued)

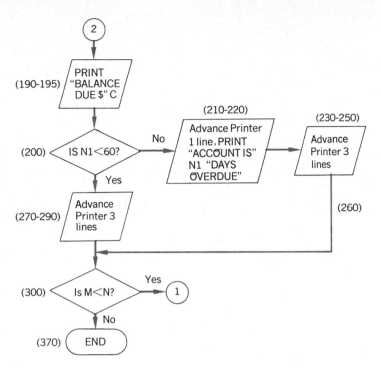

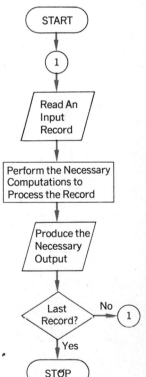

Figure 12-24   RPG object program processing logic

cause the program to perform certain specified operations. On line 030, the value of NDAYS is compared (CØMP) to thirty days. If NDAYS is < thirty days, resulting indicator 02 is set on (line 030, columns 56 to 57). Line 040 shows that when indicator 02 is on, program control is to then branch to a line that has the TAG or label "CØMPUT." The calculations below a TAG line are then performed in sequence. Since CØMPUT on line 130 has no following calculation specifications, the basic RPG processing logic automatically takes over to produce any appropriate output that might be needed. Should this occur in our example, i.e., should a record that is < thirty days overdue be mistakenly included in the input file, lines 010 to 070 of the *output* specification sheet would be used to produce the appropriate output. Why? Because should this situation occur, indicators 01 and 02 would be set on. Indicator 01 is set in an on condition for each input record by the entry on line 010, columns 19 to 20, of the *input* specification sheet. And we have just seen how indicator 02 is set on by the comparison operation on the calculation sheet. Thus, when indicator 01 is on, lines 010 to 030 of the output sheet specify the appropriate action to take. "CUSTØMER STATEMENT FØR" NAME would be printed on the output document according to the formats specified

IBM

INTERNATIONAL BUSINESS MACHINES CORPORATION

REPORT PROGRAM GENERATOR FILE DESCRIPTION SPECIFICATIONS

IBM System/360

Form X24-3347-3
Printed in U. S. A.

Date 1/26/70

Program ACCOUNTING PENALTY PROCEDURE

Programmer JOHN Q PROGRAMMER

Punching Instruction	Graphic							
	Punch							

Page (1 2) 01

Program Identification (75 76 77 78 79 80)

Line (3 4 5)	Form Type (6)	Filename (7–14)	File Type: I/O/U/C (15)	File Designation: P/S/C/R/T (16)	End of File: E (17)	Sequence: A/D (18)	File Format: F/V (19)	Block Length (20–23)	Record Length (24–27)	Mode of Processing: L/R (28)	Length of Key Field or of Record Address Field (29–30)	Record Address Type: K/I (31)	Type of File Organization: I/D/T (32)	Overflow Indicator (33–34)	Key Field Starting Location (35–38)	Extension Code E/L (39)	Device (40–46)	Symbolic Device (47–52)	Labels (S, N, or E) (53)	Name of Label Exit (54–59)	Extent Exit for DAM (60–65)	File Addition: A (66)	No. Tracks for Cylinder Overflows (67)	No. of Extents (68–69)	Tape Rewind: N/U (70)	(71–74)
0 1 0	F	CARD	I	P													MFCM1									
0 2 0	F	OUTPUT	O														PRINTER									
0 3	F																									
0 4	F																									
0 5	F																									
0 6	F																									
0 7	F																									
0 8	F																									
0 9	F																									
1 0	F																									
1 1	F																									
1 2	F																									
1 3	F																									
1 4	F																									
1 5	F																									
	F																									
	F																									
	F																									
	F																									
	F																									

E076510MSP

Card Electro Number ______

Figure 12-25

IBM

INTERNATIONAL BUSINESS MACHINES CORPORATION

REPORT PROGRAM GENERATOR INPUT SPECIFICATIONS

IBM System/360

Form X24-3350-1 U/M025
Printed in U.S.A.

Date 1/26/70

Program ACCOUNTING PENALTY PROCEDURE

Programmer JOHN Q. PROGRAMMER

Punching Instruction	
Graphic	
Punch	

Page (1 2) 02

Program Identification (75 76 77 78 79 80)

Line (3 4 5)	Form Type (6)	Filename (7–14)	Sequence (15 16)	Number (1-N) (17)	Option (O) (18)	Resulting Indicator (19 20)	Record Identification Codes 1: Position (21–24)	Not (N) (25)	C/Z/D (26)	Character (27)	Record Identification Codes 2: Position (28–31)	Not (N) (32)	C/Z/D (33)	Character (34)	Record Identification Codes 3: Position (35–38)	Not (N) (39)	C/Z/D (40)	Character (41)	Stacker Select (42)	Packed (P) (43)	Field Location From (44–47)	Field Location To (48–51)	Decimal Positions (52)	Field Name (53–58)	Control Level (L1-L9) (59 60)	Matching Fields or Chaining Fields (61 62)	Field-Record Relation (63 64)	Field Indicators Plus (65 66)	Field Indicators Minus (67 68)	Field Indicators Zero or Blank (69 70)	Sterling Sign Position (71–74)
010	I	CARD	AA			01	2	N	C																						
020	I		.																		1	2	0	NDAYS							
030	I																				3	10	2	UNBAL							
040	I																				11	25		NAME							
05	I																														
06	I																														
07	I																														
08	I																														
09	I																														
10	I																														
11	I																														
12	I																														
13	I																														
14	I																														
15	I																														
	I																														
	I																														
	I																														
	I																														
	I																														

E086624MSP

Card Electro Number

Figure 12-25 (Continued)

INTERNATIONAL BUSINESS MACHINES CORPORATION

REPORT PROGRAM GENERATOR   CALCULATION SPECIFICATIONS

IBM System/360

Date 1/26/70

Program _ACCOUNTING PENALTY PROCEDURE_

Programmer _JOHN Q. PROGRAMMER_

Punching Instruction — Graphic / Punch

Page 03

Line	Form Type	Control Level (L0-L9, LR)	And (Indicators)	And (Indicators)	Factor 1	Operation	Factor 2	Result Field	Field Length	Decimal Positions	Half Adjust (H)	Compare High 1>2	Compare Low 1<2	Compare Equal 1=2
010	C					SETOF						02	03	04
020	C					SETOF						05		
030	C				NDAYS	COMP	30							02
040	C		02			GOTO	COMPUT							
050	C				UNBAL	COMP	200.					03		
060	C		03		UNBAL	MULT	0.05	PENLTY	5	2				
070	C		03		UNBAL	GOTO	PNLIZE							
080	C				UNBAL	MULT	0.02	PENLTY	5	2				
090	C				PNLIZE	TAG								
100	C				UNBAL	ADD	PENLTY	CACCNT	5	2				
110	C					SETON						04		
120	C				NDAYS	COMP	60					05		05
130	C				COMPUT	TAG								
14	C													
15	C													

Program Identification

Card Electro Number _____

Figure 12-25   (Continued)

394

IBM

INTERNATIONAL BUSINESS MACHINES CORPORATION

REPORT PROGRAM GENERATOR OUTPUT-FORMAT SPECIFICATIONS

IBM System/360

Form X24-3352-1 U/M 025
Printed in U.S.A.

Punching Instruction	Graphic	
	Punch	

Date __1/26/70__

Program __ACCOUNTING PENALTY PROCEDURE__

Programmer __JOHN Q. PROGRAMMER__

Page __04__ (1 2)

Line	Form Type	Filename	Type (H/D/T)	Stacker Select	Space Before	Space After	Skip Before	Skip After	Output Indicators Not	And Not	And Not	And	Field Name	Zero Suppress (Z)	Blank After (B)	End Position in Output Record	Packed Field (P)	Constant or Edit Word	Sterling Sign Position
01	0	OUTPUT	D			2													
02	0								01							24		'CUSTOMER STATEMENT FOR '	
03	0		D			3							NAME			39			
04	0		D			1			02							21		'ACCOUNT NOT INCLUDED'	
05	0								02							2		'-'	
06	0		D			2			04										
07	0																		
08	0												CACCNT			19		'BALANCE DUE $'	
09	0								N05	N02						25		0.	
10	0		D			2			N05							2		'-'	
11	0																		
12	0		D			3			05							12		'ACCOUNT IS '	
13	0																		
14	0												NDAYS	Z		14			
15	0															27		'DAYS OVERDUE'	
16	0		D			1			05							2		'-'	
17	0																		
18	0																		

Program Identification: 75 76 77 78 79 80

Card Electro Number ____

Figure 12-25 (Continued)

395

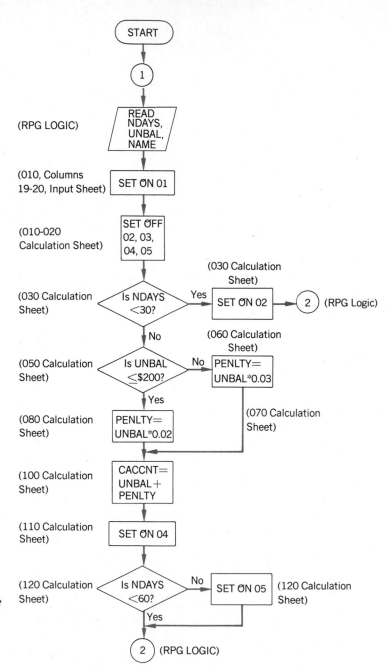

Figure 12-26 Accounts receivable penalty procedure (RPG) coding (numbers in parentheses refer to line numbers on the indicated specification sheets)

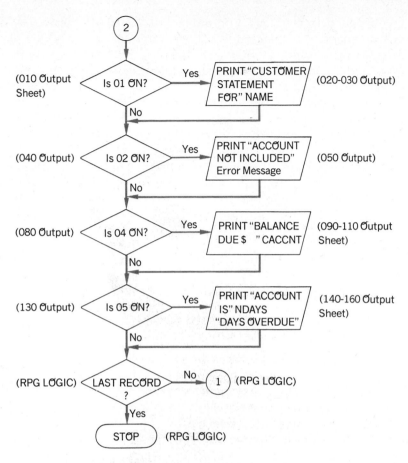

Figure 12-26 (Continued)

in columns 42 and 43 of lines 020 to 030. The printer is advanced according to the instructions specified in columns 17 and 18 of the output sheet. When indicator 02 is also on (line 040), the error message "ACCOUNT NOT INCLUDED" is printed (line 050).[23]

Referring back to the calculation sheet, if NDAYS had *not* been < 30, program control would have moved in sequence to line 050 where the value of UNBAL would have been COMPared to $200. If UNBAL is > $200, indicator 03 is set (line 050, columns 54 and 55) and PENLTY is calculated by multiplying UNBAL times 0.03 (line 060). If UNBAL is =< $200, PENLTY is assigned a value equal to UNBAL * 0.02 (line 080). On line 100, UNBAL is added to PENLTY, the result

[23]The purpose of lines 060 to 070, 110 to 120, and 170 to 180 on the output sheet is to advance the printer the desired number of lines. Since the limit of a single entry is three, we have had to add another entry to obtain the desired four spaces after "ACCOUNT NOT INCLUDED" and "ACCOUNT IS _____ DAYS OVERDUE" (see Fig. 12-2).

is assigned to CACCNT, and indicator 04 is then SETON (line 110). A comparison is then made between NDAYS and sixty days, and if NDAYS > 60 indicator 05 is set on (line 120). Since there are now no additional calculation specifications, the RPG processing logic takes over to produce the necessary output. This output is specified on the Output sheet depending on which indicators are on. The RPG program flowchart in Fig. 12-26 summarizes the above comments. The numbers in parentheses refer to line numbers on the individual specification forms.

RPG is the primary language on small business-oriented processors such as IBM's System/3. Because the programmer does not write statements that represent the sequence of all the steps to be followed in the program, the initial reaction of some is that RPG is a confusing language. Actually, however, it is relatively easy to learn. Of course, it is not suitable for scientific applications, but commercial computer-center operators who process business applications for many small customers have found it to be an extremely valuable language.

SUMMARY

A brief overview of five popular programming languages has been presented in this chapter. The purpose has been to acquaint you with the general structure of each language and to introduce you to some of their characteristics. Each language has strengths and weaknesses. COBOL, for example, is better suited than FORTRAN for data processing applications that involve the manipulation of large business files. FORTRAN, on the other hand, is probably easier to learn than COBOL and is well suited to processing scientific applications. There are published standard versions of both of these languages.

PL/I combines features of both FORTRAN and COBOL and introduces additional features not found in either of those languages. Although it is more difficult to learn in its entirety than most other languages, a programmer need not know the entire language to prepare application programs of a particular type. Also, the PL/I modular procedure blocks are efficiently handled by the operating system in a multiprogramming environment.

BASIC resembles FORTRAN in many ways; it is the easiest language of the five to learn and use. Output format need not be specified. It is a popular language, and its popularity appears to be growing. RPG is a limited purpose language used to process business applications. As in the case of PL/I and BASIC, there is currently no standard version of RPG.

1. (a) In FORTRAN, what is an integer number? (b) A real number?
2. (a) What is meant by *floating-point notation?*
    (b) What is the fixed decimal equivalent of .175E+04?
    (c) What is the fixed decimal equivalent of .175E−02?
3. What is a variable name?
4. What will the computer do in executing the following FORTRAN statements:
    (a) READ (1,10)J,HELP
    (b) IF (HELP-OUCH)10, 10, 30
    (c) DO 30 I=1,8,1
5. Identify and put in proper order the four divisions of COBOL.
6. What is meant by:
    (a) AR-NAME PICTURE IS X(40).
    (b) AR-AMOUNT PICTURE IS 9(6)V99.
7. (a) What is the purpose of the DECLARE statement in PL/I?
    (b) Of the GET . . . EDIT statement?
    (c) Of the PUT . . . EDIT statement?
8. What is the meaning of the following PL/I statement: END SEX;
9. What will the computer do in executing the following BASIC statements:
    (a) 010 READ A,B,C,D,E
        200 DATA 025, 200, 300
        210 DATA 060, 150, 175, ... , 125
    (b) 120 PRINT A,B,C
    (c) 020 PRINT TAB (10); "HELP"
    (d) 050 IF N < = 50 THEN 100
    (e) 130 FOR J = 1 TO 10 STEP 2
        .
        .
        .
        170 NEXT J
10. What are the four basic specification sheets used in RPG?
11. "Every object program generated by the RPG compiler follows a basic processing cycle." What is the general form of this cycle?

The following texts are arranged according to language. Most of the materials are business oriented.

SELECTED REFERENCES

Fortran II

Anton, H. R., and W. S. Boutell: *FORTRAN and Business Data Processing*, McGraw-Hill Book Company, New York, 1968.

Emerick, P. L., and J. W. Wilkinson: *Computer Programming for Business and Social Science,* Richard D. Irwin, Inc., Homewood, Ill., 1970.

Kazmier, Leonard J., and A. Philippakis: *Fundamentals of EDP and FORTRAN,* McGraw-Hill Book Company, New York, 1970.

McCameron, Fritz: *FORTRAN Logic and Programming,* Richard D. Irwin, Inc., Homewood, Ill., 1968.

Fortran IV

Anderson, Decima: *Computer Programming: FORTRAN IV,* Appleton-Century-Crofts, New York, 1966.

Couger, J. Daniel, and L. E. Shannon: *FORTRAN IV: A Programmed Instruction Approach,* Richard D. Irwin, Inc., Homewood, Ill., 1968.

Lee, R. M.: *FORTRAN IV Programming,* McGraw-Hill Book Company, New York, 1967.

McCameron, Fritz: *FORTRAN IV,* Richard D. Irwin, Inc., Homewood, Ill., 1970.

Cobol

McCameron, Fritz: *COBOL Logic and Programming,* rev. ed., Richard D. Irwin, Inc., Homewood, Ill., 1970.

Melichar, P.: *COBOL for IBM System/360,* Science Research Associates, Inc., Chicago, Ill., 1968.

Spitzbarth, L. M.: *Basic COBOL Programming,* Addison-Wesley Publishing Company, Inc., Reading, Mass., 1970.

PL/I

Scott, R. C., and N. E. Sondek: *PL/I for Programmers,* Addison-Wesley Publishing Company, Inc., Reading, Mass., 1970.

Sprowls, R. Clay: *Introduction to PL/I Programming,* Harper & Row, Publishers, Incorporated, New York, 1969.

Weinberg, G. M.: *PL/I Programming Primer,* McGraw-Hill Book Company, New York, 1966.

Basic

Farina, M. V.: *Programming in BASIC,* Prentice-Hall, Inc., Englewood Cliffs, N.J., 1968.

Gately, W. Y., and G. G. Bitter: *BASIC for Beginners,* McGraw-Hill Book Company, New York, 1970.

RPG

Brightman, R. W., and J. R. Clark: *RPG I and RPG II Programming,* The Macmillan Company, New York, 1970.

Management
and
Computers:
An
Orientation

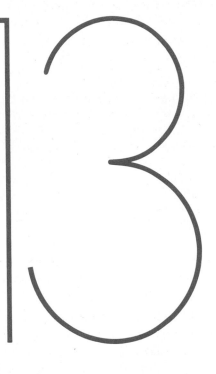

In Chapter 1 it was pointed out that the first objective of this text was to provide a general orientation to the computer for students of business. This orientation has now been completed. In earlier chapters we have seen what a computer is, what it can and cannot do, and how it operates.

The second text objective is to focus attention on the impact that computers have had (and are having) on business managers and on the environment in which managers work. In the remaining pages of this book we shall concentrate attention on this second objective.

The purpose of this chapter is to provide a broad orientation to the managerial implications of computer usage. Some implications, of course, have been suggested in previous chapters. For example, the ability of a manager to access online files in search of answers to queries carries definite planning and control overtones. In this chapter we shall first briefly summarize the *functions of management*. We shall then gain an overall perspective on the remaining chapters of this text by looking at the impact that the introduction and use of computers can have in the areas of *planning and making decisions, organizing, staffing,* and *controlling. Economic implications* will also be considered.

MANAGEMENT FUNCTIONS

What is management? For our purposes, *management* is defined as the process of achieving organizational objectives through the efforts of other people. Three important points of this definition may be emphasized. The first point is that management is a *process;* i.e., *management consists of a number of interrelated steps or functions,* which, when satisfactorily performed, lead to the achievement of goals. The second point is that without the establishment of specific objectives, the effective practice of management is most difficult, if not impossible, The third point is that the successful practice of management involves people working together in harmony to achieve desired results. The availability of quality information is, of course, a requirement for a smoothly functioning operation.

The business manager is a practitioner of the art and science of management. It is his job to carry out the basic management functions necessary to attain company goals. Of course, the objectives pursued vary according to the manager's mission. The goal of a production manager may be to produce a specified number of units in a certain time period; the goal of a marketing manager may be to meet a sales quota; and the goal of the company president may be to see that the firm earns a satisfactory profit on the capital invested. But although objectives sought by managers vary, the managerial functions or activities that they perform in the course of their work are common to all. In other words, the activities of *planning, organizing, staffing,* and *controlling* are performed by all managers.[1]

Planning

The planning function looks to the future; to plan is to decide in advance a future course of action. Thus, *planning* involves making decisions with regard to (1) the selection of both short- and long-run business strategies and goals, (2) the development of policies and procedures that will help accomplish objectives or counter threats, (3) the establishment of operating standards that serve as the basis for control, and (4) the revision of earlier plans in the light of changing

---

[1]This is not necessarily an exhaustive list of *all* the functions performed by managers. It is, rather, those functions that we shall be referring to in this text.

conditions. The steps followed in *planning and in arriving at rational decisions are:*

1. *Identifying the problem or opportunity.* Meaningful planning may begin when a manager understands and has correctly defined the problem or opportunity that he faces. Information is needed to bring about awareness.
2. *Gathering and analyzing relevant facts.* To plan and make decisions, managers must have information that possesses the desirable characteristics outlined in Chapter 1.
3. *Determining suitable alternatives.* The manager must seek out the most attractive possible courses of action. The appropriateness of the options selected is determined by the manager's skill and the quality of his information.
4. *Evaluating and selecting the most appropriate alternative.* The manager must weigh the options in light of established goals and then arrive at the plan or decision that best meets the company needs. Again, the correctness of this choice depends upon managerial skill and information quality.
5. *Following up on decision.* Broad plans may require supporting supplementary plans. For example, if the result of the above steps is a decision to acquire a computer, then additional plans must be made to (a) locate the new computer department in the organization and (b) staff it with operating personnel.

Organizing

The organizing function involves the grouping of work teams into logical and efficient units in order to carry out plans and achieve goals. In a manufacturing company, employees may be grouped formally into production, marketing, and finance divisions. In each of these divisions, workers may be further organized into smaller units. The marketing division, for example, might consist of advertising, direct selling, and marketing research departments. Salesmen might be further organized by territory, products sold, and type of customer contacted. Managers at each organizational level receive formal authority to assign goal-directed tasks; they then must motivate and coordinate employee efforts if goals are to be achieved. To sum up, *organizing* is ". . . the grouping of activities necessary to accomplish goals and plans, the assignment of these activities to appropriate departments, and the provision for authority delegation and coordination."[2]

[2]Harold Koontz and Cyril O'Donnell, *Principles of Management,* 3d. ed., McGraw-Hill Book Company, New York, 1964, p. 205.

Staffing

One aspect of the *staffing* function consists of selecting people to fill the positions that exist in the organizational structure of the business. The staffing activity also includes (1) the training of employees to meet their job requirements, (2) the preparation of employees for promotion to positions of greater responsibility, and (3) the reassignment or removal of employees when such action is required.

Controlling

Unlike planning, which looks to the future, the *control* function looks at the past and the present. It is a follow-up to planning; it is the check on past and current performance to see if planned goals are being achieved. The *steps in the control function are:*

1. *Setting standards.* Proper control requires that predetermined goals be established by planners. These standards may be expressed in *physical terms* (e.g., units produced, quantities sold, or machined tolerances permitted) or in *monetary terms* (e.g., operating-cost budgets or sales-revenue quotas). The setting of realistic standards requires quality information.
2. *Measuring actual performance.* Timely and accurate performance information is essential to control.
3. *Comparing actual performance with standards.* Comparison information is action oriented. Computers can provide this information to managers on an *exception basis only* when performance variations are outside certain specified limits.
4. *Taking appropriate control action.* If performance is *under control,* the manager's decision may be to do nothing. However, if actual performance is not up to the standard, it may be because the standard is unrealistic. Therefore, replanning may be necessary to revise the standard. Unfavorable performance may have to be corrected by reorganizing work groups or adding more employees. Thus, the control actions taken may require further planning, organizing, and staffing activities. If outstanding performance is noted, the appropriate action may be to reward the individuals or groups responsible.

The process of management is a continuing one. The *order* of the four managerial functions presented here (planning, organizing, staffing, and controlling) is a logical one, and we shall use this order as the basis for the presentation of the material in the next four chapters. In practice, however, managers carry out these functions simultaneously. "Plans beget subordinate plans, old plans require modifications, and new plans develop while old ones are in effect.

Thus, it is impractical to insist on a special time sequence for the various functions."[3]

We saw in Chapter 1 (and in Fig. 1-4) that quality information could support good decisions; good decisions should lead to effective performance of managerial functions; and effective functional performance should lead to the attainment of organizational goals. It is not surprising, therefore, that the acquisition and use of a computer (or any tool that promises to dramatically improve the quality of information) may have important managerial implications.

We can consider this broad topic from at least three viewpoints. *First,* it is possible to look at the implications involved in *planning for computers. Second,* we can look at the impact of *planning with computers.* (Planning *for* computers should not be confused with planning *with* computers. The first subject deals with the *introduction* of the system; the latter deals with its subsequent *use.*) Finally, we can look at some computer-oriented *decision-making techniques* that are now being used.

Planning for computers   In light of the importance of information in the decision-making process, it would be logical to assume that top executives have always actively participated in the planning and implementation of new systems that would influence their future decisions. Alas, such leadership has often been lacking! In the past, many executives have apparently felt that the introduction of a computer was primarily a technical problem. They were content to define the goals of the new system vaguely and then to turn the entire project over to data processing specialists. Such abdication ignored the far-reaching personnel and organizational implications of the undertaking. Without precisely defined managerial information needs and without the backing at the top echelons that is often required to secure cooperation and overcome resistance to procedural and organizational change, the specialists could be excused if their efforts resulted in marginal results. And only marginal results have been obtained in a number of firms. For example, a conclusion of a study of 36 large firms conducted by the management consulting firm of McKinsey & Company was that

> From a profit standpoint, our findings indicate, computer efforts in all
> but a few exceptional companies are in real, if often unacknowledged,

[3]*Ibid.,* p. 39.

**MANAGERIAL
IMPLICATIONS OF
COMPUTERS**

**Planning and
Decision-making
Implications**

trouble. Faster, costlier, more sophisticated hardware; larger and increasingly costly computer staffs; increasingly complex and ingenious applications: these are in evidence everywhere. Less and less in evidence, as these new applications proliferate, are profitable results.[4]

Top managers should realize that their serious involvement in planning for computers is perhaps the most important single factor determining the success or failure of a computer installation. They should also be aware of the magnitude of the problems that will have to be overcome. Firms that have been successful in making computers pay off have been thorough in the initial planning stages. A careful *systems study* (to be covered in Chapter 14) is required to answer such questions as:

1. What data processing improvements are needed; i.e., what are the data processing objectives of the firm?
2. Has proper attention been given to systems review and redesign?
3. Is computer usage the best way to achieve all of the objectives? Have noncomputer alternatives been evaluated?
4. Have all computer alternatives been considered? (A firm need not acquire or use its own machine in all situations. The use of computer centers or multisubscriber timesharing services are possible options.)
5. If acquiring an initial computer or a new replacement model is called for, have all feasible machines and vendors been considered?
6. Have different acquisition methods (rental, lease, or purchase) been studied?

If, as a result of careful study and planning, a decision is made to order a new computer and/or implement new applications, then the following additional plans must be developed:

1. *Technical preparation plans.* Prior to the delivery of hardware, the computer site must be laid out and prepared and programs must be written and tested. This subject is also considered in Chapter 14.
2. *Organizing plans.* It is important that adequate attention be given to the composition and location of the computer department. The subject of organization and the computer is covered in Chapter 15.
3. *Personnel preparation plans.* Staffing plans should be made to fill any new jobs that will be created. In an organization acquir-

---

[4]McKinsey & Company, Inc., "Unlocking the Computer's Profit Potential," *Computers and Automation*, April, 1969, p. 25.

ing its first computer, for example, the selection and training of programmers should obviously take place without delay so that they may begin preparing the initial programs. Plans should also be made to alleviate the hardships brought about by the elimination of jobs. These personnel topics are developed further in Chapter 16.

4. *Control plans.* The quality of the information produced must be controlled. The accuracy of input data must be considered. And internal controls should be created to minimize error and disclose fraud when and if it occurs. The subject of computer controls is considered in Chapter 17.

Planning with computers   Information played an important part in the successful completion of each of the steps in the planning procedure that was presented earlier. Generally speaking, computer usage can improve planning by providing effective information, which (1) leads to problem awareness, (2) supports problem analysis and selection of alternatives, (3) influences the choice of the most appropriate option, and (4) permits feedback on the implementation of decisions. More specifically, *the use of computers can have an impact on the planning function by:*

1. *Causing faster awareness of problems and opportunities.* Computers can quickly signal out-of-control conditions requiring corrective action when actual performance deviates from what was planned. Masses of current and historical internal and external data can be analyzed by the use of statistical methods, including trend analyses and correlation techniques, in order to detect opportunities and challenges. Planning data stored online may permit managers to probe and query files and receive quick replies to their questions.

2. *Enabling managers to devote more time to planning.* Use of the computer can free the manager of clerical data-gathering tasks and permit him to concentrate more attention on analytical and intellectual matters. The computer is an intelligence amplifier that broadens man's time dimension.

3. *Permitting managers to give timely consideration to more complex relationships.* The computer gives the manager the ability to evaluate *more* possible alternatives (and to consider *more of the internal and external variables* that may have a bearing on the outcome of these alternatives). It makes it possible for managers to do a better job of identifying and assessing the probable economic and social effects of different courses of action. The

awareness of such effects, of course, influences the ultimate decision. In the past, oversimplified assumptions would have to be made if resulting decisions were to be timely. More complex relationships can now be considered and scheduled. In addition to broadening man's time dimension, the computer can furnish him with planning information that could not have been produced at all a few years ago or that could not have been produced in time to be of any value.

4. *Assisting in decision implementation.* When decisions have been made, the computer can assist in the necessary development of subordinate plans that will be needed to implement these decisions. Computer-based techniques to schedule project activities have been developed and are now widely used. Through the use of such techniques, business resources can be utilized and controlled effectively.

Decision-making techniques A number of quantitative managerial aids have been introduced, which utilize computers to provide the framework for decision-producing analyses.[5] These techniques (which are often classified under the headings of *operations research* or *management science*) can be used to (1) speed up problem or opportunity awareness, (2) permit more timely consideration of increasingly complex relationships, and (3) assist in decision implementation. In particular, the computer-based techniques of *network analysis, mathematical programming, and simulation* have managerial implications.

Network analysis Both PERT (Program Evaluation and Review Technique) and CPM (Critical Path Method) are network models which are used to plan, schedule, and control complex projects. The basic concepts of PERT and CPM are similar.[6] The following procedure is used to set up a network model:

1. *All* the individual *activities* to be performed in the project must be identified.
2. The sequence of each activity must be determined; i.e., it must be known what elements have to be completed prior to the start

---

[5]We know, of course, that computers do not "make decisions." Rather, they follow program decisions made earlier by managers and programmers. Much of planning will remain judgmental or heuristic in nature because it is man who defines problems, selects strategies to follow, and formulates hypotheses and hunches. However, computer-produced information can improve the effectiveness of managerial planning and decision making for the reasons listed above.

[6]One difference is that CPM uses one activity-time estimate while PERT incorporates *optimistic, pessimistic,* and *most-likely* activity-time estimates.

of a particular activity and what tasks cannot commence until after its completion.

3. The *time interval* required to complete each activity must be estimated.

4. The *longest sequence* of events in the project must be identified. The sum of the individual activity times in this sequence becomes the total project time, and this sequence of activities is known as the *critical path*.

Network models have gained widespread acceptance. The Department of Defense requires that they be used on all major defense contracts, and major construction projects employ them. They have proven quite effective in helping manage the transition to computer data processing systems. The use of PERT and CPM improves the *planning* function because it forces managers to identify *all of the project activities that must be performed*. *Control* is also improved because attention can be focused on the sequence of activities in the critical path. Managers quickly become aware of potential problems. If a critical activity begins to slip behind schedule, steps can be quickly taken to correct the situation. By trading project cost against project time, several alternative paths can initially be computed to help in planning. By a greater commitment of resources, managers can often reduce the time required to complete certain activities in the critical path (and thus reduce total project time). The effect of a greater resource commitment, however, is often higher project cost. Network models can simulate the effects on time and cost of a varying resource mix. Computations for small networks can be produced manually, but a computer is needed with networks of any significant size. Most computer manufacturers have PERT and CPM packaged programs available, and they are also available in the online program libraries of many multisubscriber timesharing services.

Mathematical programming   The purpose of mathematical programming is to find the best strategy from among a large number of options. Most mathematical programming work involves the use of *linear programming*. Not to be confused with computer programming, linear programming models are used to find the *best combination* of limited resources to achieve a specified objective (which is, typically, to maximize profit or minimize cost). One important class of linear programming applications is in blending operations, where the objective is often to minimize the cost involved in the production of a given amount of blended product. For example, cattle feed may be a mixture of minerals, grains, and fish and meat products. The prices of these ingredients are subject to change, so the least expensive blend required to achieve specified nutritional requirements is subject to variation. Linear programming can help managers quickly determine the correct blend to use to minimize cost while meeting product specifications.

In addition to blending, linear programming is being used for such diverse purposes as scheduling manpower, selecting media for advertising purposes, determining minimum transportation costs from given supply points to specified points of delivery, and determining the most profitable product mix that may be manufactured in a given plant with given equipment. Practically all linear programming applications require the use of a computer. As a powerful *planning* tool, linear programming enables a manager to select the most appropriate alternative from a large number of options. It is also a technique that may aid the manager in carrying out his other functions. Its use in scheduling manpower, for example, has definite staffing implications.

Simulation   In the physical sciences, experiments may be performed in a laboratory using small models of a process or an operation. Many complex variations may be possible in these tests, and the results show the scientist what happens under certain controlled conditions. Simulation is similar to scientific experimentation in that managers may evaluate proposed strategies by constructing business models. They can then determine what happens to these models when certain conditions are given. Simulation is thus a trial-and-error problem-solving *approach;* it is also a *planning* aid that may be of considerable value to executives.

Simulation models have helped top executives decide, for example, whether or not to expand operations by acquiring a new plant. Among the dozens of complicating variables that would have to be incorporated into such models are facts and assumptions about (1) present and potential size of the total market, (2) present and potential company share of this total market, (3) product selling prices, and (4) investment required to achieve various production levels. Thus, simulation has helped top executives in their strategic planning and decision-making activities.

Simulation may also be helpful to middle-level managers in tactical planning and decision making.[7] For example, simulation models are used to improve inventory management. The problem of managing inventories is complicated because there are conflicting desires among organizational units and what is best for one department may not be best for the entire firm. To illustrate, the purchasing department

[7]Strategic and tactical planning were discussed in Chapter 4.

may prefer to buy large quantities of supplies and raw materials in order to get lower prices; the production department also likes to have large inventories on hand to eliminate shortages and make possible long—and efficient—production runs; and the sales department prefers large finished-goods inventories so that sales will not be lost because of out-of-stock conditions. The finance department, on the other hand, views with concern large inventory levels since storage expense is increased, risk of spoilage and deterioration is increased, and funds are tied up for longer periods of time. Through the use of simulated inventory amounts and simulated assumptions about such factors as reorder lead times and cost of being out of stock, managers can experiment with various approaches to arrive at more profitable inventory levels.[8]

In short, we see from this brief summary of simulation that it can aid in planning by permitting managers to give timely consideration to complex relationships. Of course, in many respects there is nothing new about simulation. As Franklin Lindsay points out:

> A corporate planner who sets forth half a dozen alternative investment schemes, together with the costs and expected return from each, is simulating each alternative so that his board of directors can judge their relative merits. But the new mathematical tools, together with high-speed computers, extend tremendously the capabilities of simulation processes.[9]

Organizational Implications

The organizational framework of a business is structured on the work to be done and the human and physical resources to be committed. However, with the introduction of a computer and/or with the conversion of existing applications to computer processing, *significant changes* are likely to be made in data processing activities and thus in those departments that are engaged in informational activities. When this happens, it is often desirable to restructure the organization in the interests of greater efficiency. Work groups may be realigned; tasks formerly assigned to a number of departments may be eliminated or consolidated in a single new computer department; and existing departments may be eliminated or the scope of their operations may be sharply curtailed. Basic changes of this nature require the attention of top executives.

We have seen earlier that broader information systems are now

---

[8] Several programming languages have been developed for the purpose of preparing simulation programs. Two of the most popular are SIMSCRIPT and GPSS (General Purpose Systems Simulator).

[9] Franklin A. Lindsay, *New Techniques for Management Decision Making*, McGraw-Hill Book Company, New York, 1963, p. 60.

being designed and implemented. Related to this trend is an organizational issue of fundamental importance. The issue to be decided is to what extent the new systems should concentrate or *centralize* authority and control in the hands of the top-level managers. With a computer, a greater degree of centralized control *can* be supported in a business because top managers can be furnished with information from outlying divisions in time to decide on appropriate action. Without computers, such action must be determined by a lower-level manager because of time, distance, and familiarity factors. But although greater centralized control *can be supported* with a computer, it is *not necessarily a requirement*. The degree of centralized authority and control that *should* exist in the new system is determined by managerial philosophy and judgment and not by computer usage. The impact of the path chosen on future organizational structure, basic company philosophy and policies, and managerial authority of managers below the top echelons will be great. Certainly, decisions of this magnitude require the serious consideration of top executives; they are just too fundamental to be left to data processing specialists or lower-level managers. We shall look more closely at the questions of computer department organization and the centralization of decision-making authority in Chapter 15.

Staffing Implications

Data processing changes often bring about organizational stress. The introduction and use of a computer also requires employee adjustments. Staffing decisions are necessary to (1) select and train workers for new jobs (and then retain these workers) and (2) deal with employees whose jobs have been eliminated or reduced in content or appeal. Resistance may be expected from employees and managers because of significant changes occurring in the alignment of work groups, the content of individual jobs, and the methods of performing data processing tasks. Proper planning and leadership can reduce this resistance. We shall look into this matter again in Chapter 16.

In addition to considering the implications of filling new jobs and coping with resistance to change, top executives should also realize that it does no good to attempt to install sophisticated systems if company managers at all levels are unable to (1) define their information needs, (2) develop analytical planning, decision-making, and control procedures, (3) state specifically these analytical procedures, and (4) interpret and make use of the output of the sophisticated systems. If the machines are to be effectively utilized, it will generally be necessary to undertake an educational effort to acquaint managers with computer capabilities and the analytical tools that will make use of those capabilities.

Control Implications

Several ways in which computer usage can affect the control function have already been pointed out, and so we need not dwell long on the subject here. The *control implications of computer usage* include the facts that:

1. Computers can quickly signal out-of-control conditions, thus bringing about faster awareness of problems. Going a step further, programmed analyses may be carried out by the computer to present recommended courses of action to managers.
2. Triggered control reports, based on the *principle of exception*,[10] may be prepared only when actual performance varies from planned standards. Managers are thus relieved of much routine paper shuffling and are free to concentrate on more important personnel and environmental matters.
3. Computer-based techniques such as PERT and CPM may permit more effective control of business resources.
4. Computer systems make it possible to centralize authority and control previously delegated to lower echelons because of time, distance, and familiarity factors.
5. Internal control and auditing techniques will generally have to be revised to accommodate computer systems. Internal control and auditing will be examined in Chapter 17.

Economic Implications

From an economic standpoint the acquisition of an initial or replacement computer cannot be taken lightly. An investment decision involving many thousands of dollars (or a few million) must be made. It is the duty of top executives to determine if a new computer can be justified economically.

This has never been an easy task. We know from Chapter 1 that a computer *can* improve the firm's economic position by reducing the ratio of expenses to revenues in tangible and intangible ways. But there is no guarantee that profits *will* be improved merely because a computer is installed. On the contrary, many firms have invested

---

[10]In chapter 18 of Exodus, Jethro gives good advice when he tells Moses to delegate some of his routine leadership duties to subordinates and concentrate his attention on the more important exceptions, which the subordinates are unable to handle. This idea is called *"the principle of exception"* in management literature.

large sums in computers and have received returns of *less* than a dollar for each dollar spent.[11] (Of course, merely to recover the initial investment is hardly sufficient either, for the money invested in a computer could be put to use in an alternate manner that might prove to be quite profitable.)

The computer feasibility studies conducted in the early and middle 1960s were usually made to determine whether or not money could be saved, i.e., the decision to acquire a new computer was often based on estimates of cost displacement.[12] We know, however, that the firm's profit picture may also be enhanced if information is provided that will enable managers to make better decisions and give better service to customers. Unfortunately, it is difficult (if not impossible) to assign a precise dollar value to such revenue-raising activities. Yet it is the opinion of several authorities[13] that the information systems that designers are now working on are often more than merely data processing systems and thus they should not be justified solely on the basis of earlier tangible cost displacement criteria. Rather, it is argued, the value of information should be determined by what managers can do with it instead of what it costs to produce. In short, many of the important benefits of these new systems will be intangible, and although by definition intangible benefits are not subject to precise quantitative measurement, designers and managers are still faced with the problem of assigning approximate values to them, for they represent implicit future dollar values. But in quantifying intangibles, there is always the danger that errors in assumptions and judgment will lead to economically unsound systems decisions.

To summarize, then, computer acquisition and use require executives to make decisions involving large sums of money; the investment of this money may lead to profitable results, but this end is by no means assured; and greater consideration may need to be given to qualitative or intangible factors (with the risks involved) in future computer systems decisions. In light of the possible economic consequences of unwise computer decisions, a top executive might be

---

[11] The economic results of past computer usage are mixed. Some firms are achieving substantial returns. But the McKinsey & Company study quoted earlier in this chapter showed that several large firms were achieving marginal results, and a survey of 2,500 companies conducted by the Research Institute of America "disclosed that only half the companies with in-house computers could give an unqualified 'yes' to the question of whether they were paying off or not, while only 28 percent believed that the machines were doing a good job." See Tom Alexander, "Computers Can't Solve Everything," *Fortune,* October, 1969, p. 126.

[12] Such estimates were frequently found to be in error; e.g., the level of expenditures required to initially acquire the computer system and sustain computer operation was (and is) frequently underestimated.

[13] See, for example, John Diebold, "Bad Decisions on Computer Use," *Harvard Business Rev.,* January-February, 1969, pp. 27-28.

tempted to have nothing to do with computers. But this course of nonaction might be the most hazardous of all because the executive must also consider the possible economic implications of *not keeping pace with competitors* in the development and use of new information systems.[14]

SUMMARY

Managers achieve organizational objectives through the efforts of other people. To do this they are required to perform the managerial activities of planning, organizing, staffing, and controlling. These activities are interrelated; in practice, a manager may be carrying out several functions simultaneously.

The top-level managers of a business should support and actively participate in the design and installation of new management information systems. In many cases, of course, they will have to rely on the advice of data processing specialists. But the decision to introduce (and use) computers in an organization has managerial *implications that go far beyond* the mere acquisition of a piece of technical equipment. Information vital to the support of planning and control decisions is affected by the computer system that develops; the entire organizational structure may undergo stress and alteration; the nature and number of jobs is affected; the economic consequences are often hard to predict; and the decision-making techniques that have been used by managers in the past may have to be changed.

In the chapters that follow, we shall examine some of the managerial problems associated with the introduction and use of computers. In so doing we shall also focus attention on the impact that computers have had (and are having) on managers and the environment in which they work.

DISCUSSION QUESTIONS

1. (a) What is management?
   (b) What activities or functions must be performed by managers?
2. (a) What is involved in the planning function?
   (b) What steps must be followed in planning?
3. Explain what is involved in (a) the organizing function and (b) the staffing function.

[14]Furthermore, failure to keep pace might result in stockholders filing a lawsuit against a corporation and/or an executive. " 'I have no doubt,' says Milton Wessel, an attorney who specializes in computer law, 'that in the near future, failure to use computers will be the subject of a lawsuit. The failure to use the latest technology is frequently the subject of stockholder derivative actions.' " See Stanley H. Lieberstein, "The Computer and the Law," *Dun's Rev.,* March, 1970, p. 58.

4. Identify and discuss the steps in the control function.
5. (a) What is the distinction between "planning for computers" and "planning with computers"?
   (b) What are the managerial implications of planning for computers?
   (c) Of planning with computers?
6. What are the managerial implications of computer-based decision-making techniques?
7. (a) Discuss the possible organizational implications of computer usage.
   (b) What are the possible staffing implications?
8. (a) What are the possible control implications of computer usage?
   (b) The economic implications?

SELECTED REFERENCES

Burch, Jr., John G.: "Business Games and Simulation Techniques," *Management Accounting,* December, 1969, pp. 49–52.

Coughlan, John W.: "Linear Programming," *Journal of Data Management,* March, 1970, pp. 30–34.

Dean, Neal J.: "The Computer Comes of Age," *Harvard Business Review,* January–February, 1968, pp. 83–91.

Diebold, John: "Bad Decisions on Computer Use," *Harvard Business Review,* January–February, 1969, pp. 14–16ff.

Horowitz, Joseph: "Effective Planning with CPM," *Journal of Systems Management,* March, 1970, pp. 27–29.

McKinsey & Company, Inc.: "Unlocking the Computer's Profit Potential," *Computers and Automation,* April, 1969, pp. 24–33.

Schoderbek, Peter P., and James D. Babcock: "At Last—Management More Active in EDP," *Business Horizons,* December, 1969, pp. 53–58.

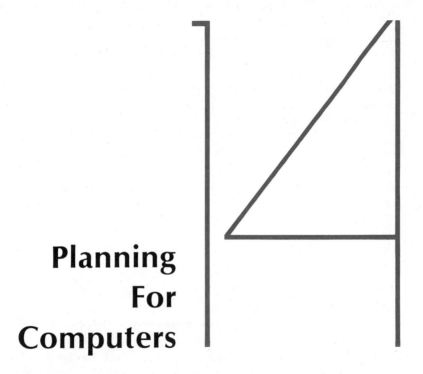

Planning
For
Computers

As used in this chapter, *planning for computers* involves the possible introduction of computing hardware and/or software into an organization for purposes of solving problems (or realizing opportunities) that may exist in the organization's information systems.

Technical, economic, and *operational* aspects must be considered in planning for computers. In a technical sense, most contemplated business systems are feasible, the job *can* be done, and hardware and software exist (or can be prepared) to implement the systems. Whether such implementation would be economical, of course, is another matter that should be evaluated. Finally, a system may fail to achieve company goals (even though it is technically and economically feasible) if company personnel are not sold on it and do not want to make it work. We shall briefly look at technical and economic aspects in this chapter. Operational aspects will be deferred to Chapter 16.

Planning for computers is accomplished through *systems studies*.

417

An information systems study may be initiated in response to many types of business problems. For example, the purpose of a study in a smaller organization may be to redesign noncomputer systems and determine the feasibility of installing a first computer. In organizations with existing computer facilities, the purpose of a systems study may be to (1) revise and update existing procedures using currently available hardware, (2) develop new applications for existing hardware, or (3) determine the feasibility of redesigning and converting existing systems to new hardware.

In this chapter we will first examine the *essential nature of the systems study,* then we will look at a generalized *systems-study approach.* Since a study that involves equipment evaluation and selection is generally broader in scope than one that deals with systems revision and with the development of new applications in an existing equipment environment, we shall emphasize the broader type of study. Of course, factors to consider in conducting more limited systems studies are *included in* the broader approach.

ESSENTIAL NATURE OF THE SYSTEMS STUDY

A *systems study* is the investigation made in an organization to determine and develop needed informational improvements in *specified* areas. In the context of this chapter, the needed improvements will involve using a computer to achieve specific objectives. There are at least three reasons for making a systems study. First, as we saw in the closing paragraphs of the last chapter, substantial investment may be involved in using a computer, and *a proper study reduces the risk of loss.* Second, many of the common *pitfalls associated with inadequate planning may be avoided.* Finally, *the study may point the way to substantial benefits.*

Reducing Economic Risk

Computer usage seems to be justified only when one or more of the following conditions is present:

1. When greater processing speed is both desired *and necessary*
2. When complexities of data processing require electronic methods
3. When computer investment is offset by tangible or intangible economic benefits

The last of these conditions is of paramount importance to a business, for, as Richard H. Hill, vice-president of Informatics, Inc., has observed: *"A computer installation in an economic enterprise can never be justified except in economic terms."* [1]

---

[1] Richard H. Hill, "Computer Economics," *Data Processing Digest,* May, 1966, p. 3.

Yet we have seen that there are numerous examples of businesses that *have not* achieved any economic gains from their computers. One authority has estimated that (1) about 40 percent of all computer-using organizations have not received economic benefits equal to their investments and (2) this 40 percent "failure" rate may be expected to continue for the next five years. He goes on to say that "it has further been estimated that some 90 percent of all new data-processing installations exceeded their initial budget and failed to meet their installation schedule."[2] Benjamin Conway, a senior systems consultant with IBM, concludes that almost invariably costs are understated, savings are overstated, and, without tight control, the savings that are actually possible tend to melt away.[3]

These gloomy facts support the contention that computer acquisition and use can be risky. The costs associated with acquiring and using a computer can be hard to predict. The difficulty is not caused by hardware rental or purchase costs, for such costs are known. Rather, the difficulty is caused by the unpredictability of software and operating costs (which are likely to be larger than hardware costs). And, of course, when expenses are hard to pin down, tangible savings resulting from computer usage become equally difficult to predict. A properly conducted systems study will not eliminate economic risk, but it can substantially reduce it.

Avoiding Common Pitfalls

We have just seen that financial loss may be an *end result* of failure to conduct an appropriate systems study. In the past, numerous mistakes made by managers have contributed to this undesirable end. These same snares will undoubtedly serve as the future *means* by which unwary managers (through their failure to conduct a proper study) will bring about economic losses for their firms. Several of the more *common pitfalls to be avoided are presented below:*

1. *Lack of top management support.* As noted in Chapter 13, converting to a new system carries with it many managerial implications of a nontechnical nature. In the past, top executives have often failed to provide the needed leadership.
2. *Failure to specify objectives.* A systems study should be directed toward achieving *specific* objectives. It is the responsibility of managers to specify what they want in the way of quality management information. Computer usage should be considered *only* when goals can best be reached by electronic means. Failure to

[2]See Dick H. Brandon, "The Need for Management Standards in Data Processing," *Data & Contr. Syst.,* p. 27, September, 1966.
[3]See Benjamin Conway, "The Information System Audit: A Control Technique for Managers," *Management Rev.,* March, 1968.

specify needs and objectives is a planning blunder that occurs more often than might be expected.

3. *Excessive reliance on vendors.* Computer manufacturers can provide many valuable services. But it is unrealistic to expect them to be objective if (as has sometimes been the case in the past) they are given the job of conducting a systems study to determine the feasibility of acquiring a new computer.

4. *Lack of awareness of past estimation-error patterns.* The following error patterns are among those that have been common in the past: (1) initial program preparation time and difficulty of training programmers has generally been underestimated; (2) the degree of employee resistance to change has been "surprisingly" high; (3) program running times have been unexpectedly long (this error can lead to the selection of inadequate hardware); and (4) costs have been understated while savings estimates have been too optimistic.

5. *The crash-program pitfall.* It typically requires from fifteen to thirty months to complete an initial conversion to a magnetic tape computer system. Yet it is not uncommon for managers to attempt a crash program in much less time because (1) they do not appreciate the magnitude of the task; (2) they have neglected the old system until an urgent solution is needed; (3) they wish to achieve immediately the benefits that the computer is supposed to provide; and (4) they can get hardware delivery in, perhaps, six months, and so this future date arbitrarily dictates the conversion time available. The data processing system produced in a crash program generally leaves much to be desired. It often fails to meet company needs; it requires that a disproportionate amount of time be taken to correct errors and oversights; it encounters resistance from personnel who were not properly prepared for it; and it costs more to operate than had been expected.

6. *The hardware-approach pitfall.* Executives have been known to contract for a new computer first and then to decide on how it can be used. The hardware approach typically dispenses with any meaningful systems study; an elusive intangible called prestige is its goal; and the effects of change on personnel are given little consideration.

7. *The improper-priority pitfall.* One of the consequences of a lack of top management support and of failure to specify objectives clearly has been that critical application areas have been ignored. Processing emphasis is placed on lower-priority tasks. A thorough systems study should identify the critical functions.

8. *The piecemeal-approach pitfall.* During a systems study, careful attention should be given to *redesigning* procedures for greater

efficiency. Excellent results are seldom achieved, for example, when manual records are simply converted and processed on a computer. Yet failure to redesign applications has been common. Although a step-by-step[4] approach to system integration is followed by most firms, new systems that will impede future consolidation efforts should not be designed. Also, the newly designed systems should incorporate, whenever possible, externally produced data.

9. *The inadequate-staffing pitfall.* Members of the study team should have an intimate knowledge of the business, and/or they should be competent in the technical aspects of systems and data processing. Although their talents are often in demand elsewhere in the organization, these people must be released from other duties if a proper study is to be made. Entrusting the study effort to an "average" group yields only average results at best.

Study Benefits

A primary benefit of the systems study is that it enables a company to steer clear of many of the pitfalls described above and is thus able to reduce the possibility of financial loss. In addition, the *time and money invested in a systems study may yield the following benefits:*

1. *Current systems savings may be achieved* by the cleaning up of outdated procedures that have evolved over long periods of time. Obsolete reports and duplication can often be eliminated; significant cost reductions may thus be possible regardless of whether or not a computer is installed. In fact, it is likely that the cost reductions attributed to many computers are more probably the result of systems improvement.

2. *A healthy reevaluation of company purpose and goals may result.* The major problems and opportunities of the business may be made explicit, perhaps for the first time. Long-range planning is likely to be encouraged by this definition. Operating personnel may better understand what is expected of them; they may better appreciate the problems of other departments of the organization, and this appreciation can lead to better cooperation and coordination of effort.

The above pages have demonstrated the essential nature of the systems study in planning for computers. Let us now look at an approach to be followed in conducting such a study.

[4] The step-by-step approach is the strategy of converting specific applications to the computer while moving gradually toward greater integration. Although integration is generally desirable, some firms have attempted studies that were *too broad* in view of their personnel and financial resources.

SYSTEMS-STUDY APPROACH

A systems study is conducted to provide information for decision-making purposes. You will recall from Chapter 13 that the questions to be decided in planning for computers include: (1) What data processing improvements are needed? (2) Has proper attention been given to systems review and redesign? (3) Is it desirable to use a computer to achieve data processing objectives? (4) If new equipment is required, what computer system should be selected?

Answers to these and other questions will be sought during the systems study. In arriving at their answers, the team[5] making the study should follow the planning and rational decision-making steps presented in Chapter 13. In other words, the steps or stages in the systems-study approach are to (1) *accomplish planning prerequisites and identify the objectives*, (2) *gather data on current operations*, (3) *analyze current operations and determine suitable solutions*, (4) *decide on the most appropriate solution*, (5) *implement the solution*, and (6) *follow up on the decisions made*.

Planning Prerequisites and Identification of Objectives

The account of an early well-managed survey is found in the Bible in chapter 13 of the Book of Numbers. A team of 12 "analysts" was sent by Moses to spy out the Promised Land and report back their findings. Three *important prerequisite principles* were observed in this survey:

1. *The survey had implicit support at the highest levels.* God told Moses: "Send men to spy out the land of Canaan . . . from each tribe of their fathers shall you send a man, every one a leader among them." Such top-level support is a prerequisite.
2. *The survey team consisted of highly respected individuals.* Only tribal leaders were sent on the mission. Systems study members are often selected for the offsetting talents they can bring to the job. It is common to find at least one team member who possesses a knowledge of the information needs of the business and another who is familiar with systems and the technical side of data processing. The participation of a knowledgeable auditor in the design phase so that proper controls may be built in is a wise precaution. The team leader must have the respect of the company personnel. He should be chosen on the basis of proven managerial ability, for he must plan, organize, and control the project. It is his job to (1) understand the scope, purpose, and goals of the study, (2) schedule and coordinate the team effort and keep interested

[5]In broader systems studies involving extensive redesign of existing procedures, a team approach is generally followed; in less complicated systems projects the "team" may shrink to one analyst.

parties informed of the team's progress, (3) secure the cooperation of company employees who can contribute to the study, and (4) achieve the end objectives. Although study personnel are generally employees of the organization, it is possible to employ independent consultants to perform the investigation.

3. *The scope and objectives of the survey were clearly stated.* Moses specifically told the 12 to investigate the richness of the land, the physical and numerical strength of the occupants, and the defensibility of their cities. In a systems study, the nature of the operation(s) that is (are) to be investigated should also be specifically stated at the outset; the relationship of the study to other company projects should be noted; the organizational units in the company that are to be included and excluded should be identified; the responsibility for survey review must be established; and the degree to which efforts should be made to consolidate data processing procedures should be clarified. Following the definition of the study's scope and direction, it is then important to specify the objectives that are to be pursued. Figure 14-1 summarizes some goals that are commonly sought. Goal selection, of course, should be based on the work that *needs to be done* and not upon the work that a computer is capable of doing. When

Expense reduction objectives
(Benefits of a tangible nature)

1. Reduce clerical labor expense
2. Reduce supervisory and other nonclerical labor expense
3. Reduce equipment expense
4. Reduce space and overhead expense
5. Reduce supplies expense
6. Reduce inventory carrying expense

Revenue raising objectives
(Benefits which are usually intangible)

1. Shorten processing time
2. Increase processing capacity to expand marketing efforts
3. Acquire more accurate information
4. Acquire more comprehensive information
5. Improve operating control
6. Improve customer service
7. Acquire new information (sales analyses, cost analyses, etc.)
8. Achieve better planning through the use of operations research techniques

Other objectives

1. Attain prestige and a progressive image
2. Meet clerical labor shortages
3. Prepare required government reports

Figure 14-1 Common systems study objectives

multiple objectives are sought, priorities should be assigned to guide the study team.

The biblical survey team returned to Moses after forty days. There was agreement on the richness of the land (and this report was "documented" with examples of the fruit that it produced). There was lack of agreement, however, on the strength of the people occupying the Promised Land. Sessions were held during which the differing viewpoints were presented.

It is usually desirable for the team members to hold preliminary sessions with the managers of all departments that the study will affect. Such *design sessions* allow the managers to participate in setting or revising specific systems goals. This participation is logical; it enables those most familiar with existing methods and procedures to make suggestions for improvement. Furthermore, these managers are the ones whose performance is affected by any changes, and they are the ones whose cooperation is needed if the study is to yield satisfactory results.

Before concluding this discussion of goal definition, it is appropriate to point out that a repeating or *iterative process* may be necessary before this first study step is considered complete. There is no definite procedure to be followed before detailed data gathering can begin. A top executive may believe that a systems study is needed because of informational deficiencies; he may prepare a general statement of objectives and then appoint a manager to conduct the study. A number of design sessions may be held to translate general desires into more specific goals; the scope of the study may be enlarged or reduced; objectives may be similarly changed as more facts are gathered. When it appears that tentative approval has been reached on objectives, the study leader should put these goals *in writing* and send them to all concerned for approval. If differences remain, they should be resolved in additional design sessions. Although repeating such sessions may appear to be unproductive to those who are impatient to get on with the study, their costs "most often end up being small relative to later costs caused by incomplete, and possibly erroneous, definition and directions."[6]

Before the more detailed investigation begins, the team leader should prepare a *written charter* for approval by the individual or group in charge of the overall data processing program. This charter, when approved, should include (1) a detailed statement of the study's scope and objectives, (2) a grant of authority to permit the team to cross departmental lines and receive top priority on the working time

---

[6] Marvin W. Ehlers, "Management's Blunder Buffer," *Business Automation*, March, 1966, p. 40.

of specified individuals (who should be informed of this authority grant by a high-level executive), and (3) a schedule giving a target date for the completion of the survey recommendations and interim dates for the presentation of progress reports to the executive or steering committee in charge. (Many well-managed studies have made use of PERT-CPM networks for scheduling and control purposes.)

The study-team members must first gather data on current operations before they can design suitable alternatives to achieve specified goals. In short, they must find out *where they are* before they can determine *where they want to go.* In identifying objectives, it is likely that preliminary data were gathered. But more details are now needed to determine the strengths and weaknesses of current procedures. As a result of information brought to light during this study phase, it may be desirable to revise the scope and goals of the investigation. The iterative process may be continued.

Gathering Data on Current Operations

The data gathered must be accurate, up to date, and sufficiently complete, for they will become the input to the design stage. On the other hand, however, if the analysts are not careful, they may become so mired down in relatively unimportant details at this stage that time schedules cannot be met. The data to be collected will vary from one study to another, but in most cases the following questions about the operations being studied should be answered: (1) What source information is used? (2) What work is done? (3) What business resources are being used? (4) What results are achieved? Figure 14-2 provides a list of more specific questions that may be asked in the course of gathering data.

Many well-managed firms base their ultimate decision to acquire new systems on a *return-on-investment* analysis. The profit improvement expected to result from computer usage is compared with the required hardware and software investment to see if the investment appears to be justified. Anticipated profit improvement is affected, in part, by the comparison of current processing costs with the similar costs of proposed alternatives. Thus, the team must gather data about the *current costs* to process a given volume of information. Information about processing *volume* is also needed to determine the complexity and cost of proposed alternative methods. The following cost figures related to the operations under study should be collected: (1) charges for payroll and associated fringe benefits; (2) cost of processing equipment (in the form of rental and/or depreciation charges); (3) charges for office materials, supplies, forms, etc.; and (4) overhead charges (office space used, insurance, utilities, etc.).

What source information is used?

　　What source documents are received?
　　What source documents are used?
　　Where do they originate?
　　What is the frequency of input—daily, weekly or monthly?
　　What is the maximum volume received? The minimum? The average?

What work is done?

　　What records and files are being kept to support the operation?
　　How frequently—daily, weekly, or monthly—is the operation being performed?
　　What is the volume or magnitude of work in each phase of the operation? What
　　volume fluctuations occur in the operation? What is the cause of these fluctuations?
　　What is the flow of work, i.e., what sequence of steps is followed to perform the
　　operation?

What business resources are used?

　　What departments are involved in the operation? What place in the organization
　　do they occupy? What is the primary function of these departments?
　　How many people are involved? What are their skill levels?
　　How many man-hours are needed?
　　How much time is required to complete each step?
　　What equipment is being used? For how long?
　　What materials and supplies are being used?
　　How much does it cost to perform the operation?

What results are achieved?

　　What output reports are prepared?
　　What is their purpose?
　　Who uses the reports?
　　What use is actually being made of the reports?
　　How accurate are they?
　　How timely are they?

Figure 14-2　Data-gathering questions

　　The following tools and techniques are among those that may be useful in gathering data:

1. *Design sessions.* Early participation of operating managers can serve to focus attention on important areas. Furthermore, these managers represent a storehouse of information on current methods. This knowledge can reduce the analysts' data-gathering task.
2. *Systems flowcharts.* Beginning with source-document inputs, each operation step is charted using the proper symbols. Files and equipment being used are identified, the processing sequence is shown, the departments involved are located, and the output results are indicated.

3. *Questionnaire forms.* These forms are often keyed to steps in a flowchart.[7] They give the details of processing frequencies, input and output volumes, workers performing each activity, time required to complete each step, and materials and supplies used.

4. *Personal interviews.* Interviews are needed to gather the information, prepare the flowchart, and fill in the questionnaire forms. Interviews also serve as a check on the reliability of procedures manuals and other existing systems documentation. To verify the accuracy and completeness of interviews, an analyst may take an input document and "walk it through" the processing procedure. A walk-through also presents an opportunity for the analyst to obtain suggestions from employees about ways in which procedures might be improved. Interviews must be conducted with skill and tact. The analyst should (1) carefully plan his questions, (2) make advance interview appointments, (3) explain the purpose of the interview, and (4) avoid being openly critical of current approaches. He must realize, in other words, that preoccupation with technical matters at the expense of proper human relations will quickly ruin any chance of real achievement.

5. *Operational review.* When the analysts feel that they have gathered all the data that are necessary, they should, as a final check on their accuracy and completeness, present these facts to operating personnel for verification and approval.

During the fact-finding stage, emphasis was placed on *what* was being done; now the team is interested in (1) learning *why* these activities are being performed and (2) designing the alternative ways in which these operations can be improved.[8] Perhaps the first alternative that should be considered is a *modified and improved* version of present methods.[9] There are at least two reasons for updating current operations. *First,* other possible alternatives should *not* be compared with obsolete and outdated procedures. It is quite possible that an option that is attractive when compared with outdated methods might not be the best choice when compared with redesigned procedures. And

Data Analysis and Determination of Alternatives

---

[7]The IBM booklet entitled *Documentation Techniques* (IBM Corporation, Manual C20-8075) is an element in that firm's Study Organization Plan series. This booklet is an excellent data-gathering guide, which provides examples of useful forms.

[8]The Accurately Defined Systems (ADS) technique developed by NCR provides forms to specify what a new or revised system must do. These forms cover system outputs, inputs, files, computations, and logic. A manual entitled *A Study Guide for Accurately Defined Systems* has been prepared by NCR, Dayton, Ohio, 45409.

[9]This course of action might include acquiring new equipment other than a computer. Often, however, savings can be realized with little or no additional investment.

second, an updating of current operations may prevent useless forms, reports, and records from being preserved in a conversion to an alternative.

Data gathered in the fact-finding stage are analyzed to detect weaknesses and determine the real informational needs of the business. The team's objective here is to develop an efficient set of data processing specifications for each area of study. Figure 14-3 lists some of the possible questions that should be answered during this review and design stage. However, the variety of different processing systems, the difficulty of describing these systems, the wide range of mechanical and electronic equipment that can be used, the speed with which equipment changes, the lack of static testing conditions caused by a rapidly changing business environment—all of these factors prevent the formulation of exact rules to follow in systems analysis and design.[10] Such factors also limit the number of alternative designs that can be manually evaluated. The questions in Fig. 14-3 may be presented as a *guide.* But the success of the project is dependent upon the ingenuity of the team in arriving at answers that satisfy company needs.

The following tools and techniques may be helpful in analyzing current procedures and in designing alternatives:

1. *Additional design sessions.* Operating managers can explain *why* activities are being performed, and they can answer most of the procedural questions presented in Fig. 14-3.
2. *Systems flowchart analysis.* Flowchart analysis may disclose bottlenecks; unnecessary files may be discovered (e.g., the charts may show a file where information is stored but from which little or nothing is being removed); and duplications and omissions may be identified. From the systems flowcharts *program flowcharts* and/or *decision tables* will evolve.
3. *Input/output charts.* These charts show the relationship that exists between system inputs and outputs. Input source documents are listed in rows on the left of a chart (see Fig. 14-4), while the output reports produced by the system are identified in the chart columns. An "x" is placed at the intersection of a row and column when a particular source document is used in the preparation of a specific report. For example, in Fig. 14-4 form A is needed in the preparation of reports 1 and 4. The input/output or *grid chart* enables the analyst to identify and isolate inde-

[10] In the last few years there has been a veritable explosion of alternative processing approaches from which to choose. In Chapters 3 and 4 we saw that the rapid expansion of hardware and software options, the availability of timesharing facilities, and the complications caused by unbundling have added additional challenges to the task of information systems design.

Procedural considerations

1. Are documents being produced relevant to the needs of the business? When were they originated? Who originated them? For what purpose?

2. Is faster reporting desired? Is faster reporting necessary? Can the processing sequence be improved? What would happen if the document were delayed? If it were eliminated?

3. Is greater accuracy needed? Could less accuracy be tolerated, i.e., is the expense involved in error checking greater than the cost of committing the error? Is adequate control maintained over document preparation? Does excessive control add to expense?

4. What monetary value would the user place on the document? Would he be willing to have his department charged with part of the cost of preparation?

5. Is the document in a useful form? Has writing been minimized? When were forms designed? Who designed them? For what purpose?

6. Does an output document cause action when it is sent to a manager? If not, why is it sent? If it does, what decisions are made?

7. Is the document filed? If so, for how long? How often is it referred to? Does the filing cost exceed the value of having the document available?

8. Can documents be combined? Is the same information duplicated on other reports? In other departments? If so, can procedures be integrated?

9. Is there any part of the document which is ignored? Are unnecessary facts recorded? Are additional facts needed? Are the correct number of copies prepared?

10. Is exception reporting feasible? Do current reports clearly point out exceptions?

11. Are additional documents needed? What additional documents? Is computer processing required? Are packaged programs available which will meet the needs of the business?

12. Is system capacity adequate? Do bottlenecks exist? Is overtime required? What can be done to eliminate peak loads?

13. Is customer service adequate?   What improvements can be made?

Personnel and organizational considerations

14. Are documents being prepared in the proper departments? By the right people? Could departments be combined? Could any work units be eliminated? What effects would organizational change have on personnel?

15. What effect will procedural change have on personnel? Are personnel agreeable to such change? What has been done to reduce resistance to change? What will be done with workers whose jobs are eliminated or changed? If new jobs are created, has proper consideration been given to selecting and training workers to staff these vacancies?

Economic considerations

16. What will be the cost of processing data with revised current procedures? What will it cost to satisfy company needs by other alternatives? If the cost of using the computer is greater, are intangible benefits available which are worth the extra expense?

Figure 14-3   Questions for analysis and design

Input source documents	Output reports							
	1	2	3	4	5	6	7	8
Form A	x			x				
Form B		x		x				
Form C			x					
Form D					x			
Form E		x		x				
Form F			x				x	
Form G					x		x	

Figure 14-4   Input/output chart

pendent subsystems quickly for further study. This is done by (1) drawing a vertical line down any *single* report column and *then* (2) drawing a horizontal line across any row with a covered x, etc., until further vertical and horizontal lines are impossible. For example, if we draw a line down column 1, we cover only one x—the one indicating that form A is used in preparing report 1. If we then draw a horizontal line along the form A row, we cover the x in column 4. We then draw a vertical line down column 4 and a horizontal line along any row with a covered x. The result of this procedure is that forms, A, B, and E and reports 1, 2, and 4 combine to form an independent subsystem.

4. *Electronic evaluation of computer alternatives.* Only a limited number of alternative system designs can be *manually* evaluated. Fortunately, however, if a new computer system appears to be justified, a computer can be given the firm's processing requirements and can then *simulate* the performance of these requirements using cost/performance models of selected computer alternatives. In other words, *a computer is used to evaluate other computer hardware and software configurations.*

It is assumed at this point that the study team has analyzed the current operations, prepared a detailed set of written (documented) systems specifications to achieve the study goals, and settled on the alternatives that it feels will best achieve those goals. *The prepared specifications should include:*

1. *The input requirements.* Included in the input specifications should be the source documents to be used, the means of preparing and transmitting those documents, the frequency of preparation, and the volume figures expected.
2. *The processing specifications.* The new procedures must be defined. How the inputs will be used to prepare the desired

outputs should be clearly indicated. All files and records to be used and maintained should be identified, frequency of file usage must be known, and processing volumes (both current and expected) associated with the files should be specified.

3. *The output requirements.* The output specifications should include the form, content, and frequency of reports. Volume figures are also needed.

4. *Control provisions.* The steps to be taken to provide the necessary internal control should be specified. This will be the task of the auditor, who should be a member of the study team.

5. *Cost estimates.* Preliminary estimates of (1) setup costs and (2) annual operating costs using new systems approaches should be made.

Decision Making: Study Team

Computer usage is justified when the tangible and intangible economic benefits to be gained are greater than comparable benefits received from other alternatives. The type and number of alternatives to be considered vary, of course, from one systems study to another. In some situations, noncomputer options may be preferable; and for many organizations the results of a study may indicate that the use of a computer center or a timesharing service would be the best solution.

In selecting a computer center, the study team would consider such factors as: (1) the proximity, reputation, and financial stability of the center, (2) the quality of center personnel and their experience in dealing with similar systems, (3) the care exercised in safeguarding documents and providing backup facilities, and (4) the costs of using the center.

In choosing a timesharing service, the study team would be interested in such factors as: (1) the reputation and financial stability of the service, (2) the quality of service personnel and their ability to assist in systems implementation, (3) the reliability of the service, e.g., its loading and therefore its response time, and its backup facilities, (4) the controls available to protect the security and integrity of user data and programs maintained in online storage, (5) the availability of programming languages and accurate library programs, and (6) the costs associated with using the service.

Regardless of whether a computer center or a timesharing service is chosen, the team should be required to present its findings and the economic basis for its recommendations to a top executive or steering committee for the final decision. For the remainder of this chapter we shall assume that the team believes that a new in-house computer installation is justified. However, portions of the material that follows may be appropriate in a study that does not result in the acquisition of new equipment.

Once the decision to concentrate attention on an in-house installation has been made (with the approval of top executives), there are a number of other questions that should be studied by the team members before they present their final recommendations. These questions include:

1. Which computers should be considered? What hardware/software package would best meet company needs? Can consultants help in equipment evaluation and selection?
2. Which hardware/software package offers the greatest return on investment? Can the company afford the investment at this time? Would other investment opportunities available to the firm yield a greater return?
3. Have all possible acquisition methods (rent, lease, or buy) been evaluated?
4. Have organizational and personnel aspects received proper consideration? (These topics will not be considered at this time but will be discussed in the next two chapters.)

Equipment Evaluation and Selection   To select is to choose from a number of more or less suitable alternatives. Evaluation should be based on the ability of several machines to process the detailed set of written systems specifications that have been prepared. With the availability of whole families of computers from different manufacturers, evaluation and selection is, of course, a complicated task. Furthermore, with the separate pricing of hardware and software brought about by unbundling, the process of selecting the best hardware/software package has probably become even more complicated in recent years. *The following selection approaches have been widely used:*

1. *Single-source approach.* This noncompetitive approach merely consists of choosing the hardware/software package from among those available from a selected vendor. Sometimes the vendor participates in the systems study and recommends the package. There is a lack of objectivity in this approach; unfortunate results have been produced; but it has often been used in the "selection" of smaller in-house packages.
2. *Competitive-bidding approach.* Systems specifications are submitted to vendors with a request that they prepare bids. Included in the bid request may be a requirement that cost and perform-

Economic factors

1. Cost comparisons
2. Return on investment
3. Acquisition methods

Hardware factors

1. Hardware performance, reliability, capacity, and price
2. Presence or absence of modularity
3. Number and accessibility of backup facilities
4. Firmness of delivery date
5. Effective remaining life of proposed hardware
6. Compatibility with existing systems

Software factors

1. Software performance and price
2. Efficiency and reliability of available software
3. Programming languages available (not promised)
4. Availability of useful and well-documented packaged programs, program libraries, and user groups
5. Firmness of delivery date on promised software
6. Ease of use and modification

Service factors

1. Facilities provided by manufacturer for checking new programs
2. Training facilities offered and the quality of training provided
3. Programming assistance and conversion assistance offered
4. Maintenance terms and quality

Reputation of manufacturer

1. Financial stability
2. Record of keeping promises

Figure 14-5   Equipment selection factors

ance figures be prepared for a specified "benchmark" processing run. The vendors select what they believe to be the most appropriate hardware/software packages from their lines and submit proposals. The team then evaluates these proposals and makes a decision. Some of the evaluation factors to be considered are shown in Fig. 14-5. Sometimes this bidding approach yields excellent results. But frequently vendors do not prepare the proposals they are capable of making—this is especially true when a vendor representative feels that his chance of receiving the order is marginal or if the order itself is likely to be small. Other possible shortcomings in bidding include the facts that: (1) systems specifications may be altered to improve procedures or, perhaps, place the vendor's package in the best possible light (the study team must then compare bids based on different specifications—a most difficult comparison indeed, as the vendors well know); and (2) program running (or throughput) times may be underestimated in the bids because inadequate allowance is made for house-keeping and setup times.[11]

3. *Consultant-evaluation approach.* Qualified data processing consultants can assist businesses in selecting the hardware/software package. Consultants can bring specialized knowledge and experience and an objective point of view to bear on the evaluation and selection problem.

4. *Simulation approach.* We have already discussed the use of simulation programs for evaluation purposes. These programs are capable of comparing the input, output, and computing times required to process specific applications on all available commercial computers made in this country. The General Services Administration, a housekeeping agency of the federal government, has used a family of simulation programs known as SCERT[12] (Systems and Computers Evaluation and Review Technique) to help in the selection of 10 large-scale computer systems for its regional offices. Simulation provides fast, accurate, and objective evaluation. However, as might be expected in view of the benefits obtained, the use of proprietary simulation models is not inexpensive.

Regardless of the approach used, the study team must compare the quantitative and qualitative factors listed in Fig. 14-5 to further limit the choices. At this point (or perhaps at an earlier point) a return-on-investment analysis should be made for economic justification and analysis purposes.

Estimated Return on Investment[13]   The costs associated with the options remaining should be compared with the cost of improved current methods of performing the work. Let us assume that as a result of one cost comparison it is expected that there will be negative effects on after-tax earnings for the first three years but that after this initial period substantial positive returns are anticipated. It is known that top executives believe that the computer should yield a satisfactory return over a six-year period or it should not, at least for the

---

[11] Throughput-time estimates are also subject to complicating variations caused by differences in software and programmer efficiency. Of course, shorter program running-time estimates give the impression of economy in the bids, but such estimates can also lead to the acquisition of hardware with inadequate capability to meet expanding needs.

[12] SCERT was prepared by and is the property of COMRESS, Inc., a Washington, D.C., consulting organization.

[13] For further details on the subject of capital-investment analysis and the concept of the time-adjusted return on investment, see chap. 19 of Robert N. Anthony, *Management Accounting*, 3d ed., Richard D. Irwin, Inc., Homewood, Ill., 1964.

time being, be acquired. Since the company can earn a 10 percent return on investments made in plant and equipment, it is also the feeling of top managers that the computer investment should be postponed if it cannot produce a similar return.

Armed with this information, the study team prepares the following table:

Year	1 Effects on Cash Flow of Acquisition	2 10% Discount Factors*	3 Present Value of Cash Flow
1	$-100,000	0.9091	$-90,910
2	- 75,000	0.8264	-61,980
3	- 25,000	0.7513	-18,782
4	+ 50,000	0.6830	+34,150
5	+100,000	0.6209	+62,090
6	+150,000	0.5645	+85,675
		Total	$+10,243

*SOURCE: Billy E. Goetz, *Quantitative Methods: A Survey and Guide for Managers*, McGraw-Hill Book Company, New York, 1965, p. 526, Table 8a.

Column 1, the effects on cash flow, represents the economic effects expected by the team if updated current procedures are replaced by a selected computer system. In other words, this column shows the expected effects of the acquisition on net income plus depreciation. Column 2 shows the *present value* of $1 received in years 1, 2, 3, etc., when the required rate of return is 10 percent. At the end of one year, 10 percent interest on $0.9091 is $0.0909. Thus, the present value ($0.9091) plus the interest ($0.0909) gives $1 at the end of a year. Column 3 is the product of column 1 multiplied by column 2. The *time-adjusted* return on investment is exactly 10 percent if the total of column 3 is zero. A negative total means that the 10 percent return cannot be expected. In our example, the estimated return is found to *exceed* 10 percent.

Before leaving the subject of return on investment, it is appropriate to note that 20 of 33 "outstandingly successful" manufacturing companies studied by the consulting firm of Booz, Allen & Hamilton make use of formal return-on-investment analyses in their computer decisions.[14]

[14]See James W. Taylor and Neal J. Dean, "Managing to Manage the Computer," *Harvard Business Rev.,* vol. 44, p. 107, September–October, 1966.

Acquisition methods[15]   It is the job of the study team to evaluate acquisition methods and recommend the one best suited to the company. *Computers may be acquired in the following ways:*

1. *Renting.* Hardware in about three-fourths of the computer installations is rented from the computer manufacturer. This is a flexible method that does not require a large initial investment. It is also the most expensive method if the equipment meets company needs for four or five years or longer.

2. *Purchasing.* Although the rental method is the most popular, there is evidence of a trend toward greater equipment purchasing. This is especially true of the federal government, which, in recent years, has substantially reduced the percentage of rented installations. Greater interest in purchasing is due to (1) the fact that it is the least expensive method when hardware is kept for several years, (2) the greater reliability, longer physical life, and greater expected residual value of third-generation hardware, and (3) the belief of some managers that the risk of becoming "locked-in" to a particular configuration is reduced by their ability to do a better job of long-range systems planning.

3. *Leasing.* Under the typical leasing arrangement, the user tells the leasing company what equipment is desired. The leasing organization arranges for the purchase of the equipment and then leases it to the user for a long-term period (usually three to five years). This method combines some of the advantages of both renting and purchasing.

Figure 14-6 summarizes the advantages and disadvantages of each acquisition method. The study team should weigh these merits and faults carefully before making its choice. At the time of this writing, the *program products* of unbundled manufacturers are acquired through rental agreements between manufacturer and user. Packaged programs may also be acquired from independent software firms through rental and/or purchase agreements.

Presentation of Recommendations

Guided by a written charter, which defined the scope and direction of their efforts, the study team has analyzed the relevant facts; from this analysis has come a detailed set of systems specifications designed to achieve the study goals. After careful consideration of alternatives, the team has concluded that computer usage is justified. Return-on-

[15]For further details on this subject, see Irving I. Solomon and Laurence O. Weingart, *Management Uses of the Computer,* Harper & Row, Publishers, Incorporated, New York, 1966, pp. 187–198.

Rental

Advantages

1. No large purchase price required.
2. Risk of technological obsolescence reduced.
3. Maintenance included in rental charges.
4. Agreement may be cancelled without penalty after brief period.
5. Greater flexibility in changing equipment configurations.
6. Possibility of applying some part of rental charges to later purchase.

Disadvantages

1. Most expensive if equipment is used for long period of time.
2. Rental charges remain same throughout life of agreement.
3. Rental charges may increase when monthly usage exceeds a specified number of hours.

Lease

Advantages

1. Less expensive than rental over life of the lease.
2. No large purchase price required.
3. Maintenance is included in the lease charges.
4. No additional charges when equipment is used beyond a specified number of hours monthly.
5. Lease charges decline after specified period.
6. Possibility of applying part of lease charges toward later purchase.

Disadvantages

1. User contracts for equipment over long time period.
2. Reduced flexibility—user is obligated to pay a contracted charge if lease is terminated prior to end of lease period.

Purchase

Advantages

1. Generally least expensive if machine is kept over long time period.
2. No additional charges when equipment is used beyond specified number of hours monthly.
3. Certain tax advantages accrue to the purchaser.

Disadvantages

1. Equipment maintenance not included in the purchase price.
2. Risk of technological obsolescence—of being ''locked-in'' to a system which does not continue to meet changing company needs.
3. A large initial capital outlay is required.

Figure 14-6 Factors to consider in equipment acquisition

investment analyses have been made; a particular hardware/software package has been chosen; and the best acquisition method for the company has been agreed upon. The team has made many decisions. But the *final* decisions are made by top-level managers. It is the job of the team to recommend; it is the responsibility of top executives to decide.

The report of the systems-study team should cover the following points:

1. A restatement of study scope and objectives
2. The procedures and operations that will be changed
3. The anticipated effects of such changes on organizational structure, physical facilities, and company information
4. The anticipated effects on personnel and the personnel resources available to implement the change
5. The hardware/software package chosen, the reasons for the choice, and the alternatives considered
6. The economic effects of the change, including cost comparisons, adequacy of return on investment, and analysis of acquisition methods
7. A summary of the problems anticipated in the changeover
8. A summary of the benefits to be obtained from the change

Decision Making: Top Managers

Top executives must evaluate the recommendations made by the team to detect any evidence of bias[16] and decide whether the benefits outweigh the disadvantages. Suspicion of bias or of an inadequate effort may be justified if the points outlined above are not included in the recommendation. For example, suspicion is probably warranted if little or no mention is made of the personnel or organizational aspects of the change, if the alternatives considered are really just "straw men," which are obviously inadequate, or if feasibility depends solely on vaguely defined and suspicious intangible benefits.

If the decision is to accept the recommendations of the team, top executives should then establish subsequent project performance controls. Personnel must be selected to do the work; a conversion schedule should be drawn up, and periodic reports on implementation progress should be required. In the following section we shall look at some of the technical conversion questions that will have to be considered; in following chapters we shall examine organizational and personnel problems that will have to be dealt with.

If the decision is *not* to acquire and/or use a computer, a follow-up on this decision may be needed at a later time. Rising labor costs, reduced computing costs, and other factors may make the use of a computer more attractive in a very short period. To the "no" decision perhaps should be added "not yet."

---

[16]After all, if the change is made, some members of the study team may expect to move into positions of greater influence.

Since a decision has been made to acquire a new computer, the next order of business for top administrators is to deal with those organizational and personnel matters that now take on immediate importance. The organizational location of the computer must be reviewed; a computer implementation officer must be appointed; and an effort should be made to inform employees of the effects, if any, that the change will have on their jobs and opportunities.

Systems Conversion

Depending upon organizational decisions, the computer implementation officer may be a top-level executive, a member of the computer steering committee, and/or a data processing manager who will be in charge of the computer department. He must be given the authority to plan, organize, staff, and control the conversion phase of the systems project. His first duties will be to (1) review the policies, objectives, and target dates that have been established by top management to control the project, (2) submit an implementation plan for top-level approval, which outlines conversion time and cost elements, and (3) select the computer personnel needed to carry out the conversion. From this point on the manager will be involved in planning and scheduling the many jobs that must be completed. A multitude of preparation tasks will go on simultaneously: additional workers may be selected; training must take place; programming and systems-analysis standards should be developed; file conversion must be initiated and carried out; programs must be prepared, debugged, and made ready for conversion; and the physical computer site must be readied. The total time needed for these activities varies, of course, but many months are generally required. To illustrate graphically the complexity of computer-systems implementation, Figure 14-7 presents a network-conversion model.[17] The boxes represent activities; solid lines indicate time consumption; broken lines indicate necessary sequence but do not involve time usage; and the heavy lines show the critical path. The activities listed in many of the boxes will be considered in the following paragraphs. Remaining activities are covered in later chapters.

Program preparation and conversion[18] The following overlapping activities are performed during this phase of the project.

[17] From David H. Li, *Accounting/Computers/Management Information Systems,* McGraw-Hill Book Company, New York, 1968, p. 155. See chap. 13 for a review of planning and control by means of critical-path scheduling. In a systems study conducted for the purpose of putting new applications on existing hardware, the general implementation procedure presented here (and in Chapters 10 and 11) is appropriate, although, of course, those activities relating to hardware factors will not be included.

[18] A review of materials found in Chapter 11 might be appropriate here.

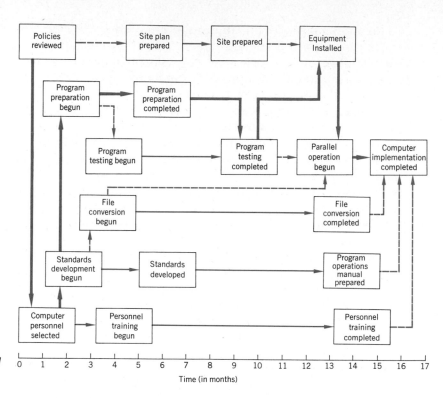

Figure 14-7   Network model for conversion

1. *Program analysis.* The systems specifications defined during the feasibility study must be broken down into the detailed arithmetic and logic operations required to achieve the goals. *Program flow-charts* and/or *decision tables* are generally prepared during this activity.

2. *Standards development.* Standardized flowcharting symbols should be decided upon and consistently used; standard programming procedures and the use of standardized symbolic names to describe company data should be prescribed.[19] Developed standards promote consistency, reduce future program maintenance problems, and make it easier for others to take over the work of a programmer who decides to leave the company.

3. *Program preparation.* Once the necessary arithmetic and logic operations have been identified, they must be translated, or coded, into a language and form acceptable to the processor that has been ordered. In the event that replacement hardware is being acquired, the conversion of existing programs to the new equip-

[19]The importance of standard data definitions in the development of broader systems has already been mentioned.

ment may be facilitated by the techniques described in Chapter 11.

4. *Debugging and testing*. Program *bugs* must be removed and the coded programs must be tested before the programmed procedures can be considered ready for use.

5. *File conversion*. Current files must be changed into a form acceptable to the processor. This can be a tremendous task, and it is one that is often underestimated. Files should be consolidated and duplicate records eliminated; errors in current files must be detected and removed; and file inconsistencies must be found *before* the changeover rather than later when they can cause system malfunctions. Also, new manual methods that are to be developed and new forms that are to be designed must receive attention.

6. *Changeover*. When the computer arrives, there should be a shakedown period during which applications are processed by both currently used and new procedures as a final check before the cut-over to the new system occurs. A *parallel running* check involves the processing of *current* input data by old and new methods. If a significant difference appears, the cause must be located. A *pilot testing* approach is sometimes substituted for parallel running. Input data for a *previous* month's operations are processed using new methods, and the results are compared with the results obtained from existing operations. Preliminary pilot tests can be run on the vendor's equipment prior to delivery of the user's hardware. Thus, debugging and testing are facilitated through the use of actual input data, and it may be possible to reduce the time (and costs) associated with maintaining two different systems at a later date. Regardless of the checking approach, final conversion to computer production runs comes from satisfactory performance during this shakedown period.

The activities associated with the program preparation and conversion phase may represent 50 percent or more of the total human effort expended from the inception of the systems study to conversion completion. Because of the time and complexities involved, this phase must begin as promptly as possible. You will recall that earlier in the chapter it was estimated that installation schedules are not met 90 percent of the time. Difficulties with program preparation and debugging almost always contribute to slipped schedules. Good management can help to avoid schedule slippage. For example, by incorporating *application-program packages* whenever possible, the project manager may help speed up the program-preparation activity. It is during this activity, too, that many firms have made valuable use of the specialized knowledge and experience of *software consulting organizations.* Finally, the manager should, in the interests of programming schedule and cost control, establish a formal procedure to evaluate systems-change requests occurring after a *freeze point* has been reached.

If program-preparation schedules begin to slip, there is a tendency to slight programming documentation. But time made up at the expense of good documentation is likely to be a very temporary gain; it will be lost at high cost in a later period when programs must be tested and when program corrections and changes must be made.

The conversion time is almost always a period of personnel and organizational strain. Data processing employees may work long hours and be subjected to pressure to complete the conversion. Unforeseen problems, last-minute corrections, and the disruption of data processing services to using departments, customers, suppliers, etc., may contribute to these pressures. It is at this time that cooperation is badly needed between data processing specialists and personnel of affected departments. Yet it is precisely at this time that cooperation frequently breaks down because of managerial preoccupation with technical conversion matters at the expense of proper personnel preparations.

Site preparation　　The cost of site preparation can range from a modest figure to hundreds of thousands of dollars, depending on the wishes of top executives and the extent of remodeling or construction required. *The following factors must be considered during site planning and preparation:*

1. *Location.* From an economic standpoint, the computer location should probably be chosen for its accessibility to those company departments that will be closely associated with computer operations. But factors other than economics are often given top priority. Company executives may want a "show case" installation enclosed in glass, expensively furnished, and located where it can be seen by large numbers of people. Location planning must take into account a structure's ability to support the weight of the hardware. Also, soundproofing will probably be required to control internal and external noise levels.

2. *Space and layout.* The physical dimensions of the equipment to be housed, the location and length of power and connecting cables, the space needed to allow service access to this hardware, the data-movement patterns; the storage room needed for input/output media, supplies, spare parts, and maintenance equipment,

and the number and size of work areas, offices, and conference rooms—all these factors must be considered in determining the space requirements and the layout of the site. Future expansion needs should also be taken into account.

3. *Air-conditioning.* Earlier computers needed large amounts of air-conditioning to dissipate the heat generated by vacuum tubes. Although heat generation has been significantly reduced through the use of solid state components, air-conditioning is still needed for employee productivity and dust, temperature, and humidity control.

4. *Power and lighting.* Hardware electrical requirements must be met. If rewiring is called for (and it is usually needed), the job should be done by qualified electricians in accordance with building codes and fire-insurance rules. Adequate illumination of the site is a detail which should not be overlooked.

5. *Cable protection.* Numerous cables interconnect hardware units and supply electrical power. Yet attractive sites have no unsightly cables lying around on the floor to impair safety. The usual practice is to install a raised or false floor and then run the cables beneath this floor.

6. *Fire protection.* Since much of the data stored on cards and tapes may be irreplaceable, fireproof materials should be used wherever possible in the site preparation. Hardware and media fire-insurance protection is available. A fireproof vault to store vital records, programs, etc., might be a wise investment. Adequate fire-alarm facilities and emergency power cutoffs should be provided, but a sprinkler system is generally not recommended because of the water damage to media and electrical equipment that might result from its use.

Vendor Assistance   The computer manufacturer stands ready to provide a number of services of a technical nature to help the customer make the transition to computer usage. Prior to unbundling, most of these services were offered to customers at no extra charge. Now, a separate pricing policy is followed for many of these services. *The following services are commonly offered:*

1. *Training.* The vendor has introductory training classes available for the selected programmer candidates. Included in this training are details about the specific processor model ordered and the programming languages that will be employed. Brief executive seminars may also be held to acquaint managers with a few of the basic computer concepts. The subject of training will be considered further in Chapter 16.

2. *Program preparation.* The vendor has systems representatives available to help with program preparation. The representative knows the computer and how to program it, and he can furnish on-the-job training to the user's programmers. But it is risky (and expensive) to place too much reliance on the systems representative because company personnel may then not be adequately prepared to take over program preparation and maintenance when he leaves. Of course, the competency of systems representatives varies. And even the best ones may not know much about the user's business.

3. *Programming aids.* Program preparation is aided by the software that the vendor can furnish. The availability and efficiency of subroutines, packaged programs, operating systems, compilers, etc., are important considerations.

4. *Debugging and testing.* Most vendors make debugging and testing time available (the amount varies) on equipment similar to the user's hardware prior to its arrival time. The systems representative, of course, is also available to help with the predelivery debugging and testing of prepared programs. A larger amount of machine time may be furnished for these purposes after the hardware is installed.

5. *Site preparation and installation.* Vendors are of considerable help in site preparation. They have had extensive experience in this matter, and in this case their interests and the interests of the customer are usually the same. Both are interested in efficiency, safety, ease of maintenance, and attractiveness. Vendor engineers, of course, install the hardware and make the necessary tests to be sure it is operating properly before it is turned over to the user.

Consultant assistance   We have seen that during the earlier systems-study stages consultants can often be used to advantage by alert managers to assist in such areas as systems design and hardware-software selection. Prior to systems conversion, they can offer sound advice on personnel and organizational matters associated with the forthcoming changes. And we have seen that packaged application programs, available from software consulting organizations, may be used during the implementation stage to shorten the disruptive conversion period. In addition, consultants are frequently retained during the conversion stage because: (1) the firm's computer staff is too small to finish the mammoth transition job on time; (2) the firm's staff lacks the necessary training, knowledge, and experience to complete the job satisfactorily without some type of assistance; (3) consulting organizations can provide needed training in systems analysis and programming (and they can recommend and incorporate the use of data processing standards and controls into such training); and (4) it is judged to be more economical to "farm out" certain activities than to attempt to complete them internally.

Once the system has been implemented and is in operation, a thorough appraisal or audit should be made.[20] This follow-up is commonly conducted by internal auditors and others who have an independent viewpoint and are not responsible for the development and maintenance of the system. Among the questions that should be considered in the audit are:

Follow-up on Systems Decisions

1. How useful is the system to company decision makers? How enthusiastic are they about the service they receive? Do they receive reports in time to take action?
2. Are planned processing procedures being followed? Are all new procedures being processed on the computer? Have old procedures been eliminated? If not, why not?
3. Is the information processing function properly organized?
4. Are responsibilities of data processing personnel defined and understood? Are training programs of acceptable quality?
5. Have programming standards been established? Are testing procedures adequate?
6. Are systems controls being observed? Is documentation complete? Have procedures to control program changes been established? Are these control procedures being enforced? Are any modifications or refinements indicated as a result of operating experience? If so, are they being made? How are they being controlled?
7. How do operating results compare with original goals and expectations? Are economic benefits being obtained? If variations exist, what is the cause? What can be done to achieve expected results?

Planning for computers is accomplished through systems studies. An information systems project may be initiated in response to many types of business problems. Technical, economic, and operational aspects must be evaluated during such a study. Failure to plan properly for computers subjects the organization to probable financial loss; careful study, on the other hand, may yield positive benefits and may help the firm avoid common mistakes.

SUMMARY

[20] Data processing personnel should know in advance that such a follow-up will be made.

The steps in the systems-study approach are to (1) identify the scope of the problem and the objectives to be gained, (2) gather the facts on current operations, (3) analyze current operations and determine suitable solutions, (4) decide on the most appropriate solution, (5) implement the solution, and (6) follow up on the decisions made.

If, during the course of a systems study, the decision is made to acquire a new computer, a bewildering number of technical preparation tasks must be accomplished before the conversion can be completed. Personnel must be trained; programs must be written (or converted), debugged, tested, and documented; file conversion must be considered; the physical site for the equipment must be readied; and the actual changeover must be accomplished. Many months are required to perform these tasks. Computer vendors and consultants may assist by helping to perform some of the necessary jobs.

DISCUSSION QUESTIONS

1. (a) What is a systems study? (b) Why are they essential?
2. What pitfalls may be avoided by conducting a proper systems study?
3. What benefits may be obtained from systems studies?
4. Identify and briefly explain the steps in the systems-study approach.
5. What are the prerequisite principles that should be observed in making a systems study?
6. What objectives are commonly sought from computer usage?
7. (a) What is a design session? (b) An iterative process? (c) Why is a written charter needed by the study team?
8. (a) What questions should be answered during the fact-finding stage of the systems study? (b) During the analysis and design stage?
9. (a) What tools and techniques are useful during the data-gathering stage? (b) During the analysis and design stage?
10. (a) What factors should be considered in selecting a computer center? (b) In choosing a timesharing service?
11. (a) Discuss the equipment-selection approaches that may be employed. (b) What factors should be considered in equipment selection?
12. Why should a return-on-investment analysis be made during the systems study?
13. (a) Discuss the possible computer acquisition methods. (b) What are the advantages and disadvantages of each method?
14. What technical preparation matters must be considered before the arrival of the computer?

15. Identify and explain the activities that are performed during the program preparation and conversion phase of the project.
16. Distinguish between parallel running and pilot testing.
17. Why is proper documentation necessary?
18. What factors must be considered during site planning and preparation?
19. (a) How may the computer vendor assist the customer during systems conversion? (b) How may consultants be of assistance?

SELECTED REFERENCES

Amato, Vincent V.: "Computer Feasibility Studies: The Do-It-Yourself Approach," *Management Review,* February, 1970, pp. 2–9.

Canning, Richard G.: "Management of Systems Analysis," *EDP Analyzer,* July, 1968, pp. 4–10.

Chaplin, Joseph E.: "A Feasibility Study Guide," *Journal of Systems Management,* July, 1969, pp. 20–26.

Dorn, Philip H.: "How to Evaluate a Time-Sharing Service," *Datamation,* November, 1969, pp. 220–221ff.

Freed, Roy N.: "Get the Computer System You Want," *Harvard Business Review,* November–December, 1969, pp. 99–108.

Hammersmith, Alan G.: "Selecting a Vendor of Time-Shared Computer Services," *Computers and Automation,* October, 1968, pp. 16–22.

Hillegass, John R.: "Systematic Techniques for Computer Evaluation and Selection," *Management Services,* July–August, 1969, pp. 35–38.

Martin, B. A.: "Guidelines for Contracting for Computer Related Services," *Computers and Automation,* April, 1970, pp. 18–25.

McCarn, Davis B.: "Getting Ready," *Datamation,* August 1, 1970, pp. 22–26.

Plummer, John: "Will Your Computer Pay Its Way?," *Business Horizons,* April, 1969, pp. 31–36.

Schroeder, Walter J.: "If You Can't Plan It, You Can't Do It," *Journal of Systems Management,* April, 1969, pp. 4ff.

Schwartz, M. H.: "Computer Project Selection in the Business Enterprise," *Journal of Accountancy,* April, 1969, pp. 35–43.

Totaro, J. Burt: "How to Get Your Money's Worth With Consultants," *Data Processing Magazine,* April, 1970, pp. 18–21ff.

Weiser, Alan L.: "Automatic Data Processing Systems—Physical Installation Considerations," *Computers and Automation,* November, 1969, pp. 44–46ff.

Organization and the Computer 15

In this chapter we come to grips with the question of the present and potential consequences of computers on the environment in which managers work, i.e., the impact of computers on the organizational structure of business. Furthermore, since managers work in such an environment, it is clear that anything that affects organizational structure is also of vital interest to them. Following a brief discussion of a few *organization fundamentals,* we shall study *the organization of data processing activities* and *the computer's impact on future organization.*

ORGANIZATION FUNDAMENTALS

The organizing function, you will recall, involves the grouping of work teams into logical and efficient units in order to carry out plans and achieve goals. If work units are to operate efficiently, each unit mem-

**Organizational
Structure**

ber must know what his job includes and what position he occupies. The *formal*[1] organizational (or *authority*) structure is represented by an *organization chart,* which indicates, by position titles, the place in the organization of each job, the formal lines of authority and reporting relationships among positions, and the assigned role of the work unit in the total structure. Figure 15-1 shows the organizational chart of a hypothetical manufacturing firm. In this example, work units are grouped by *type of work* (finance, marketing, and production), *geographic area* (regional and district sales offices), and *product line.* Of course, a logical and efficient organizing scheme for one company may not be desirable for another.

An organizational structure must be flexible because of constantly changing technological, social, and economic factors. We saw in Chapter 3 that such factors may bring about the introduction of new products and processes, cause changes in markets and buying habits, and result in company growth or decline. When a computer is introduced into an organization, it may take over a large part of the work of several departments. When there is no longer a valid reason for some units to continue to exist, changes should be made in the organization to avoid duplication and waste. Unless careful planning precedes such changes, however, they are likely to produce efficiency-robbing employee resistance in the affected departments.

**Centralization or
Decentralization**

The level in the organization structure where significant decisions are made can vary. The concept of *centralization of authority*[2] refers to a concentration of the important decision-making powers in the hands of a relatively few top executives. *Decentralization of authority,* on the other hand, refers to the extent to which significant decisions are made at lower levels. In very small organizations, *all* decision-making power is likely to be centralized in the hands of the owner-manager; in larger firms, the question of centralization or decentralization *is a matter of degree*—i.e., it is a question of how much authority is held at different levels. The extent to which authority is delegated to lower levels depends, in part, on such factors as: (1) the managerial philosophy of top executives; (2) the growth, size, and complexity of the business; (3) the availability of qualified subordinates; and (4) the availability of quality information and adequate operating con-

---

[1] There is also the important concept of the *informal* organization. This type of organization occurs naturally and voluntarily as a result of the interaction of employee groups. Although this subject is generally beyond the scope of this text, we will have some points to discuss about informal organization in Chapter 16.

[2] *Authority* is defined here as the right to give orders and the power to see that they are carried out.

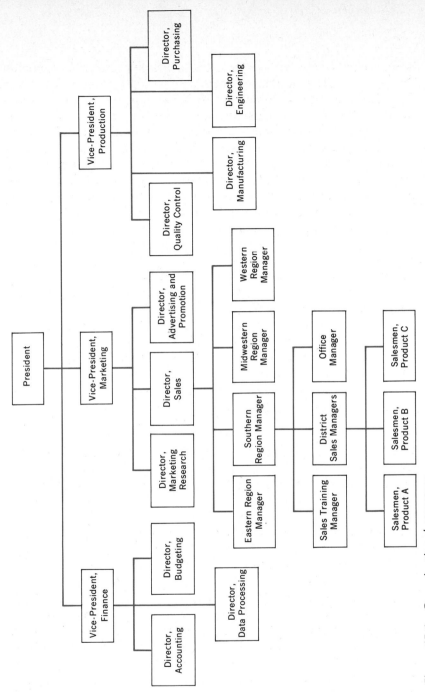

Figure 15-1 Organizational structure

trols. Since change may occur in all of these factors, it is apparent that the degree of authority centralization is also subject to revision.

In addition to centralization or decentralization of *authority,* it is also possible to use these terms in connection with (1) company operations in a *geographic sense* and (2) *activities to be performed.* In the discussions that follow, *it is important to remember that an organization may be centralized in one sense of the term and not in others.* For example, it is possible for the *data processing activities* of a business to be concentrated at a central point to economize by using a large-scale computer. But this approach may have *little* or *no effect* on the degree of authority or geographic concentration. To illustrate, a sales manager, located a thousand miles from corporate headquarters, may have the authority to make important decisions. With the availability of quick-response systems, however, it may not matter to him that the information that supports those decisions was prepared by a centralized computer. Thus, in this case we have centralization of data processing activities combined with geographic and authority decentralization.

ORGANIZATION OF DATA PROCESSING ACTIVITIES

Prior to the introduction of computers, data processing activities were generally handled by manufacturing, marketing, and finance divisions on a separate and thus decentralized basis. But such developments as (1) the creation and improvement of online storage devices, (2) the introduction of quick-response systems, (3) the direct connection of remote stations to distant processors by means of high-speed data-communication facilities, and (4) the design of broader systems, which cut across organizational lines, have made it possible to centralize data processing activities *if* company needs are best served by such action. Thus, many firms must now decide to what extent (if any) they will centralize their data processing operations. Should small computers be used by individual organization units, or should these units furnish input to (and receive output from) one or more central computer centers, which can be established to process data originating at many points?

Advantages of Centralized Data Processing

The considerations in favor of the centralized approach are as follows:

1. *It permits economies of scale.* With adequate processing volume, the use of larger and more powerful computing equipment may result in reduced operating costs. A lower unit cost for each item

processed may be achieved by lower total charges for personnel and equipment.

2. *It permits other economies.* Duplication in record storage and program preparation may be eliminated; less expensive standardized forms can be used; and site preparation costs may be reduced since fewer sites are involved.

3. *It facilitates necessary systems integration.* For example, achieving companywide agreement on customer code numbers is a necessary step in integrating the procedures required to process customer orders. Such agreement is more likely to occur for efficiency reasons when order processing is handled at a central point. We have also seen that an integrated, central corporate data bank makes it possible for managers to probe files and obtain timely information.

4. *It has certain personnel advantages.* It may be possible to concentrate fewer skilled programmers at a centralized site and thus make more effective use of their talents. A sizable operation may offer more appeal to highly qualified computer specialists. Thus, recruiting may be simplified and a professional group will be available to help train new personnel.

5. *It permits better utilization of processing capability.* With a centralized operation, *companywide* priorities can be assigned to processing tasks. Those jobs that are of greatest importance are, of course, completed first. With a decentralized approach, however, low-priority work may be processed in one division with excess capacity while in another division a higher-priority application may be left unfinished because of inadequate processing capability.

In view of these benefits, it might seem that a decision to follow a centralized approach would be automatic. Yet there are limiting factors in centralization, which may cause a company to follow a more decentralized path. These limitations are implicit in the following discussion of the advantages of decentralization.

Included among the possible advantages of decentralization are the following:

Advantages of Decentralized Data Processing

1. *Greater interest and motivation at division levels.* Division managers in control of their own computers may be more likely to (a) maintain the accuracy of input data and (b) use the equipment in ways that best meet their particular operating needs. Greater interest and motivation, combined with greater knowledge of

division conditions, may produce information of higher quality and value even though the unit processing costs may be higher.

2. *Better response to user needs.* The systems standardization typically required for centralized processing may not be equally suitable for all divisions. With decentralization, special programs can be prepared to meet exact divisional needs. In addition, although a smaller machine will probably be slower than the centralized equipment, it should be remembered that central machine time must be allocated to several users. Information considered important to one division may be delayed because higher priority is given to other processing tasks. Thus, the fact that a smaller machine allows for prompt attention to a given job may lead to faster processing at the division level.

3. *Reduced downtime risks.* A breakdown in the centralized equipment or the communications links may leave the entire system inoperative. A similar breakdown in one division, however, does not affect other decentralized operations.

Trend Toward Centralization of Data Processing Activities

There is no general answer to the question of whether or not a company *should* centralize or decentralize its processing. In the final analysis the decision usually involves a trade-off between motivational values and responsiveness to division needs, on the one hand, and operating costs on the other. A centralized system may reduce costs, but it is sometimes less responsive to user needs. The reverse is true in the case of decentralization.

It is appropriate to mention here, however, that the present trend is toward the creation of *central computer centers* to achieve the advantages outlined earlier. Smaller firms have little choice in this matter since their organizational units do not have sufficient volume to justify separate machines. Because of the difficulties involved, very large organizations have generally not created single, huge, installations. Rather, they have often achieved a greater degree of centralization by establishing several regional data centers. Some executives who choose to follow the *centralization* route are hopeful that online terminals will give operating managers a sense of control over their information needs and will encourage them to take a proprietary interest in data processing. Firms with centralized hardware may also achieve greater interest and motivation at operating levels by maintaining some systems-analysis operations on a more decentralized basis. This can be a logical arrangement because (1) divisional systems analysts may have a better understanding of the information needs of the division and (2) this approach can effectively counter the argument from division managers who hold that since systems design was beyond their control, they cannot be held accountable for design results. Finally, some organizations with centralized corporate files and a larger central computer are using small and minicomputers at the operating levels for preprocessing and offline activities.

Each business must determine the proper organizational location for its computer department. What is "proper" depends, in part, on the size of the organization, the applications to be processed, the degree of systems integration achieved and sought and the importance attached to information systems by top executives. Figure 15-2 shows a simplified version of the chart presented in Fig. 15-1. Three possible locations for the computer department are designated. Let us look at each of these arrangements.

Computer Department Organizational Location

Location Number One The computer department is found to be a part of the finance function in a majority of businesses. The reason for the popularity of this location is not hard to understand. Historically, the accounting department was often the first to see that a computer could be used to process large-volume applications such as customer billing. Since most of the early applications were of a financial nature, the computer was most often placed under the control of financial managers. Of course, in businesses engaged in large-scale scientific and engineering projects, a computer may be located in research and engineering departments because these departments recognized the advantages of computer usage. To a con-

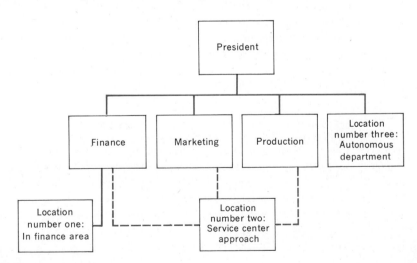

Figure 15-2 Alternative computer department locations

siderable extent, then, the organizational location of the computer depends on its original sponsor.

As long as the processing requirements of the financial area are sufficiently large to keep the computer busy and as long as no other departments have the need or desire to use the computer, then location number one is satisfactory. However, with modern equipment it is unlikely that one area can utilize all the computing capacity, and it is also unlikely that nonfinancial departments will not have a need for information that the computer can deliver. Therefore, the computer department is usually required to process nonfinancial applications.[3]

The following are possible drawbacks associated with the finance-area location:

1. *Possible lack of objectivity in setting job priorities.* Computer-department personnel may tend to concentrate on accounting applications at the expense of important nonfinancial jobs. The data processing manager is likely to give more attention to the wishes of his boss, a financial officer, than he does to the heads of marketing or production.
2. *Possible limited viewpoint.* The computer department may continue to be staffed and managed by people whose viewpoint is limited primarily to accounting. A corporatewide orientation may be lacking.
3. *Possible lack of organizational status.* Organizational status and authority are lacking when the top computer executive is interred several echelons down in one functional area of the business. A firm can expect little in the way of needed systems integration when the data processing manager has little or no power to bring about interdepartmental changes and compromises. As John Diebold, a leading consultant, writes:

> Assistant controllers equipped with the best computers in the world are not going to make the vision of applied information technology a reality very often. They are buried too deep in one leg of the business. They lack status. They lack authority. . . . But most important of all, they lack the entrepreneur's view of the enterprise as a whole.[4]

[3] In some companies, *each* functional area may support a computer on a decentralized basis (although this tends to defeat systems-integration goals and is more costly). But when a corporate division is a relatively *self-contained* operating unit, i.e., when the division manager is responsible for finance, production, and marketing activities, and when a single computer is to serve the entire division, then the organizational situation may be comparable with that of the majority of computer-using firms.

[4] John Diebold, "ADP: The Still-Sleeping Giant," *Harvard Business Rev.,* vol. 41, p. 63, September-October, 1964.

Location number two   One approach which can avoid the lack of objectivity in setting job priorities is to establish a company "service center" to handle the various tasks. Each department may be charged its proportionate share of center costs. While the center manager may report to a neutral top-level executive or an executive committee, the service center basically occupies a position that is on the periphery of or outside the main organizational structure.

The main limitation of this type of organizational arrangement for business data processing is that the center manager generally has little status or authority outside his own department. Thus, little attempt is made to initiate systems improvements or develop integrated systems; a fragmented, every-department-for-itself approach may be expected.

Location number three   In order to realize the full potential of the computer, a majority of information-processing authorities believe that an independent computer department should be established as shown in location three of Fig. 15-2. Such factors as company size, the extent of computer usage, the managerial personalities involved, and the existing spirit of cooperation make it impossible to state that location three is best for all firms. But there are persuasive reasons for concluding that this is perhaps the most desirable location in the case of medium-sized and larger concerns that seek to develop effective systems integration. Three of the reasons that can be given to support this conclusion are that this location:

1. *Reflects the corporatewide scope of information.* Independent status is needed to give impartial service to all organizational units that receive processed information. An interdepartmental viewpoint is required of data processing personnel.
2. *Confers organizational status.* The top computer executive should have a strong voice in determining the suitability of new and existing applications, should probably set processing priorities, and should study and make necessary changes in corporatewide systems and procedures in order to achieve better integration. To perform these duties, the information manager must have the cooperation of executives at the highest operating levels. In the event of significant change, such cooperation may not be received unless the information manager occupies a position that is no lower in the organization than the highest information-using department. Furthermore, in the event of a dispute, the information manager should report to an executive who is at a higher level than any of the disputing parties. Since the parties who resist

significant integration changes may be vice-presidents, the top computer executive should probably report to the president (or to the top executive of a division in the case of a decentralized processing department), or an executive or administrative vice-president. One computer department head, with the title of administrative services manager, told the author that when several changes were made in his company, there was a great amount of corporate politics involved as well as resistance from several vice-presidents. The administrative services manager reported directly to the president, however, and the president backed the changes.

3. *Encourages innovation.* Personnel of an independent department can be encouraged to recommend improvement and change whenever and wherever the opportunity arises. They may also be encouraged to introduce, for the greatest total benefit, fresh ideas that may upset certain conventional approaches.

Composition of Computer Department

The composition of the computer department depends on the scope and magnitude of the data processing work that must be performed and the extent to which this work is carried out by the computer department. It is usual to include the activities of systems analysis and design, program preparation, and computer operation in the computer department. Although other logical arrangements might possibly be used, Fig. 15-3 provides us with an organizational framework from which combinations or further subdivisions of activities may be made as needed.

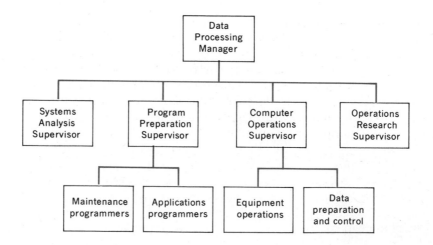

Figure 15-3 Possible composition of computer department

Systems-analysis section Because of the close cooperation that must exist between programmers and systems analysts, it is generally desirable that both groups report to the same executive to minimize friction. The systems-analysis section acts as the vital interface between outside operating departments and the other sections in the computer organization. As noted earlier, it may be desirable to maintain systems analysts in the operating divisions of large firms with centralized computer centers.

Program-preparation section There is no reason why a single supervisor could not be in charge of both systems analysis and program preparation. In medium-sized and larger organizations, however, a separate supervisor is frequently found. The programming function is sometimes subdivided into (1) the preparation of new applications and (2) the maintenance of existing programs. Authority may also be given to one or more individuals to make sure that proper standards and documentation levels are maintained.

Computer-operations section The function of this section is to prepare the input data and produce the output information on a continuing production basis. Multiple shifts may be required. The control of equipment time and the scheduling of processing activities are an important part of the duties of the operations supervisor. Controls must also be established to make sure that input data are accurate. Computer operators, operators of peripheral equipment, keypunch operators, and media librarians are found in this section. The total number of employees may be large, and turnover is likely to be high; thus, personnel-management considerations may occupy a significant part of the operations supervisor's time.

Operations-research section This section may logically be assigned to some other corporate planning element concerned with the overall study of company operations. But since the use of computers and data files is required to support many of the mathematical models that OR personnel create, there may be good reasons for assigning them to the computer department for coordination purposes. Certainly, the work of the OR and systems-analysis groups should be closely coordinated. As H. Warren White points out:

> Experience indicates that the design of mathematical models, for example, must be accomplished through close liaison with the systems specialist, as models can serve a useful purpose only if the systems provide the necessary data to fit in the model.[5]

[5] H. Warren White, "Electronic Data Processing: A 10-year Perspective," *NAA Bull.*, vol. 45, p. 13, April, 1964.

THE COMPUTER'S IMPACT ON FUTURE ORGANIZATION

We saw earlier in the chapter that the trend today is toward centralization of data processing *activities*. But a broader issue, and one which should be of particular interest to those business students whose careers lie before them, is what effect computer usage will have on the centralization or decentralization of managerial *authority*. It is this issue that will receive our attention for the remainder of the chapter.

Before computers came along, the general trend was toward *greater decentralization* of authority. To some top managers decentralization was more a matter of necessity than of choice. They often found themselves in a position where they could (1) wait for the necessary supporting information to arrive from lower levels before making a decision (in which case company reaction time suffered and opportunities were lost), (2) place their trust in experience, intuition, and their horoscope and make the decision without proper supporting information, or (3) delegate the authority to make the decision to a lower-level manager who was closer to the situation calling for the decision and who could thus be expected to react in a prompt and more informed manner. Given these alternatives, it is understandable that as businesses grew in complexity, the third path was frequently chosen.

With the introduction of quick-response computer systems, however, information may be processed and communicated to top executives at electronic speeds; reaction time may be sharply reduced; and thus the *need* for decentralization of authority may be lessened. But although new systems may make it possible to reconcentrate at the upper echelons authority and control previously held at lower levels, there is *no reason* why the information output cannot be disseminated to lower-level managers to provide them with better support for decision-making purposes. Professor Glenn Gilman expresses this point succinctly when he writes:

> The computer can serve equally well to support a move toward greater decentralization as toward greater centralization. If change in either direction develops, it will be the result of managerial choice, as it always has been. The computer's role in this respect is neutral—except as it offers the possibility to do what ought to be done in any case.[6]

Computer usage has thus far supported both a centralized and a decentralized organizational philosophy. But what will be the future effects on organizational structure as more sophisticated management information systems are developed? In making their "managerial choice," will it seem clear to top executives that one approach has

[6]Glenn Gilman, "The Computer Revisited," *Business Horizons,* vol. 9, p. 89, Winter, 1966.

definite advantages over the other? In other words, will the organizational preferences and philosophies that are valid and suitable today be equally valid tomorrow when there will be widespread use of the revolutionary business information systems described in Chapter 4? Will top executives with a decentralized organizational philosophy have the necessary time and expertise to switch to the greater-centralization-of-authority approach if the total information needed to make an important decision is consolidated at one place? Or will such information be communicated to several managers for separate decisions?

There cannot, of course, be any final answers to such questions at this time. Still, it is possible and desirable that we have an understanding of the conflicting viewpoints, speculations, and predictions that surround these questions. It is no understatement to say that the future career of every business student will be affected in some way by the ultimate answers.

There are three schools of thought on the question of the effect that computer usage will have on the centralization or decentralization of managerial authority. The first school believes that the computer *need have little effect* on organizational structure; the second school believes that *greater decentralization* of authority may be encouraged; and the third group takes the position that *recentralization* of authority is inevitable. Let us examine each of these positions.[7]

Centralization or Decentralization of Authority?

No-necessary-change school After looking at the inconclusive effects of computer usage up to the present time, the proponents of this viewpoint maintain that the computer is essentially neutral with respect to the organizational structure.[8] It is their position that the computer can act as a catalyst to help a firm move in whatever direction it feels it must go. The factors influencing the direction include market changes, competitive changes, organizational flexibility, and managerial philosophy.

In the short run, and as long as the computer is used primarily for the purpose of processing more or less routine applications, the available evidence seems to indicate that the viewpoints of this school will remain correct. However, proponents of other views are assuming that more sophisticated uses of computers will be developed. New

[7] More detailed statements in support of these positions may be found in Charles A. Myers (ed.), *The Impact of Computers on Management*, The M.I.T. Press, Cambridge, Mass., 1967.
[8] Most authorities agree that *the hardware itself is, indeed, neutral*. The point being disputed, however, is that *the emerging systems* that the computer will support *may not be so neutral*.

systems, it is felt, will cause significant changes in competitive positions, organizational environment, and the philosophy of top executives. Such changes, so the argument goes, will persuade top executives that it *is necessary* to move in a specific direction; and such changes, it is held, will produce pronounced authority trends that are not now apparent.

Decentralization school   Some writers believe that the future trend may be toward decentralization of authority. The availability of adequate controls is a factor in determining the extent of authority delegation. Managers are more likely to delegate decision-making powers to subordinates when they can be reasonably sure that the delegated authority will be handled properly. The computer makes it possible for systems to be designed that can quickly indicate to top executives when actual performance deviates from what was planned. Thus, by providing better control, the computer may make it possible to eliminate one important objection to decentralization. Furthermore, as the computer relieves them of certain routine aspects of their jobs, the subordinate managers are able to concentrate on their more important duties. The net effect will be that upper-echelon executives will have greater confidence in (1) the ability of subordinates and (2) their own ability to control subordinate performance properly. The conclusion of this school, therefore, is that the decentralization philosophy will be reinforced.

Centralization school   This group believes that the computer makes it possible for those executives whose leanings are toward centralized management to bring back under their own jurisdiction the authority that they were forced to delegate as a matter of necessity. There is little argument against this point. More controversial, however, is this group's belief that when *other* top executives realize that their new management reporting systems[9] can uncover problems at lower levels and can place at their fingertips vital decision-supporting data, they will be unable to resist making operating decisions even if they had no intention of doing so when the systems were designed.[10] Subordi-

---

[9] The types of reports included in these new systems may be: (1) periodic *monitoring reports,* which compare actual performance with planned expectations; (2) nonscheduled *triggered reports,* which are prepared only when actual performance deviates too much from plans; (3) *demand reports,* which answer managerial probings (by means of, perhaps, online consoles and/or visual display stations) about the causes of triggered reports and about other special problems; and (4) *planning reports,* which seek to identify trends, opportunities, and appropriate courses of action. See Richard G. Canning, "New Management Reporting Systems," *EDP Analyzer,* vol. 5, January, 1967, pp. 7-8.

[10] This point is disputed. If true, it could present problems if lower-level decisions absorbed too much top-executive time so that higher-level planning activities were slighted.

nate managers will thus be bypassed, not as many of them will be needed, and delegated authority will be recovered. Since the new systems will be capable of taking over various functions previously performed by subordinate managers, there will be a need to consolidate the remaining functions to produce new positions. The result of this reorganization will be to produce a *more flattened organizational structure;* i.e., there will be fewer managerial levels between the lowest supervisor and the top company executive.

Future changes in the organizational structure of business will have a direct bearing on managers who occupy places in that structure. Obviously, however, if there is controversy about future organizational patterns, there will also be disagreement about the effects of new computer systems on managers.

Effects on Managers?

High-level executives, of course, will be affected; they may reassume some of the decision-making powers previously delegated to subordinates (centralization school); or they may, with a greater feeling of confidence, delegate additional authority to subordinates (decentralization school). The primary role of top managers lies in formulating company objectives and policies and planning and guiding overall company strategy. Computer-based systems should help to remove some of the uncertainties from the usually unique and ill-structured problems that top executives face. But substantial changes in this top management role are generally not expected.

If significant reductions are made in clerical and/or production workers because of computer usage, it is to be expected that lower-level supervisory reductions will also occur. However, the *foreman's* role of providing face-to-face communication, direction, and leadership to production-oriented employees is not expected to change, although the computer can relieve him of many of his clerical duties.

This leaves us then with the *middle-management* positions,[11] around which has been centered the bulk of the published speculation and argument. Although there are some who believe that computer usage will have no major or lasting effect on middle managers, it is possible to classify most of the comment into three categories.

[11]*Middle managers* may be defined as those who are above the lowest level of supervision and below the highest level of a self-contained operating organization, i.e., they occupy positions between foremen and first-rung supervisors, on the one hand, and company presidents, executive vice-presidents, and division managers of larger corporations, on the other. Thus, the term *middle manager* is rather nebulous and is applied to a number of levels. The difficulties of generalizing about such a wide range of positions should be recognized; it is not at all certain that the paths leading from all middle-management levels will lead in the same general direction.

There are (1) those who believe that middle-management positions will be *more rewarding and challenging* in the future; (2) those who see the prospects in a much more *pessimistic* light; and (3) those who occupy a *middle position* between optimism and pessimism.

The greater-challenge viewpoint Those holding to this viewpoint believe that future middle managers will be better educated, will be more creative, more confident, and better prepared to cope with rapid change, will be more mobile, and will tend to place their own professional standards above values deemed to be important by the organization that employs them.

Middle managers, like all managers, perform the functions of planning, organizing, staffing, and controlling. Optimistic prophets point out that less time will have to be spent on the controlling function because the computer can take over many of the clerical control activities; e.g., it can signal with a triggered report whenever actual performance varies from what was planned. Time saved in controlling will enable middle managers to devote more attention to planning and directing the work of subordinates. More accurate and timely information supplied by the computer will enable middle managers to spend more time identifying problems, recognizing opportunities, and planning alternate courses of action. In this respect, then, their jobs will more nearly resemble those of chief executives. With more time to devote to departmental employee matters, improved morale may be expected and better communication should result. Furthermore, with more timely information at the middle managers' disposal, top managers will expect them to react more rapidly. This may call for frequent face-to-face coordinating conferences between managers. Such meetings foster better interdepartmental communication.

In summary, a number of writers agree with Professor Peter F. Drucker:

> The computer will force us to develop managers who are trained and tested in making the strategic decisions which determine business success or failure. I doubt that the computer will much reduce the number of middle management jobs. Instead the computer is restructuring these jobs, enabling us to organize work where it logically belongs and to free middle managers for more important duties.[12]

The pessimistic viewpoint The pessimistic group takes the position that (1) middle-management job content will be *less* challenging

[12] Peter F. Drucker, "What the Computers Will Be Telling You," *Nation's Business*, vol. 54, p. 89, August, 1966.

because of computer usage and (2) the *number of* such managers will be *substantially reduced.* The argument of this group is as follows:

1. Many middle-management decisions are highly structured and repetitive and are thus programmable on a computer.
2. Therefore, many planning and decision activities will move from middle managers and will be handled by the data processing systems.
3. The need for middle managers will be greatly reduced, and the content of the remaining jobs at the middle levels will be less challenging, more routine, and more formalized than before.
4. Why will remaining jobs be less challenging? Because the tasks of middle managers will be divided. Duties requiring less judgment and skill will remain with middle managers; other tasks requiring the skilled interpretation of systems information will move toward the top levels.
5. Three administrative organizational layers may emerge. There will be the production-oriented workers and their supervisors, who will prepare the computer-systems input; there will be an elite group of systems and computer specialists, who will perform the processing activities; and there will be a small group of top executives, who will analyze the facts and make the necessary decisions. There will be a minimum of personnel transfers between these layers.

An intermediate position   Some writers agree with the viewpoint that in the future middle-management jobs will be more rewarding and challenging, but they also believe that the number of such jobs will be significantly reduced. They are *optimistic about the job content* of the future middle-management position—they feel that the occupant will find more freedom and creativity in it—but they are *pessimistic about the number of such managers who will be needed.*

This is the consensus position taken in a report published by the American Foundation on Automation and Employment. The report, based on 35 extensive interviews with business, government, and academic leaders, states that computers have "already cut deeply into the need for middle managers." And although there is as yet no evidence of widespread displacement in their ranks, the report warns that "the middle manager's job stability . . . is subject to a far more serious threat and open to greater possibilities than past experience and expected trends in the immediate future would suggest."[13]

---

[13] From a report entitled *Automation and the Middle Manager, What Has Happened and What the Future Holds,* published by the American Foundation on Automation and Employment. Quotations appear in *Administrative Management,* p. 54, June, 1966.

Those who are optimistic about *both* job content and number of positions generally belong to the *authority decentralization school*. Those who foresee a trend toward *centralization* of authority *may or may not* agree about the outlook for job content, but they usually do concur in the belief that the number of such jobs will be reduced.

It is fair to conclude that a majority of the published predictions at least agree that the future middle manager will function in a setting that is more intellectually demanding. Unlike the Dodo bird, he will not become extinct, although his numbers may become proportionately lower. The manager of today must upgrade his abilities if he is to meet the sterner challenges of tomorrow. And the business student of today must acquire an understanding of business systems and the uses and limitations of computers if he is to compete effectively in the future managerial environment.

SUMMARY

In this chapter we have looked at the present and potential consequences of computers on managers and the environment in which managers work. We have seen that the data processing activities of a business may be centralized or decentralized; we have seen that the computer can be established in one of several locations; we have looked at the composition of the computer department; and we have examined the computer's impact on (1) future organization and (2) those managers who occupy positions in that organization.

A number of variables must be considered by each business before it decides whether to centralize or decentralize data processing activities. The present trend, however, is toward the creation of centralized computer centers in the interest of reducing operating costs. Each firm must also decide where in the organizational structure the computer department should be located. A location within the finance function is currently the most popular; however, for many companies a preferable alternative might be to create an independent department. Regardless of the organizational location, the department itself usually consists of systems-analysis, program-preparation, and computer-operations sections. An operations-research staff may also be included.

The effects that computers will have on the centralization or decentralization of managerial authority is unresolved. Thus far, the computer has supported a change in either direction. But speculation and controversy surround the unanswered question of what will happen to authority delegation when more sophisticated computer uses are perfected. Will any trends then be discernible? And, if so, what will the direction be?

Answers to these questions will obviously affect the future of managers at all levels. For the foreseeable future, it seems fair to conclude that middle managers will function in a setting that will become more challenging, more demanding, and more competitive.

DISCUSSION QUESTIONS

1. (a) Why must an organizational structure be flexible?
    (b) What is an organization chart?
2. (a) What is meant by centralization of authority?
    (b) What factors determine the extent to which authority is delegated to lower-management levels?
3. "An organization may be centralized in one sense of the term and not in others." Discuss this statement.
4. (a) What developments have made it possible to centralize data processing activities?
    (b) What are the advantages of centralized data processing?
    (c) What are the possible advantages of decentralized data processing?
    (d) Why is the trend in the direction of centralization of data processing activities?
5. (a) Identify and discuss three possible organizational locations for the computer department.
    (b) What reasons can be given to justify the establishment of an independent computer department?
6. What activities are usually included in the computer department?
7. (a) Why has the general trend in the past been in the direction of decentralization of authority?
    (b) How can computer usage reduce the need for decentralization?
8. (a) Discuss the positions taken by the three schools of thought on the question of centralization or decentralization of authority.
    (b) Which school do you believe has the best argument?
    (c) Why?
9. (a) Are you optimistic or pessimistic about the prospects for future middle managers?
    (b) How do you think computer usage is likely to affect your career?

SELECTED REFERENCES

Brink, Victor Z.: "Top Management Looks at the Computer," *Columbia Journal of World Business,* January–February, 1969, pp. 77–85.

Caruth, Donald L.: "How Will Total Systems Affect the Corporation," *Journal of Systems Management,* February, 1969, pp. 10–13.

Gilman, Glenn: "The Computer Revisited," *Business Horizons,* Winter, 1966, pp. 77–89.

Hofer, Charles W.: "Emerging EDP Pattern," *Harvard Business Review,* March–April, 1970, pp. 16–22ff.

Jackson, Robert S.: "Computers and Middle Management," *Journal of Systems Management,* April, 1970, pp. 22–24.

Myers, Charles A. (ed.): *The Impact of Computers on Management,* The M.I.T. Press, Cambridge, Mass., 1967.

Schoderbek, Peter P., and James D. Babcock: "The Proper Placement of Computers," *Business Horizons,* October, 1969, pp. 35–42.

Whisler, Thomas L.: *Information Technology and Organizational Change,* Wadsworth Publishing Company, Inc., Belmont, Calif., 1970.

Withington, Frederic G.: "Data Processing's Evolving Place in the Organization," *Datamation,* June, 1969, pp. 58–68.

Staffing and the Computer 16

There are a bewildering number of tasks, involving both technical and personnel issues, that must be performed concurrently in the many months between the time a decision is made to install a computer system and the time the conversion to electronic data processing is completed. You will recall that in Chapter 14 we looked at the technical conversion steps that must be taken to develop and install new electronic systems. Before these technical matters can be concluded in a way that will satisfactorily achieve company goals, however, serious attention must also be given to personnel considerations. More specifically, staffing consideration must be given to (1) *selecting employees for new jobs,* (2) *training selected employees,* (3) *motivating computer department personnel,* (4) *reducing employee resistance to changes,* and (5) *alleviating hardships caused by job displacement.*

**SELECTING
EMPLOYEES
FOR NEW JOBS**

A most important aspect of staffing for computers is, of course, to select capable people to fill new data processing jobs. After all, the quality of the information systems that are developed is directly dependent upon this staffing effort. It is possible to classify the new positions created into the following occupational categories: (1) *information-systems management*, (2) *systems analysis and design*, (3) *program preparation*, and (4) *computer operation*. After a brief description of each of these job categories, we shall look in this section at the *recruitment of job candidates* and the *selection procedures* that may be used.[1]

**Information Systems
Management**

It is particularly important that a competent information-systems (or data processing) manager be appointed. This manager—like all managers—must perform the management functions of planning, organizing, staffing, and controlling. He must plan the activities of his department so that it provides a quality, timely, and economical product. Careful *planning* is required to schedule installation activities and to provide the basis for control of the project. To be able to plan effectively and then *control* the activities of his department, the manager should possess technical competence in addition to managerial ability. But too much emphasis on technical competence at the expense of managerial ability should be avoided. Too often in the past, the most skilled technician became the manager, only to demonstrate, very soon, incompetence in the techniques of management. The manager selected should understand the company's business, its purpose and goals, and its data processing procedures; he should be able to motivate people; and he should possess the poise, stature, and maturity to command the respect of other company executives as well as data processing employees.

The data processing manager must *organize* the human and physical resources of his department to achieve company objectives in a smooth and efficient manner. He must *staff* his department by selecting and then training competent employees; he must encourage these employees to keep up with rapid new developments occurring in their specialties; he should develop quantity and quality job-evaluation standards for control purposes; and he must attempt to motivate and retain good employees.

Increasingly, people planning to seek a career in information

---

[1] For a good presentation of the personnel management process as it relates to data processing, see Dick H. Brandon, "Personnel Management—Missing Link in Data Processing," *J. Data Manage.*, June, 1968, pp. 50–52ff.

systems management must first acquire a college degree. Courses in business administration, economics, data processing, and statistics are desirable. If a company has a manager with the proper qualifications or if it has a systems analyst with demonstrated managerial ability, it is fortunate; if it does not have such a person (and if it is felt that no present manager should be trained to take the job), it will have to be willing to overcome spirited competition in order to hire one from outside the organization. If one *is* hired from outside, he should be brought in far enough in advance to learn the business and to gain the respect of other managers before the conversion begins.

Systems Analysis and Design

Although there is no generally accepted job description for the position of *systems analyst,* the job basically consists of (1) gathering facts about and analyzing the basic methods and procedures of current business systems, (2) determining company information needs, and (3) modifying, redesigning, and integrating these existing procedures into new systems specifications as required to provide the needed information. In addition to making the most effective use of existing data processing equipment, the analyst may also (as in the case of the systems study) recommend justifiable equipment changes.

The systems analyst must be familiar with the specific firm—he must know its objectives, its personnel, its products and services, its industry, and its special problems. Also, he must know the uses and limitations of computers as well as other types of data processing equipment, for he is the interpreter between managers and data processing specialists. He must understand programming basics; he must be able to determine which jobs are candidates for computer processing; he must have logical reasoning ability; he must have initiative and the ability to plan and organize his work since he will frequently be working on his own without much direct supervision; and he must be able to communicate with and secure the cooperation of operating employees and supervisors.

Educational backgrounds vary, but a college degree or the equivalent is generally desired. Courses that have proven valuable to the types of systems analysts described above are the same ones mentioned for data processing managers. An analyst with a good grounding in management techniques is often a prime candidate for promotion to more responsible management positions both in and out of data processing because of his broad knowledge of the business. As we saw in Chapter 4, there is a severe and worsening shortage of qualified analysts.

Program Preparation

To summarize briefly, the job of the typical company *programmer* (as defined in this book) is to take the broad systems designs of the analysts and transform these specifications into workable, coded machine instructions. However, there are different programmer categories, and their duties vary in different organizations. In some companies, for example, a person with the title of "programmer" may perform *both* the systems-analysis and programming functions.[2] In other firms, a programmer may carry the work from the broad systems specification stage through the program flowcharting stage and then turn the task of writing the actual machine instructions over to a *coder*.

Because programmer job descriptions vary, there are also varying opinions about the educational background required of business programmers. Such factors as the duties of the programmer, the degree of separation between the systems-analysis and programming functions, the complexity of the data processing systems, and the industry in which the business operates should probably be considered by the company in establishing educational standards. As the programmer's job is defined here, a college degree is not necessarily a condition for employment in most organizations. What *is required,* however, is that the programmer have (1) analytical reasoning ability, (2) the ability to remember and concentrate on small details, (3) the drive and motivation to complete programs without direct supervision, (4) the patience and perseverance to search for small errors in programs, (5) the accuracy to minimize the number of such errors, and (6) the creativeness to develop new problem-solving techniques. Such people are in short supply relative to the rapidly growing need for their services.

Computer Operations

The duties of the *computer operator* include setting up the processor and related equipment, starting the program run, checking to ensure proper operation, and unloading equipment at the end of a run. Some knowledge of programming is needed. A high-school education is often acceptable, although additional educational levels may be specified. *Keypunch operators,* a media *librarian* who maintains control over master tape and card files, a *scheduler* who plans the daily

---

[2]The degree of separation of systems analysis and programming has depended upon the size and complexity of the company and its data processing systems, the ability of data processing personnel, and the desire of high-level executives to reduce communication problems and fix responsibility for each application on a single person. The lack of general agreement on the definition and description of systems-analyst and programmer positions poses severe personnel management problems for the data processing manager, who is expected to recruit, select, train, evaluate, and compensate the employees who occupy these positions.

flow of work to be accomplished and assigns the necessary personnel, and various other clerks and operators of peripheral equipment may be needed in the operations area. The staffing of operations positions generally presents less of a problem.

A prerequisite to sound staffing procedures is the preparation of job descriptions and job specifications for the new positions to be filled. A *job description* defines the duties that must be performed and the equipment that is used, indicates the degree of supervision that is given and received, and describes the working conditions associated with the position. A *job specification* identifies the qualifications that candidates for each job should possess. Job specifications include the levels of education, experience, and training considered necessary to perform each job adequately. Also included is a statement outlining the physical and communication skills needed as well as the personality traits desired. In summary, job descriptions deal with the work itself, while job specifications deal with the human qualifications needed by those who are to do the work. Brief descriptions and specifications were outlined above for the more important new jobs. These facts are useful for (1) staffing purposes (since both the recruiter and the candidate must know what is needed and expected), (2) wage purposes (in determining the relative worth of the new job), (3) job evaluation purposes, and (4) manpower planning purposes (it is desirable to hire new employees with potential to move into more responsible positions).

Recruiting Potential Candidates

Two general procedures are often used to recruit candidates for new jobs. *One procedure* is to review personnel records and supervisory recommendations (or application forms and references in the case of nonemployee candidates) to compile a selective list of people qualified. People on this screened list are then contacted to see if they might be interested. The main weakness of this approach is that qualified candidates may be overlooked. *A second "reserve pool" procedure* is to announce the openings to all employees and invite them to make application if interested. Those applicants who appear to possess the necessary qualifications join the pool from which initial and subsequent openings are filled. Printed advertisements, college placement offices, outside employment agencies, contacts made at professional meetings, the knowledge of vendor representatives—all of these resources can be used to secure nonemployee applications.

The information systems manager may sometimes be hired from an outside source to supervise an initial computer installation. The big disadvantage of this approach is that the person hired has little knowledge of the firm or of the personnel with whom he must work. Perhaps a preferable choice would be to appoint someone in the company who has the managerial qualifications and give him the required technical training. In staffing other vacancies, too, most firms prefer to select suitable candidates from within and to train them in the necessary skills. This approach is particularly valid in the case of systems analysts who must be familiar with company operations.

Programmers are more likely to be recruited from outside than analysts and other data processing employees. This may be especially true when the programming job is considered to be basically coding and includes little in the way of systems work. In staffing programming jobs requiring some degree of systems analysis, a firm may give technical training to people possessing a knowledge of the business or it may hire experienced programmers (or programmer trainees) and school them in company policies, problems, and operations. Businesses have usually found that *when suitable candidates are available,* the first approach is preferable.[3] Furthermore, with the shortage of skilled computer technicians becoming more intense, the recruitment of experienced personnel will become a more expensive and less dependable way of meeting future staffing requirements. In spite of these considerations, however, hiring experienced programmers may help speed up the conversion process. Many organizations have found that programmers skilled in the use of the hardware ordered for the new system are a valuable complement to company trainees.[4]

Selection Procedures

Once possible candidates have been identified, it is then necessary to balance and compare their qualifications with those listed in the job specifications. Sorting out the "best" applicants is a difficult job. The screening process generally involves the use of such selection devices as *aptitude tests, personal interviews,* and careful *examination of records* indicating the candidate's educational background, experience, and work habits. A frequently used approach in the selection of analyst and programmer trainees is to give candidates an aptitude test and then to follow up with interviews and careful record exami-

[3] There are several *advantages associated with internal selection:* (1) employees have a better understanding of the business; (2) their work habits and personality traits are easier to appraise; (3) having demonstrated some degree of company loyalty, they may be less inclined to leave the firm after they are trained; and (4) internal selection can improve employee morale. In some situations, too, union contract agreements may specify that selections be made internally.

[4] Of course, there is always the danger that they may select an "experienced" programmer who is interested in keeping one jump ahead of his past mistakes.

nations on all who receive satisfactory test scores.[5] In the selection of *experienced* programmers, personal interviews and personal or telephone contacts with parties familiar with the work of the candidate are of particular importance. Proficiency tests are sometimes used to check on the ability of a candidate to program a test problem.

A *programmer aptitude test* is a form of general intelligence test that *attempts* to measure the ability of a person to acquire whatever skills are needed to become a successful programmer. Although there is lack of agreement about the ability of these tests actually to measure what they claim to measure, when carefully used they may give an indication of a person's ability to reason in arithmetic and abstract terms. Since this ability is considered to be an important prerequisite for many data processing jobs, the test may serve as a screening aid. But good test performance alone does not necessarily mean that the candidate will be a successful programmer. The tests do not measure motivation, and they may not begin to measure all the other qualities that may be required. In short, programmer aptitude tests may provide clues, but they should not be the only selection device employed. Tests are also used in the selection of computer-operations personnel. These tests measure manual dexterity, mechanical aptitude, clerical aptitude, etc., and they generally yield satisfactory results.

Selection decisions follow the testing, interviewing, and background-investigation phases. The chosen candidates must then be trained to prepare them for their new duties.

TRAINING SELECTED EMPLOYEES

Before looking at the approaches taken to train data processing personnel, it is proper to mention here that *noncomputer personnel* should also receive exposure to data processing concepts. It is especially desirable that top executives, operating managers, and other key employees be introduced to (1) the basic fundamentals of systems, computers, and data processing, (2) the uses and limitations of modern information systems, (3) the new concepts associated with the information-processing revolution, and (4) the implications of computer usage for managers and the managerial environment. Such an exposure will enable noncomputer personnel to see how their operating needs can be served; it may serve to show them why knowledge of information processing is important; and it may help to reduce resistance to changes being made in processing procedures. Training

[5] Is it logical, however, to attempt to measure a candidate's aptitude for a particular job in the absence of a job definition and description? Can a test measure a person's aptitude to perform in an undefined capacity?

seminars for noncomputer personnel are conducted by consulting organizations, professional associations, equipment vendors, colleges and universities, and company employees.

Extensive training must be given to those selected to be systems analysts and programmers. In addition to having a *knowledge of the business and the industry,* the systems analyst must also understand the *techniques of systems analysis and design.* There is lack of uniformity at the present time in the methods used to train (*educate* is probably a better word) analysts to meet the latter requirement. A good grounding in the "core" courses found in collegiate schools of business combined with further emphasis on accounting systems, communication skills, mathematics, and statistics are felt by many to be prerequisites to more specialized systems training. There are several universities that offer degree programs in computer science; courses in systems analysis are sometimes included in their curricula. Vendors will contract to teach machine-dependent skills to their customer trainees, but since systems analysis is independent of machines, they have only recently begun to offer programs in formal systems training.[6] (Their systems representatives, of course, may also provide some on-the-job training in systems-analysis techniques.) Consulting firms, private institutes, and organizations such as the American Management Association conduct systems-analysis seminars on a limited basis. Correspondence courses in systems work are offered by the Association of Systems Management and others. Also, an in-house systems training program utilizing senior analysts as instructors has proved to be effective.[7]

A third requirement of the analyst is that he possess a *general understanding of computer hardware and software.* The formal training given to analysts in this area may parallel or be identical with the formal training received by programmers. One method employed to introduce analyst and programmer students to hardware and software concepts is to enroll them in the vendor's programming classes. These classes introduce the students to the vendor's hardware and software that can be used. Such courses vary in length from one to six weeks, they are usually offered at the vendor's educational center, and they generally emphasize coding. Following satisfactory completion of the vendor's course, the students may receive additional on-the-job instruction from other experienced programmers who may be available.

[6]See Richard G. Canning, "Developments in System Analyst Training," *EDP Analyzer,* September, 1970, pp. 9-13.

[7]For further information on in-house systems training programs, see the two articles by John J. Anderson appearing in the July, 1969, and August, 1969, issues of the *J. Data Manage.*

Prior to unbundling and before separate charges were placed on "customer education" services by unbundled vendors, the above approach was the most popular. It is, of course, still very popular; however, there is reason to believe that larger computer users will establish and/or expand their own in-house educational operations to perform some of the training previously conducted by the vendor.[8] Courses offered by independent training organizations may also receive greater consideration in the future.

Programmer training is a continuous, lengthy, and expensive process. To the surprise (and dismay) of many executives, it has been found that *at least six months* is generally required before programmers attain a *minimum* level of proficiency. Training costs per programmer may run into the thousands of dollars. In addition to the training available from vendors and through in-house activities, programming skills are also taught by consultants, professional organizations, colleges and universities, and vocational schools.

Equipment manufacturers and vocational schools also offer brief courses to train operators of peripheral equipment. On-the-job training is often the only preparation required. Because of their need to know some programming, computer operators are often sent to the vendor's programming course or they receive the necessary in-house training.

Selecting and training employees for new positions are, of course, important aspects of staffing. But executives cannot concentrate all their attention on these personnel aspects if they hope to achieve organizational goals. Proper consideration must also be given to the questions of (1) motivating computer personnel, (2) reducing employee resistance to change, and (3) alleviating hardships that can be caused by job displacement. We shall briefly consider these matters in the remainder of this chapter.

MOTIVATING COMPUTER PERSONNEL

It is a distressing fact that many computer department managers annually lose and must replace a large number (up to 40 percent) of their skilled employees. Of course, locating and training replacements are time-consuming and expensive activities. Furthermore, department productivity may suffer seriously because of the departure of key personnel. It is therefore important for computer managers to keep turnover to a minimum. Psychologists have outlined the needs and factors that *influence* and *motivate* human behavior. Since moti-

[8] See Stanley Sawyer, "Unbundling's Impact on Training of Programmers," *J. Data Manage.* March, 1970, pp. 23-26.

vated employees are less likely to leave an organization and are more likely to be highly productive members of a department, the manager should be aware of these important behavioral concepts.

What are the needs and factors that influence and motivate behavior? What is likely to cause job satisfaction and dissatisfaction among computer staff members? Behavioral scientists tell us that human needs may be classified into a series of ranks or levels as follows:[9]

1. *Physiological needs.* Included in this lowest-level category are the needs for food, clothing, shelter, and sleep. They are necessary for survival and thus receive first priority. When thwarted, these needs override in importance all others in influencing behavior; when regularly satisfied, they cease to direct human behavior.

2. *Safety needs.* The needs for protection against danger, threat, or deprivation begin to dominate man's behavior when the physiological needs are satisfied.

3. *Social needs.* When the above needs are satisfied, social needs, i.e., the need to belong to a group, associate with, and be accepted by others, become important influencing factors.

4. *Ego needs.* When the first three need levels are reasonably satisfied, ego needs become important in behavior motivation. There are two kinds of egoistic needs: (1) those that relate to the *self-esteem* of an individual, e.g., the needs for self-confidence, achievement, and independence, and (2) those that relate to the *reputation* of an individual, e.g., the needs for status, recognition, and respect. "Unlike the lower needs, these are rarely satisfied; man seeks indefinitely for more satisfaction of these needs once they have become important to him."[10]

5. *Self-fulfillment needs.* The final level in the need hierarchy reflects the desire of an individual to realize his own potential, continue to develop, and be creative.

Professor Frederick Herzberg of Case Western Reserve University has made a distinction between those factors that motivate and those that only influence behavior. The *motivating* factors are such high-level needs as (1) the need to *achieve* something useful, (2) the need to be *recognized* for such achievement, (3) the need to have the *work itself be meaningful,* (4) the need to be *responsible* for making decisions, and (5) the need to *grow and advance.* In short, job satisfaction, high production, and low employee turnover are related to the self-fulfillment of people on the job.

[9]See Douglas McGregor, *The Human Side of Enterprise,* McGraw-Hill Book Company, New York, 1960, pp. 36–39.
[10]*Ibid.,* p. 38.

The lower-level *physical, security, social,* and *status* needs are sometimes called *maintenance* factors. According to Herzberg, the presence of these factors, along with economic and employee-orientation factors, does *not* necessarily motivate workers because such factors tend to be taken for granted. (This may be especially true among skilled programmers and analysts, whose services are in such short supply.) The *absence* of one or more of these factors, however, may have an *adverse influence* on employee behavior and may result in job dissatisfaction, low production, and high turnover.

The information-systems manager must therefore look beyond the lower-level needs in motivating his staff. These needs *must* be satisfied, of course, but frequent raises and private offices may not be enough to reduce turnover and produce motivated employees. What is likely to be more important in achieving these desirable ends is (1) the promise of challenging work, (2) the assignment of greater responsibility to staff members, and (3) giving employees the opportunity to grow and develop through such means as carefully planned training programs. It is such motivators as these, in fact, that have helped several facilities management firms build highly qualified staffs.[11]

It was observed early in Chapter 14 that "a system may fail to achieve company goals (even though it is technically and economically feasible) if company personnel are not sold on it and do not want to make it work." In too many cases, however, company personnel *have not been convinced* of the merits of the changes taking place and no attempt has been made to counter this attitude. Why not? One reason is that executives and data processing specialists have too frequently become so preoccupied with systems problems of a technical nature that they have ignored the human factors involved in the transition. In short, the emphasis has too often been placed on work rather than on workers.

Personnel preparations should receive considerable attention during the systems-study period and at the same time that technical preparations are being made so that employees will accept changes with a minimum of resistance.

EMPLOYEE RESISTANCE TO SYSTEMS CHANGE

[11] For more information on the subject of employee motivation, see Frederick Herzberg, "One More Time: How Do You Motivate Employees?," *Harvard Business Rev.,* January–February, 1968, pp. 53–62; Richard G. Canning, "Job Enrichment in Data Processing," *EDP Analyzer,* January, 1969, pp. 1–13; and Richard G. Canning, "Designing the Reward System," *EDP Analyzer,* August, 1969, pp. 1–11. Canning's articles supply further references.

Forms of Resistance

Resistance to change is the rule rather than the exception, and it may appear in many forms. The extreme forms are explained by Heckmann and Huneryager in these words:

> At one extreme people suffer a temproary disequilibrium in need satisfaction, ask a few questions about the change, quickly adjust to it, and resume their previous behavior. At the other extreme, reaction can take the form of open opposition, rebellion, and even destruction.[12]

Between these extremes may be found a number of other symptoms, including the following:

1. *Withholding data and information*. It is not uncommon during the systems study for employees to withhold information about current operations. Even after the new system is installed, input data may be withheld or turned in late.
2. *Providing inaccurate information*. Input data containing known inaccuracies are submitted to sabotage processing results.
3. *Distrusting computer output*. Some employees continue to maintain old methods after the conversion is made. In one case it was found that "the payroll supervisor was insisting that his clerks recalculate the pay of the company's 1,000 hourly workers after each payroll had been completed by the IBM 1401."[13]
4. *Showing lowered morale*. A general lowering of employee morale may result in lack of cooperation, sullen hostility, sloppy effort, an attitude of indifference, jealousy among workers, etc.

Although employee reaction to change depends, of course, on the individual, it also depends on answers to such questions as: (1) What are the nature and magnitude of the changes? (2) Why are they being made? (3) Who is backing them? (4) Who will administer them? (5) When will they take place? (6) In what departments will they be felt? (7) What has been the extent of personnel preparation? (8) Does the firm have a history of good personnel relations? (9) Does the firm have a reputation for innovation and change?

Reasons for Resistance

It is not too difficult to compile a list of motivating forces that may stimulate one or more individuals to seek business changes. Included in such a list are (1) dissatisfaction with the *status quo* together with a desire for greater knowledge and understanding, (2) the desire to create, to excel, to be a leader in the use of new techniques and in

[12] I. L. Heckmann, Jr., and S. G. Huneryager, *Human Relations in Management*, South-Western Publishing Company, Cincinnati, Ohio, 1960, p. 425.
[13] George Berkwitt, "Middle Managers vs. the Computer," *Dun's Rev.* November, 1966, p. 42.

the development of new products and services, and (3) the pursuit of economic benefits.

But the changes sought by some may appear to others to be a *threat*—a threat that prevents them from satisfying certain basic needs or one that decreases the level of their need satisfaction. That a proposed change *does not* actually affect an employee's need satisfaction may be irrelevant from a resistance standpoint. *What is relevant* in this situation is that if the employee *believes* that he is threatened by the proposed change, he will no longer feel secure. "Only when he recognizes that the change will not affect his need satisfaction, or when he adapts himself to a change that in fact does decrease or prevent the satisfaction of a need, will equilibrium return and resistance disappear."[14]

Some of the *reasons why people may resist computer systems changes are:*

1. *The threat to safety-need satisfaction*. Computers have a reputation for replacing people; therefore, there is the understandable fear of loss of employment and/or of reduction in salary.

2. *The reduction in social-need satisfaction*. The introduction of a new system often calls for a reorganization of departments and work groups. When change causes a breaking up of compatible human relationships and a realigning of personnel, it also causes a reduction in social-need satisfaction. Resistance to such a proposed change may be anticipated; it diminishes to the extent that the displaced individual forms new friendships in, associates with, and is accepted by the new group.

3. *The reduction in ego-need satisfaction*. The individual needs to feel self-confident; but self-confidence may be shaken by the lack of knowledge about and experience with the new system. The equipment is strange to him, and he may fear that he will be unable to acquire the new skills necessary to work with it. In short, the individual's self-esteem may suffer as a result of the change; therefore, the change may be resisted. Egoistic needs relating to the reputation of the individual are also threatened by change. Fear of loss of status and/or prestige is an important reason for resistance by both managers and employees. For example, if the change threatens to reduce the number of employees in and the importance of a department, then the department manager may oppose the change because to admit that the change is needed is to admit that he has tolerated inefficiency—an admission that can hardly be expected to enhance his reputation. An employee

[14]Heckmann and Huneryager, *op. cit.*, p. 421.

who has the respect of fellow workers because of his knowledge of the old system may also suffer a loss of prestige. When new procedures are installed, he is no longer looked to for information because his knowledge of the new procedures may not be any greater than that of other workers.

Employees Who Resist

It is generally conceded that nonsupervisory employees may resist change because they fear they will (1) lose their jobs or be downgraded, (2) be transferred away from their friends, (3) be unable to acquire the needed new skills, and/or (4) lose status and presitge. A greater obstacle to successful computer operations, however, may be *managerial* resistance to change. Although a manager may suffer economic loss because of the change to computer processing,[15] the more usual motivating force behind his resistance, as we have just seen, is the threat of a reduction in ego-need satisfaction. Many managers feel that their positions are being threatened (and indeed this is sometimes the case). In a very real sense, those who may be most affected by the change are being asked to help plan and implement it. But it is unrealistic to expect a manager to be enthusiastic about changes that threaten his position. Proper personnel preparation must include managers as well as nonsupervisory employees.

Suggestions for Reducing Resistance

Unfortunately, there is no simple formula that prevents resistance and ensures a successful systems transition. But there are some guidelines and suggestions that have been developed as a result of practical experience and social research, which may, when used with care, help to reduce the level of employee opposition. Included in these suggestions are steps to:

1. *Keep employees informed.* Information relating to the effects of the change on their jobs should be periodically presented to personnel at all levels. Topics discussed should include loss of jobs, transfers, the extent of necessary retraining, the reasons for (and the benefits of) the change, the effect on various departments, and what is being done to alleviate employee hardships. Basic company objectives should be reviewed; the motives behind these objectives should be identified; and the contribution that the change makes to goal achievement should be explained. When possible, employees should be assured that the change will not interfere with the satisfaction of their personal needs.

[15] And the pessimistic predictions being made by some writers about the number of future middle-management positions does little to relieve the apprehension some managers may have about the possibility of economic loss.

2. *Seek employee participation.* Employees are more likely to support and accept changes that they have a hand in creating. In addition to yielding valuable information during the systems study, design sessions also help reduce later resistance by allowing managers to have a say in the planning of the project. Psychologists tell us that participation has three beneficial effects. First, it helps the employee satisfy ego and self-fulfillment needs. Second, it gives the employee some degree of control over the change and thus contributes to a greater feeling of security. And third, the fear of the unknown is removed. The *participation of supervisors and informal group leaders* may greatly reduce the level of resistance. But participation is not a gimmick to manipulate people. Employees asked to participate must be respected and treated with dignity, and their suggestions must be carefully considered.

3. *Use managerial evaluation.* Make their ability to handle change one of the criteria for evaluating supervisors' managerial capability. Let them know that this criterion has been established.

4. *Consider the timing of the change.* Do not set unreasonable conversion deadlines. Give personnel time to get used to one major change before another is initiated.

PLANNING FOR DISPLACEMENT

Do computers cause widespread unemployment among white-collar workers? Printed sources could be cited to support this position. But other printed sources could also be quoted that take the position that the computer (and technological change in general) provides increased job opportunities. To some extent the controversy is fed by a failure on the part of some writers to make a distinction between unemployment and displacement. Those who are optimistic about the effects of computers on employment are generally looking at the effect of technological change on the *total employment* picture; i.e., they are looking at the effect on the *total number of jobs* in the labor market. Those who view the picture pessimistically are frequently looking at the short-run effects of *displacement* on *specific occupational categories;* i.e., they are looking at the reduction in the number of jobs in a specific segment of the labor force.

Unemployment and displacement are not the same. Unemployment refers to the total number of people involuntarily out of work. *Displacement* occurs when the jobs of individual workers are eliminated as a result of technological change. *If* these displaced workers cannot find similar jobs elsewhere and *if* they cannot find work in other occupations, then there is, indeed, an increase in the unemployment figures. But has the development of the computer caused a larger number of people to be unemployed than would otherwise have been the case? In other words, have computers reduced the total number of jobs available in the total labor market? Professor Yale Brozen, University of Chicago economist, expresses the views of most authorities when he writes:

> The reigning economic myth is that automation causes unemployment. It has only a slight element of truth—just enough to make the proposition plausible. Automation does cause displacement. A few become unemployed because of it. However, it does not create unemployment in the sense that a larger number are unemployed than would have been if no automation had occurred. . . . Many persons point to specific persons unemployed as a result of [automation]. What they fail to do is point to the unemployed who found jobs because of automation or to those who would have joined the jobless if new technology had not appeared.[16]

It is beyond the scope of this book to go into the economic causes of unemployment. We may conclude this topic by mentioning that most economists are of the belief that (1) displacement must not be prevented and (2) unemployment is best avoided by high levels of capital investment, unhampered mobility of capital and labor, and a continuing high level of technological progress. The alternative to technological progress is economic stagnation.

Although technological change is beneficial to the nation as a whole and in the long run, this does not mean that the short-run effects of displacement on particular individuals are not a matter of importance. A displaced person may understand the long-run benefits, but he is likely to be in greater sympathy with the famous economist who noted wryly that "in the long run we are all dead." It is true that displacement must not be prevented; but leaders in business, government, and labor must make every effort to see that displacement does not lead to unemployment.

Business Displacement Experience

Studies have shown that computer usage can displace large numbers of people. For example, in a study of 32 companies, Ernest Dale found some substantial changes. He reported reductions of 4,000 people in an insurance company and 1,000 people in an oil company. All except three of the 32 firms ". . . used fewer people for the same amount of work or found that the same number of people could do more work than before."[17] Although other examples could be given, this

---

[16]Yale Brozen, "Putting Economics and Automation in Perspective," *Automation*, vol. 11, p. 30, April, 1964.

[17]Ernest Dale, *Management: Theory and Practice*, McGraw-Hill Book Company, New York, 1965, p. 678.

one serves to show that many jobs can be eliminated. This fact, of course, is not surprising; as you will remember, a reduction in clerical labor costs is often an objective sought by businesses.

But a number of other examples could be cited that would show little or no displacement. The extent to which displacement actually occurs and the significance of the problem in particular cases depend in large measure on the following factors:

1. *The rate of growth of the firm and the economy.* If the company is growing rapidly so that more work must be done to handle the expanding business, then there may be little or no effect on the number of clerical workers employed. The use of a computer enables workers to be more productive, but increases in the demand for a company's output can prevent a layoff problem. Reassignment of surplus workers to different departments may, of course, be required. If a worker must be laid off, he will have greater opportunity to find employment elsewhere if the economy is in a period of prosperity. It is fortunate that most computer installations have occurred during relatively prosperous periods.

2. *The objectives sought.* Is the company introducing a computer system for processing purposes that could not otherwise be considered? Is the goal to do more work with present employees? Or is it to save money by eliminating existing jobs? Objectives obviously play a part in determining the degree of displacement.

3. *The care in planning and preparation.* Business executives should give careful thought to the displacement problems that they are likely to encounter. It should be remembered that fear of displacement is a cause of resistance to change. If displacement is not expected, employees should be so informed; if jobs are to be eliminated, plans should be made to protect present employees as much as possible. Employees in departments where reductions are expected can be given the first chance to fill vacancies occurring elsewhere in the company. Vacancies in affected departments can be left unfilled, they can be filled by new employees who have the ability to adjust quickly to different positions, or they can be filled with temporary outside help. Special programs can be established to train soon-to-be-surplus workers in skills needed in other areas.

4. *The type of occupations threatened.* Up to the present time, most of the jobs that have been eliminated have been of a clerical nature and have usually been held by young women who can be transferred to other departments without too much difficulty. In the past, few clerical workers were laid off in larger businesses

when job reductions occurred.[18] This was possible because those workers in affected departments who quit during the many months between the time the computer order was placed and the time the conversion was completed were simply not replaced. Thus, a potentially serious layoff problem often has not developed. (However, employables who have a minimum amount of training and who seek *to enter* the clerical labor force may face shrinking opportunities because of the leveling off in the rate of growth of certain clerical job categories in the past several years.) When the affected jobs are *not* of the clerical type, the displacement problem is likely to be much more severe. Attrition and turnover, in these situations, may not be of much help. The affected workers may be older employees or lower-level managers whose skills are no longer needed. They are not likely to quit, but they may find it difficult to retrain for jobs at an appropriate level. Such personnel problems can be perplexing; and in the future, as computer applications become more sophisticated and move into more operating areas, they can be expected to occur with increasing frequency.

SUMMARY

Before the conversion to new computer systems can be made in a way that will satisfactorily achieve company goals, attention must be given to the staffing function.

Plans must be made to recruit and select personnel to fill positions that computer usage may create. A prerequisite to sound recruitment and selection is the preparation of job descriptions and job specifications. Positions may be filled from a pool of present employees or from candidates recruited from external sources. Most businesses have found that when suitable employee candidates are available, it is preferable to give them the necessary training to prepare them for the data processing jobs. However, when suitable candidates are not available internally, the company must resort to external sources. Workers are usually selected on the basis of aptitude-test scores, personal interviews, and background records.

The most extensive training, of course, must be given to analysts and programmers. But it is desirable that noncomputer personnel receive exposure to data processing concepts. Training given for equipment operators may consist of formal classes combined with on-the-job training or on-the-job training alone.

[18]Small firms have not been as successful in preventing layoffs possibly because there may not have been other departments to which surplus workers could be reassigned.

If highly trained and skilled computer employees are to be retained as productive and motivated members of the organization, their personal needs and aspirations must be given serious consideration. Lower-level physiological, safety, and social needs must be satisfied, and economic rewards must be adequate. But frequent raises and pleasant facilities may not be enough because psychologists point out that job satisfaction, high production, and low employee turnover are related to the self-fulfillment of people on the job.

Resistance to the change to new computer systems is the rule rather than the exception. This resistance may appear in many forms when employees perceive that the change threatens the satisfaction of certain personal needs. Resistance may come from all employee levels—from clerks to vice-presidents. But by knowing and following certain guidelines and suggestions with care, the changers may be able to reduce the level of opposition.

If jobs are to be eliminated or changed, executives should plan at an early date to reduce the personnel hardships that can occur. Although technological change is desirable for the nation as a whole, the effects of displacement on particular individuals can be serious. Business, government, and labor leaders must make every effort to see that displacement does not cause an individual to be involuntarily thrown out of work.

DISCUSSION QUESTIONS

1. Explain the job functions of the following data processing personnel:
   - (a) Information systems managers
   - (b) Systems analysts
   - (c) Programmers
   - (d) Computer operators
2. What qualifications should candidates for the above jobs possess?
3. (a) What is a job description? A job specification?
   (b) Why are job descriptions and specifications needed?
4. Discuss the possible procedures that may be used to recruit candidates for new jobs.
5. What selection procedures may be used to fill data processing positions?
6. (a) Why should noncomputer personnel receive data processing training?
   (b) What kind of training should they receive?
7. What are the needs which influence and motivate human behavior?

8. (a) What is likely to cause job dissatisfaction among computer staff members?
   (b) What is likely to motivate employees?
9. In what forms may personnel resistance to change appear?
10. (a) Why do managers resist change?
    (b) Why do employees resist?
11. How may resistance to change be reduced?
12. What is the distinction between displacement and unemployment?
13. What factors influence the significance of the displacement problem when computers are introduced into businesses?

SELECTED REFERENCES

Anderson, John J.: "Developing an In-House Systems Training Program," *Journal of Data Management,* July, 1969, pp. 26–31.

Bower, James B., and J. Bruce Sefert: "Human Factors in Systems Design," *Management Services,* November–December, 1964, pp. 39–50.

Brabb, George J.: "Education for Systems Analysis: Part Two," *Systems & Procedures Journal,* March–April, 1966, pp. 38–43.

Brandon, Dick H.: "Personnel Management—Missing Link in Data Processing," *Journal of Data Management,* June, 1968, pp. 50–52ff.

Canning, Richard G.: "Designing the Reward System," *EDP Analyzer,* August, 1969, pp. 1–11.

_____: "Developments in System Analyst Training," *EDP Analyzer,* September, 1970, pp. 1–14.

Data Processing Digest: The October, 1969, to October, 1970, issues contain articles in a series entitled "The EDP People Problem," which deal with staffing considerations.

Davis, Sidney: "Internal Recruitment and Training of Data Processing Personnel," *Computers and Automation,* September, 1969, pp. 38–39.

Emery, James C.: "Training the Systems Designer," *Wharton Quarterly,* Fall, 1968, pp. 25–29.

Greenwood, Frank, and Erwin M. Danziger: *Computer Systems Analysts,* American Management Association, No. 90, New York, 1967.

Herzberg, Frederick: "One More Time: How Do You Motivate Employees?," *Harvard Business Review,* January–February, 1968, pp. 53–62.

McMurrer, J. A., and J. R. Parish: "The People Problem," *Datamation,* July 15, 1970, pp. 57–59.

Murdick, Robert G., and Joel E. Ross: "Management Information Systems: Training for Businessmen," *Journal of Systems Management,* October, 1969, pp. 36–39.

Sawyer, Stanley: "Unbundling's Impact on Training of Programmers," *Journal of Data Management,* March, 1970, pp. 23–26.

Williams, Edgar G.: "Changing Systems and Behavior," *Business Horizons,* August, 1969, pp. 53–58.

Control
and the
Computer

17

In this chapter we consider two aspects of the subject of control and the computer. *First,* we shall briefly review some ways in which information produced by computer systems *can help managers control business operations.* Of course, if managers are to perform this function of the management process satisfactorily, the information upon which control decisions are based must be of high quality. Therefore, the *second* major consideration in this chapter will be the examination of the *controls that are applied to processing techniques and procedures* in order to produce a high-quality information output. More specifically, the topics covered in connection with this second consideration are *internal control, administrative controls,* and *data controls.*

491

MANAGERIAL CONTROL: A REVIEW

The control function of the management process is a follow-up to planning activities; i.e., it is the check on current performance to determine if planned goals are being achieved. Thus, control activities are involved in the day-to-day administration of a business. You will recall that the general control procedure consists of several steps: (1) the establishment of predetermined goals or standards, (2) the measurement of performance, (3) the comparison of actual performance with the standards, and (4) the making of appropriate control decisions.

The information output of the computer can help the manager carry out this procedure in many ways. First of all, better information about such things as the effectiveness of the firm's sales and distribution efforts, the quality and cost of the firm's products and services, and the strengths and weaknesses of the company's financial position can lead to better planning and the creation of *more realistic standards.* Computer simulation can assist managers in setting goals by showing them the effects of various alternate decisions when certain conditions are assumed; and computer-based network models such as PERT and CPM can improve planning (and therefore control) by forcing managers to identify all project activities that must be performed.

Computer processing systems can also help managers control by gathering, classifying, calculating, and summarizing *actual performance data* promptly and accurately. Once performance data are read into the computer, it is possible for the machine to *compare* the actual performance with the established standards. Periodic reports showing this comparison can be prepared; in some systems, triggered reports may be furnished to the manager only when variations are outside certain specified limits.

It is also possible to program the computer so that it signals when *predetermined decisions* should be carried out. For example, a program may specify that when the inventory of a certain basic part falls below a given level, an output message signals the need to reorder and indicates the reorder quantity. By thus relieving man of many of the routine operational control tasks, the computer frees him to devote more time to (1) planning future business moves and (2) leading the all-important human resources of the organization. Such a man-machine relationship, in other words, makes it possible for man to concentrate more of his attention on the heuristic area of intellectual work—an area in which he is far superior to the machine—while the machine is permitted to take over the well-structured control tasks.

Of course, an assumption underlying everything said in the above paragraphs is that the *information produced* by the computer system

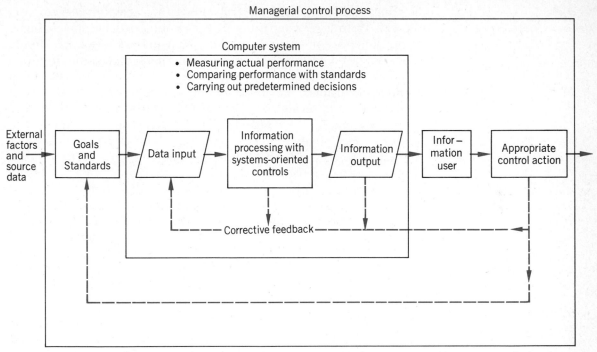

Managerial control process

Computer system
- Measuring actual performance
- Comparing performance with standards
- Carrying out predetermined decisions

External factors and source data → Goals and Standards → Data input → Information processing with systems-oriented controls → Information output → Information user → Appropriate control action

Corrective feedback

Figure 17-1 Control and the computer

is of high quality.[1] If it is, total business operations may be well controlled; if it is not, inadequate managerial performance may be expected. Internal control arrangements are therefore needed to assure managers that accurate and proper information is being produced by the computer system. Figure 17-1 is a generalized illustration showing the place of a computer system in the overall control process. In the remainder of this chapter we shall concentrate on computer-system controls.

Internal control is the total of all the control arrangements adopted within an organization to: (1) check on and maintain the accuracy of business data; (2) safeguard the company assets against fraud and other irregularities; (3) promote operating efficiency; and (4) encourage compliance with existing company policies and procedures.[2]

INTERNAL CONTROL

[1]You may wish to review the desired properties of quality information presented in Chapter 1.
[2]This definition is based on the one prepared by the American Institute of Certified Public Accountants. See *Auditing Standards and Procedures,* Statements on Auditing Procedure, no. 33, p. 27, AICPA, 1963.

**Need for
Internal Control**

In noncomputer systems the data processing activities are typically separated into several departments, with a number of employees being responsible for some portion of the total activity. For example, in the processing of a customer order, credit approval may come from one location, control of the inventory of ordered items may reside in another department, customer billing may be handled by a third department, and receipt of payment for items shipped may be in a fourth location. Thus, the organizational structure separates those who authorize and initiate the order from those who record and carry out the transaction. And both of these groups are separated from those who receive payment for the order. Such a division of data processing activities makes it difficult for fraud to go undetected since several people from different departments would have to be a party to any deception. Also, personnel in each organizational unit can check on the accuracy of others in the course of their routine operations.

But as pointed out in Chapter 15, the tendency is for data processing *activities to be centralized* as a result of computer usage. Centralization of activities, along with greater integration of processing steps, may make it possible for a single department to perform all the steps required to process a customer order. In the past, internal control has been achieved by the reviews and cross-checks made by personnel at separate points in the organizational structure. In other words, *internal control was employee oriented.* With fewer departments involved, however, and with the likelihood that fewer people are cross-checking data, it *may appear* that, even though source documents originate outside the computer department, the use of computer systems results in a reduction of internal control. Such a reduction *can occur* in an *inadequately controlled* centralized computer department in several ways:

1. *Through theft of money or goods.* Several reports of criminal manipulations involving money or goods have appeared in print in recent years. For example, a bank programmer installed a program *patch,* which prevented the computer from revealing that he was writing "hot" checks. Unfortunately for the programmer, the computer system broke down one day and a clerk processing accounts by hand caught the overdraft. In another case, a vice-president of a Wall Street brokerage company embezzled $50,000 a year over a five-year period by increasing the credit balances of his and his wife's personal brokerage accounts and reducing an interest income account by a similar total amount. A third example involved the Human Resources Administration, a New York antipoverty agency. Nearly $2 million in phony Youth Corps

payroll checks was issued by the agency's computer during 1968. An illegally parked car led to the discovery of a batch of processed checks. Other techniques used by computer-wise thieves include (a) deducting a few cents in excess service charges, interest, taxes, or dividends from thousands of accounts and writing themselves a check for the total amount of the excess deductions and (b) reporting inventory items as broken or lost and then transferring the items to accomplices.[3]

2. *Through misrepresentation of facts.* Major stockholders, for example, could distort the financial facts produced by computer systems in order to obtain illegal gain. Overvalued assets, understated liabilities, and other false representations could be used in criminal manipulations.

3. *Through careless handling of media.* Improper handling of tapes, cards, and disk packs can cause damage with a resulting loss of data. Faulty control procedures (or failure to follow correct procedures) may result in the erasure of entire files stored on magnetizable media.

4. *Through sabotage.* In addition to being exposed to careless handling, important files centrally stored in a computer center are also vulnerable to deliberate destruction. In one case, a disgruntled employee "used magnets to destroy virtually every file and program that his company possessed. He accomplished this in practically no time at all, but reconstructing the data will take a very long time indeed. At last report, in fact, the auditors were not sure whether they could reconstruct enough information to keep the company in business."[4]

5. *Through industrial espionage.* An unscrupulous outsider might be willing to go to considerable trouble and expense to gain access to the secrets and confidential records that are stored in a firm's computer system. Information about secret processes, research in progress, customers, mailing lists of prospective customers, management-simulation programs, etc., would be of considerable value to a competitor. Included among the tools of the industrial spy are: (a) the bribing of insiders to make duplicate copies of master tapes (which can be done in a few minutes

[3] For other examples of embezzlement, see the following articles: Sheldon Dansiger, "Embezzling Primer," *Computers and Automation,* November, 1967, pp. 41–43; Roy N. Freed, "Computer Fraud—A Management Trap," *Business Horizons,* June, 1969, pp. 25–30; Alan Adelson, "Whir, Blink—Jackpot! Crooked Operators Use Computers to Embezzle Money from Companies," *Wall Street Journal,* April 5, 1968; Brandt Allen, "Danger Ahead! Safeguard Your Computer," *Harvard Business Rev.,* November–December, 1968, pp. 97–101.
[4] Brandt Allen, "Danger Ahead! Safeguard Your Computer," *Harvard Business Rev.,* November–December, 1968, p. 99.

without leaving any incriminating evidence); (*b*) electronic devices that pick up electromagnetic radiations given off by computing equipment and convert these radiations into humanly readable form (in one demonstration, receiving devices coupled to a printer were placed in a truck, the truck was parked next to an unshielded computer center, and the output being produced by the computer's printer was received and copied in the truck); (*c*) the use of wire taps on data transmission lines (an attempt may be made to penetrate online systems through the use of wiretaps and bootleg terminals); and (*d*) reading discarded carbon paper, output listings, and other documents. In short, an outsider with motivation, financial resources, and access to computer skills may attempt to acquire and use the information found in a firm's computer center.[5]

In spite of the possible dangers inherent in an inadequately controlled computer system, however, *there is no reason why a company should have less internal control because of computer usage.* On the contrary, there is no reason why *systems-oriented controls,* in the form of computer programs, cannot be substituted for the employee-oriented controls of manual systems. Also, there is no reason why the separation of duties and responsibilities cannot be maintained *within* the computer department to safeguard the integrity of the systems-oriented controls. In fact, there is no reason why a firm cannot achieve better control because of (1) the computer's ability to follow policies and execute processing procedures uniformly, (2) the difficulty of changing and manipulating, without detection, proper programmed systems controls, and (3) the computer's inherent accuracy advantage when given correct input data.

Organization and Internal Control

Separation of activities *within* the computer department can help maintain the integrity of systems-oriented controls. One important control principle is that there should be an organizational separation between those knowledgeable employees who design and prepare the new systems and those who prepare the input data and operate the equipment. In other words, analysts and programmers should design, maintain, and make necessary changes (according to specified procedures) on programs, but they *should not* be involved with

[5] For further information on industrial espionage, see the following articles: Richard G. Canning, "Data Security in the CDB," *EDP Analyzer,* May, 1970, pp. 1–14; Harold K. Mintz, "Safeguarding Computer Information," *Software Age,* May, 1970, pp. 23–25; Timothy A. Davidson, "Computer Information Privacy," *The Office,* August, 1969, pp. 10–12ff; Dennie Van Tassel, "Information Security in a Computer Environment," *Computers and Automation,* July, 1969, pp. 24–25ff.

day-to-day production runs; equipment operators, on the other hand, should not have unrestricted access to completed computer programs, nor should they be involved with making changes in data or programs. Completed programs and their supporting documents should be kept and controlled by a librarian who is not engaged either in planning or maintaining programs or in operating processing equipment. These programs and documents should be issued to interested parties only upon proper authorization.

Business information systems undergo periodic examinations or *audits* by *internal auditors* (employees of the firm) and by *external auditors* (independent certified public accountants employed by the board of directors or stockholders). The evaluation of internal control arrangements is the point of departure in auditing. Although no exact audit procedure is used, the auditors seek to determine, by observation, inquiry, and review of charts and manuals (1) whether a proper organizational separation of duties has been made and (2) whether adequate controls have been created to maintain accuracy, safeguard assets, etc.

Auditing and Internal Control

During the course of the examination, attention is turned to the *audit trail* to determine if controls are effective and if reported procedures and policies are being followed. The audit trail begins with the recording of a transaction, winds through the processing steps and through any intermediate records which may exist and be affected, and ends with the production of output reports and records. By selecting a representative sample of previously processed source documents and following the audit trail, the auditor can trace these documents through the data processing systems to their final report or record destinations as a means of testing the adequacy of systems procedures and controls. In a manual system, original transactions may be recorded in one or more books of original entry; from there they may be connected to the final output by means of ledgers, documents, and summary totals. A visual and readily traceable trail is thus created.

With the introduction of computer systems, however, the *form* of the trail has changed. Of course, *it cannot be eliminated* because of the desire for good internal control and because of tax and legal requirements. The Internal Revenue Service, in a 1964 report on the use of EDP equipment, said that "the audit trail or the ability to trace a transaction from the general ledger back to its source document must not be eliminated."[6] Nevertheless, intermediate steps in the

[6]See Benton Warder, "An Auditor Looks at Data Processing," *J. Data Management,* vol. 5, p. 17, February, 1967.

information systems that were previously visible *have seemed to vanish* into reels of magnetic tape, magnetic disks, and magnetic cards and strips. To those auditors not familiar with computer systems, a portion of the audit trail "disappeared" at the entrance to the computer site. Since a "lost" audit trail is naturally a serious control matter, accounting literature is full of articles on this subject.

Nor will the audit trail become more visible in the future. The increased use of online direct-access storage devices to hold intermediate data and the substitution of online processing techniques for batch processing will result in an even greater decrease in the visible portion of the trail. For example, source documents may be replaced by machine-language recordings made with transaction recording equipment; input data will originate from widely dispersed locations through the use of remote terminals (again, no paper documents need be involved); and a reorder message for a basic part may be transmitted by the computer to the supplier through the use of data-communications facilities, with no paper documents being prepared. In examining such systems, the auditor must be satisfied that adequate controls are incorporated to prevent unintentional or deliberate damage to "invisible" files and records stored in an erasable medium.

In a majority of the past electronic systems audits that have been made, the *around-the-computer* approach has been used.[7] In this approach, the assumption is that if the input data to the computer are correct and if the output is properly handled, then the intermediate processing must be correct. This approach owes much of its popularity to its simplicity and familiarity to the auditor.

An alternative is the *through-the-computer* approach, where the auditor verifies that (1) the input data are correct and (2) internal processing is properly conducted. He then assumes that output is correct. The through-the-computer approach may employ the following techniques:

1. *The use of test data.* Just as the programmer uses simulated input data to check his programs during the debugging and testing stage, so, too, may an auditor use test decks to check on program accuracy and controls. Both valid and invalid transactions are included in the test data. The auditor will likely ". . . concentrate on developing invalid data and control violations. The error input should relate directly to the specific system controls which are critical to his objective of being assured that he can rely on the

---

[7]The expression *auditing around the computer* may carry the implication that the auditor can ignore the machine. This, of course, is false. The expression is used here because it has appeared extensively in accounting literature.

system as an information source."[8] Of course, the fact that a program passes the auditor's test does not mean that the tested program always receives accurate input data or is always the one that is used during processing. Reasonable but incorrect input data may be supplied, and a fraudulent patch may be inserted into the program during subsequent processing runs. Thus, organizational, administrative, and data controls must also be examined by the auditor.

2. *The use of auditor-prepared programs.* It is possible for the auditor to test and analyze the firm's data processing records and accounts *with the computer itself* through the use of special programs that have been prepared under his supervision. In other words, the auditor uses his *own* program and the firm's computer to process the firm's records for auditing purposes. The output of this operation may signal items requiring further attention and may provide analytical data for further study. However, the preparation of a special audit program to analyze accounts would probably not be economically feasible if there are relatively few records to be analyzed.

3. *The use of packaged audit programs.* Rather than prepare his own special analytical programs, the auditor may choose to use standardized programs that are available for a number of auditing purposes. Various audit routines to perform specific operations (e.g., to analyze accounts-receivable records to determine (a) the validity of the record amounts and (b) the collectibility of the accounts) may be adopted to the auditor's purpose by the use of specification sheets from which program cards are punched. The data on the cards may then be read into the computer and combined with the package instructions to complete the program for the particular test being processed. The Auditape system of the accounting firm of Haskins & Sells is an example of the available packaged programs.[9]

The around-the-computer approach may be suitable for audits made during the initial phases of a computer changeover and for some low-volume, uncomplicated systems; the through-the-computer method is frequently preferable for larger, more sophisticated procedures. Many auditing authorities recommend that a combination of approaches be employed.

The *function* of the auditor will probably not change in the future,

[8]Michael R. Moore, "EDP Audits: A Systems Approach," *Arthur Young J.*, Winter, 1968, p. 13.
[9]See W. Thomas Porter, "Generalized Computer-Audit Programs," *J. Accountancy*, January, 1969, pp. 54–62.

but his *techniques* will certainly be subject to revision as a result of computer usage. One of the greatest challenges facing the systems designer and the auditor will be to devise ways of preserving an audit trail that (although it may seem to be nearly invisible) must be readily retraceable. Furthermore, this trail must be kept as simple as possible, and it must not require great masses of supporting printed detail. To perform their function properly, auditors will need to understand computer systems. A psychological barrier will be removed with understanding, and concern about an invisible audit trail will abate. As T. W. McRae writes:

> The fact that the records are not visible is a psychological rather than a practical handicap. . . . The problem is not that the records are invisible but rather that the auditor is dependent on the computer room staff for translating coded tape into a printed format.[10]

On the basis of the definition of internal control given earlier, we can separate the *types of controls that should be developed* into two categories. In the first category are *administrative controls* designed to (1) promote the operating efficiency and (2) encourage employees to comply with existing company policies and procedures. In the second category are *data or procedural controls,* which are created to check and maintain the accuracy of business data. Prevention of fraud and other irregularities is controlled by organizational separation of duties and by administrative and data controls. In the remaining pages of this chapter we shall briefly survey some of the computer-related administrative and data controls that the auditor may look for during his examination.

ADMINISTRATIVE CONTROLS

In checking operational efficiency and procedural consistency, the auditor is interested in techniques that have a direct bearing on *systems design, programming, and computer operation.*

Systems-design controls

We have seen in earlier chapters that systems and program *documentation* is needed to provide a means of recording, analyzing, and communicating information. Good documentation promotes operating efficiency; it also *provides the basis for the evaluation and control of new and existing computer systems*. New system specifications should be designed (and documented) with audit and control considerations in mind. (It is expensive to ignore control aspects and then

---

[10]T. W. McRae, *The Impact of Computers on Accounting,* John Wiley & Sons, Inc., New York, 1964, p. 165.

have to revise and rework a designed system. The participation of a knowledgeable auditor in the design phase so that proper controls may be built in and so that the audit trail does not vanish in fact as well as in appearance is thus a wise precaution.) Without good supporting documents and flowcharts on existing systems, managers and auditors will probably not know if and when systems changes have been made. In short, poor documentation represents a basic internal control weakness. Therefore, one of the most important controls that can be exercised over systems design is to assign authority to one or more individuals to make sure that systems and program flowcharts, decision tables, manuals, etc., are correctly prepared *and maintained*. Specifically written control procedures should be established for this purpose, and, as noted in Chapters 10 and 14, standardized charting symbols and methods should be used.

Programming Controls

A detailed explanation of the purpose of each program together with copies of all related documents should be kept in a *program file*. A manual containing *standard programming procedures* should also be prepared and kept up to date.[11] The operating policies and approaches that are to be followed by personnel should be specified. Among the topics to be covered are program documentation methods and standards, program testing and modification procedures, magnetic tape labeling and retention policies, and the use of standardized symbolic names to describe company data. Such specified procedures promote consistency, reduce program maintenance problems, and make it easier for others to take over the work of a programmer who decides to leave the company.

A definite procedure should be formulated to handle *program changes*. Changes should be made only after written approval is given by someone in a position of authority, e.g., the manager of the affected department. It is sometimes a good policy to postpone making a number of minor changes until the end of an accounting cycle so that data handling remains consistent throughout the accounting period. Changes in programs should be made by authorized programmers and not by computer-operating personnel. All changes should be charted and explained in writing; when completed, they should be reviewed and cleared by someone other than a maintenance programmer. All documents related to the change should be made a part of the permanent program file.

[11]For an in-depth treatment of the topic of data processing standards, see Dick H. Brandon, *Management Standards for Data Processing*, D. Van Nostrand Company, Inc., Princeton, N. J., 1963.

Computer-operation Controls

Computer-operation controls may be maintained in the following ways:

1. *By the use of appropriate manuals.* A standard *operating manual* should include an explanation of the procedures established to deal with such things as the issuance and return of program and data tapes and cards and the means of scheduling and keeping records of equipment operating time. A manual of *program operating instructions* should be available to tell the operator how each program should be run. These instructions can specify the peripheral equipment to use, the console-switch settings to make, the action to take on all program halts, the exceptions to standard procedures and routines that may be needed, the input data to use, and the disposition of the output information obtained.
2. *By the creation of a data-security program.* Definite controls should be established to safeguard programs and data from fire and water damage or destruction. Duplicate program and master file tapes may have to be kept at a location away from the computer site. A fireproof storage vault at the computer site is a wise precaution. The importance of proper identification of and control over library tapes, cards, disks, and blank forms cannot be overemphasized. Adequate insurance protection should be provided. A waste-disposal procedure to destroy carbon papers and other media containing sensitive information should be followed. And proper shielding of equipment to reduce electromagnetic radiation is necessary in some situations.
3. *By control over console intervention.* It is possible for the computer operator to bypass program controls. He has the ability to interrupt a program run and introduce data manually into the processor through the console keyboard. With organizational separation of program preparation and computer operation and with operators having access to object programs and not source programs, it is unlikely that an operator will have enough knowledge of the program details to manipulate them successfully for improper purposes. But the possibility of unauthorized intervention should be reduced in a number of ways. Since, for example, the console typewriter may be used to print out a manual intervention, the paper sheets in the typewriter can be prenumbered and periodically checked. Other approaches using locked recording devices may be employed. Additional control techniques include rotating the duties of computer operators and having them account for computer operating time (manual intervention is slow, and manipulation can thus result in processing times that are longer than necessary for affected runs).

4. *By controlling access to the computer site.* Only authorized
    personnel should be allowed access to equipment, data files, and
    programs. Easy access invites fraud and/or damage. To illustrate,
    one visitor to an insurance company computer center (a member
    of a touring garden club) was so impressed by the blinking lights
    and spinning tapes that she decided to take home a souvenir.
    "She later said, 'I hope I didn't do anything wrong. There were
    all those boxes of cards on the table, and I just reached into the
    middle of a box and took one.'"[12]

Data controls are concerned with the accuracy and propriety of the
data flowing through a processing system; therefore, let us consider
these controls at the *input, processing,* and *output* stages.

DATA CONTROLS

The purpose of input controls is to make sure that (1) *all* authorized
input transactions are identified, (2) these transactions are *accurately
recorded* in a machine-usable form at the *right time,* and (3) *all* these
transactions are then sent to the processing station. Among the control
techniques that may be adopted are:

Input Controls

1. *The use of prenumbered forms.* Whenever possible, a simple and
    effective control is to use serially numbered forms so that docu-
    ments may be accounted for. A missing number in the sequence
    signals a missing document.
2. *The use of control totals.* When batch processing is used, certain
    totals can be computed for each batch of source documents. For
    example, the total dollar-sales figure may be computed on a batch
    of sales invoices prior to, perhaps, keypunching. The same calcu-
    lation can be made after keypunching to see if the figures com-
    pare. Control totals do not have to be expressed in dollars. They
    can be the totals obtained from adding figures in a data field that
    is included in all source documents being considered. A simple
    count of documents, cards, and other records is an effective
    control total. For example, the number of cards processed in the
    computer-operating department can be compared with the count
    of the number of cards that are delivered for processing. Similar
    comparisons between records read on magnetic tape and the
    number of input source documents may be possible. Of course,
    with control totals as with other data controls, the volume of
    transactions and the importance of the data should determine the

[12] Allen, *op. cit.,* p. 100.

degree of control and the amount of money that is spent to maintain that control.

3. *The use of transcription methods.* One means of controlling data transcription is to have knowledgeable clerks conduct a preaudit of source documents prior to recording the transactions in a machine-usable form. If input is by means of punched cards, the card verifier can be used. Transaction recording devices are available that can reduce errors caused by recopying, keypunching, illegible records, and loss of documents.

4. *The use of programmed checks on input.* Program instructions can be written to check on the reasonableness and propriety of data as they enter the processing operation. For example, program checks can be written to determine if (1) certain specified limits are exceeded, (2) the input is complete, and (3) a transaction code or identification number is active and reasonable. When online processing is used, lockwords or passwords may be required from remote stations before certain files can be made accessible.

Processing Controls

Processing controls are established to (1) determine when data are lost or not processed and (2) check on the accuracy of arithmetic calculations. These controls may be classified into *hardware* and *software* categories. Important hardware controls include parity checks (i.e., checks that test whether the number of digits in an array is odd or even) and the use of dual reading and writing heads in input/output equipment. Although not a built-in hardware control, a definite program of *preventive maintenance* can pay big dividends by reducing the number of machine malfunctions.

Software or programmed controls include the input checks mentioned above. The number of possible programmed controls that may be used is limited only by the programmer's imagination.[13] Some of the possibilities include:

1. *The use of record count.* As a check against a predetermined total, the computer can be instructed to count the number of records that it handles in a program run.

2. *The use of tape labels.* The *external* labeling of magnetic tapes should be carefully controlled. These outside labels may give those interested such information as the tape contents, program identification number, and length of time the contents should be retained. As we saw in Chapter 6, *internal* header and trailer

---

[13] But the value of the controls must be weighed against the additional programming expense and the cost of additional computer running time.

control labels may also be recorded on the tapes themselves. The first (or *header*) record written on the tape gives the program identification number and other information. Before actual processing begins, then, a programmed comparison check may be made to make sure that the correct tape reel is being used. Since information on a master file will be erased if the file should accidentally be written upon, this is an important precaution. The last (or *trailer*) record contains a count of the number of other records on the tape.

3. *The use of sequence check.* In batch processing, the records are in some kind of sequence, e.g., by employee number or stock number. Programmed checks to detect out-of-sequence and missing cards and records prevent a file from being processed in an incorrect order.

4. *The use of structural check.* A test of the transactions to be processed can be made to determine whether the debits and credits called for represent acceptable combinations. Transactions with unacceptable debit and credit combinations are rejected.

Output Controls

Output controls are established as final checks on the accuracy and propriety of the processed information. Among the output control methods that may be employed are:

1. *The use of control totals.* How do the control totals of processed information compare with the input control totals? For example, is there agreement between the number of records that were delivered for processing and the number of records that were actually processed? A basic output control technique is to obtain satisfactory answers to such questions.

2. *The review of interested parties.* Feedback on a regular basis from input-initiating and output-using departments points out errors that slip through in spite of all precautions. Follow-up action must be taken to correct any file inaccuracies that may be revealed.

3. *The use of systematic sampling.* Internal auditors can check on output by tracing randomly selected transactions from source documents through the processing system to the output destination. This should be done on a regular and systematic basis.

4. *The use of prenumbered forms.* Certain output forms should be prenumbered and accounted for in the same manner as input documents. Blank payroll-check forms, for example, should be closely guarded.

SUMMARY

Information produced by computer systems helps managers plan and control business activities in a number of ways. Of course, the information produced by computers must be of high quality if business operations are to be well managed. The purpose of internal control is to maintain an accurate and proper information output.

In manual systems, employee-oriented controls are established. Although processing efficiency is often low, the review and cross-checking of documents by several employees at separate organizational points provide a measure of internal control. When computers are used, systems-oriented controls may be substituted for some of the employee checks. Internal control need not suffer because of this substitution; in fact, it may quite possibly be improved. Separation of duties within the computer department is an organizational technique that can help maintain the integrity of systems-oriented controls.

Internal and external auditors periodically check on the adequacy of the internal control arrangements that have been made. During their examinations, auditors trace transactions through the processing systems as a means of testing the accuracy of information and the adequacy of procedures and controls. Computer usage has changed the form of this audit trail; its visibility has been reduced by the elimination of paper documents. New techniques have been developed because of audit trail changes; additional changes in audit methodology will be required in the future.

During the audit, the auditor checks to see if a proper organizational separation of duties has been made. He also wants to know if adequate administrative and data controls have been created. Several control methods are presented in the last pages of the chapter.

DISCUSSION QUESTIONS

1. How can computer systems help managers control business operations?
2. (a) What is internal control?
   (b) Why is it needed?
3. What is meant by (a) *employee-oriented* controls? (b) *systems-oriented* controls?
4. Of what significance is organizational structure in maintaining internal control?
5. (a) Distinguish between internal and external auditors.
   (b) What is the function of the auditor?

6. (a) What is the audit trail?
   (b) Why is it needed?
   (c) Can it be eliminated?
7. "The audit trail will become less visible in the future." Discuss this statement.
8. Identify and describe the approaches which are used to audit computer information-processing procedures.
9. (a) What is the purpose of administrative controls?
   (b) Into what three categories may administrative controls be classified?
   (c) Give some examples of administrative controls.
10. (a) What is the purpose of data controls?
    (b) Into what three categories may data controls be classified?
    (c) Give some examples of data controls.

SELECTED REFERENCES

Allen, Brandt: "Danger Ahead! Safeguard Your Computer," *Harvard Business Review,* November–December, 1968, pp. 97–101.

Davis, Gordon B.: *Auditing & EDP,* American Institute of Certified Public Accountants, Inc., New York, 1968.

John, Richard C., and Thomas J. Nissen: "Evaluating Internal Control in EDP Audits," *Journal of Accountancy,* February, 1970, pp. 31–38.

Moore, Michael R.: "EDP Audits: A Systems Approach," *Arthur Young Journal,* Winter, 1968, pp. 4–15.

Porter, W. Thomas: "Generalized Computer-Audit Programs," *Journal of Accountancy,* January, 1969, pp. 54–62.

Thorne, Jack F.: "The Audit of Real-Time Systems," *Journal of Data Management,* May, 1970, pp. 14–19.

Wasserman, Joseph J.: "Plugging the Leaks in Computer Security," *Harvard Business Review,* September–October, 1969, pp. 119–129.

Tomorrow's Outlook

In spite of the profound warning contained in an old Danish proverb ("Prediction is difficult, particularly when it pertains to the future . . . ."), in this final chapter we shall attempt to summarize briefly some of the computer developments that may be expected in the future.

The discussion in this chapter is limited, however, for two reasons: (1) in earlier chapters speculation about future trends was presented as particular subjects were discussed; and (2) the time period involved is, for the most part, "tomorrow," i.e., the next five years or so, rather than the "day after tomorrow."[1] Thus, this chapter attempts to summarize some of the developments that may logically be expected in the next few years based on the current state of the art in the elec-

---

[1] The literature is not lacking in guesses about the effects that computers will have on business twenty or more years in the future. When appropriate, sources of longer-range predictions are footnoted for the benefit of the interested reader.

tronic data processing field. The topics to be considered can be classified as (1) the *hardware outlook,* (2) the *software outlook,* (3) the *outlook for management-information systems,* and (4) the *outlook for managers.*

THE HARDWARE OUTLOOK

Trends in Input/Output

It is likely that considerable progress will be made in data *input* methods. Since input has generally been a limiting factor in business data processing, a great deal of attention has been and will continue to be focused on improved input performance. The bulk of the computer input in the next five years will continue to be in the form of punched cards or magnetic tape. However, keyboard-to-magnetic-tape input systems are likely to grow in popularity at the expense of keypunching systems. Tape-recording densities will increase in the future, and storage costs will thus be reduced. But there will be a trend toward recording data in machine-usable form at the point of origin through the greater use of online terminals. Remote I/O consoles, transaction recorders, input tablets and light pens, CRT-equipped display stations—all these online instruments will become less expensive and will be used much more often in the future.[2] When such a direct man-machine interface is possible, the need for a data-recording medium may not be required. The direct input techniques, then, will also help to reduce the keypunching of cards from source documents—a laborious translating operation.

Optical character recognition of machine-printed characters and hand-printed marks and numbers will also increase in importance at the expense of manual keypunching. The cost of using OCR has been dropping and will continue to decline, and reliability will be improved by a movement toward standardization of paper, inks, and type fonts. Research will continue on the development of machines that will read handwritten letters and machines that will accept voice input. Such equipment will not be in widespread use in the next five years but could become important at a later date.

The high-speed printer will continue to be the primary *output* device when information is to be used directly by man. Dramatic improvements in impact printers will not be forthcoming; however, they will become more reliable and somewhat less expensive. There will be a trend in the direction of lessening the role of the printer.

[2]In 1960, all peripheral equipment accounted for about 30 percent of the cost of hardware. By 1975 it is expected that terminal devices alone will represent 35 percent of a much greater total hardware sales amount. The Diebold Group estimates that terminal sales will increase from $1.6 billion in 1970 to $5.5 billion in 1975.

It will be bypassed by the use of online stations, which will give the information requested directly to the user. (Of course, if the remote station is equipped with a typewriter, a printed document will be produced; but if the station has a CRT, no printed document may be prepared.) The computer-output-to-microfilm (COM) approach discussed in Chapter 7 may also reduce the role of the printer. Better systems design and the utilization of the *management-by-exception* principle may result in fewer and more concise reports. The use of voice output will grow in those specialized situations where an audio response can be given to predictable queries.

Rapid changes may be expected in the next five years in the *size, speed, cost, information storage capacity,* and *reliability* of the central processor. Although it is now possible to crowd well over 100,000 basic electronic components on a square inch wafer, future circuits will once again be reduced in *size*. In fact, future LSI circuits are now being mentioned that would have packaging characteristics approximating the compactness and complexity of the circuits in the human brain.[3] Anticipated size reductions will mean shorter distances for electric pulses to travel, and thus processor *speed* will again be increased. Single users will be hard pressed to use the capabilities of the larger of these new processors in an efficient manner. Thus, greater emphasis will be placed on using them in timeshared, multiple-access systems.

Trends in the Central Processor

Dramatic changes will also occur in the area of *costs*. In the past, there have been substantial cost reductions for given levels of computing power; this trend will continue in the future. For example, we saw in Chapter 3 that the cost to provide internal storage capacity for 1 bit had declined from $2.61 in 1950 to 20 cents in 1965; the comparable cost in 1970 was from 5 to 10 cents, while the 1975 figure is expected to be $\frac{1}{2}$ cent. A few years ago, the central processor represented 75 percent and the input/output and other peripheral equipment made up the other 25 percent of the total value of an installation's hardware. By the mid-1970s this situation will have reversed because of cost reductions in LSI circuits.

In addition to being smaller, faster, and much less expensive, computer storage devices will have larger *storage capability*. Equip-

[3]Such developments are beyond our five-year period. See F. G. Heath, "Large-Scale Integration in Electronics," *Sci. Amer.,* February, 1970, pp. 22–31. See also David Brand, "Electronic Chips Offer Advances in Computers and Consumer Goods," *Wall Street Journal,* June 22, 1970, pp. 1ff.

ment will be available with the number of bytes of primary storage measured in the tens of millions. Much of the equipment produced in the next five years will use magnetic core primary storage techniques. But the trend appears to be in the direction of such noncore storage forms as LSI circuits, planar thin films, and plated wires—all of which hold out the promise of being easier to fabricate than magnetic core planes. Research making use of laser beams and cryogenics (a branch of physics relating to the production and effects of very low temperatures) is being conducted to develop storage devices with improved characteristics.

Self-repairing computers were discussed in Chapter 3. Although *reliability* will be improved in the next five years through the ability of multiprocessor systems to (1) perform self-diagnosis of difficulties and (2) reconfigure to do the work at lower efficiency levels, the appearance of a self-repairing commercial computer must wait until LSI circuit technology makes it possible to produce redundant parts at low cost. Future business machines will benefit greatly from the reliability research currently being conducted by military and space agencies.

The future of smaller, freestanding computers has been a matter of some dispute. Although these machines represent the majority of the present installations, there are some who believe that the future will see a decline in their *number* in favor of large timesharing equipment. In other words, it is felt that remote terminals connected to timesharing facilities will *replace* smaller computer installations. Some organizations will follow this route in the next five to seven years, but during this period, there will not be a discernible trend in this direction.

The number of computer installations is expected to increase from 90,000 in 1970 to 200,000 in 1975. Obviously, most of these new machines will *not* be large timesharing systems; rather, most of them will be small machines and minicomputers. However, we should keep the distinction between the *number* of machines and the *computing capability and value of each installation* clearly in mind. A majority of the computers installed in the 1970s will be "small." (The growth in the number of minicomputers in the next few years will be dramatic.) But the number of large timesharing installations will grow rapidly, and each of these large installations will have the computing capability of a number of smaller machines. By 1975 about 50 percent of the total United States computing capability may be found in timeshared installations.

During the 1970s there will be an increase in the number of both large and small hardware systems. There will be *increasing compati-*

bility between smaller machines and larger timeshared ones. This compatibility will eventually (the Swami is now looking further into the future than five years) help bring about a size polarization: on the one hand, there will be large, centralized computing facilities used on a timeshared basis; and, on the other hand, there will be large numbers of small and relatively inexpensive computers used independently to satisfy the particular special requirements of the user. Furthermore, many of these small, freestanding computers will be compatible with, will be connected to, and will communicate with, the larger timeshared facilities. Such communication among computers will not be limited to single organizations; rather, it will cut across company boundaries.

The trend toward compatible families of machines and modular design will continue. We saw in Chapter 11 that *microprograms* (also called *firmware* or *stored logic*) were used to make the smaller models in a family of machines hardware compatible with the larger models. Computer technology in the 1970s will make much greater use of firmware. Functions currently being performed with software will be converted into microprograms and stored for use in a read-only control storage device. The microprograms may be (1) wired into LSI circuit modules and made a permanent part of the CPU, (2) wired into circuit modules, which can be "plugged in" to a machine to specialize it for better performance of specific applications, or (3) read directly into a reloadable control storage section in the CPU through the use of specialized equipment and procedures designed specifically for the purpose.[4] The effect will be to replace expensive software with more efficient hardware—a resource that is becoming less expensive.

Most computers today are designed with single control, storage, and arithmetic-logic units in the CPU. But it is likely that this traditional architecture will be modified more frequently in the future. (As we saw in Chapter 5, multiprocessor, concurrent, and parallel designs are also possible.) It is also likely that the *distributed-computer* concept will gain in popularity; i.e., it is likely that more of the processing functions previously handled by the CPU will be shifted to peripheral equipment. For example, with appropriate built-in circuitry, an online station may make some of the programmed input control checks described in the last chapter before transmitting the data to the central processor. Many input terminals will, in fact, become satellite minicomputers doing preliminary processing before transmitting data to the central processor.

---

[4]This last approach is now used in the IBM 370/145 computer. A small read-only disk cartridge supplied by IBM contains the microprograms needed for a specific installation. These microprograms are loaded into an integrated-circuit control storage section in the central processor.

**Trends in
Online Storage**

Online secondary storage devices will continue to use magnetic cores, drums, disks, and cards or strips. The use of replaceable cartridges gives an open-ended storage capability to magnetic disks and cards or strips at the present time. But in the future the use of higher recording densities will make it possible for each disk, strip, or card to hold more data. Online storage capacity will therefore be expanded, and direct-access times will also be improved. There will be a continuation of the inverse relationship that currently exists between direct-access time and storage capacity; e.g., strips or cards will have the slowest access time along with the largest storage capability. Beyond five years, magnetooptical mass storage systems utilizing a magnetic storage medium, an optical scanning and tracking network, and a laser light source may be widely used to achieve mass stores with much greater data-recording densities.

**THE SOFTWARE
OUTLOOK**

As we have just seen, future hardware will become much more powerful. The bottlenecks in future management-information systems will be almost entirely associated with software. Because of this fact, software designers may be willing in the future to adopt methods that will be relatively less efficient in terms of hardware usage. Such brute-force processing methods, which could not have been tolerated in the past because of more limited hardware capabilities, may be more acceptable in the future if they lead to software with the attributes of simplicity, reliability, and generality. Of course, some current software functions will be taken over by hardware or firmware in the future.

Language Trends

Procedure-oriented languages such as those described in Chapter 12 will continue to dominate applications programming for the next several years. Compilers will be further improved, and machine-oriented assembly languages will continue to decline in use. Because of the huge investment in such languages as FORTRAN and COBOL, they will be maintained and updated. Standard versions of PL/I and BASIC may be agreed upon.

The use of simplified *conversational programming languages* will become common in the 1970s. When such a programming approach is used (timeshared terminals are needed), the computer itself keeps track of the acceptable vocabulary of the language and displays permissible alternate terms and statements to the user until the problem is satisfactorily formulated. The machine then computes the answer to the problem. In short, the user's major skill will lie in his ability to state problems. He will be assisted by a "dialogue" with the computer as it attempts to find out what he wants to say. "Under the tutelage of the computer (for here the machine will be part teacher, part learner), the problem will be formulated until it is in a form for which a useful solution can be 'programmed' by the computer itself."[5]

In a business setting, conversational programming may be a feature of *data management software*. As we saw in Chapter 4, such software, together with direct-access timesharing facilities, permit managers to probe file contents in order ultimately to obtain answers to questions that initially were vague and/or poorly defined. This file processing software "manages" the stored data items and assembles the items needed from the data base in response to the query or instruction of a manager who is not a programming specialist. To summarize, the availability of data management systems will (1) enable managers to seek out for themselves answers to unique problems and (2) thereby save the time of systems analysts and programmers. There will be greater emphasis on the development and use of conversational languages and data-management software in the future.

Growth of Packaged Programs and Software Specialists

The number of firms preparing and marketing proprietary program packages has increased significantly in the past few years. Demand for their products is growing because of the reasons listed in Chapter 3 and because unbundled manufacturers are now charging for the program products previously supplied at no charge to customers. In the next five years, packaged programs for common applications will be improved, and new packages for more specific tasks will be offered by computer manufacturers, computer users and user groups, commercial service centers, facilities-management firms, timesharing companies,[6] and independent software speciality organizations. Smaller businesses will obtain lower-cost processing services from service centers, timesharing firms, and others through the use of these packaged programs. Because of the growing importance of packages, more attention must be given in the future to the need for legal safeguards to protect against the unauthorized use of proprietary programs.

[5]John W. Carr, III, "Programming in the 1970's," in *Data Processing*, Data Processing Management Association, Park Ridge, Ill., 1965, VIII, p. 151.

[6]Some package developers will market their products *wholesale* to timesharing companies who, in turn, will *retail* the programs to their subscribers. Royalties may be paid to the developer on the basis of program usage.

Today there are hundreds of independent software speciality companies in existence. The growth of the better managed of these firms will be substantial. Many new companies will be formed in the early 1970s, but many existing software houses will cease to exist in a few years. A significant number of those that fail will do so not because of lack of technical capability but because of managerial deficiencies. For example, "a lack of marketing know-how will prove fatal to many companies with otherwise estimable software skills."[7]

THE OUTLOOK FOR MANAGEMENT INFORMATION SYSTEMS

Trend toward Quick-response Systems

It should be noted at the outset that batch processing is economical, is suited to many types of applications, and will continue to account for the bulk of the processing work for some time to come. But because they allow managers to react more quickly to changes in the external environment and because they give quicker answers to inquiries, there is a trend in the direction of the judicious use of quick-response systems. Of course, the degree of quickness needed will vary; therefore, the needs of each business will determine the speed with which records are updated.

Real time processing will become increasingly common in those applications where immediate updating of records is justifiable. When the time limitations are not so severe, online processing, with periodic updating of records, will be frequently used in place of traditional batch-processing methods. Source-document data will be keyed directly into the computer; thus, the use of intermediate cards or tapes will be eliminated, and the computer can be programmed to check input and develop control totals. The source documents that may be required will be accumulated for short periods of time, but sorting can be eliminated, batch sizes can be smaller, and data flow can be steadier.

The growth of timesharing   During the decade of the 1970s there will be substantial and accelerating growth in the number of large timesharing facilities, and these facilities will represent an increasing proportion of the total computer investment. The reader should not be surprised at this conclusion. Many of the predictions made in this final chapter depend in whole or in part on the use of timesharing equipment. A number of future trends—e.g., (1) the greater use of online I/O devices to provide a direct man-machine interface, (2) the greater communication between large machines and multitudes of

---

[7]Robert V. Head, "Twelve Crises—Comments on the Future of the Software Industry, *Datamation*, March, 1970, p. 125.

smaller compatible ones, (3) the rapid increase in the use of data communications facilities, (4) the growth of conversational programming, (5) the trend toward quick-response systems, and (6) the development of broader intracompany and intercompany data systems—are all intimately associated with and generally based upon the growth of timesharing systems. Hardware manufacturers expect that half of their equipment sold in 1975 will be destined for use in a timesharing environment. Therefore, much of their design effort is currently being directed toward minimizing the deficiencies that exist in the hardware and software of present timesharing systems.[8]

Many timeshared systems installed in the next five years will be for the use of a single organization. These systems may be small, general purpose machines capable of serving a relatively small number of users and costing less than $20,000, or they may be multimillion dollar systems. In addition, of course, more multisubscriber *information utilities* will be established and will prove to be economical and successful. Beyond the five-year period, the size polarization of computing equipment mentioned earlier in this chapter will begin to take shape. The speed with which information utilities appear on the scene will depend upon the speed with which formidable software and data communication obstacles can be overcome.

Data communications developments   With increased emphasis being placed on timesharing, the trend will obviously be toward greater use of data communications facilities. Data communication will account for at least half of the traffic on the telephone network by the end of the 1970s. Western Union has predicted that 60 percent of the computers sold by 1975 will be linked in some way to a data communications network.

Improved technology and greater usage of data transmission facilities will combine to reduce gradually the cost of long-distance data communications. Such reductions may not be substantial. Laser research and the use of communications satellites may eventually result in more economical transmission but not in the next five years. It is quite possible, in fact, that most of the costs associated with processing a task originating at a remote station will be directly attributable to communications charges. Such charges will result in the construction of more company-owned communication systems. But most of the data transmission facilities will, of course, be furnished by regulated telephone and telegraph companies. Teletype and voice-grade telephone channels will continue to transmit most of the data; however, as we saw in Chapter 4, there is some doubt that the

[8]The existing timesharing problems are outlined in Chapter 4.

telephone network can expand rapidly enough to meet the data transmission needs of the computer field. More foreign attachments desired by computer users will be permitted on the network; and new interstate data communications services may be authorized by the F.C.C.

Touch-Tone telephones, with push-button input and audio output, will become a common low-cost I/O device in the next five years. Data will be transmitted directly to a computer by "keying" the Touch-Tone buttons. In the more distant future, Picturephones and cable television sets may be combined with computers to provide an integrated voice-data-picture communications system for society. Ultimately, it may be possible for professionals such as managers, teachers, engineers, etc., to perform their jobs in offices located in their homes. Thus, the transmission of information may be substituted for the transportation and concentration of humans. The need to crowd together into cities may be reduced; communities of interest and interaction may be linked electronically rather than by geographic boundaries.[9]

Movement toward Broader Systems

In the next five years companies will increase their efforts to find ways and means of consolidating data processing activities into broader and more integrated systems. A large number of organizations will be moving in this direction, but because of the complexities involved, the movement will be gradual. Firms will increasingly seek to define and classify certain types of basic data commonly so that better integration will be possible. Developmental work on corporate data banks, which will replace a multitude of the independent files maintained at the present time, will receive greater attention. Hopefully, the issue of the potential threat to an individual's right to privacy (which has been raised by the recommendation to create a National Data Center, and which was discussed in Chapter 4) will also receive greater attention and will be satisfactorily resolved.[10]

The purchase of financial and marketing information in the form of cards or magnetic tape will grow; as a result, agreement in data coding methods between information supplier and customer will become more important and will, in some cases, lead to standardized data descriptions.

[9] For more information on these intriguing possibilities, see the following articles: William A. Lape, "The Home Office of the Future," *J. Syst. Manage.*, April, 1970, pp. 28–32; Charles Winston, "New Horizons for Communications," *J. Data Management,* June, 1969, pp. 66–68; and W. E. Sims, "Preview of 1979: Communications and the Computer," *J. Data Management,* September, 1969, pp. 20–23.

[10] For further discussion of the privacy issue, see Ralph Nader, "Computers and the Consumer," *Computers and Automation,* October, 1970, pp. 14–21.

It is likely that, eventually, many data systems that cross company lines will be linked together by compatible computer networks. Buyers and sellers may integrate their systems, and firms that perform similar services (in addition to airlines) may be connected by intercompany networks. In the realm of account billing and payment there may eventually be a substantial reduction in the use of currency and checks drawn on banks. The "cashless-checkless society" might operate in an individual's case as follows: (1) his pay would be credited to his account in the banking system automatically on authorization by his employer; (2) at the end of (or during) the month, the bills he owes would be entered (in the form of claims) into a banking central-clearing operation by his creditors; (3) he would approve the valid claims and authorize the banking system to make payment (perhaps by using a Touch-Tone telephone); (4) payment would be handled automatically by the banking-system computers. One or more "money cards" would reduce the need for cash, and the need to prepare and mail checks would be largely eliminated. If all this sounds pretty farfetched to you, consider this fact: A special committee has been organized by the American Bankers Association (a sober group) to give serious thought and study to such concepts. By 1977, the American Bankers Association predicts that 86 percent of the bills that the typical consumer now pays by check may be handled by electronic transfers.

In the operation of their businesses, managers must contend with the rapid scientific, social, and economic movements that are taking place in this nation and in the world. Scientific advances will result in the development of new products and the appearance of new processes, and population growth will result in more people to feed, clothe, house, educate, employ, and transport. Markets will change to accommodate changing tastes, the greater mobility of the population, and the changes in age composition.

THE OUTLOOK FOR MANAGERS

The managerial implications of such changes are clear—the manager must be prepared to make continuous readjustments in his plans. He must make decisions about new markets and the channels of distribution to use, and he must determine how a more flexible capital investment structure can best be acquired. Furthermore, he must make these decisions within the limits of a reaction-time period that is constantly shrinking![11] If he is to compete effectively in the future,

[11]President Thomas J. Ready, Jr., of Kaiser Aluminum and Chemical Corporation, has stated in this connection: "A major change now that could take place over a three-year period could occur in a year or less, five years hence." (Quoted by Jack B. Weiner in "What's Ahead in Management?" *Duns Review*, January, 1965, p. 32.)

he must receive information that is accurate, timely, complete, and pertinent. Because of difficulties experienced with traditional information systems, businesses have developed quicker-reacting and more integrated systems as a means of meeting their informational needs. Much more will be done along these lines in the future.

The computer is the tool that will provide needed information for managers of the future. It "will help open as many new business opportunities tomorrow as past technology has occasioned today. And it will reap obsolescence in the same fashion for many businesses that are alive today."[12] If present and future managers want to prevent their firms from possibly being numbered among the obsolescent businesses, they will have to prepare for a successful working relationship with computerized information processing. And they will have to learn to adapt their operations to include the use of computer-dependent decision-making techniques. The middle manager who is able to apply the coming technological and systems developments in his job should have no fear about his future. He will not become extinct; rather, he will be in demand and will function in a setting that will be more challenging and stimulating.

The computer cannot and will not make difficult managerial decisions. "But it will greatly multiply the ability, the effectiveness and the impact of those people of intelligence and judgment who take the trouble to find out what the computer is all about."[13] And that is the message with which we began this book. You now have found out something about what a computer is, what it can and cannot do, and how it operates; and you now have an idea of the broad impact that computers have (and will have) on businesses and on the people who manage them. By continuing to build upon this foundation, you will be preparing for the challenging and competitive business environment of tomorrow.

SUMMARY

Significant advances will be made in hardware in the next five years. The bulk of computer input will continue to be in the form of punched cards and magnetic tape but, with increasing emphasis being placed on timesharing, there will be greater use made of online I/O terminals. The use of optical character readers will grow.

[12]James H. Binger, "The Computer: Engine of the Eighties," *Advanced Management J.,* January, 1967, p. 27. This article, written by the Chairman of the Board of Honeywell, Inc., delves into some of the broader social changes that may appear in the 1980s.
[13]Peter F. Drucker, "What the Computer Will Be Telling You," *Nation's Business,* vol. 54, p. 90, August, 1966.

Improvements in integrated-circuit technology will result in smaller, faster, and more reliable central processors; circuit improvements will also make it possible in some situations to replace expensive software with microprograms and additional hardware elements. Substantial cost reduction for a given level of computing power will be forthcoming, and storage devices will have larger storage capability. Higher recording densities will improve the performance of tapes, disks, cards, and strips. The number of small computers will grow as will the number of large timeshared machines. With the growth in timesharing will come greater communication between large machines and compatible smaller ones and increased use of data transmission facilities.

Procedure-oriented languages will become more dominant. Managers will make routine use of simplified conversational programming languages and data management software. Compilers will be improved, and machine-oriented symbolic languages will continue to decline in use. Applications packages will grow in popularity as will the use of services provided by software, facilities management, and computer-center organizations.

Although batch processing will continue to account for the bulk of the work done for some time to come, more systems with quick-response features will be designed and implemented in the next five years. Companies will increase their efforts to find ways of consolidating data processing activities into broader and more integrated systems. These trends are developing because of dissatisfaction with the traditional ways of processing information. Ultimately, the transmission of information may be substituted in part for the transportation and concentration of humans.

Managers will face a rewarding and challenging future—*if* they plan and prepare for it. They will have to make decisions in a more complex and dynamic setting, and they will have less time to react to problem situations. But they can have access to higher-quality information upon which to base their decisions.

DISCUSSION QUESTIONS

1. What future hardware developments are expected to support the growth of timesharing?
2. "Rapid changes may be expected in the size, speed, cost, storage capacity, and reliability of the central processor." Discuss this statement.
3. What is meant by the distributed-computer concept?

4. (a) What is conversational programming?
   (b) What is the purpose of data-management software?
   (c) Why are these software concepts of interest to managers?
   (d) How do these concepts relate to timesharing?
5. What is meant by the "cashless-checkless society"?

SELECTED REFERENCES

In addition to the references suggested in the chapter footnotes, the interested reader might examine the following sources:

Amdahl, Lowell D.: "Architectural Questions of the Seventies," *Datamation,* January, 1970, pp. 66–68.

Diebold, John: "When Money Grows in Computers," *Columbia Journal of World Business,* November–December, 1967, pp. 39–46.

Head, Robert V.: "Obsolescence in Business Organization and Management," *Datamation,* January, 1969, pp. 29–33.

Whisler, Thomas L.: *Information Technology and Organizational Change,* Wadsworth Publishing Company, Inc., Belmont, Calif., 1970.

Withington, Frederic G.: "Trends in MIS Technology," *Datamation,* February, 1970, pp. 108–110ff.

Glossary

The communication of facts and ideas in the dynamic field of information processing is dependent on a mutual understanding of the technical terms used. Recognizing the need for a common information processing vocabulary, a Subcommittee of the American National Standards Committee, X3, on Computers and Information Processing, working under the Operating Procedures of the American National Standards Institute, Inc., prepared the "American National Standard Vocabulary for Information Processing." The Standards Institute approved and published this standard in 1970.[1] The abridged glossary of terms that follows has been excerpted from this most authoritative of sources. Those words that are printed in *italics* are defined elsewhere in this abridged vocabulary, and those definitions that are preceded by the symbol "SC1" are definitions that have been dis-

[1] This standard is a revision of the USA Standard X3.12-1966.

cussed and agreed upon at meetings of the International Organization for Standardization.

This material from "American National Standard Vocabulary for Information Processing," X3.12-1970, copyright 1970, has been reprinted by permission of the American National Standards Institute. Copies of the complete standard may be purchased from the American National Standards Institute at 1430 Broadway, New York, N.Y. 10018.

Absolute Address   (1) An *address* that is permanently assigned by the machine designer to a *storage location*. (2) A pattern of *characters* that identifies a unique storage location without further modification. (3) Synonymous with machine address, specific address.

Absolute Coding   Coding that uses *machine instructions* with *absolute addresses*. Synonymous with specific coding.

Absolute Error   (1) The amount of *error* expressed in the same units as the quantity containing the error. (2) Loosely, the absolute value of the error, i.e., the magnitude of the error without regard to its algebraic sign.

Abstract Symbol   In *optical character recognition*, a *symbol* whose form does not suggest its meaning and use; these should be defined for each specific *set* of applications.

Access   See *direct access, immediate access store, random access, remote access, serial access.*

Access Arm   A part of a *disc storage* unit that is used to hold one or more reading and writing *heads.*

Access Mode   In *COBOL,* a technique that is used to obtain a specific *logical record* from, or to place a specific logical record into, a *file* assigned to a *mass storage device.*

Access Time   (1) The time interval between the instant at which *data* are called for from a *storage device* and the instant delivery begins. (2) The time interval between the instant at which data are requested to be stored and the instant at which storage is started.

Accounting Machine   (1) A keyboard actuated machine that prepares accounting *records.* (2) A machine that *reads data* from external *storage* media, such as cards or tapes, and automatically produces accounting records or tabulations, usually on continuous forms.

Accumulator   A *register* in which the result of an arithmetic or logic *operation* is formed.

Accuracy The degree of freedom from *error,* that is, the degree of conformity to truth or to a rule. Accuracy is contrasted with precision. For example, four-place *numerals* are less precise than six-place numerals, nevertheless a properly computed four-place numeral might be more accurate than an improperly computed six-place numeral.

Accuracy Control Character A *control character* used to indicate whether the *data* with which it is associated are in *error,* are to be disregarded, or cannot be represented on a particular device. Synonymous with error control character.

Actual Key In *COBOL,* a *data item* that may be used as a *hardware address* and that expresses the location of a *record* on a *mass storage device.*

Adapting See *self-adapting.*

Adder (1) A device whose *output* is a representation of the sum of the quantities represented by its *inputs.* (2) See *half-adder.*

Adder-subtractor A device whose *output* is a representation of either the arithmetic sum or difference, or both, of the quantities represented by its *inputs.*

Address (1) An identification, as represented by a name, *label,* or number, for a *register,* location in *storage,* or any other *data* source or destination such as the location of a station in a communication network. (2) Loosely, any part of an *instruction* that specifies the location of an *operand* for the instruction. (3) See *absolute address, base address, content addressed storage, direct address, effective address, immediate address, indexed address, indirect address, instruction address, machine address, multiaddress, relative address, single address, symbolic address.*

Address Format (1) The arrangement of the *address parts* of an *instruction.* The expression "plus-one" is frequently used to indicate that one of the addresses specifies the location of the next instruction to be executed, such as one-plus-one, two-plus-one, three-plus-one, four-plus-one. (2) The arrangement of the parts of a *single address,* such as those required for identifying *channel, module, track,* etc. in a disc system.

Address Part A part of an *instruction word* that specifies the address of an *operand, instruction,* or *result.* Contrast with *instruction address.*

Address Register A *register* in which an *address* is *stored.*

ALGOL   ALGOrithmic Language. A *language* primarily used to express *computer programs* by *algorithms.*

Algorithm   (SC1) A prescribed set of well-defined rules or *processes* for the solution of a problem in a finite number of steps, e.g., a full statement of arithmetic procedure for evaluating sin *x* to a stated *precision.* Contrast with *heuristic.*

Algorithmic Language   A *language* designed for expressing *algorithms.*

Allocation   See *storage allocation, dynamic storage allocation.*

Alphabet   (1) An ordered set of all the *letters* and associated marks used in a *language.* (2) An ordered set of *symbols* used in a language, e.g., the Morse code alphabet, the 128 characters of the *ASCII* alphabet.

Alphabetic Code   (SC1) A *code* whose *code set* consists only of *letters* and associated *special characters.*

Alphabetic String   A *character string* consisting solely of *letters* from the same *alphabet.*

Alphabetic Word   (1) A *word* consisting solely of *letters.* (2) A word consisting of *characters* from the same *alphabet.*

Alphameric   Same as *alphanumeric.*

Alphanumeric   Pertaining to a *character set* that contains *letters, digits,* and usually other *characters* such as punctuation marks. Synonymous with alphameric.

Alphanumeric Character Set   A *character set* that contains *letters, digits,* and usually other *characters.*

Alphanumeric Code   (SC1) A *code* whose *code set* consists of *letters, digits,* and associated *special characters.*

Analog   (1) (SC1) Pertaining to representation by means of continuously variable physical quantities. (2) Contrast with *digital.*

Analog Computer   (1) (SC1) A *computer* in which *analog* representation of *data* is mainly used. (2) A computer that operates on analog data by performing physical processes on these data. Contrast with *digital computer.*

Analysis   (1) The methodical investigation of a problem, and the separation of the problem into smaller related units for further detailed study. (2) See *numerical analysis, operations analysis.*

Analyst   (SC1) A person who defines problems and develops *algorithms* and *procedures* for their solution.

Annotation   An added descriptive comment or explanatory note.

Argument   An independent variable. For example, in looking up a quantity in a *table,* the *number,* or any of the numbers, that identifies the *location* of the desired value.

Arithmetic Shift   (1) A *shift* that does not affect the *sign position.* (2) A *shift* that is equivalent to the multiplication of a *number* by a positive or negative integral power of the *radix.*

Arithmetic Unit   The unit of a computing system that contains the circuits that perform arithmetic *operations.*

Array   An arrangement of elements in one or more dimensions.

Artificial Intelligence   The capability of a device to perform functions that are normally associated with human intelligence, such as reasoning, learning, and self-improvement. Related to *machine learning.*

Artificial Language   A *language* based on a set of prescribed rules that are established prior to its usage. Contrast with *natural language.*

ASCII (American National Standard Code for Information Interchange, X3.4-1968)   The standard *code,* using a coded *character* set consisting of 7-bit coded characters (8 bits including *parity check*), used for information interchange among *data processing systems,* communication systems, and associated equipment. The ASCII set consists of *control characters* and *graphic characters.* Synonymous with USASCII.

Assemble   To prepare a *machine-language program* from a symbolic language program by substituting *absolute operation codes* for symbolic operation codes and *absolute* or relocatable addresses for *symbolic addresses.*

Assembler   A *computer program* that *assembles.*

Associative Storage   A *storage device* in which storage *locations* are identified by their contents, not by names or positions. Synonymous with content addressed storage. Contrast with *parallel search storage.*

Asynchronous Computer   (SC1) A *computer in which each event* or the performance of each *operation* starts as a result of a *signal* generated by the completion of the previous event or operation, or by the availability of the parts of the computer required for the next event or operation. Contrast with *synchronous computer.*

Automatic (SC1) Pertaining to a process or device that, under specified conditions, functions without intervention by a human operator.

Automatic Check A *check* performed by equipment built in specifically for checking purposes. Synonymous with built-in check, hardware check. Contrast with *programmed check*.

Automatic Coding The machine assisted preparation of *machine-language routines*.

Automatic Computer A *computer* that can perform a sequence of *operations* without intervention by a human *operator*.

Automatic Data Processing (1) (SC1) *Data processing* largely performed by *automatic* means. (2) (SC1) By extension, the discipline which deals with methods and techniques related to data processing performed by automatic means. (3) Pertaining to data processing equipment such as *electrical accounting machines* and *electronic data processing* equipment. Abbreviated ADP.

Automatic Programming The process of using a *computer* to perform some stages of the work involved in preparing a *computer program*.

Automation (1) (SC1) The implementation of processes by *automatic* means. (2) The theory, art, or technique of making a process more *automatic*. (3) The investigation, design, development, and application of methods of rendering processes *automatic,* self-moving, or self-controlling. (4) (SC1) The conversion of a procedure, a process, or equipment to *automatic* operation.

Auxiliary Operation An *offline operation* performed by equipment not under control of the *central processing unit*.

Auxiliary Storage (1) A *storage* that supplements another storage. Contrast with *main storage*. (2) In *flowcharting,* an *offline operation* performed by equipment not under control of the *central processing unit*.

Background Processing The *automatic* execution of lower priority *computer programs* when higher priority programs are not using the system resources. Contrast with *foreground processing*.

Backspace To move back the reading or display *position* according to a prescribed format. Contrast with *space* (4).

Band (1) A group of circular recording *tracks* on a *storage device* such as a drum or disk. (2) In communications, the frequency spectrum between two defined limits.

Bank See *data bank*.

Base (1) A reference value. (2) A *number* that is multiplied by itself as many times as indicated by an *exponent*. (3) Same as *radix*. (4) See *floating-point base*.

Base Address A given *address* from which an *absolute address* is derived by combination with a *relative address*.

Batch Processing (1) Pertaining to the technique of executing a set of *computer programs* such that each is completed before the next program of the set is started. (2) Pertaining to the sequential input of *computer programs* or *data*. (3) Loosely, the execution of *computer programs* serially.

Beginning-of-tape Marker A marker on a *magnetic tape* used to indicate the beginning of the permissible recording area, e.g., a photo reflective strip, a transparent section of tape.

Benchmark Problem A problem used to evaluate the performance of *hardware* or *software* or both.

Bias The amount by which the average of a set of values departs from a reference value.

Binary (1) Pertaining to a characteristic or property involving a selection, choice, or condition in which there are two possibilities. (2) Pertaining to the *number representation system* with a *radix* of two. (3) See *column binary, row binary*.

Binary Card A card containing *data* in *column binary* or *row binary* form.

Binary Cell A *storage cell* of one *binary digit* capacity, e.g., a single-bit re*gister*.

Binary Code A *code* that makes use of exactly two distinct characters, usually 0 and 1.

Binary-coded Decimal Notation *Positional notation* in which the individual *decimal digits* expressing a *number* in *decimal notation* are each represented by a *binary numeral,* e.g., the number 23 is represented by 0010 0011 in the 8-4-2-1 type of binary-coded decimal notation and by 10111 in *binary notation*. Abbreviated BCD.

Binary Digit (1) In *binary notation,* either of the characters 0 or 1. (2) *Abbreviated bit*.

Binary Notation *Fixed radix notation* where the *radix* is two. For example, in *binary notation* the *numeral* 110.01 represents the number 1 × 2 squared plus 1 ×2 to the first power plus 1 × 2 to the minus 2 power, that is, $6\frac{1}{4}$.

Binary Number Loosely, a *binary numeral.*

Binary Numeral A *binary* representation of a *number,* e.g., "101" is a binary numeral and a "V" is the equivalent Roman numeral.

Binary Search A *dichotomizing search* in which the number of items of the set is divided into two equal parts at each step of the process. Appropriate adjustments are usually made for dividing an odd number of items.

Bionics A branch of technology relating the functions, characteristics, and phenomena of living systems to the development of *hardware* systems.

Bistable Pertaining to a device capable of assuming either one of two stable states.

Bit (1) A *binary digit.* (2) Same as Shannon. (3) See *check bit, information bits, parity bit, sign bit.*

Bit String A *string* of *binary digits* in which the position of each *binary digit* is considered as an independent unit.

Blank A part of a *medium* in which no *characters* are recorded.

Block (1) A set of things, such as *words, characters,* or *digits* handled as a unit. (2) A collection of contiguous *records* recorded as a unit. Blocks are separated by *block gaps* and each block may contain one or more records. (3) A group of bits, or n-ary digits, *transmitted* as a unit. An encoding procedure is generally applied to the group of bits or n-ary digits for error-control purposes. (4) A group of contiguous characters recorded as a unit.

Block Diagram A diagram of a *system,* instrument, or *computer* in which the principal parts are represented by suitably associated geometrical figures to show both the basic functions and the functional relationships among the parts. Contrast with *flowchart.*

Block Gap An area on a *data medium* used to indicate the end of a *block* or *record.* Synonymous with interblock gap.

Block Length A measure of the size of a *block,* usually specified in units such as *records, words, computer words,* or *characters.*

Block Transfer   The process of *transmitting* one or more *blocks* of *data* where the data are organized in such blocks.

Boolean   (1) Pertaining to the *processes* used in the algebra formulated by George Boole. (2) Pertaining to the operations of *formal logic*.

Bootstrap   A technique or device designed to bring itself into a desired state by means of its own action, e.g., a machine *routine* whose first few *instructions* are sufficient to bring the rest of itself into the computer from an *input device*. Contrast with *initial program loader (IPL)*.

Branch   (1) A set of *instructions* that are executed between two successive *decision instructions*. (2) To select a branch as in (1). (3) A direct path joining two *nodes* of a network or graph. (4) Loosely, a *conditional jump*.

Branchpoint   A place in a *routine* where a *branch* is selected.

Breakpoint   A place in a *routine* specified by an *instruction,* instruction digit, or other condition, where the routine may be interrupted by external intervention or by a *monitor* routine.

Buffer   (1) A *routine* or *storage* used to compensate for a difference in rate of flow of *data* or time of occurrence of events when transmitting data from one device to another. (2) An isolating circuit used to prevent a driven circuit from influencing the driving circuit.

Bug   A *mistake* or *malfunction*.

Built-in Check   Same as *automatic check*.

Burst   (1) To separate continuous-form paper into discrete sheets. (2) In data transmission, a sequence of *signals* counted as one unit in accordance with some specific criterion or measure.

Bus   One or more conductors used for transmitting *signals* or power.

Business Data Processing   (1) (SC1) Use of *automatic data processing* in accounting or management. (2) *Data processing* for business purposes, e.g., recording and summarizing the financial transactions of a business. (3) Synonymous with administrative data processing.

Byte   A sequence of adjacent *binary digits* operated upon as a unit and usually shorter than a *computer word*.

Calculator   (1) (SC1) A *data processor* especially suitable for performing arithmetical *operations* which requires frequent intervention by a human *operator*. (2) Generally and historically, a device for carrying out logic and arithmetic digital operations of any kind.

Call   (1) To transfer control to a specified *closed subroutine*. (2) In communications, the action performed by the calling party, or the operations necessary in making a call, or the effective use made of a connection between two stations. (3) Synonymous with cue. (4) See *subroutine call*.

Calling Sequence   A specified arrangement of *instructions* and *data* necessary to set up and call a given *subroutine*.

Card Column   A single line of *punch positions* parallel to the short edge of a $3\frac{1}{4}$- by $7\frac{3}{8}$-inch *punched card*.

Card Hopper   The portion of a card processing machine that holds the cards to be processed and makes them available to a card feed mechanism. Contrast with *card stacker*.

Card Row   A single line of *punch positions* parallel to the long edge of a $3\frac{1}{4}$- by $7\frac{3}{8}$-inch *punched card*.

Card Stacker   The portion of a card processing machine that receives processed cards. Contrast with *card hopper*.

Carriage Return   The operation that prepares for the next *character* to be printed or displayed at the specified first position on the same line.

Central Processing Unit   (SCI) A unit of a *computer* that includes the circuits controlling the interpretation and execution of *instructions*. Synonymous with main frame. Abbreviated CPU.

Central Processor   A *central processing unit*.

Chad   The piece of material removed when forming a hole or notch in a *storage medium* such as *punched tape* or *punched cards*. Synonymous with chip.

Chained List   A *list* in which the *items* may be dispersed but in which each item contains an *identifier* for locating the next item to be considered.

Chaining Search   A *search* technique in which each *item* contains an identifier for locating the next item to be considered.

Chain Printer   A printer in which the type slugs are carried by the links of a revolving chain.

Channel   (1) A path along which *signals* can be sent, e.g., *data* channel, *output* channel. (2) The portion of a *storage medium* that is accessible to a given reading or writing station, e.g., *track, band*. (3)

In communication, a means of one way transmission. Several channels may share common equipment. For example, in frequency multi-plexing carrier systems, each channel uses a particular frequency band that is reserved for it. Contrast with *circuit*. (4) See *input channel, output channel*.

Character (1) A *letter, digit,* or other *symbol* that is used as part of the organization, control, or representation of *data*. A character is often in the form of a spatial arrangement of adjacent or connected strokes. (2) See *accuracy control character, check character, control character, graphic character, illegal character, numeric character, print control character, special character*.

Character Printer A device that prints a single *character* at a time. Contrast with *line printer*.

Character Recognition The identification of graphic, phonic, or other *characters* by *automatic* means. See *magnetic ink character recognition, optical character recognition*.

Character Set A set of unique representations called *characters,* e.g., the 26 *letters* of the English *alphabet,* 0 and 1 of the Boolean alphabet, the set of signals in the Morse code alphabet, the 128 characters of the *ASCII* alphabet.

Character String A *string* consisting solely of *characters*.

Check (1) A *process* for determining *accuracy*. (2) See *automatic check, built-in check, duplication check, echo check, hardware check, parity check, programmed check*.

Check Bit A *binary check digit,* e.g., a *parity bit*.

Check Character A *character* used for the purpose of performing a *check*.

Checkpoint A place in a *routine* where a *check,* or a recording of *data* for *restart* purposes, is performed.

Circuit In communications, a means of two-way communication between two points, comprising associated "go" and "return" *channels*. Contrast with *channel*.

Clear To place one or more *storage* locations into a prescribed state, usually zero or the space character. Contrast with *set*.

Clock (1) A device that generates periodic *signals* used for synchronization. (2) A device that measures and indicates time. (3) A *register* whose content changes at regular intervals in such a way as to measure time.

Closed Shop   Pertaining to the operation of a *computer* facility in which most productive problem *programming* is performed by a group of programming specialists rather than the problem originators. The use of the computer itself may also be described as closed shop if full-time trained *operators* rather than user-programmers serve as the operators. Contrast with *open shop*.

Closed Subroutine   A *subroutine* that can be stored at one place and can be linked to one or more calling *routines*. Contrast with *open subroutine*.

Coalesce   To combine two or more *files* into one file.

COBOL   (COmmon Business Oriented Language) A *business data processing* language.

Code   (1) (SC1) A set of unambiguous rules specifying the way in which *data* may be represented, e.g., the set of correspondences in the standard code for information interchange. Synonymous with coding scheme. (2) (SC1) In telecommunications, a system of rules and conventions according to which the *signals* representing *data* can be formed, transmitted, received, and processed. (3) (SC1) In *data processing*, to represent data or a *computer program* in a symbolic form that can be accepted by a *data processor*. (4) To write a *routine*. (5) Same as *code set*. (6) Same as *encode*. (7) A *set of items*, such as abbreviations, representing the members of another set. (8) Same as *code value*. (9) See *alphabet code, alphanumeric code, binary code, computer code, excess three code, gray code, hamming code, instruction code, machine code, numeric code, object code, operation code*.

Coder   (SC1) A person mainly involved in writing but not designing *computer programs*.

Code Set   (SC1) The complete set of representations defined by a *code*, e.g., all of the three-letter international identifications for airports. Synonymous with code (5).

Code Value   (SC1) One element of a *code set*, e.g., the eight-binary digit code value for the delete character. Synonymous with code (8).

Collate   To combine *items* from two or more ordered sets into one set having a specified order not necessarily the same as any of the original sets. Contrast with *merge*.

Collating Sequence   An ordering assigned to a set of *items* such that any two sets in that assigned order can be *collated*.

Collator   A device to *collate, merge,* or *match* sets of *punched cards* or other *documents.*

Column   (1) A vertical arrangement of *characters* or other expressions. (2) Loosely, a *digit place.*

Column Binary   Pertaining to the *binary* representation of *data* on cards in which the *significances* of *punch positions* are assigned along *card columns.* For example, each column in a 12-row card may be used to represent 12 consecutive *bits.* Synonymous with Chinese binary. Contrast with *row binary.*

Command   (1) A control *signal.* (2) Loosely, an *instruction* in *machine language.* (3) Loosely, a mathematical or logic *operator.*

Communication Link   The physical means of connecting one location to another for the purpose of transmitting and receiving *data.*

Compile   To prepare a *machine-language* program from a *computer program* written in another *programming language* by making use of the overall logic structure of the program, or generating more than one *machine instruction* for each symbolic *statement,* or both, as well as performing the function of an *assembler.*

Compiler   A program that *compiles.*

Complement   A *number* that can be derived from a specified number by subtracting it from a second specified number. For example, in *radix notation,* the second specified number may be a given power of the *radix* or one less than a given power of the radix. The negative of a number is often represented by its complement.

Computer   (1) (SC1) A *data processor* that can perform substantial computation, including numerous arithmetic or logic operations, without intervention by a human *operator* during the *run.* (2) See *analog computer, asynchronous computer, automatic computer, consecutive sequence computer, digital computer, general purpose computer, hybrid computer, parallel computer, sequential computer, serial computer, special purpose computer, stored program computer, synchronous computer.*

Computer Code   A *machine* code for a specific *computer.*

Computer Instruction   A *machine instruction* for a specific *computer.*

Computer Network   A complex consisting of two or more inter-connected *computers.*

Computer Program   A series of *instructions* or *statements,* in a form acceptable to a *computer,* prepared in order to achieve a certain result.

Computer Word   A sequence of *bits* or *characters* treated as a unit and capable of being *stored* in one *computer location*. Synonymous with machine word.

Concurrent   Pertaining to the occurrence of two or more *events* or activities within the same specified interval of time. Contrast with *consecutive, sequential, simultaneous.*

Conditional Jump   A *jump* that occurs if specified criteria are met.

Connector   (1) (SC1) On a *flowchart,* the means of representing the convergence of more than one *flowline* into one, or the divergence of one flowline into more than one. It may also represent a break in a single flowline for continuation in another area. (2) A means of representing on a *flowchart* a break in a line of flow. (3) See *inconnector, outconnector.*

Consecutive   Pertaining to the occurrence of two *sequential* events without the intervention of any other such event. Contrast with *concurrent, sequential, simultaneous.*

Consecutive Sequence Computer   (SC1) A *computer* in which *instructions* are executed in an implicitly defined sequence unless explicitly specified by a *jump instruction.*

Console   That part of a *computer* used for communication between the *operator* or *maintenance* engineer and the computer.

Content Addressed Storage   Same as *associative storage.*

Control   See *numerical control, sequential control.*

Control Character   (1) A *character* whose occurrence in a particular context initiates, modifies, or stops a *control operation,* e.g., a character that controls *carriage return,* a character that controls transmission of *data* over communication networks. A control character may be recorded for use in a subsequent action. It may in some circumstances have a graphic representation. Contrast with *graphic character.* (2) See *accuracy control character, print control character.*

Control Panel   (1) A part of a *computer console* that contains manual controls. (2) Same as *plugboard.*

Copy   To reproduce *data* in a new location or other destination, leaving the source data unchanged, although the physical form of the result may differ from that of the source. For example, to copy a deck of cards onto a *magnetic tape.* Contrast with *duplicate.*

Core   See *magnetic core.*

Counter (1) A device such as a *register* or *storage* location used to represent the number of occurrences of an event. (2) See *instruction counter.*

Crosstalk The unwanted energy transferred from one *circuit,* called the "disturbing" circuit, to another circuit, called the "disturbed" circuit.

Cryogenics The study and use of devices utilizing properties of materials near absolute zero in temperature.

Cue Same as *call.*

Cybernetics (SC1) That branch of learning which brings together theories and studies on communication and control in living organisms and machines.

Cycle (1) An interval of space or time in which one *set* of *events* or phenomena is completed. (2) Any set of *operations* that is repeated regularly in the same *sequence.* The operations may be subject to variations on each repetition. (3) See *search cycle.*

Data (1) (SC1) A representation of facts, concepts, or *instructions* in a formalized manner suitable for communication, interpretation, or processing by humans or automatic means. (2) Any representations such as *characters* or *analog* quantities to which meaning is or might be assigned.

Data Bank A comprehensive collection of *libraries* of data. For example, one line of an invoice may form an *item,* a complete invoice may form a *record,* a complete *set* of such records may form a *file,* the collection of inventory control files may form a *library,* and the libraries used by an organization are known as its data bank.

Data Flowchart (SC1) A *flowchart* representing the path of *data* through a problem solution. It defines the major phases of the *processing* as well as the various *data media* used. Synonymous with data flow diagram.

Data Hierarchy A *data* structure consisting of *sets* and subsets such that every subset of a set is of lower rank than the data of the set.

Data Medium (1) (SC1) The material in or on which a specific physical variable may represent *data.* (2) (SC1) The physical quantity which may be varied to represent *data.*

Data Processing (SC1) The execution of a systematic sequence of *operations* performed upon *data.* Synonymous with information processing.

Data Processor (SC1) A device capable of performing *data processing,* including desk *calculators, punched card* machines, and *computers.* Synonymous with *processor* (1).

Data Reduction The transformation of raw *data* into a more useful form, e.g., *smoothing* to reduce *noise.*

Debug To detect, locate, and remove *mistakes* from a *routine* or *malfunctions* from a *computer.* Synonymous with troubleshoot.

Decimal (1) Pertaining to a characteristic or property involving a selection, choice, or condition in which there are 10 possibilities. (2) Pertaining to the *number representation system* with a *radix* of 10. (3) See *binary-coded decimal notation.*

Decimal Digit In *decimal notation,* one of the *characters* 0 to 9.

Decimal Notation A *fixed radix notation* where the *radix* is 10. For example, in decimal notation, the *numeral* 576.2 represents the *number* 5×10 squared plus 7×10 to the first power plus 6×10 to the zero power plus 2×10 to the minus 1 power.

Decimal Numeral A *decimal* representation of a *number.*

Decimal Point The *radix point* in *decimal* representation.

Decision A determination of future action.

Decision Instruction An *instruction* that effects the selection of a *branch* of a program, e.g., a *conditional jump instruction.*

Decision Table A *table* of all contingencies that are to be considered in the description of a problem, together with the actions to be taken. Decision tables are sometimes used in place of *flowcharts* for problem description and documentation.

Deck (1) A collection of *punched cards.* Synonymous with card deck. (2) See *tape deck.*

Decode To apply a set of unambiguous rules specifying the way in which *data* may be restored to a previous representation, i.e., to reverse some previous *encoding.*

Decoder (1) A device that *decodes.* (2) A *matrix* of *logic elements* that selects one or more *output channels* according to the combination of *input signals* present. (3) See *operation decoder.*

Density See *packing density, recording density.*

Descriptor In *information retrieval,* a *word* used to categorize or index *information.* Synonymous with keyword.

Destructive Read   A *read* process that also *erases* the *data* from the source.

Detail File   Same as *transaction file.*

Diagnostic   Pertaining to the detection and isolation of a *malfunction* or *mistake.*

Dichotomizing Search   A *search* in which an ordered *set* of *items* is divided into two parts, one of which is rejected, and the process is repeated on the accepted part until the items with the desired property are found.

Digit   (1) A *symbol* that represents one of the nonnegative integers smaller than the radix. For example, in *decimal notation,* a digit is one of the *characters* from 0 to 9. Synonymous with numeric character. (2) See *binary digit, decimal digit, sign digit, significant digit.*

Digital   (1) (SC1) Pertaining to *data* in the form of *digits.* (2) Contrast with *analog.*

Digital Computer   (1) (SC1) A *computer* in which *discrete* representation of *data* is mainly used. (2) A *computer* that operates on *discrete data* by performing arithmetic and logic processes on these data. Contrast with *analog computer.*

Digit Place   In *positional notation,* the site where a *symbol* such as a *digit* is located in a *word* representing a *number.* Synonymous with symbol rank.

Digit Punch   A punch in rows 1, 2, . . . , 9 of a *punched card.*

Direct Access   (1) Pertaining to the process of obtaining *data* from, or placing data into, *storage* where the time required for such access is independent of the *location* of the data most recently obtained or placed in storage. (2) Pertaining to a *storage* device in which the *access time* is effectively independent of the location of the *data.* (3) Synonymous with random access (1). (4) Contrast with *serial access.*

Direct Address   An *address* that specifies the location of an *operand.* Synonymous with one-level address. Contrast with *indirect address.*

Disc   Alternate spelling for *disk.* See *magnetic disc.*

Discrete   (SC1) Pertaining to distinct elements or to representation by means of distinct elements such as *characters.*

Disk   Alternate spelling for *disc.* See *magnetic disc.*

Display   A visual presentation of *data.*

Document (1) A *medium* and the *data* recorded on it for human use, e.g., a report sheet, a book. (2) By extension, any *record* that has permanence and that can be read by man or machine.

Documentation (1) The creating, collecting, organizing, storing, citing, and disseminating of *documents* or the *information* recorded in documents. (2) A collection of *documents* or *information* on a given subject.

Double Precision Pertaining to the use of two *computer words* to represent a *number*.

Downtime The time interval during which a device is *malfunctioning*.

Drop Out (1) In *magnetic tape,* a recorded signal whose amplitude is less than a predetermined percentage of a reference signal. (2) In *data* transmission, a momentary loss in *signal,* usually due to the effect of *noise* or *system malfunction.*

Dump (1) To copy the contents of all or part of a *storage,* usually from an internal storage into an external storage. (2) A process as in (1). (3) The *data* resulting from the process as in (1). (4) See *dynamic dump, postmortem dump, selective dump, snapshot dump, static dump.*

Duodecimal (1) Pertaining to a characteristic or property involving a selection, choice, or condition in which there are 12 possibilities. (2) Pertaining to the *numeration system* with a *radix* of 12.

Duplex In communications, pertaining to a simultaneous two way independent *transmission* in both directions. Contrast with *half duplex.* Synonymous with full duplex.

Duplicate To *copy* so that the result remains in the same physical form as the source, e.g., to make a new *punched card* with the same pattern of holes as an original punched card. Contrast with *copy.*

Duplication Check A *check* based on the consistency of two independent performances of the same task.

Dynamic Dump A *dump* that is performed during the execution of a *computer program.*

Dynamic Storage Allocation A *storage allocation* technique in which the location of *computer programs* and *data* is determined by criteria applied at the moment of need.

Echo Check A method of checking the *accuracy* of *transmission* of *data* in which the received data are returned to the sending end for comparison with the original data.

Edit   To modify the form or *format* of *data,* e.g., to insert or delete *characters* such as page numbers or decimal points.

Effective Address   The *address* that is derived by applying any specified *indexing* or indirect *addressing* rules to the specified address and that is actually used to identify the current *operand.*

Electrical Accounting Machine   Pertaining to *data processing* equipment that is predominantly electromechanial such as a keypunch, mechanical *sorter, collator,* and *tabulator.* Abbreviated EAM.

Electronic Data Processing   (1) (SC1) *Data processing* largely performed by electronic devices. (2) Pertaining to *data processing* equipment that is predominantly electronic such as an electronic *digital computer.* Abbreviated EDP.

Eleven Punch   A punch in the second *row* from the top, on a *Hollerith punched card.* Synonymous with x punch.

Emulate   To imitate one *system* with another such that the imitating system accepts the same *data,* executes the same *programs,* and achieves the same results as the imitated system. Contrast with *simulate.*

Emulator   A device or *computer program* that *emulates.*

End-around Carry   A carry from the most significant *digit place* to the least significant digit place.

End-of-tape Marker   A marker on a *magnetic tape* used to indicate the end of the permissible recording area, e.g., a photoreflective strip, a transparent section of tape, a particular bit pattern.

Entry Point   In a *routine,* any place to which control can be passed.

Erase   To obliterate *information* from a *storage medium,* e.g., to clear, to overwrite.

Error   (1) Any discrepancy between a computed, observed, or measured quantity and the true, specified, or theoretically correct value or condition. (2) See *absolute error, inherited error, rounding error, truncation error.* (3) Contrast with *fault, malfunction, and mistake.*

Error Ratio   The ratio of the number of *data* units in *error* to the total number of data units.

Event   An occurrence or happening.

Excess Three Code   A *binary coded decimal notation* in which each *decimal digit* N is represented by the *binary numeral* of N plus three.

Executive Routine   A *routine* that controls the execution of other routines. Synonymous with supervisory routine.

Exponent   In a *floating point representation,* the *numeral,* of a pair of numerals representing a *number,* that indicates the power to which the *base* is raised.

Fault   (1) A physical condition that causes a device, a component, or an element to fail to perform in a required manner, e.g., a short circuit, a broken wire, an intermittent connection. (2) Contrast with *error, malfunction, mistake.*

Feedback Loop   The components and processes involved in correcting or controlling a system by using part of the *output* as *input.*

Feedback System   See *information feedback system.*

Fetch   To locate and *load* a quantity of *data* from *storage.*

Field   In a *record,* a specified area used for a particular category of *data*, e.g., a group of card columns used to represent a wage rate, a set of *bit* locations in a *computer word* used to express the *address* of the *operand.*

File   (1) A collection of related *records* treated as a unit. For example, one line of an invoice may form an *item,* a complete invoice may form a *record,* the complete set of such records may form a file, the collection of inventory control files may form a *library,* and the libraries used by an organization are known as its *data bank.* (2) See *detail file, logical file, master file, transaction file.*

File Gap   An area on a *data medium* intended to be used to indicate the end of a *file* and possibly the start of another. A file gap is frequently used for other purposes, in particular, as a *flag* to indicate the end or beginning of some other group of data.

File Layout   The arrangement and structure of *data* in a *file,* including the *sequence* and size of its components. By extension, a file layout might be the description thereof.

File Maintenance   The activity of keeping a *file* up to date by adding, changing, or deleting *data.*

Fixed-cycle Operation   An *operation* that is completed in a specified number of regularly timed execution cycles.

Fixed-point Part   In a *floating-point representation,* the *numeral* of a pair of numerals representing a *number,* that is the fixed-point factor by which the power is multiplied.

Fixed-point Representation   A *positional representation* in which each *number* is represented by a single set of *digits,* the position of the *radix point* being fixed with respect to one end of the set, according to some convention.

Fixed Radix Notation   A *positional representation* in which the significances of successive *digit* positions are successive integral powers of a single *radix.* When the radix is positive, permissible values of each digit range from zero to one less than the radix and negative integral powers of the radix are used to represent fractions.

Fixed Storage   *Storage* whose contents are not alterable by *computer instructions,* e.g., *magnetic core* storage with a lockout feature, photographic disc. Synonymous with nonerasable storage, permanent storage, read-only storage.

Flag   (1) Any of various types of indicators used for identification, e.g., a wordmark. (2) A *character* that signals the occurrence of some condition, such as the end of a *word.* (3) Synonymous with mark, sentinel, tag.

Flip-flop   A *circuit* or device containing active elements, capable of assuming either one of two stable states at a given time. Synonymous with toggle (1).

Floating-point Base   In *floating-point representation,* the fixed positive integer that is the *base* of the power. Synonymous with floating-point radix.

Floating-point Representation   A *number representation system* in which each *number,* as represented by a pair of *numerals,* equals one of those numerals times a power of an implicit fixed positive-integer *base* where the power is equal to the implicit base raised to the *exponent* represented by the other numeral.

Common Notation
0.0001234 or (0.1234) $\times$ (10^{-3})

A Floating-point Representation
1234 -03

Contrast with *variable-point representation.*

Flowchart   (1) (SC1) A graphical representation for the definition, analysis, or solution of a problem, in which *symbols* are used to represent *operations, data,* flow, equipment, etc., Contrast with *block diagram.* (2) See *data flowchart, programming flowchart.*

Flowchart Symbol   (SC1) A *symbol* used to represent *operations, data,* flow, or equipment on a *flowchart.*

Flowchart Text   The descriptive information that is associated with *flowchart symbols.*

Flow Direction   (SC1) In *flowcharting,* the antecedent-to-successor relation, indicated by arrows or other conventions, between *operations* on a *flowchart.*

Flying Spot Scanner   In *optical character recognition,* a device employing a moving spot of light to scan a sample space, the intensity of the transmitted or reflected light being sensed by a photoelectric transducer.

Font   (1) A family or assortment of *characters* of a given size and style, e.g., 9-point Bodoni Modern. (2) See *type font.*

Foreground Processing   The *automatic* execution of the *computer programs* that have been designed to preempt the use of the computing facilities. Usually a *real time* program. Contrast with *background processing.*

Formal Logic   The study of the structure and form of valid argument without regard to the meaning of the terms in the argument.

Format   (1) The arrangement of *data.* (2) See *address format.*

FORTRAN   (FORmula TRANslating system) A *language* primarily used to express *computer programs* by arithmetic formulas.

Frame   (1) An area, one recording position long, extending across the width of a magnetic or paper tape perpendicular to its movement. Several *bits* or *punch positions* may be included in a single frame through the use of different recording positions across the width of the tape. (2) See *main frame.*

Function   (1) A specific purpose of an entity, or its characteristic action. (2) In communications, a machine action such as a *carriage return* or *line feed.*

Function Table   (1) Two or more *sets* of *data* so arranged that an entry in one set selects one or more entries in the remaining sets, e.g., a tabulation of the values of a function for a set of values of the variable, a dictionary. (2) A device constructed of *hardware,* or a *subroutine,* which can either *decode* multiple *inputs* into a single *output* or *encode* a single input into multiple outputs.

Functional Design   The specification of the working relations between the parts of a *system* in terms of their characteristic actions.

Functional Diagram   A diagram that represents the functional relationship among the parts of a *system.*

General Purpose Computer   (SC1) A *computer* that is designed to handle a wide variety of problems.

Generate   To produce a *program* by selection of subsets from a *set* of *skeletal coding* under the control of parameters.

Generator   A controlling *routine* that performs a *generate* function, e.g., report generator, *I/O* generator.

Graphic   A *symbol* produced by a process such as handwriting, drawing, or printing.

Graphic Character   A *character* normally represented by a *graphic.* Contrast with *control character.*

Gray Code   A *binary code* in which *sequential* numbers are represented by *binary* expressions, each of which differs from the preceding expression in one place only. Synonymous with reflected binary code.

Group Mark   A mark that identifies the beginning or end of a set of *data,* which could include *words, blocks,* or other *items.*

Half-Adder   A combinational *logic element* having two *outputs,* S and C, and two *inputs,* A and B, such that the outputs are related to the inputs according to the following table.

Input		Output	
A	B	C	S
0	0	0	0
0	1	0	1
1	0	0	1
1	1	1	0

S denotes "Sum Without Carry," C denotes "Carry." Two half-adders may be used for performing *binary addition.*

Half Duplex   In communications, pertaining to an alternate, one way at a time, independent transmission. Contrast with *duplex.*

Halfword   A contiguous sequence of *bits* or *characters* that comprises half a *computer word* and is capable of being addressed as a unit.

Hamming Code   A *data code* that is capable of being corrected *automatically.*

Hardware   (SC1) Physical equipment, as opposed to the *computer program* or method of use, e.g., mechanical, magnetic, electrical, or electronic devices. Contrast with *software.*

Hardware Check   Same as *automatic check.*

Head   A device that *reads, writes,* or *erases data* on a storage *medium,* e.g., a small electromagnet used to read, write, or erase data on a *magnetic drum* or *tape,* or the set of perforating, reading, or marking devices used for punching, reading, or printing on paper tape.

Header Card   A card that contains *information* related to the *data* in cards that follow.

Heuristic   Pertaining to exploratory methods of problem solving in which solutions are discovered by evaluation of the progress made toward the final result. Contrast with *algorithm.*

Hexadecimal   Same as *sexadecimal.*

Hit   A successful comparison of two *items* of *data.* Contrast with *match.*

Hollerith   Pertaining to a particular type of *code* or *punched card* utilizing 12 *rows* per *column* and usually 80 columns per card.

Hybrid Computer   (SC1) A *computer* for *data processing* using both *analog* representation and *discrete* representation of *data.*

Identifier   A *symbol* whose purpose is to identify, indicate, or name a body of *data.*

Illegal Character   A *character* or combination of *bits* that is not valid according to some criteria, e.g., with respect to a specified *alphabet* a character that is not a member.

Immediate Access Store   A *store* whose *access time* is negligible in comparison with other *operating times.*

Immediate Address   Pertaining to an *instruction* in which an *address part* contains the value of an *operand* rather than its *address.* Synonymous with zero-level address.

Inclusion   A logic *operator* having the property that if P is a statement and Q is a statement, then P inclusion Q is false if P is true and Q is false, true if P is false, and true if both statements are true. P inclusion Q is often represented by $P > Q$. Synonymous with IF-THEN, implication.

Inconnector   In *flowcharting,* a connector that indicates a continuation of a broken *flowline*. Contrast with *outconnector*.

Incremental Representation   (SC1) A method of representing a *variable* in which changes in the values of the variable are represented, rather than the values themselves.

Index   (1) An ordered reference list of the contents of a *file* or *document* together with *keys* or reference notations for identification or location of those contents. (2) To prepare a list as in (1). (3) A *symbol* or a *numeral* used to identify a particular quantity in an *array* of similar quantities. For example, the terms of an array represented by X_1, $X_2, \ldots , X_{100}$ have the indexes $1, 2, \ldots , 100$ respectively. (4) To move a machine part to a predetermined position, or by a predetermined amount, on a *quantized* scale. (5) See *index register*.

Index Register   A *register* whose content may be added to or subtracted from the *operand address* prior to or during the execution of a *computer instruction*. Synonymous with b box.

Indexed Address   An *address* that is modified by the content of an *index register* prior to or during the execution of a *computer instruction*.

Indirect Address   An *address* that specifies a *storage* location that contains either a *direct address* or another indirect address. Synonymous with multilevel address. Contrast with *direct address*.

Information   (SC1) The meaning that a human assigns to *data* by means of the known conventions used in their representation.

Information Bits   In *telecommunications,* those *bits* that are generated by the *data source* and that are not used for error control by the *data transmission* system.

Information Feedback System   In *telecommunications,* an *information transmission* system that uses an *echo check* to verify the *accuracy* of the transmission.

Information Processing   (SC1) Same as *data processing*.

Information Retrieval   (SC1) The methods and *procedures* for recovering specific *information* from stored *data*.

Information Theory   The branch of learning concerned with the likelihood of accurate *transmission* or communication of *messages* subject to transmission failure, distortion, and *noise.*

Inherited Error   An *error* carried forward from a previous step in a *sequential* process.

Inhibiting Signal   A *signal* that prevents an *operation* from taking place.

Initial Program Loader   The procedure that causes the initial part of an *operating system* or other *program* to be loaded such that the program can then proceed under its own control. Contrast with *bootstrap.* Abbreviated IPL.

Initialize   To set *counters, switches,* and *addresses* to zero or other starting values at the beginning of or at prescribed points in a computer *routine.* Synonymous with prestore.

Input   (1) Pertaining to a device, process, or *channel* involved in the insertion of *data* or states, or to the data or states involved. (2) One, or a sequence of, *input states.* (3) Same as *input device.* (4) Same as *input channel.* (5) Same as *input process.* (6) Same as *input data.* (7) See *real time input.*

Input Area   An area of *storage* reserved for *input.* Synonymous with input block.

Input Channel   A *channel* for impressing a state on a device or *logic element.* Synonymous with input (4).

Input Data   *Data* to be processed. Synonymous with input (6).

Input Device   The device or collective set of devices used for conveying *data* into another device. Synonymous with input (3).

Input/Output   Pertaining to either *input* or *output,* or both.

Input Process   (1) The process of receiving *data* by a device. (2) The process of transmitting data from *peripheral equipment,* or external *storage,* to internal storage. (3) Synonymous with input (5).

Input State   The state occurring on a specified *input channel.*

Inquiry Station   *Data* terminal equipment used for inquiry into a *data processing* system.

Installation Time   Time spent in installing and testing either hardware or software, or both, until they are accepted.

Instruction   (1) A *statement* that specifies an *operation* and the values or locations of its *operands*. (2) See *computer instruction, decision instruction, logic instruction, machine instruction, macro instruction, repetition instruction*.

Instruction Address   The *address* that must be used to *fetch* an *instruction*. Contrast with *address part*.

Instruction Code   Same as *operation code*.

Instruction Control Unit   In a *digital computer,* those parts that effect the retrieval of *instructions* in proper *sequence,* the interpretation of each instruction, and the application of the proper *signals* to the *arithmetic unit* and other parts in accordance with this interpretation.

Instruction Counter   A *counter* that indicates the *location* of the next *computer instruction* to be interpreted.

Instruction Register   A *register* that stores an *instruction* for execution.

Instruction Repertoire   The set of *operations* that can be represented in a given *operation code*.

Integrated Data Processing   (SC1) *Data processing* in which the coordination of *data* acquisition and all other stages of data processing is achieved in a coherent system, e.g., a *business data processing* system in which data for orders and buying are combined to accomplish the functions of scheduling, invoicing, and accounting. Abbreviated IDP.

Interblock Gap   Same as *block gap*.

Interface   A shared boundary. An interface might be a *hardware* component to link two devices or it might be a portion of *storage* or *registers accessed* by two or more *computer programs*.

Interleave   To arrange parts of one *sequence* of things or events so that they alternate with parts of one or more other sequences of things or events and so that each sequence retains its identity, e.g., to organize *storage* into banks with independent *busses* so that sequential *data* references may be overlapped in a given period of time.

Internal Storage   Addressable *storage* directly controlled by the *central processing unit* of a *digital computer*.

Interpreter   (1) A *computer program* that *translates* and executes each *source-language* statement before translating and executing the next one. (2) A device that prints on a *punched card* the *data* already punched in the card.

Interrecord Gap   Same as *record gap*.

Interrupt   To stop a *process* in such a way that it can be resumed.

ISO   International Organization for Standardization.

Item   (1) In general, one member of a group, e.g., a *record* may contain a number of items such as *fields* or groups of fields; a *file* may consist of a number of items such as records; a *table* may consist of a number of items such as entries. (2) A collection of related *characters* treated as a unit.

Job   A specified group of tasks prescribed as a unit of work for a *computer*. By extension, a job usually includes all necessary *computer programs, linkages, files,* and *instructions* to the *operating system*.

Job Control Statement   A *statement* in a *job* that is used in identifying the job or describing its requirements to the *operating system*.

Jump   (1) A departure from the normal sequence of executing *instructions* in a *computer*. Synonymous with *transfer* (1). (2) See *conditional jump*.

Justify   (1) To adjust the printing positions of *characters* on a page so that the lines have the desired length and that both the left- and right-hand margins are regular. (2) By extension, to *shift* the contents of a *register* so that the most or the least significant *digit* is at some specified position in the register. Contrast with *normalize*. (3) See *left-justify, right-justify*.

K   (1) An abbreviation for the prefix kilo, that is 1,000 in decimal notation. (2) Loosely, when referring to storage capacity, 2 to the tenth power, 1,024 in *decimal notation*.

Key   (1) One or more *characters* within an *item* of *data* that are used to identify it or control its use. (2) See *actual key, search key*.

Keypunch   A keyboard actuated device that punches holes in a card to represent *data*.

Label   One or more *characters* used to identify a *statement* or an *item* of *data* in a *computer program*.

Language   (1) A set of representations, conventions, and rules used to convey *information*. (2) See *algorithmic language, artificial language, machine language, natural language, object language, prob-*

lem-oriented language, procedure-oriented language, programming language, source language, target language.

Latency The time between the completion of the interpretation of an *address* and the start of the actual transfer from the addressed *location*. Latency includes the *delay* associated with access to *storage devices* such as *magnetic drums* and *delay lines*.

Left-justify (1) To adjust the printing positions of *characters* on a page so that the left margin of the page is regular. (2) By extension, to *shift* the contents of a *register* so that the most significant *digit* is at some specified position of the register. Contrast with *normalize*.

Letter A *graphic,* which, when used alone or combined with others, represents in a written *language* one or more sound elements of the spoken language; diacritical marks used alone and punctuation marks are not letters.

Level The degree of subordination in a hierarchy.

Library (1) A collection of organized *information* used for study and reference. (2) A collection of related *files*. For example, one line of an invoice may form an *item,* a complete invoice may form a file, the collection of inventory control files may form a library, and the libraries used by an organizaton are known as its *data bank.* (3) See *program library*.

Library Routine A proven *routine* that is maintained in a *program library*.

Line Printer A device that prints all *characters* of a line as a unit. Contrast with *character printer*.

Line Printing The printing of an entire line of characters as a unit.

Linear Programming (1) (SC1) In *operations research,* a procedure for locating the maximum or minimum of a linear *function* of *variables* that are subject to linear constraints. (2) Synonymous with linear optimization. Abbreviated LP.

Linkage In *programming, coding* that connects two separately coded *routines.*

List (1) An ordered set of *items*. (2) See *chained list, pushdown list, pushup list.*

List Processing A method of processing *data* in the form of *lists.* Usually, *chained lists* are used so that the logical order of *items* can be changed without altering their physical locations.

Load   In *programming,* to enter *data* into *storage* or working *registers.*

Load-and-go   An operating technique in which there are no stops between the *loading* and execution phases of a *program* and which may include *assembling* or *compiling.*

Location   (1) Any place in which *data* may be *stored.* (2) See *protected location.*

Logical file   A collection of one or more *logical records.*

Logical Record   A collection of *items* independent of their physical environment. Portions of the same logical *record* may be located in different physical records.

Logic Design   The specification of the working relations between the parts of a system in terms of *symbolic logic* and without primary regard for *hardware* implementation.

Logic Diagram   A *diagram* that represents a *logic design* and sometimes the *hardware* implementation.

Logic Element   A device that performs a logic function.

Logic Instruction   An *instruction* that executes an *operation* that is defined in *symbolic logic,* such as AND, OR, NOR.

Logic Symbol   (1) A *symbol* used to represent a *logic element* graphically. (2) A *symbol* used to represent a logic *operator.*

Loop   (1) A *sequence* of *instructions* that is executed repeatedly until a terminal condition prevails. (2) See *feedback loop, magnetic hysteresis loop.*

Machine Address   Same as *absolute address.*

Machine Code   An *operation code* that a machine is designed to recognize.

Machine Instruction   An *instruction* that a machine can recognize and execute.

Machine Language   A *language* that is used directly by a machine.

Machine Learning   (SC1) The ability of a device to improve its performance based on its past performance. Related to *artificial intelligence.*

Machine-readable Medium   A *medium* that can *convey data* to a given sensing device. Synonymous with automated data medium.

Machine Word   Same as *computer word.*

Macro Instruction   An *instruction* in a *source language* that is equivalent to a specified *sequence* of *machine instructions.*

Macroprogramming   *Programming* with *macro instructions.*

Magnetic Card   A card with a magnetic surface on which *data* can be *stored* by selective magnetization of portions of the flat surface.

Magnetic Core   A configuration of magnetic material that is or is intended to be placed in a spatial relationship to current-carrying conductors and whose magnetic properties are essential to its use. It may be used to concentrate an induced magnetic field as in a transformer induction coil, or armature, to retain a magnetic polarization for the purpose of *storing* data, or for its nonlinear properties as in a *logic element.* It may be made of such material as iron, iron oxide, or ferrite and in such shapes as wires, tapes, toroids, rods, or thin film.

Magnetic Disc   A flat circular plate with a magnetic surface on which *data* can be *stored* by selective magnetization of portions of the flat surface.

Magnetic Drum   A right circular cylinder with a magnetic surface on which *data* can be *stored* by selective magnetization of portions of the curved surface.

Magnetic Hysteresis Loop   A closed curve showing the relation between the magnetization force and the induction of magnetization in a magnetic substance when the magnetized field (force) is carried through a complete cycle.

Magnetic Ink   An ink that contains particles of a magnetic substance whose presence can be detected by magnetic sensors.

Magnetic Ink Character Recognition   The machine recognition of characters printed with magnetic ink. Contrast with *optical character recognition.* Abbreviated MICR.

Magnetic Storage   A *storage device* that utilizes the magnetic properties of materials to *store data,* e.g., *magnetic cores, tapes,* and *films.*

Magnetic Tape   (1) A tape with a magnetic surface on which *data* can be *stored* by selective polarization of portions of the surface. (2) A tape of magnetic material used as the constituent in some forms of *magnetic cores.*

Magnetic Thin Film   A layer of magnetic material, usually less than 1 micron thick, often used for logic or storage elements.

Main Frame   (SC1) Same as *central processing unit.*

Main Storage   The general purpose *storage* of a *computer.* Usually, main storage can be *accessed* directly by the operating *registers.* Contrast with *auxiliary storage.*

Maintenance   Any activity intended to eliminate *faults* or to keep *hardware* or *programs* in satisfactory working condition, including tests, measurements, replacements, adjustments, and repairs.

Malfunction   The effect of a *fault.* Contrast with *error, mistake.*

Management Information System   (1) (SC1) Management performed with the aid of *automatic data processing.* Abbreviated *MIS.* (2) An *information system* designed to aid in the performance of management *functions.*

Map   To establish a correspondence between the elements of one set and the elements of another set.

Markov Chain   A probabilistic model of events in which the probability of an event is dependent only on the event that precedes it.

Mark Sensing   The electrical sensing of manually recorded conductive marks on a nonconductive surface.

Mass Storage Device   A device having a large *storage capacity,* e.g., *magnetic disk, magnetic drum.*

Master File   A *file* that is either relatively permanent or that is treated as an authority in a particular *job.*

Match   To *check* for identity between two or more *items* of *data.* Contrast with *hit.*

Mathematical Model   A mathematical representation of a process, device, or concept.

Matrix   (1) In mathematics, a two-dimensional rectangular *array* of quantities. Matrices are manipulated in accordance with the rules of matrix algebra. (2) In *computers,* a logic network in the form of an array of *input* leads and *output* leads with *logic elements* connected at some of their intersections. (3) By extension, an array of any number of dimensions.

Matrix Storage   *Storage,* the elements of which are arranged such that access to any *location* requires the use of two or more coordinates, e.g., cathode-ray storage, *magnetic core* storage.

Medium (1) The material, or configuration thereof, on which *data* are recorded, e.g., paper tape, cards, *magnetic tape*. Synonymous with data medium. (2) See *data medium, machine-readable medium*.

Memory Same as *storage*.

Merge To combine *items* from two or more similarly ordered sets into one set that is arranged in the same order. Contrast with *collate*.

Message An arbitrary amount of *information* whose beginning and end are defined or implied.

MICR *Magnetic Ink Character Recognition.*

MIS *Management Information System.*

Mistake A human action that produces an unintended result. Contrast with *error, fault, malfunction*.

Mnemonic Symbol A *symbol* chosen to assist the human memory, e.g., an abbreviation such as "mpy" for "multiply."

Modem MOdulator-DEModulator. A device that modulates and demodulates signals transmitted over communication facilities.

Module (1) A *program* unit that is discrete and identifiable with respect to *compiling,* combining with other units, and *loading,* e.g., the *input* to or *output* from an *assembler, compiler, linkage* editor, or *executive routine*. (2) A packaged functional *hardware* unit designed for use with other components. (3) See *object module, programming module*.

Monitor *Software* or *hardware* that observes, supervises, controls, or verifies the operations of a *system*.

Move Same as *transfer, transmit*.

Multiaddress Pertaining to an *instruction format* containing more than one *address part*.

Multiplex To *interleave* or simultaneously *transmit* two or more messages on a single *channel*.

Multiprocessing (1) Pertaining to the simultaneous execution of two or more *computer programs* or *sequences* of *instructions* by a *computer* or *computer network*. (2) Loosely, *parallel processing*.

Multiprocessor A *computer* employing two or more processing units under integrated control.

Multiprogramming Pertaining to the *concurrent* execution of two or more *programs* by a *computer*.

Natural Language   A *language* whose rules reflect and describe current usage rather than prescribe usage. Contrast with *artificial language*.

Nest   To imbed *subroutines* or *data* in other subroutines or data at a different hierarchical level such that the different levels of routines or data can be executed or accessed recursively.

Node   The representation of a state or an *event* by means of a point on a diagram.

Noise   (1) Random variations of one or more characteristics of any entity such as voltage, current, or *data*. (2) A random *signal* of known statistical properties of amplitude, distribution and spectral density. (3) Loosely, any disturbance tending to interfere with the normal operation of a device or *system*.

Nondestructive Read   A *read* process that does not *erase* the *data* in the source. Abbreviated NDR.

Normal Direction Flow   (SC1) A flow in a direction from left to right or top to bottom on a *flowchart*.

Normalize   (1) To multiply a *variable* or one or more quantities occurring in a calculation by a numerical coefficient in order to make an associated quantity assume a nominated value, e.g., to make a definite integral of a variable or the maximum member of a *set* of quantities equal to unity. Contrast with, *justify, left-justify, right-justify*. (2) Loosely, to *scale*.

Normalized Form   The form taken by a *floating-point representation* of a *number* when the *fixed-point part* lies within some prescribed standard *range,* so chosen that any given number will be represented by a unique pair of *numerals*. Synonymous with standard form.

Null String   The notion of a *string* depleted of its entities or the notion of a string prior to establishing its entities.

Number   (1) A mathematical entity that may indicate quantity or amount of units. (2) Loosely, a *numeral*. (3) See *binary number, random numbers*.

Number Representation   (SC1) The representation of *numbers* by agreed *sets* of *symbols* according to agreed rules. Synonymous with numeration.

Number Representation System   An agreed set of *symbols* and rules for *number representation*. Synonymous with numeral system, numeration system.

Number System   Loosely, a *number representation system*.

Numeral   (1) A discrete representation of a *number*. For example, twelve, 12, XII, 1100 are four different numerals that represent the same number. (2) A numeric word that represents a *number*. (3) See *binary numeral, decimal numeral*.

Numeric   (SC1) Pertaining to *numerals* or to representation by means of numerals. Synonymous with numerical.

Numerical   Same as *numeric*.

Numerical Analysis   The study of methods of obtaining useful quantitative solutions to problems that have been expressed mathematically, including the study of the *errors* and bounds on errors in obtaining such solutions.

Numerical Control   (SC1) *Automatic* control of a process performed by a device that makes use of all or part of *numerical data* generally introduced as the *operation* is in process.

Numeric Character   Same as *digit*.

Numeric Code   (SC1) A *code* whose *code set* consists only of *digits* and associated *special characters*.

Numeric Data Code   A *code* consisting only of *numerals* and *special characters*.

Numeric Word   A word consisting of *digits* and possibly *space* characters and *special characters*. For example, in the universal decimal classification system, the numeric word 621.39 + 897 is used as an identifier for a class of literature.

Object Code   *Output* from a *compiler* or *assembler* that is itself executable *machine code* or is suitable for processing to produce executable machine code.

Object Language   Same as *target language*.

Object Module   A *module* that is the *output* of an *assembler* or *compiler* and is *input* to a *linkage* editor.

Object Program   A fully *compiled* or *assembled program* that is ready to be *loaded* into the *computer*. Synonymous with target program. Contrast with *source program*.

OCR   *Optical character recognition.*

Octal   (1) Pertaining to a characteristic or property involving a selection, choice or condition in which there are eight possibilities. (2) Pertaining to the *number representation system* with a *radix* of eight.

Offline   Pertaining to equipment or devices not under control of the *central processing unit.*

Offline Storage   *Storage* not under control of the *central processing unit.*

Online   (1) Pertaining to equipment or devices under control of the *central processing unit.* (2) Pertaining to a user's ability to interact with a *computer.*

Online Storage   *Storage* under control of the *central processing unit.*

Openended   Pertaining to a process or system that can be augmented.

Open Shop   Pertaining to the operation of a *computer* facility in which most productive problem *programming* is performed by the problem originator rather than by a group of programming specialists. The use of the computer itself may also be described as open shop if the user/programmer also serves as the *operator,* rather than a full time trained operator. Contrast with *closed shop.*

Open Subroutine   A *subroutine* that is inserted into a *routine* at each place it is used. Synonymous with direct insert subroutine. Contrast with *closed subroutine.*

Operand   That which is operated upon. An operand is usually identified by an *address part* of an *instruction.*

Operating System   (SC1) *Software* that controls the execution of *computer programs* and that may provide scheduling, *debugging,* input/output control, accounting, *compilation, storage* assignment, *data* management, and related services.

Operation   (1) A defined action, namely, the act of obtaining a result from one or more *operands* in accordance with a rule that completely specifies the result for any permissible combination of operands. (2) The *set* of such acts specified by such a rule or the rule itself. (3) The act specified by a single *computer instruction.* (4) A *program* step undertaken or executed by a *computer,* e.g., addition, multiplication, extraction, comparison, *shift, transfer.* The operation is usually specified by the *operator* part of an instruction. (5) The event or specific action performed by a *logic element*. (6) See *auxiliary operation, fixed-cycle operation, parallel operation, sequential operation, serial operation.*

Operation Code   A *code* that represents specific operations. Synonymous with instruction code.

Operation Decoder   A device that selects one or more control *channels* according to the *operator* part of a *machine instruction.*

Operations Analysis   Same as *operations research.*

Operations Research   The use of the scientific method to provide criteria for decisions concerning the actions of people, machines, and other resources in a system involving repeatable operations. Synonymous with operations analysis. Abbreviated OR.

Operator   (1) In the description of a *process,* that which indicates the action to be performed on *operands.* (2) A person who operates a machine.

Optical Character Recognition   The machine identification of printed *characters* through use of light-sensitive devices. Contrast with *magnetic ink character recognition.* Abbreviated *OCR.*

Optical Scanner   (1) A device that scans optically and usually generates an *analog* or *digital signal.* (2) A device that optically scans printed or written *data* and generates their *digital representations.*

Order   (1) To arrange *items* according to any specified *set* of rules. Synonymous with sort. (2) An arrangement of items according to any specified set of rules.

Outconnector   In *flowcharting,* a *connector* that indicates a point at which a *flowline* is broken for continuation at another point. Contrast with *inconnector.*

Output   (1) (SC1) Pertaining to a device, *process,* or *channel* involved in an *output process* or to the data or states involved. (2) One or a sequence of *output states.* (3) Same as *output device.* (4) Same as *output channel.* (5) Same as *output process.* (6) Same as *output data.* (7) See *real time output.*

Output Area   An area of *storage* reserved for *output.*

Output Channel   A *channel* for conveying *data* from a device or *logic element.* Synonymous with *output* (4).

Output Data   (SC1) *Data* to be delivered from a device or *program,* usually after some processing. Synonymous with *output* (6).

Output Device   (SC1) The device or collective set of devices used for conveying *data* out of another device. Synonymous with *output* (3).

Output Process   (SC1) The *process* of delivering *data* by a system, subsystem, or device. Synonymous with *output* (5).

Output State   The state occurring on a specified *output channel*.

Overflow   (1) That portion of the result of an *operation* that exceeds the capacity of the intended unit of *storage*. (2) Pertaining to the generation of overflow as in (1). (3) Contrast with *underflow*.

Overlay   The technique of repeatedly using the same blocks of internal *storage* during different stages of a *program*. When one *routine* is no longer needed in storage, another routine can replace all or part of it.

Overlay Supervisor   A *routine* that controls the proper *sequencing* and positioning of *segments* of *computer programs* in limited *storage* during their execution.

Pack   To compress *data* in a *storage* medium by taking advantage of known characteristics of the data in such a way that the original data can be recovered, e.g., to compress data in a storage medium by making use of *bit* or *byte* locations that would otherwise go unused.

Packing Density   The number of useful *storage cells* per unit of dimension, e.g., the number of bits per inch stored on a *magnetic tape* or drum track.

Parallel   (1) Pertaining to the *concurrent* or *simultaneous* occurrence of two or more related activities in multiple devices or *channels*. (2) Pertaining to the simultaneity of two or more *processes*. (3) Pertaining to the simultaneous processing of the individual parts of a whole, such as the *bits* of a *character* and the characters of a *word,* using separate facilities for the various parts. (4) Contrast with *serial*.

Parallel Computer   (1) A *computer* having multiple arithmetic or logic units that are used to accomplish *parallel operations* or *parallel processing*. Contrast with *serial computer*. (2) Historically, a computer, some specified characteristic of which is *parallel,* e.g., a *computer* that manipulates all *bits* of a *word* in parallel.

Parallel Operation   Pertaining to the *concurrent* or *simultaneous* execution of two or more *operations* in devices such as multiple arithmetic or logic units. Contrast with *serial operation*.

Parallel Processing Pertaining to the *concurrent* or *simultaneous* execution of two or more *processes* in multiple devices such as *channels* or processing units. Contrast with *multiprocessing, serial processing.*

Parallel Search Storage A *storage device* in which one or more parts of all storage *locations* are queried *simultaneously.* Contrast with *associative storage.*

Parameter A *variable* that is given a constant value for a specific purpose or *process.*

Parity Bit A *check bit* appended to an *array* of *binary digits* to make the sum of all the binary digits, including the check bit, always odd or always even.

Parity Check A *check* that tests whether the number of ones (or zeros) in an *array* of *binary digits* is odd or even. Synonymous with odd-even check.

Pass One *cycle* of processing a body of *data.*

Patch (1) To modify a *routine* in a rough or expedient way. (2) A temporary electrical connection.

Pattern Recognition The identification of shapes, forms, or configurations by *automatic* means.

Peripheral Equipment (SC1) In a *data processing* system, any unit of equipment, distinct from the *central processing unit,* that may provide the system with outside communication.

Permanent Storage Same as *fixed storage.*

Plugboard A perforated board into which plugs are manually inserted to control the *operation* of equipment. Synonymous with *control panel* (2).

Position (1) In a *string* each location that may be occupied by a *character* or *binary digit* and may be identified by a serial number. (2) See *punch position, sign position.*

Positional Notation (SC1) A *numeration system* in which a *number* is represented by means of an ordered *set* of *digits* such that the value contributed by each digit depends upon its position as well as upon its value. Synonymous with positional representation.

Postmortem Pertaining to the analysis of an operation after its completion.

Postmortem Dump   A *static dump,* used for *debugging* purposes, performed at the end of a machine *run.*

Precision   (1) The degree of discrimination with which a quantity is stated. For example, a three-digit *numeral* discriminates among 1,000 possibilities. (2) See *double precision.*

Predefined Process   A process that is identified only by name and that is defined elsewhere.

Preset   To establish an initial condition, such as the control values of a *loop.*

Print Control Character   A *control character* for print *operations* such as line spacing, page ejection, or *carriage return.*

Problem Description   (1) (SC1) In *information processing,* a statement of a problem. The statement may also include a description of the method of solution, the procedures and *algorithms,* etc. (2) A statement of a problem. The statement may also include a description of the method of solution, the solution itself, the transformations of *data* and the relationship of procedures, data, constraints, and environment.

Problem-oriented Language   A *programming language* designed for the convenient expression of a given class of problems.

Procedure   (SC1) The course of action taken for the solution of a problem.

Procedure-oriented Language   A *programming language* designed for the convenient expression of procedures used in the solution of a wide class of problems.

Process   A systematic *sequence* of *operations* to produce a specified result. See *input process, output process, predefined process.*

Processor   (1) In *hardware,* a *data processor.* (2) In *software,* a *computer program* that includes the *compiling, assembling, translating,* and related functions for a specific *programming language, COBOL* processor, *FORTRAN* processor. (3) See *data processor, multiprocessor.*

Program   (1) (SC1) A series of actions proposed in order to achieve a certain result. (2) Loosely, a *routine.* (3) To design, write, and test a program as in (1). (4) Loosely, to write a *routine.* (5) See *computer program, object program, source program, target program.*

Program Library   A collection of available *computer programs* and *routines.*

Programmed Check A *check* procedure designed by the *programmer* and implemented specifically as a part of his *program*. Contrast with *automatic check*.

Programmer (SC1) A person mainly involved in designing, writing and testing *computer programs*.

Programming (1) (SC1) The design, the writing, and testing of a *program*. (2) See *automatic programming, linear programming, macroprogramming, multiprogramming*.

Programming Flowchart (SC1) A *flowchart* representing the sequence of *operations* in a *program*.

Programming Language A *language* used to prepare *computer* programs.

Programming Module A discrete identifiable set of *instructions*, usually handled as a unit, by an *assembler*, a *compiler*, a *linkage* editor, a *loading routine*, or other type of routine or *subroutine*.

Protected Location A *storage* location, reserved for special purposes, in which *data* cannot be stored without undergoing a screening procedure to establish suitability for storage therein.

Punch (1) A perforation, as in a *punched card* or paper tape. (2) See *digit punch, keypunch, eleven punch, twelve punch, zone punch*.

Punched Card (1) A card *punched* with a pattern of holes to represent *data*. (2) A card as in (1) before being *punched*.

Punched Tape A tape on which a pattern of holes or cuts is used to represent *data*.

Punch Position A defined *location* on a card or tape where a hole may be *punched*.

Pushdown List A *list* that is constructed and maintained so that the *item* to be retrieved is the most recently *stored* item in the list, i.e., last in, first out.

Pushup List A *list* that is constructed and maintained so that the next *item* to be retrieved and removed is the oldest item still in the list, i.e., first in, first out.

Quantization The subdivision of the *range* of values of a *variable* into a finite number of nonoverlapping but not necessarily equal subranges or intervals, each of which is represented by an assigned value within the subrange. For example, a person's age is quantized for most purposes with a *quantum* of one year.

Quantize   To subdivide the *range* of values of a *variable* into a finite number of nonoverlapping but not necessarily equal subranges or intervals, each of which is represented by an assigned value within the subrange.

Quantum   A subrange in *quantization.*

Queued Access Method   Any access method that automatically synchronizes the *transfer* of *data* between the *program* using the access method and *input/output* devices, thereby eliminating delays for input/output *operation.*

Radix   (SC1) In *positional representation,* that integer, if it exists, by which the *significance* of the *digit place* must be multiplied to give the significance of the next higher digit place. For example, in *decimal notation,* the radix of each place is 10; in a biquinary code, the radix of the fives place is 2. Synonymous with *base* (3).

Radix Notation   A *positional representation* in which the *significance* of any two adjacent *digit positions* has an integral ratio called the *radix* of the less significant of the two positions; permissible values of the digit in any position *range* from zero to one less than the radix of that position.

Radix Point   In *radix notation,* the real or implied *character* that separates the *digits* associated with the integral part of a *numeral* from those associated with the fractional part.

Random Access   (1) Same as *direct access.* (2) In COBOL, an *access mode* in which specific *logical records* are obtained from or placed into a *mass storage file* in a nonsequential manner.

Random Numbers   (1) A series of *numbers* obtained by chance. (2) A series of *numbers* considered appropriate for satisfying certain statistical tests. (3) A series of *numbers* believed to be free from conditions which might *bias* the result of a calculation.

Range   (1) The *set* of values that a quantity or *function* may assume. (2) The difference between the highest and lowest value that a quantity or *function* may assume.

Read   (1) To acquire or interpret *data* from a *storage device,* a *data medium,* or any other source. (2) See *destructive read, nondestructive read.*

Read-only Storage   Same as *fixed storage.*

Real Time   (1) Pertaining to the actual time during which a physical *process* transpires. (2) Pertaining to the performance of a computation during the actual time that the related physical *process* transpires in order that results of the computation can be used in guiding the physical process.

Real Time Input   *Input data* inserted into a *system* at the time of generation by another system.

Real Time Ouput   *Output data* removed from a *system* at time of need by another system.

Record   (1) A collection of related *items* of *data,* treated as a unit, for example, one line of an invoice may form a record; a complete set of such records may form a *file.* (2) See *logical record, variable-length record.*

Record Gap   An area on a *data medium* used to indicate the end of a *block* or *record.* Synonymous with *interrecord gap.*

Recording Density   The number of *bits* in a single linear *track* measured per unit of length of the recording *medium.*

Record Layout   The arrangement and structure of *data* in a *record,* including the *sequence* and size of its components. By extension, a record layout might be the description thereof.

Record Length   A measure of the size of a *record,* usually specified in units such as *words* or *characters.*

Register   (1) A device capable of *storing* a specified amount of *data* such as one *word.* (2) See *address register, index register, instruction register, shift register.*

Registration   The accurate positioning relative to a reference.

Relative Address   The *number* that specifies the difference between the *absolute address* and the *base address.*

Relative Coding   *Coding* that uses *machine instructions* with *relative addresses.*

Reliability   The probability that a device will perform without failure for a specified time period or amount of usage.

Relocate   In *computer programming,* to *move* a *routine* from one portion of *storage* to another and to adjust the necessary *address* references so that the routine, in its new *location,* can be executed.

Relocation Dictionary   The part of an *object module* or *load module* that identifies all *addresses* that must be adjusted when a relocation occurs.

Remote Access   Pertaining to communication with a *data processing* facility by one or more stations that are distant from that facility.

Remote Station   *Data terminal equipment* for communicating with a *data processing* system from a *location* that is time, space, or electrically distant.

Repertoire   See *instruction repertoire.*

Repetition Instruction   An *instruction* that causes one or more instructions to be executed an indicated number of times.

Rerun   A repeat of a machine *run,* usually because of a correction, an *interrupt,* or a false start.

Reset   (1) To restore a *storage device* to a prescribed initial state, not necessarily that denoting zero. (2) To place a *binary cell* into the state denoting zero.

Restart   To reestablish the execution of a *routine,* using the *data* recorded at a *checkpoint.*

Right-justify   (1) To adjust the printing *positions* of *characters* on a page so that the right margin of the page is regular. (2) To *shift* the contents of a *register* so that the least *significant digit* is at some specified *position* of the register. Contrast with *normalize.*

Rollback   A *programmed* return to a prior *checkpoint.*

Roll-in   To restore in *main storage data* that had previously been *transferred* from *main storage* to *auxiliary storage.*

Roll-out   To record the contents of *main storage* in *auxiliary storage.*

Rounding Error   An *error* due to *roundoff.* Contrast with *truncation error.*

Roundoff   To delete the least *significant digit* or digits of a *numeral* and to adjust the part retained in accordance with some rule.

Routine   (1) (SC1) An ordered set of *instructions* that may have some general or frequent use. (2) See *executive routine, library routine, service routine, subroutine, supervisory routine, tracing routine, utility routine.*

Row   A horizontal arrangement of *characters* or other expressions.

Row Binary   Pertaining to the *binary* representation of *data* on cards in which the *significances* of *punch positions* are assigned along *card rows.* For example, each row in an 80-column card may be used to represent 80 consecutive *binary digits.* Contrast with *column binary.*

Run   A single, continuous performance of a *computer program* or *routine*.

Sampling   (1) Obtaining the values of a *function* for regularly or irregularly spaced *discrete* values of the independent *variable*. (2) In statistics, obtaining a sample from a population.

Scale   To adjust the representation of a quantity by a factor in order to bring its *range* within prescribed limits.

Scan   To examine *sequentially,* part by part.

Search   (1) To examine a set of *items* for one or more having a desired property. (2) See *binary search, chaining search, dichotomizing search*.

Search Cycle   The part of a *search* that is repeated for each *item,* which normally consists of locating the item and carrying out a comparison.

Search Key   *Data* to be compared to specified parts of each *item* for the purpose of conducting a *search*.

Segment   (1) To divide a *computer program* into parts such that the program can be executed without the entire program being in *internal storage* at any one time. (2) A part of a *computer program* as in (1).

Selective Dump   A *dump* of one or more specified *storage locations*.

Self-adapting   (SC1) Pertaining to the ability of a *system* to change its performance characteristics in response to its environment.

Sequence   (1) An arrangement of *items* according to a specified set of rules. (2) See *calling sequence, collating sequence, consecutive sequence computer*.

Sequential   Pertaining to the occurrence of *events* in time *sequence,* with little or no simultaneity or overlap of events. Contrast with *concurrent, consecutive, simultaneous*.

Sequential Computer   A *computer* in which *events* occur in time *sequence* with little or no simultaneity or overlap of events.

Sequential Control   A mode of *computer operation* in which *instructions* are executed in an implicitly defined *sequence* until a different sequence is explicitly initiated by a *jump instruction*.

Sequential Operation   Pertaining to the performance of *operations* one after the other.

Serial   (1) Pertaining to the *sequential* or *consecutive* occurrence of two or more related activities in a single device or *channel*. (2) Pertaining to the *sequencing* of two or more *processes*. (3) Pertaining to the *sequential processing* of the individual parts of a whole, such as the *bits* of a *character* or the characters of a *word,* using the same facilities for successive parts. (4) Contrast with *parallel.*

Serial Access   (1) Pertaining to the *sequential* or *consecutive transmission* of *data* to or from *storage*. (2) Pertaining to the *process* of obtaining *data* from or placing *data* into *storage,* where the *access time* is dependent upon the *location* of the data most recently obtained or placed in storage. Contrast with *direct access.*

Serial Computer   (1) A *computer* having a single arithmetic and logic unit. (2) A *computer* some specified characteristic of which is *serial,* e.g., a computer that manipulates all *bits* of a *word* serially. Contrast with *parallel computer.*

Serial Operation   Pertaining to the *sequential* or *consecutive* execution of two or more *operations* in a single device such as an arithmetic or logic unit. Contrast with *parallel operation.*

Serial Processing   Pertaining to the *sequential* or *consecutive* execution of two or more *processes* in a single device such as a *channel* or processing unit. Contrast with *parallel processing.*

Service Routine   A *routine* in general support of the *operation* of a *computer,* e.g., an *input/output, diagnostic, tracing,* or *monitoring routine.* Synonymous with utility routine.

Servomechanism   (1) (SC1) An *automatic* control *system* incorporating feedback that governs the physical *position* of an element by adjusting either the values of the coordinates or the values of their time derivatives. (2) A feedback control *system* in which at least one of the system *signals* represents mechanical motion. (3) Any feedback control system.

Set   (1) A collection. (2) To place a *storage device* into a specified state, usually other than that denoting zero or space character. Contrast with *clear.* (3) To place a *binary cell* into the state denoting one. (4) See *character set, code set, preset, reset.*

Setup   (1) (SC1) In a *computer* that consists of an assembly of individual computing units, the arrangement of interconnections between the units and the adjustments needed for the computer to solve a particular problem. (2) An arrangement of *data* or devices to solve a particular problem.

Sexadecimal (1) Pertaining to a characteristic or property involving a selection, choice, or condition in which there are 16 possibilities. (2) Pertaining to the *numeration system* with a *radix* of 16. (3) Synonymous with hexadecimal.

Shift (1) A movement of *data* to the right or left. (2) See *arithmetic shift.*

Shift Register A *register* in which the *stored data* can be *moved* to the right or left.

Signal (1) (SC1) A time-dependent value attached to a physical phenomenon and conveying *data.* (2) The *event* or phenomenon that conveys *data* from one point to another. (3) See *inhibiting signal.*

Sign Bit A *binary digit* occupying the *sign position.*

Sign Digit A *digit* occupying the *sign position.*

Significance (SC1) In *positional representation,* the factor, dependent on the *digit place,* by which a *digit* is multiplied to obtain its additive contribution in the representation of a *number.* Synonymous with weight.

Significant Digit A *digit* that is needed for a certain purpose, particularly one that must be kept to preserve a specific *accuracy* or *precision.*

Sign Position A *position,* normally located at one end of a *numeral,* that contains an indication of the algebraic sign of the *number.*

Simulate (1) (SC1) To represent certain features of the behavior of a physical or abstract *system* by the behavior of another system. (2) To represent the functioning of a device, *system,* or *computer program* by another, e.g., to represent the functioning of one *computer* by another, to represent the behavior of a physical system by the execution of a computer program, to represent a biological system by a *mathematical model.* (3) Contrast with *emulate.*

Simulation (SC1) The representation of certain features of the behavior of a physical or abstract *system* by the behavior of another system, e.g., the representation of physical phenomena by means of *operations* performed by a *computer* or the representation of operations of a computer by those of another computer.

Simulator (SC1) A device, *system,* or *computer program* that represents certain features of the behavior of a physical or abstract system.

Simultaneous   Pertaining to the occurrence of two or more *events* at the same instant of time. Contrast with *concurrent, consecutive, sequential.*

Single Address   Pertaining to an *instruction format* containing one *address part.* Synonymous with one address.

Skeletal Coding   *Sets* of *instructions* in which some *addresses* and other parts remain undetermined. These addresses and other parts are usually determined by *routines* that are designed to modify them in accordance with given *parameters.*

Skip   To ignore one or more *instructions* in a *sequence* of instructions.

Snapshot Dump   A *selective dynamic dump* performed at various points in a machine *run.*

Software   (SC1) A set of *computer programs, procedures,* and possibly associated *documentation* concerned with the *operation* of a *data processing system,* e.g., *compilers, library routines,* manuals, circuit diagrams. Contrast with *hardware.*

Solid State Component   A component whose *operation* depends on the control of electric or magnetic phenomena in solids, e.g, a transistor, crystal diode, *ferrite* core.

Sort   (1) To segregate *items* into groups according to some definite rules. (2) Same as *order.*

Sorter   A person, device, or *computer routine* that *sorts.*

Source Language   The *language* from which a *statement* is translated.

Source Program   A *computer program* written in a *source language.* Contrast with *object program.*

Space   (1) A site intended for the *storage* of *data,* e.g., a site on a printed page or a *location* in a *storage medium.* (2) A basic *unit* of area, usually the size of a single *character.* (3) One or more space characters. (4) To advance the *reading* or *display position* according to a prescribed *format,* e.g., to advance the printing or display position horizontally to the right or vertically down. Contrast with *backspace.*

Special Character   A *graphic character* that is neither a *letter,* nor a *digit,* nor a space character.

Special Purpose Computer   (SC1) A *computer* that is designed to handle a restricted class of problems.

Statement (1) In *computer programming,* a meaningful expression or generalized *instruction* in a *source language.* (2) See *job control statement.*

Static Dump A *dump* that is performed at a particular point in time with respect to a machine at the end of a run.

Step (1) One *operation* in a *computer routine.* (2) To cause a *computer* to execute one *operation.*

Storage (1) Pertaining to a device into which *data* can be entered, in which they can be held, and from which they can be retrieved at a later time. (2) Loosely, any device that can *store data.* (3) Synonymous with memory. (4) See *associative storage, auxiliary storage, content addressed storage, fixed storage, internal storage, magnetic storage, main storage, parallel search storage, permanent storage, read-only storage, temporary storage, volatile storage, working storage.*

Storage Allocation (1) The assignment of *blocks* of *data* to specified blocks of *storage.* (2) See *dynamic storage allocation.*

Storage Capacity The amount of *data* that can be contained in a *storage device.*

Storage Cell An elementary *unit* of *storage,* e.g., a *binary cell,* a *decimal* cell.

Storage Device A device into which *data* can be inserted, in which they can be retained, and from which they can be retrieved.

Storage Protection An arrangement for preventing access to *storage* for either *reading,* or *writing,* or both. Synonymous with memory protection.

Store (1) To enter *data* into a *storage device.* (2) To retain *data* in a *storage device.* (3) A *storage device.* (4) See *immediate access store.*

Stored Program Computer (SC1) A *computer* controlled by internally stored *instructions* that can synthesize, *store,* and in some cases alter instructions as though they were *data* and that can subsequently execute these instructions.

String (1) A linear *sequence* of entities such as *characters* or physical elements. (2) See *alphabetic string, bit string, character string, null string, symbol string, unit string.*

Subroutine (1) A *routine* that can be part of another routine. (2) See *closed subroutine, open subroutine.*

Subroutine Call   The *subroutine,* in *object coding,* that performs the *call function.*

Supervisory Routine   Same as *executive routine.*

Switch   A device or *programming* technique for making a selection, e.g., a *toggle,* a *conditional jump.*

Symbol   (1) A representation of something by reason of relationship, association, or convention. (2) See *abstract symbol, flowchart symbol, logic symbol, mnemonic symbol.*

Symbolic Address   An *address* expressed in *symbols* convenient to the *computer programmer.*

Symbolic Coding   *Coding* that uses *machine instructions* with *symbolic addresses.*

Symbolic Logic   The discipline that treats *formal logic* by means of a formalized *artificial language* or symbolic calculus, whose purpose is to avoid the ambiguities and logical inadequacies of *natural languages.*

Symbol String   A *string* consisting solely of *symbols.*

Synchronous Computer   (SC1) A *computer* in which each *event,* or the performance of any basic *operation,* is constrained to start on, and usually to keep in step with, *signals* from a *clock.* Contrast with *asynchronous computer.*

System   (1) (SC1) An assembly of methods, *procedures,* or techniques united by regulated interaction to form an organized whole. (2) (SC1) An organized collection of men, *machines,* and methods required to accomplish a *set* of specific *functions.* (3) See *information feedback system, management information system, number representation system, number system, numeral system, operating system.*

Table   (1) A collection of *data* in which each *item* is uniquely identified by a *label,* by its *position* relative to the other items, or by some other means. (2) See *decision table, function table, truth table.*

Table Look-up   A *procedure* for obtaining the *function* value corresponding to an *argument* from a *table* of function values.

Tabulate   (1) To form *data* into a *table.* (2) To print totals.

Tag   (1) One or more *characters* attached to an *item* or *record* for the purpose of identification. (2) Same as *flag.*

Tape Deck   Same as *tape unit.*

Tape Drive   A device that moves tape past a *head*. Synonymous with tape transport.

Tape Unit   A device containing a *tape drive,* together with *reading* and *writing heads* and associated controls. Synonymous with *tape deck,* tape station.

Target Language   The *language* to which a *statement* is *translated.* Synonymous with *object language.*

Target Program   Same as *object program.*

Telecommunications   Pertaining to the *transmission* of *signals* over long distances, such as by telegraph, radio, or televison.

Temporary Storage   In *programming, storage locations* reserved for intermediate results. Synonymous with *working storage.*

Terminal   A point in a *system* or communication network at which *data* can either enter or leave.

Timeshare   To use a device for two or more *interleaved* purposes.

Timesharing   Pertaining to the *interleaved* use of the time of a device.

Toggle   (1) Same as *flip-flop.* (2) Pertaining to any device having two stable states.

Tracing Routine   A *routine* that provides an historical record of specified *events* in the execution of a *program.*

Track   The portion of a moving *storage medium,* such as a drum, tape, or *disk,* that is accessible to a given *reading head position.*

Transaction File   A *file* containing relatively transient *data* to be processed in combination with a *master file.* For example, in a payroll application, a transaction file indicating hours worked might be processed with a master file containing employee name and rate of pay. Synonymous with *detail file.*

Transducer   A device for converting energy from one form to another.

Transfer   (1) Same as *jump.* (2) Same as *transmit.*

Translate   To transform *statements* from one *language* to another without significantly changing the meaning.

Transmission   (1) The sending of *data* from one *location* and the receiving of data in another location, usually leaving the source data unchanged. (2) The sending of *data.* (3) In *ASCII* and communications, a series of *characters* including *headings* and *texts.*

Transmit To send *data* from one *location* and to receive the data at another location. Synonymous with *transfer* (2), *move*.

Truncate To terminate a computational *process* in accordance with some rule, e.g., to end the evaluation of a power series at a specified term.

Truncation Error An *error* due to truncation. Contrast with *rounding error*.

Truth Table A *table* that describes a logic *function* by listing all possible combinations of *input* values and indicating, for each combination, the true *output* values.

Turing Machine (1) A *mathematical model* of a device that changes its internal state and *reads* from, *writes* on, and moves a potentially infinite tape, all in accordance with its present state, thereby constituting a model for *computer*-like behavior. (2) See *universal turing machine*.

Twelve Punch A *punch* in the top row of a *Hollerith punch* card. Synonymous with *y punch*.

Type Font Type of a given size and style, e.g., 10-point Bodoni Modern.

Underflow Pertaining to the condition that arises when a machine computation yields a nonzero result smaller than the smallest nonzero quantity that the intended *unit* of *storage* is capable of storing. Contrast with *overflow*.

Unit (1) A device having a special *function*. (2) A basic element. (3) See *arithmetic unit, central processing unit, tape unit*.

Unit String A *string* containing only one entity.

Universal Turing Machine A *turing machine* that can *simulate* any other turing machine.

Unpack To recover the original *data* from *packed* data.

USASCII Same as *ASCII*.

Utility Routine Same as *service routine*.

Variable A quantity that can assume any of a given *set* of values.

Variable-length Record Pertaining to a *file* in which the *records* are not uniform in length.

Variable-point Representation   A *positional representation* in which the position of the *radix point* is explicitly indicated by a special *character* at that position. Contrast with *floating-point representation*.

Verify   (1) To determine whether a transcription of *data* or other *operation* has been accomplished accurately. (2) To *check* the results of *keypunching*.

Volatile Storage   A *storage device* in which stored *data* are lost when the applied power is removed, e.g., an acoustic delay line.

Word   (1) A *character string* or a *bit string* considered as an entity. (2) See *alphabetic word, computer word, halfword, machine word, numeric word*.

Word Length   A measure of the size of a *word,* usually specified in *units* such as *characters* or *binary digits*.

Working Storage   Same as *temporary storage*.

Write   To record *data* in a *storage device* or a data *medium*. The recording need not be permanent, such as the writing on a cathode ray tube *display* device.

X Punch   Same as *eleven punch*.

Y Punch   Same as *twelve punch*.

Zero Suppression   The elimination of nonsignificant zeros in a *numeral*.

Zone Punch   A *punch* in the eleven, twelve, or zero row of a *punched card*.

Index